THE ITALIANS
Social Backgrounds of an American Group

The Italian Ghetto. Lower East Side,
New York City, c. 1915

THE ITALIANS

Social Backgrounds
Of An American Group

FRANCESCO CORDASCO

and

EUGENE BUCCHIONI

AUGUSTUS M. KELLEY • PUBLISHERS
CLIFTON 1974

First published 1974 by
AUGUSTUS M. KELLEY, PUBLISHERS
Clifton, New Jersey 07012

Library of Congress Cataloging in Publication Data
Cordasco, Francesco, 1920- comp.
   The Italians; social backgrounds of an American group.
   Bibliography: p.
   1. Italians in the United States—Addresses, essays, lectures. 2. United States—
Emigration and immigration—Addresses, essays, lectures. 3. Italy—Emigration and
immigration—Addresses, essays, lectures.
I. Bucchioni, Eugene. II. Title.
E184.I8C65   917.3'06'51   74-3151
ISBN 0-678-01366-7

PRINTED IN THE UNITED STATES OF AMERICA
by SENTRY PRESS, NEW YORK, N. Y. 10013
Bound by A. HOROWITZ & SON, CLIFTON, N. J.

In Memory of

Carmela Madorma Cordasco

1883-1962

Giovanni Cordasco

1883-1953

Who were part of the great migrations

No one can follow the fortunes of the Italians abroad without being struck by a sort of contempt in which they are often held. "Dago," "gringo," "carcamano," "badola," "cincali," "macaroni"—how long the list of epithets might be! "Italy feeds nobody and is everybody's guest" was the widely quoted utterance of a Frenchman. Whether such names and such opinions originate in the laborer's resentment of competition or in the citizen's easy association of objectionable or misunderstood personal attributes with the idea of the foreigner, they but emphasize the discomfort of the Italians and stir up a sense of shame in Italy. In the Parliament at Rome frequent reference has been made to the dislike in which Italians have been held in the United States, and such men as San Giuliano and Tittoni believed there were reasons for it. Those who have most lauded the Greater Italy of the emigrants have realized its circumscriptions. Money confers a respect and an influence (that of England for example in Argentina) to which toil cannot attain. The Greater Italy is an empire— but a proletariate empire. It bestrides the world like a Colossus—but a Colossus arrayed in rags.

Robert F. Foerster, *The Italian Emigration of Our Time* (1919).

TABLE OF CONTENTS

ix

xii

ILLUSTRATIONS

The photographs are from the Leonard Covello Collection of reports, papers, correspondence and memorabilia on the East Harlem, New York City, Italian community.*

(1)   The Italian Ghetto. Lower East Side,   *Frontispiece*
      New York City, c. 1915

> *The following illustrations grouped as a separate section will be found following page 300*

(2)   Italian East Harlem, New York City, late 1920's

(3)   Italian District, Lower East Side, New York City, 1920's

(4)   Our Lady of Mt. Carmel Feast Day, early 1930's. Italian East Harlem, New York City

(5)   Italian East Harlem, New York City, early 1930's

(6)   Italian Street Vendor, Greenwich Village, New York City, late 1930's

(7)   Italian Street Vendor, Italian East Harlem, New York City, mid-1930's

(8)   Italian East Harlem, New York City, 1942

(9)   Italian Espresso Shop, New York City, mid-1930's

(10) Italian Scavenger, Italian East Harlem, New York City, 1930's

(11) Italian Fruit and Vegetable Vendor. Italian East Harlem, New York City, 1930's

(12) Italian District, Greenwich Village, New York City, mid-1920's

(13) March For Better Housing. Italian East Harlem, New York City, early 1940's

*See No. 768, F. Cordasco, *Italians in the United States: A Bibliography of Reports, Texts, Critical Studies, and Related Materials* (New York: Oriole Editions, 1972).

PREFACE

There can be little doubt that the new interest in ethnicity in America derives from the civil rights movement of the last two decades, and the new Black consciousness which accompanied it. In a very real sense, the emergence of a white ethnic consciousness (Irish, Jewish, Polish, Italian, Slavic, etc.) is to be understood as a reaction to the special "minority status" accorded over the turbulent 1960's to Blacks, Indians, and Hispanics (incongruously lumping together Mexican-Americans, Puerto Ricans, and Cubans); to the Johnsonian War on Poverty and the Federal interventions in behalf of the newly discovered minorities; and to the concomitant egalitarianism which was viewed as a threat to white ethnic status: this last is acutely witnessed in the resistance to "affirmative action" criteria for faculty recruitment of minorities in the colleges and universities and is pointedly articulated by Paul Seabury.[1]

Yet all of this (however it be understood) obscures the more important issue of the neglect in the past by *academia* of ethnicity in American life. If ethnic subcommunities were generally neglected by American academicians, the Italian experience in America (when it was noted at all) was, as I have observed elsewhere, subjected to the ministrations of social workers who concentrated on the sociopathology inevitable in a matrix of deprivation and cultural conflict, or to the probings of psychologists who sought to discern and understand the dynamics of adjustment.

It was not unanticipated, in the floodtide of this new ethnic awareness, that the Italian experience in America would be given a prominent attention; and it is hardly fortuitous that Italian-American academicians (until the 1960's in little evidence in the

[1]Paul Seabury, "HEW and the Universities," *Commentary*, February, 1972, pp. 38-45; and correspondence, *Ibid.*, May, 1972.

xv

universities and colleges) have discovered a cultural *ethos* which relates them to both an enviable minority status and the new egalitarianism, and that they have begun exploring the vast, unchartered expanses of their American experiences. In recent years, the academic community has witnessed a proliferating number of works which attest to these explorations, and which suggest an impatience in clearing away the neglect of past decades.[2]

But one *great* need (among a multiplicity of others) must be met if the Italian experience in the United States is to be studied in an organized way: and that need is the provision of a sourcebook of documents and other materials which recreates the period of the great migrations to America and describes, in all their verisimilitude, the "Italian American Colonies" (to use Antonio Mangano's felicitous phrase) at the time of their existence as vast interstitial communities. It is this need which *The Italians: The Social Backgrounds of an American Group* attempts to provide.

That a sourcebook on the Italian American experience was not done in the past is probably due, in part, to the neglect (as noted above) by *academia* of ethnicity in American life; yet, for Italians in the United States, the reasons may be intricately more complex: the reasons (in whatever rank order one assigns them importance) comprehend (1) generally speaking, the absence of cooperative ethnic activity amongst Italians, itself deriving from that phenomenon which is *campanilismo,* that village-mindedness or provincialism which dominated the world of the immigrant and entrapped his progeny; (2) the extreme poverty which was endemic in the Italian-American enclaves; (3) the apolitical tradition which impeded Italian civic progress; (4) the return migration to Italy, a phenomenon which not only arrested Italian assimilation in American society but equally hardened the obduracy of the unsympathetic greater society; (5) and, within the restricted time frame, the arrival of Italians in such vast numbers that they inundated American cities: their huge numbers, at once, judged inimical to American culture and interests. It is this last factor which explains the intensity of the prejudice against Italians, and their tardy emergence as an ethnic group, clearly distinguishable in the American social-cultural mosaic. The talented journalist, Erik Amfitheatrof (born in Milan of a Russian father and Italian mother, and resident in the United

---

[2]See, in the Bibliography, entries for Andrew F. Rolle (1968; 1972); Humbert S. Nelli (1970); Joseph Lopreato (1970); Alexander DeConde (1971);Leonard Covello (1967; 1972); Lydio Tomasi (1972); Erik Amfitheatrof (1973).

States since age seven), conceptualizes the elusive subtleties of Italian American alienation in his *The Children of Columbus:*

> The fact is that Italian-Americans have always been notoriously defensive about their ethnic heritage. A proud people, they have had to struggle—like other minorities—against a debilitating sense of always having to measure themselves by Anglo-Saxon values and standards. Often, this process has meant rejecting one's own Italian past, or one's parents. The over fourteen hundred mutual aid societies that flourished among Italian-Americans in the early years of the century served in part as gathering places where successful Italian immigrants could meet and remind one another that they came from *Italia!* the heartland of art, beauty, knowledge. At innumerable smoke-wreathed dinners, speakers rose to proclaim the glorious achievements of Italian civilization and to sound the names of Dante, Leonardo, Michelangelo, Raphael, Galileo, Manzoni, Marconi—names that fused into a drum roll of reassurance against the scorn of haughty Anglo-Saxons and, all too often, alas, of the immigrants' own American-born, American-educated children . . .
>
> In truth, Italian-Americans have a right to feel misunderstood. Except for the Indians, they are actually the oldest of all Americans. Yet, ironically, the Italians were the last people to emigrate to America in great numbers, and they have yet to make those numbers count in the running of America. Their record in this New World discovered by their navigators remains opaque, confusing. In the days of the Sacco-Vanzetti trial, Italian workmen were regarded as subversives. Now, to suspicious liberals, they are angry flag-waving hard-hats. As Professor Richard Gambino pointed out recently in the New York *Times Magazine,* not even the Chinese are more mysterious to Main Street than are the Italian-Americans.[3]

The scope and variety of materials available for a sourcebook on Italian Americans are indescribably diverse; my recent *Italians in the United States: A Bibliography*[4] attests this rich diversity: in a strict sense, the present work is a companion volume to the *Bibliography.* Structurally (and in a lesser thematic sense), it is modeled on Marshall Sklare's invaluable *The Jews: Social Patterns of an American Group* (1958/1966), a fortuitous emulation, despite the historic relations of Jews and Italians in the period of the great migrations; and the differences in thematic structuring in the Sklare book and the present

[3]Erik Amfitheatrof, *The Children of Columbus: An Informal History of the Italians in the New World* (Boston: Little, Brown, 1973), pp. 4-6.

[4]Francesco Cordasco, *Italians in the United States: A Bibliography of Reports, Texts, Critical Studies, and Related Materials* (New York: Oriole Editions, 1972).

volume are an index of the contrasting experiences of different peoples in the United States. Professor Sklare's attention to the Jew in contemporary America rests on the unbroken continuum of the study of Jews in the United States (and in a greater sense, on the unique assimilative/acculturative processes which exist for the Jewish community in any society); for the Italian, that historical continuum of attention does not exist, and the new ethnicity which has engulfed the Italian American community is still an evolving and elusive phenomenon. For my volume, a thematic structure had to be articulated within a chronological framework (*circa* 1890-1940), essentially congruent with the period of the great migrations and the existence of large Italian American communities, which provided the social backgrounds against which the Italian Americans and the new ethnic consciousness were to be understood. The Jews know who they are; Italian Americans are in the process of discovering themselves.

I have adopted a framework for the text sufficiently flexible to permit the inclusion of a broadly representative literature; with very few exceptions, the literature is drawn from the very period or phenomenon to which it is addressed: more often than not it is by Italian observers in the ethnic ghetto, itself; or it is drawn from those major resource depositories (*e.g.*, the progressive social journal, *Charities*, sponsored by The Charity Organization Society of New York) which, written by sympathetic observers, recreate the Italian subcommunities (if, on Anglo-Saxon terms) at the height of their existence. In this sense, the text is truly a retrospective sourcebook providing social backgrounds and impinging directly on contemporary contexts. I make no apology for the exclusion of the literature of nativistic and abrasively racist clamor which culminated in the restrictive legislation which ended the mass migrations. If one of its main targets was the Italian, it was also directed at the exclusion of Eastern Europeans and others, and as an historical corpus, this *genre* is better sought elsewhere. I am, also, cognizant of that vast neglected literature in Italian which responded to the Italian experience in the United States, written by literate Italian immigrants of every persuasion (political pamphleteers and ideologues, religious reformers, journalists, chroniclers, etc.) which awaits translation into English and sourcebooks of its own.[5]

Part I (*Emigration: The Exodus of a Latin People*) is built on the

---

[5]See my *Bibliography*, generally. Representative titles include Gaetano Conte, *Dieci Anni in America: Impressioni e Recordi* (1903); Adolfo Rossi, *Nel Paese dei Dollari: Tre Anni a New York* (1893); Gaspare Nicotri, *Dalla Conca d'Oro all' Golden Gate: Studi e Impressioni di Viaggio in America* (1928); Alfredo Bosi, *Cinquanti 'Anni di Vita Italiana in America* (1921).

conceptual historicism of Grazia Dore, the multitudinous detail drawn out of Robert F. Foerster's classic work, and a variety of contemporary vignettes; Part II (*Italian Communities in America: Campanilismo in the Ghetto*) is a dimensionally rich mosaic of pieces which recreate the Italian interstitial community, and directly intrude into that "round of life" which was the Italian ethnic enclave; Part III (*Responses to American Life*) deals with the twin dynamics of assimilation and acculturation, and tangentially with crime: it is herein that I have drawn from the work of a modern scholar, Francis A. J. Ianni, in dealing with the byzantine and elusive *Mafia;* Part IV (*Employment, Health and Social Needs*) provides a context in which the *padrone* system, the exploitation of Italian workers, and occupational trends, are to be understood: and it vividly delineates the social conditions under which Italians lived, the deleterious health problems (particularly, the scourge which was tuberculosis), and the ministrations, however inadequate, to the social needs of Italians; and Part V (*Education: The Italian Child in the American School*) sketches the verisimilitude of the American schools in which the Italian child was not spared the alienation of segregated schools, the bitter rejection of a middle-class society, or the haunting ambivalence of undefined identity. For the millions of American children born of Italian mothers in an alien land, the school was a cruel stepmother whose middle-class ministrations were magisterial and remote. At best, it remained a mixed blessing.

Although this sourcebook makes available to libraries a basic collection of materials on an important American ethnic group, its use is more broadly intended. It provides a basic reference text for use in a wide gamut of academic courses: in the proliferating ethnic studies; ethnic relations; minority groups in the United States; the sociology of immigrant groups; immigrant history; and urban sociology. It should be of value to a wide constituency outside traditional academic contexts, and to a broad lay readership.

My dear friend and colleague, Leonard Covello, furnished a major motivation for the volume's completion, and my first indebtedness is to him; Eugene Bucchioni shares in the volume's early conceptualization, but its final design, selections, introductory vignettes, and bibliography are mine, and any of the text's faults must be be attributed to me: it may be of interest to note that I initiated the text's early discussion with Dr. Bucchioni in contexts of urban deprivation while engaged in work amongst the contemporary poor, a fact not unrelated to our own wellsprings of identity with a world we nostalgically revisited in the familiar present-day urban scenarios of human neglect and destitution.

I am indebted, too, to a wide range of individuals both within and outside academic communities whose work I have used (at times, inattentively); to Dr. Silvano Tomasi; Rev. Lydio Tomasi; Professor Ernest S. Falbo; Professor Andrew F. Rolle; Dr. Salvatore Mondello; Dr. Luciano J. Iorizzo; Professor Humbert S. Nelli; Dr. Alexander DeConde; and Erik Amfitheatrof; and to that extraordinary Sicilian American, Giovanni E. Schiavo. As in most of my books of recent years, Angela Barone Jack assumed the role of patient assistant, tirelessly attending to the multitudinous details with which any effort is surrounded. For her, *un 'abbraccio.*

FRANCESCO CORDASCO
West New York, N.J.
October 1973

I

Emigration

The Exodus of a Latin People

INTRODUCTION

The Italian emigration of modern times is one of the great mass migrations of a people; in size, in the multiplicity of its destinations, and in the complexity of the forces which brought it into being (what the economist Robert F. Foerster felicitously simplified as *"l'imperialismo della povera gente*), it may well be without parallel in the annals of modern history. It has been estimated that no fewer than 26 million Italians emigrated between 1861 and 1970, and that since 1900 more than 10 million Italians have left their country permanently.[1] The journalist, Erik Amfitheatrof, has graphically caught the sense of this extraordinary phenomenon: "The exodus of southern Italians from their villages at the turn of the twentiety century has no parallel in history. Out of a total population of fourteen million in the South [of Italy] at the time of national unification in 1860-1870, at least five million—*over a third of the population*—had left to seek work overseas by the outbreak of World War I. (In Italy as a whole, over eleven million people, a quarter of the population, emigrated at least once in the thirty-year period between 1881 and 1911. The land literally hemorrhaged peasants."[2]

The population of the United States includes, amongst all countries, the greatest number of persons of Italian origin: how many exactly nobody knows. Estimates run as low as seven million and as high as twenty million and more.[3] The magnitude of the Italian emigration to the United States is indicated in some of the annual statistics. Between 1900 and 1910, over two million Italians arrived in the United States; in 1907, 285,000 entered; on the eve of World War I, in 1914, 296,414 made their way through American ports.

[1]See generally Giuseppe Lucrezia Monticelli, "Italian Emigration: Basic Characteristics and Trends with Special Reference to the Post-War Years," in S.M. Tomasi and M.H. Engel, eds., *The Italian Experience in the United States* (New York: Center for Migration Studies, 1970), pp. 3-22.

[2] Erik Amfitheatrof, *The Children of Columbus: An Informal History of the Italians in the New World* (Boston: Little, Brown, 1973), p. 138.

3

By 1920 there were more than 1.5 million persons of Italian birth in the United States. In the thirty year period from 1891 to 1920, some four million Italians entered the United States.[4] In whatever time-frames, the magnitude of Italian migration to the United States is staggering; and only its magnitude can explain the restrictive quotas of the 1920s which were reactions (cast in the social Darwinism of the period) to the fears of Anglo-Saxons expressed by population statisticians who attempted to show "what disastrous results awaited a country in which 50 Roumanian or Italian peasants would have a perfect army of offspring in several generations whereas the stock of 50 Harvard or Yale men would probably be extinct within the same length of time."[5]

Grazia Dore is correct in noting that significance of Italian emigration is to be fully understood by examining the social and historical environment from which it developed, and her perceptive analyses represent a starting point from which the extraordinary emigration is to be approached. The conceptual framework in which she studies organized emigration from the Italian peninsula following unification, the new institutions needed to effect this process of emigration, the twin dynamics of "emigration to nationalism," and the future which would "impede 'the great proletarian nation' from pushing its sons to emigrate," remains (allowing its neo-Marxian subtleties) the best introduction to a complex historical phenomenon.[6] Robert F. Foerster's "Coming of the Italians" is drawn from his classic *The Italian Emigration of Our Times* (1919) which still remains the basic work on Italian emigration to all parts of the world

---

[3] "It is not easy to ascertain the number of Italo-Americans, and different figures are given according to different criteria of calculation. For example, *Il Popolo Italiano*, a Philadelphia newspaper, and *Fra Noi*, a Chicago newspaper, seem to have estimated in 1963 and 1969 that, if one included the generations after the second (with which official statistics stop) there would be 21 and a half million persons of Italian descent, half of whom are living on the Eastern Coast (New York, New Jersey, Pennsylvania, Connecticut, and Massachusetts). However, according to an interesting demographic study by Massimo Livi-Bacci, *L'immigrazione e l'assimilazione degli Italiani negli Stati Uniti secondo le statistiche demografiche Americane* (Milano, 1961) in 1950, there were in the United States no fewer than 7 million people, belonging to three generations, who have at least one Italian grandparent. No doubt closer to the truth seems the figure of 15 to 16 million Americans who consider themselves to be Italian Americans." Giuseppe L. Monticelli, *loc. cit.*, p. 18.

[4] Manlio A. D'Ambrosio, *Il Mezzogiorno d'Italia e l'Emigrazione negli Stati Uniti* (Roma: Athenaeum, 1924).

[5] Carl Wittke, *We Who Build America: The Saga of the Immigrant* (Englewood Cliffs, N.J.: Prentice-Hall, 1939), p. 406. For nativism and restrictive immigration policy, see John Higham, *Strangers in the Land: Patterns of American Nativism, 1860-1925* (New Brunswick, N.J.: Rutgers University Press, 1955); and the same author's "Another Look at Nativism," *Catholic Historical Review*, 44 (July 1958), pp. 147-158. A very useful study of American immigration policy is Robert A. Divine, *American Immigration Policy, 1924-1952* (New Haven: Yale University Press, 1957).

for the period it covers. Foerster is, of course, a man of his time, and he surveys all that he sees with the cold objectivity of the economist; but he is not without a condescending sympathy for the objects of his study. At the end of his *magnum opus,* he plaintively observed:

> "Among ten illiterate emigrants, only two perhaps will ɔucceed in clearing themselves a path to moderate gains," Sig. Franzoni once declared, and he recommended that the illiterate be prevented from emigrating. But illiteracy is only one evidence of ill preparedness. The tragedy of emigration lies precisely in this, that it exacts energetic and well directed effort of a mass generally ill fitted therefor. The fact that a man wishes to sally forth is no proof that all is well. There is no one "emigration" by which he can gauge his chances of success; there are emigrations—to Buenos Aires, to Delaware, last year, this year, by one kind of person or another—and the variability of circumstances, according as one year or country or collection of personal attributes is taken, makes any inference from others' fortunes difficult. Italy, we have seen, has recognized the blindness to which the emigrant masses are heir by so far assuming responsibility for their decisions as, from time to time, to suspend emigration to particular regions. But it is by no means certain that the responsibility should not be exercised oftener and in more diverse ways.

> No one can follow the fortunes of the Italians abroad without being struck by a sort of contempt in which they are often held, "Dago," "gringo," "carcamano," "badola," "cincali," "macaroni"—how long the list of epithets might be! "Italy feeds nobody and is everybody's guest" was the widely quoted utterance of a Frenchman. Whether such names and such opinions originate in the laborer's resentment of competition or in the citizen's easy association of objectionable or misunderstood personal attributes with the idea of the foreigner, they but emphasize the discomfort of the Italians and stir up a sense of shame in Italy. In the Parliament at Rome frequent reference has been made to the dislike in which Italians have been held in the United States, and such men as San Giuliano and Tittoni believed there were reasons for it. Those who have most lauded the Greater Italy of the emigrants have realized its circumscriptions. Money confers a respect and an influence (that of England for example in Argentina) to which toil cannot attain. The Greater Italy is an empire—but a proletari-

----

[6]Beyond the article included in the text (one of the few pieces by Dore in English), reference should be made to her elaborate study, *La Democrazia Italiana e L'Emigrazione in America* (Brescia: Morcelliana, 1964) which includes a vast bibliography on the history of Italian emigration to America.

ate empire. It bestrides the world like a Colossus—but a Colossus arrayed in rags. (pp. 503-504)

Beyond the invaluable materials by Dore and Foerster, I have chosen to include a variety of other pieces which establish multi-dimensional perspectives from which the human phenomenon which was the emigration is to be viewed. G. E. DiPalma Castiglione and Gustavo Tosti furnish official Italian views; and if Tosti's views (as Italian Consul-General in New York) are the circumspect observations of the official abroad, DiPalma Castiglione's micro-analysis of Italian immigration for the years 1901-1904 is a superb orchestration of overwhelming data. Gino C. Speranza, who was later to become a super American nationalist and a restrictionist, is better seen in the posture of the searching examination of the Italian Emigration Department as it existed in 1904, and in his interview of Adolfo Rossi.[7] Actually, it is in the short kaleidoscopic vignettes which I have brought together that the human experience of what emigration was is best seen: in the impressionistic pieces by Charles B. Phipard, William E. Davenport, Willard Price, and Victor Von Borosini; in "An Italian's Advise to Italian Immigrants;" and in Signorina Cesarina Lupati's poignant plea for steerage reform: "When the ship touched the dock and the crowd, eager for deliverance, rushed to the gangway, I saw them—ragged, begrimed—in sullen violence or apathetic stupor unaware of their destiny—I saw them, ashamed for Italy for whom we toil, pray or die—Italy never to be truly glorious and great till she heeds the silent groan from her peasants' bitter lips."

---

[7]Gino C. Speranza (1872-1927), who was Secretary of the Society for the Protection of Italian Immigrants, is a neglected figure who deserves a full scale study; his letters and papers are deposited in the New York Public Library. See his *Race or Nationality: A Conflict of Divided Loyalties* (Indianapolis: Bobbs Merrill, 1920).

GRAZIA DORE

SOME SOCIAL AND HISTORICAL ASPECTS OF ITALIAN EMIGRATION TO AMERICA*

In order to understand fully the significance of Italian emigration it is necessary to make a brief examination of the social and historical environment from which it developed. This environment imprinted certain characteristics on emigration so strongly that they persisted throughout the entire period in which the phenomenon of emigration occurred.

In the first place, organized emigration from the Italian peninsula began only after Unification, in a moment when the Italian government, torn by civil strife, was entirely preoccupied with maintaining its very existence and therefore could not give the emigrants more than superficial, desultory attention. Thus before the central power became aware of the exodus and concerned itself with the rural areas, emigration was occurring in an original, autonomous and individual way without the aid of politicians, technicians, experts or the educated, drawing only upon rural experience and popular culture. New in-stitutions were not needed to effect this process of emigration which until a few years before had been so unexpected and unimaginable. Indeed, the characteristics of the old rural community structures were so solid and at the same time so resilient that no subsequent provisions of the Italian or the American governments succeeded in replacing them. One might venture to say that some typical village social relations which observers in the past century had already judged relics of another age, destined soon to disappear, proved, on the contrary, to be so useful in emigration that sometimes Italian communities in America showed a certain regression in their cus-toms even in comparison to the rustic world from which they had come.

Thus it is impossible to understand the first emigrants, those who typified so much of the Italian presence across the ocean, without first knowing who the peasants of the peninsula were.

To the young Italian nation, this very question was among its most agonizing problems: how to understand its rural areas and to be

Journal of Social History (Winter, 1968), pp. 95-122. Reprinted with permission.

7

understood and accepted by them. The ruling classes wondered how the very religious Northerners, for example, or the Southerners who were also passionately bound to their religious traditions, would be able to respect the authority of a state which now, after the conflict with the Church, bore the responsibility for its total desecration.

Another fear was added: The government and its opposition, moderates and democrats, were blaming each other for the alleged lack of participation on the part of peasants in the struggles for Unification. The democrats said that the moderates had excluded the peasants in order to prevent the fight for Unification from assuming a revolutionary character; the moderates retorted that the opposition's propaganda was based on abstract democratic principles rather than concrete concern for the populace. Moreover, no one was forgetting how Garibaldi's promise of land distribution had carried the masses in the South and had not yet been accomplished. Therefore it was inevitable to fear that mass emigration could assume dangerous political significance.

Yet there were those who pointed out that the peasant's acceptance of Italian Unification was undeniable, since Unification could not have been accomplished if the peasants, the enormous majority of the Italian population, had not wanted it. However, those unfamiliar with the peasants found it difficult to evaluate the peculiar ways in which the peasants expressed themselves, since their world appeared so reserved and isolated.

The Italian village was a community in which ties among the inhabitants were so close and complex that the village resembled a cooperative association rather than a town hall government. Often each region had a style of dressing that, by means of some variation in colors and ornaments, served to distinguish it from even its closest neighbors. These visible signs indicated membership in a particular group inside of which more restricted relations and neighborhoods were formed, linked together by diverse types of bonds. The struggles, for whatever appearance of power or prestige, were very violent. The detailed rules which regulated agrarian contracts, the relationships between various categories of peasants, shepherds, laborers and the enrollments for seasonal work constituted, in themselves, a field of knowledge which gave to the humble experts, even when they were illiterates, an envied authority which was never transgressed. In the South, above all, despite the easy use of violence, one is struck by the deferential attitude toward those who, often simply because they knew how to read and write, were in a position to act as mediators between the peasants and the government. These, whom we can call the intellectuals of the village, not because of their possession of any kind of culture, but for the functions which they exercised, did not at this time think of abandoning their clients, as they did later when the immense development of state bureaucracy furnished them with a myriad of small jobs, distorting their relationship with the rural areas. At that time they were an integral part of peasant life: They were relatives, neighbors, and associates. Many solicited the emigrants to leave, while others accompanied them to America and became their "padroni."

Italian agriculture, which had appeared prosperous before the agrarian revolution overthrew the old rural economies, could no longer sustain the confrontation with more progressive nations. It had become conscious of its poverty and feared the future. Not only, in fact, was there a lack of necessary capital to undertake new methods of farming, but, in a country still without industries, all the fiscal burdens fell upon the agriculturists. Their resources were so sparse that the population of the peninsula, which in 1861 slightly exceeded 20 million inhabitants, was already beginning to seem excessive in relation to income from the land. In addition, the constant rhythm of Italy's demographic growth was a growing worry.[1]

The rural areas were therefore a political, economic and social unknown. There was an awareness of the pressing need to provide for their integration, their direct participation in national life, but even this was feared and an attempt was made to delay the process. The rural areas were excluded in practice by confining the electorate to those who could demonstrate a knowledge of reading and writing and who possessed some, even if a modest, income. This, it must be remembered, was at a time when the illiteracy rate was extremely high.

Quite often signs of impatience and anger appeared in the rural areas and between 1860 and 1865 brigandage ran rampant in the South. Almost everywhere, disorder and unrest, which were usually rapidly quelled, would blaze and then die out. A law passed in 1867 affecting the consumption of bread exacerbated the situation still further. At the end of that year it was noted that in the port of Genoa peasants appeared, more numerous than usual and without any explanation of what had brought them, not only from the arid zone of the South, but also from fertile regions of Lombardy and Emilia. Everybody was embarking for the Americas.[2]

---

[1]For the conditions of agriculture and the Italian peasants after Unification, see especially the *Atti della Giunta Parlamentare per l'inchiesta agraria e sulle condizioni delle classi agricole* (Rome, 1881-1886).

[2]These and other reports, though all incomplete, on the first period of emigration are found scattered through the newspapers of the period and in a vast number of publications, among which are the *Atti* cited above and Leone Carpi's *Delle colonie e dell'emigrazione italiana all'Estero* (Milan, 1874).

The first alarm was sounded in Parliament on January 30, 1868: "These people," said a deputy from the Lombard region, "are leaving Italy cursing and in tears." In reality, the true feeling of those who were departing was only partially expressed by such lamentations. The Italian rural world, formerly like a frozen, immobile stream on which time had designed bizarre incrustations of archaic customs and magic rites, survivors of the death of the culture which had created them, was beginning to manifest deep breaks and to flow, at first slowly, then more impetuously, in unprecedented directions.

Nonetheless, the movement of emigration continued, within moderate bounds, during the first decade of the Italian Kingdom and according to projections, not completely accurate, reached the massive figure of 22,201 emigrants in 1869.[3] It is necessary to note, however, that not everyone left simply in search of land or work. Secret recruiters, scattered here and there throughout Italy before 1870, enrolled robust young men for the agricultural military colonies in Latin America where there was a need not only for colonists, but also for soldiers. This was not altogether distasteful to public opinion, since it corresponded to a tradition represented by Garibaldi himself, the beloved national symbol, who as a fighter in South America and worker in the United States exemplified the first wave of emigration, among many other things, and gave it a certain stamp of popular approval.

Many hoped that eventually Latin America, especially the Plata, would offer opportunities to the Italians not inferior to those offered elsewhere to Anglo-Saxons, even if very different. There, claimed these publicists, Italians could show the world an entirely new model of peaceful colonization, as new as they wished Italy to be—not only a nation newly-born but a nation inspired by fresh concepts and actions. Consequently, in the region of the Plata, according to ardent idealists, there should have arisen "a greater Italy" bound to the peninsula by undefined ties of idealism which would have excluded any kind of subjection whether economic or political.[4]

Perhaps it is difficult today to realize how dear to the souls of men, above all to the democrats of the time, was the hope that Italy would not become just another state in a Europe already overcrowded with states, but a better and different one, even if they did not succeed in defining exactly the ways in which she was to be different. Unfortunate-

[3]All the statistical reports are contained in the *Annuario statistico dell' emigrazione italiana dal 1876 al 1925*, published under the direction of the Commissariate for Emigration (Rome, 1926).

[4]See Attilio Brunialti, *Le colonie degli Italiani* (Turin, 1897); Luigi Einaudi, *Un principe mercante, Studio sull'espansione coloniale italiana* (Turin, 1900).

ly, precision has never been a characteristic of generous ideas. Even the governing powers showed some interest in the conditions of compatriots overseas and, beginning with the first census of the Italian Kingdom in 1861, they sought to determine their numbers. They were not called emigrants, but rather Italians abroad, and it was assumed that their presence would help develop trade with the countries where they settled. For this purpose, the Sardinian government in 1853 had encouraged Genoese shipowners to establish regular lines which would connect Buenos Aires with Genoa every month, touching Rio de Janeiro and New York. For the moment the project was unsuccessful and no one could have foreseen the incessant tide of men who within a few years would disembark on the shores of the Atlantic, following the course of the first precarious transports and of the Sicilian and Neopolitan sailing ships which trafficked with the United States bringing citrus fruit, sulphur, and sumach.

It was rather the necessity of substituting steamships for sailing boats which induced a shipbuilder of Palermo to call upon the English Anchor Line, which later actively competed in the traffic of emigrants from Sicily. Along with this, companies of navigation suddenly appeared in the ports of the peninsula, where their agents assembled the peasants prepared for embarkation.[5]

The interest of the ruling classes, however, remained solely concerned with relations with Plata, and one must note the preference given to this generic appellation rather than to the precise titles of Argentina and Uruguay. This preference was due certainly to the region's geographical vagueness which permitted thinking of the country as still undefined and therefore without a real national designation. Subsidies were therefore granted to the shipowners Thomas Pertica and to the Marittima G. B. Lavarello Company, to increase travel to the *Italo Platense;* the latter company for some time made regular trips.

Another reason for the partiality for the Plata was soon added: The community of the Plata seemed the only one destined in the future to acquire enough political prestige to compensate for Italy's lack of participation in the conquest of Africa, then underway among the European powers, which was condoned by one section of public opinion and condemned by another. Furthermore, in that first period only Northerners poured into the Plata territory, coming from those Italian regions which were deemed most capable of becoming part of mod-

---

[5]No complete study on the trade of the emigrants exists. One can usefully consult the *Inchiesta parlamentare sulla Marina Mercantile* (Rome, 1882-1883) and the Parliamentary discussion on the December 30, 1888 law (19th legislature) and the January 1, 1901 law (21st legislature).

ern civilization—a modern civilization which even those Italian states which had been poor and decrepit wished now to enter resolutely, forcing, so to speak, the doors of history which for a long time had confined them to the borders of Europe. As to the Southerners, those who doubted their ability to "make Italy" believed much less that they could "make America."

The illusions about a colonizing emigration, encouraged but not controlled by the government whose liberalism was inconsistent with direct intervention, were soon contradicted by the facts, for the apparent disorderliness of the emigration greatly surprised observers. The peasants did not appear, unexpected in their imaginative attire, solely in places of embarkation in the peninsula with which the rural areas had had periodic interests and contacts. For example, the Prefect of Turin in 1872 signalled the passage of from fifty to eighty persons per day who arrived from the South, especially from Potenze, and went to France to embark for the Americas.[6]

The most difficult and painful decision was to leave one's own village to which, by comparison, all other countries appeared equally strange. It should be remembered that the diversity of dress, traditions and language among the Italian provinces was great in a world which loved to differentiate itself at least as much as it wishes today to conform. Much depended therefore on leaving Italy and until nuclei of compatriots were established, who could be joined overseas, many abandoned their choice of destination to shipping agents. They completed incredible voyages in their total ignorance of geography and distances. A certain man—Bonelli, of whom little is known except that he was an agent—was able in 1874 to conduct a frightened herd of about 150 emigrants from the small village of Lucania to Lima.

Entire families poured into the stations of Venetia with the unmistakable signs of poverty on their faces. In 1876, it was above all the hope of free land across the ocean which led to the departure of many small proprietors from the peninsula. After having sold everything else, they were permitted to bring with them 150 lire per person and from 400 to 800 lire per family. These groups travelled toward Brazil and even toward Venezuela. Mayors and other persons in authority tried in vain to dissuade them although there were also some, among their own poverty-striken pastors and medical men, who encouraged them to leave.

One Genoese recruiter alone succeeded in encouraging hundreds to emigrate before some pretext was found to arrest him. Some of the

---

[6]Reports of the prefects in Carpi, *Statistica illustrata dell'emigrazione italiana all'Estero*, for the three-year period from 1874 to 1876 (Rome, 1878) pp. 82-112.

peasants even told of a palace replete with delicacies where a queen would welcome them in Marseilles. Such force did these stories have that, in 1876, out of 3233 Venetian emigrants, 1146 embarked at this port, suspecting that those who gave them contrary advice were in league with the very wealthy who wished to ruin the poor people.

The pain of departure was surpassed by a vigorous vital impulse, by the enthusiastic conviction of accomplishing an altogether new act, and by the invigoration of finally choosing one's own destiny after centuries of passivity. In 1877, emigrants crossed Venice on the way to the point of embarkation with the cry, "Viva l'Italia, Viva Vittorio Emanuele. To America, to America!"

The liberation from Austria for some regions, the unification of the peninsula for all, gave concrete proof of how much the will of the people could accomplish. Nations could be made as Italy had been made, according to the expression common in those years in Europe. In other words, destiny was no longer determined and immutable. Many young people questioned by those collecting information on the emigration movement replied that they were going to make themselves Americans, but this did not conflict with their national pride since it was also a sign of the liberty achieved by the new Italian state.

By contrast Lombardy, which within a brief period would see agrarian strikes and peasant associations with socialistic overtones, presented quite a different picture. Around 1877 in the provinces of Cremona, Crema and Montova, families who had previously never heard of Argentina or Brazil decided to go there through means which seemed downright insurrectionary to the landed proprietors. They rioted, set fire to dairy farms, and protested violently against the delay in the release of passports. The habitual cry of "To America" rang menacingly to the great Lombard proprietors, who had not forgotten their old fear of the rural areas when Austria tried to restrain their desire for independence by threatening an agrarian reform which would have placed them in opposition to the peasants. In fact, these proprietors were among the first to ask for governmental precautionary measures against the emigrants, despite the fact that these never reached significant numbers in Lombardy and indeed soon decreased because of the region's agriculture, to which enormous capital investments flowed.

Ligurians and Piedmontese meanwhile continued to set out— traditionally by now—toward the Plata and free passages pushed the most destitute peasants, primarily Venetians, in the direction of Brazil. Among their poor belongings a handful of seeds was often jealously guarded, which would serve to lessen the strangeness of that unknown land. From Central Italy emigration was still insignificant, but the mysterious South increased relations with the United States to such an extent that it was already noted in 1869 that of 148 Italian ships arriving in New York, 100 had come from the South.

Until 1876 the emigrants remained limited in number; at most 19,610 had gone to the Americas, of whom 14,724 were from Northern Italy, 1,067 from Central Italy and 3,809 from the South. What worried the ruling class, however, was that the state was taking no role at all. There was reason to fear that the break between the state power and the agriculturalists, between the religious regions and the cities, between the ideology of laymen and official culture would broaden, since, in fact, underneath the superficial uniformity of the Italian laity fermented a cultural and social agitation which could neither be explained or suppressed. It was also true that the abstention of Catholics from voting made many urban centers as politically impotent in practice as the peasants were.

Any move stirring in the decrepit agricultural world greatly alarmed property owners, convinced that their decayed systems could only be maintained through immobility and that changing one thing would mean the breakdown of all. It was thought that only the low cost of manual labor due to an abundance of man power could assure profits to the proprietors. Whenever, then, a diminution in the number of cultivators occurred and resulted in a rise in salaries, the land could no longer produce enough to compensate for the trouble of owning it. The proprietors therefore insisted that it was necessary to impede the departure of men.[7]

Nonetheless, many voices arose in defense of peasant liberty, and in the great 1870 Inquiry into conditions of land laborers, the sad history of the agriculturalist was observed: slaves during the major part of the Roman Empire, later serfs, then freed but subjected to every kind of imposition, as miserable in their civil status as in the very unhappy conditions of their daily lives. Their civil inferiority compelled them to endure dire poverty, but now their equality under the law, their participation in the establishment of the state, and their defense of it by obligatory conscription—indeed the whole tendency of the dominant, liberal ideals—had awakened in them the aspiration to become "something" and to count in proportionate measure to their capacities. It can now be added that the votes of the South, which represented the most impoverished agriculture, in effect contributed to the downfall of the Historical Right *(Destra storica)* in 1876.

[7]The relation between emigration and the landowners is illustrated, in particular, by F. S. Nitti, *L'emigrazione italiana e i suoi avversari* (Turin, 1888).

The classical traditions which dominated Italian culture maintained the necessity, considered perpetual, of sacrificing the farm areas to the power of the city, agriculture to industry. This theme, dominant in the works of the historians and Latin poets, was very much alive in the memory of those who governed and had been nurtured in these studies. But they interpreted the basic elements of this theme to suit themselves. The antithesis appeared as intolerable as it had been when the country was called a Republic or an Empire, humble Italy or Grand Rome. And those interests which formed around emigration were powerful and militant also, no less so than those of the big agrarians.

The group which began to oppose the Societies of Navigation was obviously tied to the growing big industry and the small rural bourgeoisie on one side and the landowners on the other, but the conflict between them was still too recent to allow a clear realization of the significance that emigration would soon acquire. Broadening of the suffrage was, by now, inevitable and moved toward completion with the reform of 1882. The electoral weight of the big property owners was less than was commonly thought since they often lived in the city and did not have as direct a contact with the villages as did the small peasant bourgeoisie of middlemen, who had been taught by Italian history to be compromisers. Ultimately, it was the rural bourgeoisie who provided and handled the clientele. The rich *signore* was so utterly dependent on this peasant bourgeoisie that in many localities he could impose his will directly only by outright violence and the use of mace-bearers and other armed men.

It was not until January 12, 1888 that the first emigration law was approved, however inadequate and incomplete. Until then the property owners had only obtained the issuance of two circulars by the Minister of the Interior, one on January 18, 1868, and the other on January 18, 1873, as oppressive as they were useless.[8] These required that the emigrant, whose irremediable misery was well known, had to demonstrate a natural ability to support himself, an assured occupation abroad, and a solvent person who would assure in writing his willingness to pay for a return voyage should it become necessary for the emigrant to come back.

In Parliament there were protesters from many sides who claimed that the government had arbitrarily intervened in favor of the landowners to impede the freedom of work contracts and an eventual rise in agricultural salaries which even then would be insufficient for

[8]*Raccolta di circolari e istruzioni ministeriali dal I gennaio 1861 al 30 settembre 1904* (Rome, 1905).

the most miserable conditions of existence. The facts proved them right: The number of clandestine emigrants, who came primarily from agriculture, rose from 1,768 in 1873 to 3,471 in 1876, according to partial and inexact calculations.

In fact, however, with few exceptions the local authorities made very moderate use of the regulations and the thousands of departures continued, leaving now from Marseilles, Le Havre or Antwerp rather than from Genoa or Naples.

Even if they had not feared to abandon their liberal and democratic convictions openly, the ruling ranks would have hesitated to irritate the rural areas beyond tolerable limits anyway. Nothing seemed so terrifying as their possible revolt in those years when public opinion feared the thesis of the famous anarchist Michael Bakunin, that revolutionary socialism was ingrained in the Italian peasant. And it was also observed how frequently priests guided the peasant struggles in which tumultous processions raised images of the Madonna and the Saints. Whoever wanted to employ persuasion, regardless of how secular his convictions, had to use a language with religious intonation, which was the only erudite and therefore prestigious language known to the peasants and one which, in fact, had been adopted by the pioneers of socialism in the rural areas. Universal Catholicism worried some as international socialism worried others. Still, the overwhelming fact was the constant increase in population—26,801,-154 Italians in 1871, 28,459,626 Italians in 1881. Many observers were convinced that it was better for excess people to leave the country, though public opinion was saddened when, in 1872, there were 33,-552 emigrants and the common regret was repeated in Parliament: "Italians are leaving!"

The press of the time repeated that there was a name on the lips of many—Ireland—as if the Italian rural areas were occupied by a hostile foreign power which was called "the royal conquest." However, none of the many polemical efforts concerning emigration and no party zeal succeeded in proving that those who emigrated had a deliberate desire for political protest. Rather, one was astonished by their naive patriotism, the totally Italian and often brutally disillusioned conviction that they would not be considered foreigners in any part of the world. Supporting this belief was a single, precise fact: everywhere they had been preceded by men of their "blood." There was not a region on the globe in which street peddlers and hawkers in their intrepid poverty had not arrived, from where they could not have returned or could not have sent word through obscure channels unknown to official communication. And finally, there is the Italian proverb, half skeptical and half optimistic, which claims that "you will find the same village the world over."

Meanwhile, discussions on the emigration movement among economists, politicians and students of the social sciences grew heated. There were those who demanded the intervention of the state administration, citing the example of the admired or detested Germany, where the government undertook the professional preparation of the emigrants, supervised recruitment and embarkation operations and favored the use of capital in undertaking colonization.[9] Others feared that the state, preoccupied with political rather than economic issues, would favor the departure of those who were considered undesirables, without taking their productivity into account. Some calculated the loss in human capital in statistics or dwelt on the advantages to be derived from trade with the cities to which the peasants emigrated. Unanimously the impossibility of resolving the problem of emigration while the agricultural problem remained unsolved was admitted when the agrarian crisis which had hit Europe in 1874 was felt in Italy in 1880, after a delay due to Italy's slight ties with world commerce.

It seemed that the only hope for the salvation of the peasants lay in the search for new lands which should establish a secure, close and complementary relation with the land of origin. Therefore, said the supporters of colonial policies, emigration should not be directed toward America, where the Italians dispersed and vanished, as it were, but to Africa and, moreover, peacefully, because to Italy, until a short time before a conquered country, the idea of armed occupation was still repugnant.

Instead, it was France which proclaimed its protectorate of Tunisia in 1881 and the borders of Africa seemed lost to Italian colonizers and fishermen who formerly had operated there. There was much bitter resentment. The fear that Italy had become a nation too late to be able to compete with the already strong states of the West, too late indeed not to be suffocated by them, expressed itself in irrational and perilous forms of panic, resentment and a spirit of spite culminating ultimately, in a word, in fascism.

Soon unprecedentedly audacious actions were attempted; commercial penetration was considered, a political influence in Ethiopia. On January 26, 1887 an Italian column was caught by surprise and destroyed by the Abyssinians at Dogali. Italians could not penetrate into Africa save by weapons, blood, and sorrow. The disgust with what had happened gave greater force to those who maintained that the overabundant population should be encouraged to emigrate

[9]For all this see F. Manzotti, *La polemica sulla emigrazione nell'Italia Unita* (Milan, 1962).

to America. The time had come for a regulatory law on emigration.

But the emigration movement was by now a vital and complete system which would not tolerate changes, and those who had first provided its leadership made it quickly understood that they were not disposed to concede to anyone, much less to the state, either the gains or the obscure power which they believed had been tacitly delegated to them once and for all by the ruling classes. In effect, it did not escape the more alert observers that it was these leaders who were the true holders of political power in the South and as such they demonstrated a tactical capacity for compromise and resistance that prevented their defeat. Their defense was desperate. The customs tariff of 1887 had favored the new powers of industry and the farming of cereals, which was the most backward area of Italian agriculture, that of extensive cultivation and the latifundia. The transformation of Northern Italy from a purely agricultural country to an industrial one was facilitated, but the backwardness of the South was further aggravated by specialized cultivation, confined to an inadequate production of cereal that did not even guarantee sufficient bread for the area's own consumption.

The large latifundia owners of the South had discovered a dangerous community of interests with Northern capitalists and hoped, by the increase in tariffs, to impose a barrier on American competition and on emigration which would have rendered it difficult to abandon the rural areas. But at this point interests diverged: the departures were necessary for the merchant marine, the shipyards and the industries tied to them, and were one of the very few resources of Naples.

In Parliament no significant voice arose to defend the proposals of the agrarians. The December 30, 1888 law officially guaranteed the freedom of emigration, attempting however to impose some restraint on the activity of those without legal authorization who, whether as business agencies or as private individuals, and often secretly, completed arrangements concerning the choice of American countries, the sale of tickets for the voyage and transportation to points of embarkation.[10] The heads of the agencies had now to request a government license to qualify as emigration agents or their deputies as subagents. The government affirmed its right to control and limit recruitments, in regard both to the provinces in which they were undertaken and to the countries of destination. De-

[10]See *La legislazione sull'emigrazione*, treated by the Commissariato per l'emigrazione (Rome, 1913). For emigratory Italian politics, see Grazia Dore, "La politica dell'emigrazione dall'Unita al fascismo" in *La democrazia italiana e l'emigrazione in America* (Brescia, 1964), pp. 31-108.

tailed rules were to safeguard emigrants from eventual frauds, against which the possibility of free legal recourse was provided. The connection between the peasants and the subagents of the villages was so distinctive, however, that very few appeals were presented despite frequent and open violations of the law.

It was clear that the state for the moment renounced the creation of a viable emigration service of its own, one capable of replacing the system formed in an anarchy of interests without any moderating authority in the society of the time. Although there was a tendency toward centralization of power in Italy, public opinion allowed historical forces, independent of the state, to operate autonomously and thus escape the general leveling trend. The Italian rural areas, in this as in other cases, showed a very particular tenacity in their refusal to become objects of complete administration, and consequently the same people continued to do things as before although accusations of indoctrinating and manipulating the masses and pushing them to expatriation did not cease.

During the decade which preceded the law the methods by which emigration agents operated had been investigated and described empirically and efficiently. The observation of social phenomena, much in vogue in those years, did not yet possess a technique but rather expressed the attempt to approach reality with a new scientific spirit, both directly and individually, without the apparatus of preliminary studies, consultations, reports, and committees. We know from these modest but acute and tireless observers that the instruments being used by the American republics, the navigation society and the agencies, were all extremely simple.[11]

Posters were sent to the South, even to the smallest communities, indicating the price and date of voyages to the Americas. The most varied people took it upon themselves to convince the future emigrants and to sell them tickets: auditors, priests, pharmacists, postmen and copyists. These latter served as secretaries for the illiterates on those occasions when it was essential to know how to read and write. In the zones where education was more widespread, the posters were even placed around farmsteads. Everywhere men went about—to market places and fairs—to approach the peasants and convince them of the fortunes of America. If and when the peasants were also warned of the difficulties they would encounter, they chose not to listen, especially if they suspected that the warning came from people interested in keeping them tied to their landlords.

---

[11]Many reports are contained in *Statistica dell'emigrazione italiana all'Estero,* ed. Direzione Generale della Statistica (Rome, 1881-1888).

It is unquestionable that the propaganda had to display a strong social tenor, a summons to ancient utopian motives. It is not a coincidence that the years in which the emigration of the masses began were also the years of the first libertarians, of agitators and anarchists, of Bakunin but also of David Lazzaretti. America was the promised land to the poor, as opposed to the old world where land was denied the peasant.

But since secrecy was the pivot of social relationships in Southern society, even the existence of agencies was denied as much as possible in the South and they masqueraded under different names. In Campania, Calabria and Lucania, where secrecy dominated customs with particular force, the people hired to explain matters of booking and recruitment were secretly notified by letter.

A fund of information came in incessantly from the countryside around Naples and Genoa. Rural society had always been accustomed to providing its own means of existence. It did not occur to the peasant to seek help elsewhere to arrange his affairs before his departure, to procure the necessary money, to complete his indispensable business or to procure information on the cities of destination. There were qualified people in the village. They performed the tasks necessary to obtain passports, negotiated for the sale of the peasant's meagre house or small fields and directed the emigrant to small hotels in the port while awaiting embarkation. Scarcely then had a small group of fellow villagers formed a nucleus of compatriots across the ocean than the peasants reconstituted their old customs, the old mediations appeared again, the frightening rural usury followed them, providing labor contracts and assuring the first terrifying relations with the ensnaring bankers, bosses or "padroni."

The school teachers, the postal directors, the pharmacists, the landlords, the emigration agents, the many people in the South equipped with a modest education but without work had been looking for over a generation for such a complex activity which, however, never forced them to alter their former social functions or the techniques of persuasion and mediation which they had always used. Although they were often the objects of cruel exchanges, the emigrants considered these agents an integral and necessary part of their society. They saw them living in the village and sharing in their own destiny. From time immemorial they had been accustomed to being represented before the outside world and therefore preferred these agents to a functionary who, by comparison, would have represented exactly that world in all its strangeness.[12]

The state had not succeeded in intervening in time. So the rural

[12]Dore, pp. 38-54.

areas, which had opposed the attempt to destroy their social structures, brought them almost intact to America and the approved law
was rendered practically inoperative.

Many studies had been made, besides those on the persons
promoting emigration, on the causes of the emigration movement.[13]
The landowners, as we have seen, maintained that it was an artificial movement created to satisfy the interests of speculators. Their
contentions were based on the apparent immobility of the rural
world and on its presumed inexperience in any form of organization. They did not see, nor did they wish to see, how Italian agriculture in some regions, especially those from which emigration
was greatest, paradoxically remained almost nomadic, with a structure based on this nomadism. Often the peasants did not live on the
fields they cultivated but travelled long distances to reach them.

They emigrated from the mountains to the plains at the peak of
the harvest season or crossed the sea, as the Calabrese did who
went to reap in Sicily. Hearing that there were other grounds for
sublease in better conditions, they would leave the key under the
door of their miserable huts in which no one could have found
anything to rob and even travel out of the province. Public labor
jobs had accustomed them to activity beyond the purely traditional;
long lines of laborers and barrow pushers had gone into the construction of railroads and into land reclamation. Therefore, the
agricultural classes had a different relationship with the land from
that generally acknowledged. They preferred an immediate salary
to a long range gain. Their proletarianization had increased enor-
mously and they sought more immediate gains, however slight, in
money rather than precarious ones from insufficient property; even
the very poorest small proprietors sought employment. Old customs,
furthermore, had trained them in the discipline of contractual dealings assigned to the experts of the villages. The study of techniques
of emigration contracts and recruitment among the agriculturalists
can show not only the tyranny to which the peasants were constantly subjected but also the methods by which they always attempted, even if within fiercely restricted limits with feeble means,
to defend some essential rights and even to pursue insofar as they
could their own economic policies, precisely as they did in emigration. The poverty of the results and the apparent disorder with which
they accomplished all this sometimes casts undeserved discredit on
the ability and the tenacity of the resistance of rural areas, which on

[13]It is impossible to cite the vast bibliography, primarily composed of polemical
pamphlets. Most important is the *Inchiesta* cited above and the parliamentary
discussions.

the contrary revealed their true effectiveness in this case; when the peasants, in spite of everything, wanted to cross the seas, they did so without undergoing any modification in the structure of their society—in fact, they did so by virtue of this structure.

Responding to the investigations that the Director General of Statistics made annually from 1878 on, the majority of the prefects indicated that the determining factors in the exodus were destitution, the absence of property owners from their land, the speculations of subtenants, insufficient salaries, and the flight of capital from agriculture to the dominant cities. Whether he went elsewhere in Europe or to the Americas, there seemed only one law for the emigrant, superior to any psychological incentive which came from the agencies or from the summons of intimates who had already left: the disproportion between earnings and the necessities of existence, between economic conditions in the cities of emigration and those offered by the cities of immigration.

The problem of the peasants—the fear that the religious rural areas would reject the state with its liberal institutions having disappeared—was no longer political but social, and the same groups which at first had wanted to put obstacles in the way of emigration were now eager to facilitate it. Socialism was the new spectre for the ruling classes after the first strike of land laborers, which occured in Mantovano in 1872. Other strikes followed and the peasant movement was beginning to organize. Now the formerly feared emigration was considered by many as a downright "savior."

Still, no economic calculation, no effort to obtain the tranquil enjoyment of well-being at any cost could be made without somebody shouting scandal against the inhumane system of recruitments, which lacked any guarantee for the emigrants with whom recruiters insisted on unjust contracts.

Usually the propaganda in favor of Argentina was excluded from the criticisms although the exorbitant promises which sometimes accompanied it did awaken some alarm (as for example in a manifesto published in Naples in 1871 on behalf of a French Navigation company). In 1871 51,106 Italians lived in Argentina, 254,388 in 1881, 452,000 in 1891 and so on in swelling numbers. Hope continued that the Plata was the country of Italian "colonies without a flag" and that the incredibly great power of the General Italian Navigation Society was able in any case to support the interests of a policy of settlement in the region. There was no objection therefore when entire families of workmen were hired for the construction of the city of Plata for the building of Argentine railroads.

There were some reservations about the United States: for example, the enrollment in 1881 of Lombard laborers for road work in the distant, unknown state of Texas caused objections. Above all, the unpredicted flight of Southerners toward North America was certainly not justified by any similarity of civilization, language or race which, on the other hand, did recommend their exodus to the Latin countries. But here the perilous equilibrium of the South was involved and the emigrants' choice could not be upset when the ruling classes had no alternatives to offer. In addition there was the invincible cohesion of the rulers' familiar clientele and electoral supporters who would have imposed respect for their interests.

There remained Brazil toward which emigration was incredibly intense. The movement became a veritable mass exodus in Venetia where 71,796 departures occurred in 1888 and 70,010 in 1891.

It was true that recruitment occurred for all the American countries and even Argentina used it, largely through Ligurian shipowners. It was effected in such a manner that emigration toward the Plata appeared spontaneous. Workers were also signed up for the United States, though provisions that the United States government had to take to restrain them should be noted. But for North America the system of formal recruitment was due to the need to industrialize the overabundant Southern masses, who were forced to turn abroad because of the incapacity of Italian industry to absorb them. It was always Southern society that retained direction and control with the old corporals and "padroni" who maintained these titles even across the ocean.

The recruiters for Brazil were reproached for providing for the population of these immense regions without any regard for public opinion. The first big Venetian exodus, occuring in 1888 when the wound of the abortive penetration of Africa was still fresh, could have appeared as a painful confirmation of Italian inability to resolve the problems of agriculture, either outside the peninsula or within its borders, and the exodus had certainly contributed to the approval of the emigration law. However, it is more important to note that from the beginning the choice of Brazil seemed to many observers less completely free than the initial choice of the Ligurians for the Plata and of the Southerners for the United States, responding to the interests of these respective societies, even if the speculations on the departures for North America and for Argentina were often no less impartial and merciless than those for Brazil.

There was news of colossal contracts, of recruiters scattered everywhere, of huge profits, infinitely greater than those acknowledged. Through the navigation societies, agencies, or individual recruiters, the money for the voyage and maintenance until emigrants found work was advanced to those signed up, with the obligation to repay from future earnings. The usury claimed was such, however, that sometimes the debt remained inextinguishable and it was not unknown for an emigrant to have to repay 100 ducats in paper with 150 ducats in gold. Typical contracts drawn up for Brazil or for other countries stipulated that those leaving had to form a group, composed for the most part of eight or ten persons jointly responsible to the creditor, so that if one of the group should die en route or in America, those remaining were liable for the dead man's debt with its matured or maturing interest. The creditor could even be granted the authority to confiscate money being sent to an emigrant's family from the post office if he failed to make payment.

All this, as we have noted, was not peculiar to the Brazilian states since enlistments with paid voyages were the usual form wherever emigrants were going. The method assumed major proportions in that recruitment which, in order to beat the competition with the various American republics, turned to the most poverty-stricken and destitute of the masses.

The suffering of the emigrants, apparent to all, had neither defeated nor softened the coalition of interests formed at their expense or the selfishness of the ruling classes. No serious attempt had been made to protect the emigrants when, in 1887, news came that the Holy See was studying a way to provide for their material and spiritual interests and later the Bishop of Piacenza, Giovanni Battista Scalabrini, publicly intervened to help them and was given national acclaim for this charitable work.[14]

The prohibition against participation in elections and thus in the official politics of the country had divided Catholics into intransigents and compromisers and while the former wished to identify Italy solely with the people but not with the Italian state, the latter, among whom was Monsignor Scalabrini, were attempting a method of conciliation which, though still difficult in the peninsula, was being realized abroad wherever it was possible: this time in America.

The matter is less paradoxical than it seems since the difficulties with the church did not revolve, as they did in every other Catholic area, on the theoretical principle of the Papacy's temporal power, but rather on the Papacy's physical location within the boundaries of the Kingdom and of Rome. It was almost as if the dispute, absurdly, had geographical limits; outside of these the encounter

---

[14]G. B. Scalabrini, *L'emigrazione italiana in America* (Piacenza, 1887) and *Il disegno di legge sull'emigrazione* (Piacenza, 1888).

became easier. However, the Holy See had never, in fact, claimed that the population would resist with complete intransigence, especially the poor for whom, above all, isolation appeared very dangerous while the intervention of the State in their favor (an intervention which the State had so long been reluctant to offer) appeared increasingly necessary. The clergy often defended emigrants' rights, and this was also a way of affirming its true affiliation to the Italian people, substituting as best they could for the lack of state assistance, as did the two conciliatory bishops Scalabrini for transoceanic emigration and Bonomelli for temporary emigration in Europe.

Religion and emigration, according to the Bishop of Piacenza, could together prevent an immense catastrophe in the future, by both granting the excess population the possibility of living elsewhere and relieving their exile with faith. Charity, the real truce of God, could have quieted the wrath of the parties. The *Osservatore Romano*, the official organ of the Holy See, confirmed the significance of opening relations with the Italian state implicit in the welfare institutions for the emigrants, asserting that it would demonstrate how the concerns of religion and those of the nation were one and the same. Their "providential" reconciliation was one of the major benefits that these poor exiles could contribute to the fatherland.

Even the state authorities were pleased with this and with other missionary initiatives which followed, among which those of the Salesians and of Mother Cabrini can be recalled. There was no lack of dissent in the usual lay polemics which in some cases, however, had a mere ritual function, like someone completing a job which had become pure routine.

Perhaps the practical accord which we have mentioned was due to the fact that in America, among the Italo-Americans, there was no Catholic opposition to the Italian government which was in any way comparable to that of the peninsula. On the other hand, the secular and the Southern oppositions which controlled the Italian press abroad were vigorously represented. Every now and then when political events compelled the exile of republicans, democrats, anarchists and socialists, those among them who had some journalistic experience took part in establishing periodicals in the Americas which for a long time had a strong anticlerical tenor. Those who had no means of expressing themselves were the apolitical and religious multitudes, and one of the least studied and least noted aspects of their problem was the difficulty they encountered precisely because of their faith.

Many commonplaces concerning the alleged paganism of the Italian peasant have long existed and were widely current in the period of emigration. Exuberant popular ritual was enriched over a long period of centuries with ceremonies, devotions, processions and pilgrimages. Religion was the only cultural and artistic form in which peasants, excluded from the official culture, could express their timeless sociability. But under the luxuriant vestment of images there was a simple, austere faith, as was demonstrated by the fidelity to a sacred feeling for life and to the heavy sacrifices of everyday existence.

Nothing they had known in Italy could prepare the emigrants for what they had to experience across the ocean. Their religious piety was alarmed by the solitude of South America, where clergy was so scarce. They sent word that they were terrified of living "like animals," asking that their Italian priests be sent to them. Many unfortunates had been signed up with the promise of being led to the land where Jesus Christ had been born and died and instead, they wrote, these places were Hell.

Even more painful was the clash with other Catholic groups of different ethnic origin who accused the Italians of belonging to the country which had taken Rome from the Pope, a charge of which the peasant emigrants felt wholly innocent. The aggressive Irish Catholicism which predominated in the United States and which did not tolerate rivalry was sometimes unsympathetic toward the Italians' faith, which for its part was devoid of any nationalistic tenor. Perhaps the end of temporal power scandalized the Catholics of other countries more than it did the Italians, accustomed as they were to see it not in abstract terms but in the garb of a state in increasing decadence. It is probable, too, that no one then in America felt the universality of the Church as the Italian emigrants did and certainly no one was further from the temptations of a nationalistic Catholicism. The doubts now encountered even in this area and the bitterness expressed toward them caught the Italians by surprise and they were at first totally unprepared to defend themselves, even though the Holy See had recommended them to the compassionate understanding of the United States bishops.

In Italy, meanwhile, in the decade following the 1888 law it had become clear that the desired results could not be obtained from those who had agreed to check recruitment. On the contrary, though in 1890 emigration had been predominantly steered toward Argentina, from 1891 to 1897 Brazil had prevailed with its colossal contracts which drove 288,853 emigrants from Venetia alone. Least of all had the abuses of the agencies ceased. One still found Italians in European ports who, convinced that they had departed for America, had been traitorously disembarked and were begging for alms to continue their journey. Others, after having paid for a voyage on a steamship, had been forced to remain up to six months on a sailing boat in shocking conditions of filth and malnutrition. The examples of cruel deceptions were innumerable.

But Italian democracy, which in the last decade of the nineteenth century had surmounted very difficult trials, finally felt more sure of itself and better able to provide for the genuine control of emigration. For the second time a defeat in Africa, at Adua in 1896, had suggested the alternative of America to the ruling classes, although this was nothing new to the rural areas, which had never accepted any other solution, even if the South was vaguely aware of a political power that could somehow compensate for its perennial poverty. Nevertheless, years of parliamentary discussion were needed before the law was approved on January 30, 1901.

The South was alarmed. Some years before there had been a diversity of interests among the agrarians, who earned their income from agriculture, and the small bourgeoisie, accustomed to drawing profits from the peasants in proportion to their productive capacities and also, during the period of emigration, to procuring money for the emigration agents. The alarm had later quieted down when experience proved that not even the exodus across the ocean served to change significantly either the salaries from agriculture, which were miserably low, or the social relations in agriculture, which sorely needed reform. Irremediable, instead, was the opposition that grew, slowly and crudely becoming clearer with the years, between the societies of navigation and the shipowners of the North on one side, and the South on the other. The competition for enlistments and the cargo charges had stiffened and had pushed the South against the North, Naples against Genoa.

From 1887 transoceanic emigration had prevailed over transitory emigration in Europe, primarily because of the growing preference accorded it by the Southerners. Departures from the South reached 208,874 in 1901 as opposed to 34,496 leaving from the North and 34,806 from Central Italy. The exodus to America was characteristic of the South and yet Naples did not have a mercantile fleet nor a navigation society. There was not even a naval shipyard for construction or repairs; no big ship builder had established offices there. In this large Mediterranean port there existed hardly any commerce except that of the emigrants. Along the antiquated street of the Marina, navigation agencies were opening, workers and ship brokers were bustling about, from the provinces subagents and recruiters were gathering, followed by their poor people. Numerous miserable lodging houses closely connected with the agencies gave lodging to those awaiting embarkation while in the meantime the emigrants were besieged by a famished horde of small Neopolitan merchants. All this world, now gone, feared for its survival when it began to feel the threat of the Italian General Navigation Society (founded in 1881 by the merger of Rubattino and Florio with minor navigation societies) and so resolved now to solicit a new emigration policy. From 1888 the General Navigation Society had placed itself at the head of successive coalition leagues aiming to abolish the institution of agencies, the intervention of which had become, so it appeared to the navigation society, superfluous. An elaborate network of subagents covered the entire peninsula, who would have been willing to deal directly with the shipowners without the mediation of the agencies, particularly since the agencies had been accused of raising the price of the voyages with the percentage that was paid to them. It was known, in fact, that the agents offered the emigrants to Italian or foreign companies which were willing to pay the highest rates, 20, 25, or 30 lire for each person who embarked. To these accusations, the Southern agencies, in lively disputation in Parliament and the press, answered that the South also had the right to retain for itself a part of the earnings on cargo so that the exodus from the region would not serve once again to enrich the North.

We do not know if the profit that the colossal exploitation of the emigrants brought to the shipowners, the charterers, the agents and subagents has ever been calculated with sufficient accuracy; this calculation could illumine an interesting page of history, not only Italian, but European and American as well. Brief mention will be made of what happened in Italy.

Owing to old relations with the Ligurians, the departures for South America of that emigration which was called "favored" with semigratuitous voyages, or that called "recruited" (arruolata) with free voyage came mostly from Genoa. Italian ships offered to the various republics the transportation of emigrants at prices judged unacceptable by foreign shipowners, competition with whom was therefore very violent. Naples, for her part, intended to reserve what was called "spontaneous" emigration—that is, a voyage paid by the person who was leaving and who was, in most cases, going to the United States. This voyage was paid, as is known, at a price of such inhuman usury that it brought a form of real slavery to the peninsula and across the ocean. Upon this immense traffic the

General Navigation Society, strong through subvention and state privileges, attempted to impose its monopoly. To force it to lower the freight charges for the United States the Neopolitan agencies had called to their side the English Anchor Line but the Navigation Society had finally forced the Line to an agreement. The agents had successfully turned to the Fabre, then to the Nationale, both of Marseilles. One and the other yielded, however, entering the "pool" for an additional increment. The agencies therefore turned to the German companies and, not having succeeded immediately in curbing them, the General Italian Navigation Society retired for some time from the New York route. Not resigned, however, to this defeat, it had reappeared unexpectedly bringing a steep decrease in cargo charges which rose nonetheless soon after, due to a new and formidable trust concluded in Paris among all the companies involved in the transportation of emigrants. Nor was it possible to escape its empire because had the agencies tried to send the emigrants from non-Italian ports, they would have been compelled, on the basis of the Paris agreement, to pay an extra twenty lire on the price established for the emigrants of other cities in Europe.[15]

Even more painful than this brazen juggling of their misery was the cynical indifference with which the Northern shipowners sent the peasants on to agricultural colonizations, exposing them without any shelter to all the economic and political uncertainties of South America while at the same time the Southern agencies were brutally casting them on the markets of the big cities in the United States. It was hoped that the law passed in 1901 would establish some control over the brazen speculations of the Navigation society and the agencies. The emigrants were placed under state tutelage, under a commissariate to which was entrusted the supervision over cargo, over the embarkation operation, the voyages and recruitment. In spite of this, Italian emigration remained essentially an autonomous process, as desired by the agricultural populations in the South more decisively than elsewhere, resigned to undergo any exploitation but not to renounce their transmigration across the ocean or to change their destinations for motives extraneous to the more fundamental reasons for their choices.

After 1901 therefore, emigration continued in even greater proportions than in the preceding years. However, the push to leave, resulting less at this point from difficulties within Italy or the necessity for populating the American continent, came now because of the diverse conditions of the Italian settlements abroad, from their

[15]*Atti Parlamentari, Camera dei Deputati*, 3d session 1899. *Atti*, s 97 and 97 bis.

search for a better equilibrium within the republics of which they intended to become an integral part. Italians therefore emigrated less toward Argentina and Brazil where Italians had attained a numerical strength, compared to the other ethnic groups, sufficient to avoid being threatened but still not great enough to appear as a threat. Instead, there was an increase in emigration to the United States toward which Italians (particularly the Sicilians, accustomed to a characteristic politics of group power) arrived in increasing measure, though only after compatriots had established the necessary structure for their collective life. Therefore Compania, the Neopolitan port leading in numbers of departures until 1904, yielded in 1905 to Sicily, which had an emigration figure of 91,709 in 1906, increasing to 111,159 in 1913.

But at this point the numerical displacement in favor of one or another region with a community overseas ceases to be Italian history and instead becomes American history. Anyone who observed them from the peninsula could only with difficulty succeed in understanding the decrease or the increase of the groupings of the different Italian provinces within the states of the new world and many of their movements appear indecipherable unless seen in American "key." From the beginning, some consistent data acquired immediate importance in the eyes of observers. The Italians used to unite everywhere in unnumbered minute associations which gathered together men from the same province or even from the same village, and they were reproved for not setting up more potent national associations. Instead the emigrants had justifiably sensed the danger of presenting themselves as a single national entity and that, no less crucial, of losing their culture in a dispersion of the regional groups—a culture that they had to preserve at any cost before they could feel ready to receive American culture and to make America willing to accept the most important of the precious cultural elements which they had brought with them. To discern from among these elements those which would be most suited to become an integral part of the historical and social web of the Plata, Brazil or the United States was long and fatiguing work and no one in the peninsula or in the new world was in a position to help the emigrants hastily complete the proper choice. However, it should not be said, that there exist choices which are relatively more profitable. Rather each choice should be considered as right in itself.

Meanwhile, with the beginning of the present century Italians were beginning to ask, with somewhat different feelings from those of the preceding years, exactly what Italy gained or lost from emigration, attempting to make an initial and summary evaluation.

Perhaps serious social disturbances had been avoided. The demographic pressure had certainly though not adequately been alleviated. Well over 8,863,000 Italians had gone across the ocean. What the emigrants had left or sent back had often aided the government's treasury although it had not altered the Italian economy. Those who returned to Italy, in order to invest the sum of money scraped together in America, found no other opportunity than once again to buy a small piece of property in the same deteriorated rural economy from which they had thought, when they left, they had escaped for all time.[16]

Some sectors of public opinion expressed harsh dissatisfaction with the political results of emigration. One heard expressed, confusedly but not without rancor, that the power of America, even though it was not yet using the conventional instruments of power, already threatened to overwhelm Europe by its forces of attraction which had shaken every man within the most remote regions of the peninsula.

Many emigrants, it is true, had been successful, unexpectedly becoming industrialists, bankers, or politicians. The greater part had achieved a condition of well-being and what was more important, and more painful to an increasing nationalism, had become part of America. There were those who recalled as an offense to Italian national dignity the fact that Italians had so frequently been used for the most menial tasks. The distrust and suspicions to which they had been subjected were well remembered. The delusions of emigration for those who did not consider their American destiny, but rather the advantage which they had hoped to derive from it for the peninsula, fed the propaganda of the nationalists and they created the slogan, "From emigration to nationalism." The Tripoli war in 1911 made apparent the existence, and unfortunately not for the last time, of the "mirage" of a conquest which in the future would impede the "great proletarian nation" from pushing its sons to emigrate.[17]

In reality, if emigration had not created the change of fortune for Italy that many had imagined it would at the beginning, it had contributed to the construction of the new world. The emigrants were well aware of this and of the suffering with which they had paid, and they were proud; they stated as much in the bitter sweetness of their songs: "How many tears this America costs." The changes brought about by the emigration movement were, however,

[16]For the effects of emigration on the South, see *Inchiesta Parlamentare sulle condizioni dei contadini nelle provincie meridionali e nella Sicilia* (Roma, 1909-1910).

[17]Enrico Corradini, *Dall'emigrazione al nazionalismo* (Il Carroccio, 1916).

and essentially remain the results of the integration of one continent with another, of the mingling of their cultures, all part of an incessant and changing future, even if the tools used in affecting this and the ascertainable results are not as yet fully known.

ROBERT F. FOERSTER

COMING OF THE ITALIANS*

Throughout the nineteenth century, the immigration of Italians into South America exceeded that into North America. In the twentieth, although the current has poured much more copiously into the northern continent than into the southern, the difference has not yet been made up. Any attempt to find in the history of the Italians in Argentina and Brazil a clew to their fortunes in the United States is bound to fail, partly because the Italians who came were mainly of a different sort and partly because their destination was a broadly different country. It needs a knowledge of the Italian experience in the United States to complete an understanding of the work and fortunes of the emigrants from modern Italy.

That part which the Italians played in Argentina during the second half of the nineteenth century is one which in the United States fell to immigrants who preceded the Italians and to natives of the seaboard. With opening up the country, geographically speaking, they had little to do. The early westward movement was accomplished by Easterners who, to the number of half a million, entered western New York and Virginia, Tennessee and Kentucky, between the American Revolution and the year 1800. A score of years later Americans had settled the Ohio Valley; by 1840, the cotton states of the Southwest, and Illinois and Indiana; by 1860, the eastern portion generally of the Mississippi Valley. The tumultuous settlement of California in the years of gold discovery was followed by the gradual development of the entire Pacific coast, coincident, in great part, with the peopling of the western portion of the Mississippi Valley.

The swift course of migration and settlement was hastened, if it was not indeed made possible, by two momentous forces. One is the improvement in transportation. The twenty-five years in the course of which the steamboat was proved practicable, the Erie Canal opened, and the Baltimore and Ohio Railroad begun, constitute an epoch. Rapidly thereafter the mileage of railways

*The Italian Emigration of Our Time (Harvard University Press, 1919; reprinted, with an introductory note by F. Cordasco, New York: Russell & Russell, 1968), pp. 320-341. Reprinted with permission.

was redoubled, pushed into the West even faster than settlers
would go. In the first ten or twenty years of the century, pressed
on by political and military contingencies, the factory had
crowded out the domestic system; but the incessantly ripening
chances of securing cheap land in the West tended, by abstracting
the population, to limit the expansion of manufactures. This
tendency was itself, however, partly held in check by the second
momentous force of the period. The immigration of European
settlers, never, since colonial days, wholly arrested, but fluctuating with the years and fed by shifting currents, supplied the places
of many Americans who moved West. At times, as in the decade
1810-20, the population of some important eastern cities and
states was hardly more than maintained; but as the stream of
immigrants became heavier the places of those who went West
were more than filled.

Between 1840 and 1890 (while Italians were going to South
America) fifteen million immigrants entered the United States.
They were mainly English, Scotch, Irish, Welsh, Swedes, Nor-
wegians, Danes, and Germans. By predilection they established
themselves in the cities and states of the seaboard; for then, as
now, the immigration was of persons whose means were slender
and who sought an easy adaptation to the country. A courageous
minority, Swedes and Norweigians largely, made pioneer settlements in the agricultural West and Northwest, displaying much of
that independence of character that had marked the Easterners
who went West. Only in the most indirect way—the contrast with
Brazil is emphatic—could it be shown that the collapse of slavery
had anything to do with the coming of the foreigners.

Yet even the movement of these immigrants into the West depended first of all upon the railway building of the country. In a
few years after the Civil War the length of the rail course doubled,
touching 52,000 miles in 1870; after a great boom it was 93,000 in
1880, and 166,000 in 1890. Almost wholly this great saddling of
the continent, an indispensable means to the rearing of a great
nation, was the performance, as to common labor and largely
even as to skilled, of the incoming foreigners. Digging and con-
structing, in the opening country, they received something at
least of that harsh contact with a virgin natural environment
which in earlier years had conferred upon the frontier settlers
some of their most valuable traits. The first results of the extension of the railways were quick to appear. To the riches of cotton
and tobacco were added the astounding harvests of wheat and corn.

In the early years of the century the men who created the country's wealth were, characteristically, self-dependent owners of their farms and shops. Such they could be because the acquisition of a farm on the public lands was a universal alternative to employment by others. Of the arriving immigrants, however, most found that they could make their start with the greatest security not by independent ventures but by entrance into a hired class. The creation of an opportunity for them was the outstanding accomplishment of the second half of the century. In the first half, manufactures had unfolded slowly but had found an expanding market in the opening West, and after the Civil War received a tremendous impetus. Coincidently, mining developed. No longer was agriculture the country's one great industry. By 1880, 30 per cent of the entire population were of foreign birth or were the children of foreign parents. The sixfold increase in the capital invested in manufactures between the outbreak of the Civil War and the year 1890, a period in which the population of the country doubled was largely made possible by the inpouring of immigrants. Now social classes could be discerned. They were the fruit of the modes of employment that modern industrial systems impose and were the surest sign that a primitive phase of the history of the United States had come to an end, bringing a modern state. Rich as are still the untouched resources of the country, the land frontier—which as late as 1860 was the Mississippi Valley—could not be said to exist after 1890. Henceforth, to do well by himself, a man must meet the tests laid down, not by Nature, but by his fellows.

The days of turnpike and stagecoach were only a memory when the Italians began to come. In all the time before 1850, their immigration had none of the marks of a mass movement. Between 1820 and 1850 less than 4500 were counted and a third of these came by way of unexplained exception (or statistical error) in one year, 1833. When the census first distinguished nationalities, in 1850, 3645 were in the country. To these in 1850-60, 8940 were added by further immigration—the merest ripple compared with the mighty wave then sweeping in from western Europe—and in 1860 those still alive and in the country numbered 10,518. In 1861-70, 12,206 disembarked in our ports; in 1870, 17,157 were living here. In 1871-80, 55,759 came and in 1880, 44,230 were still in the United States.

Before 1860 the immigration appears to have been of persons who desired permanent settlement. That could be readily explained, without going further, by the difficulties of transportation. Chiefly the arrivals were North Italians, and they included, besides traders, many Lucchese vendors of plaster statuary and street musicians with monkeys—fantastic vanguard of the brawny army to follow. Because they were few, they escaped the attention, certainly the ire, of the anti-immigrant agitators of the time. In the miscellany of the Italians were a slight but precious group of political refugees, and it is a fact still enshrined in the bosoms of Italians that chief of these was the ubiquitous Garibaldi who lived on Staten Island while he made candles in a shop on Bleecker Street.[1] Some sprinkling of Italians there had been in the cities of the eastern seaboard since early colonial days. Although a few individuals came to the western coast as early as 1830, larger numbers were drawn by the gold fever, to their very mediocre profit.[2]

Between 1860 and 1880, as the fresh arrivals increased, the immigration assumed a much more definite character. Where before there had been individuals there were now types and classes. From small beginnings the contingent from South Italy had swelled to substantial proportions. After 1870, for the first time, it became evident that, following a somewhat indeterminate stay, many repacked their chattels and went home again. No previous immigrants into this land of promise had done that!

The New York colony was passing through a curious phase. To the Genoese merchants who had come in earlier years were added, after 1860, Palermitan merchants who dealt in the citrous fruits and oil. But still other immigrants, of a startling sort, had perched and nestled in the section called Five Points. Not so much the novelty of the type as the number and persistence of those who embodied it made it conspicuous even in the cosmopolis. In large tenement houses these everlasting organ grinders and sellers of statuettes dwelt—how, is authoritatively described by that rare spirit in American philanthropy, Charles Loring Brace:

> In the same room I would find monkeys, children, men and women, with organs and plaster-casts, all huddled together; but the women contributing still, in the crowded rooms, to roll their dirty macaroni, and all talking ex-

[1]The experiences of one refugee are described in the anonymous "Letters of an Italian Exile," *Southern Literary Messenger*, December, 1842, pp. 741-748.

[2]Some recollections of the Italians of the early fifties are in C. Dondero, "L'Italia agli Stati Uniti ed in California," *L'Italia Coloniale*, June, 1901, pp. 9-22. C. Gardini relates a romantic legend—with doubtless a basis in fact—of how in 1858, 300 Italian miners gaily went nine miles, with gifts, to greet the first Italian woman who came to California. *Gli Stali Uniti* (2 vols., Bologna, 1887), ii, p. 224.

citedly; a bedlam of sounds, and a combination of odors from garlic, monkeys, and dirty human persons. They were, without exception, the dirtiest population I had met with. The children I saw every day on the streets, following organs, blackening boots, selling flowers, sweeping walks, or carrying ponderous harps for old ruffians. [They did not, he adds, go to school and rarely went to church, and many were indentured to masters.] The lad would frequently be sent forth by his *padrone* late at night, to excite the compassion of our citizens, and play the harp. I used to meet these boys sometimes on winter nights half-frozen and stiff with cold.[3]

About 1870 there was a considerable diversity of types in the United States. They were largely North Italians, it would seem, and were perhaps more evenly scattered over the country than their people were ever again to be. Some were grocers, or keepers of barrooms and restaurants—mainly Ligurians who had settled in New York. Some were in market gardening, especially about New Orleans, or in other branches of agriculture. Many were successful stonecutters; others were masons. In the South and West, fishermen had established themselves. In many cities were waiters, street musicians, and sellers of casts. There were sundry important groups of Sicilians (they had a settlement in Alabama, for instance) and Neapolitans were numerous. Though many disappointed miners had departed from California, other sorts of workers had stayed there.[4] Generally, however, in the western states where "the inhabitants live armed to the teeth to fight Indians and wild beasts," as a contemporary wrote,[5] Italians were few.

A decade later the New York colony numbered 12,223—including the children, possibly 20,000. So it was materially larger than before, though otherwise not greatly changed. In one of the few pictures we have of the time, Charlotte Adams noted "the child musicians and the wandering minstrels . . . who pass their summers playing on steamboats and at watering places," the adult organ grinders, and the makers of macaroni, of art things,

[3]C. L. Brace, *The Dangerous Classes of New York* (3d ed., New York, 1880), pp. 194f. The first edition was in 1872. In 1855 Brace helped to establish a remarkable school among these Italians; he relates its vicissitudes before 1867. Florenzano (pp. 154 f.) gives the text of an agreement made in 1866 between a Viggiano father and an exploiter who took his boy to New York; see also, on the situation of such boys in New York, pp. 161-164. Cf. Carpi, ii, p.121.

[4]Carpi, ii, pp. 131, 225-267. Carpi followed a consul's lead in estimating at 55,000 a population that the census presently figured at 17,157. Even though it doubtless included American-born children, the estimate was much too high.

[5]Florenzano, p. 311.

confectionery, artificial flowers. The Genoese girls studied needle-
work at night schools. The North Italians repudiated kinship
with the Neapolitans and Calabrians. Italian workmen of the unskilled sort were "everywhere," but that is Miss Adams' only
pronouncement touching a group that was every day becoming
more prominent. One sentence was prophetic: "That the Italians are an idle and thriftless people is a superstition that time
will remove from the American mind."[6]

Adolfo Rossi, who came to the United States in this period, was
an adventurous youth, with keen powers of observation and a
capacity for vivid, even poignant, narrative. The South Italians
he found to be the dominant type. Country folk they had been in
Italy but now they inhabited the dirtiest part of New York City,
dwelling often more than one family to a room. "Men, women,
dogs, cats, and monkeys eat and sleep together in the same hole
without air and without light." They buy stale beer at two cents
a pint from a rascally Italian in a basement, and they break into
endless brawls. During the summer they work on the railroads
and in the fields; "in the winter they return to fill the streets of
New York, where the boys are bootblacks and the men either are
employed at the most repulsive tasks, scorned by workmen of
other nationalities—carrying offal to the ships and dumping it in
the sea, cleaning the sewers *et similia*—or they go about with
sacks on their shoulders rummaging the garbage cans, gleaning
paper, rags, bones, broken glass." The Five Points are the center of
that species of slavery exercised by Italian bosses or *padroni*.
These fellows know English, hire workmen in herds (being paid by
the employers), charge them enormous commissions, having already advanced to many their passage money for the journey
from Italy, sell them the necessaries at high prices, and deduct
heavy commissions from the savings which they transmit to Italy.
"And while the workmen fag from morning to evening, the bosses
smoke tranquilly and superintend them with rifles at their sides
and revolvers at their belts. They seem—and are—real brigands."
Whoever tells these natives of Avellino, of the Abruzzi, of Basilicata,
that they are being cheated, loses his words. *"Signorino,"* they reply,
"we are ignorant and do not know English. Our boss brought us here,
knows where to find work, make contracts with the companies. What
should we do without him?" The Camorra flourishes as in the worst
Bourbon times and "the Italian, illiterate, carrying the knife, de-

---

[6]C. Adams, "Italian Life in New York," *Harper's Monthly*, April, 1881, pp. 676-
684.

frauded and fraudulent, is more despised than the Irish and the Chinese." Rossi made a journey across the continent with a squad of Italians, two-thirds of them from the South, who were engaged in New York by the Denver and South Park Railway. To them fell the gang tasks while the Irish and the Americans wielded authority.[7]

By 1880 the formative years of Italian immigration may be said to have been completed. Then its main characteristics were apparent. It was largely from South Italy, was increasingly disposed after a time to return to Europe, had taken up a certain range of vocations in the United States, and had developed the institution of the padrone, unknown previously among immigrant peoples. In later years no new elements appear, but the old assume many forms, of deep significance. If some of the newer immigrants came while yet the country had a frontier, it retreated westward before they could reach it. A heavy immigration after 1880 left a population of 182,580 in 1890. Henceforth, those who came were to find a full-grown nation, with all good lands preëmpted.

In 1900 the Italians were a population of 484,027, or nearly three times their number of ten years before. This increase is impressive, not only because it was exceptional, but because it took place during a period disturbed by industrial collapse. It is partly explained by the fact that in South Italy the decade had been one of intensified hardship and of desperate desire to escape. But why should the South Italians come to the United States? Perhaps the knowledge prevailed that South America was the hunting ground of the North Italians; more likely, it seemed most natural to follow in the footsteps of those South Italians who had done well in the United States. Whatever the reason, the influx was heavy.

In 1900-10, years of prodigious industrial expansion in the United States, 2,104,309 Italians arrived. So many, however, had gone home again that the enumeration of 1910 found only 1,343,125. But these were nearly three times the number present a decade earlier. Having been less than 5 per cent of the foreign population, they had become 10. Together with their American-born children they now numbered 2,098,360. Their stock had increased faster since 1900 than that of any other large group, except the Russians. Among the foreign-born Italians two in three were men, a proportion not nearly approached by any other

---

[7]A. Rossi, *Un italiano in America* (3d ed., Treviso, 1907). My citations are drawn more especially from pp. 65-71, 80, 217 ff., 301. Comparison with Jacob Riis' picture in *How the Other Half Lives* (New York, 1890), chs. v-vii, suggests that no advance had taken place in ten years either in occupation or mode of living.

important group in the country, and reflecting better than any
other circumstance the fact that they had come to earn.[8]

After the initial stage of settlement of any immigrant nationality at its chosen destinations, some scattering, however gradual,
invariably ensues. Thus one expects subsequent censuses to show
less geographical concentration. As the Italian immigration,
however, increased in volume and the predominance of the Southern element became greater, its concentration became actually
more marked. In 1850 just half the Italians were within the area
included in the census of 1790, but in 1900 three-quarters were.[9]
And in 1910 they were distributed as follows, in the several groups
of states:

New England 13.2%		East South Central 0.7%	
Middle Atlantic 58.6		West South Central 3.0	
East North Central 10.8		Mountain 2.4	
West North Central 2.6		Pacific 6.0	
South Atlantic 2.6			

It is a strange result.[10] In the state of New York were about
as many Italians as the whole country had contained ten years
earlier. Two out of five of all the newcomers, in some recent
years, have gone thither. Of those in the state in 1910, nearly
two-thirds dwelt in its metropolis, 340,770—such a number as
would make one of the largest cities in Italy; and if their children
were added, the colony would exceed in population every Italian
city, except possibly Naples. No two cities of Basilicata together, to make but one further illustration, contain so many
natives of that province as does this American city. And in
New York no foreign people, save only the Russians, are so
strongly represented.

In New Orleans, in 1910, the Italians exceeded all other for-

---

[8]The statistical data for these observations, and those that follow, are available in *Thirteenth Census—Abstract of the Census* (Washington, 1913).

[9]The percentages are 49.6 and 74.9. In the New England states, in 1850, were
7.2 of all the Italians, in 1900, 12.7. In the Middle States the percentages were
28.2 and 60.3; and in the Southern, 14.2 and 2.0. Bureau of the Census, *A Century
of Population Growth, 1790-1900* (Washington, 1909), p. 131.

[10]In the states where the Italians chiefly went, they numbered in 1910:—

New York............472,201	Michigan.................16,861	Oregon.......................5,538
Pennsylvania.........196,122	Colorado.................14,375	Vermont....................4,594
New Jersey.............115,446	Washington 13,121	Florida......................4,538
Massachusetts..........85,056	Missouri....................12,084	Nebraska...................3,799
Illinois 72,163	Minnesota.................9,669	Kansas.......................3,520
California.................63,615	Wisconsin 9,273	Maine........................3,468
Connecticut.............56,954	Texas 7,190	Utah..........................3,117
Ohio.........................41,620	Maryland 6,969	Delaware....................2,893
Rhode Island 27,287	Indiana 6,911	District of Columbia .2,761
Louisiana.................20,233	Montana 6,592	Alabama....................2,696
West Virginia...........17,292	Iowa 5,846	Oklahoma..................2,564

eigners. But in no other large city except New York were they either first or second in rank among the immigrants. Philadelphia and Chicago each had about 45,000, Boston had 31,000—subsequently (by the Massachusetts census of 1915) 43,000. Newark in 1910 had 20,000 San Francisco 17,000. The other large centers were, in order, Pittsburgh, Jersey City, Buffalo, Cleveland, New Orleans, St. Louis, Detroit, Baltimore. About four-fifths of all the Italians were classed by the census as urban, twice as high a proportion as that for the country's population as a whole.

The emigration of Italians into the countries of Europe has for the most part been specialized according to the understood requirements of those countries. That into Brazil and Argentina has aimed either to fulfill a need or to take advantage of unexploited resources and opportunities. What likelihood has there been that the great outpouring from South Italy would find itself suited to the conditions of the United States? By what occupations have the immigrants tried to earn a living? And what has been their accomplishment?

That some notion of fitness to prosper in the future articulately or inarticulately precedes the decision to emigrate, might be inferred from the action of that "professional proletariat" which so abounds in Italy. Because of the language barrier and the specialized nature of their training, such persons can ordinarily expect to serve only their fellow countrymen. Hence they have been few, relatively far fewer than among immigrants from English-speaking countries or from those nearer to the United States in institutions and ways.

To this rule there has been one very notable exception. With the musicians, training, where it exists, is of advantage, and language does not matter since their art is universal. Training may indeed be absent; and if there is only an inborn love of music and the impulse to play, then the *organetto* and the tambourine, the resonant voice and the rhythmic legs, contribute all that is needful. Gains do not depend upon length of residence in America; a too facile assimilation to established ways may even make profit less easy. So it happens that musicians have been plentiful among these immigrants, constituting about half of all Italian professional persons in the United States. With the lapse of time, they have undergone some changes. In city and suburb the hurdy-gurdy has displaced the harp, violin, and old-time hand organ. The street types as such are less than they once were, and the band players in the great cities more. But all together, humble types, high, and highest, they contend for the primacy in numbers among foreign musicians.

Less favorably circumstanced, the physicians, lawyers, teachers, actors, priests, and their kin have had to contemplate taking one of two courses. Either they must settle in some "Little Italy" or an isolated cluster of Italians anywhere, or they must sink into unskilled work. Let such persons avoid this country, an Italian consul-general at New York recommended a quarter century ago. "Hardly have they landed when they discover that America is not for them. Wanting knowledge of the language, and every other resource, they come to the consulate to ask succor in repatriation. How many think themselves lucky if they can find employment as waiters on board a vessel bound for Italy!"[11] A colony must have attained a certain size and stability before it can maintain a priest. Teachers may find posts in parochial schools. Doctors, when they have duly passed examinations or had their diplomas validated, can still only secure a patronage among their compatriots. On the other hand, where the demand is meager, the supply may also be meager. Among a thousand Italians in Richmond in 1909 there was said to be not one professional person.[12] And in 1882, when the first Italian daily paper was started, "not only," says Rossi, its first news-gatherer, "were there in New York no Italian reporters by vocation, but it was extremely hard even to find an Italian who could write his own tongue with accuracy."[13] The consuls have not ceased to discourage professional immigration. In the most prosperous epoch of the Italian coming, the Labor Information Office, with its seat in New York, said of teachers, under-officials, accountants, and others in liberal professions: "All of them meet bitter disillusionment and are often forced to take up humble and arduous occupations, not always well paid."[14] Despite many fluctuations a persistent decrease in the professional element has taken place. In the immigration of 1910 it had relatively only one-fifteenth the importance it had had in 1875.

A vastly broader place has been occupied by those who are conveniently styled skilled workmen and by certain types that have successfully defied our statisticians' capacity in classification and been dubbed "miscellaneous." These together have not neces-

[11]G. P. Riva in *Emig. e Col.*, 1893, p. 438. Cf., on the same period, G. Conte, *Dieci anni in America* (Palermo, 1903), pp. 58-61.

[12]L. Villari, "Gli italiani negli stati di Virginia, Carolina del Nord e Carolina del Sud," *Boll. Emig.*, 1909, No. 8, p. 58.

[13]Rossi, p. 179.

[14]Note in *Boll. Emig.*, 1907, No. 2, p. 116. Cf. *Boll. Emig.*, almost at random, e.g., 1903, No. 4, p. 47; No. 5, p. 45; No. 11, p.12; also G. Preziosi, *Gl' italiani negli Stati Uniti del Nord* (Milan, 1909), p. 40.

sarily either more intelligence and skill or less than the professional immigrants; but they satisfy different wants: they provide
generally the material things of life and the physical services, and
if they touch aesthetic or liberal interests at all it is incidentally.

The proportion of skilled workmen—leaving aside for the
moment the miscellaneous group—has risen appreciably in the
last thirty or forty years, and recently has been about an eighth of
all.[15] The percentage is lower than that of the immigrants from
western Europe—the Germans, Irish, English, Scotch, Scandi-
navians, French—but is much higher than that of the Croatians
and Slavonians, the Slovaks, Lithuanians, Magyars, and Balkan
peoples. One recalls that North Italian skilled emigrants have
played some part in the countries from which these eastern immigrants come. Yet our Italians are of the South, where skill is less
than in the North; hence the proportion of skilled among them
approaches more nearly the low ratios of the eastern peoples of
Europe than of the western, and it has actually, in most years, been
less than the proportion for all immigrant nationalities together.

What is peculiar in the Italian contingent can be brought out
by some simple comparisons. In 1907, for example (a year when
the immigration from all countries was very heavy, and when that
from Italy was one-fourth of the total, and when Italian skilled
workers were a fifth of all skilled immigrants), Italian plumbers
were one in 150 arriving plumbers, locksmiths one in 74 of their
kind, milliners one in 48, painters and glaziers one in 16, clerks
and accountants one in 23, plasterers one in 26, saddlers one in 18,
machinists one in 38, tailors one in 8. Extremely few likewise
were the butchers, bookbinders, iron and steel and other metal
workers, hat makers, woodworkers, and wheelwrights. And
generally these immigrants originated in North Italy. In a different group of occupations, the Italians have been much more
numerous. Of blacksmiths, bakers, millers, in some years miners,
their representation has been near the average of all peoples. It
fell but little below such an average in 1907 in the case of cabinet-
makers, carpenters, dressmakers, gardeners, and metal workers
(other than in iron and steel), but in some years has exceeded the
average.[16]

[15]By quinquennia, beginning with 1876-80 and ending with 1906-10, the percentages were 7, 9, 6, 8, 14, 13, 11. Since no figures are to be had for 1896, I have
made the fifth period cover four years only.

[16]The figures are compiled from statistics in the *Report of the Commissioner-
General of Immigration for the Fiscal Year 1906-1907*, but the reports for other
years are of similar tenor.

The peculiarities of representation are in no sense fortuitous. In one or two instances, the grounds are wanting for such heavy emigration as other countries show. Tailors and locksmiths seem few chiefly because in the Russian Jewish exodus they abound— the consequence of centuries of trade specialization. In some occupations language creates a difficulty. Others have in Italy had no material basis for growth; hence, iron and steel workers, for example, come rather from Germany and England. Since bakers and carpenters exercise trades as universal as they are ancient, nothing in the Italian rate of their coming is characteristic. Miners are mainly from North Italy, where their history has been long.

Unique interest attaches to those trades in which the Italian representation is high. Here fall the stonecutters, mechanics, mariners, masons, barbers, seamstresses, and shoemakers. Commonly one-half or more of all arriving masons are Italian, and in some years a third to a half of all the stonecutters. In deforested Italy, with its rocky vertebrae of Alps and Apennines, stone and cement are used to an exceptional degree in building. It is the countries from which in general many skilled workmen come— Germany, Great Britain, Scandinavia—and not the eastern countries, that chiefly rival Italy in sending masons and stonecutters. Mariners have always been numerous—the Genoese maintain an old tradition. Were the Hebrew seamstresses excluded, the Italian portion, now commonly a fourth to a third of all, would rise substantially. The prominence of this type argues at once the Italian women's need of earning and their proficiency with an implement universally manipulated by women. The amazingly heavy representation of shoemakers reflects the persistence in South Italy of a traditional village craftsman, working by hand. In the United States, the *calzolaio* must change. Strangest of all, Italian barbers and hairdressers are actually one-half to two-thirds of all arrivals of such workmen! Indeed, these artists have long stood forth prominently in our immigration from Italy and over many years have increased in number. They derive largely from South Italy, where in truth men's beards grow heavy and where the narrow range of possible employments has made for concentration in the standard sorts.

Consider some other types. Italian fishermen are often half of those who come from all countries; for Italy is bordered by fish-abounding seas, supplying, in a country where meat is expensive, one of the most valued of foods. Draymen, teamsters, and their allies are often a third to a half of all who come; for Italy is a land of few railroads and fewer navigable streams. Did not England and Germany, and still more the Jewish populations of central Europe, send extraordinary numbers of merchants and dealers, those that flock from the simple communities of South Italy, the more numerous because of the small scale of their operations, would eminently stand forth. Many immigrants have been servants at home, but their general proportion in the whole shrivels because very great numbers have come from two or three other countries. In particular, there have been many farm servants. Farmers, finally, that is, persons who have had an independent position in agriculture and have not been mainly hired by others, have been few. From Germany, in the days of her great emigration, which was yet materially inferior to that from Italy in recent years, five to ten times as many farmers came annually as have come from Italy in the years of amplest immigration; and even several other western countries have sent more. In late years while immigration from these countries has been dwindling, their farmers have still exceeded or have nearly equalled those from Italy. For this strange situation the explanation is first of all that the innumerable Italian proprietors of farm land have also been laborers; and at one time it was true that our officials did not carefully distinguish farmers from farm laborers.

Passing by for the moment the more purely industrial types, let us scan more closely the careers of the rest. In part these people work for wages, in part they are made independent, each man a center unto himself, by the circumstances of their trade. Training and apprenticeship may be necessary for some, for others reliance is mainly on personal resources, even upon qualities that one is encouraged to call social.

The bootblacks, humblest of all, have not, save in rare instances, plied their trade in Italy. But they found it open to them here (or occupied mainly by negroes) and they brought to it a pride in neat work which is in some sense a national attribute. In goodly numbers they entered the trade very early, at the time in fact when the street musicians, with their bears and monkeys, and the rag pickers, were still the conspicuous types; and they were one in sixteen of all bootblacks counted five years after the Civil War had ended.[17] Twenty years later, in those quarters of New York where the foreign population dwelt, 473 out of the 474 foreign bootblacks enumerated were Italians—and the native

---

[17]*Ninth Census*, iii, p. 833; later censuses have ignored their vocation.

workers numbered 10![18] Subsequently, though no statistics exist, the frequent references to their kind in Italian consular reports fortify the opinion that in the cities they were exceedingly numerous.[19] Especially in early days they patrolled the streets, carrying their implements; but the evolution of their industry has brought to the fore the chair and stand, sometimes the shop, whose owner now and then is self-styled "professor" or "artist." In New Orleans, they appear to have outgrown their trade some years ago, being superseded by negroes.[20] In the great eastern cities, Greeks, Jews, and others have cut into their dominance. This is not surprising, for while men past middle life often are bootblacks, the majority are youths, who expect to turn to other things.

Of the barbers and hairdressers, few abandon their vocation here, while many for the first time enter it. In 1870 only the French had a higher proportion of barbers.[21] In 1890, when the Italian population was still small, the actual number of Italian barbers exceeded the total of British, Irish, Scandinavian, and French, and was nearly a third the number of all German barbers, although German workpeople in general were twelve times as many as Italian.[22] In 1900, the 12,289 Italian barbers were half as many as the Germans; they were one in twenty-five occupied males—a rate nine times as great as that for the entire country.[23] In New York today they may be nearly as numerous as all other

[18]Seventh Special Report of the United States Commission of Labor, *The Slums of Baltimore, Chicago, New York, and Philadelphia* (Washington, 1894), pp. 188 f.

[19]The following references touch different parts of this country and Canada. V. Manassero di Castigliole, *Emig. e Col.*, 1893, p. 451; G. Marazzi, *ibid.*, p. 478; A. Dall' Aste Brandolini, "L'immigrazione e le colonie italiane nella Pennsylvania," *Boll. Emig.*, 1902, No. 4, p. 6z; R. Michele, "L'immigrazione italiana in . . . Connecticut," *"Boll. Emig.*, 1902, No. 5, p. 11; G. P. Baccelli, "Gl'italiani in . . . Albany," *Boll. Emig.*, 1902, No. 5, p. 16; Serra, "Gl' italiani in California ed in altri stati della costa del Pacifico," *Boll. Emig.*, 1902, No. 5, pp. 45, 51; E. Rossi, "Delle condizioni del Canada rispetto all' immigrazione italiana," *Boll. Emig.*, 1903, No. 4, p. 9; L. Villari, "L'emigrazione italiana nel distretto consolare di Filadelfia," *Boll. Emig.*, 1908, No. 16, p. 26.

[20]G. Saint-Martin, "Gli italiani nel distretto consolare di Nuova Orleans," *Boll. Emig.*, 1903, No. 1, p. 12.

[21]*Ninth Census, loc. cit.*

[22]*Eleventh Census*, ii, p. 485. Among the Irish, barbers were amazingly few— one in a thousand occupied males; among the Italians one in thirty-four.

[23]*Twelfth Census, Special Report on Occupations*, pp. ccii, 65. The *Thirteenth Census* unfortunately did not give occupational statistics by nationality.

[24]Cf. New York, *Report of the Commission on Immigration* (Albany, 1909), p. 134; J. Daniels, *In Freedom's Birthplace* (Boston, etc., 1914), p. 324; F. G. Warne, *The Immigrant Invasion* (New York, 1913,) p. 174.

barbers together. Before their numbers and their proficiency the negroes and Germans have in many centers lost command of the trade.[24]

Figaro must learn American styles of hair cutting and the use of American instruments. That is not difficult. The system by which in Italy customers often pay by contract is rare in this country, a less personal relationship being the rule. In the great cities the barber patronizes one of the numerous towel supply houses (often Italian) instead of washing his towels himself. Quick fingers and a sense of neatness and finish are dependable natural assets which he brings with him. American requirements and a bit of English, the fresh immigrant learns in an established shop. Presently his wage is $9—14 per week. What his next and final fortune will be depends on his skill and his proficiency in English. Innumerable are the one-chair or two-chair shops using a basement or narrow room, serving mainly Italian or other immigrants, and charging rates much lower than those of the established shops, whether union or non-union. In the more flourishing concerns six or eight competent men are employed: and the ablest of all can count on being welcomed in the great hotels.

Italian shoemakers and shoe repairers were found to be very numerous both in 1870 and 1890. In 1870 the Germans were relatively much more numerous, but in 1900, after the great South Italian influx, their proportion was only a third that of the Italians.[25] Makers of shoes though they had been in Italy, they became in this land of machine-made shoes chiefly repairers, invading the patronage of others. Many of the residents of our cities have beheld the German repair shop disappear—through the death of the cobbler or transformation by his children into a store—and the Italian, humbly beginning, take its place. More, apparently, than the barbers, the shoemakers have courted a general patronage, reaching out into the suburbs and into parts of cities where Italians are scarce, and managing their affairs with the barest knowledge of English. In one person or in one family bootblack and shoemaker may be united. Expensive machinery is sometimes used, electrically propelled. But the Italians who have successfully undertaken the general sale of boots and shoes are still few.

Traders and dealers, like barbers and cobblers, have not been

[25]*Twelfth Census, Report on Occupations, loc. cit.* I shall not, in the remainder of this account, detail my references to the Ninth, Eleventh, and Twelfth censuses.

wont to abandon their vocations after arrival. As early as 1870, dealers in groceries, wines, liquors, and other commodities, and hucksters, were one in nine of all occupied Italians. Then the Italian consul-general estimated, I suspect rather liberally, that in New York three-fifths of all street sellers of peaches and pears —or in the winter, of apples and chestnuts—were Genoese or Sicilian; and in the larger and stabler forms of trade, some considerable fortunes were said to be in the making.[26] Twenty years later there were over 10,000 dealers. As hucksters and pedlars, only the German and Russian Jews were more numerous. Many were wholesalers, and a goodly number, for the most part Sicilians, imported lemons and other fruits and wine. In 1892 the consul-general in New York reported to his government that Italians owned most of the fruit stands in the metropolis and ran them profitably; in Boston also were many. In the Far West, during the period of the gold excitement, the dealers had more success trading in the camps than their brethren had digging in the mines. Subsequently they rose to considerable importance in San Francisco and elsewhere in the coast states, selling wines and liquors, groceries, fruits, and vegetables—in the last two departments, apparently unrivalled. In New Orleans, long a center for trade with Sicily, the Sicilians had achieved a leading position in the sale of fruit, vegetables, and oysters. In part their specialty grew out of their prior employment, as seamen and longshoremen, in unloading fruit from Italian sailing vessels. In the face of the operations of the United Fruit Company, the Italian shipping was destined to decline, but the retail trade was to continue long in Italian hands. In Texas, Alabama, and Mississippi, in Colorado and the adjacent parts, and in the Central States, sellers of fruit and other commodities were reported to be numerous in the nineties.[27]

The new century has brought a still more extensive field of operations, with substantial outposts even in Canada, and has set the general characteristics of Italian trade into sharper relief. In 1900, retail dealers numbered 17,640, wholesale dealers 369, hucksters and pedlars 7209—with the German and Russian Jews in relatively much the same position as ten years earlier.

[26]Carpi, ii, p. 231.

[27]See the reports in *Emig. e Col.*, 1893, pp. 442, 449-453, 462, 464, 475-479. Note the prominence of dealers in the directory of Fratelli Metelli, *Guida Metelli della colonia italiana negli Stati Uniti per l'anno 1885* (New York, 1884), pp. 265-311. See also C. Ottolenghi, "La nuova fase dell' immigrazione del lavoro agli Stati Uniti," *Giornale degli Economisti*, April, 1899, p. 381; Saint-Martin, p. 4.

The tremendous increment of the immigrant population since 1900, all unmeasured statistically as to occupation, has certainly boosted the Italian participation in trade. For we must remember that many general laborers, miners, and others are tempted to enter "bisinisse," and that they can do so by learning fifty words of English and buying a fruit stand. Sometimes the wife manages the shop or stand while the husband continues at his work. In New York many men have begun with a pushcart, then got the privilege of a stand, then a concession to sell garden produce in connection with a grocery store, and finally have set up a shop of their own.[28] In small towns and at railroad stations many Italian fruit stands are now to be found. The Italians' love of their trade, bringing an eagerness to have fresh fruits and to display them in comely arrangements, has undoubtedly somewhat stimulated the fruit consumption of the American people. In recent years, the Greeks and Syrians—the latter already met as competitors in Brazil—have challenged the Italian dominance in the fruit trade, not merely in New York, but as far away as Galveston.

A common type in our foreign communities is the coal and wood or coal and ice dealer, observed half a century ago in San Francisco. In some places he has been the successor of the Jews, as these have succeeded the Irish. The business is simple enough: one rents an unused basement, constructs crudely in the rear a bin or bunk, then hangs out a sign or peddles small portions in the tenements.

In the specifically Italian districts are many shops providing a single class of wares, such as Italians are likely to seek. Nothing sells so well as food. A sufficiently modest shop is styled, in Italo-English, a *"grande grosseria italiana."* Here a window displays voluminous round cheeses, or strings of sausages, or tinned eels; there are loaves of bread thirty inches from end to end, or great round loaves with holes in the center like gigantic doughnuts. Confetti or macaroni tempts one in another window. Dealers in alcoholic and soft drinks are many. Here, in combination, are a *"caffe e pasticceria,"* there a bank sells coal. Some shops become so diversified as to approach the "general merchandise" stores of our rural districts. Capitalizing the timidity which the Italian often shows about trusting many people with his affairs, a versatile fellow will be at once a barber, banker, undertaker, wholesale and retail dealer, perhaps also a real estate and employment

---

[28]H. B. Woolston, *A Study of the Population of Manhattanville* (New York, 1909), p. 94.

agent—yet even such a grotesque association of activities can hardly be incomprehensible to American patrons of tourists' agencies abroad!

Powerful firms and individuals have arisen. New York, Chicago, and San Francisco have their Italian chambers of commerce, composed, to an extraordinary degree, of bankers, fruit and wine merchants, and importers of fruits, wines, oil, and raw silk. The heavy Italian importations into New York and into New Orleans are mainly in Italian hands. In passing, it may be noted that the California fruit trade has cut deeply into the trade in Italian fruits. Of the large firms many are outgrowths of firms previously successful in Italy, while others have sprung from small beginnings here.[29]

Other city types are prominent, little less so in the inland centers than on the seaboard (east, south, and west). Sometimes the restaurant keeper had exercised his vocation in Italy, but as often, I suspect, he has first sold only to customers who took their purchase home; so wine merchants come to sell for consumption on the premises. The many cooks, almost always North Italians, were conspicuous as early as half a century ago. Genoese, in the early days, and many others recently, have been waiters, finding a haven often in the largest hotels. It is not necessary that they should have learned their calling in Italy. Nimble hands they may count upon, also such courtesy and deference as centuries have wrought into their fiber—centuries of abounding state and religious ceremony, maintained in an old civilization. Before the influx of Italian and other white waiters, the negroes have lost their former prominence. Confectioners are many, from northern and central Italy, and bakers have been a leading South Italian type. Dressmakers and tailors have been innumerable.

Of Italian fishermen there has been a wide scattering. In Boston is an old colony which used to moor its gaudy craft along time-honored "T Wharf." At several points in Florida, notably at Tampa, there have been settlements, the men sometimes owning their ships, sometimes manning those of other persons; most are from Sicily, but many are from Tuscany and the Marches. An old colony—it can count fifty years—is at New Orleans. The fishermen of Galveston, who sell their fish under contract, have been chiefly from the isle of Elba. On the Pacific coast are

---

[29]The chambers of commerce (subsidized by the Italian government) have issued various publications. On trade see a contribution by G. Rossati to the comprehensive volume *Gli italiani negli Stati Uniti* (New York, 1906), pp. 54-59; I have drawn freely upon the consular reports.

several collectivities, one for instance in Oregon (Astoria), but all shrink in importance before that at San Francisco.

As early as 1870, the Italians were supplying much of San Francisco and part of the adjacent interior with fish. In the early eighties it was said that a majority of the resident Italians were fishermen or fish merchants. Generally they came from North Italy, but their successors have been largely Sicilians. About a third of all the emigrants from Augusta (province of Syracuse) have been fishermen. And they have gone chiefly to California and Alaska. Still others of the San Francisco colony have come from the Isola delle Femmine or from the Sicilian settlements in Tunisia. Mending their nets or returning with their catch, they have made a considerable part of San Francisco picturesque by their presence. Their industry was not abated after the earthquake. On the Sacramento River, not far from San Francisco, there is an Italian fishermen's town. Some 1250 a year, it is said, go to Alaska for the April-September season, during the rest of the year fishing from motor boats owned by themselves or by companies. For the Alaska campaign they are enrolled by half a dozen South Italian "bosses," who make a pretty pile in pay from the salmon companies, in commissions from the fishermen, and in their profit on the sustenance they provide. The fishermen make their catch with nets at the mouths of the streams on Kodiak Island, in Bristol Bay, and on the west coast of Alaska Peninsula, receiving for the season $100 in "run money" and 3½ or 4 cents per head of fish caught, say $450 for five months.[30]

[30]Carpi, ii, pp. 132, 225, 237; *Guida Metelli*, p. 183; *Emig. e Col.*, 1893, pp. 462, 464, 478; Ottolenghi, p. 381; G. B. Cafiero, "Gli italiani nel distretto consolare di Nuova Orleans, III, Florida," *Boll. Emig.*, 1903, No. 1, p. 21; Fara Forni, "Gl' interessi italiani nel distretto consolare di Nuova Orleans," *Boll. Emig.*, 1905, No. 17, pp. 6, 16; G. Moroni, "L'emigrazione italiana in Florida," *Boll. Emig.*, 1913, No. 1, p. 73; Corbino, p. 24; F. Daneo, "I pescatori italiani nell' Alaska," *Boll. Emig.*, 1915, No. 4, pp. 39-44; H. A. Fisk, "The Fishermen of San Francisco Bay," in *Proceedings of the Thirty-second Annual Conference of Charities and Correction*, 1905, pp. 383-393; E. Patrizi, *Gl' italiani in California* (San Francisco, 1911), *passim*.

G. E. DI PALMA CASTIGLIONE

ITALIAN IMMIGRATION INTO THE UNITED STATES 1901-4*

At this time Italian immigration has reached the highest point yet attained, and perhaps to be attained in the future.

The Italians, who until 1879 had contributed but a meager part to the mass of energy which immigration represents, since that year, have gone on giving an element more and more relevant to the general body of immigration. In the last three years they have taken the lead among the diverse nationalities of the Old World which furnished men to this, the younger nation of the New World. This is shown in the following table, which indicates, by decades, the proportion of the Italian element to the entire immigration into the United States:

TABLE I

Decades	Total	Yearly Average	Percentage
1821–30	408	41	0.25
1831–40	2,258	226	0.37
1841–50	1,870	167	0.09
1851–60	9,231	923	0.17
1861–70	11,728	1,173	0.50
1871–80	55,759	5,576	1.98
1881–90	307,309	30,731	5.85
1891–1900	655,668	65,567	17.05
1901–4	741,986	185,496	27.86
1821–1904	1,786,217		

The increase of Italian immigration into the United States, rather than depending upon the general increase of the emigration from Italy, is the effect of a change of direction of the mass of Italian immigrants, as is shown in the next table, which gives the percentage represented by the Italian emigration to the United States as compared with the entire emigration from Italy:

American Journal of Sociology, Vol. 11 (September, 1905), pp. 183-206.

TABLE II

Year	Per Cent.
1891	23.46
1892	37.00
1893	35.25
1894	28.34
1895	20.56
1896	27.28
1897	27.01
1898	40.74
1899	44.14
1900	48.73
1901	40.12
1902	61.20
1903	61.91
1904	67.28

As is clearly seen from these figures, it is only during the last few years that the Italians represent a large percentage of general immigration into the United States. This fact is accounted for, in part if not entirely by the diminution of property in the South American republics, where, because of the greater similarity of climate, and race, customs, and language, the Italians have always preferred to emigrate.[1] For some time, however, the South American labor markets have been traversing periods of depression, which at present show no signs of disappearing; and consequently they have had, and still have, an immediate and strong repercussion upon the human current which flows in that direction. Moreover, the Italian emigration, which was formerly subventioned and encouraged by the Brazilian government, has been restrained by the Italian authorities because of the insufficiency of legislation in Brazil for the protection of the Italian laborers, who were unable to exact the payment of their wages from the masters of the haciendas, to the plowing and cultivation of which they devoted their labor. Recently, however, a remedial law has been approved by the Brazilian parliament, and it is probable that in a short time the Italian government will withdraw its opposition, and that Brazil will again take up the work of encouraging Italian immigration. In such event, the immigratory current toward the United States will undergo a cer-

[1] It is a well-known fact that in the Argentine Republic and contiguous states, and to a certain extent in Brazil, the Italians represent the predominating factor of the foreign population, and in these countries, especially the first-named, they have succeeded in imprinting their own national character upon many of the social manifestations of these communities.

tain change, and necessarily diminish. It may be foreseen, therefore, that the succeeding years will bring into the United States a progressively decreasing number of Italians. Nevertheless, even in view of these facts, it will be of interest to study in detail the present immigration into the United States. The analysis of this immigratory current will form a basis for a true conception by American public opinion of its greater or less desirability, and, by showing its component parts and its distribution over the areas of the United States, will indicate what is necessary to be done, either by private enterprise or by the government, to utilize the qualities and energies which it brings into the country.

For the sake of brevity, and also because it is only in recent years that Italian immigration has assumed important proportions, the four years 1901-4 have been selected for the purposes of this study. It is thought that this limitation will not be prejudicial to a general conception to the entire Italian immigration, as in the preceding years it was composed of similar elements.

According to the statistics compiled by the Bureau of Immigration, the entire Italian immigration, from the point of view of its derivation, has been divided, in the last three years, as follows:

TABLE III

Year	Northern Italy	Southern Italy	Total	Per Cent. of Southern Italians
1901	22,103	115,704	137,807	83.23
1902	27,620	152,915	180,535	84.70
1903	37,429	196,117	233,546	83.97
1904	36,699	159,329	196,028	81.28

It is southern Italy, which furnishes the greater number of immigrants. The southern element represents more than 80 per cent of the total. This fact is explained by the geographical position of Italy. While the exuberance of the northern Italian population can overflow toward the north of Europe, in Switzerland, Germany, and Austria, the overplus of southern Italians has only the North African coast and the Americas. To Africa, and especially Tripoli, where they have founded flourishing agricultural colonies, the Sicilians from the southern and eastern part of their island direct their steps, while to America, North and South, turn those who come from the territory south of Tuscany, to the extreme point of Calabria and the northern part of Sicily. In this portion of Italy clusters a closely packed population which presents an average density to the square kilometer sometimes superior to the average density of the whole of Italy (113). This mass of people, generally very prolific, has no industries, its only source of production being agriculture, which in these last decades has suffered severe crises, one more violent than the other, principally those which have affected the sale of wine and oranges.

Submerged in their prolification, impoverished by the decline of agriculture, and discouraged by the unjust distribution of taxes between the north and the south, to these people emigration offers the only relief, and they desert the land which produces in abundance the good things of the earth, for which there is little demand, and at first temporarily, but afterward permanently, abandon their native country to establish themselves in others where they find conditions sufficient for their maintenance.

The emigration from the southern provinces of Italy is destined to continue until the general conditions are changed, or until a diminution of the birth-rate establishes equilibrium between production and population. As neither of these solutions is probable before a period yet remote, emigration must necessarily remain a permanent feature for a long time to come, and, what is more important—a point which the reader should note particularly—it must assume more and more the character of definitive emigration to the countries where these people have found means to live and prosper. From this it will readily be seen that the cry of danger, which many Americans still repeat, is without foundation in fact. That the accusation, so readily made against the Italians, that they come here only for a time, and return to their home country with their accumulated gains, has no substantial basis, is well established by the American consul at Naples in his reports, which state that, if the southern Italian emigrant returns once, or even a second time, to Italy, he finally gives up repatriation, and, together with his wife and family, goes back to the United States with the firm idea of remaining there permanently.

Such conclusion is favored also by the consideration of two other series of data, which indirectly re-confirm it: (1) the number of immigrants who have been in the United States before, and (2) the number of those leaving to return to Mediterranean ports. The following table is an extract from the figures gathered by the Bureau of Immigration:

TABLE IV

IMMIGRANTS WHO HAVE BEEN IN THE UNITED STATES BEFORE

Year	Northern Italians	Southern Italians	Total
1901	3,017	11,524	14,524
1902	3,475	11,829	15,304
1903	4,452	12,619	17,071
1904	5,163	14,870	20,033

Of 741,986 who came to the United States during the four years, 66,932 had been here before. They had therefore decided not to repeat the experiment of repatriation.

Before giving the figures collected for (2) it must be noted that they were furnished by the reports of the conferences of the different transportation companies which serve between the ports of the United States and the Mediterranean, from the agents of the Compania Transatlantica of Barcelona and the Compagnie Transatlantique Française; and, also, that these data include not only Italians, but all third-class passengers for Mediterranean ports and Havre. How many among these may be Italians is difficult to determine, but, considering that these companies touch not only at Italian ports, but also at French and Spanish, and remembering that eastern and southern Europeans return generally by way of Italy, and Belgians by way of Havre, it cannot be far from the truth, after deducting 15 per cent from the companies' figures to consider the balance as the approximate number of Italians who during the three years have left the United States. Proceeding in such manner, we have the following table, in which the calendar and not the fiscal year is used:[2]

TABLE V

Year	Italians Sailed from the United States	Italians Arrived
1901	32,266	143,071
1902	48,684	201,260
1903	83,333	235,088
Total.......	164,283	579,419

The number of Italians, then, who left the United States in the three years represents, as the largest approximate number, a little more than one-fourth of the total number arrived in the same period.

Uniting the data derived from the last two tables with the general considerations, it may be seen that Italian immigration is not temporary in character, but a permanent contribution to the American population. Observation and knowledge of general conditions in those regions of Italy whence flows the stream of immigration into the United States, as well as into the other parts of the globe toward which the Italians direct their emigration, strengthen the opinion already expressed. It is certain that among the enormous mass of Italians arrived and arriving in this land there are some who, temperamentally unadapted to struggle in new climatic and social conditions, or already too advanced in life to take root in new soil, prefer to finish their life where it began, and decide to return to Italy. Apart from the fact that this phenomenon is common to all immigratory currents, it should be considered a fortunate circumstance, and not a cause of comtempt for Italians, since of all who come here, only those remain permanently who are more adapted to be absorbed in the new environment, and such represent the very large majority of Italian immigrants.

An analysis of Italian immigration in respect to sex gives the following results:

TABLE VI

YEAR	NORTHERN ITALIANS		SOUTHERN ITALIANS		TOTAL	
	Male	Female	Male	Female	Male	Female
1901.....	17,852	4,251	90,395	25,309	108,247	29,560
1902.....	22,425	5,195	124,536	28,379	146,961	33,574
1903.....	30,477	6,952	158,939	37,178	189,416	44,130
1904.....	28,784	7,915	122,770	36,559	155,554	44,474

[2]From the official publications of the Italian government for the calendar years 1902 and 1903 we have the following data in regard to the passengers arrived at the ports of Naples and Genoa from the United States:

	1902	1903
Arrived at Genoa.....................	7,859	5,571
Arrived at Naples	44,357	72,662
	52,216	78,233

These figures include all passengers landed in Italy, either Italians or foreigners. The totals are different from those derived from the calculation made upon the figures supplied by the navigation companies, but they only tend to confirm our conclusion in regard to the small number of Italian immigrants in the United States who go back to Italy.

A glance at these figures is sufficient to perceive the large preponderance of males. To bring out this fact more clearly, a table showing the percentage of females in the total number of immigrants coming from the north and south is here appended:

TABLE VII

Year	North	South	Total
1901........	19.23	21.87	21.44
1902........	18.20	18.55	18.59
1903........	18.57	18.95	18.03
1904........	21.56	23.00	22.68

Among immigrants from the north as well as among those from the south we find the males in the same large proportion, which proves the strength of the Italian immigration, in that it consists almost entirely of individuals who must work for their living, and not of women, who, to a certain extent, must depend upon others. This is explained by the work they are called to perform—a kind of work where the presence of women would be a hindrance and not an aid. The Italian women belonging to this class, should they come in large numbers, would be unable to find work, and would be obliged to depend upon the men, who, employed as day laborers and paid small wages, would find it difficult to maintain families, which in America requires large means.

The vigor of Italian immigration is further demonstrated by the abundance of individuals between the ages of fifteen and forty-five. The figures are given in the table below:

TABLE VIII

Years	Northern Italians		Southern Italians		Total	
	Under 14 Years	45 Years and Over	Under 14 Years	45 Years and Over	Under 14 Years	45 Years and Over
1901.....	1,830	1,117	14,794	9,593	17,624	10,710
1902.....	2,215	1,376	16,954	12,216	19,169	13,692
1903.....	3,404	1,419	21,619	9,837	25,023	11,256
1904.....	3,633	1,537	20,895	9,443	24,528	10,980

PERCENTAGE

1901.....	8.22	5.05	13.64	8.29	12.79	7.71
1902.....	8.01	4.98	11.08	7.98	10.61	7.52
1903.....	9.09	3.79	11.02	5.00	10.71	4.00
1904.....	9.89	4.18	13.11	5.92	12.51	5.60

Referring to the above tables, it can be seen that the number of boys and old men does not surpass 20 per cent of the entire immigration, except in the year 1901, and then but slightly. The great majority, then, is composed not only of individuals who can procure directly the means of subsistence, but of young men who are physically capable of working immediately upon landing.

The physical integrity of Italian immigration is also shown by the negligible number refused access to the United States by the immigration authorities at the ports. The small number deported, besides proving the florid health of the Italian immigrants, shows also the infinitely few excluded for political, economical, or moral reasons. The figures below demonstrate the exactness of these observations:

TABLE IX

NUMBER OF DEBARRED

Cause of Rejection	1901			1902			1903			1904		
	North	South	Total	North	South	Total	North	South	Total	North	South	Total
Idiots..........	..	2	2	..	..	..	..	..	..	1	3	4
Insane.........	..	4	4	..	5	5	..	8	8	1	8	9
Paupers........	51	1292	1343	51	2049	2100	160	2164	2324	141	1396	1537
Dangerously ill..	10	30	40	..	7	7	9	147	156	35	235	270
Convicts	..	2	2	..	..	..	3	46	49	..	25	25
Prostitutes	..	..	..	..	..	..	..	1	1	..	..	..
Contract laborers	67	125	192	11	100	111	71	447	518	83	425	508
Total........	128	1455	1583	78	2235	2313	243	2813	3056	261	2092	2353

To bring out more clearly the extremely small number refused access, the percentage of the total number of immigrants is here given:

TABLE X

PERCENTAGE OF THE DEBARRED IN TOTAL ITALIAN IMMIGRATION

Year	Northern Italians	Southern Italians	Total
1901........	0.57	1.25	1.14
1902........	0.28	1.36	1.28
1903........	0.60	1.43	1.30
1904........	0.71	1.31	1.20

As is shown, the number of deported does not exceed 1.3 per cent of the total number of immigrants. This is the result of severe legislative action in Italy, which forbids emigration to all persons comprised in the categories excluded by the American laws. The Italian government has established special offices at every port of departure to enforce the laws of emigration. Another safeguard is the inspection by the salaried physicians attached to the American consulates in Italy. These physicians, with the acquiescence of the Italian authorities, and furnished with the permission of the navigation companies, inspect one by one all the departing emigrants, and prevent those from leaving who, according to their opinion, would not be allowed to land in America. Thus it is seen that, by the Italian government's work, all elements which could menace law and order in the United States are removed from the emigratory stream, while the consular physicians see to it that it is freed from those individuals who might imperil the public health. The insignificant number refused access by the United States authorities is composed of the few who at times succeed, owing to the enormous number embarking, in eluding the vigilance of the Italian authorities and the inspection of the consular physicians.

The preceding data therefore authorize the statement that the Italian immigration into the United States is vigorous and desirable from the physical point of view, and pure and healthy from the moral point of view.

The question of education now presents itself. Analytical investigation of the Italian immigration from this point of view gives the following results:

TABLE XI

YEAR	ILLITERATES OVER FOURTEEN YEARS			PERCENTAGE OF ILLITERATES IN TOTAL IMMIGRATION		
	Northern Italians	Southern Italians	Total	Northern	Southern	Total
1901.....	3,122	58,493	61,615	14.12	50.55	45.44
1992.....	3,556	76,529	80,085	12.87	50.00	44.35
1903.....	4,283	84,512	88,795	11.45	43.09	38.01
1904.....	4,150	74,889	75,039	11.31	47.00	40.32

The progressive improvement in regard to primary instruction is evident. The year 1901 shows a proportion of over 45 per cent of illiteracy; the year 1904, about 40 per cent. Nevertheless, illiteracy remains a characteristic disadvantage of the Italian immigrants, especially those from southern Italy. The difference of intellectual conditions between the north and south of Italy is the result of long years of misgovernment and neglect in the provinces of southern Italy. Although in these provinces, as well as in the whole of Italy, the law of compulsory elementary education is now in force, yet complex circumstances, among which may be named low financial conditions and lack of administration in the communes, have hindered the southern populations from enjoying the fruit of legislative action in the same proportion as the northern populations have been able to do. Healthier economic conditions, the communes administered by more modern classes than the governing officials in the south, have, in a little more than forty years of national life, almost obliterated the plague spot of illiteracy in the northern parts of Italy. Illiteracy must diminish as in fact it has always diminished, among the immigrants; but it remains in relatively large proportion because improvement in this respect is necessarily slow. The question arises then: Is the illiteracy of the Italian immigrants a menace to those countries—especially the United States—to which they betake themselves?

Many writers upon immigration have given this question first place when speaking of the greater or less desirability of the same, but a closer view of the subject cannot but disclose the exaggeration of those who maintain that a heavy percentage of illiteracy is a grave peril for the United States. In the first place, illiteracy is not a new fact, nor can it be affirmed to be a characteristic of Italian immigration alone, because we ignore the number of illiterates in the great immigratory currents which in the past fifty years have inundated this country. Only during the last few years has it become a feature of immigration statistics to take note of illiteracy. Given the relative recency of the acceptance of the principle of compulsory popular education in European states, and keeping in mind the origin of the Irish and German immigrants (who formed the bulk of the immigration into the United States in the past), coming, as they did, from the least developed regions of their respective countries, it is not difficult to believe that the proportion of illiterates was, if not equal, at least little inferior, to that which the Italian immigration actually presents. As is well known, the Irish and Germans became elements of force and prosperity in the new country in which they settled. What, then, are the criteria for judging the desirability of immigrants? First, the possibility of utilizing the qualities of the newcomers, and, second, the facility of absorption, with the loss of the distinctive character of their national origin.

When the Italian may be utilized in the development of the country's mines, the culture of its lands, and the embellishment of its cities, his grammatical attainments in his own language may well be a negligible quantity. A country in its period of development has need of brawn as well as brain, and the vigor of the Italian as a laborer cannot be placed in doubt; and, therefore, considered in the light of the first criterion for judgment, the Italian immigration cannot be held to be undesirable.

In regard to the facility of absorption, illiteracy should be an advantage in the work of Americanizing newcomers. The individual who cannot read brings fewer impressions and ideas from his native country than one who has been able through education to observe the movements in which he was born and bred. The illiterate man, in some respects, and especially if he comes from the rural regions, is more like a child. While deficient in past impressions, he has an intellectual freshness and curiosity. His adaptability to a new environment, therefore, will be accomplished more rapidly and with greater ease, like that of a child's. Moreover, instruction does not necessarily include the idea of intelligence, and when the observations made upon the physical force and vigor of the Italians are joined to those made upon their intellectual brightness (Italians of southern Italy are noted for their quickness of perception and other strong mental qualities), one is forced to the conclusion that the percentage of illiteracy among the Italians cannot constitute a peril for the United States, and, further, that this defect may even become an aid to the work of assimilation.

Instead of meditating exclusion for the illiterate immigrant, it would be much more logical and just to add to the conditions demanded for obtaining citizenship the obligation, not only of stammering a few English words, but of speaking and writing English. In such manner the intellectual youth of the illiterate immigrant would come to be exploited effectively for the advancement of his Americanization. Apart from this, however, it is useful to note that the illiteracy existing among the immigrants is reduced only in small proportion among their children. The census of 1900 establishes this fact. On the other hand, the same census shows that the children of new immigrants manifest greater diligence in study, and greater profit from it, than do the children of parents born in America. Seventy-five per cent of the first-mentioned class, and 65 per cent of the second, frequented the schools. Of 30,404,762 persons of ten years and over, born of American parents, 1,737,803, or 5.7 per cent, were illiterates;

while of 10,958,803 persons born of foreign parents, only 179,384, or 1.67 per cent, were in the same condition. It is necessary only to cite, in regard to Italian immigration, the deductions made by Mr. R. P. Falkner with respect to all immigration from southern Italy: "From the foregoing analysis it should, I think, be clear that the evidence of a declining average of intelligence and capacity, which has been alleged to characterize recent immigration, is just as inconclusive as that brought forward to show an increasing volume."

The usefullness of a body of immigration, as has been pointed out before, can be judged only by the mass of capacities it brings into countries, and the relation of the same to the work demanded by the country's needs. As an immigration of learned people into an undeveloped country could be a detriment rather than an advantage to its interests, so an immigration of laborers into a country already well provided in that respect might be held to be perilous for its economic and social order.

Taking up this part of the subject, it is necessary to ascertain what kind of work the Italians know how to do, and what productive capacities they possess; and from this can be seen in what numbers they may be utilized in the United States.

The following table shows the three larger categories of Italian immigration constituted of farmers, farm laborers, and laborers:

TABLE XII

	1901			1902		
	North	South	Total	North	South	Total
Farmers	23	7	30	9	140	149
Farm laborers......	311	26,566	29,877	6,455	39,128	45,583
Laborers	8,735	43,210	51,945	10,143	38,396	68,539
Total..........	12,069	69,783	81,852	16,607	97,664	114,271

	1903			1904		
	North	South	Total	North	South	Total
Farmers	200	678	878	260	269	529
Farm laborers.	6,462	32,391	38,853	5,154	42,471	47,625
Laborers	15,622	85,682	101,304	13,526	42,502	56,028
Total..........	22,284	118,751	141,035	19,940	85,242	104,102

All of this part of the immigration originates in the rural districts of Italy; even those classified by the Bureau of Immigration as laborers are in fact peasants. The enormous majority comes from the south, and, as is shown by the statistics published by the Italian government, the urban population in general, and that of the south in particular, does not emigrate except in very small proportion. It is misleading to consider the laborers as distinct from the farm laborers; actually they form but one class, and, with the tillers of the soil, represent the total agricultural element. They constitute more than one-half of the entire immigration, and, as the gross figures do not bring out clearly the characteristic note of the observation, it can be seen by the percentage table below:

TABLE XIII

PERCENTAGE OF THE AGRICULTURAL ELEMENTS IN TOTAL ITALIAN IMMIGRATION

Year	Northern Italians	Southern Italians	Total
1901........	54.60	60.21	59.39
1902........	60.12	63.86	63.29
1903........	61.14	60.55	60.38
1904........	51.60	53.50	53.14

In the three years under consideration—except the first—the urban population, made up of skilled workmen and professionals, represents less than 40 per cent; the remainder consists of farm laborers more or less skilled in the art of agriculture. Thus it is readily seen that the Italians in large majority should find their way to the fields of agriculture, the ground adapted to the development of their activities. There they would find the greatest advantage with the least proportionate sacrifice, and at the same time would be able to contribute most effectively to the increasing productivity and wealth of the United States.

Before observing the actual direction taken by the Italians once disembarked, it is well to note what capital, in addition to their personnel, they bring with them. This investigation gives the following results:

TABLE XIV

Year	Amount of Money Shown by the Italian Immigrants	Average per Capita
1901	$1,523,284	$12.67
1902	3,018,641	14.47
1903	2,123,625	13.09
1904	3,100,664	20.00

The figures reported show a progressive improvement in the amount of money brought by the Italians. These figures, it must be observed, cannot be considered exact, because the Italian peasant in general, and the southern Italian in particular, is diffident toward strangers and obstinate in refusing to make known his personal affairs, and still more so when it is a question of money in his possession. It can well be imagined, then, that a large number of immigrants have kept hidden the exact amount of money they possessed; so much the more so owing to the widespread opinion among them that $10 is a sufficient sum to own up to at the port in order to obtain admittance into the country.

Allowing for this, however, it is but just to say that the Italian immigration is composed principally of poor people in the strictest sense of the word—people who have not enough money to pay transportation expenses from the ports of disembarkation, and who must find work immediately upon disembarking.

Having examined in detail the ethnic and demographic composition of the Italian immigration, and having seen the conditions, physical, economic, social, and financial, which it presents, it remains to study the direction taken by the immigrants toward the different parts of the country. The figures below indicate the percentage of Italian immigrants who have directed their steps toward the different geographic divisions of the United States, according to the origin of the immigrants, during the four years under consideration:

TABLE XV

	NORTHERN ITALIANS				SOUTHERN ITALIANS				TOTAL			
	1901	1902	1903	1904	1901	1902	1903	1904	1901	1902	1903	1864
North Atlan. Div.	61	28	59	56	88	86	86	85	83	82	82	80
North Centr. Div.	16	18	18	17	6	8	8	8	7	9	10	10
South Atlan. Div.	1	1	1	2	1	1	2	3	2	1	2	2
South Centr. Div.	2	2	2	3	3	3	3	3	3	3	2	3
Western Division	20	21	20	20	2	2	1	1	5	5	4	5
	100	100	100	100	100	100	100	100	100	100	100	100

The percentages are referred to as approximative, exact figures not being necessary to show the objective points.

By these data it is seen that the northern states of the Union absorb more than 90 per cent of the Italian immigration, less a small fraction from the north of Italy, which goes to the western states. The great majority of the Italians remain in the vicinity of the ports of disembarkation; and even those who travel west, instead of dispersing in the eleven states and territories which form that division, concentrate mostly in California, which fact is set forth in the following figures:

TABLE XVI

PERCENTAGE OF NORTHERN ITALIANS DIRECTED TO CALIFORNIA OF ALL NORTHERN ITALIANS WEST-BOUND

1901..................................63.14
1902..................................64.95
1903....................................70.76
1904..................................72.61

Neglecting to consider this tendency of a part of the northern Italian immigrants to concentrate in California, precisely the most populous point of the Western Division, it is well to return to the principal deductions to be made from Table XV; i.e., the enormous prevalence of Italians in the states of the North Atlantic and North Central Divisions. The figures below set forth that in these divisions the great majority of the Italians are concentrated in a few states:

TABLE XVII

NORTH ATLANTIC DIVISION

	1901	1902	1903	1904	1901	1902	1903	1904	1901	1902	1903	1904
New York.........	50.44	46.17	42.91	44.28	60.57	60.68	53.82	56.15	59.37	59.10	53.09	5,445
Pennsylvania	30.87	30.15	33.87	31.96	20.58	24.79	25.31	22.29	21.78	21.37	26.30	2,350
New Jersey........	5.00	6.84	5.22	5.17	5.79	3.47	5.91	7.76	5.70	5.70	5.83	744
Massachusetts.....	8.64	9.43	10.13	10.46	7.25	9.00	7.41	8.03	7.41	7.41	8.32	861
Connecticut	32	6.13	5.63	6.46	3.67	3.38	3.34	3.47	3.34	3.34	3.95	386

NORTH CENTRAL DIVISION

	1901	1902	1903	1904	1901	1902	1903	1904	1901	1902	1903	1904
Illinois............	39.53	47.56	47.75	43.20	50.16	45.99	41.61	39.89	42.69	46.48	43.41	4,099
Michigan	25.62	21.14	18.25	12.51	8.32	7.16	9.85	7.26	14.36	11.50	12.27	895
Ohio	6.05	7.49	7.57	9.92	26.74	34.50	33.67	35.47	19.52	26.11	26.06	2,646

The data are wanting for showing what centers of population in the states considered become the final destination of the immigrants, or in what proportions they are scattered in the different parts of these states. It can be assumed, however, that the mass of Italians cannot spread in the farming lands, since these farms are already occupied, and it may be affirmed that the immigrants go to augment the population of the cities, and principally the large cities. This idea is favored by common observation, by the census of 1900, and by the conclusions of Dr. Tosti in his study of the Italian population of New York state. According to the census of 1900, 62.4 per cent of the Italians established in the United States were settled in centers whose population was greater than 25,000. According to Dr. Tosti who secured data up to December, 1903, of 486,175 Italian residents in New York state, 382,775, or 78.7 per cent, were established in New York city.

The conclusion, then, from the figures reported is that more than 80 per cent of the Italians settle in the states of the northern divisions, and that from 75 per cent to 85 per cent of these concentrate in the large cities. Remembering now the arts and trades of the Italians, as established by the data given previously, it is seen that, while more than 60 per cent of them are peasants and farmers, instead of going to the agricultural districts, they come to increase the urban populations of the United States.

The concentration of the Italians in the large cities is as detrimental to themselves as it is to the United States. The peasant who establishes himself in a large American city cannot be anything but a laborer; all of his technical qualities are lost both to himself and to the country which harbors him. The Italian peasant, who has had centuries of experience in tilling the land, who understands all kinds of cultivation, who is not only expert in viniculture, but also in the culture of all the vegetables and fruits of his new country, is giving but the minimum part of his productive habits, i.e., his physical force.

The evils of concentration do not consist only in this dispersion of energy, or rather this mistaken employment of forces; they are not only economic evils, but they extend also to the moral and political fields. In fact, the Italian immigrant as a laborer, alternating only between stone-breaking and ditching, remains an alien to the country. The immigrant, to whatever nationality he may belong, does not feel himself a part of the collectivity as long as no ties, first economic, then moral, are formed to attach him to the new soil. The laborer cannot form these ties while he remains a machine, pure and simple, furnishing only brute force and no special interest can be felt in the work he accomplishes. Thus the Italian immigrant, thrust into the large cities, surrounded and outclassed by those who do not understand him and whom he does not understand, shuts himself in with his fellow-countrymen and remains indifferent to all that happens outside of the quarters inhabited by them. Although renouncing the idea of repatriation, because he knows the economic conditions in his own country forbid, and becoming an American citizen, he remains always a stranger to the new country.

The crowding into the large American cities brings other harmful effects. The cost of living in the northern states, and especially in the large centers, is very high, while the wages, on account of the greater competition, are relatively low. This lack of equilibrium imposes upon the Italian large material sacrifices which deplete him physically and lower him socially. The high rents force him to live in the worst quarters and in restricted space. In the Italian quarters of New York and Philadelphia can be seen the alleged lodging-houses, with seven or eight or even ten persons occupying one bedroom. Families of seven or more members crowd into houses containing only two rooms, one of which is the kitchen. This mode of existence, apart from the fact that it is fruitful in the development and extension of infectious diseases, renders the people vile in their personal habits, and, as has been alluded to before, makes them appear repulsive to the Americans. If these material conditions influence the Italians to feel no sincere or profound attachment to the adopted country, on the other hand they influence the native American to disdain the newcomers, thus causing a reciprocal psychologic state of mind which is a powerful obstacle in the way of assimilation.

But the influence of this agglomeration of the Italians goes still farther, for, besides the evils already spoken of, it furnishes an effective stimulus for the development and deepening of moral corruption. Among Italian immigrants, as among all others, there are certain elements which belong to no class, having lived the life of all, with no trade or capacity for honest work of any kind. Such people have no moral curb or scruple, and prey upon the others. They find in the swarming Italian quarters of the large American cities fruitful fields in which to exercise their baneful powers for the despoliation of their countrymen, who, ignorant and ingenuous, become their ready victims. In the guise of agents, solicitors, or journalists, they extort money. As founders of gambling dens and houses of ill-fame, they organize schemes of blackmail and other crimes. It is among these people that the ward politicians find their agents. The existence of people like these depends upon the crowded conditions referred to. The number of such individuals is not large, but they are indefatigable propagators of corruption among the immigrants.

Thus are conditions formed which, while placing obstacles in the way of reciprocal advantage, ruin the Italian immigrant morally, materially, and physically.

It is not the large number of Italian immigrants which constitutes a peril for the United States. The immigrants are young, honest, strong, and overflowing with energy; they possess potentially all the factors to represent an increase of development of the American people. The real danger is their concentration in the large cities, their defective distribution in the territory of the republic, which renders impossible their proper utilization, and forms an ever-increasing plethora of labor in the more populous states, while at other points there is a large and unsatisfied need of laboring-men.

The problem is not, as some are inclined to think, to find means for limiting or stopping the immigratory current, but to avoid the evils of concentration, and to find a way effectually to distribute the mass of immigration.

What causes provoke the concentration of Italians in the large cities? Why is it that these peasants prefer to live in crowded centers, rather than to scatter over the country, where they would be able to continue the art of agriculture and find the most appropriate outlet for their energies? Looking for the causes of this phenomenon will aid powerfully to solve the problem, and a brief survey of present and former conditions reveals the two principal causes: (*a*) the poverty of the Italian immigrants; (*b*) their previous mode of existence.

As has been demonstrated, the average amount of capital of the newcomer is a sum which, at the most enables him to live without work ten or twelve days. If work be not found in that limited period, he must turn for help to his countrymen or to public charity. He has no time—aside from all other difficulties encountered, such as ignorance of the language, difference in all the conditions of life, etc., etc.—to study the advantage or disadvantage of points in the United States where he might be able to develop his activities. Even if he knew before landing that the South or West was adapted to his needs, his lack of funds would prevent his using that knowledge. Furthermore, the same lack of money forbids him to choose work in the fields, for, although better paid, it depends upon circumstances, which he has neither time nor money to command, and the fact that the land can be bought at a low price must be neglected, while he is glad to secure any kind of work which will provide for his present needs.

In addition to the economic causes, there is another, far more complex, because derived from habits of life which have obtained for centuries. The population of southern Italy is composed in great part of peasant farm laborers massed in large boroughs, which might be called cities, not for the perfection and complexity of their municipal and social life, but for their number of inhabitants. In order to live in these crowded haunts and mix with their fellows, the peasants walk morning and night several miles to and from the fields. They leave their homes long before dawn and return after sunset. This custom arose in feudal days, when the organization for public safety was deficient, and existed in those communities until the foundation of Italian unity, thus forming tendencies and psychological conditions in the peasant peculiar to him.

A study of the character of the southern Italians shows that they cannot live isolated; the conditions indicated above have formed in them the necessity of living in homogeneous groups, to reunite with their own kind. At the same time, they have acquired great diffidence toward the outside world of all who do not belong to the nucleus in which they were born and bred. Such are slowly passing away, but are yet strong enough to influence the deliberations of the individual, and especially in his choice of a mode of life.

This fear of isolation and this distrust of strangers become stronger and deeper in a new, strange country, and the peasant, although provided with money enough to buy and stock a small farm, finds in his own social needs a powerful obstacle to the realization of such a plan; but, joined with a sufficient number of his own countrymen in similar financial conditions, he does not hesitate to choose the farm.

These, then, are the principal reasons which account for the agglomeration of Italians in large cities. Suppressing them, the resulting evil will necessarily cease to exist.

The means best adapted to solving this problem would appear to be the formation of colonizing societies which should propose to found agricultural colonies composed of Italian peasants. It is well known that the greater part of the good arable land, once the property of the government, has been pre-empted, and has become the property of railroad companies and private indidivuals; but we are still far from the time in which all the good land will be under cultivation. Large areas await the hard and continued work of the laborer to be productive. As stated above, most of these lands belong to private corporations or individuals, and these should, in their own interests, favor the colonizing idea and aid in realizing it.

The work of the society would consist in locating the land and in providing transportation, and other expenses incident to the placing of the laborer in working contact with the land. A fixed wage-rate might be advanced, or the peasant guaranteed the living of himself and family until such time as the land became productive. The ultimate aim of the colonizing society would be (a) to render the peasant proprietor of the land he has put under cultivation, or (b) to remain proprietor of the land and administer the agricultural plant it has established. In the second case, the society would pay the laborer wages, or rent the land, exacting a part of the harvest. The choice of either of these two plans should not prejudice the practicability of success. However, the first would appear to be better adapted to invoke the ready forma-tion of colonies. Should the second plan be preferred, and the obligation to provide for the needs of the laborers and the land remain for a time, the peasants could be treated as tenants, and ten-ants with long leases, rather than as wage-earners; for only in this way could they be permanently established and attached to the land.

It is certain that such a society, organized to place Italian immigrants to the best advantage, would be able to reap large profits upon the capital invested. The Italian peasant, if not the best, is one of the best cultivators of land in Europe. Despite the drawbacks existing for ages in his own country, he has shown heroic resistance, and has confronted misfortunes and persecu-tions before which many others would have sustained ultimate defeat. In spite of all the disadvantages of climatic conditions, and the varying qualities of land, lack of capital, and wise admin-istration, ignorance of modern agricultural science and its inven-tions, he has known how to produce cultures of every kind. But in agricultural industry—different from many other forms of work—the most important factor of production is always the man. It is the capacity, the force, of the man that assures the success of a colonizing enterprise. In America, where he would find all the help he could not find in his own country, the Italian peasant would yield marvelous and remunerative results, if placed where he could prove his ability.

Now, as never before, the conditions are propitious for an experiment of this nature. After many trials the cultivation of the mulberry tree in the United States—without which the rais-ing of the silk-worm would be impossible—is an assured fact. There are numerous plantations flourishing in several states, and it can be predicted that its culture will be universal in the South and West. Every Italian peasant understands the mulberry, and knows how to foster the silk-worm with its cocoon. In Italy, anywhere except in a very few provinces, the silk culture is undertaken, at some points being the only culture made, at others subsidiary. In the United States the Italian colonies could propose the extension and exploitation of this new fountain of riches, certain that it would repay largely, especially those who would initiate it. The United States imports all raw silk needed for its manufactories, which consume immense quantities. Such culture, aided by the experience of the Italians, would absolutely assure success.

The establishment of an Italian colonization society in the United States would be looked upon favorably in both countries. Every report of the commissioner of immigration exposes the perils of concentration and exhorts Congress to adopt special precautions for a right distribution of the new immigration.[3] It is certain that the government would give moral, if not material, support to such an undertaking. In Italy, attached to the ministry of foreign affairs, is a special bureau created for the purpose of protecting and advising emigrants to seek the countries most adapted to their needs. This bureau is more than ever convinced of the necessity of aiding the formation of agricultural colonies where the Italian emigrant would be able to secure conditions more favorable to his development and assimilation.

The two governments, therefore, the one indirectly and morally, the other directly and materially, would contribute to spur on the Italian immigrant toward the destination best adapted to him by his previous mode of living and by his special aptitude for tilling the soil.

[3]See reports of the general commissioner of immigration for the years 1901-3 (Washington, D.C.).

GUSTAVO TOSTI

ITALY'S ATTITUDE TOWARD HER EMIGRANTS*

I.

The recently published report of the Commissioner-General of Immigration has given renewed impetus to the discussion, which has of late engaged public attention, of the question how to deal with foreign immigration. It may be fairly assumed that Mr. Sargent's report will, by its general trend and through certain statements it contains, afford a strong argument to those who still advocate a restrictive policy, in order to lessen the evils resulting to this country from the constant influx of certain specific foreign elements, which seem particularly obnoxious to the cultivated American of the day. I do not propose, nor have I any authority, to enter into the general discussion of the immigration problem. That is a question which concerns the American nation, and it would be entirely out of my province to express any opinion on the subject, in my official capacity as representative of the Italian Government in New York City. But there is one important aspect of Mr. Sargent's remarkable argument which seems properly to call for a word of explanation on my part. I refer to the chapters on "Inducements to Immigration" and "Naturalization and Distribution," on pages 43 and 44 of the report. Mr. Sargent contends (p. 44) that "at least one of the reasons for the existence of alien colonies in the United States," which is "the cause of the chief dangers to be apprehended from the enormous immigration of aliens," is that certain foreign governments are actively engaged in trying (p. 43):

> "to colonize their subjects who come to this country for the purpose of maintaining in them a love of their mother country. This was accomplished through agents of the home government and church sent here to keep them

*North American Review, Vol. 180 (May, 1905), pp. 720-726.

from imbibing a knowledge of, and affection for, the institutions of the United States, which might, and probably would, result in their purchase of homes here and final expatriation from their own country. That result meant a permanent loss to those countries of the allegiance and usefulness of such of their subjects as adopt our views and become American citizens, as well as loss of the enormous aggregate revenue sent back annually by those who cherish the intent of ultimately returning, buying homes and living on the proceeds of their savings."

He says further on (p. 45):

"Those foreign countries where the labors of the ever-active transportation agent have been most effective in diminishing native population have become alarmed, and have made futile attempts to check an exodus which threatens to seriously impair their self-supporting capacity. Failing in this, they have taken the next possible step, that of minimizing the evil, and, if possible, of turning it to their advantage in the long run. Hence all the political and social, and occasionally the religious, resources of these countries are being directed to one end—to *maintain colonies of their own people in this country*, instructing them through various channels to maintain their allegiance to the countries of their birth, to transmit their earnings here to the fatherland for the purchase of ultimate homes there, and *to avoid all intercourse with the people of this country that would tend to the permanent adoption of American ideals.*"

These charges, as an able student of the problem remarks, "are serious indeed and cannot be too plainly substantiated, if made at all."[1] As to the countries concerned, we are logically brought to the conclusion that they are two: Austria-Hungary and Italy. In fact, as the same critic remarks, "the countries of northwestern Europe are not in question, as immigration from them is light, and there are no dense colonies of their people to hold together. Russia is so situated toward her immigration that she could not, if she would, influence them sufficiently to hold them in colonies. There are left then, Austria-Hungary and Italy."

An additional proof that Italy is really involved in Mr. Sargent's charges is that, on page 45 of his interesting report, he mentions, among the evils resulting from the tremendous increase and racial character of foreign immigration, "the introduction into this free country of such hideous and terrifying fruits of long-

[1]Kate Holladay Claghorn, "Immigration for 1904," in *Charities*, February 4th, 1905, p. 455.

continued oppression as the mafia, the vendetta, black hand . . . "
This reference to the mafia, etc., obviously suffices to show that the
Italian Government is one of those which, in the mind of the Com-
missioner-General, pursue the line of policy deprecated by him.

II.

First of all, it behooves us to correct an erroneous impression,
which seems to dominate in certain quarters, as to the scope and
meaning of the Italian Emigration Law, of January 31st, 1901.
There is no provision in that law which might, with any fairness,
be construed as an attempt to exploit emigration by turning it to
the advantage of the mother country. The law accepts the fact
of emigration as something determined by causes which are deeply
rooted in the social and economic conditions of the country, and
which are entirely beyond the reach of empirical measures, directed to favor or to restrict the exodus. The law merely proposes
to solve a problem which is specifically forced upon the Italian
Government, *i.e.*, the problem of insuring the most efficient protection to the emigrant against all possible wrongs and abuses.
It is primarily and fundamentally a *social* law, that is, a law
destined to serve the ends of *social* justice by affording an instru-
ment of defence to those classes which are unable to protect themselves against the various forms of social parasitism.

That it never was the intention of the law to favor emigration
is conclusively shown by Section 17, through which "Carriers"—
i.e., Steamship Companies and their representatives—"are forbidden to persuade people to emigrate." The same section of the
law specifically recalls a provision of the Penal Code by which
inducement to emigration, based on the circulation of news and
statements concerning alleged conditions abroad, is considered
a misdemeanor and punished accordingly. This section of the
law is supplemented by Section 31, by which a fine of 1,000 lire is
imposed upon the Carrier (Steamship Company) who "shall
introduce between himself and the emigrant any middleman who
shall not be his own representative." The same penalty is by the
same section of the law imposed upon the "Carrier," or his
representative, "who shall pass off as spontaneous emigrants,
having paid their own passage, any parties who shall in fact
travel at the expense, total or partial, of any foreign government
or private enterprise," such fine to be increased to 2,000 lire in
case of recurrence. It is clear that the law has aimed at eliminating the possibility of any artificial attempt to favor or facilitate

emigration. Under the above-mentioned provisions of our law, it is difficult to conceive the possibility of the abuses denounced in the report of the Commissioner-General, through which "violations of our [American] laws, particularly of those that are directed against aliens under agreement to work here, continuously occur" (p. 43). The business of inducing emigration to this or any other country is considered an illegal one in Italy; and, therefore, the statement that "certain foreign countries are actively engaged in it" cannot possibly apply to Italy.

The above-mentioned provisions against any form of soliciting in connection with emigration are completed by others concerning the emigration of children under fifteen years of age, unless they have undergone a medical examination and have been granted a special permission by the local authorities, in accordance with the provisions of the Children's Employment Act. Section 3 punishes with imprisonment at hard labor up to six months, and a fine from 100 to 500 lire, "any one who shall enlist, or receive in his care in the kingdom, one or more children under fifteen years of age, with a view to employing them abroad," in unhealthy and harmful occupations. The same penalty applies to those "who send abroad, or deliver to third parties to be taken abroad, children under fifteen years of age with a view to employing them as above." In such cases, the father or guardian shall be deprived of his powers. The same penalties apply to "any one who shall induce a woman not of age to emigrate with a view to prostituting her." That the law never aimed at facilitating the dumping of paupers in foreign countries is proven by section 25, by which provision is made for the return home of indigent Italians, at the expense of the Steamship Companies, and at the rate of 10 adults per 1,000 tons register, and one for every further 200 tons or fractional 200 tons above 1,000.

But, apart from the above considerations, the mere reading of the headings of the law suffices to show that its sole aim is to assist the emigrant during the voyage, and see that he be well taken care of by the Steamship Company.

Previous to the passing of our law, emigrants were piled up like cattle in unsanitary conditions, on board of steamers which very often left much to be desired in point of safety, comfort and decency. It was our plain duty to care in that way for the hundreds of thousands of our countrymen who go abroad to work. The following is the list of the Chapters of the By-Laws issued for the enforcement of the Emigration Act:

This shows plainly that, aside from a few sections, dealing with the general question of emigration or with the organization of the emigration service, the bulk of the regulations concerns the condition of emigrants during their voyage.

III.

Mr. Sargent calls attention to the congestion of emigrants in the cities and the existence of alien colonies, which are by him assumed to be largely due to the action of the foreign Governments concerned. As to Italy, it suffices to recall that, as far back as December, 1901—that is, at the time when the great influx of Italian immigration was beginning to take place—I published a paper, in the "Monthly Bulletin" of the Italian Chamber of Commerce of New York, calling attention to the dangers resulting from the overcrowding of our immigrants in the city tenements under unhealthy surroundings. In that article, I advocated strongly the formation of a powerful Land Corporation for the purpose of favoring the agricultural distribution of our immigrants. My article was reproduced in some of the leading newspapers and magazines in Italy. It was followed in May, 1904, by another article published in the Italian number of "Charities," over my official signature. In the latter ("The Agricultural Possibilities of Italian Immigration"), I took up again the subject of urban congestion, emphasizing the necessity of organizing agricultural Italian colonies in the Southern States, where conditions, climatic and others, seemed to be most favorable. On December 29th last, I published a long article in one of the lead-

ing Italian newspapers of this city, *"L'Araldo Italiano,"* discussing at length the same question, and again concluding in
favor of a wider distribution of our immigrants in the agricultural districts. In this article, as also in a number of public
speeches, delivered on various occasions, I advocated, in unmistakable terms, the Americanization of our immigrants, strongly opposing the constitution of "alien" colonies, such as those
which Mr. Sargent justly deprecates. Perhaps it may not be amiss
to reproduce certain statements contained in the last-named
publication, which are of a nature to show exactly the trend of
thought dominating the action of the official representatives
of Italy in this country. I wrote in part:

> "The transformation of our immigrants into owners of
> land is sometimes opposed on the ground that it would
> gradually lead to their denationalization. We are thus
> confronted by a sort of nationalistic obsession . . . It is
> evident that the more active the participation of our im-
> migrants in the life of their adopted country, political
> and otherwise, the wider will be the field of action of-
> fered them. The alien colony is bound to be hampered
> by unavoidable limitations in its possibilities of life and
> action. In a group materially separated from the coun-
> try of origin, and yet kept deliberately apart from any
> intimate contact with the country of adoption, all the
> originary racial deficiencies cannot but be intensified
> through the action of a well-known psychological law.
> The colonialistic conception ends in an imitation or
> caricature of the type of civilization represented by the
> mother country. And against this form of nationalism,
> narrow-minded, intolerant and fanatic, we cannot protest
> with sufficient energy in the interest of our emigration.
> The conception of enforced exoticism must be replaced
> by that of a free and unhampered fusion of the immi-
> grant with the indigenous element."

IV.

On the evidence thus submitted, it is difficult not to see that the
efforts of the official representative of Italy in New York—that
is, in the most important place of landing of our immigrants,—
have been persistently and systematically directed toward the
attainment of the very ends which the Commissioner-General has
in view. The agricultural distribution of the newcomers, the
gradual and natural disintegration of the so-called "alien" colonies
and the blending of their members with the communities in which
they have established their new home, such are the corner-stones

of a programme which has been asserted on every occasion and with every means at our disposal. It is hardly necessary to point out that this line of action was in perfect harmony with the general policy pursued by the Italian Government concerning the immigration problem. A most striking proof of this is afforded by the fact that, when Signor Adolfo Rossi, a member of the Italian Department of Emigration, was sent here last winter to make a thorough study of the question, the first object to which his attention was directed by his Government was the overcrowding of immigrants in the cities, and the means to favor their agricultural distribution. If the central idea of our law is to leave emigration entirely free from any attempt at artificial inflation, and merely to perform in regard to the individual emigrant certain specific duties of help and assistance, the central idea of our policy concerning the Italian emigration to this country must necessarily be to let the assimilation of our immigrants go on unhampered. By pursuing that policy, we will assist our immigration in becoming an active factor in the life of this great country.

GINO C. SPERANZA

THE ITALIAN EMIGRATION DEPART-MENT IN 1904*

The Possibility Of Its Co-operation With The Immigration Department Of The United States

The report recently made by Signor Egisto Rossi, acting commissioner-general of emigration, to the Italian Parliament on the work of his department contains matters of interest to the American observer of Italian immigration to our country.

The Italian Emigration Department was founded to look after the interests of the half million yearly exodus from Italy. The report shows that this vast and important work is being ably and intelligently carried on.

It may surprise some to learn that Italian emigration has been falling off in the last three years, the maximum of 533,245 reached in 1901 having gradually decreased to 506,731 in 1904. Of this last total, the largest number was furnished by the northern provinces of Piedmont and Venetia, with the southern provinces of Sicily and Campania following. Of the north Italian emigrants the majority, however, emigrated to European countries or to South America.

In relation to the population (*i.e.*, counting one emigrant for every 100,000 inhabitants), the highest figures are given by the southern provinces of Calabria (2,544, per 100,000) and Basilicata (2,416 per 100,000). Sicily and the Puglie showed a marked decrease during 1904. Of the total who emigrated from the kingdom, 82.31 per cent were males, of which 6.56 per cent were below the age of fifteen. The small percentage of women and children would seem to confirm the growing belief that Italian emigration all over the world is becoming more and more temporary in character.

Of the total emigration to transoceanic countries, 67.29 per cent

Charities, Vol. 15 (1906), pp. 114-116.

came to the United States. The actual decrease during 1904 of those coming here was about 70,000. This, the department ascribes to the industrial uncertainty of the "presidential year" and to the unusually long and severe winter here. While these causes will also explain the very large number of Italians who returned to the mother country during 1904 (129,231), such large repatriation is further evidence of the temporary character of such emigration.

The report does not mince matters regarding the attitude of Americans towards Italian emigration. It plainly says:

> Despite the admittedly progressive improvement in our emigrants, they are still considered in some respects by Americans as little desirable. They are mostly day-laborers and peasants, an active and useful element, but considered unstable and not susceptible of being assimilated. The proportion of those unable to read and write among our emigrants is still high . . . The Italians, moreover, tend to crowd in the great urban centers, where they live a life apart, with habits of possibly too great economy, in contrast with the habits of Americans.

We are glad to see the advice given repeatedly and unconditionally in this official document that the Italian should go to the agricultural states, such as Virginia, Georgia, Louisiana and Texas. Such distribution is stated to be "one of the most pressing problems" of the department. Towards its solution the department will probably endeavor to establish labor-bureaus here, and to cooperate in any of the various plans for distribution which are being discussed in this country.

This would seem to offer a splendid opportunity to our government to call an international conference on immigration.

Of special interest is that part of the report which treats of the schools which have been opened for intending emigrants in those parts of the kingdom from which the emigration is heaviest. In 1903 the minister of public instruction proposed to the Emigration Department to contribute financially towards the support of such schools. Thereupon, the department appropriated 50,000 lire for the purpose. This increased the total of 3,000 schools opened for the instruction of the illiterates in the evening and on Sundays by 450. Of these 450 schools for the special instruction of emigrants, the largest number was opened at Avellino (70), where the percentage of illiteracy is 73.9, and 62 at Teramo, where the percentage is 74.9.

The department also prepared a mural chart of the United States, especially for the use of such schools. The chart gives the number of Italians living in each state of the Union, and the proportion of

Italians to the total population of each state, while special marks are used to indicate those cities having the largest Italian populations, and where an Italian consular officer resides. At the bottom of the chart are printed data and suggestions which may be of profit and use to the emigrant coming to this country.

The department calls attention to the difficulty of controlling clandestine emigration. As a possible basis for arriving at the number of such emigrants to the Americas, the report cites the difference between the number of those who sail, as given by the emigration statistics of the department, and the number of those who land on the other side, according to the statistics of immigration. This difference amounts to over 25,000 yearly. Such discrepancies are especially marked as regards the statistics for the United States. Thus, the excess of tabulated arrivals of Italians here over tabulated departures from Italy, was +13,180 in 1902, +27,806 in 1903 and +14,437 in 1904. These large differences do not represent clandestine emigration (which the department, however, believes to be several thousand a year) but are mostly made up of Italian emigrants sailing from foreign ports over which the department can exercise no jurisdiction.

Obviously this is another matter for international control.

The department justly complains of the increasing number of emigrants sailing on what are known as "prepaids," that is, on tickets bought, for example, in the United States and sent to Italy. The financial advantages which we may gain by having the tickets bought here cannot be offset against the obvious abuses of such a system. In 1904 the number of such prepaids was 57,754, while during the first five months of 1905 the number rose to 45,881.

The activity of the department in enforcing the strict provisions of the Italian Emigration Law is shown by the number of proceedings brought against authorized agents of steamship companies, sub-agents and other persons, which in three years amounted to 1,254. The department complains, however, that the courts have been too lenient in emigration proceedings and urges greater severity. To the above total of penal proceedings should be added 637 civil actions brought on behalf of emigrants against steamship companies, upon which (1902-1904) judgments aggregating 58,-000 lire were secured.

As regards the work of societies founded outside the kingdom for the protection of Italian immigrants, and which are subsidized by the department, the report is somewhat non-committal. It recognizes the importance of such societies, especially in the United States, and of increasing their number and strengthening those already in existence. It appears that the largest subsidy (35,000 lire) is paid to the Society for Italian Immigrants of New York, founded by Americans, while the Italian Benevolent Institute, of the same place, and the Immigrants' Aid Society of Buenos Ayres, come as close seconds (25,000 lire each). The Italian Benovolent Institute appears to have the largest outlay (95,458 lire) as well as the largest income (102,112 lire) of any such society.

The part of the report relative to the money carried by emigrants and the amounts sent by immigrants is instructive. The Bank of Naples is the authorized financial agent of the department for the transmission of the money of emigrants. Yet it is doubtful whether it handles even one-half of the total business. Hence, the figures cited can represent at most only one-half of the amounts going from and coming to Italy. The bank now issues at its Naples office drafts payable in the United States in dollars. The number of such drafts during 1904 was 25,868 for a total of $366,030.85.

During the same year there were sent from the United States to Italy through the Bank of Naples 125,133 drafts, totaling over twenty-two millions of lire. It is safe to say that at least thirty million lire were sent through other channels.

The reading of the entire report shows not only that the Italian Emigration Department is engaged in a great, useful and beneficent work, but also (and this is of special importance to us) that it appreciates the American viewpoint regarding Italian immigration and is willing to meet us half way.

The problem of the immigrant, as I have recently insisted, is an international one. Italy is as much interested as we are that her peasant-emigrants shall settle in our agricultural sections rather than crowd in unhealthy city quarters. She is aware that it is in her interests as well as in ours that the character and condition of her emigrants here shall be acceptable to us. She has repeatedly and officially advised her subjects here to become American citizens and to take part in our political life.

On our part, we must change the often trying attitude of suspicion, doubt and even discourtesy towards a friendly power such as Italy, with whom we are at peace.

Let us call an international conference and come to an international understanding of benefit to all concerned.

THE EFFECT OF
EMIGRATION
ON ITALY*

An Interview with Adolfo Rossi

When the papers announced that Adolfo Rossi would visit the United States, many an Italian here prepared joyfully to bid welcome to an old friend. Many an expatriate remembered him during his first visit to this country in the varied experiences which he afterward described in his two books: *The Land of the Dollar* and *An Italian in America*. An even larger number looked toward to his coming as to that of a friend—though they had never seen him. They knew him and loved him because he typified modern Italy, and because in his twenty years of quasi-public life he had brought honor to his country.

There are probably few living Italians more widely known among his people in Italy than Adolfo Rossi. As a journalist he gained prominence not merely by his up-to-date methods of gathering news, but by the fearlessness with which he expressed his views. As war correspondent in the disastrous Italian campaign in Abyssinia, he kept his countrymen fully informed of every bad move on the part of the commanding officers, no less than of every heroic deed of the subalterns. As the result of the former he was expelled from Africa; as a consequence of the latter he won the love of his people. Wherever he went as correspondent or investigator, he won laurels and friends—whether it was in the Graeco-Turkish war, in the investigation of the coffee plantations of Brazil, or in the Transvaal. A man of the people, modest and reserved, the casual observer would never imagine in seeing him that he had followed royalty and been at home with the Papal Court. Above all it is his geniality with its subtle Venetian charm that makes him a general favorite at home.

It was in the beginning of 1902, shortly after the Italian emigration law went into effect, that Adolfo Rossi, now raised to the dignity of Cavalier Rossi, was appointed *inspettore* or supervisor of the emigration department. His wide knowledge of conditions in Italy and abroad, his keen power of observation and his tremendous activity qualified him in an unusual degree to fill the duties of his

*Gino C. Speranza, *Charities*, Vol. 12 (1904), pp. 467-470.

new office. These consist mainly in visiting the various points where Italian emigration is marked, studying conditions there, examining how the emigration law is enforced and ascertaining whether emigrants have fair play. And that is one reason why Adolfo Rossi is here.

"There seems to be a widespread belief here," he told me, "that the Italian government is encouraging emigration."

"Well," I said, "it is a fact that Italy is overcrowded and that, therefore, the government must favor the outflow of the overplus."

"I do not deny," said Rossi seriously—and when he is serious he is very serious—"that Italy has been overcrowded. Its population increases at the rate of about half a million a year, and this is approximately the number of those who emigrate during such a period. The right to emigrate is an inalienable right and my government cannot deny that right. Your own statutes," he added with a twinkle in his eye taking up a paper, "declare that 'expatriation is a natural and inherent right of all the people.' But the government can and does interfere with forced or artificial emigration, such as that stimulated by certain steamship lines. You see, these steamship companies have invested large capital in steamers for the emigration trade. Unless they get full shiploads for every trip they don't make a profit. Our emigration law of 1901, and its subsequent amendments, are aimed especially at such forced methods of emigration. If Americans would only examine that law they would see that my government is not aiding any process of dumping her sons here."

"Are the Italian steamship lines mainly responsible?" I asked.

"Let it be said to the honor of Italian capital that it has not lent itself to depopulate Italy by the method pursued by many of the foreign steamship companies," he answered.

"But people here," I prodded him on, "believe that while there may be a very drastic law on the statute books in Italy, yet this outpour from your country is too good a thing for Italy to expect that any law that would check it would be enforced."

"The curse of Italy seems to be that outsiders never judge her by her present; foreign opinion seems generally based on facts at least ten years old."

Adolfo Rossi knows present conditions in Italy too well to sympathize with ignorance on the subject. "I'll tell you exactly what the facts are to-day," he went on, "and I will explain to you how far emigration is a blessing and where the blessing stops and begins to become a curse."

He began moving his fingers as if he were writing, which is always a sign that he is going to tell you a long story. "Of course, for a time," he began in that persistent drawl that is characteristic of Venetians, "emigration was a safety valve for the tremendous increase in the population of Italy. It also brought in money from those in America who had families in Italy. A good deal of money came in that way. Then undoubtedly it decreased crime—not because we sent you our criminals, but because many of the crimes committed, especially in the country, were due to over-population and poverty. Another good effect of emigration has been to increase wages all over Italy from one-third to one-half."

"Isn't that a whole list of blessings you owe to emigration?" I dared interrupt.

"Yes, but that's only one side of the picture, and the only side that seems to be known here. What you overlook is that the character of the emigration has changed in recent years. It is not hard conditions or starvation that now sends Italians to America; they come because they are eager for more money. A mason earning four lire a day in southern Italy, can live there comfortably, but he has heard that he can earn six a day in America. So he emigrates, and in such numbers that in certain parts of Sicily, Basilicata and Calabria, it amounts to a general exodus. This large emigration has been irregular or uneven in its distribution, that is, it has not been a few men from a number of villages, but all the able-bodied men of one village, for instance, have gone. In some places the village priest and the doctor, having lost their flock, have followed them to America. Certain municipalities have had to be consolidated and the parish church abandoned. You can see some decided disadvantages for Italy in this situation. First, it works harm to the land-owners because despite the increase of wages they can't get laborers. Laborers have actually to be imported from Messina to Termini-Imerese during the olive-picking season. Many wheat farms have to-day become mere pasture lands from lack of hands to cultivate them. Sicily, called from ancient times 'the granary of Italy,' to-day does not produce sufficient wheat for its own consumption and has to import some."

"But above all this excessive emigration is working a harm to the nation at large in that it takes from us the flower of our laboring class, which leaves Italy, not to seek a living, but greater comfort. To this, naturally, contributes the selection exercised by your immigration laws which let in only the good and reject the bad. My government allows the American commission of physicians of your own selection at Italian ports a pretty free hand. They do examine the emigrant not only for trachoma, but make a fairly thorough ex-

amination for hernia, for diseases due to senility, etc., thus adding
a potent artificial selection.

"Then I notice that the newspapers write of the influx of a lot of
poverty-stricken Italians. Just look at the facts: 84 per cent of Italians
coming here are between 18 and 45 years of age. That means that 84
per cent of such immigrants belong to the working age. They are, in
other words, producers. You get this product without the expense
incurred in its raising. Every Italian of 18, for instance, costs his
country, at the very lowest, $1,000 to bring him up. At 18, he begins
to be a producer, but by leaving Italy, the 1,000 invested by his country in him is lost. This 'human capital' of fresh, strong young men is
the contribution of Europe to the new land. We spend a thousand
dollars to bring up and develop a young man and then you reap the
profits on the investment. We give you a good laborer, but I find you
pay him less than other laborers. If it were not for his sobriety and
thrift, he could not live on his hire. I think this is a manifest unfair-
ness; first, because the Italian does not produce cheap work; and second, because you take advantage of his ignorance to underpay him.
And then people think that he is underbidding other laborers."

"Don't these immigrants return to Italy in large numbers after they
have laid aside a little sum?" I asked.

"That is another ten-year-old fact," he answered. "Many go back
on a visit, but not to settle there. They go to bring their family or to
find a wife; or they go back with a smattering of bad English to look
over their 'estates' and be looked up to, and then come back. In some
parts of Sicily, if a well-dressed stranger, even an Italian, goes on a
visit, the villagers will say, 'He's from America.' But they do not remain, though they can live there comfortably. Four or five years of
America seem to unfit the Italian immigrant for a return to live in
Italy."

"But what is their idea of America—do the majority of them look
upon it merely as a place to go to make money?" I asked.

"I believe that among many Italian peasants, America stands for
more than the land of the dollar, even though they know little
about it. I will tell you a story bearing on this point, and with it I shall
insist on closing this interview, as I am leading a strenuous life. Some
time ago, in a Sicilian village, a lot of peasants became dissatisfied
with the mediaeval agricultural methods of the local 'feudal lord.'
These peasants felt that they were neither chattels going with the land
nor serfs. So one fine morning they gathered in front of the lord's
house, bunched their shovels in a heap, and on top placed the following notice: 'Sir do your farming yourself—we are going to America.'
And unless the immigration officials at New York have refused ad-

mission to these independent peasants, out of fear that they might become public charges, you will find them working on some of your railroads.''

And, with a smile, Signor Rossi closed the interview.

CHARLES B. PHIPARD

THE PHILANTHROPIST— PADRONE*

What Is Being Done To Raise The Standard Through Competition And Example

The majority of the 1,000,000 and over Italians who have come to this country since 1893, have had little or no capital, are uneducated, and, in consequence, manual labor is all they can do. In addition to this, the most of them, having been peasants at home, naturally drift to work in the open air with pick and shovel when they come to this country.

There is an abundance of this kind of work to be done and the Italian seems to be particularly fitted for it, but some medium is necessary by which he can be brought in contact with the employer and his work; this is done by the padroni or labor contractors. These men make it their business to supply laborers in any numbers. They are thus useful to employers, who as a universal rule would not themselves know how to get Italian laborers in any numbers, and who would find it impossible to proceed by picking up one man at a time.

The padrone has been very useful also, all in all, to the Italian laborer. The immigrant, in his ignorance of the language, could not find employment and could not look after himself in any way if he did. The padrone steps in and finds him employment, boards and lodges him while at work, collects his wages, writes his letters, acts as his banker, and engineers any and all dealings which the laborer may have with the concern for which he may be working. The padrone has therefore served a very useful purpose to both employer and laborer, and also to the public.

But the padroni as a class—for there are some honest and intelligent men among them—are not scrupulous in their dealings with the laborers with whom they come in contact. Many of them engage in mean and petty swindling of one kind and another. Universally they overcharge the laborer for what they do for him. They never do anything to improve the condition of the laborer or to teach him to better his own condition for himself. They are ignorant

*Charities, Vol. 12 (1904), pp. 470-472.

men trying to make as much money as possible out of other ignorant men, who from their inability to speak the language and their
foreignness, are peculiarly helpless. And there can be no great difficulty in judging the result.

To alter or remedy these conditions is no easy task, for it is necessary to possess some method of getting together the laborer and the
work to be done, while improving the evil attributes of the padrone.
Worse evils than those existing would ensue if the padrone were
wiped suddenly out of existence.

It would seem that the best remedy for cases of actual swindling is
through the criminal laws, and in these cases the laborer should
have the assistance of public officials, charitable societies, etc.
Even then, and with such assistance, his ignorance will be constantly a hindrance to his obtaining justice.

Overcharging arises from the dependence of the laborers on the
padrone for provisions. In the majority of cases where a padrone
places a gang of men at work, he conducts the commissary; and in
such commissaries, where the work is located out of town, the padrone
carries everything in stock which is necessary to the needs of the
laborer, in the way of both provisions and clothing; and in a great
many cases, or, perhaps, we should say the majority of cases, the
prices charged to the laborer are exorbitant. Also, short weight or
count is given, or the goods are of an inferior grade but sold at the
prices of first-class goods.

This matter of overcharging could in part be regulated by passing
laws to control the price of board, supplies and medical service
to laborers when in contractors' camps. But overcharging cannot
be prevented wholly except by the growth of a higher conception of
their duty to the laborer on the part of employer and padrone. And it
must be in this same way, too, that the general neglect and indifference to the laborer's welfare in other matters than overcharging on
the part of the employer and padrone, can be rectified. The public
is interested in preventing laborers from being treated like machines
and allowed or forced to live like brutes. In a republic everything
like this tends to debase the average character of the people, on which
alone the welfare of the republic depends.

Accordingly, the Society for the Protection of Italian Immigrants
has actively entered into the business of supplying employers with
laborers and of conducting labor camps through trustworthy agents
of its own. In these camps, the laborer will not be overcharged, and
every effort will be made so that he can lead a healthful life, and not
be brutalized in any way. Naturally, the entrance of the society into

this field has been difficult of accomplishment on account of the opposition which it has met from the unscrupulous padrone and through the ignorance of the laborers, who do not as yet fully understand and appreciate that the society is doing this work solely for the betterment of existing conditions. Employers, also, have been hard to reach, as, for the past fifteen or twenty years, they have been in the habit of getting such uneducated labor as they have needed from the padroni, and they naturally look at the matter from a strictly business point of view. So long as the padroni can supply them with the desired number of men at the right time, they are not over particular, and in fact cannot be, as to the treatment accorded the men in the camps. The society has had the opportunity of demonstrating to both employers and laborers that labor camps can be conducted decently and on a legitimate business basis, and it has hopes that eventually its place in the regard of laborers will become firmly fixed. The main difficulty in weaning the ignorant laborer from his padrone is his habit of believing that the padrone is the only one who can supply his needs. This is repeatedly proved by the fact that no matter how badly one of these padroni may treat his followers they return to him for employment and advice in preference to all others. The padrone fully realizes this weakness and makes the most of it on every occasion. In consequence of this blind belief, it has been extremely difficult to win the confidence of the laborer, thereby making it additionally hard to demonstrate to the employer that the society can render him as good service in the matter of getting him men at short notice as do the padroni. The society feels confident, however, from experience, and from the growing interest by the particular laborers with whom its representatives have come in close contact in labor camps, that the desired object will be accomplished—that the laborer and the padrone will both become sufficiently educated and enlightened so that the laborer will look out better for himself, and the padrone for him.

WILLIAM E. DAVENPORT

THE EXODUS OF A
LATIN PEOPLE*

While it would be an exaggeration to say that any section of Italy has been depopulated by emigration, it is true that many towns in Calabria and Basilicata have lost one-tenth of their residents within the past two years, and one-fifth in a somewhat longer period.

The result of extensive emigration from any given section is usually advantageous to the institutions of the region in question and to the families of the emigrants remaining in Italy. The earnings of the father or older brother are largely sent back to the old land, and both the family and the village profit by this influx of money from abroad. At the same time the withdrawal of a great proportion of the able-bodied and enterprising men of a village or country place causes a certain unrest and dissatisfaction, and during the harvest seasons especially the need of these laborers is severely felt.

On every hand I heard the complaint that large land-owners suffer because it is difficult to find men enough to work their lands—and, of course, this means only that they must pay higher wages. The result has been in many sections that the pay of field laborers has risen from a lira (twenty cents) a day to twice that amount.

Occasionally a landed man will buy modern agricultural machinery to make good the lack of hands, but the inertness of these men in general passes all understanding. Many of them are selling off their lands piecemeal and others are living a life of idle discouragement while their holdings practically go to waste. This suicidal course seems to be common in Basilicata and parts of Calabria and even in the Abruzzi.

Meanwhile, the income received from America suffers no diminution and is regarded as second in importance only to the agricultural receipts from whole sections. The number of large families who withdraw permanently from the country is now on the increase, and this will mean in time smaller receipts from the United States. Perhaps then more of the communes will be obliged to purchase the land of

Charities, vol. 12 (1904), pp. 463-467.

wealthy proprietors and rent it at low rates to the villagers, as they are now doing in some cases.

The problem of the agricultural districts is a very knotty one, mainly because the communal taxes are often so high that the produce when brought to town scarcely pays the farmer the cost of production. In some towns the rate on wine amounts to one-quarter or even one-third of its retail selling price. The physical difficulties to be overcome, in sections where the farms lie eight and ten miles from the villages, are enormous. Often the laborer reaches the field only after four hours of hard walking. Large sections are so steep and rocky that the yield must of necessity be light.

Realizing all these things, the Italian peasant lends a ready ear to the tales of prosperity in America. He does not expect, like his predecessors from western Europe, to dig up gold in the streets of New York, but is really well acquainted with conditions here and knows the rate of wages he may expect. His going causes little excitement outside his own family circle, because to go to America is the ordinary, almost the popular, thing to do. He is almost as much in a rut when he leaves for the steamer at Naples as when he followed his antique plow in the uplands of Calabria.

Sixty percent of the Italian immigrants in the United States come from the Abruzzi, Basilicata and Calabria. A very large percentage of them—almost all of them, in fact—have been farm laborers, or men holding small tracts of land through inheritance. The conditions which they leave behind seem almost impossible to an American. Even where the man owns his little farm, the income is so small that he must work for a larger owner, while his wife and children care for his own place. His average wage is thirty cents a day, although during harvest time it may rise to two lire, or forty cents. The conditions under which he is employed involve practically all of his working hours. All of the houses are in the villages, and the fields are often miles away. So the workman must trudge for hours before he reaches his field. At work he is a digger, not at all a farmer in our sense of the word. Many of the owners believe that it is better to cut the earth with a spade or tear it with a mattock, than to turn it with a plow. The laborer spends his day digging over a small plot which an American plow would finish up in a few moments. On his own little place his wife swings a heavy mattock over her head and jerks out lumps of sod just as sturdily and for just as many hours as does he.

Italy has been called the garden land of Europe, but at least in these three provinces the term has no significance. They are mountainous, with sharply sloping fields full of rocks and incapable of fair returns.

This, of course, is not true of all land in these provinces, for here are many of the best vineyards and olive groves in Italy. But from the physical conditions alone the farmer is doomed to work which is un-remunerative, or at best, uncertain.

In Sicily, sending over twenty per cent of the emigration of this country, the soil, once rich, has been exhausted. This is largely due to the deforesting of the mountains and consequent diminution of the water supply. For six months in the year central Sicily looks like the barren lands of Arizona and New Mexico. I saw little rills trickling pitifully in the center of wide river beds, which had once held streams a quarter of a mile wide. In March and April there is a little rain, but none again until October or November. The principal crop here is wheat. An American farmer could feel only pity for the sickly, sparse, stunted crops and the gleaners cutting them with sickles as they did in the days of Ruth.

Sicily has probably the richest sulphur mines in the world, but here, too, primitive methods keep down proceeds and wages. The ore is carried up from the mines on the shoulders of boys who pass in long files up and down stairways cut in the rock. Some of the mines, I was told, have introduced machinery, but I did not visit any where other than hand tools were in use. In Sicily, also, are the richest groves of oranges and lemons.

These are the physical and economic conditions which the Italian leaves behind him to emigrate. His social condition is no less a marked contrast to ours. His house is nothing to him but a place to sleep. If it has a bed nothing else is needed; he has not felt the want of running water in it, or even near it, and sends his wife to the fountain in the morning and at sunset, for water. For everything except sleeping he uses the piazza, or public square.

The thought and pride which we expend on our own homes, the Italian contadino lavishes on his piazza and his village, his "paese," which is really all the world of which he has any knowl-edge. This is true not only of the contadino, but of many in the middle classes as well. On the piazza are the social club, the work-ing-man's club, the cafe, the fountain, the pharmacy, the tobacco shop, the postoffice and the church. It is there that he receives his friends, talks politics and transacts business. The *circolo sociale,* the social club, has been transplanted to New York with slight varia-tion from its original form. The piazza is the one place which is faithfully swept out every day.

Next to the civic pride is the pride in the local church. Very likely it was built in the open country and the village grew up around it.

For centuries the church was first in the villagers' affections, but gradually it has been eclipsed by the love of the village itself, as a whole. When I met men whom I had known in New York, in Italy, they asked me first, "Have you seen my village?" Then, "Have you seen my church?" Not one asked if I had seen his house. It is this feeling which makes possible the handsome buildings and churches in villages where ninety per cent of the houses are barren.

I was strongly impressed with the evident growing away from the church, as an institution rather than as a religion, of many of the educated fraction of the population. Both religious ceremonial and priestly activity are constantly on men's tongues, and as constantly denied their former influence. This is partly due to the influence of the social clubs, where modern literary and scientific notes are discussed, and a general impatience with what are regarded as the pretensions of the church is freely expressed. Shocking as it is to Americans, nothing is more common than to hear educated Italians refer to the church as "the shop." Unquestionably, too, the position of antagonism maintained by the Vatican toward Italian unity wounds the Italian's pride and seriously affects his confidence in and esteem for the ecclesiastical organization.

This, indeed, is freely, though regretfully, admitted by leading churchmen. Whether or not it is a good thing that such a condition exists, is a matter on which there is naturally the greatest difference of opinion.

The Italian is infinitely bettered industrially by emigrating, but socially he suffers a loss. In his own village he may have been of some small importance, but here he must long be content with a position at the bottom of the social ladder, as a laborer or factory worker. This social loss would be even greater were it not that families from the same province group themselves here in the same neighborhood. Thus, in the space of two blocks on Elizabeth street dwell several hundred households from the Sicilian town of Sciacca; while in South Brooklyn, in close proximity, scores of Falernitan families have bought homes of their own and form a community by themselves. The continuity of this social life is conserved by constant accessions from the old land, by the frequent departure of grown sons (who came here in infancy) to serve in the Italian army, by the Mutual Aid Society, membership in which is based on one's nativity in a specific province or township, and finally by the local Italian news published in the great Italian-American newspapers. I had an illustration of this social loss in the case of a young man whom I knew in Brooklyn. He was of good family and standing at home, graduate of a school, and ambitious. When he came to New York he worked in a factory at seven dollars a week for a time and later was out of work. He became discouraged at the lack of work, and at the kind of work which fell in his way and returned. Political influence, following a passing of very rigid examinations, secured him a place in a post-office in a small village. The position demanded an expert telegrapher, and in addition he speaks French and is familiar with the classics. His salary is fifteen dollars a month. He pays ten dollars a month to live in the best hotel in the village, and his official position assures him social recognition. He has been convinced, however, that when he becomes a master of ready English his telegraphy will bring him seventy-five dollars a month in New York, and he told me that he should come back to stay. In the Italian post-office his first advance in salary, probably five dollars a month, may not come for many years.

I have in mind a household in Brooklyn which is an even better illustration of the industrial side of emigration. Just around the corner from our settlement four Italian men eat and live and sleep in one room which costs them five dollars a month. Two are brothers, the other two a father and son. They work as street cleaners, or diggers, and earn seven or eight dollars a week, perhaps more. The living for all four costs less than three dollars a week. Taking out all expenses, they have been able to send home fifty or sixty dollars a month, or thirty dollars to each of the two families. In the little villages where they came from this is a fabulous sum and quickly makes the rounds of the piazza. The mother or sister brags that Tony is paid seven lire a day. The brother at home earns two lire. Living as they do, the cost of living here is not high, and certainly is low in comparison with the wages. Is it any wonder that others follow quickly on?

The reports issued by the government undoubtedly stimulate emigration by a bare recital of facts. For instance, a report from the royal consul at New Orleans tells of the number of Italians in the city and state, their principal occupations, their wages, the average cost of living, the social and benevolent and church organizations. It is, in fact, a complete catalogue of answers to the questions which a prospective emigrant would naturally ask. When the head man of a village is asked for information of America, or of the best place to settle in America, he hands out the latest report. It has been my observation that these reports are carefully compiled and accurate, but the bare statement that for the same work, and probably shorter hours, a man receives from five to ten times as much wages, cannot fail to send ever increasing numbers.

These, briefly, are the points which I shall cover in my report to the Brooklyn Italian Settlement of over three months spent in Italy during the winter and early spring. From my observation both here and abroad, it seems to me that the needs of the Italian at our hand, after he has secured work—and he generally does secure work very soon—are educational. He must be taught English and he must be taught our customs and history. Public work attracts very large numbers of Italians, from its character and from the wages, so that they become citizens with alacrity. The right kind of instruction is essential to their becoming good citizens. Beyond this their pressing needs are chiefly for clubs and other substitutes for the piazza life and to fill in the time until their wives and families are brought to join them.

WILLARD PRICE

WHAT I LEARNED BY TRAVELING FROM NAPLES TO NEW YORK IN THE STEERAGE*

"Isn't it queer we can't see the big hoop the sun goes 'round on?"

Giuseppe, seated on an overturned macaroni bucket on the steerage deck, was gazing intently at the great, red apoplectic sun settling down for the night behind the black, little island of Madeira.

"Hoop?" I questioned with interest. "Do you mean to say that the sun goes around the earth on a hoop?"

"Certo!" replied Giuseppe. "Just after a rain you can sometimes see it in the sky—all different colors—but not now," and he strained his eyes toward the west in search of the sun-hoop.

Here was an interesting conception indeed! Without betraying the fact that my astronomical theories did not precisely coincide with his, I asked Giuseppe further questions, and found that he believed the earth is flat, that the sun is about two kilometres away and *almost* as large as the ship upon which we were sailing, and that he sympathized with a local Sicilian tradition to the effect that the stars are ornaments painted on the dome of Heaven by a wonderful Italian artist of former ages.

Giuseppe's is by no means an isolated case. Conversation with hundreds of his Italian compatriots in the steerage—and there was plenty of time for such conversation during the long voyage from Naples to New York and the five days in quarantine—revealed the fact that with regard to so-called "matters of common knowledge" their notions were usually quite as primitive as Giuseppe's. To be sure there were exceptions—a few tall, graceful, keen-eyed Italians from Genoa and Milan who possessed some slight measure of intelligence and culture. But the vast majority of those on board were Southern Italian laborers, so densely ignorant as to fill with despair

World Outlook, Vol. 3 (October, 1917), pp. 3-5, 14.

anyone not possessed of the strongest faith in the regenerating power of American civilization.

It was after completing a ride of two thousand miles through Europe on a bicycle that I resolved to cap off a most interesting year of social exploration by taking passage in the Italian steerage for New York. I wanted to study the immigration problem at close range.

The White Star office in Naples, after much delay and objection, finally granted me a steerage ticket, and I was bundled off to the Pest House, where all steerage passengers must be quarantined five days before sailing, as a precaution against cholera.

I have never spent five days more enjoyably.

Half starved, unkempt and vermin ridden, the only American in the company of 1500 of the grimiest Italians, still I found the experience of such fascination and value that I shall never look back upon it except with the keenest interest and pleasure.

Like the others, I was examined, vaccinated, tattooed, fumigated, disinfected, put through medical gymnastics, dosed with this and that, and at last stamped approved. Then the five hundred of us intended for the White Star boat were marched in a most carefully guarded procession through the streets to the docks and on board the Cretic.

I shall not attempt to describe the conditions in the Italian steerage, first, because the words necessary for such a description haven't been invented yet; second, and chiefly, because the subject would be foreign to the purpose of this article. I wish to confine myself not to a discussion of the mere temporary, physical surroundings of the immigrant while on board but to the *spirit* of the steerage, the *heart* of the immigrant, the mental and moral make-up of these prospective Americans.

There are certain facts that are soon borne in irresistibly upon the observer in the Italian steerage.

One of the first of these is that the Italian of the first generation— that is, the Italian who lands on our shores as an immigrant—is deplorably crude material out of which to build an American citizen.

The old saying is, "A bad beginning maketh a good ending." So it seems to be with the Italian immigrant. His descendant of the second or third generation ultimately climbs the ladder of success; but the immigrant himself must start from the lowest rung with the shackles of ignorance, superstition and foreign custom heavy upon him.

When you see the bewilderment of some of these would-be Americans when asked to spell their own names, notice their surprise when they hear that the same language is spoken in England as in America, observe the way they swaddle up their babies from chin to toe in tight bandages, making many of them cripples for life, hear them marvel at the fact that the ocean is larger than their own Mediterranean, mark their perfectly blank look when you mention any country or city outside of Italy (always except New York, which every one of them knows a great deal about) and watch them, for a while, eating and sleeping and living in their sensual, animal-like way, you begin to realize how enormous is the task America assumes when it undertakes to transform this grimy, stupid riff-raff of Europe into intelligent, self-respecting American citizens.

But that is what America does. And perhaps the most potent factor in the transformation is the Italian's own tumultuous eagerness to be transformed. He is predisposed toward Americanizing influences. He is anxious to become American as rapidly as possible. The new country, which offers him a fresh lease on life claims his profoundest admiration, his respect and—even before he reaches its shores—his love. And after he has visited America and returned to Italy he will not rest until he responds again to the lure of the wonderful country of whose exhilarating life he has had a taste.

The ordinary comments of my steerage companions on the land left behind were anything but complimentary. "Italy no good," was their ultimatum. Among the half thousand Italians on board constant inquiry failed to disclose one who had any intention of returning to Italy to live. Almost thirty per cent of the men planned to go back to Italy, but it was merely to get their families and their earthly possessions and then recross the Atlantic and establish a permanent home in America.

"Oh, but wait!" I said to one man who had been expressing the universal disgust for the toiler's lot in Italy. "So you say now; but after a few years of hard work in America you will get lonesome and homesick and you will be returning to sunny Italy."

"No, Signore!" he expostulated. "I'll never go back to that accursed place. Italy is a beautiful country for kings and tourists, but a bad hole for a man who must earn his own living. The wages are next to nothing, while the cost of living is not very much lower than it is in America. I can live in New York almost as cheaply as in Naples and make three times as much money. Then, too, we have regular hours in America. We stop at the toot of the whistle. In Italy, if we are in the middle of a job when quitting times comes, we have to continue working until the job is finished. In America we are paid every week, or every two weeks, regularly. In Italy we are paid whenever it suits our employer's convenience—perhaps not for months at a time. Italy is old, careless, lazy. But America—" He brought out the name with such enthusiasm and such a comprehensive gesture of approval that he found it quite unnecessary to complete the sentence with mere words.

He leaned on the rail, looking out longingly over the sea, not toward his own Italy, but into the west. Presently he whispered very softly, almost inaudibly, "Viva l'America, viva il Paradiso!"

The Italian's greatest deprecator is the Italian. He has scant respect for his own race. He distrusts his fellow countrymen far more than he does his American associates. The Italian immigrants, with their characteristic humility, fully realize that they themselves are dishonest, hot-blooded, ignorant and dirty. Against a stranger they will defend themselves hotly; but to one who has gained their confidence they will speak in open disparagement of their own race. Especially the Italian who has lived in America long enough to contrast his compatriots with native born Americans comes to hold his own people in very slight esteem. To be sure, he still clings to them— simply because Americans will not have him. They call him a "dago" and bar him out of their society. So while he remains, perforce, in his Italian companionships, he longs to pull free of old-world customs, learn English, become an American, and stand on a par with native born American citizens.

A young man saw me lend my fountain pen to an Italian friend, and he drew me aside to furnish me with some kindly advice.

"Don't you trust nobody!"—his accent was that of the East Side— "nobody! I'm Eye-talian myself, but I got t' say dis: De Eye-talians is de most dishonest people on de face o' de eart'! I wouldn't trust my dearest friend 'f he was a Eye-talian!"

"Dat's why I want to go back to 'Merica," he continued, his eyes sparkling with anticipation. "Where I live in New York up on 116th Street there ain't none of these dirty dagoes, but all clean, edicated people—'Mericans, Irishes, Germany and Dutches!"

The proudest Italian in the steerage was one who possessed his American naturalization papers proclaiming him a full citizen of the United States. When he first showed me his papers—he produced them upon every possible occasion during the voyage—I saw with astonishment that they were made out to "James Carter." He beamed with delight at my surprise. "I change my name," he said. "Wish to be American. My old name was Giacomo Caravaggio."

There is greater loyalty to America among our Italian immigrants than among the majority native-born American citizens. The contrast is vivid between the lackadaisical patriotism of the ordinary American and the blazing enthusaism for things American that consumes the heart and mind of the incoming Italian. When the Statue of Liberty is at last sighted his joy knows no bounds.

So the immigrant reaches the land of his dreams. He is finally passed through Ellis Island—if he is fortunate—and steps into New York at the Battery. He enters a tenement, he lives amid the most squalid and unhealthful surroundings in order to save money, he works hard and learns English little by little.

Unfortunately, the first phrases of English he learns are usually the American curses. I have heard Italians who could not say "Good morning" in English discharge a perfect tornado of American curses that, as a lingual accomplishment, would have done credit to the most professional American-born hooligan. The Italian is decidedly unmoral in thought, but he is not so immoral and criminal in action as yellow journalism would have us suppose. Police experts state that the Black Hand in America is more a matter of newspaper imagination than of fact. There is a much lower percentage of criminality, immorality and insanity among the Italians then among many other immigrant races. As for dependency, statistics for a representative year showed that out of every 28,000 Italians in the city of New York there was only one in the almshouse on Blackwell's Island, while out of every 28,000 Irish in New York there were 140 in the almshouse. Mr. James Forbes, chief of the Mendicancy Department of the C.O.S., says he has never seen or heard of an Italian tramp. Italian beggars are also exceedingly rare. There are practically no drunkards among the Italians, and no abstainers.

The immigrant from Italy proves to be a faithful and cheerful worker. When a contractor engaged in building a city sewer was asked why he had only Italians in his employ, he replied, "Because they are the best workmen, and there are enough of them. If an Italian down in the ditch has a shovelful of earth half way up when the whistle blows for dinner, he will not drop it; he will throw it up; the Irishman and the French Canadian will drop it. And when the lunch hour is over, when the clock strikes, the Italian will be leaning on his shovel ready to go to work, but the Irishman will be out under that tree and he will be three minutes getting to his job, and three minutes each, for 150 men, is not a small item."

The Italians are industrious, good-natured, very affectionate toward children, courteous and polite often to the point of dishonesty, generous and self-sacrificing. But the impulse of these excellent qualities is offset by the Italian's dense ignorance which sentences him to spend the rest of his life after he reaches America in the drudgery of unskilled labor.

But then comes the second generation. The immigrant's American-born son goes to school. He comes back with that small amount of learning which is proverbially dangerous. He disrespects his parents because they know less than he does, they speak English poorly, and, most condemning fact of all, they are "dirty dagoes," while he—he is an American! In the Pest House in Naples a little fellow who had been born in America and who had gone to an American school, but whose parents were Italian, came running out of the men's dormitory one morning complaining to me very indignantly that his father had whipped him. "Well," I said, "hasn't your father a right to whip you when you're naughty?" "No," he exclaimed. "I'm an American. I'm not going to be whipped by a *foreigner!*"

It is small wonder that these young Americans soon become unruly. From disregard of parental authority it is an easy step to violation of civic authority. They become turbulent and lawless, and are the despair of the police. But this is only a step, and fundamentally a forward step, in the assimilation of the Italian.

Out of this class emerges a third generation, and here the final fruition of the slow process of Americanization can be seen. The members of this generation are of creditable character, industrious, intelligent and valuable to American society in every way. They are so different from the newly-arrived immigrant that it is almost impossible to detect from their speech manners or appearance the fact that they come originally of Italian stock. According to the report of the investigation of the Federal Commission on Immigration, even the bodily form of the Italian race undergoes radical and far-reaching changes in America. Physically, as well as mentally and morally, the Italian is remoulded to conform to that little understood standard, the American type. The Italians of the third generation crowd into the professions, and we have Italian teachers, doctors, architects, engineers, lawyers and judges.

The immigrant from Italy, illiterate, ignorant, superstitious and simple-minded, is, then, of tremendous value to us, not for what he is, but for what America can make of him.

The spirit of the steerage! Ah, it's a yearning spirit, a fervent spirit, a spirit of fire and devotion, of loyalty to the new land; a spirit of willingness to toil and suffer, to take the bitter with the sweet, kissing the hand of the nation that has given both. It is a spirit of the pioneer, courting difficulties, unafraid of obstacles. It would be well if every phase of the life of America were as full of hope and promise as is the spirit of the steerage.

AN ITALIAN'S ADVICE
TO ITALIAN
IMMIGRANTS*

No other foreign land is so vitally interested in the new restrictive law regarding emigration to the United States as is Italy, for the stream of Italian emigration has not only been an outlet for a surplus population that would not find profitable occupation at home, but has also provided a notable addition to the annual revenue of the country from the large sums remitted by the expatriated Italian workers. Hence it is recognized in Italy as most important to forestall as far as may be any check to the renewal of emigration after the war that might result from the new law.

This question is very impartially examined by Dr. G. B. Nicola in the *Rivista Internazionale*. The main grounds for the law against the admission of illiterates are acknowledged to be that the illiterate immigrant will be satisfied with low wages; that he is easily imposed upon and prone to seek revenge in crimes of violence, and that he is necessarily held aloof from the influences of the American educational system. Dr. Nicola finds that before protesting against this law and seeing in it a proof of hatred toward the Italians, it should be carefully weighed, and if its provisions are found reasonable it should be cordially accepted.

He rejects as a wholly childish expedient the proposal of certain Italian journals that the tide of emigration should be diverted to Asia Minor, as though the Italian laborers were tourists in search of pleasurable emotions, who could vary their journeys at will, and were not invincibly bound by a tissue of complex interests, of family relations and social requirements, not to be disturbed.

The strongest current of Italian emigration has set toward the United States. In the quinquennial period 1909-1913 the annual average was 278,000, representing 41 per cent of the total number of Italians who went to foreign lands, and 68 per cent of those who crossed the sea. In the year 1913 as many as 377,000 went to America.

*Review of Reviews, Vol. 56 (1917), p. 100.

The writer believes that the military service of Italians born after 1900 will hardly be needed in the war, and he finds that the proper education of this new generation, even apart from serving to overcome the obstacles to immigration interposed by the United States, would render those who remained in Italy more productive.

Naturally the education given to prospective emigrants should not stop at the ability to read thirty words, as demanded by the American law. It should embrace a minimum of knowledge regarding the State and national constitutions and the geographic divisions of the United States, as well as a familiarity with the standards of weight and measurement. Scarcely less essential would be an elementary knowledge of Italian conditions, so that when questioned as to these by an American, the Italian would be able to give intelligent answers.

In conclusion Dr. Nicola gives some useful hints to those of his fellow-countrymen who intend to establish themselves in the United States. They are urged to keep in mind the notable differences between the customs and ways of thinking of the two countries. Of this he says:

> If, for example, two boys coming out of school begin to pummel each other and a friend of one of them runs up to help him, this will be looked upon as cowardly; the two boys ought to be left to fight it out with each other; but two against one, when all are of about the same strength, is not to be allowed, is not to be thought of for a moment, is almost inhuman in American eyes.
>
> Another principle is the so-called eleventh commandment: "Mind your own business!" This is a national attitude foreign to the Latin temperament of to-day, a lively and expansive temperament, ready to give aid, but also sometimes, in spite of all good intentions, animated by an importunate curiosity that may give offense.
>
> At first sight it might seem that this should be especially applicable to Englishmen and Germans and that the American is almost anarchical. But this is altogether untrue. Take your stand at the corner of Broadway and Wall Street, or at any other center of intense traffic, and remark how at a single sign of the policeman's "magic wand" hundreds of vehicles are instantly arrested in their course, and this without the slightest thought of remonstrance. We are accustomed to call America the land of liberty, meaning that kind of liberty that borders on license. This is all wrong. Liberty among equals is indeed perfect, but all must submit to authority. The President of the United States exercises an executive power more autocratic, one might almost say more absolute, than does the King of Italy with his ministers. Lastly, in America, with but few exceptions, all are re-

ligious. There is full freedom in the choice of this or that confession, but national custom and trend of thought require the profession of some religion, demand that some form of worship, however simple, shall be practised. The open conflict with the primary principles of the Christian religion, so frequent in Latin countries is entirely inadmissible.

VICTOR VON BOROSINI

HOME-GOING ITALIANS*

The present Italian emigration is mostly transoceanic, and has lost to a large extent its former seasonal character. The average proportion of men to women emigrants is 78.5 per cent to 11.5 per cent, the proportion of emigrant families being smallest from south Italy. Seventy-four per cent of the emigrants from northern Italy return to their native villages, while the South sees again only 41 per cent of those who leave. The proportion of returning women is smaller than of men. Of the native Italians who return to Sicily, Campagna, Abruzzi, Latium, and Apulia, from 75 to 90 per cent come from the United States. As three-fourths of the men are between sixteen and forty-five years of age, their most productive period, the total loss Italy suffers by emigration is not very large.

The death rate among Italian emigrants is not known, but is probably, on account of bad working and housing conditions, higher than at home. Most Italians remain in the United States from two to five years, the northern Italians not staying as long as their southern compatriots, in all probability because as skilled and better educated laborers they immediately command higher wages in the New World, and work steadily, while the illiterate southerner works at low wages and is often unemployed during the winter.

Returning emigrants are in much improved economic circumstances, their average savings being from $250 to $1,000. This money is placed in postal savings or co-operative banks until it is used to buy land, cattle, and machinery, or for building. The increasing demand of the returning emigrant has raised land values, especially in the South, where land jobbers and large proprietors make immense profits by dividing estates and selling plots to the land-hungry crowd.

Emigrants returning from small American communities show more markedly than those from large cities the influence of decent surroundings in their standard of living. One lesson they all take home is the knowledge of how great a handicap is illiteracy in the strug-

*Survey, Vol. 28 (September, 1912), pp. 791-793.

gle for existence. Hence, they favor strongly obligatory instruction
for their children, and co-operate willingly to extend the system. With
their wider experience their political interest increases and frequently they try to introduce into public life methods of American
politics—not a wholly desirable importation.

North Italians tend to become more tolerant toward other
churches and more indifferent toward their own, while even five
years in the United States fails to eradicate the superstitions of the
southerner. The latter do, however, become not infrequently ad-
herents of radical ideas, such as Socialism and Syndicalism, already current among the North Italians before emigration.

Criminal statistics reveal a curious phenomenon. As a consequence of better economic conditions crimes against property decrease, while those against persons and propriety increase, the men
having adopted the dangerous habit of carrying pistols and drinking heavily.

One reason for these crimes is immorality caused by the long-continued separation of husbands and wives who part at a period when
sexual instincts are strong. Frequently the husband, emigrating soon
after marriage, leaves a robust, young, and pregnant wife in the
care of parents or relatives. He does not lead a chaste life, but demands absolute faithfulness from her. But women in Italy have
the same inborn tendencies as men—they are not satisfied with the
regularly arriving money order. As a consequence illegitimate
children, child murder and abortion are increasing alarmingly
as are acts of vengeance committed by wronged husbands. While
abroad men often acquire venereal diseases, and after their home
coming they infect the whole family. The mother country is much
concerned in the physical condition of returning emigrants. Statistics are incomplete, as many return on lines which do not report to
the government, and besides only a small percentage comes under
medical care on board. Sometimes appalling illnesses are neglected,
because the men do not know that that the Italian law makes special
provisions for free treatment on board. Though some leave the ships'
hospital improved, in 1909 over 1,500 were landed in a serious condition. Chronic tuberculosis and venereal diseases are acquired in
the United States, while from Latin America emigrants bring
trachoma and hookworm.

Each year the consuls send back a number of invalids who are no
longer of use to the country, which exploited their labor power to
the utmost. The most desperate of these cases are treated in the marine
hospitals of Palermo, Naples, and Genoa. Their capacity is not,
however, sufficient for all cases and many patients are sent to their

homes in out-of-the-way places, where there is great lack of physicians, hospitals, and general hygienic provisions, and where, in their ignorance, they become a dangerous source of infection to the whole community. Italy proposes to increase her hospital sanatorium service, and to teach therein the elements of hygiene and sanitation. She plans also to inaugurate an information service by which the authorities at home can be warned of the impending arrival of a diseased citizen and told of the proper steps to be taken for the protection of others.

ITALIAN EMIGRANTS EN ROUTE: A PROPOSED STEERAGE REFORM*

The national conscience of Italy is very much concerned of late with the emigration problem; but reform projects have until now received such inadequate financial support that the results have been somewhat discouraging. As to the aid to be given to the emigrants it is generally admitted that the home government owes its wandering poor preparation in the primary schools, surveillance of the emigration agencies, care on the voyage to North and South America; and in their new country, the establishment of employment offices, mutual aid societies, schools, libraries, etc. The preparatory aid in Italy and the guardian care in America give ample material for study, new projects and parliamentary debates, but the assistance on board the steamers seems to have been neglected, although the expenses of improvements would be light and the results immediate.

Signorina Cesarina Lupati, writing in the *Nuova Antologia*, studies the question of assisting the steerage passengers more efficiently at a minimum cost to the Italian authorities. Under prevailing conditions there is on board every ship a royal commissioner—almost invariably a marine surgeon—sent to protect the rights of the emigrants from possible encroachments on the side of the company, to keep good order and superintend the embarking and landing. After sailing, the commissioner's duties are confined to aiding the ship doctor in promoting hygiene and maintaining discipline. The greater part of his day is free and he is able to amuse himself with the first-class passengers and entertain the ladies. For the purpose of protection against the company, the commissioner's presence would seem superfluous, as the first and second class have no need of championship, and the third even less for the good reason that they form the company's most numerous and constant clientele, and when land-

Review of Reviews, vol. 44 (1911), pp. 348-350.

ed, the best advertising agents. It is regrettable that this excessive precaution is not expended on the lodging-houses at Naples and Genoa,
where the peasants from the interior often spend several days before
sailing and arrive at the ship in a half-starved, dirty and dejected
state. Several million lire have been waiting for years to be applied to
the building of official hotels to meet this crying need, but it was
decided at the commission's last sitting that the idea was impractic-
able because the emigrants' stay in port is too short to justify the
expenditure. The boarding-house harpies will continue to prepare the soil for epidemics and all the other ills to which the
emigrants are especially exposed in their crowded quarters below
deck.

Signorina Lupati complains that the commissioners do not enforce personal cleanliness, and replies to the objection that there
are only six or eight bathrooms for over a thousand people, that
by barrack discipline, every emigrant could at least have one bath
on board. This reform could be begun by obligatory baths for mothers and children. As regards food the majority fare better on board
than at home, but the chief hardship for the better class of emigrants
is the dark-brown sacking and cover for the mattresses and the
stifling dormitories to which the women and children are sent shortly after sunset. If the payment of twenty lire additional could secure
coarse white sheets, it would be a welcome substitute for the "preferred" class at table which only encourages departure from hardy
abstemiousness. Decency would be furthered by the subdivision of
the dormitories into four or six beds instead of the present huddled
masses of hale and infirm side by side.

The emigrants pass the time that they are not violently ill in complete idleness, some half-somnolent, others gambling and quar-
reling, but rarely in conversation. Schools have been proposed,
but they would prove of little use as the numbers are too great and
reading or writing could not be taught in fifteen or twenty days, supposing the pupils always able to attend. But the example of a young
second officer suggested to Signorina Lupati the best way to prepare
the peasants for their new citizenship even at the eleventh hour. The
officer was explaining the compass to an animated group, each of
whom took it in his hands with child-like eagerness, and when the
officer had gone, all the circle discussed his friendliness and their
newly-acquired knowledge. Afterwards, when congratulated on
his success, the young man answered that the emigrants were always interested and it pleased him to make up a little for the unfair
difference between the second and third classes. Proceeding from this
experience, Signorina Lupati proposes a series of conferences

which should primarily appeal to the good common sense which is the liveliest faculty of the illiterate. These talks could be held every day in good weather, or if possible, twice a day, to two groups. Without formal pretensions, the instructor could carry out a short program on the necessity of hygiene, on obedience to the stewards and officers' vaccination, superstitions, temperance, respect for women, economy and honesty; personal inquiry as to motive of emigration, name, age, trade and destination; the new country, its population, important cities, customs, language, inhabitants and chief laws concerning foreigners—and finally, how Italy is represented in the new land, the consuls, the ambassador, newspapers, mutual aid and employment societies, the need for absolute respect of the laws of the hospitable country and the duty to Italy that every Italian should make himself respected and welcomed in the place where he is going to become a breadwinner if not a citizen.

As these talks with the emigrants would only take up two hours daily, the task could be entrusted to the commissioners, to whom the government could pay a slight additional salary. Their zeal could be insured by the institution of medals of honor or advancement by the Emigration Commission, which would first award recompense to the disinterested pioneers of the movement—the young officers of the merchant marine who have devoted their leisure moments to the mitigation of the chief ill—ignorance.

On the sad lack of dignity shown by the emigrants, Signorina Lupati observed that the principal cause was their ignorance of law except the atavistic law of blood-thirstiness—their hostility and suspicion of superiors engendered by the oppression of several generations. That the Western courts of justice do not take in consideration this heriditary burden, but condemn all Italians for each semi-irresponsible act of violence, is shown by the labor riots in Louisiana and more recently in Brazil. Signorina Lupati closes her humane exposition of the wrongful neglect of her unfortunate countrymen by an appeal to Italy that at least the last days passed in the emigrant ships under her flag floating from the mast should bestow encouragement and strength for the unequal struggle.

> When the ship touched the dock and the crowd, eager for deliverance, rushed to the gangway, I saw them— ragged, begrimed—in   sullen violence or apathetic stupor unaware of their destiny—I saw them, ashamed for Italy for whom we toil, pray or die—Italy never to be truly glorious and great till she heeds the silent groan from her peasants' bitter lips.

II
Italian Communities in America
Campanilismo in the Ghetto

INTRODUCTION

What was life like in the Italian communities in America (what Antonio Mangano called "Italian colonies in America") during the period of the great migrations? What were those forces which were main determinants of behavior? At best, life was indescribably hard for the Italian immigrant in the cities of America. The journalist reformer Jacob Riis provides a vivid description (*circa* 1890) of life in the Mulberry Street slum in lower Manhattan which housed a great congregation of Italians:

> With the first hot night in June, police dispatches that record the killing of men and women by rolling off roofs and window sills while asleep, announce that the time of greatest suffering among the poor is at hand. It is in hot weather, when life indoors is well-nigh unbearable, with cooking, sleeping, and working, all crowded into the small rooms together, that the tenement expands, reckless of all restraint. Then a strange and picturesque life moves upon the flat roofs. In the day and early evenings mothers air their babies there, the boys fly their kites from the house-tops, undismayed by police regulations, and the young men and girls court . . . In the stifling July nights, when the big barracks are like fiery furnaces, their very walls giving out absorbed heat, men and women lie in restless, sweltering rows, panting for air and sleep. Then every truck in the street, every crowded fire-escape, becomes a bedroom, infinitely preferable to any the house affords. A cooling shower on such a night is hailed as a heaven-sent blessing in a hundred thousand homes.
>
> Life in the tenements in July and August spells death to an army of little ones whom the doctor's skill is powerless to save. When the white badge of mourning flutters from every second door, sleepless mothers walk the streets in the grey of the early dawn, trying to stir a cooling breeze to fan the brow of the sick baby. There is

no sadder sight than this patient devotion striving
against fearfully hopeless odds.[1]

Erik Amfitheatrof (himself, a journalist), who uses Riis as his
major source in recreating the Italian urban ghetto of the period,
adds the following grim observations: "In one block in Mulberry
Street, in 1888, the death rate for adults and older children was 15.78.
For infants and children below the age of five it was 136.70. In
perpetually dark, airless rear tenements, as many as a third of all
babies born died before their first birthday. In summer, Riis wrote,
despite the efforts of special teams of doctors and nurses, 'the grave-
diggers in Calvary work over-time, and little coffins are stacked
mountains high on the deck of the Charity Commissioners' boat
when it makes its semi-weekly trips to the city cemetery.' But the
Italian peasant survived in this "sort of purgatory—if not in the
[Mulberry] Bend then in similar slums in Boston, Philadelphia,
or Chicago."[2]

A key to the life of Italian community in America is an understanding of the phenomenon known as *campanilismo*. The word
campanilismo derives from the words *campana* (bell) and *campanile*
(church tower), and "refers to a view of the world that includes reluctance to extend social, cultural, and economic contacts beyond points from which the parish or village bell could still be
heard."[3]

Campanilismo was the single most potent force operating in the
universe of the southern Italian peasant (who constituted the bulk
of the migration) in the urban ghettoes of the United States; and it
was strengthened by the mores of the family which was the social
world of the southern Italian *contadino* (peasant) society. Leonard
Covello has best capsuled the basic concept of the family which the
Italian transplanted to America:

> The concept of family that prevailed in South Italy
> was that of a social group which included all blood and

---

[1]Quoted by Erik Amfitheatrof, *The Children of Columbus: An Informal History
of the Italians in the New World* (Boston: Little, Brown, 1973), p. 167. See generally,
Francesco Cordasco, ed., *Jacob Riis Revisted: Poverty and the Slum in Another
Era* (New York: Doubleday, 1968). The harsh portraits of Riis (which span the years
1890-1903) are not overdrawn. For the Italian immigrant, life in American cities
continued to be unduly severe across the next four decades (exacerbated by the
great depression of the 1930's), relieved by the restrictive immigration quotas of the
1920's, by the social reforms of President Franklin D. Roosevelt's "New Deal," and
by the abrupt break with the past initiated by World War II and its aftermath.

[2]Amfitheatrof, *Ibid.*

[3]Joseph Lopreato, *Italian Americans* (New York: Random House, 1970), p. 104.

in-law relatives up to the fourth degree. To the southern Italian, the family was an inclusive social world, of and by itself. In a *contadino* community the population consisted of a number of familial groups. There were frequent instances where one familial set-up embraced the entire population of a village; that is, all the inhabitants were related by blood or by marriage. In such a *contadino* community, the social interaction actually amounted to relationship between a limited number of marriage units.

The family, then, as applied to the *contadino* class, may be considered as made up of a number of integrated units, each unit consisting of parents and their children (a marriage unit), each evolving toward greater stability and wider importance. The marriage unit reached the highest stage when it was the oldest living household group within the larger family group. Thus the *famiglia*, as conceived by the *contadino* did not limit itself to one domicile, but might embrace several households even though scattered over the territory of the village or town.

The fundamental familial concept was based on a communal family relationship similar to that among Polish peasants, among whom this solidarity

> . . . cannot be converted into any other type of group relationship nor reduced to a personal relation between otherwise isolated individuals. (This bond) manifests itself both in assistance rendered to, and in control exerted over, any member of the group by any other member representing the group as a whole . . . And again, the familial solidarity and the degree of assistance and of control involved should not depend upon the personal character of the members but only upon the kind and degree of their relationships; the familial relation between two members admits no gradation as does love or friendship.

To the southern Italian *contadino* this was indeed the idea of family and family relations. It was the only concept of family that he had, and the only form of family relationship that he knew. That there could be other forms was absolutely beyond his conception, and only upon arrival in America did he experience the perception of other forms.[4]

And Covello further notes: "The southern Italian immigrant in America naturally sought to perpetuate this traditional family pattern in his adopted country. The congregation of Italian immigrants in 'little Italys,' where the continuation of traditional family pat-

---

[4]Leonard Covello, *The Social Background of the Italo-American School Child: A Study of the Southern Italian Family Mores and their Effect on the School Situation in Italy and America*. Edited and with an Introduction by Francesco Cordasco (Leiden, The Netherlands: E. J. Brill, 1967; reprinted, Totowa, N.J.: Rowman and Littlefield, 1972), pp. 149-50. Covello is quoting from William I. Thomas and Florian Znaniecki, *The Polish Peasant in Europe and America* (Boston: The Gorham Press, 1919, I pp. 89-90).

terns was more or less practicable, accounts for a major aspect of the conflict with their new environment."[5]

Life in the "Italian Colonies in America" can be recreated from a variety of sources; but the very plethora of materials makes necessary their careful differentiation and definition. The materials I have assembled are, indeed, diverse: they range from the idyllic, solicitous portraits (themselves, part of voluminous reform literature born of philanthropic ideal and 19th century evangelical piety) of Charlotte Adams to the ascerbic observations of Gino C. Speranza. Their sentiments (however contrasting, and separated by a generation), are, nonetheless, responses to the same world: Adams: "A little kindly guidance and teaching can mould them into almost any form;" Speranza: "This congested living, this communal life is so intimately close that it might seem well nigh useless to hope that the breeze of American views will blow through its narrow ways and alleys."

Antonio Mangano's "The Associated Life of the Italians in New York City" is a more gentle portraiture but still a fully dimensional overview of the immigrant Italian community;[6] and it is essentially congruent with the professionally incisive observation of Alberto Pecorini, and the constellation of articles drawn together in a special issue of the reform journal *Charities* ("The Italian in America") in which the American progressive reformers of the settlement house movement (*e.g.*, Jane Addams, Robert A. Woods, Bertha

[5]Covello, *op. cit.*, p. 238. There is some controversy on the continuing influence of *campanilismo* and old world culture in the lives of Italian immigrants in the American urban communities. Obviously, a great amount of adaptation to the new milieu took place, and the Italian immigrant experienced, no less than other new arrivals, the culture conflicts out of which adaptive responses arose, but the adaptation was cast in the mould of *campanilismo* and family structure which shaped the responses: there was no attenuation of the basic cultural determinants. For the contrary view, see Humbert S. Nelli, *The Italians in Chicago: A Study in Ethnic Mobility* (New York: Oxford University Press, 1970), e.g., "the process of re-creating the homeland did not, and could not, take place in the Chicago environment of mobile population, absence of tradition, impersonal relationships, and acceptance of change. Ironically, the old world community intimacy that Italians in America 'recalled' so nostalgically originated in the new world as a response to urban surroundings." (p. 6)

[6]Antonio Mangano was Director of the Italian Department of Colgate Theological Seminary in Brooklyn. He was one of a handful of Italian born Protestant ministers proselytizing among Italian immigrants, if with little success. His *Sons of Italy* (1917) is one of the best contemporary accounts available in English. His book is full of wry comments of which the following is typical: "The south Italian is illiterate, but not unintelligent. Traces of the 'divine fire' of a race largely Pelasgic in south Italy, a race that has produced the greatest genius the world has ever seen persist and only await favorable environment to flash out and enrich our life. Said a hardheaded business man to Professor Steiner, 'These dagos are an ignorant lot.' 'Yes' was the reply, 'but they are the same race as Tasso, Dante, Verdi, Garibaldi, and Cavour.' 'Oh, come now, they aren't Tassos or Garibaldis.' 'No; neither are you George Washington or Lincoln.' " (p. 113)

Hazard, Florence Kelley) viewed the Italians in their midst.[7] Enrico C. Sartorio's sensitive observations on "Americanization" are the invaluable insights afforded by an Italian Protestant minister who tried to explain his countrymen's needs: "I am only acquainted with the knowledge of America which exists among Italians, but that which I know is sad enough."[8] A different view of "Americanization" is that of Aurelio Palmieri whose animadversions intrude into the volatile contexts of the Roman Catholic Church and the Italian immigrants;[9] and there is in the melioristic pieties of Edward Corsi a rebirth of the simplistic optimism of Charlotte Adams, if removed by a half century of conflict and enforced acculturation.

The full "round of life" of the Italian subcommunity is in the comprehensive commentaries of Marie J. Concistrè, and I have drawn heavily from her unpublished work. In describing the East Harlem (New York City) Italian community, she provides detailed vignettes of Italian traditions and heritages; the Italian family; language difficulties of immigrant groups; the Italian and politics; economic status and housing; mobility and social effects; and of the multiplicity of Italian religious institutions which flourished. Unlike the participant-observer who, more often than not is from outside the community he studies, Concistrè was indigenous to the East Harlem community she describes, and her narrative has all of the verisimilitude which gives it authenticity and truth; and it suffers

[7]See generally, Allen F. Davis, *Spearheads for Reform: The Social Settlements and the Progressive Movement, 1890-1914* (New York: Oxford University Press, 1967); and for a corpus of late 19th and early 20th century texts, F. Cordasco, ed., *The Social History of Poverty: The Urban Experience* (New York: Garrett Press, 1969-1970, 15 vols.) which reprints works by Jacob Riis, Robert Hunter, John Spargo, Hutchins Hapgood, Robert A. Woods, Helen Campbell, Carroll D. Wright, and Edward N. Clopper, all of whom (in one way or another) intruded into the world of the Italian immigrant.

[8]Enrico C. Sartorio (not unlike Antonio Mangano) was, as I have noted in the reissue of his *Social and Religious Life of Italians in America* (1918; 1973), one of a group of "bright young Italian men who found in the Protestant missions working amongst Italians those opportunities commensurate with their talents and skills which were denied them elsewhere in American society; and this is not intended to impugn their integrity or to question their religious conviction: it is only to reaffirm a truism in American social history—the existence of that burgeoning hospice which liberal Protestantism extended to the urban poor of another era; the social settlements and progressive movements which Allen F. Davis has called 'spearheads for reform' and of which the immigrant poor were often the beneficiaries."

[9]The best introduction to the evolving relationships of Italian peasants and the American Catholic Church is Rudolph J. Vecoli, "Prelates and Peasants: Italian Immigrants and the Catholic Church," *Journal of Social History*, vol. 2 (Spring 1969), pp. 217-268. See also (for a different view, and a modification of the Vecoli position), S. M. Tomasi, *Assimilation and Religion: The Role of the Italian Ethnic Church in the New York Metropolitan Area, 1880-1930* (unpublished Ph.D. dissertation, Fordham University, 1972).

little if any attenuation because of the multitudinous detail in which it is encapsulated.[10]

It is East Harlem (the largest Italian community in the United States, at that time) which is the setting of Leonard Covello's autobiography from which I have drawn several chapters. Covello's reminiscences of the "Italian colony" are, perhaps, the most sensitive extant; and it was he, more than any other individual, who sought to preserve the records and *disjecta membra* of a world which was rapidly disappearing as changes engulfed Italian immigrants and their progeny.

[10]Concistrè's work carries with all of the ponderous baggage of the American doctoral dissertation, and the work is mistitled. Although the work is entitled *Adult Education in a Local Area: A Study of a Decade in the Life and Education of the Adult Italian Immigrant in East Harlem, New York City,* Concistrè actually (in the "statement of the problem") studied "the cultural patterns and attitudes of the local immigrant group in its relation to the American milieu, and the processes involved in the synthesis of both Italian and American cultures in the Americanization of the immigrant." Her decade is 1932-1942, the period in which the East Harlem Italian community was at its height and on the eve of its dispersal across the two decades which were to follow.

CHARLOTTE ADAMS

ITALIAN LIFE IN
NEW YORK*

The fact that Italian immigration is constantly on the increase in
New York makes it expedient to consider both the condition and
status of these future citizens of the republic. The higher walks
of American life, in art, science, commerce, literature, and society,
have, as is well known, long included many talented and charming
Italians; but an article under the above title must necessarily deal
with the subject in its lower and more recent aspect. During the year
1879 seven thousand two hundred Italian immigrants were landed
at this port, one-third of which number remained in the city, and
there are now over twenty thousand Italians scattered among the
population of New York. The more recently arrived herd together
in colonies, such as those in Baxter and Mott streets, in Eleventh
Street, in Yorkville, and in Hoboken. Many of the most important
industries of the city are in the hands of Italians as employers and employed, such as the manufacture of macaroni, of objects of art, confectionery, artificial flowers; and Italian workmen may be found
everywhere mingled with those of other nationalities. It is no uncommon thing to see at noon some swarthy Italian, engaged on a
building in process of erection, resting and dining from his tin
kettle, while his brown-skinned wife sits by his side, brave in her
gold earrings and beads, with a red flower in her hair, all of which at
home were kept for feast days. But here in America increased wages
make every day a feast day in the matter of food and raiment; and why,
indeed, should not the architectural principle of beauty supplement-
ing necessity be applied even to the daily round of hod-carrying?
Teresa from the Ligurian mountains is certainly a more picturesque
object than Bridget from Cork, and quite as worthy of incorporation
in our new civilization. She is a better wife and mother, and under
equal circumstances far outstrips the latter in that improvement of
her condition evoked by the activity of the New World. Her children
attend the public schools, and develop very early an amount of

Harper's Magazine,, vol. 62 (April, 1881), pp. 676-684.

energy and initiative which, added to the quick intuition of
Italian blood, makes them valuable factors in the population. That
the Italians are an idle and thriftless people is a superstition which
time will remove from the American mind. A little kindly guidance
and teaching can mould them into almost any form. But capital is the
first necessity of the individual. It is to be wondered at, therefore,
that the poor untried souls that wander from their village or mountain homes, with no advice but that of the parish priest, no knowledge of the country to which they are going but the vague though daz-
zling remembrance that somebody's uncle or brother once went to
Buenos Ayres and returned with a fortune, no pecuniary resource
but that which results from the sale of their little farms or the wife's
heritage of gold beads, and no intellectual capital but the primitive
methods of farming handed down by their ancestors, should
drift into listless and hopeless poverty? Their emigration is frequently in the hands of shrewd compatriots, who manage to land
them on our shores in a robbed and plundered condition.

On the other hand, the thrifty *bourgeois* who brings with him the
knowledge of a trade, and some little capital to aid him in getting a
footing, very soon begins to prosper, and lay by money with which
to return and dazzle the eyes of his poorer neighbors, demoralizing
his native town by filling its inhabitants with yearnings toward the
El Dorado of "Nuova York." Such a man, confectioner, hairdresser,
or grocer, purchases a villa, sets up his carriage, and to all appearance purposes spending his life in elegant leisure; but the greed
of money-getting which he has brought back from the New World
surges restlessly within him, and he breaks up his establishment,
and returns to New York to live behind his shop in some damp, unwholesome den, that he may add a few more dollars to his store,
and too often his avarice is rewarded by the contraction of a disease which presently gives his hard-earned American dollars into
the hands of his relatives in Italy. There is an element of chance in
the success of Italians which makes emigration with them a matter
of more risk than with other nationalities of more prudence and
foresight. The idyllic life of an Italian hill-side or of a dreaming
mediaeval town is but poor preparation for the hand-to-hand struggle for bread of an overcrowded city. Hence the papers of the peninsula teem with protests and warnings from the pens of intelligent
Italians in America against the thoughtless abandonment of home
and country on the uncertain prospect of success across the ocean.

The fruit trade is in the hands of Italians in all its branches, from
the Broadway shop with its inclined plane of glowing color, to the
stand at a street corner. Among the last the well-to-do fruit-merchant

has a substantial wooden booth, which he locks up in dull times, removing his stock. In winter he also roasts chestnuts and pea-nuts, and in summer dispenses slices of water-melon and *aqua cedrata* to the *gamins* of the New York thoroughfares, just as he once did to the small lazzaroni of Naples or the fisherboys of Venice. With the poorer members of the guild the little table which holds the stock in trade is the family hearth-stone, about which the children play all day, the women gossip over their lace pillows, and the men lounge in the lazy, happy ways of the peninsula. At night the flaring lamps make the dusky faces and the masses of fruit glow in a way that adds much to the picturesqueness of our streets. These fruit-merchants are from all parts of Italy, and always converse cheerfully with any one who can speak their language, with the exception of an occasional sulky youth who declines to tell where he came from, thereby inviting the suspicion that he has fled to escape the conscription. That they suffer much during our long cold winters is not to be doubted, but the patience of their characters and the deprivations to which they have always been accustomed make them philosophic and stolid. As soon as they begin to prosper, the fatalism of poverty gives place to the elastic independence of success, and their faces soon lose their characteristic mournfulness. I have seen young Italian peasants walking about the city, evidently just landed, and clad in their Sunday best—Giovanni in his broad hat, dark blue jacket, and leggings, and Lisa with her massive braids and gay shawl, open-eyed and wide-mouthed in the face of the wonderful civilization they are to belong to in the future. The elevated railroad especially seems to offer them much food for speculation—a kind of type of the headlong recklessness of Nuova York, so unlike the sleepy old ways of the market-town which has hitherto bounded their vision.

There are two Italian newspapers in New York—L'Eco d' Italia and *Il Republicano*. There are also three societies for mutual assistance—the "Fratellanza Italiana," the "Ticinese," and the "Bersaglieri." When a member of the Fratellanza dies, his wife receives a hundred dollars; when a wife dies, the husband receives fifty dollars; and a physician is provided for sick members of the society. It gives a ball every winter and a picnic in summer, which are made the occasion of patriotic demonstrations that serve to keep alive the love of Italy in the hearts of her expatriated children. Many of the heroes of '48 are to be found leading quiet, humble lives in New York. Many a one who was with Garibaldi and the Thousand in Sicily, or entered freed Venice with Victor Emanuel, now earns bread for wife and child in modest by-ways of life here in the great city. Now and then one of the king's soldiers, after serving all through the wars, drops down in his shop or work-room, and is buried by his former comrades, awaiting their turn to rejoin King Galantuomo.

There is something pathetically noble in this quiet heroism of work-day life after the glory and action of the past. I met the other day in a flower factory, stamping patterns for artificial flowers, an old Carbonaro who had left his country twenty-two years before— one of the old conspirators against the Austrians who followed in the footsteps of Silvio Pellico and the Ruffinis. He was gray-haired and gray-bearded, but his eyes flashed with the fire of youth when we talked of Italy, and grew humid and bright when he told me of his constant longing for his country, and his feeling that he should never see it again. It was a suggestive picture, this fine old Italian head, framed by the scarlet and yellow of the flowers about him, while the sunlight and the brilliant American air streamed over it from the open window, and two young Italians, dark-eyed and stalwart, paused in their work and came near to listen. It was the Italy of Europe twenty years back brought face to face with the Italy of America to-day. In another room, pretty, low-browed Italian girls were at work making leaves—girls from Genoa, Pavia, and other cities of the north, who replied shyly when addressed in their native tongue. Italians are especially fitted for this department of industry; indeed, their quick instinct for beauty shows itself in every form of delicate handiwork.

In the second generation many Italians easily pass for Americans, and prefer to do so, since a most unjust and unwarranted prejudice against Italians exists in many quarters, and interferes with their success in their trades and callings. It is much to be regretted that the sins of a few turbulent and quarrelsome Neapolitans and Calabrians should be visited upon the heads of their quiet, gentle, and hardworking compatriots. All Italians are proud and high-spirited, but yield easily to kindness, and are only defiant and revengeful when ill-treated.

There are two Italian Protestant churches in the city, various Sunday-schools, mission and industrial schools, into which the Italian element enters largely, established and carried on by Protestant Americans, chiefly under the auspices of the Children's Aid Society. The most noteworthy of these, as being attended exclusively by Italians, adults and children, is the one in Leonard Street.

Some four hundred boys and girls are under instruction in the afternoon and night schools, most of them being engaged in home or industrial occupations during the day. The building is large and airy, containing school-rooms, bath-rooms, a reading-room, and printing-offices, where work is furnished to Italians at the usual wages, and those seeking instruction are taught. There is a class of twenty-four girls who are taught plain sewing and ornamental needle-work, including lace-making. I visited this class, and found a number of little girls employed with lace cushions, and the manufacture of simple artificial flowers. With these last they were allowed to trim the new straw hats that had just been given them. They were plump, cleanly little creatures, much better off in the matter of food and raiment than their contemporaries of the peninsula. The lace class has been in existence but a short time, and the specimens are still somewhat coarse and irregular, but there is no reason why it should not become as important a branch of industry among the Italian women of America as among those of Europe. The only wonder is that instruction in a calling which exists by inheritance in Italy should be needed here, as these girls are mostly from the villages of Liguria, of which Genoa is the sea-port, and might fairly be supposed to know something of the craft which has made Rapallo and Santa Margherita famous. Shirts for outside orders are also made in the school, and the girls receive the same wages for their labor as are offered by the shops. The attendants upon the school are mostly Ligurians, and repudiate indignantly all kinship with the Neapolitans or Calabrians, whom they refuse to recognize as Italians, thereby showing how little the sectional sentiment of Italy has been affected by the union of its parts under one ruler.

Under the guidance of a lady connected with the school, I explored Baxter and contiguous streets, nominally in search of dilatory pupils. Here and there a small girl would be discovered sitting on the curb-stone or in a doorway, playing jackstones, with her hair in tight crimps, preparatory to participation in some church ceremony. An Italian feminine creature of whatever age, or in whatever clime, stakes her hopes of heaven on the dressing of her hair. Her excuse for remaining away from school was that she had to "mind the stand," or tend the baby, while her mother was occupied elsewhere, and her countenance fell when she was reminded that she could have brought the baby to school. It was noticeable that all these children, who had left Italy early or were born here, had clear red and white complexions, the result of the American climate. We passed through courts and alleys where swarthy Neapolitans were carting bales of rags, and up dark stairs where women and children were sorting them. Some of their homes were low, dark rooms, neglected and squalid; others were clean and picturesque, with bright patchwork counterpanes on the beds, rows of gay plates on shelves against the walls, mantels and shelves fringed with colored paper, red and blue prints of the saints against the white plaster, and a big nosegay of lilacs on the dresser among the earthen pots. Dogs and children were tumbling together on the thresholds just as they do in the cool corridors of Italian towns. On the first floor of one of the houses I found an establishment for the repairing of hand-organs, where a youth was hammering at a barrel of one, and a swarthy black-bearded man, to whom it belonged, was lounging on a bench near by. Against the smoke-blackened wall an armful of lilacs stood in a corner, filling the room with sweetness, and lead-ing naturally to the thought that with the spring and the flowers the organ-grinder prepares for a trip into the country, playing his way from one watering-place to another, accompanied perhaps by his family, or at least a child or two. In answer to an inquiry con-cerning monkeys, we were directed to a large double house op-posite, said to be inhabited entirely by Neapolitans, who were swarm-ing about the windows in all their brown shapeliness. In the hall-way, above the rickety outer stairs, lounged several men with red shirts and unkempt heads and faces. One of them was the proprietor of the monkey establishment, and his *farouche* manner disappeared with our first words of interest in his pets. He led us into the little room adjoining, where some six or eight half-grown monkeys were peering through the bars of their cages, evidently pleading to be let out. The most creditably schooled monkey was released first, hand-ed his cap, made to doff and don it, and shake hands, orders being issued both in Italian and English. Some of the others—small brown things with bright eyes, and "not yet quite trained," said the Nea-politan—were allowed a moment's respite from captivity, at which they screamed with joy, and made for the dish of soaked bread, dipping their paws into it with great greediness, while the *padrone* laughed indulgently. A properly trained organ-monkey is worth from twenty to thirty dollars.

In the great house known to Baxter Street as the "Bee-hive," we found the handsome *padrona* whose husband rents organs and sells clocks, which latter articles appear to be essentials to Italian house-keeping, in default of the many bells of the old country. The *padrona* was at first by no means eager to give information, as she supposed, in good broad American (she was born in New York), that it "would be put in the papers, like it was before." It would appear that the ad-vantages of communication with the outer world are not appreciated by the inhabitants of Baxter Street. The *padrona* finally informed me that the rent of an organ was four dollars a month, and that they had hard work getting it out of the people who hired them, "for they always told you they had been sick, or times were bad, or their children had been sick; and when the Italians came over they expected you to give them a room with a carpet and a clock, else they said you had no kindness." I saw in the cluster of eight houses that form the "Beehive" various humble homes, from the neat and graceful poverty adorned with bright colors, and sweet with the bunch of lilacs brought from the morning's marketing (the favorite flower of the neighborhood), to the dens of one room, in which three or four families live, and take boarders and lodgers into the bargain. They told me that the building contained a thousand souls, and that cases of malarial fever were frequent. It is true that the odors of Baxter Street are unhealthy and unpleasant, arguing defective drainage; but those of Venice are equally so, and exist for the prince no less than the beggar. As for overcrowding, no one who, for example, has spent a summer in Genoa, and has seen the stream of pallid, languid humanity pour out of the tall old houses of the Carignano district, can find food for sensationalism in the manner of life common to Baxter Street. It must be remembered that the standard of prosperity in America is not that of Italy, and that a man is not necessarily destitute nor a pauper because he prefers organ-grinding or rag-picking to shoemaking or hod-carrying, and likes macaroni cooked in oil better than bakers' bread and tough meat.

I fail to find that Italians here retain their national habits of enjoyment or their love of feast-day finery. True, I have seen *contadine* in gold beads and ear-rings sitting on their door-steps on Sunday afternoons, and I have watched a large family making merry over a handful of boiled corn, just as they did at home, and I have seen the Genoese matrons dress one another's hair of a Sunday morning in the old fashion. But the indifferentism and stolidity of the country react upon them. There seems to be little of the open-air cooking, the polenta and fish stalls, the soup and macaroni booths, that breed conviviality in the Italian streets. They apparently eat in their own homes, after the New World fashion.

Undoubtedly much of the recklessness with which Italians are charged in New York is the result of the sudden removal of religious influences from their lives. At home there is a church always open and at hand, and the bells constantly remind them of the near resting-place for soul and body. When their homes are noisy and uncomfortable, they can find peace and quiet in the cool dark churches; and when they are on the verge of quarrel or crime, and the hand involuntarily seeks the knife, the twilight angelus or the evening bell for the dead softens the angry heart and silences the quick tongue. Here the only escape from the crowded rooms is in the equally crowded yard, or the door-step, or the rum-shop. The only entirely Italian Catholic church in New York, I believe, is that of San Antonio di Padova, in Sullivan Street, attended by a superior class of Italians, all apparently prosperous and at peace with their surroundings.

In the days of political persecution and struggle in Italy, America was the republican ideal and Utopia toward which the longing eyes of all agitators and revolutionists turned. When self-banished or exiled by government, they were apt to seek their fortunes in America, often concealing their identity and possible rank, and taking their places among the workers of the republic. Among these was Garibaldi, who passed some time here in the suburbs of New York, earning his living like many another honest toiler, and awaiting the right moment to strike the death-blow at tyranny. To study the Italian character in its finer *nuances,* the analyst should not limit his investigations to the broad generalizations of the Italian quarters, but should prosecute his researches in out-of-the-way downtown thoroughfares, where isolated shops with Italian names over their doors stimulate curiosity. In these dingy places, among dusty crimping-pins, pomatum-pots, and ghastly heads of human hair, half-worn clothing, the refuse of pawnbrokers' shops, you may meet characters that would not have been unworthy the attention of Balzac, and would eagerly have been numbered by Champfleury among his "Excentriques." I have one in my mind whose short round person, tall dilapidated hat, profuse jewelry, red face, keen gray eyes, and ready tongue fully qualify him for the title of Figaro of Canal Street.

Another interesting class of Italians is found in the people attached to the opera—the chorus-singers and ballet-dancers, engaged also for spectacular dramas. It is in a measure a migratory population, crossing the ocean in the season, and recrossing when the demand for its labor ceases. Many chorus-singers who remain in New York follow different trades out of the opera season, and sing sometimes in the theatres when incidental music is required. By singers New York is regarded chiefly as a market in which they can dispose of their talents to greater pecuniary advantage than in Europe, and they endure the peculiar contingencies of American life simply in order to lay by capital with which to enjoy life in Italy. A season in America is always looked forward to as the means of accumulating a fortune, and not for any artistic value. I have heard of more than one Italian who, after a successful engagement in New York, has invited sundry compatriots to a supper at Moretti's, and announced his intention of **shaking the dust of America** from his shoes for evermore, being satisfied to retire on his gains, or to sing only for love of art and the applause of artists in the dingy opera-houses of Italy. The climate of America with its sudden changes kills the Italian bodies, and the moral atmosphere chills their souls—notably among artists. The "Caffè Moretti" has for years been the *foyer* of operatic artists, and no review of Italian life in New York would be complete without a mention of it. For many years they have dined, and supped, and drank their native wines in this dingy, smoke-blackened place, forgetting for the nonce that they were in America, and coming away, have left their portraits behind them, large and small, fresh and new, or old and smoke-dried, hanging side by side on the wall to cheer the hearts of the brother artists who should follow after them to the New World, and find a moment's respite from homesickness over Signor Moretti's Lachryma Christi and macaroni cooked in the good Milanese fashion. In view of the general assimilation of Italians with their American surroundings, it is surprising and delightful to find a place that retains so picturesque and Italian a flavor.

Since the abolishment of the *padrone* system one sees few child-musicians, and the wandering minstrels are chiefly half-grown boys and young men, who pass their summers playing on steamboats and at watering-places. It is gratifying to feel that one of the disgraces of modern and enlightened Italy has been wiped from the national record by the strong hand of governmental authority.

GINO C. SPERANZA

THE ITALIANS IN
CONGESTED DISTRICTS*

The great though unsuspected evil effect of congestion on Italians is psychological even more than physical. By this I mean that the suggestion of the worst or of the weakest is spread easily over the congested mass, whereas it would be sterile of results in a freer environment. Many an Italian who never would have thought of doing any other labor than that in the open air, some fine day hears that a neighbor of his is working in a cigar factory. Ninety-nine chances in one hundred that cigarmaker is a weakling who could not handle pick and shovel and, conscious of his physical deficiency, probably boasts what easy money factory work yields, where a man sits down all day and after work "goes home with the factory girls." The idea strikes the shoveller as novel and worth considering. The greater wage with the pick may for a while hold him, but if a day of temporary discontent or lassitude comes he digs up the factory ideal. I remember, a year ago, sending home a gang of strong, enduring Italian laborers from North Carolina, where they could perform hard work in the labor camps where I had found them, but one of them, just the one who was undersized and lazy, got a job in a factory on his return to the city. That entire gang is at the factory now.

I dwell on this psychological side of the influence of congested living, as we will see it especially active in influencing the civic relations of the Italian.

But so far, industrially, it is the Italian woman that has suffered most through congestion. The Italian wives or sisters, who in Italy used to work around the house or in the fields, never receiving compensation, see the "girl on the lower floor" go out every day and earn good money that gives her, what appears to the newcomer, not only splendid independence, but even the undreamed of joy of wearing Grand street millinery. The home becomes hateful, the traditional restraint which was considered a domestic virtue becomes a symbol of slavery, and the domestic woman will become a factory hand. Un-

Charities and the Commons, vol. 20 (1908), pp. 55-57.

used to such so-called freedom, she will misuse it as a starved man who overeats.

Congested living, working its evil spell on the morals of the Italians among us, in so far as it leads women to industrial work is, in my opinion, a greater evil, for it tends to destroy one of the finest of the Italian traditions, the unity of family life, and leads to the destruction of the Italian ideal of the home.

So likewise, in the civic relations of the Italian, our congested living works varied evils. One bad idea, one wrong notion, spreads by contagion over the mass, and it is the shrewd and often the dishonest that take advantage of this vehicle of contagion, which, under certain conditions, might be made a vehicle for good. The first to profit by it is the so-called Italian banker. I am not one of those who think all things bad of the Italian banker and of the Italian *padrone*. I think he has been and is an absolute necessity in the life of the expatriated Italian peasant. It will take years and years to obviate the economic necessity of the Italian *padrone;* we will have and we are having better and better *padroni*. The aim of those who wish to help Italians here should be to improve the quality of the *padroni* rather than to destroy them; to imitate their methods and use such methods to good end. It is against the abuse of the powers exercised by the banker that I appeal. Urban congestion is the very condition of life for the banker and the *padrone;* in exact ratio with the topographical nearness of his clients and *paesani* does he control them for good or bad. Each street has its particular region of Italy; Elizabeth street is claimed by the Western Sicilian; Catharine and Monroe streets by the Eastern Sicilian; Mulberry by the Neapolitans; Bleeker by the Genoese; MacDougal by the North Italians. The more crowded the street on which the bank is, the better for the banker; better yet, the more crowded is the block where the bank has its habitat; best of all, the more crowded with *paesani* the tenement in which operates the banker. Americans at times wonder how quickly a *padrone* can supply a large demand for laborers; it is simply that the *padrone* lives with them—and at his order the regiments of *paesant* turn out of the barracks of his tenement. Surely the *padrone* is not going to help you spread out his constituents.

Likewise, the average Italian banker could not do the varied kind of business he does unless he had his clientele under close physical vigilance. He could not take the risk, even for a larger consideration than he gets now, to go bail for his clients who are in trouble; he could not, as he undoubtedly often does, make advance on wages and render services of value where the compensation is contingent on his client's work in the future.

This power to control a mass, which through its very congestion is more like a large family than a healthy community of independent units, is shrewdly used not only by the banker and the *padrone* but by the politician. The voter among this controllable and controlled mass is the easy prey of the political boss, an easily worked political machine.

The intimacy, I might say, gossipy nature of such congested districts massed according to the towns or villages in Italy, while it is a religiously closed book to the outsider, is too open a book for the insider; none of its members can do anything that it does not become the property of the entire community. If this stopped at harmless gossip—it would merit no attention. But the fact is, that it is taken advantage of in two important ways by the criminally inclined in the community. If Antonio puts $100 in the bank, if Giuseppe's barber shop shows evidence of prosperity, if Gaetano especially pampers his children and dresses them well, if Michele gets a little extra money from some unexpected source, all the *paesani* in the crowd know it. And very likely the day after Antonio has made his bank deposit or Michele has got his extra cash, each will receive what is picturesquely called a Black Hand demand. Or perhaps Gaetano, who has shown his fondness for his children too much and is also prosperous, one fine day will find that his little Beppino is missing.

Not only this, but the close knowledge of each other in these congested communities is not merely limited to the present status of its members but to their family histories. Therefore, if in the past Gaetano has had some trouble, big or little, with the police or otherwise, that fact is known to the community—he is vulnerable or invulnerable according to the willingness of the members of the community to let the past be dead. I am thoroughly convinced that with very few exceptions, so called Black Hand threats are never made against an irreproachable person—that is against one who either in the past or the present has not something, not necessarily criminal or immoral, but something in his life that he would prefer to keep hidden.

The other way in which this close intimacy is a culture bed for crime, is that differences between individual members lead to divisions into criminal feuds. If Antonio insults Giuseppe and it remained between them, they might often settle it if not forgive it. But everybody knows of the insult passed and it would seem cowardly to submit before such a large audience. This may lead to divisions into partisans for the offender and for the offended—and a quarrel between two becomes a war between two parties. That same communal spirit nourished into a spirit of intimate fellowship results into other dangerous principles; that if any member of the community commits a crime the community must protect him; above all will he be hid and sheltered from the outsider, from the police officer and the detective.

This congested living, this communal life is so intimately close that it might seem well nigh useless to hope that the breeze of American views will blow through its narrow ways and alleys. The tendency to congregate, especially in a strange land, is natural, neither this conference, nor any man or body of men can hope to find means of preventing it—it would be like fighting instinct or nature. But while it is in vain to fight such a tendency, we may hope to destroy or minimize its almost absolute segregation. Every city, even in Utopia, will have districts where the rich live apart from the poor, the scholars from the market men, the lovers of freedom from the lovers of comfort, there will be aggregations of tastes if not of conditions; but even these separate units must constitute one great whole; there must be one municipal spirit, its denizens must constitute one people and not distinct clans. So the danger of our Little Italies, which in no way reflect the beauty and greatness of real Italy, lies not in their physical congestion, as much as in their spirit of aloofness, in the lack in their denizens of a sense of joint responsibility with all the people, not merely with some of them. These aliens must learn that they do not merely live their physical existence in New York, but constitute jointly with others the life of the city; that they must and can aid to make New York, not a bad copy of some ancient little Italian feudalism, but a great cosmopolitan city, different from other great centers in this essential regard—that its cosmopolitanism has its origin and life in the cosmopolitanism of the working classes.

ANTONIO MANGANO

THE ASSOCIATED LIFE OF THE ITALIANS IN NEW YORK CITY*

It is generally supposed by those unfamiliar with actual conditions, that the Italian colony of the Borough of Manhattan is a well-organized and compact body of people, having a common life and being subject to the absolute control and leadership of some one person or group of persons. To the reader of popular articles describing Italian life and customs, in these days so frequently appearing in newspapers and magazines; to the enthusaistic and romantic slum visitor, who walks through Mulberry street, and possibly peeps into the dark and dismal hallway of some dilapidated tenement and feels that he knows just how Italians live and act; to the theoretical sociologist, to whom all Italians look alike and in whose estimation all Italians are alike, think alike, and act alike—to such persons the mere mention of the Italian colony inevitably suggests unity of thought and action as well as of mode of life on the part of all who belong to that colony. And yet nothing is farther from the real truth.

Although many of the people of the Italian colony could not tell what the word *republic* means, and while none of them prior to coming to America have ever breathed the atmosphere created by republican institutions, it must be said that the love of freedom and the spirit of independence are elements inherent in the Italian character. Countless battlefields, made sacred during many centuries by the blood of those who rather than be subject to tyranny or foreign dominion offered their lives, as well as their substance, as a sacrifice, are unmistakable witnesses to the love of Italians for freedom and for liberty. When the Italian lands upon our shores and catches the spirit of the independence which prevails here, his own nature finds itself in a congenial atmosphere and begins to expand along those lines. Under the social and economic conditions in his own country, he could not assert himself; he was timid; he did not dare say his soul was his own for fear of being deprived of the means of sub-

Charities, vol. 12 (1904), pp. 476-482.

sistence. Here a very different state of affairs prevails. He somehow catches the idea that if he works faithfully and behaves himself, he need fear no man. This means an appeal to his manhood.

No one will deny that development along this line is good and wholesome. But, unfortunately, the good is accompanied by a shadow of evil. The spirit of independence seems to go to seed. The members of the Italian colony have a certain element in their general make-up which has rendered it virtually impossible for them to act unitedly and harmoniously. Each man feels that he is a law unto himself; each small group of men are a law unto themselves. They appreciate most keenly that it is their right and privilege to do as they see fit—providing they do not interfere with other people's rights— but they lose sight of this other great fact equally important, that personal rights and privileges should be modified by consideration for the welfare of the community—the only condition under which men can live together in any proper and mutually helpful relation.

But, now, if we are asked whether any plausible reason can be advanced as to why the Italians seem to lack natural capacity for a large co-operation, we would answer that they have for centuries lived in the midst of an evnironment which has tended to develop in them a spirit of division and sectional feeling. Prior to the formation of the present Italian kingdom, the country was divided into numerous dukedoms and principalities among which there was constant rivalry and bitter feeling, if not open warfare. As a natural consequence, the people not only have lacked sympathy for those outside of their particular principality or dukedom, but even have nursed a strong feeling of hostility toward them. Added to this, there is the spirit which prevails to-day in many parts of Italy—a clearly marked rivalry between two towns or two cities within the same province. Doubtless such contention has its good effect in inducing rival towns to put forth every effort for their improvement; but on the other hand, division and dissension are unconsciously fostered under the guise of a false patriotism.

The New York colony is composed of persons coming from nearly every nook and corner of the old peninsula. It is by no means strange, then, that they should bring with them local prejudices and narrow sympathies; it is not to be wondered that they feel that highest duty consists in being loyal to the handful who come from their immediate section and in manifesting opposition toward those who come from other localities. Thus it comes to pass that while a man may be known as an Italian, he is far better known as a Napoletano, Calabrese, Veneziano, Abbruzese, or Siciliano. This means that the Italian colony is divided into almost as many groups as there are sections of Italy represented.

There are, however, many signs which unmistakably point to a decided change for the better in the near future. There are certain forces at work which have for their ultimate object the development of a larger spirit of co-operation, which will enable the Italians as a whole to unite for the attainment of specific objects. The main purpose of this article, therefore, is to point out the chief Italian institutions which indicate the lines along which Italian organized effort is directed, and to describe briefly their operation.

Among the agencies which have for their ideal united Italian action, there are none more potent than the Italian Chamber of Commerce. This organization, founded in 1887 with but a few members, to-day embraces in its membership of 201 a majority of the Italian business men in Greater New York. The objects for which it was established may best be stated by translating a few articles from its constitution and by-laws:

(1) *a.* To promote, develop and protect commercial relations between Italy and the United States.
b. To facilitate and protect orderly interests, both commercial and industrial, which the Italians residing in the United States of America may have with other countries, and especially with Italy.

(2) *a.* To act as interpreter to the Italian government, to public or private officials, foreign or domestic, in regard to all matters concerning the development of Italian commercial interests in the United States.
b. To study the existing commercial and industrial reports between Italy and the United States; indicate the causes which hinder the development and suggest remedies.
c. To transmit to the Italian government all such inmation which may be of value in matters commercial and industrial between the mother country and the United States.
d. To compile a general annual directory of all Italian merchants in New York City and in the principal centres of the American union.
e. In general, to lend its good offices in the settlement of any difficulties which might arise between Italians, or between Italians and other nationalities.

In addition, the chamber occupies itself with a number of other things which are not specifically stated in the constitution. It aims at increasing Italian exports to this country and American exports to Italy; it acts as a medium in suggesting to dealers, both Americans and Italians, where they can secure the particular goods desired.

But to my mind, while I would not for a moment detract from the commercial functions of the chamber, its greatest good is achieved along another line—one which is destined eventually to lead the

Italians to drop sectional feeling and rejoice in the glory of a common nationality. That the Neapolitan, the Sicilian, the Roman, can all join this organization and have as the one object the advancement of Italian interests, is a step in the right direction and toward another end which is eminently wholesome and greatly to be desired.

The Columbus Hospital is situated on Twentieth street between Second and Third avenues. Organized in 1892 and incorporated in 1895, it has been from its beginning under the direct supervision of the missionary Sisters of the Sacred Heart. Were it possible for the hospital to secure increased accommodations and better facilities, it would be of far greater service to those in whose interests it is dedicated. The following paragraph is taken from the last annual report: "During the year, 1,098 patients were admitted, and of this number only sixty-three paid full board. When we consider that the hospital is devoid of endowment, annuity, or permanent fund for its maintenance, depending entirely upon the energies of the sisters and the voluntary contributions of those who have its well-being at heart, it becomes a problem which those unacquainted with the management would find difficulty in solving."

Columbus Hospital is generally known as an Italian institution, yet of the twenty-one physicians on its medical and surgical staff not one is an Italian, but the sisters who carry it on are all native Italians, and ninety-five per cent of the patients treated are of that race.

The Society for the Protection of Italian Immigrants was founded three years ago, and since then has, without a shadow of a doubt, rendered more practical assistance to the thousands flocking to our shores than any other institution working in the interest of Italians.

Speaking of the conditions in which Italians find themselves on arrival, Eliot Norton, president of the society, says in his annual report: "These immigrants are landed at Ellis Island, where they are examined by United States officials. From there some go into the interior of the country and some remain in New York. Almost all of them are very ignorant, very childlike, and wholly unfamiliar with the ways, customs and language of this country. Hence, it is obvious that they need friendly assistance from the moment of debarcation at Ellis Island. Those who go into the interior of the country need to be helped in getting on the right train, without losing their way or money; while those coming to New York City need guidance to their destination and, while going there, protection from sharps, crooks and dishonest runners, and thereafter to have advice and employment."

The society is constantly enlarging its activities. It has had the hearty co-operation of Commissioner Williams and of the police department. Its officials are stationed at Ellis Island and act as interpreters for the newcomers. With such immigrants as have friends either on Ellis Island or on the New York side, awaiting them, the society does not concern itself. Its attention is fully occupied in attending to those who have no friends and who have not the remotest idea as to the place for which they are bound. These are taken directly to its office, at 17 Pearl street, and later turned over to its guards or runners. For this service the immigrant is charged a nominal fee. During the first two years and a half, 7,293 friendless immigrants were conducted to their destinations, in or about New York City, at an average cost of thirty-two cents apiece, as against an average expenditure of from $3.00 to $4.00, which immigrants formerly were forced to pay by sharpers.

Closely associated with the work of the Society for the Protection of Italian Immigrants is the Italian Benevolent Institute. Within the past two years it has taken on new life. The work was encouraged by gifts from many quarters, the most noteworthy one being from His Majesty the King of Italy, which amounted to 20,000 lire. One of its encouraging features is the fact that it is maintained almost exclusively by Italians.

The institute has its headquarters in a double house, 165-7 West Houston street, which is intended as a place of refuge for the destitute. It often happens that newcomers, bound for interior points, land in New York without a cent in their pockets, expecting to find at the post-office or some bank the sum necessary to carry them to their destination; it also often happens that the money expected does not arrive in time. To such persons as these the Benevolent Institute opens its doors. Then, too, there are immigrants who come with the intention of settling in New York. Such persons may have $8 or $10, but unless they find work at once they too are compelled to seek aid from some source. Further, New York has become, in a sense, a central market for Italian labor, and of those who go to distant points in search of work some fail to find it, and return to the city.

Attention has already been called to the fact that the Italian is lacking in the spirit of unity, and of association in a large sense. The last few years, however, have witnessed a few noteworthy victories in the interest of larger sympathy—mainly through the efforts of a few leading spirits who have been prominent in the affairs of the colony. If one can prophesy, in the light of tendencies already at work, the day is coming when the Italian colony will recognize its responsibilities, and, throwing aside petty jealousies, will launch out upon such a policy as will best enhance the interests of the Italians as a whole.

If we were asked, therefore, whether there is any bond which unites the Italian colony as a whole, we must answer no. Even the Roman Church cannot be considered such a unifying factor in the attitude of indifference taken toward its claims.

It must be observed, however, that the Italian manifests a strong tendency toward organization with small groups for social ends and for the purpose of mutual aid. There are in Manhattan alone over one hundred and fifty Italian societies of one sort or another. "The moral disunity of the old peninsula is transplanted here."

The Italian does not lack the instinct of charity or mutual helpfulness; but at present he lacks the instinct in a broad sense. He would take the bread from his own mouth in order to help his fellow townsman; there is nothing he will not do for his *paesano;* but it must not be expected from this that he will manifest such an attitude toward *all Italians.* Notwithstanding, were it not for this strong feeling, even though limited to small groups, we should have many more calls upon public charity on the part of the Italians than we now do.

In matters of amusement and recreation, the Italian stands in great contrast with his American cousin who too often goes to extremes and excesses. When the Italian goes off for an afternoon's or evening's outing, he does not demand horse racing, cock fights, vulgar exhibitions or other forms of violent excitement. He finds boundless pleasure in comparatively simple things. Gathered about a table sipping coffee or wine, listening to some music, a stroll up and down the street, a game of cards in a saloon or in some friend's house—these are the chief amusements of the masses. Italian temperance along this line might well teach the American a wholesome lesson.

The Italian is fond of the theatre, and it is the better class of plays which appeal to him. The one distinctly Italian theatre, *Teatro Drammatico Nazionale,* which furnishes nightly performances in New York, is situated on the Bowery in the heart of the Italian population, and is fairly well supported. But there are numerous small places throughout the colony, mainly in connection with saloons, where light comedies and bits of tragedy are given. There is also the little marionette theatre in an upper room on Elizabeth street, with its doughty knights and plaintive spokesman, and the clash of arms in its battles royal to the crooning of a violin.

It is music, however, which appeals most strongly to the Italian character. He is not carried away with our slam-bang-band music, nor do you hear him whistling and humming the so-called popular songs of the day. Negro melodies are pleasing to him because of their combined elements of sweetness and sadness. But it is the opera which lifts him to the third heaven. The favorite operas of Verdi, Puccini and Mascagni, always draw large Italian audiences at the Metropolitan, especially so if the leading artists are Italians, and often such is the case. With the love of music is joined a sentiment of patriotism. I have in mind a young barber—and he one of a class who earns less than ten dollars a week—who rarely, if ever, misses one of the great Italian operas. During the season—it is a common experience to hear shoe-blacks, and even day laborers, discussing the merits of this or that singer, and giving their reasons why this or that opera pleases them.

Italians from every nook and corner of the tenements largely make up the great crowds which listen to the park concerts at Mulberry Bend.

It is the custom of each of the small group societies to give an annual festival, and it is in connection with such festal occasions that the Italian manifests his love for show and pomp, uniforms, banners, music, elaborate discourses. Eating and drinking are the chief features, and order generally prevails.

On religious holidays the greatest and most extravagant celebrations take place. They, as a rule, occur in midsummer, when prodigal decoration, street illuminations—such as one sees so frequently in Italy, fireworks, processions, etc.—are indulged in. No inducement could tempt the Italian to miss these festivals. At such a one held three years ago in "Little Italy," in honor of one of the saints, it was claimed that no less than fifteen thousand men paraded up and down the streets each day, bearing banners on which were pinned offerings of money. In the three days, the contributions were said to have amounted to something over $20,000.

If the Italian is anything he is convivial. Nothing gives him more pleasure than to meet with his friends. In this strong desire within him for companionship may be found a cause of the herding of Italians together in certain "quarters" and of his reluctance to seek employment on farms where he would have far better opportunity for rearing his children.

As one passes through the Italian quarter and observes the number of windows displaying the sign "Banca Italiana," he is naturally led to think that the Italians do nothing but deposit money. I am told on very good authority that in Greater New York the number of so-called "banks"—distinctively Italian—is beyond three hundred. It should be said, however, that ninety per cent of these banks are nothing more or less than forwarding agencies. They are constantly springing up to meet the needs of this or that group of persons, coming from a particular town or village. For example, here is a group of people from Cosenza. They want a place where they can have their letters directed. They need some one who can assist them in the matter of sending home money now and then. They look for information regarding new fields of labor which are developing. It is in response to these needs that the larger part of these so-called banks have been brought into existence. They are generally attached to a saloon, grocery store, or cigar store—sometimes to a cobbler shop. The "banker" is always a fellow townsman of the particular group that does business with him, and this for the simple reason that the *paesano* is trusted more, no matter how solid, financially, another bank may be.

The one real substantial Italian bank, incorporated in 1896 under the laws of the state of New York, is the Italian Savings Bank, situated on the corner of Mulberry and Spring streets. It has to-day on deposit $1,059,369.19. Its report shows open accounts to the number of 7,000, and books up to date to the number of 10,844. The moneys deposited in this bank, as might be supposed, are generally in very small sums, but the figures show an average sum on deposit of about $170. The depositors as a rule are Italians, but persons of any nationality may open accounts if they wish.

This institution was started at a time when small Italian banks were failing, and when there was special antagonism to such institutions, both on the part of those who had lost money through the failure of the smaller banks and on the part of those of the small banks which continued to do business. But through determination and perserverance on the part of the officers under the lead of Cav. J. N. Francolini, who was chosen president, and who for two years gave his services free of charge, the institution was placed upon a firm foundation, and is to-day a credit to the colony.

Any discussion of the associated life of the Italians would be incomplete unless some mention were made of religious organizations. There are on Manhattan, 23 Roman Catholic churches which are entirely or in part devoted to the Italians. As one enters these churches, he is struck by a certain warmth and artistic display which are lacking in many of the other churches. The Italian has had centuries of training in the matter of artistic cathedral decorations and, taking into account the fact that so much of his life has been centered about the church, it is but natural that his places of worship should embody all that art and aesthetic natures can contribute. The church does work for Italians along the lines of parochial schools, and maintains a home in the lower part of the city for female immigrants.

In Manhattan, there are four regularly organized evangelical churches—maintained by the Presbyterian, Methodist, Protestant Episcopal and Baptist denominations. With the exception of the beautiful little Episcopal church on Broome street, the evangelical churches may be said to lack altogether the very elements which the Italian, in view of his past training, deems most essential to his environment for worship. And yet notwithstanding this, these churches are well attended. There are several other missions established for Italians, but results of their work cannot easily be seen, simply because they lack the organization necessary to hold together the people whom they reach in a more or less effective manner.

Probably the institution which has done more than any other for the Italian colony in an educational way is the school on Leonard street, devoted exclusively to Italians and maintained by the Children's Aid Society. This school, with its faithful body of teachers, has exerted a strong influence upon the Italian colony. The day sessions are conducted precisely along public school lines, mainly for children who do not enter the public schools for a variety of reasons. A night school is conducted in the same building, which aims primarily at giving instruction in the English language. There is an average attendance of men and boys at these classes of about three hundred. Besides this, there is a department of Italian instruction. A teacher who has this work in charge is supported by the Italian government. The building is also used for social purposes, and entertainments are held during the winter every Friday evening.

As an evidence of the esteem felt by Italians who have come under the influence of this school, a movement is now on foot among them to secure funds—$3,000 has already been raised—for the establishment of a similar school for the Italians in "Little Italy."

ALBERTO PECORINI

THE ITALIANS IN
THE UNITED STATES*

There are something like 2,000,000 Italians in the United States, and of these considerably more than 500,000 are living in the City of New York, so that the Italian problem—if, indeed, an Italian problem exists—may be said to be centered here. The Italian population of New York is increasing at the rate of at least 50,000 per year, while the approximate 4,000,000 of other nationalities, native and foreign, grows at the rate of only 200,000 per year. This increase among the Italians began with the year 1903, and continued until 1907. One effect of the bank panic of that year was to cause an exodus to Italy, as a result of which the Italian population of the city remained stationary until last year. In 1909, however, the increase was again approximately 50,000; and, similar conditions as at present continuing to exist, the same annual growth is likely to continue for at least ten years more. It is probable, therefore, that taking the natural growth of the present population with the increase from Italy into consideration , the Italian population in 1917 or 1918 will number 1,000,000 of the potential 6,000,000 residents of New York City, or one-sixth of the population, instead of one-eighth, as they are to-day. It is more difficult to predict the growth of the Italian population in the United States outside of New York City, but the ratio is likely to remain about the same as at present.

The Italians are here; they are coming, and it is worth while to consider what effect this great tide of immigration of one nationality is likely to have upon the well-being of New York City in particular and the country in general. I believe that the United States have derived benefit from the coming of the hundreds of thousands of my countrymen who are already here, and that that benefit will become increasingly manifest with the advent of additional hundreds of thousands. The average American to-day, however, feels somewhat uneasy when he thinks of the immense number of Italian immigrants crowding into New York and other large cities of the East, although

The Forum, Vol. 45 (January, 1911), pp. 15-29.

there was a time when the Italian immigrant was received with open arms in the metropolis. During the years which preceded the Italian revolution, Italy was not a safe place for Italian patriots; and, although the majority of them preferred to follow Mazzini to England, many came to America. In 1849, as soon as the news of the liberal policy adopted by Pius IX reached New York, a mass meeting was held at which several of the greatest living Americans were present to help the cause of the unification of Italy. Those were what may be called the heroic times of Italian immigration—when Garibaldi lived in a poor frame house on Staten Island and worked as a candle maker in a shop in Bleecker street. Before 1879 most of the Italians of New York were from Northern Italy, but after that year immigrants from the South and from Sicily came in very large numbers, and with the recent rapid growth of the Italian population attention has been attracted by the condition of the Italian quarters, by the personal appearance of the Italian laborer, and by the headlines in the newspapers about Italian criminals. Thus the former sympathy with the Italian disappeared to a large extent, and many Americans have gone to the other extreme and actually oppose Italian immigration.

Before coming to a definite conclusion as to the value of the Italian in the community, is it not well that the American people should know all the facts concerning him in order that final judgment may be impartial? It is only by facts that a clear interpretation of the life of the whole mass of the members of the race, as distinguished from that of only a small part of it, may be had.

Conditions existing in New York may be said to approximate those of the other American cities in which the Italians have made their homes. In New York, although they are scattered throughout the five boroughs, there are several quarters that may be considered as distinctively Italian, of which three are in Manhattan, two in the Bronx, and five in Brooklyn. In manhattan there are two Italian settlements in the lower part of the city, one on the east side with its centre in Mulberry street, and the other on the west side with its centre in Bleecker street; uptown the Italian quarter is known as "Little Italy," and its centre is Jefferson Park in Harlem. The population both of "Little Italy" and the Mulberry Street settlements are almost entirely from Southern Italy and Sicily, while in that centering on Bleecker street there are a large number of Italians from the North. In the Bronx are two Italian quarters: one with its centre in Morris avenue near 150th street, and the other near Bedford Park and 200th street. In Brooklyn the oldest Italian quarter is to be found between Atlantic avenue and Hamilton avenue, and the others are in Navy street; in Williamsburg; in Flatbush, and at the west end of Coney Island.

Life in these Italian settlements is to a large extent explained by the composition of the population. Four-fifths of the Italians of New York come from centres of less than 10,000 population, and are therefore entirely new to the active and exciting life of a great city. American students of social conditions have referred to the Italian settlements of New York as cities within a city. As a matter of fact, they are a collection of small villages, with all the characteristics of village life. In one street will be found peasants from one Italian village ; in the next street the place of origin is different and distinct, and different and distinct are manners, customs and sympathies. Entire villages have been transplanted from Italy to one New York street, and with the others have come the doctor, the grocer, the priest, and the annual celebration of the local patron saint. The acute rivalry between village people, who have not developed and can scarcely be expected to develop in a short period what may be called "city consciousness," is perhaps the most important cause of the lack of coherence in the Italian mass, which makes impossible united and persistent effort on its part in any direction, economic, social or political.

In the Italian quarters the life is that of the tenement. The families are usually large, and in most of them boarders are taken with a view to eking out the payment of the rent. There are tenements occupied by Italians in New York in which eight and ten men sleep in one room, with not more than 1,500 cubic feet of air to breathe, for eight or nine hours. Very often a whole family occupies a single sleeping room, children over fourteen years of age sleeping with their parents or with smaller brothers and sisters. The first consequence of this overcrowding is an astonishing decline in physical strength. Thousands of Italians who come to New York robust and healthy go back every year to their native country to die. The records of the Board of Health show that the death rate among the Italians in New York is higher than that of any other nationality, being no less than 36.43 in the thousand, as against an average of 18.71, the next highest being that of the Irish, 23.55, and the lowest that of the Germans, 12.13, while that of native Americans is 13.98. Consumption and bronco-pneumonia are the most fatal diseases among adult Italians, and diphtheria and measles (both easily cured if treated in time) the principal causes of the high death rate among the children, because of the ignorance of the Italian mothers.

Ignorance is, indeed, the cause of most of the evils of Italian immigration in this country. Almost 50 per cent of all Italian adults in New York are illiterate; and, as a whole, they form a mass of faithful and honest workers—the most useful, and in a certain sense the most needed, if not the most desirable. These are the men who excavate the subways, clean the streets, work at the cement foundations of the sky-scrapers, and build the great railway stations. Their ignorance, however, creates a number of problems that otherwise would not exist. Not being able to make their own contracts, they must depend on some boss or "padrone"; they work when and where he sends them, and take what he gives them. Not being able to read or write, they must hire somebody to indite letters to Italy and send money to the family there. This somebody is the "banker"—a curious product of the Italian quarter. The banker receives the mail of his clients, who are usually from the same village as himself; he writes their letters sends their money, sells them steamship and railway tickets, acts as notary public; he goes with them to the Italian consulate to arrange matters for them there; he is, in fact, advisor of the ignorant Italian in all his business affairs. Quite a number of these bankers have absconded with the money of their patrons, and the marvel is, when the ignorance of the Italian mass is taken into consideration, that so many of the bankers are honest. Perhaps the circumstance that a victimized Italian, more particularly if he is from the South, is likely to take the law into his own hands when he finds his despoiler rather than hale him into court, may have some bearing on this phase of the matter. Very often the banker and the padrone, as well as the grocer and the real estate man, are themselves half-illiterate, though they have a decided advantage over the laborer in that they have lived longer in the country and have some knowledge of their invironment and of American methods. With the increase of their business, however, they are compelled to employ educated assistants—and Italian professional talent is cheap in New York. There are Italian lawyers and professional men, with diplomas from renowned universities, acting as clerks to half-illiterate bankers and contractors at salaries of from $6 to $10 per week.

Aside from the professional men, the half-illiterate man of business, and the laborer, there is still another intermediate Italian-American type, somewhat above the others in education, but not sufficiently cultivated to associate with the university graduates. He is the son of the little merchant in Italy, who has been through the elementary schools, but could not meet the requirements of the high school; the man who served three years in the army, and went to prison for making fun of his peasant corporal, and who finally landed in America without any trade, and, what is worse, with no inclination or intention to work. A new land, a new environment, often works wonders, and some of these derelicts find fields of honest activity in trade and industry, but a large number of them unite with the few criminals escaped from Italy, and form a class of half-educated malefactors—the "Black Handers," if you care thus to term them. To these outlaws the poor, illiterate laborer and his prosperous half-illiterate boss fall an equally easy prey, and on them they manage to subsist. The laborer they exploit and swindle at every turn, and occasionally succeed in robbing him of all his savings as he is about to take the steamer home. The boss is duped and despoiled in many ingenious ways. These predal opportunists flatter him in magnificent articles published in weekly newspapers and magazines that are born and die in the Italian quarters with wonderful rapidity; they get money for subscriptions to and advertisements in newspapers that are never published at all; they take his part in foolish quarrels with equally vain competitors for the presidency of a society, perhaps, or over a decoration expected from the Italian Government; and, after all other expedients have been employed, they demand money with threatening letters, kidnap his children, or put a stick of dynamite in his cellar.

In another way does ignorance among the Italians in this country breed criminals. The children born in this country of the Italian illiterate laborer never see a book or a newspaper in their homes, until they bring them there from the public schools. These children cannot help making comparisons between the palatial surroundings of the school and the squalid tenements in which they live; between the intelligence, knowledge and grace of the teachers and the ignorance and bad manners of their own parents. The illiterate Calabrian or Sicilian has a much larger grounding of sound common sense than his American child who has studied history, geography, arithmetic, and a number of other beautiful things, but the youngster who has reached the eighth grade becomes vain of his knowledge and too often looks with disdain upon his unlettered parents. If the illiterate father succeeds in swearing falsely as to the age of his child, and sends him to work at the age of twelve, the chances are that he will make of him an honest and industrious worker and a second-rate citizen. If, however, the boy goes on to the ninth grade, he too often breaks from the influence of his parents, when he begins a career of idleness in the pool-room, continues it in the saloon, and ends in the reformatory or the jail. The breaking up of family ties results even more disastrously in the case of girls, but fortunately natural instinct keeps them more securely under the influence of the mother. The young American-educated Italian criminals already constitute a much graver problem than the uneducated criminal from Italy, or the older Italian criminals created by environment in this country.

What proportion of the 50,000 Italian pupils of the public schools in New York, and of the 5,000 in the parochial schools, are subject

to the process of demoralization described above, it is difficult to estimate. Even in well-to-do Italian families, however, there are not a
few parents who complain bitterly of the system of American education, and of the degree of liberty manifested by children in their relations with fathers and mothers. There are, of course, many Italian
children who take advantage of the opportunities offered them in
this country that would never have been theirs in Italy. A number
of young Italians have been graduated from Columbia University,
and there is even a society of Italian students, most of them attending
Columbia and the City College, that numbers a hundred members.
On the whole, nevertheless, the Italians of the second generation in
America pay more heavily than the second generation of settlers
from north-western Europe that preceded them, the price of the
sudden change from the environment of their parents. The relatively
few successful youths of Italian parentage and American birth and
education are lost to the Italian population of New York; they are not
interpreters of American life and American ideals, as they should be.

At this point I feel that I ought to make an apology to the Italians
of America. They may justly say that I have drawn a dark picture;
that I have presented the very worst features of Italian life here. This
I have done purposely, for, thus far, one of the most discouraging features of the situation has been the lack of serious and zealous study,
by the Italians, of conditions among themselves in the new land.
On the whole, however, the Italian outlook in the United States is
encouraging. First of all, Italian immigration is improving. The day
of the organ-grinder, once the only representative of his race, has
passed forever, and that of the ignorant peasant is rapidly passing.
Illiteracy is diminishing, and with it the evils of which it has been the
principal cause. The Italians who have come to New York in recent
years—and, as has been noted, conditions among the Italians here are
approximately those in other American cities—have not all been
mere manual laborers, but in a large measure representatives of the
different trades. There are to-day in the city fifteen thousand Italian
tailors, many of them employed in the best establishments of Fifth
avenue and Broadway, earning from $40 to $100 per week. Almost
one half of the barbers in New York are Italians, and satisfaction with
their cleanliness and skill is general. There are thousands of printers,
mechanics, bricklayers, electricians and carpenters at work here, and
their employers will testify that they are among the most sober, honest and industrious of workmen.

The rising movement among the Italians has been noticed especially in trade and industry. The retail fruit business is to a large
extent, and the artificial flower industry almost entirely, in their

hands. Italian hotels and restaurants are popular with Americans, and the Italian 50-cent *table d'hote* is conceded to be the best to be had for that amount. Italians are prominent in the contracting business, although contractors generally can not be considered the most desirable class of Italians, many of them being utterly uneducated and taking advantage of the ignorance of the laborers of their race. Italian importers and merchants are no longer small storekeepers, importing a few barrels of wine or boxes of macaroni from their native villages, to be distributed among purchasers from the same villages; they are members of well-organized and powerful firms, with offices on Broadway and elsewhere side by side with those of important American merchants and importers. Four-fifths of all the trade between Italy and the United States, which amounts to $100,000,000 per year, passes through New York, and the greater part of it is controlled by Italians, from the importation of raw silk to that of lemons, olive oil and macaroni.

The number of Italian bankers doing a legitimate business among their countrymen in New York, especially since the enactment of the law compelling them to give a bond to the state, is increasing every day. There are at present more than a hundred of these bankers in New York; and, while most of their business is that of steamship agents and notaries public, there are several important financial institutions among them. One of these, founded in 1865, occupies fine quarters in Wall street. The number of the bankers of the old irresponsible type is rapidly decreasing, partly on account of the decrease of ignorance among the Italian masses, but more particularly because of the establishment here of the Italian Savings Bank and of an agency of the Bank of Naples. On the first of the year the Savings Bank held total deposits of $2,395,750.71, divided among 11,170 depositors. The agency of the Bank of Naples, which was established by the Italian Government to facilitate the transfer of money from Italian immigrants here to their families at home, under normal conditions sends to Italy $5,000,000 annually—and about $2,000,000 is sent each year through the Post Office. Italian business men have in the banking field, as their particular financial organ, the Savoy Trust Company, founded five years ago as the Italian-American Trust Company. This institution has a capital of $500,000; and, although during the panic of 1907 its deposits dwindled to an insignificant amount, it weathered the storm, and is prospering today in its handsome offices on Broadway, with deposits of $2,000,000. An institution that is inspiring and directing Italian trade in New York is the Italian Chamber of Commerce, which, in existence for many years, has recently been reorganized and is now controlled by younger and more capable men.

Italian professional men are involved in the general uplift. The lawyers of to-day, although many of them are bad enough, are a great improvement upon their fellows of only ten years ago. Formerly, when actions were brought for damages in case of accident, the lawyer who appeared for the complainant was in the pay of the individual or corporation responsible for the casualty; he would accept ridiculously small compensation on behalf of his client, and then divide that with the unfortunate laborer who had been injured, or with his family in the event of his death. This practice, once the rule, still exists as an exception. There are almost 400 Italian physicians in New York, and by far the majority of them are respectable and able men. Competition among them has been somewhat severe in the past, and it is yet to some extent. However the Italian Medical Association of New York was recently formed, with headquarters in the Metropolitan Building, and at its first annual banquet, held at the Hotel Astor, the Italian doctors demostrated that vast possibilities exist among them for serious, organized effort for the good of the Italian masses.

The professional men suggest the artists. There are, of course, the Italian operatic "stars," who are attracted by the high prices offered by the American impresarios, but who do not come to stay. Those artists who remain are the musicians, the teachers of music and the decorators. The musicians have already made their presence felt, having practically abolished the monopoly held for years by German bands and orchestras; the decorators are already asserting themselves as against artists of other nationalities, and their work may be seen in the handsomest theatres and the finest hotels. And among the artists, may I be pardoned if I mention the cooks? They claim that theirs comes first among the *beaux arts*, and a great many of us agree with them. Well, Italian cooks are already employed in large numbers in the most fashionable restaurants and hotels, and the day is not far off when they will destroy the monopoly of the French *chefs des cuisines* as they ended that of the German musicians.

That the Italian Government has done a great deal for the Italian immigrants in America cannot be denied. The Society for Italian Immigrants, which protects ignorant arrivals from thieves and swindlers and gives them food and shelter for 50 cents a day until they may find work, is largely subsidized by the Italian Government, as is the Home for Italian Immigrants, established by the St. Raphael Society under the presidency of Archbishop Farley. The Italian Government also maintains an Italian labor bureau in New York for the distribution of immigration, and an Italian inspectorate of immigration informs the Government at Rome of the conditions of labor in this country. The Italian Government further has subscribed $60,000 toward the fund for the erection of an Italian hospital in New York.

The Roman Catholic Church is, of course, the most important religious agency among the Italians in America. There are about fifty Italian churches of this denomination and more than eighty priests in New York. Various Protestant denominations have also established churches and missions throughout the Italian quarters, twenty of which are now in operation. Grace Episcopal Church, the Methodist Episcopal Church of Jefferson Park, and the Presbyterian Church in University Place, have been particularly successful in social work among the Italians. Settlement work exclusively among Italians, both in Manhattan and Brooklyn, has had a far-reaching influence, the Richmond Hill House in the former borough being a centre of activity.

The most important educational centre for Italians in New York at present is the great English and trade school, recently established by the Children's Aid Society in the two large buildings formerly used by the Five Points House of Industry, in Worth street. Here nearly 500 Italians of both sexes may be found every evening. There are classes in English, stenography, typewriting, sewing, cooking, sign painting and printing, as well as a gymnasium, club rooms, a library and a large auditorium. The Young Men's Christian Association has also done a great deal in the way of evening classes for Italians, half the membership of the Bowery branch, for instance, being of that race. The Italians are further receiving efficient help from the Board of Education in the matter of evening schools and lectures in Italian, and it is a cause for regret that these schools and lectures are not patronized as are those in the Jewish quarters. For the last eight years there has been an Italian member of the Board of Education.

It is to be regretted that the Italian press, by reason of a mistaken idea of patriotism, is not serving as an interpreter of American life and ideals to its constituency. Nevertheless the Italian press has followed the general movement forward, though it has not led it. There are six Italian daily newspapers in New York with a circulation varying from 10,000 to 30,000 copies per day. About half of these newspapers have a larger circulation out of than in the city, and all have special agents hunting for subscribers in the smaller towns, the mining districts and the labor camps. The first Italian newspapers consisted merely of translations from American journals and even now the Italian press has no local news service of its own, while almost every daily imposes upon itself a great sacrifice for its cable service from Italy. While a great part of the advertising of the Italian newspapers comes from steamship companies, professional men, importers and merchants, there is still too large a proportion from fake doctors, real estate swindlers, and alleged brokers who sell to the immigrant the stock of companies that do not exist. However, there are two Italian dailies that enjoy the distinction of having refused money offered for political support at the last municipal election, and of having helped the Fusion cause without recompense—a startling reform in Italian journalism. It is to be hoped that in the future the Italian press may not confine its benevolent activities to the providing of the city with monuments to Italian worthies, but that it will attempt to instruct the Italian masses with regard to their duties in their new environment.

That Italians to-day are coming to America in families in much larger numbers than ever before is a most encouraging sign. Accustomed and attached to family life, the Italian is lost without it. The proportion of Italian women coming to the county is much greater then it was, and Italian life in American cities is little by little losing the appearance of impermanence it presented when a small number of families, each with a large number of men boarders, was the rule. Another encourgaing feature of the situation is that Italian books are coming into the United States in much larger quantities than in the past, one dealer in Broadway having imported as many as a million volumes last year, three-fourths of which were fairy tales and popular novels, the literary pabulum of artisan families in Italy. The Italian uplift in New York may further be said to have found expression in the formation of an up-to-date men's club, with a handsome house near Fifth avenue. The Italian Club has more than 350 members, with an initiation fee of $100, and it boasts of having sold $600 worth of champagne to its members last New Year's Eve—thus measuring a long step forward in the arts of civilization.

So much for the urban Italian. One of the arguments urged against the race, that they are a failure in the United States, because, having been engaged in agricultural pursuits at home they turn to other labor here, is rather proof of their value to their adopted country. On this point may be cited an interesting paradox in the history of immigration, to be found in the fact that during a decade of agricultural expansion in the United States, from 1870 to 1880, her greatest immigration was from the industrial countries of north-western Europe, Great Britain and Ireland, Norway, Sweden and Germany, while, during a like period of industrial expansion, from 1895 to 1905, her principal immigration was from south-eastern Europe,

Greece, Italy, Austria, Hungary, Poland and Russia. The riddle is easily read: forty years ago the crying need of the country was for agricultural workers; hence the immigrants from north-western Europe went to the West and settled there. Immigration from south-eastern Europe, and particularly from Italy, was at its height at the time of the demand here for mill workers and unskilled laborers of all kinds in the building industries fifteen years ago, and hence the Italians crowded into the large cities of the north-east, and were employed chiefly in manufactures. The Italian working population of the United States today is approximately 1,200,000, of whom 67 per cent were engaged in agriculture at home, while only 6.60 per cent of them are actually engaged in agriculture here. If, then, the Italian immigrants have been an agricultural failure in the United States, they have been an industrial success, and moreover have proved their capacity to "make good" in either pursuit, the fact being that their occupation here depends upon economic conditions, and not upon any particular preference of their own.

The small percentage of Italians engaged in agriculture in this country have developed in three distinct fields—truck farming, extensive agriculture, and fruit raising. During the last ten years a considerable number of farms, abandoned by Americans who have gone west or entered business in the cities, have been occupied by Italians in Western New York and the New England States. Truck farming has been carried on to a greater extent, however, in New Jersey, Pennsylvania and the Carolinas. In Ohio there are Italian truck farmers in the vicinity of Cincinnati and Cleveland, and fruits are raised by Italians in large quantities near the former city. The vicinity of Chicago, in Illinois, has also a large number of Italian farmers, many of whom make sausages after the Italian fashion, which, being sold in the east, seriously menace the trade in the imported Italian kind. Recently the Long Island railroad has established an experimental agricultural station, where Italians have been successfully raising vegetables. Long Island, like New Jersey, Western New York and the lower part of the Connecticut Valley, will in the next few years see an even greater number of Italian farmers raising vegetables on land neglected or abandoned by native Americans.

The second field in which the Italian has been tried out as an agricultural laborer in the United States is in what I have termed extensive agriculture. Italians are not numerous in the wheat and corn fields of the Dakotas and Kansas, but they have gone in considerable numbers to the cotton, sugar cane, and tobacco fields of the south and south-west. Of the 30,000 Italians in Louisiana, about one-half are working on sugar and cotton plantations. Reports from the famous farm colony of Sunny Side, in Arkansas, founded by the late Austin Corbin, in which many Italians are employed, show that in spite of adverse conditions they are much more than holding their own in competition with the negro. Very few Italians have penetrated into Alabama, although they are raising vegetables and tobacco in two agricultural colonies in that state. Texas, on the contrary, is a wide open and inviting field for the Italian, and already 15,000 of them are engaged in agriculture there.

It is, however, in fruit culture that the Italian agriculturist has been the most successful in the New World. Almost every Italian owning a farm raises fruit to some extent, but the great fruit-bearing country for them is California, in which state are 60,000 Italians, of whom fully one-half are engaged in agriculture. Vines of all kinds have been imported from the most celebrated wine-producing districts of Europe, and for the last few years the American tourist has been drinking London claret produced by the Italian in California.

As to the future of the Italian engaged in agriculture, the country need have no misgivings; for he loves the soil and his most ardent desire is to own his little piece of land as soon as possible. The need of the urban Italian is a civic need. There are only a little more than 15,000 voters among the half million Italians in New York, approximately 3 per cent., while the proportion among other foreign nationalities varies from 15 per cent to 25 per cent. The naturalized Italians are mostly of the class of laborers, small storekeepers and petty contractors. The better elements have not as yet identified themselves with the community in which they live, in which their children were born, in which they own millions of dollars' worth of real estate, and pay millions annually in taxes. There is not an Italian holding an important municipal office. These conditions are abnormal, unhealthful, and they may become disastrous; they must be changed. Desirable Italian residents must become American citizens, and must take away the direction of their politics and the protection of their interests from the dealers in votes. Thus far relations between the Italian voter and the political parties have existed only at election time, and the better class of Italians have lost confidence in them.

To get votes is political propaganda; to make citizens an educational process. Citizens are needed far more than voters. To organize all educational agencies at present working among the Italians, and make them transform this inert, dead mass into a living progressive force, is an immediate necessity. A million unassimilated Italians in New York, with three millions in the United States, only a few years hence, will not tend to lessen the burden of government in the city or the nation. The problem of making a citizen of the Italian is not an insoluble one. It is only a question of going to work with a sincere desire to help, not to exploit; recognizing the bad side of Italian-American life, but giving full credit for the good. The Italian is certainly capable of contributing his full quota to the best life of the Republic, and it should be the task of earnest Americans to bring that consummation about. Only thus may what seems now a peril be made a blessing.

THE ITALIAN IN
AMERICA, 1891-1914*

THE PHILANTHROPISTS' VIEW

Charities in this number enters upon a new field, of which the first fruits, we are confident, will be found by our readers to be both appetizing and rich with promise. The influx of immigrants of various races and nationalities brings the social worker into contact with peoples whose histories, characteristics, virtues and weaknesses it is important for him to know. It is our purpose to present some of the salient facts in regard to these various groups of strangers within our gates, not as they are viewed by unfriendly outsiders, whether of a little earlier arrival or of native stock; but as seen from the inside by those who know intimately the colonies that have been formed within our cities and states, and who, through sympathy and intimate knowledge, are in a position to lay bare the obstacles to complete assimilation. It is the purpose of these studies to prevent needless friction; to do what we can to insure that racial aptitudes which are worth preserving are not needlessly sacrificed either by ignorance on the part of the newcomers, or by misinterpretation on the part of their American neighbors.

It often happens that our conception of a foreign type is based upon a caricature. *Mickey, sheeny, dago,* have a terrible power of impressing themselves in places where the Irishman, the Jew and the Italian are entitled to stand with no shadow of a caricature behind them. Neither the opera singer across the footlights, nor the padrone-worked ditch digger, is, in any complete sense, the Italian in America; and the value of the Italian laborer is no more to be judged offhand from his looks, than is that of the singer, especially if the judge is one whose standard of physical beauty happens to be rigid adherence to a Saxon type. We have therefore sought, in this Italian number of *Charities,* and have obtained, the generous and most valuable co-operation not only of representatives of the Italian government, but of Americans of Italian origin, men who, knowing both Italy and America, elect to become and

Charities, Vol. 12 (1904), pp. 443-455.

remain American citizens, but who, knowing both Italians and Americans, are able to speak authoritatively of the former and instructively to the latter; and the co-operation also of American writers who have entered most fully into the peculiar hardships and dangers and successes of Italian immigrants who are struggling with the conditions of what is to them a new country.

It is clear that certain obligations rest upon American communities toward recent immigrants. What those are in reference to Italians is shown clearly in some of the papers which we publish. That there shall be a courteous reception to those who are invited to come—and in this respect Mr. Speranza is right in pointing out that permission to come is an invitation—a reception such as is advocated and typified by the Society for the Protection of Italian Immigrants; that child labor and garment making in tenement-houses shall be prevented; that the common laborer shall have the equal protection of the law; that there shall be strict sanitary inspection and a suitable provision for light and air in living and sleeping rooms—these are among the elementary obligations assumed by American communities, not primarily in the interests of the Italians, but from which, incidentally, direct benefit will come to them.

There is no one solution for the problem so keenly and fruitfully analyzed from the inside by our various contributors this month. Restriction, as is pointed out by Adolfo Rossi, the royal supervisor of emigration, in the significant and interesting interview which we publish, introduces an artificial selection very favorable, at least from a physical standpoint, for America. Arguments for further restriction were fully presented in the February magazine number of *Charities* and need not be repeated. Suffice it to say that we are not likely to have such a degree of restriction as will in any way affect the importance of the subjects which we are now discussing.

Neither will agricultural dispersion prove a safe sole reliance. Dr. Tosti, indeed, suggests that the Italian agricultural laborer may supplant the negro in the more diversified and intensive cultivation of land which is to be a characteristic feature of the new South, and the same suggestion was made by Cyrus L. Sulzberger in an article which *Charities* published two weeks ago. Mr. Sulzberger thinks that migration from southern Italy may result in bringing into our southern states a people who shall operate upon the negro "as migrations have always operated, either to lift him up to a higher communal walk, or to cause his dispersion over the entire country." In effect, however, this would mean the migration of negroes to the cities, a process already far advanced with results not calculated to awaken enthusiasm.

If the dispersion of every Italian colony now to be found in American cities, and the closing down of the gates of Ellis Island against Italians as effectively as against the Chinese, were effected, it is doubtless true that the problems of the city would be simplified. If, however, that were accomplished at the sacrifice of American appreciation and American sympathy for the hardships, the struggles and the achievements of Italians in their own peninsula and on the Western continent, the relief would be too dearly bought. To use an Italian saying, "the world is one country." Breadth of sympathy and a feeling of the unity of the human race are worth infinitely more than economic ease and freedom from anxiety. It might, or might not, be better that the American people should be homogeneous. It is certain that in our American cities we are that, and are not likely to become so otherwise than by assimilation.

We shall continue to think aloud about our country's guests in so far as their presence contributes to our social problems, but it need not follow that this thinking aloud must be of such a character as to be unpleasant to the guests. It is far from being to their interests that we shall begin to think in whispers; but they may rightly ask that we think justly, intelligently and fraternally. *Charities* takes great satisfaction in becoming the medium through which most valuable contributions to this end are made.

Last July, on the initiation of Commendatore Giovanni Branchi, consul general, The Italian Chamber of Commerce appointed a committee on statistics which should make an investigation into the numbers and economic condition of the Italian population in the state and city of New York. The committee is composed of Signori G. Granata, D. A. Maffei, E. Mariana, and Prof. G. Rossati. Signor Branchi, who had been chosen chairman, transferred his office to the first vice-consul, Cav. Gustavo Tosti, under whose direction the work has been done.

The investigation of the committee, as outlined at its first meeting, will include the following points:

(1) The Italian population.

(2) Occupations, professions, participation in political life.

(3) Real estate owned by Italians.

(4) Savings, including money sent back to Italy, and accumulation of capital.

In the March number of the *Bulletin of the Chamber of Commerce* is given the first section of the committee's report.

The estimate arrived at of the Italian population is derived from these elements:

	N.Y. State	N.Y. City
Population in 1900	272,572	225,026
Excess of births over deaths	18,322	14,121
Excess of arrivals over departures, 1901-1903	195,281	143,628
Total Italian population January 1, 1904	486,175	382,775

With a complete registration of births and of deaths and with a complete list of arrivals, not only from Europe, but from other places in the United States, as well as of departures to other points in the country as well as to Europe, no fault could be found with the method employed. The most serious source of error is to be found in the number of departures. There are no figures to show the number of Italians who leave New York, either city or state, by rail—nor is there any method of estimating how many such there are. This number, while not large, is undoubtedly sufficient to deserve consideration.

Nor is the number of arrivals, indicated merely by the declared destination of immigrants, quite satisfactory. This number includes, on the one hand, many persons whose immediate goal is New York, but who, within a few weeks or months, go on farther into the country, thus forming the class of departures just mentioned. It omits, on the other hand, Italians drifting back to the New York colony after a more or less prolonged stay in some other state. These are probably so few in number, though there are some, as to be a negligible quantity. The net addition made to the population of the city and state is, therefore, probably less than is indicated by the difference between the immigrants who give New York as their destination and the persons who go back from New York to Italy, because of our inability to trace the movement of the population from year to year within our own country.

The large excess of births over deaths among the Italians is testimony to a high degree of vitality, and the large percentage of men, and of both men and women below forty-five years of age, is an indication of the economic possibilities, and value, of the group. In this age-composition of the Italian population, showing a very high proportion of men and women at the reproductive ages, may be found one explanation for the remarkably high birth-rate, noted in the report, among the Italians in America—much higher than is found in Italy. Immigration of the youth of the country works in both directions to bring about this difference, since it reduces the birth-rate in the old country, at the same time that it raises it in the new. To a certain large extent, also, the high birth-rate in America is a response to the easier conditions of life found here, for, however hard the conditions of the average Italian immigrant may appear to the average spectator, they are undeniably less hard than his life under the feudal customs of agrarian Italy.

Not the least impressive point found in the report under discussion is the revelation made therein that the sum of the information contained in the United States census of 1900, in regard to the Italians of New York city and of New York state, is merely their number. More descriptive information may be found about the whole group of Italians in the United States as well as about the whole group of the foreign born in New York, but about the Italians alone in any particular state or city, there is nothing more than the mere number. The courtesy with which Dr. Tosti alludes to this deficiency in our census, as well as the deficiency itself, deserves reflection.

From an altogether different source comes evidence that Italian workingmen not only appreciate the evils of the congested quarters of the larger cities, but that they apprehend that the overcrowding of certain industrial grades will be accompanied by further and more effective animosity on the part of American workers. *Il Proletario*, an Italian Socialist paper published in New York, has called attention to the reputed utterance of a delegate from the American Federation of Labor at a meeting of English unionists in Lancaster. It was especially toward southern Italians that he directed his attack in inveighing "against the torrent of the unhappy which yearly overflows this land, seeking for bread and labor."

In essaying to "point out the duty of the Italian government in the presence of these constant American threats," *Il Proletario* urges a line of action surprisingly in accord with the thought of Chicago settlement workers, with the recommendation of government experts in this country, and with the opinion advanced by the representative of Italy in New York—fresh example, this, of the fact that, however radical be the general panaceas they may advocate, an increasing number of working people are thinking—thinking hard and in some measure sanely—at the problems which stare society in the face. To translate from *Il Proletario:*

"The news from Italy shows no prospect of the rapid decrease of our emigration. Many years, if not decades, must pass before the yearly departure will cease of hundreds of thousands from our country, driven out by the sad material and economic conditions; and even when these are improved, if ever they are, the enormous fecundity of our race will force some of those born in Italy to seek elsewhere the means of subsistence."

"The seriousness of a possibly increased restriction of admittance to the United States becomes more evident when we recall that other places of refuge have already been closed or limited. We refer to the Argentine Republic and Brazil. The first, suffering from an economic and financial crisis, drives every year a larger number of its new inhabitants from its territory; the second is . . . a land of slaves and not of free and civilized men."

"The only country then which offers a sure and happy refuge for our people is North America, and it is from here that more and more are rising the cries of alarm against them."

"The southern Italian is disliked and despised because he stops in the great centers of industry, where he lowers the wages of labor, and offends by habits and customs too much in contrast with those of the majority of American citizens. Wherever our emigrant can find occupation in his own proper business of worker on the soil he is more acceptable and better liked."

"The duty then of the Italian state is to favor the formation of agricultural colonies in the United States."

The discussion, by Dr. Brindisi of Boston and Dr. Stella of New York, of the health problems of the Italians in America, especially emphasizes two points. It is clear that the Italian immigrant brings with him health and strength. It is equally clear that he finds in large cities conditions which even his peasant constitution can not long withstand.

Statistics of deaths are the only general index there is to the health of the various elements of a population. But, in the case in hand, these records fail to reveal the undue measure of sickness among the immigrants themselves, partly because, as Dr. Brindisi points out, strong constitutions and temperate habits have helped Italians to recover in an unusually large proportion of cases, and partly because, especially if stricken with tuberculosis, Italians go back home to die. Dr. Stella's many years of experience among the Italians of New York gives weight to his testimony in regard to the prevalence of tuberculosis. It is necessary to conclude both that the amount of general sickness among the "first generation" is greater than is indicated by the deathrates, and that tuberculosis is far more prevalent than the very low death-rate would attribute. It is also necessary to conclude that it is our part to modify the conditions, as far as they are responsible and remediable, whcih make for physical deterioration among the peoples coming to us. What this means in a concrete searching way is revealed by Miss Dinwiddie's study of the housing conditions of an Italian neighborhood in Philadelphia. This obligation is somewhat emphasized by the reflection that the Italian government, in its emigration disinfection station at Naples, does its part in seeing that its departing sons and daughters start for the new world aseptically clean.

In an interview, published on another page Cav. Adolfo Rossi, royal inspector of emigration from Italy, pointedly calls attention to the Italian emigration law about which hitherto so little has been generally known in this country. Those who have been somewhat skeptical about the enforcement of that law by the Italian Government will have to admit that the opening of the emigration disinfection station at Naples is in the nature of evidence against them.

Among the provisions of this emigration law passed by the Italian Parliament in 1901, was one bearing directly on the hygienic conditions and safeguards of the emigrant and his baggage immediately before his embarkation.

The Department of Emigration naturally turned its attention first to the port of Naples, the chief point of departure. The plant is near the Maritime Station and within easy reach of all the steamship piers. On the ground floor are to be found disinfecting plant, special rooms for the vaccination of emigrants, and the office established by the Bank of Naples for the issuance of emigrants' drafts. The rest of the space is given up to waiting rooms. The emigrant, after delivering his baggage in the vestibule, passes out into the large portico on one side of the station to wait until his turn comes to receive it again. In the interval it has been opened, the contents inventoried and disinfected. The plant itself consists of two large steam sterilizers with a capacity for over two hundred pieces of baggage an hour. There is, moreover, a separate laboratory for formalin disinfection. At the extreme west end of the building are three vaccination rooms, with a common waiting hall but separate exits, thus insuring rapidity and preventing confusion.

A plentiful supply of water from the Serino is an added item for the "purification of the emigrant." Two large fountains are in the portico outside and smaller ones, with sinks and lavatories, are scattered throughout the building. Artificial light is supplied when needed, by an electrical plant in the basement feeding 100 incandescent lamps and six ten-ampere arc lights. The building, with all its accessories, is the product of Italian industries. The total cost was only about twenty-five thousand dollars.

"With the completion of this disinfecting and vaccination station," writes Signor Coen Gagli, the supervising engineer, "we have provided for one of the most urgent needs of the emigrant at the port of Naples." Then, with the splendid optimism and serious purpose-fulness that seem to characterize the awakening of modern Italy, he concludes his report. "But this is only the first part of the extensive program."

Reference is made in several articles in this number to abuses among Italian workmen. Evidence of what is meant was gathered by an agent of the New York Society for the Protection of Italian Immigrants, who investigated in detail into the labor conditions of his countrymen in West Virginia. There he found them in isolated camps, shut off from the outside world by high mountains; many, barbers and waiters, were unfit for the heavy work to which they had been sent under false pretenses by agents receiving so much per man sent—"dumped into West Virginia by the brokers in white slavery of the larger cities," the investigator called it. A boy of sixteen, "the incarnation of fatalism," answered "of course" when asked if he had ever been struck. Fifteen dollars carfare was invested by the contractor in every laborer taken out from New York, to be deducted from his wages. If the laborer attempted to leave when he found conditions not as represented, intimidation and force were resorted to hold him.

Armed guards were frequent. A man turned over to the boss after a fight was locked up in a shanty under a guard of negroes. In the night a shot was heard. The man was not seen again. One Italian made affidavit of being pursued by armed guards when he attempted escape, driven back at a run under the muzzle of a rifle, and made to lift alone so heavy a stone that he suffered a severe rupture. The contractor gave him one dollar when he went away for treatment. A gatling gun on a hill overlooked one camp. The contractors and their men carried revolvers and some rode with rifles in their hands.

An Italian who is qualified to speak on the subject of criminality among his people both by his experience as a lawyer practicing among them and by his membership in the New York Prison Association, writes as follows:

"I am convinced of two things:

"First, that while the proportion of crimes against the person may be somewhat greater in our Italian population than among natives, yet the proportion of all crimes to the population is less."

"Second, that a large percentage of Italians convicted for crime here do not have a fair trial."

"This second point is of great social importance as it constitutes a quasi justification for the alleged disposition of the Italians to take the law into their own hands. The causes which militate against a fair trial are many. There is, first, the popular belief about the criminal tendencies of my countrymen. I have heard a judge charge from the bench that there is a presumption that Italians carry concealed weapons. A city magistrate was recently quoted as saying from the bench, 'It seems incredible that Italians would fight with their fists. Didn't they have knives or revolvers?' To which the accusing policeman replied, 'No.' The judge expressed the popular belief; the witness testified to the fact. A second cause is the ignorance of the accused regarding both the language and his rights under the law. There is further, among certain police officers, a pretty free use of the 'third degree.' This doubtful method of obtaining evidence becomes a source of positive abuse with a people as imaginative and sensitive as the Italians."

"Finally, I do not hesitate to say that the character of some of the lawyers who defend my countrymen is an important factor in the miscarriage of justice. If a serious investigation were made of the methods used by certain lawyers in the Tombs, who practice fraud upon their clients and upon the court, we would have some startling revelations."

"The problem of excessive criminality, if it exists, must be solved, like every other social problem, not by palliatives, but by the slow method of social therapeutics—by education and good example."

"In conclusion let me say this: About seventy-five per cent of all crimes in the United States go unpunished, while of the crimes committed by Italians here I believe that, on account of their open character, seventy-five per cent are punished."

Columbus Day—October 12—has been celebrated by Italians in America for half a century. Bills have been before the last two sessions of the New York legislature, but whether or not Columbus Day will be added to the already long list of legal holidays in New York state, its observance by Italians is increasing in significance.

It was in the 40's or early 50's that a club of young men in the Leonard street school started what was called the Columbo Guard. The membership was largely made up of Genoese, and for years their parades in uniforms suggestive of the *bersaglieri*, with feathered hats and blue suitings, paid a picturesque tribute to their historic fellow townsmen.

In the 70's, the United Italian Societies was organized as a representative body to celebrate the 20th of September, a date observed in commemoration of the unification of Italy. In 1897, the Sons of Columbus Legion was founded, and the following year observed October 12 with parade and picnics. Since then, both societies have participated in keeping both dates—celebrations which are not only patriotic in character, but bring before the colony the benevolent purposes for which these societies stand.

Madonna del Carmine, San Rocco, and the innumerable other saints' days give many opportunities for the festival spirit. But these are more or less local, or limited in their allegiance to the people of one church or from one part of Italy; and, on the other hand, the church does not officially particiapte in the observance of the 20th of September.

In Columbus Day, Italians in America have a festival which, it may be anticipated, in the future even more than in the past, will serve as an opportunity for all to unite in a common observance.

HULL HOUSE AND ITS NEIGHBORS
Jane Addams

The settlement which endeavors to reveal large foreign colonies to the rest of its city naturally pursues two methods:

The first is to secure speakers, teachers, club leaders from the more prosperous districts of the city, who shall form acquantances and friendships as naturally as possible with the residents of the neighborhood.

The second is to provide for the various foreign colonists opportunities for self-expression, one of the most natural of these being through the drama. Plays have been given at Hull House in Bohemian, Yiddish, Italian and Greek, not only to the very great pleasure of the groups of colonists who heard them, but often to the surprise and always to the edification of their English-speaking auditors. These plays often serve a most valuable purpose, in so far as they help reveal the older people of the foreign colonies to the younger, and do something toward bridging the distance between fathers and sons.

The mass of the colonists, however, have no such means of expression. It was in the hope of giving them an opportunity that the Labor Museum at Hull House was started. It began with the methods of spinning and weaving, which we were able to collect from the neighborhood and to put into some historic sequence and order—the Assyrian, the Greek, the Italian, the Dutch, the Irish, the Colonial. Something of the same was done in weaving. The demonstration which takes place every Saturday evening attracts visitors from every part of the city, notably students from the normal schools and colleges. The children of the peasant women are much amazed at the attention their mothers receive and at the admiration which is given to the hand-made kerchiefs and petticoats. This, for the first time, breaks into their ideal of department store clothes. I recall a little Italian girl who came to the cooking class the same night and in the same building that the mother came to the Labor Museum demonstration. But she always took pains to deliver her mother at one door, while she entered another, not wishing to be too closely identified with the peasant who spoke no English and could not be induced to wear a hat. One evening she heard a number of teachers from the School of Education, of the University of Chicago, much admiring the quality of her mother's spinning, and she inquired whether her mother was really the best spindle-spinner in Chicago. On being assured that she probably was, because she had lived in a village on the edge of a precipice down which the women had dropped their spindles, and that therefore the village had developed a skill beyond its neighbors, she was much impressed, and regarded her mother with a new interest, being able, apparently for the first time, to give her a background and a setting beyond that of the sordid tenement in which she lived. At any rate, from that time forth, they entered at the same door.

During one of the Christmas seasons a number of Russian women who were working in a charitable sewing-room heard that there was to be a "party" at Hull House, and unexpectedly arrived, to the number of thirty. There happened to be no festivity on at the moment, although the disappointment was so obvious that every effort was made to produce one on demand. Music, photographs, even coffee, made but little impression upon the over-worked, hard-pressed women, but a visit to the Labor Museum produced an instantaneous effect. They at once began to try the spindles and the looms, to tell each other and their hostesses what was done in each particular family and in each special part of Russia, to exhibit specimens of the weaving and knitting of the clothing which they wore. In short, they began to be the entertainers rather than the entertained, to take the position which was theirs by right of much experience and long acquaintance with life. Their pleasure was most touching, and perhaps only their homely implements could have evoked it.

The old German potter takes great pleasure each week in demonstrating his skill, as do workers in silver and copper, and in wood mosaic. After all, the apprentice system, as a method of instruction, has much to commend it, and a well-trained workman can easily teach not only his own and his neighbors' children, but "swells" from other parts of the town, with a consciousness that his skill is but receiving its natural recognition. In a few years, we shall doubtless establish schools in America in which the children and grandchildren of these men may be trained in the crafts. In the meantime they lose the heritage which is theirs, the transmission of which would be of mutual benefit to both fathers and children, and do much toward restoring the respect which is often lost. Under existing conditions of factory work, it slips away without result or use to anyone. "I was a silver-smith in Bohemia, but I have carried pig-iron ever since I came to this country." or "I was a glass-blower in Vienna, but of course nobody wants such work in Chicago," are the significant remarks which one constantly hears. The shops at Hull House offer at least the space, tools, and material to the men who care to work in them, and are but a feeble beginning toward restoring some balance between the attainments of various sorts of people.

NOTES ON THE ITALIANS IN BOSTON

Robert A. Woods

There is some question as to how the Italians will thrive physically in the New England climate. The death-rate among them increases with the second generation. This is no doubt largely the effect of extremely close tenement quarters upon people who belong out of doors and in a sunny land. Their over-stimulating and innutritious diet is precisely the opposite sort of feeding from that demanded by our exhilarating and taxing atmospheric conditions. This fact suggests the first and perhaps the chief step in bringing about the adaptation of the Italian type to life in America. On the other hand, it is undesirable that the Italians should be in any considerable degree educated away from their love of the open air and their satisfaction in rural existence. Many Italian families have been sent from Boston into the country, with excellent results. The New England farmers are at first suspicious of them, but soon come to regard them as good neighbors.

The large majority of the Italians in Boston are industrious and thrifty. They carry on several kinds of small trade with commendable assiduity. Over two million dollars' worth of real estate in the Italian district is held in the names of Italian owners. The unskilled laborers sustain themselves by accepting a low wage standard; and still lay by money because they have an inconceivably low standard of living. In both of these respects—and particularly the latter—they do a real injury to the community, and give grounds for the enmity which their industrial competitors among the older immigrant elements feel toward them.

The artisan and the small trader among the Italians do not in general make very rapid economic progress. They show a certain lack of self-reliance and "push." Jewish artisans secure the low-grade building work, and the Greeks often get the best fruit and candy stands away from them. We have had Italian barbers for a long time. They increase in number but their shops do not seem to rise to a higher grade as to service and price.

The children of the early north Italian immigrants have now been through the public schools. Many of the stumbling-blocks which embarrassed their parents have been removed for them. They are beginning to take their proportionate place in the skilled trades, in commercial establishments and in the professions. One important industry which has had an educational effect upon the whole country and for which Boston has been the center, that of making plaster casts of the work of great sculptors—has been developed wholly by Italians. A few young people show signs of that genius for which no race has been more distinguished that the Italian.

There is a particular need and opportunity among the Italians for friendly and helpful influence. With no nationality does the right sort of encouragement bring more valuable results. A lack of force of will in their case goes often with unusual skill, intelligence and constructive imagination.

The new generation is many times hindered by the ignorant conservatism of the elders. One way of breaking the unfortunate tradition of illiteracy which exists particularly among the south Italians, and which leads them to put their children to work as soon as possible, will be to provide in the public schools greatly increased opportunities of manual and technical training along with book work. The tendency of parents to take their children away from the schools is in part a just judgment upon the narrow abstract character of the school curriculum.

There is danger in Boston that with the gradual withdrawal from the Italian colony of the more progressive members who lose themselves in the general community, there will be left a distinct slum residuum. Not much degeneracy is yet evident among the Italians. But there is a steady continuance of a certain amount of violent crime. Among the large number of men without family connections there is gambling, beer-drinking, and licentiousness. The amount and variety of profanity which seems needed in order to promote the street games of some Italian boys is beyond belief.

These evils are to a considerable extent the result of city conditions. The laborers are without work for much of the year. They are huddled together so that self-respect and peace of mind are lost. It would be the work of a moral as well as an industrial reformer to transport the large surplus of Italian laborers to the agricultural regions of the south, and then to secure at least such restriction of immigration as would prevent new immigrants from creating a new city surplus.

When all is said, there is sound reason to believe that the Italians will prove a valuable factor in our composite population. They are beginning to appreciate and take to themselves our industrial standards and our political loyalties. We ought to begin to be deeply thankful for what they bring of sociability, gayety, love of nature, all-around human feeling. The continental peasant has much to teach us. At his best he is a living example of that simple life which too many of us have so far lost that the words of two recent writers—one an Alsatian, the other a Swiss—seem like a breath of inspiriation from some other sphere.

A Working Colony as a Social Investment

Bertha Hazard

Is it not possible that the Society for the Protection of Italian Immigrants, or some group of allied workers, should begin to offer in a somewhat extended manner systematic opportunities for the founding of Italian colonies here in America, as an aid in the process of distribution?

Questions such as this come naturally to mind in thinking of the make-up of the Italian quarter in the vicinity of Hull House.

They press with special significance just now because of the pent-up agricultural enthusiasm of a young Italian belonging to one of the Hull House English classes. This Mr. N. is a graduate, I believe, of one of the best of the Italian universities. At two other he has taken special courses in mathematics and agriculture, and has, as he says, a "passion" for farm-life. He claims to have had practical experience in working on a small estate belonging to his family, he speaks English fairly well, and he seems to be adapted, personally, for the direction of men and things. Some weeks ago he took a fortnight's holiday from his present work in a factory, and, attracted by the advertisements of a Southern railroad which wishes to sell land, he went to the coast of Mississippi to see what promise there might be there for him and for some of his 'connazionali.' On the Gulf shore he found a small town, well situated, having good transportation facilities; there were canneries needing workmen, a lumber company wanting more hands, much vacant land which could be bought cheap, and various officials who would find it useful to have an Italian colony started in the neighborhood. The wages offered for day-laborers were less than can be earned during the summer in the neighborhood of Chicago, so that it would be useless to expect men to go so far to undertake work which might not prove permanent. But to found a colony, Mr. N. thinks that he could easily find here in Chicago a number of families who would be willing to go South with him in October, prepared to work hard for a mere living, until the first crops should have been gathered. On the one hand, therefore, we have desirable and inexpensive land; on the other, there are sober and industrious men who now add their share to the crowded and unsatisfactory living conditions of a large city. Between the two stands the man with directive power and enthusiasm and experience. The money alone is lacking. For want of this there seems to be no present hope that this new centre of simple and healthy living can be formed.

In talking recently with another young man about the desirability of finding work for the summer in the country, I fell naturally into all the usual arguments by which the theorists strive to influence simple people to change their mode of living. The young man has been in America for some time; for at least one season he has worked in the country, and he knew out of his own experience whereof I was speaking. He heard me patiently to the end. Then he said, "Lady, you do not know. The city is not nice, but in the country *everybody* is bad."

In the gang where he had worked, the men had been treated like beasts, and, in this particular set, I suppose for the most part they must have acted like beasts; and this Hull House student would have no more of it. Of course I am unconvinced; naturally I do not feel that city life is better, in general. Still, even under better conditions than this young man happened to find, life among gangs of laborers must at best be hard and more or less demoralizing, and at the end of the summer, for many of them, there seems to be nothing to do except to go back to the cities, to be idle, perforce, until spring comes again; and the chances are that in many cases the family and the city are each the worse off for the long idle winter.

Efforts have been made here and there during the past few years to establish Italian colonies in different parts of the United States. Some have failed sadly, some have succeeded, all have had difficulties. Still, a study of the experience of these colonies seems to justify the belief that nothing which has been done for the Italian has led to such permanently good results. If the sporadic efforts of various interested individuals and companies can show these occasional good results which are to be found in our country, should they not encourage a more generous plan and concerted action for the better solution of this "essential problem of distribution."

THE SORDID WASTE OF GENIUS
Florence Kelley

It is the frequently recurring duty of the writer to attend meetings of women's clubs in all parts of the country. Incidentally this involves listening to the reading of the minutes of the previous meeting. Recently, in a small New England town, the minutes dealt with an afternoon devoted to music. The secretary, not a musical person, conscientiously reproduced, at forty minutes' length, and as well as a defective memory permitted, the contents of a long paper on the music of Palestrina. Now in that little town it would have been quite impossible to get together an audience to listen for an evening to the music of Palestrina, even if there had been musicians capable of rendering his compositions. But because the composer had lived some generations ago, and at a distance of some thousands of miles, the club members had an agreeable consciousness of being engaged in the pursuit of culture when they first listened to a long account of his methods of composition, written at second hand (from an encyclopedia of music translated from the German), and then listened to a long reproduction, in the minutes, again at second hand, of that first paper.

As the writer sat through the ordeal, she could but reflect upon the living genius of the Italian children, here in America, which perishes every year for want of opportunity for development. How many beautiful voices are ruined forever, crying papers! What plastic power is crushed out in early childhood by the weary drudgery of artificial flower making in the tenement-houses of New York! It was a little Italian boy who flung himself down to sleep on the railway track, on his way home at two o'clock in the morning, after his impossible toil in the glassworks, in southern New Jersey. He perished when the train came along.

It requires real love of music and real recognition of genius to discern both in the discordant cry of the dirty little chap on the sidewalk, who calls the last murder from his newspaper headlines. In one case, however, this was done by the music teacher of a settlement. The lad's parents were bought off for a stipulated sum, though they were more than ordinarily prosperous to begin with. For four years the child Angelo sang with joy to himself and to all who heard him. Here was a real contribution to the nobler enjoyments of our all too sordid work-a-day life! Here was promise of a real gift of genius from Italy to America, discerned and developed in the new country! But a presidential election came, cold and sleet threatened the troop of children who huddled in newspaper alley until one and two o'clock in the morning awaiting the latest night extras and the first editions of the morning papers. Angelo was among them—the greedy peasant family had not withstood the temptation to get both the music teacher's gift and the newsboy's earnings. Weariness, cold and wet did their work; pneumonia followed the election night and Angelo never sang again.

Mme. d'Arago, Charity Go-between

The trustfulness and simple-mindedness of many of the Italian immigrants make them—especially before they know the English language or American customs—easy victims to all sorts of decep-

tion. By reason of the same qualities, they often figure as participants in fraudulent transactions. The impositions of the
padroni, who, if they are Italian, have learned worse than Yankee
business methods, are familiar. So are the naturalization frauds,
in which the Italians themselves are generally but ignorant tools
of political leaders. There are other ways, less well known, in which
the Italian newcomers are "worked" to the advantage of more sophisticated fellow-citizens and to the detriment of their own reputation.

An example of this sort of thing is afforded by the history of a
woman who has been known to the New York Charity Organization Society for twenty years. During the last ten or twelve years
she has been living as a parasite on the Italians of the city, supporting herself by devices of unusual ingenuity, and coming, from
time to time and by various chances, to the notice of the society.

In 1889, Mme. d'Arago, as she may be called, asked for help
at a convent on the ground that she secured converts to the
Roman Catholic faith. She took with her a man—apparently a German—for whom she tried to get assistance. This is the first recorded
instance of the practice she later developed into a profession, of acting as an agent for her unfortunate acquaintances. A few years
later she began work among the Italians, by attempting to proselyte
in another direction, for she was writing to a Protestant clergyman:
"I would wish God would help me to raise an Italian chapel and
school in East New York in the Episcopal faith. I could canvass
two hundred to three hundred Italians, together with their children,
who now go to no religious worship." In a later communication
she assured him: "I am able to unite forty families and more than
two hundred Italians, to join, a more intelligent religion."

For most of the time since 1893 she has lived among the Italians,
getting a lodging and meals whenever she can, in return for
services rendered to them. It has rarely been possible to find her
"home," as the address she gives is generally a bank, a bakery, or
a saloon, where she receives her mail and meets her clients. She
says that at one time she was at service in Brooklyn. For a while she
lived at a Salvation Army lodging house under the name of Bertha
Klein, but generally she has kept to the Italian colony in which she
was found in 1893.

Her most constant source of revenue has been derived from the
profession she developed for herself. She made herself acquainted
with the workings of many charitable agencies in the city, especially institutions for children, and advised her friends where to apply for aid whenever they wanted it. If her clients succeeded in get-

ting what they asked for she would accept a fee from them; if not, she would write to the society to which they had applied, saying that they were "bad" and needed nothing. Her specialty was placing-out children. She got children into institutions for a consideration of ten or fifteen dollars apiece. She also secured the release of the child from the institution, when that was desired, for ten dollars. Unfortunately, for her prosperity, her second application to an institution was apt to arouse suspicion and start an investigation. She also found homes for children in families. This was accomplished through advertisements in the Italian papers, one of which reads:

> "A POOR WOMAN of the province of C----------------.
> left a widow with three children, six months, four and
> six years old, seeks a family which will care for them.
> They are healthy and very pretty. Address by letter, Mrs.
> d'Arago, at number 315 Margaret Street."

In 1903, she was still procuring "working papers" for children. When one mother for whom she had performed this service refused to give her as much money as she demanded, she told the little girl's employer that she had tuberculosis and thus brought about her dismissal. Another way in which she used her good offices is revealed in one of her letters asking for money. In enumerating her troubles and misfortunes she said: "And I got an Italian woman out of prison and for reward—she did not pay me."

Several letters addressed by her to the Bureau of Dependent Children seem to indicate that she used her wits against her enemies as vigorously as in behalf of her friends. These letters contain notes on families who have children in institutions, but who, she asserts, are perfectly able to provide for them at home. "Italians,"she writes, "import children daily and get them in homes; parents who have children in homes keep groceries and beer saloons; husband works at shovel—and I will send you a list next week—hundreds I know." The promised list tells how mothers "dress in fine style" and the family has "fine whiskey, beer and wines," and live "luxuriantly" while "the city has to pay" for the maintenance of their children. These letters to the Bureau of Dependent Children may be one of her devices for getting children restored to their parents at the parents' request. The fact, however, that they were written while she was living in the Salvation Army lodging-house, as Bertha Klein, point rather to another explanation, that she took this way of revenging herself on her clients who had not come up to all her demands in the way of pay. In either case it is entirely possible that she had helped to place the very children under discussion.

From time to time, in the course of these twenty years, Mme.

d'Arago has apparently become discouraged and thought of Europe with longing. Twice, it is known, she has obtained money avowedly for a return to Italy or to England, but she has used it for other purposes. In spite of her cleverness, her ingenuity and her fund of information in certain directions, she has never been prosperous. It is clear that life has been hard for her and that she has suffered much.

As for the Italians, her clients, it is difficult to estimate the harm that her good offices in their behalf have done them. By encouraging, and doubtless often suggesting, the theory that here in America the public stands ready and eager to assume the parent's duties, whenever he finds them inconvenient, this woman and others like her have had their part in creating and strengthening a characteristic for which the whole blame is generally placed on the Italian nature.

ENRICO C. SARTORIO

AMERICANIZATION*

The cry of today in America is "America for the Americans." The present war in Europe has revealed in an almost tragic way the danger in which America stood of losing its Anglo-Saxon characteristics and ideals, its democratic spirit and liberty. Rome fell chiefly because of the indifference of the Roman people towards the ever-increasing multitude of strangers that, as slaves and freemen, was crowding into its national life.

There are in America thousands of hyphenated Americans and I think I do not fall short of the mark in saying that until recently the majority of the American people were utterly indifferent to the need of Americanizing the stranger in their midst, or, if not indifferent, they wished to do it in an aggressive and superficial way. When I speak of Americanizing the foreigner I do not mean dwarfing the characteristics of one race in order to superimpose upon it the characteristics of another race. Americanization is this: making use of the best in the foreigner's nature, such as family love, religious spirit, love of country and humanity, by instilling in him a clear vision of the American nation, which was formed by men who had the same feelings that he has in his heart. Thus far America has not found to any appreciable extent the way of making itself known to the foreigner in its midst.

I am only acquainted with the knowledge of America which exists among Italians, but that which I know is sad enough. The average professional man, coming already educated and with a certain set of ideas and habits, settles down in one of the Italian colonies, arrogating to himself the right to describe America as he sees it to the multitude of immigrants who believe America to be as this leader describes it in the Italian newspaper. With few exceptions, the average Italian professional man has no way of knowing America as it really is. He lives all day long among his own countrymen, he never enters an American institution of learning to study, since he has already received his education, and on account of his financial

*Social and Religious Life of Italians in America (Boston: Christopher Publishing Co., 1918), pp. 48-75.

187

condition, he is forced as a rule to have his home either in the Italian quarter or in a rather poor American quarter. After a period of laborious study he acquires sufficient knowledge of English to read cheap American newspapers, but these papers in America are, as a rule, not good interpreters of American life. He meets in the Italian restaurants and hotels of the colony some Americans, but the American who habitually patronizes such places does more to harm America than a legion of hyphenated Americans. I have seen a large number of articles from Italian newspapers. written by Italian professional men concerning America, which, if translated and published, would open the eyes even of the blind. America is described in these articles as a ruthless, rapacious, hypocritical, puritanical country; American men are superficial, weak, ridiculous; American women are vain and prefer to have a good time rather than to be good wives and mothers; churches in America are places of business; social and philanthropic work is established to furnish fat salaries to innumerable office-holders; the political life is incurably corrupt; and everything else is termed "Americanate," meaning the quintessence of foolishness. A sensational divorce case, a scandal at the City Hall, Dowie or Billy Sunday, anything and everything is used as a pretext for a long philippic against America. I have seen Italian newspapers with laudatory articles on America written in English, which no Italian would read, and with an article in Italian in the same issue, that the American would not understand, painting America in the blackest colors. I greatly admire the campaign started under the patronage of the American Civic League in the newspaper "Il Cittadino" in which very earnest and sincere articles concerning America are published, but for one newspaper like that there are a dozen of the other kind. The depreciatory articles which appear in Italian papers are written sometimes by very sincere men whose only fault is that they do not know whereof they speak; their chief mistake is that they generalize, that is to say, they judge the whole American people by the descriptions in the yellow press and by the few wretched specimens of American manhood whom they meet in public life. There is an increasing number of Americans of Italian extraction, who, having the opportunity to know American life well, are now publishing works that will enlighten Italian immigrants on this subject.

The root of the evil does not lie, however, in the above-mentioned class. I may be too harsh in my judgment, but it seems to me the fault is to be traced to the extreme conservativeness of the best American families, whose doors are seldom opened to the educated Italian who chooses America for his new country. A few young diplomats, who after all will not remain long in America, some well-recommended artists or writers may be welcomed to the homes of the American middle and upper classes, but that is all. I still remember with what sadness a young Calabrian lawyer came to me for advice. He said, "I have been living for four years in a small city of New Jersey, an old Quaker city, and I have not yet been received by a single American family."

Among certain people there still exists the old prejudice that there must be something the matter with a foreigner. Exclusiveness on one side, loneliness on the other, do not help to interpret American life in the right spirit to the foreigner. If educated Italians thus do not know the real America, you can easily imagine what the immigrant's conception of America may be. My barber, who has been in this country twenty-eight years, was dumbfounded when I told him the other day that six people out of seven in America are Protestant. The poor fellow had gone about for twenty-eight years tipping his hat to every church, thinking that they were all Roman Catholic churches. I have found over and over again Italian couples living together in the belief that they were husband and wife, because they misunderstood American law. They had been told that in America a civil marriage was as valid as a religious one, so they went to the City Hall and by going through the process of answering questions in taking out the marriage license they thought they had been married and went happily home to live together as husband and wife. An Italian tried to explain to me the meaning of Thanksgiving Day. "You see," he said, "the word explains itself, "Tacchinsgiving Day' "; "tacchin" meaning turkey in Italian, it was, according to this man, the day on which Americans gave away turkeys.

And what opportunity has an immigrant to know this country when he sees America only at its worst? Through the gum-chewing girls whom he meets in factories, through the hard-drinking and hard-swearing "boss" who orders him about, through the dubious type of youth whom he meets at the saloon and in the dance hall, through the descriptions given in Italian newspapers and by cheap orators he comes to know America. Add to that poor wages, quarters in the slums, policemen, car conductors and ushers who laugh at him when he asks for information, "bosses" who claim a fee for securing him a job, and the sweet names of "Dago" and "Ghiny" by which the supposed American thinks himself entitled to call him, and you can imagine what a delightful feeling the average Italian has toward this country.

Where does the fault lie? In prejudice and indifference, and in the spirit of patronage. Americans who judge by appearances, who have not travelled in Italy or studied modern Italian life, scornfully turn away from the Italian immigrant because he is not as clean-shaven or as well-kempt as the American working man. Other Americans do not concern themselves with foreigners. They have a vague knowledge that there is somewhere, in some God forsaken corner of the city, a foreign population, and that is all. Still others take a sentimental view of the matter; they have somewhat the feeling that existed in the bosom of an Irishwoman, a neighbor of mine. On Saturday night,—she was always affectionate on that special night,—she would wipe her eyes and say, "Thim poor Eyetalians." This kind of person means well, but generally has zeal without knowledge.

A lady of refinement, born in a leading city of Italy, married to an Italian Protestant minister who is now at the head of an important religious movement in Italy, one day received the following letter:

> "Dear Madam,
> "We are going to have a bazaar for the benefit of Italians. Please come to help us, *dressed in the national costume that you used to wear in Italy.*"

A son of a leading lawyer of Naples came to this country and was soon holding a fine position and making a good living. He met at church an American lady who told him that she would be very glad to see him the next day at her house. At the appointed hour our young gentleman went there and handed his card to the servant. "Oh, yes," she said, "the lady gave me something for you," and she thrust into his hand a dilapidated suitcase and a note. The note read:

> "Dear Sir,
> "I have been called away suddenly, but my maid will give you the article which I intended to present to you in asking you to call. As I no longer have use for this suitcase perhaps it would serve you on your next trip to Italy.
> "Trusting to see you at church next Sunday,
> "Sincerely yours,—"

On another occasion an Italian minister was sent to a new field. A few days after he had settled down he had a telephone call from the wife of a minister of the town, who invited him to call at her house. At the appointed hour he went and was met by the servant, who gave him a newspaper bundle. The young man protested, saying that he had come to call in response to an invitation. The servant went upstairs but came back saying there was no mistake, that the lady wished that given to him. On reaching home he found that the contents consisted of cast-off clothing for his children. He bought a handsome edition of an Italian book for children translated into English, and sent it with his regards to the patronizing lady.

I could go on indefinitely with such stories, but I think that these few are enough to illustrate how zeal and a desire to do good are sometimes dangerous when wrongly applied. The indiscriminate giving away of old clothes, food, and coal among foreigners by private societies and individuals not only may offend self-respecting people but may also pauperize poor foreigners who otherwise would be perfectly self-supporting. Finding that with little effort he can secure valuable articles, the foreigner is tempted to take advantage of the opportunity. This fact any social worker is willing to admit. I appreciate the work of the Associated Charities, for there at least, so far as human knowledge goes, every case is carefully investigated and the begging type of individual is quickly detected.

Italy has no social work in the American sense. The psychological motive which fosters social work in America is the spirit of standardizing. The ready-made suit, the model two-story house are American institutions; the spirit of the country is that of making things uniform. In Italian streets one can see all kinds of types and costumes; no one pays attention to that; every man has some personal way of dressing, of wearing his hair or moustache two or three inches longer or shorter than his neighbor; no one is concerned about it, In America for a man to wear his hair hanging one inch down on his shoulder is enough to make him lose his position, or to gather a crowd in the street. The strongest argument in this country is:"This is not the way we do it," or: "I have never seen it done that way." The Italian attitude is: "Let every man act in his own way; I have no right to impose my ways upon him." Americans see among the new-comers certain methods of life that they think wrong, and they get up social organizations which, with energy and devotion, try to change them. Many of the habits and customs that they try to change are not wrong at all but just different ways of doing the same things. Italians resent this aggressive attitude; they do not understand that it is prompted by good will and would prefer to be let alone. Though many of the Italians welcome the social workers with a smile because they hate to be impolite, it would fill a volume to write what they really think of them.

Social workers sometimes make the same mistake that the old style foreign missionary used to make abroad: it was of greater interest to him and he thought more of succeeding in making a native boy adopt the European costume or eat with a fork than of bringing about a psychological development in the native life. In reading the report of a group of social workers I found a remark like this : "Not yet Americanized; still eating Italian food." I have heard Italian families complain about the aggressive, blunt way in which some social workers burst into their homes and upset the usual routine of their lives, opening windows, undressing children, giving orders not to eat this and that, not to wrap up babies in swaddling clothes, and so forth. Social workers are well-intentioned but they forget that they are dealing with human beings and not with cattle. Furthermore, it is not by forcing matters but by educating people in a kindly way that good is accomplished. The mother of five or six children may, with some reason, be inclined to think that she knows a little more about how to bring up children than the young-looking damsel who insists upon trying to teach her how to do it. As to her method of wrapping up the baby, a doctor was telling me a short time ago that there was a certain advantage in the old custom of wrapping babies in swaddling clothes when as among the immigrants, mothers have numerous children and the babies have to be carried about by a careless girl scarcely out of her teens; it has saved many a baby's spine. Fortunately the type of social worker that I have just mentioned is not in the majority and philanthropic institutions have now in their service better trained and kindly persons who, by their tact and understanding, accomplish a great deal of good.

Italians have a strong prejudice against social betterment institutions and social workers. It may be said that they are not as willing as they should be to help the more unfortunate among their own people; but in any case it is true that very few intelligent efforts are made on the part of Americans to seek the co-operation of Italians. There are always in the colonies Italian young men and women with zeal and education who could be made use of for social work, thus destroying the Italian argument against social work namely that it is done in a patronizing spirit by Americans who come down among them to civilize them as if they were barbarians. At a slight expense young Italian-Americans could in a short time be trained in American schools to be excellent and intelligent workers among their people. Is it not curious that there is scarcely one Italian at the head of a social betterment institution among his people in America? Social workers of Italian origin would understand how to avoid misunderstanding and mistakes, having the same feelings about the methods of work as the rest of their people.

I attended last year a gathering of representatives of all the Evangelical churches in Boston. The gathering was to consider extensive religious work among the foreigners of the community. Not a single representative of the different foreign colonies was invited. There are among the Russians, Greeks, Poles and Italians in Boston professional men, lawyers, doctors and even Protestant ministers; but that did not seem to matter. The good representatives of that gathering felt no need of advice from the educated leaders of the different races which they desired to influence. Would it not seem rather patronizing if a group of educated Frenchmen were to get together in Paris with the intention of doing some religious work among a certain type of Americans who live there—and there are in Paris Americans who do very queer things—without at least consulting refined and educated Americans and asking their co-operation? Yet things of this kind are aften done among Italians, many times thoughtlessly, and suggest a patronizing spirit which is bitterly resented.

Italians have been thought of by some as "an undesirable element." This "undersirable element" in South America has succeeded in becoming the leading element of civilization. Even taking into consideration the fact that Italian immigration to South America includes a larger percentage of Northern Italians than does that to North America, yet it is remarkable that in a few years the natural shrewdness of the Italian peasant should have succeeded in South America in conquering for him and his children the best positions in all fields of human activity. A writer thus sums up the situation: "The Italians in South America have a monopoly of the corn-farms, wine, wheat. These uneducated, poverty-stricken Italian peasants have built up a mighty work in a few years. An Italian has been President of the Republic; the present Ministers of Education and War are Italians. By sheer dint of industry and perseverance and native shrewdness, the men, who in the United States are condemned as useless or dangerous paupers, have carved their way to comfort or influence."

While in South America Italians have a future as a race, because they find there little competition from the Spanish, Portuguese and half-breeds, and because the language and civilization of that country are of Latin extraction, in the United States it is quite different. Educated Italians are well aware that here Italians as a race have no future. Either the Italian becomes Americanized, in which case he loses his native characteristics by adopting an entirely different language and way of living, or there is little prospect of success for him. Italians cling to their language and traditions with the tenacity which the English show for theirs. The success of Italians in the United States will depend upon their willingness to be "melted" into the Anglo-Saxon race. In South America Italians find a Latin race that regards life from a point of view similar to their own. The institutions, the laws, the ideals are practically the same; the language is a neo-Latin language like the Italian; he finds himself in his own element and rises to his opportunities. In the United States he is brought into contact with a different civilization; the laws, the institutions, the ideals of the country are foreign to him; he has to compete with work-ingmen who are as a rule better educated than he; the language is constructed in a way that does not seem to suit his way of putting things; the climate is more trying than that of his own country. To use an illustration, he was trained to fly and he must swim. He must swim or sink; he must either be absorbed into American life or suffer the fate that trees suffer when they are transplanted from their native region to another and cannot acclimatize themselves. That does not mean the obliteration of his Italian nature. I am speaking of the fu-ture of Italians in America "en masse," not as individuals. In enter-ing into American life, in adopting Anglo-Saxon ways and the Eng-lish language, the Italian will bring into American life his Latin characteristics, which will contribute toward the development of this country. "When an Italian becomes a loyal citizen of another country, he works out his individual salvation there, and lets his own native force make him the predominant element in it." His patience, his artistic feeling, his emotional temperament, his anti-puritanical spirit, his shrewdness, his instinctive knowledge of human nature, his love of family and country, will undoubtedly prove to be an equal-izing and perfecting element in the future generations of Americans.

America will find in its citizens of Italian extraction staunch up-holders of democratic principles. "The modern Italian is at heart and by instinct a democrat. Italian democracy is not aggressive, nor, except perhaps among a small and noisy band of advanced socialists, is it at all inclined to accept the untenable theory that all men are equals. That courtesy of manner and speech which is inherent in the true Latin races is equally to be found in all classes of the Italian com-munity, at all events so far as their ordinary dealings with a stranger are concerned—even if this stranger be one of themselves. The off-hand, scarcely veiled insolence of manner and bearing which the Briton of modern times so often assumes in order to demonstrate his ideas of social equality could not, I think, be found even among the roughest of Italian workmen imbued with republican or socialistic principles."

Almost all Italians come to America with the intention of staying two or three years and then going back to Italy to live, with a little money. They generally do go back, but, having lost the taste for life in a small village, having drunk the somewhat unclean waters of a large American city, they come to America again, and this time with the intention of settling here. They still have no way of enter-ing into the American life, while in many cases, as I have said, they are afraid of American life from the little they have seen of it.

There should be in the large foreign colonies organized lectures, clubs, stereoptican lectures, distribution of information, both in Italian and in English, to explain and to instruct in regard to American history, laws, institutions, and ideals. There should be free courses on a university extension plan for Italian professional men, with a view to preparing them to expound to their people in the right way the principles and standards of American life. A regular and carefully carried out campaign should be started in the Italian newspapers, with well-written articles by leading men on the subject of American life, and a careful censorship of Italian newspapers should be established to challenge every article that is unduly depreciatory of America.

Churches should be centres where American volunteers of the best kind can in deed and word represent their country to the foreigner. Churches furnish a good means to bring about Americanization. Italians are apt to move from place to place and those who become attached to Evangelical churches, besides the good which they eventually get in their own churches, are also brought into contact with American congregations, who by their example initiate them into the ways of American life.

A campaign to enlighten the immigrant as to his duties towards his new country should be started on a somewhat different basis from those already tried. The immigrant is often made to feel how great the material advantage is for him in becoming an American citizen and thus is trained to enter into American public and political life in a mercenary spirit. When I applied for citizenship papers, I received this letter from the Bureau of Naturalization, Washington, D. C.:

> "Dear Sir:
> You have just filed your petition for naturalization to become a citizen of the United States, and because of this the United States Bureau of Naturalization is sending this letter to you, as it desires to show you how you can become an American citizen. It also wants to help you to get a better position that pays you more money for your work. In order to help you better yourself it has sent your name to the public schools in your city, and the superintendent of those schools has promised to teach you the things which you should know to help you to get a better position. If you will go to the public school building nearest where you live the teacher will tell you what nights you can go to school and the best school for you to go to. You will not be put in a class with boys and girls, but with grown people. It will not cost you anything for the teaching which you will receive in the school, and it will help you get a better job and also make you able to pass the examination in court when you come to get your citizen's papers.

You should call at the schoolhouse as soon as you receive this letter so that you may start to learn and be able
to get a better job as soon as possible.

"Very truly yours,
N. N."

As you see, four times there occurs in this letter the exhortation to
become a citizen and to learn the English language in order to get "a
better job." The letter contains not a single appeal to higher motives
nor a reference to the duties and responsibilities of American citizenship, yet it is sent to every foreigner who applies for citizenship. I
think a letter of this kind is demoralizing. I wonder whether America
is better off for exhorting foreigners to become its citizens from such
motives, or whether it would not be more desirable to instruct immigrants carefully on the altruistic side as to the duty of sharing the responsibilities of American life.

It may be worth mentioning that thirty years of residence in the city
of Rome is required of any man, even of Italian birth, in order to become a Roman citizen.

Human nature, fortunately, is always longing for an appeal to its
best side. I accompanied a friend when the American citizenship was
granted to him. The judge, a man with a fine, clean-cut face, turned
toward the candidates—there were about a hundred in the room—
and told the story of the Pilgrim Fathers who, although starved and in
great distress, refused the opportunity of going back to England,
where religious and political freedom was denied them. The words
were to me an inspiration and in glancing around I saw the faces
of those present light up and show signs of emotion. Big Irishmen,
heavy-faced Slavs, small, dried-up Jews, dark Italians, small-headed
Greeks, I could see in the eyes of them all the light of men who were
seeing a vision. The appeal to the best there is in man should be the
leading thought in educating immigrants to a desire for American
citizenship.

The matter of taking out American citizenship papers is complicated by the lack of international understanding, which gives to the
foreigner who comes to America from a country where conscription
is enforced the feeling that he is either a man without a country or one
with two countries. No matter how long an Italian stays in America,
with what sincerity of heart he takes up citizenship there, he will always be considered by the Italian Government an Italian citizen with
the duty of serving in the Italian army. This is also true for the sons
of the Italian immigrant, even when born in America. If the Italian
immigrant and his sons choose not to answer the call of the Italian
Government, he and his sons cannot visit Italy without running the

danger of being arrested, and they lose the right of inheritance if ever a will is made in their favor in Italy. The Italian Government is not to blame; it is only a matter of international understanding that has not yet been taken up by the federal authorities. The American citizen of Italian extraction feels that he has the same right to visit Italy without encountering difficulties as his fellow-citizen of Anglo-Saxon extraction, and keenly resents the fact that America has not provided the means of defending him when his rights as the citizen of a free country are encroached upon.

A few months ago the American newspapers told of the case of a gentleman, born of an Italian father and an English mother. In order to avoid for himself and his children the stumbling block of being a citizen claimed by two countries for certain duties, and also in order to avert the race prejudice which falls more or less upon Americans who have Italian names, he asked the state to let him give up his father's name and call himself by the English name of his mother. So far as the main issue was concerned that did not change matters. This gentleman and his children will always be Italians to the Italian Government, which will require from them the same duties as before the change of name if ever it succeeds in getting hold of them. Would an Englishman, a Scotchman, or an Irishman be in great haste to take out his American papers if he knew that, if ever his business or his pleasure should lead him or his children into any part of the British Empire, there would be danger of imprisonment and compulsory military service, and that America could not help him, having provided no international law to cover his case? I think that now, during the war, when this problem is in its acute stage, the federal authorities should take it up and solve it once and forever.

The second generation needs special attention on the part of the best Americans, for to it belong those who stand in the greatest need of guidance. They are neither fish nor flesh. They have not the traditions and the love of the old country and they imperfectly possess the traditions and love of the new one. They may cry "Hooray for America" and be ever ready to display an American flag, but I am afraid that there is in such acts the clamorous attitude of the parvenu, who, knowing himself weak in regard to ancestral claims, is constantly and loudly referring to the greatness of his forefathers. The young men and women of the second generation have no love for heroes like Garibaldi, Mazzini and Cavour, and on the other hand they have a vague and troubled feeling that the heroes who gave their lives to make America were men of another race. It may be to quiet that feeling that they sing louder than the others "Land where my fathers died."

The result with Italians whose Americanization is brought about too rapidly is the same as with other races. An expert on Japanese life was telling me recently that the average Japanese who adopts American ways rapidly loses his racial courtesy and becomes blunt to the point of becoming offensive. The Italian youth of the second generation often times loses the simplicity, the temperance, the love of family, and the spirit of economy of his father without acquiring the generosity, the soberness of habits, the truthfulness, the sense of justice and the respect for the law of the true American. Grazia Deledda, an Italian writer, calls this degeneration "the changing of the simple, natural man into a modern barbarian." It is dangerous to give generous wine to a teetotaler. Races are not changed in one generation. American freedom is dangerous to youth of Latin blood. That is why, according to experts on immigration questions, the second generation is the one which should be most carefully trained. They represent the period of transition, they are at a critical stage of development similar to that of adolescence.

The public school trains the youth of the second generation, but the public school cannot take the place of home and religious training. The children of foreign extraction learn English and, as very little is done in school to make them keep up the language of their parents, they soon forget it, with the result that their home life is destroyed. I know of many families where the parents cannot understand what the children say and the gentle influence of home life is thus lost. Besides, in the public school the child of foreign extraction is made to feel by the other children, and sometimes by the teachers, that he is a superior little being because he was born here while his father and mother are just "Wops" and "Dagos". It is sad to notice the patronizing attitude that the child assumes towards his father and mother after a few months in the public school. The mother may be ignorant and primitive but she has the love of a mother in her heart and she can teach patience, purity and honesty to the child. The father may not know English and may be rough, but he is working hard to educate his child and his strong arm is ever ready to defend him. All the beautiful and lasting influence represented by mother, father and home is destroyed just because the child is made to look down upon his parents as inferior beings, he being "an American." When I discuss this matter with teachers in public schools, I become aware that they possess a holy horror of teaching children the language and history of Italy. In my opinion the way to preserve the home life of the children of immigrants is to teach through the language and history of their fathers that in every country the great men and women have always been ready to sacrifice their personal interest for the sake of their country. By making these children realize that they are connected by blood with a race of glorious traditions and by adoption have come to belong to a country which has also a glorious past, the love for America will be kept in their hearts without their acquiring a feeling of contempt for their fathers' country.

The innumerable clubs which are organized for young people in connection with all types of social work among immigrants are doing a great work in training the second generation to love and respect justice and honor. Unfortunately they help also to deepen the gulf between parents and children.

Unintentionally those clubs tend to train the young Italian boys and girls to stay out of the home almost every evening and to mix freely together. This may be very proper for other races, but I have had the opinion of many priests and ministers as to the results of this system among Italians and it was not very encouraging. The club-trained Italian boys and girls are easily recognized by the ease with which they get married and divorced, by their unwillingness to stay and take care of their home after they are married, by their almost insane desire to be incessantly out for "a good time," and by their lack of respect for their old people. This would not be the case if clubs were so organized as to include both the young people and their parents, keeping thus the whole family together, on the same social plane.

The church also should adapt itself both to the older and to the younger generation. Trinity Church in New York grew rapidly because it was attended by young Dutch men and women who, wishing to have services in English and not having such services provided in their own church, flocked to Trinity Church. Services in Italian for those who do not understand English and services in English for the young people should be provided, yet the wise pastor will urge parents and children to share one another's church services, and the principal service on Sunday should be alternately in English and in Italian, whith the whole family attending it. This plan should be kept up until the flood of Italian immigration ceases.

The war will be a great factor in solving the problem of the Americanization of Italians. Thousands of young men of Italian extraction have volunteered in the United States Army and Navy. Thousands more will join the colors while the war goes on. To fight for a flag and a country is the strongest and most powerful way to make a man love that country. These fighting men will come back to their homes Americans every inch of them, and will leaven the rest of the young men in the neighborhoods where they live.

To sum up, let me warn my reader of the danger which lurks behind the question of Americanization: that of "rushing things."
During the coming years, judging by the talk about "hyphens"
that is going on, America will hasten to assimilate its foreign elements. The danger will lie in assimilating too quickly material that
is in too raw a state. It is well to remember that it took the early
Anglo-Saxon settlers about two hundred years to realize that they
were Americans and even then many preferred to fight for the privilege of remaining British subjects. The process of Americanization should be one of slow and natural evolution; in hastening it
there is danger of making it an artificial and unhealthy process which
will produce a type of citizenship such as reminds one of the body of
an abnormally grown boy: plenty of legs and neck but weakness in
the lungs and heart. It is better to control, direct and educate the foreign element than to be partially controlled by it. It is better to make
a foreigner look upon American citizenship as a prize to be won by
service and devotion to his new country than to throw it at him as a
thing of no value. The proverb warns that: "Haste trips up its own
heels."

F. AURELIO PALMIERI

ITALIAN
PROTESTANTISM IN
THE UNITED STATES*

In an editorial in *Extension Magazine* (September, 1917) we read:
"The Italian problem *is* a problem, and it is *our* problem. We must
either face it now, or take the consequences of our neglect later on. We
must put up or shut up; but if we 'shut up' we shall be guilty before God of neglecting our opportunities."

These stern words cannot but impress everyone who is stirred
with a legitimate pride in the marvelous growth of American Catholicism. In this country, the Church has the mission of assimilating to
herself, under the flag of American ideals, the best religious and
civil elements of the Old World. It is a labor requiring not only
skill but patience, not only patience but disinterestedness, not only
disinterestedness but heroism and sacrifice. This task of assimilation
is pursued with perseverance by the political leaders of the United
States: it needs to be followed up in the religious field with even
greater constancy, since it is impossible to build a real and enduring
civilization upon an irreligious foundation. When the foundations
of a majestic building are weak, sooner or later the whole edifice will
collapse. Like the other races, the four millions of Italians who have
made this country their new home, have either become an efficient
part of the great American family or are slowly undergoing that process of Americanization which will enable them to give their energies,
both intellectual and moral, to their country of adoption. They are or
will be as true Americans by ideals and adoption as any who have
landed on these shores before them. They will bring to America not
only the vivid sparkle of Italian genius, but the glowing fire of Italian Catholicism. The Italian soul cannot be dissociated from its
natural inclination to the loftiest concept of fine arts; nor may it be
thought of as deprived of its Catholic traditions. Long experience
proves that Italians either are or have to be Catholics, else they will
ramble about the labyrinth of an ungodly materialism. A well-

Catholic World, Vol. 107 (May, 1918), pp. 177-189.

known Italian woman writer, Amy Bernardy, justly remarked that "when Italian immigrants have once lost their native religion, they cannot deceive themselves nor others that they can acquire another. They cannot have any other."

It is a recognized fact that almost all the Italians who come to this country, are either practically or nominally Catholics. It is also a recognized fact that as soon as they establish themselves in the United States, they are looked upon by some Protestant denominations as virgin soil to be exploited for the profit of their own religious aims. Some Protestant denominations, with the help of a whole staff of Italian pastors, exert a wide propaganda among the Italian immigrants.

What are the results? Here we meet with conflicting statements. A Catholic priest, who writes under the name of Herbert Hadley, declares that "the Italian falls an easy victim to the Protestant proselytizer," while a writer of great authority, the Rev. John Talbot Smith, affirms that "the Italians are not apostates even in the presence of temptation. Their faith is in their blood." To solve these contradictory statements, we have carefully examined and compared the statistics of Protestant workers among Italians, and we submit in these pages the results of our inquiry. It is hoped that the investigation will be of service in the difficult solution of the Italian religious problem in the United States.

Protestant propaganda among the Italian immigrants to the United States was preceded by similar work in the Italian Kingdom immediately after 1870. Italy had already a small nucleus of native Protestants, the Waldensians, who according to the latest report, number 20,519 members, 70 pastors, 6,408 Sunday-school pupils, and a theological seminary in Florence. After the fall of the temporal power, American propagandists hurried to Italy to help the Waldensians in their attempt to spread their belief among Italian Catholics. The so-called evangelical work" among Italians in Italy was inaugurated and is carried on by American Baptists and Methodists. The Southern Baptist Convention sent an active missionary, George Taylor, to Italy, who worked there thirty years, especially in Rome. Success, however, did not attend his efforts, judging by the last report of the Baptist mission in Italy. It numbers 32 ordained Italian pastors, 46 churches (rather, chapels or meeting houses), 70 stations, 1,362 members, 40 Sunday-schools with 1,144 pupils, a theological seminary, and a monthly religious review, *Bilychnis*.

The Methodist Episcopal Church inaugurated a Methodist mission in Italy in 1877, and confided it to Dr. Le Roy M. Vernon, who in 1888 was succeeded by Dr. William Burt, who was elected bishop in 1904. He was followed in his charge by Dr. N. Walling Clark and the Rev. Bertram M. Tipple. The last report of the mission shows that the Methodists have been somewhat more successful in Italy than the Baptists. Yet it cannot be denied that their results are very scanty as compared with the large sums they have spent, and the number of workers they have enrolled for their propaganda. In fact, the Methodist mission in Italy has 76 pastors and preachers, 3,212 members, 1,025 probationers, 2,811 Sunday-school pupils, a theological school, some secondary industrial and elementary schools, and a publishing house, which publishes a weekly religious paper, the Evangelista.

The Protestants inaugurated their missions in Italy at a time when the enormous growth of Italian immigration to America could not be forseen. From 1871 to 1877, about a thousand Italians came to the United States each year, and that immigration was chiefly temporary. The first increase took place in 1880. Every year several thousand Italians sailed to America. But Italian immigration reached the highest pitch in the decade 1906-1916, as is shown by the following data: in 1907, 293,061; in 1908, 135,247; in 1909, 190,398; in 1910, 223,410; in 1911, 189,950; in 1912, 162,273; in 1913, 274,147; in 1914, 926,414; in 1915, 57,217.

Hence it follows that in the course of ten years, two million Italians have entered this country. From July 1, 1916, to June 30, 1917, official statistics give 38,950 Italians as coming to America, and 13, 494 as returning to Italy, while during the same interval in 1915-1916, the number of the arrivals is calculated as 38,814, and that of departures as 72,507.

This vast mass of Italian immigrants has spread throughout the United States, especially in the States of New York, Pennsylvania, New Jersey, Massachusetts, Illinois, California, Connecticut, Ohio, Rhode Island and Louisiana. The census of 1910 gives a population of 739,059 Italians in the State of New York, 293,554 in that of Pennsylvania, 191,049 in that of New Jersey, 130,577 in that of Massachusetts, 116,685 in that of Illinois, and 102,618 in that of California. The same census numbers 544,449 Italians in New York City, 76,534 in Philadelphia, 49,753 in Boston, 35,861 in Newark, 30,000 in New Haven, 30,000 in Providence, and 30,000 in San Francisco. Of course, to estimate the present Italian population, we must increase the figures of this census by half, or even more. New York now has 700,000 Italians; Philadelphia more than 100,000; Boston, 70,000; San Francisco, 70,000; Providence, 50,000. Therefore, we would not be guilty of exaggeration if we were to say that the Italian population in the United States is not much less than four millions.

Such a large bulk of immigrants could not but attract the attention of various Protestant denominations. In fact there was danger that the continuous stream of Catholic immigrants would out-weigh in the long run the numerical superiority of Protestantism, at least in the largest American cities. A motive of self-defence, therefore, lies at the bottom of Protestant proselytism, especially among Italians. Professor Steiner writes: "There is no institution in the United States which will be so profoundly affected by the immigrant as the Protestant Church. *Without him, she will languish and die; with him alone she has a future.* The Protestant Church is called upon to lift the immigrant into a better conception of human relations both for her own sake and for the sake of the communities which she wishes to serve. This she must do even if it brings her under suspicion of proselyting. Indeed, one of the growing weaknesses of the Protestant Church is the loss of those deep convictions which make proselyting easy."

When the Catholic Church was yet unorganized in this country, Protestantism submerged many Catholic immigrants. Things have changed long since; and Protestantism now finds itself confronted by new conditions due to the slow but steady pressure of Catholic immigration. Generally, in proportion as the wave of Italian immigrants advances here or there in a town or in a State, even the oldest defences of Protestantism are deserted, and Catholic churches take their places. The reality of this fact is acknowledged by the chief of the Italian Department of Colgate Theological Seminary, Antonio Mangano: "We shall lose our place of primacy and some other nation will take the honor from us. See what is happening in greater New York. In the midst of a population of 5,600,000 people there are not over 300,000 members of Protestant Christian Churches. There are vast sections throughout the entire city where Protestant churches are being completely driven out. In one small district in Brooklyn during the past twelve years, one church a year has been pushed to the wall. It is true that synagogues and Roman churches are increasing, but can the Protestant Church afford to desert these districts without leaving a witness to what we believe to be the principles of vital Christianity? It is unnecessary for me to state that, wherever the Protestant Church goes out, the moral tone, both social and political, is greatly lowered. And yet, *wherever the foreigner moves in, the Protestant Church moves out.*"

Hence, it follows that self-defence is the chief aim of Protestant proselytism. No doubt, other reasons are set forth to justify the Protestantizing of Italian immigrants. It is not our purpose to discuss them in this article. But whatever may be said, we firmly believe that the "evangelical work" of the Protestant missionaries is inspired by apprehension of the dangers which impend over Protestantism, either from internal disintegration, or from the expansion of the Catholic Church. The religious propaganda among Italians is carried on by the Presbyterians, United Presbyterians, Methodists (Episcopal), Baptists (Northern Convention), Protestant Episcopalians, Reformed Protestants, Congregationalists, Lutherans, and by the Evangelical Associations.

"To the Presbyterian Church," writes the Methodist minister of Boston, G. M. Panunzio, "belongs the honor of being the pioneer of Christian endeavor among Italians. Beginning its work in 1881, it has been laying deep foundations. From the very first, it has laid stress upon securing and developing the best possible leadership; it has made concentrated effort and expended large sums of money; it has opened the regular churches to the Italian worshipper; it has supplied comparatively adequate quarters for the housing of the Italian Church; and has developed an organization for the individual Italian church which is, in a measure, a success." Antonio Mangano is equally enthusiastic: "In the field of Italian evangelization in this country, the Presbyterians are setting the standards for all other denominations. They are doing a most thorough and aggressive work with the most far-reaching plans for future development. The immigrant work office of the Board of Home Missions is busy making thorough surveys of Italian colonies in many States. They aim to build up a system of parishes which shall lead and minister to the entire community life." "The Presbyterians have in a special manner caught a vision of the possibilities of the future, and are spending large sums of money in every department of their work, without putting too great emphasis upon immediate results. They are cultivating the community in a sensible and scientific manner. Twenty-five years from now they will reap an abundant harvest for the Kingdom of God."

For the success of their proselytism among Italians, the Presbyterians appealed to the Waldensians. One of the leaders of the movement was the Rev. Alberto Clod, a minister born in Italy, the historian of the Waldensian colony of Valdese, North Carolina.

According to the last report, the Presbyterians in the United States have 107 churches or missions for the Italians. Italian Presbyterianism numbers 4,800 members; 8,000 pupils in the Sunday-schools; 70 Italian-speaking pastors; 23 lay workers; 32 visitors, and over 350 American volunteers. In twenty years the Presbyterian Church in America has spent $350,000 in building and equipping 28 churches and missions. Over $75,000 are spent each year for the Protestantizing of Italians, not including funds contributed by different Presbyterian institutions for the same purpose. The Director of the Presbyterian immigrant work in New York, William P. Shriver, affirms that $100,000 are contributed by the American Presbyterians "for the work of evangelization among Italians." The Italian members of the Presbyterian churches contribute over $14,000 a year to their support. It is noteworthy that in 1916 the Presbyterian Board of Home Missions devoted thirty-eight and five-tenths per cent ($32,000) of its resources to Italian immigrant work. Italian speaking pastors are trained in the Italian Department of the Bloomfield Theological Seminary. The centres of Presbyterian propaganda are the States of New York (29 churches and missions; 12 of them in New York City); New Jersey (20 churches or missions; 4 in Newark); Pennsylvania (25 churches or missions; 3 in Philadelphia); Minnesota (7 churches); Illinois (7 churches, all of them in the city of Chicago); Ohio (5 churches). The most important Italian Presbyterian churches are the Broome street Tabernacle and the Church of the Ascension in New York; the Olivet Church in Newark; First and Second Presbyterian Churches in Philadelphia; the Centre Mission and the Church of our Saviour in Chicago, and the Presbyterian Mission in Kansas City. The United Presbyterians have only eight churches in Pennsylvania, Rhode Island, California, and in the District of Columbia.

The Methodist Episcopal Church started its propaganda among Italians in 1881. An ex-vender of plaster models, Antonio Arrighi, was converted to Methodism in Des Moines, Iowa, in 1858. He studied at Ohio Wesleyan University, Dickinson College, and Boston Theological Seminary, and after a stay of several years in Rome, he returned to America and preached his first sermon at the Five Points Mission in New York City. In 1889 this mission was confided to an Italian preacher, Vito Calabrese. The Methodist theological school in Rome furnished pastors and preachers. For several years the mission was organized as an independent institution under the direction of a bishop and superintendent. In 1916 that organization was abolished. Each church and mission was placed under the care and supervision of the resident bishop and local conference.

The Methodist Episcopal Church has in the United States 60 Italian churches or missions, 5,241 members, 42 Italian schools, and 4,927 pupils in the Sunday-schools. Among the members are to be found 1,839 probationers. The centres of the movement are the States of New York (21 churches; 8 in New York City); Pennsylvania (10 churches); New Jersey (4 churches). The other churches are scattered through the States of Connecticut, Massachusetts, Ohio, Illinois,

Maryland, Indiana, Maine, Rhode Island, Delaware, Florida, Louisiana, Colorado, Montana, California, Alabama, Missouri, Texas, and West Virginia. The most important of these churches are those of Jefferson Park, New York; First Italian Church, Chicago; and the Peoples' Church, Denver, Colorado. In New York the Church of All Nations and the Five Points Mission have the largest Sunday-schools, averaging an attendance of from 500 to 800 pupils.

During this campaign of thirty-five years standing, the Methodists have spent $500,000 in building Italian churches. The Board of Home Missions and Church Extension expends $50,000 a year for the support of propaganda among Italians; but, as has been remarked by Frederick H. Wright, formerly Superintendent of the Italian Missions, if we take into account the sums spent by the local missionary societies, the Methodist Episcopal Church devotes every year $150,000 to the conversion of Italians. The Italian Methodist missions could not live without American pecuniary help. In fact, the Italians contribute to the support of their Methodist churches only the sum of $7,357 a year.

The Baptists have vied with the Presbyterians and the Methodists in spreading their beliefs among Italians. A special feature of their work is the effort to give a decided Italian character to their missions. In a recent report of a superintendent of the American Baptist Home Mission Society, we read: "We believe in the freedom of religious life according to racial type. An Italian Protestant Church will have and should have distinctive characteristics, distinguishing it from an American Protestant Church. This means the enrichment of the Protestant conception of God, and of social life. There is no Italian Gospel, but there is a Gospel for the Italian, which is the secret of his highest and best development, and the rebirth of Italian character according to the mind of Christ. *Italians will be won for the Kingdom of God only as the Gospel is interpreted to them in the terms of their own thinking. The use of the Italian language in worship and service is not primarily a matter of privilege, but of responsibility for winning the Italian people for Christ. The conversion of one or more Italians has demonstrated the possibility of reaching these people in a larger way than through the English language, and has usually been the determining factor in the employment of Italian missionaries.*"

Baptists in America started their mission work among Italians with English-speaking missionaries. In 1889, they had Italian Sunday-schools in some cities of the States of New York, New Jersey, Connecticut. The First Italian Church was established in Buffalo (New York), in 1893, and confided to the Rev. Ariel B. Bellondi, a former student of Colgate Theological Seminary. For many years the Italian Baptist churches were under the leadership of the American Baptist Home Mission Society. In 1917, the Colgate Theological Seminary organized an Italian department for the training of Italian ministers.

The Baptists (Northern Convention) in the United States have 82 Italian churches or missions, 2,750 members, and 60 Italian pastors. They expend in their Italian missions about $70,000 a year. The contribution of the Italian Baptists amounts to $9,000. The centres of the Italian Baptist missions are the States of Massachusetts (15 churches; 3 in Boston); Connecticut (13 churches; 2 in New Haven); New York (18 churches; 4 in New York, 3 in Buffalo, 2 in Brooklyn); New Jersey (8 churches); Pennsylvania (6 churches); Texas (4 churches). Lawrence, Massachusetts, was in 1910 the seat of the last convention of Italian missionaries and pastors. The most important churches are the First Italian in Buffalo, First Italian in Brooklyn, Hurlburt Chapel in Orange, New Jersey, and First Italian in New Haven. We have no data as to the number of Italian children frequenting Baptist Sunday-schools, except for New York City, where 680 pupils are registered.

The Congregationalists, according to a report of Philip R. Rose, Supervisor of Italian Congregational churches in Connecticut, "have no country-wide or denomination-wide work for Italian immigrants." With regard to the Italians, they follow "a policy of experiment." Their ideal is "not proselytism but Christian character." They wish to "cooperate with the Italian Roman Catholic Church (!) to prepare the best Italians to be the intellectual and spiritual leaders of their own race."

A striking feature of the propaganda work of Congregationalism is an instinctive distrust of foreign workers. They think that mission work established for the immigrants in their own tongue, is not acceptable to them, and is sometimes even offensive. Besides, the workers of their own nationality are looked upon with suspicion, and regarded as traitors to their own faith. Lastly, religious propaganda aims not at the grownup generation, but at the growing one; the children and the young people who can be reached more easily through the American mission than through one of their mother tongue.

Following these ideals, the Congregationalists, especially in Maine, prefer to establish missions which are branches of American churches without Italian workers. They have few regularly constituted Italian churches (thirteen in all), and few Italian pastors. These pastors are under the leadership of an American superintendent, who studied the Italian language and character in Italy. According to their latest report, they have 44 churches and missions, 983 members, 1,000 children in the Sunday-schools and 19 Italian pastors. The missions require a total expenditure of $13,279; the contribution of the Italian members is less than $1,000 a year. The centres of the propaganda are the States of Maine (14 missions), Connecticut (11 churches and missions), Rhode Island (5 missions), Illinois (4 churches and missions), New Jersey (4 missions). The most important churches are those of Davenport Settlement, New Haven and Grantwood, New Jersey.

Congregationalism is not fitted for proselytizing among Italians. Its complete doctrinal dissolution, and its lack of a central organization, exhaust its religious energies. Besides, its narrow nationalism and dry Puritan traditions, do not attract the sympathies of a foreign element.

The Protestant Episcopal Church officially professes to abstain from religious propaganda among Italians, unless they do not care to belong to the Catholic Church, or to be connected with other religious bodies. The "Italian evangelization" by the Episcopal Church began in New York forty years ago. It was inaugurated by a clergyman named Stouder. Later, the Italian mission was established in St. Philip's Church, Mulberry street, and in 1890 in a new building erected at a cost of $100,000 on Broome street.

The Protestant Episcopal Church numbers twenty-four Italian churches. Eleven of them are in New York and three in Philadelphia. In New York, they count 1,190 members, with 610 pupils in the Sunday-schools. The annual expenditure for these churches is $9,373. The sum of $1,037 represents the total contributions of Italians. The most important of the Italian Episcopal churches is Grace Parish in New York City. According to the report of its rector, Francesco G. Urbano, 1,800 Italians are connected with it in a distinctly religious manner. If this statement is true, we cannot understand why the statistics of all the Italian churches and missions of the Protestant Episcopal Church in New York (1912) give only 1,190 adult members and 610 Sunday-school pupils. Urbano attributes the success of Grace Parish among Italians to the simplicity of its Christian teaching, the dignity and sincerity of its worship, the usefulness of its work, and its recognition of the reasonableness of an Italian point of view in the administration of work among Italians. The Episcopal church of Boston has a congregation of nearly two hundred members. Worthy of special note is the interesting news that, last year, under the auspices of Bishop Lawrence, a chapel was built for the Italian Episcopalians, and was dedicated to St. Francis of Assisi!

We need not tarry long over the work of other Protestant denominations among the Italians. The Lutherans have a small Italian congregation in St. Peter's Church in Philadelphia (33 members, 60 pupils in the Sunday-school, and 80 children in the kindergarten). The Dutch Reformed Church has three Italian churches; in Newburgh and Union Hill, New York and Hackensack, New Jersey. This last town has, perhaps, the only Italian independent church in the United States, under the leadership of a suspended priest, Antonio Giulio Lenzo.

The Evangelical Association supports three Italian churches in Chicago, Milwaukee and Racine. We have no data about these churches.

From these statistics, it follows that the nursery of Protestant proselytism among Italians is New York City. In fact, according to the computation of Rev. Howard V. Yergin, New York numbered in 1912, 44 churches, 5,584 Italian Protestants, and 4,741 Italian pupils in the Sunday-schools. The annual cost of these missions exceeds $90,000 a year.

The general statistics of Protestant work among Italians gives a total of 326 churches and chapels, 13,774 members, 42 schools, 13,927 Italian pupils in the Sunday-schools, 201 Italian pastors, and a total expenditure of $227,309, not including the contribution of $31,571 by Italian Protestants. A statistical list of the Italian Protestant churches published in 1903 *(Chiese evangeliche italiane negli Stati Uniti e nel Canada)* gives only one hundred and sixty-five churches and missions.

Now, do these statistics represent the gains of Protestant propaganda among Italian Catholics in the United States? Is it true that in fifty years the above quoted denominations have been able to associate to their bodies 14,000 Italians who have left the Catholic Church? We are firmly convinced that there is exaggeration, and much exaggeration, in the figures just given.

First, the statistics include also the native Protestants of Italy. The Waldensians have several independent self-supporting churches in the United States: in New York City; Gainesville, Texas; Valdese, North Carolina; and Monett, Missouri. They are found also in the congregations of churches of the other denominations, and several pastors of these churches come from their ranks. It is an error to include the Waldensians among Italians converted to American Protestantism.

Secondly, the statistics of several Protestant churches are magnified or falsified for reasons easily understood by anyone. Lest we be suspected of bias in making this assertion, we quote from a paper by G. M. Panunzio, published in the *Fiaccola,* the official and militant organ of Italian Methodism in America: "In a certain church, under the enthusiastic leadership of a pastor, five hundred members were reported as belonging to the church. Now, *it may be set down as an axiom that whenever an Italian church reports such a large number of members, either the printer has made an error by adding a cipher, or a preacher has given the number of his constituency, and not of his members.* When a successor was appointed to that field, he labored for a year, and by taking into account every person who had been related in any vital way to the church and who could legitimately be counted as a member or even an adherent, he found one hundred and forty. Another pastor went to the same field, and accidentally discovered that fully one-third, if not more, of those members were enrolled upon the books of another denomination. By looking still closer, it was discovered that the children had caught the same spirit. Many children were attending at least three Sunday-schools; at the proper season, they went to three Christmas trees, three picnics, three entertainments, three outings, three everything. It was exactly this state of things that led an able minister, who had opportunity to observe the whole Italian situation in a large city, to make this remark: The Italian work in this city is a big farce."

We are not far from the truth then in saying that allowing for Waldensians, probationers, and the fanciful manipulation of statistics, the actual number of members of Italian Protestant churches may be computed as one-half of the official numbers. Thus, the gains of Protestant proselytism after fifty years of hard work, are reduced to hardly more than six thousand souls. No wonder an old Italian pastor, Enrico Chieri, frankly avowed in the *Churchman* (1916) that the fifty years of "evangelical work" of Protestantism among Italians had closed with a *complete failure.*

Our inquiry would naturally suggest some consideration of the religious conditions of Italian Catholics in the United States. We refrain, however, from enlarging on this theme at present. But if the Italian problem, according to *Extension Magazine,* is to be *"put up"* those who must solve that problem should investigate why 6,000 Italian Protestants in the United States have the freedom and the means of supporting 326 churches and missions, and more than 200 pastors, and why 4,000,000 of Italian Catholics have only 250 churches and an insignificant number of priests of their own race. An impartial and sincere inquiry into the causes of this strange anomaly will be the first and most necessary step to the right solution of the Italian religious problem in this country.

EDWARD CORSI

ITALIAN IMMIGRANTS AND THEIR CHILDREN*

While it was an Italian who first set foot on American soil and Italian names are both frequent and prominent in American history, the Italian is a comparative stranger in our midst. He does not belong to the pioneer era of America, but to Ellis Island and the great caravan of latter-day immigration[1]

The Italian came after the English, the Germans, and the Irish, at a time when America was changing from a rural to a modern industrial nation. Fewer than five thousand Italians entered the United States in all the years preceding the Civil War. They were not immigrants in Webster's definition of an immigrant, but refugees, tradesmen, scholars, and sheer soldiers of fortune. When the census of 1850 first distinguished the national composition of America's "melting pot," the Italians were a mere 3,645. In 1880, on the eve of the great mass movement that was to follow, the Italian population in the United States was a little more than 50,000. Italian immigrants those days were mostly from the north of Italy, from the Ligurian coast, Tuscany, and the Valley of the Po.

The later immigrant was from the south, from sun-scorched Sicily and the exhausted, overpopulated areas of Calabria, Abruzzi, and Basilicata. His coming coincided with a period of great depression in Italy and one of vast expansion in the United States. He literally poured through our gates. In one year alone, in 1907, more than 300,000 Italians entered the port of New York. In 1910 our Italian population had risen to 2,104,309.

PEASANT IMMIGRATION

The new immigrant was a peasant from the farms and villages

Annals of the American Academy of Political and Social Science, Vol. 223 (September, 1942), pp. 100-106.

[1]The late Dr. Antonio Stella points out in his *Some Aspects of Italian Immigration to the United States* that Italians have an average of seventeen years of residence in this country as compared with an average of thirty-four years for the English, fifty-one years for the Irish, and thirty-eight years for the Germans.

of his native country. Industrial or white-collar workers were few in this early migration. The skilled artisan, the merchant, the professional man, and the artist were to come later when the peasant and the laborer had already established the character of Italian life in America. The new immigrant migrated alone, leaving wife and children behind him. He was an unschooled, untrained person in a strange and often hostile environment. He sought employment wherever he could find it, at the most menial tasks and for whatever wages the market offered. It was this immigrant whom the padrone system exploited and who huddled in run-down, underprivileged areas of our cosmopolitan centers, giving rise to our Little Italies.

Today Italians in the United States and their children number more than six million.[2] They are scattered all over the country, though the majority are to be found in the large cities, in the industrial areas of the East and the Middle West, and in agricultural California. New York has the largest quota by far, approximately one-third, while New York City is the largest Italian center not only in America but in the world. Ninety-two per cent of all Italians live in thirteen states of the Union, and there are upward of three thousand Little Italies in all America.

INDUSTRIAL WORKER IN AMERICA

The Italian stands out in the United States pre-eminently as an industrial worker. There are artists, men of affairs, scientists, teachers, and lawyers in every Italian community, many of them leaders in their fields, but the Italian contribution to our national economy remains one of labor. It was to the peasant, turned railroad hand and ditchdigger, that the country looked in the past for the building of railroads, homes, and highways, and to this same sturdy worker it turns today for the hard tasks of our expanding industry. Common labor in the United States is still largely Italian. The Italians outnumber all others in the mining industry, in construction, and in railroad maintenance, where brawn and tireless energy have not been substituted by machinery.

But Italians play an increasingly important part, also, in the skilled trades, where they are more and more in demand, as, for instance, in the clothing industry, where they are fast displacing the Jews and the Germans. They are prominent in the metal trades; in the oil and chemical industries; in the textile, cotton, and shoe factories of New England. They are the most skilled of our silk

---

[2]According to the census of 1930, there were in the United States 4,651,195 Italians. This did not include the children of Italians born in the United States. If these are added, an estimate of 6,000,000 today is rather conservative.

workers, and monopolize the glove industry. In the field of construction, Italians have become the builders of homes and public edifices, the contractors of stone, cement, and sand.

The working standards of Italians have risen immeasurably since the early days of their migration. Italian labor is no longer at the disposal of strike-breakers and scab employers, as was the case a generation or two ago. Italian workers today are an integral part of the organized labor movement. They have unions and leaders of their own, particularly in the needle trades, mining, and textiles, where they set the pace for other workers. This trend toward unionization has eliminated much of the exploitation to which the Italian was subject in the past. In the needle trades it has abolished the sweatshop and the drudgery of homework with their toll of human misery, particularly among the women.

Contribution to Quality Standards

In business and agriculture the Italians have made rapid strides, no less than in the field of industry. Thrifty and enterprising, the Italian is a successful tradesman. To this end he combines his talents for color and specialization which give him a marked advantage over his competitors. Italians are still the leading restaurateurs of the country. They are prominent in the retail food trade. They are our best barbers. As farmers they stand alone in the cultivation of fruit and vegetables, as witness their highly successful farming ventures in Vineland, Fredonia, Canastota, and Valdese.

It is in California that the Italian farmer has realized his greatest prosperity. Introducing into that state the grape and olive production methods learned in Italy, the Italians have created one of the greatest wine industries in the world and are slowly crowding out of the American market the imported oils of Spain, Greece, and Italy. The Italian Swiss Colony and the Di Giorgio Fruit Corporation, both of California, are among the largest agricultural enterprises in America. The Vaccaro brothers in New Orleans are the leading fruit merchants in the South. Amedeo Obici is the peanut king of America.

One of the most remarkable achievements of the Italians in agriculture is their conversion of abandoned New England farms into profitable holdings, supporting large and thrifty families of immigrants and their children. The Italian who comes from the soil is finding his way back to the soil. He has been returning to the farm more and more in late years.

It is inevitable that this spirit of enterprise so characteristic of the Italian immigrant should bear fruit in all fields into which the

Italian has entered. In business and finance such names as Giannini, Paterno, Poli, Sbarbaro, Gerli, and Portfolio bespeak the highest material success, while the names of La Guardia, Patri, Capra, Verdi, and others known to every American, indicate how far Italians have come in the realization of American opportunity.

There are thousands of Italian physicians, lawyers, engineers, teachers, and businessmen in America, most of them the sons of immigrants who invested their savings in education for their children. American schools and colleges show a steadily increasing registration of young men and women of Italian parentage.

CONTRIBUTION TO AMERICAN CULTURE

We need not stress here the contribution of the Italian to the arts of the Nation, his work as painter, sculptor, musician, singer; the many ways in which he enriches and inspires the life of every American. To America's making he has contributed his genius for color and beauty, and a deep sense of the aesthetic. The itinerant musician of early Colonial days, the folk singer of our own day, Constantine Brunidi's frescoes in the Capitol building and Attilio Piccirilli's imposing statues, no less valuable than the music of a Toscanini or a Caruso or a Martinelli, are all part of a precious gift to the development of a more superb American democracy. The sense of buoyancy, the song, the delicate taste of the Italian, whether revealed in the construction of a state capitol or in the simple peasant celebration of a religious festival in Mulberry Street, have all gone to make America a richer, better country than the immigrant found it. It is not surprising that the American Federation of Musicians should be composed mainly of Italians, nor that the Metropolitan Opera should be conspicuously Italian in character.

SOCIAL PROGRESS OF ITALIANS

Italian progress in America is revealed in the social and living conditions of the masses more than in conspicuous examples of individual attainment. There is no attempt here to overlook the disastrous effects of the depression on the thousands of unemployed Italians in the United States, or the severe handicaps imposed on the immigrant worker who has been displaced by machinery, forced on relief, or discriminated against at this time because of his nationality. With all this, the Italian today is far better off economically and socially than he was a generation ago, and certainly, two generations ago.

The Little Italy of the nineties, so tragically described by Jacob

Riis, Loring Brace, and other writers of the time, is a thing of the past. No longer can it be said of the Italian, even the most backward Italian of today, that "his universal vice was his dirtiness; he was dirtier than the Negro, and the Bend was scarce dirtier than the Little Italy of Harlem",[3] nor that the Italians seek out "the cheapest, the oldest and worst tenements" and that "a whole family, or eight or ten men, may sleep in a single room."[4]

This sordid picture of an early immigration has given way to new standards of life which are common today even among Italians of the lowest economic strata. Indeed, the Italian has been moving away from Little Italy, and the congestion and segregation imposed on the early immigrant by social necessity are no longer in evidence, save in spots of extreme poverty. The census of 1930 revealed that 30,000 Italians had moved out of New York's East Harlem and 60,000 out of the lower East Side during the prosperous years of 1920-30. These Italians had moved to the outlying sections of the city, to Westchester and Long Island, to homes of their own, or to neighborhoods offering better housing and recreational facilities. This is true of Philadelphia, Boston, and other large centers of Italian population.

In New York fewer than 40 per cent of the Italians still live in so-called Italian sections, which are not to be confused with the slum areas, but are sections where the population is predominantly if not wholly Italian. The rest are scattered throughout the city, among all elements of the population. There are Park Avenue Italians as there are Italians of the East Side; but in all cases the tenor of life is higher than it has ever been, even if it is only in a remodeled First Avenue tenement.

Assimilating Influences

The reasons for this are obvious. The earning capacity of the Italian family has increased. The educational level of the Italian population has risen appreciably because of the younger American-schooled generation. And the immigrant himself, little though he may realize it, has been profoundly influenced by his American experience. It must be borne in mind that out of every ten Italians, six are born in the United States, while of the remaining four at least one has been here since childhood. Of 6,000,000 Italians in the United States, only 665,000 are not citizens of the country, though many of them

[3] J. A. Riis, *How the Other Half Live; The Children of the Poor* (New York 1892); *Out of Mulberry Street* (New York, 1898).

[4] Robert F. Foerster, *The Italian Emigration of Our Times* (New York, 1919).

have taken steps to be naturalized. The records of the Federal Naturalization Bureau indicate that over the past ten-year period Italians have led all other national minorities in the number of applications for citizenship.

The suspension of immigration and the natural play of assimilating influences in the life of the individual have radically changed the tone and character of Italian life in America. The immigrant is not planning to return to his native land, as was his original intention, but is here to stay. His home and children are here and his roots are in America. In the majority of cases, he has learned to read and write English. It is a fair guess that 80 per cent of the Italians in America are English-speaking, if not to the extent of using English as the home tongue, certainly to the extent of using it at work or in business. Old World habits and customs are vanishing rapidly, and all that the immigrant cherished as his own in his early years in America is either antiquated today and hence superfluous, or undergoing adaptation to present-day American conditions.

In fact, life in the Italian community today is not Italian but Italian-American, and Little Italy, or what remains of it, is not an alien offshoot on American soil, but a merging of two cultures, with the American increasingly predominating over the Italian. It is the newer, native-born generation that is causing this change. Young men and women of Italian parentage, more American than Italian, do not see eye to eye with their elders in many of the things of life. Their background and outlook are different. The older immigrant still thinks in terms of his native land and the social and religious patterns of his youth. The younger men and women march toward America.

DISINTEGRATION OF IMMIGRANT ORGANIZATIONS

This conflict is reflected in the rapid disintegration of all the institutions of the immigrant's own making in America: the foreign-language press, the immigrant's fraternal organization, the religious festival, the mutual aid society. The foreign-language press is losing strength and circulation daily, not alone, as many believe, because of the war, but because the younger generation cannot read it and will make no effort to do so. Such powerful organs as *Il Progresso* of New York and *L'Italia* of San Francisco are losing ground, and in the absence of fresher waves of immigration are bound to disappear from the scene unless, by attuning their language and policies to the exigencies of changing times, they can serve the younger generation in their respective communities.[5]

The order of the Sons of Italy in America, the largest Italian fraternal organization, once boasted a national membership of 300,000 men and women. Now it has dwindled to less than 100,000. Other Italian societies, religious, social, and fraternal, are suffering the same fate, a constantly diminishing membership which spells their doom. The younger men will not join these organizations because they feel, in most cases rightly, that the organizations are not responsive to their needs and aspirations and because of the conviction that these societies tend to draw them away from rather than toward American life. Of late, the Sons of Italy has been endeavoring to meet the younger generation halfway by a reorientation of its program, the adoption of social services, and the substitution of young leaders in place of its original founders. What success it will have remains to be seen.

The church, too, has suffered from its inability to keep pace with the demands of its younger parishioners, who do not share the ways of the old fashioned immigrant priest and the rigid discipline of an Old World interpretation of religion. The church has been aware of this, and there has been much housecleaning in the many Italian parishes throughout the country. Younger and more progressive priests have been placed in charge, many of them Italians themselves. The use of church properties as social centers and the organization of Italian youth groups have gone far in winning back to the fold many of those who seemed lost.

ACCELERATION THROUGH THE WAR

The war, naturally, has precipitated this process of disintegration. It has sharpened the conflict between old and new generations. It has confronted the older Italian with a severe test of loyalty which, be it said in fairness to him, he has met with admirable fortitude. Never dreaming of the possibility of a conflict between the country of his birth and that of his adoption, he has always divided his affection between the two countries. He has loved Italy as his motherland, has been proud of his achievements and traditions, has always retained a fond attachment to the things that he knew and loved in his youth. On the other hand, he has loved and been grateful to America as the land of his children and of his own opportunities in life. That

[5]Of late years many of the Italian-language newspapers have been introducing English into their columns as a means of attracting the younger, English-reading generation.

these two countries should now be at war is something beyond his comprehension, and he has difficulty in making up his mind. He still believes there is a way out, and he looks to America to provide the solution which will spare him the tragedy of having to choose between one love and another.

The war has brought Italians in America into closer identity with their adopted country. They have come to appreciate more than ever the real value of their partnership in American democracy. That some should go to extremes in expressing this appreciation is regrettable. As a result of the war, there is an increasing shying away, on the part of younger men especially, from those things Italian which in the interest of a broader American culture should be preserved in this country. It is reported, for instance, that attendance at Italian dramatic and musical performances has decreased substantially since Italy's declaration of war on the United States; that the number of young men and women studying Italian in high schools and colleges has fallen off. Such admirable institutions as the Leonardo da Vinci Art School and the Italian Welfare League in New York have shut their doors for lack of public support. There are Italians, sad to say, who feel that the only way to display their love of America is by a repudiation of everything Italian, including their names. Fortunately, this is not true of the great majority of Italians and their children, and certainly not of the more intelligent elements.

ITALIAN LOYALTY

There are fears in certain quarters of an Italian fifth column or of a Fascist sentiment which may interfere with America's efforts toward victory. There is no basis for these fears. To be sure, there are Fascists among Italians, but they are an impotent minority, uninclined to give expression to their sentiments and fearful of the Department of Justice which watches them closely.[6]

The overwhelming majority of Italians in America have never been Fascist nor, for that matter, anti-Fascist, but non-Fascist. They have approved of Fascism not as a political ideology or as a form of government, but as something good for Italy. The immigrant

[6]Of 665,000 Italian enemy aliens in the United States, 4,000 have been taken into custody by the FBI, and of these only 112 have been ordered interned by Enemy Alien Hearing Boards throughout the country. The numbers of Germans and Japanese interned are much higher than the number of Italians, notwithstanding that the Italians constitute more than 60 per cent of the total enemy alien population of the country.

has always approved of whatever regime or party happened to be in power in Italy. The Mussolini regime could not be an exception. On the contrary, its much advertised achievements, the praise lavished upon it by the press and leaders of public opinion in this country, added to the propaganda of Fascist spokesmen in every Little Italy in America, tended to strengthen the immigrant's impression that Italy under Il Duce had come into her own.

That there has been a profound change in this belief cannot be doubted. Italians are not only resentful of the predicament into which they have been thrown by Mussolini's unpopular alliance with Germany, but they are certain that an Axis victory can only mean the permanent subjugation of Italy to the Nazi will. They know from their friends and relatives abroad that the heart of the Italian people is not in this war and that Italian reverses in Libya and Greece are an indication of Italy's unwillingness to fight. They look to America to save the people of Italy from the consequences of a German victory, and they are doing everything in their power to aid in the triumph of American arms.

There are in the American armed forces some 400,000 young men of Italian parentage, and thousands of Italian workers are employed in defense industries. Italian committees are actively assisting the Treasury Department, the Red Cross, the USO, and other war causes.[7]

Italian immigrants and their children today are an integral part of American democracy, keenly alive to their duties and responsibilities as citizens of the country. They ask nothing of America but the opportunity to live, work, and serve as all other Americans.

[7]Italians in the New York area led all other nationality groups in the number of voluntary enlistments at the outbreak of the war.

There were 350,000 Italians in the AEF during the last war. The first American soldier killed in that war was an Italian from the District of Columbia.

MARIE J. CONCISTRÈ

ITALIAN EAST HARLEM*

ITALIAN TRADITIONS AND HERITAGES

The Italian immigrant is basically a social being, and his capacity for social interaction is a significant contribution to American life. The cheerful qualities which he possesses are recognized by the majority of students of Italian immigrants.

> The Italian is a boon companion, is always well liked, because he is happy, optimistic, lighthearted, light spirited and has an artistic intellectuality which we Americans of older generations lack, and is always surprising us with his apparently inexhaustible abundance of optimism, enthusiasm and joy of living.[1]

Sociability and the Festa

The Italian immigrant has brought with him numerous social customs which are perpetuated in the homogeneous Italian community which he finds here. One of the most popular customs is the *festa*— not *fiesta*, which is decidedly Spanish. The festa is connected with the celebration of Holy Days or Saints' Days. Every town in every province of Italy has its patron Saint. The same towns people tend to organize their patron Saint society here. The most popular festa in Harlem is the feast of the Madonna of Mount Carmel, *La Madonna del Carmine*, on July 16th. Ever since the writer can remember, this has been the biggest day of the year in the Little Italy of Harlem. The children look forward to the holiday because of the good things to eat, and of course, it always means a pretty new dress or a new suit. The religious observance is quite obscured by the real holiday spirit prevailing. Flags, American and Italian, wave gaily from windows,

---

A Study of a Decade in the Life and Education of the Adult Immigrant Community in East Harlem, New York City (Unpublished Ph.D. thesis, New York University, 1943), pp. 21-43; 270-312.

[1]Frederick P. Keppel, Columbia University, in a conversation with Dr. John H. Mariano, in January 1928.

fire escapes, store windows, pushcarts, fruit stands; pushcarts fairly creak with the weight of *torrone* (Italian taffy filled with hazelnuts); shelled nuts strung up and hanging like beads over the decorated booth-like arrangements are part of the great occasion. Watermelon, cut up into huge slices can be seen all along First avenue. The cafes are decorated with fancy almond paste (colorful fruits), *dolci* or pastry of all kinds and colors—the Sicilians' and Neapolitans' best! Sugar animals of many tints and hues are displayed in store windows, where rest the large prettily decorated Italian *torta* (something like a layer cake, only much larger and much richer).

At a certain time in the morning, usually around 10 o'clock, the parade passes in review. A band heads the parade, which is then followed by the members of the society of Monte Carmelo. The image of the Madonna is carried by four men. Immediately following the Madonna come the Verginelle (the little virgins), young girls all dressed in white wearing fine white veils, symbolic of the Madonna's virginity. Following there is a banner with an elaborately embroidered likeness of the Madonna. On this banner are pinned all the dollars which the faithful contribute. At the end of the parade march all those who claim that the Madonna has healed them of some malady or performed some other miracle for their benefit, many of whom walk barefoot through the streets of Harlem carrying wax images of the parts afflicted to be presented at the church, and to be melted down as candles. One curious characteristic of these festas is the fact that the bands have never been known to play ecclesiastical music, such as hymns or chants or any of the beautiful music of the Catholic church. Instead, popular gay tunes characterize the Saints' Day parade.

In the evening the band which has been hired for the parade always gives a concert. The musicians sit on a platform decorated with colored lights and flags. This is usually located near the shrine and sometimes is itself a part of the shrine. The shrine is always a glittering, showy affair, which resembles an altar with a niche in the background. In the niche is placed a statue or picture of the Saint or Madonna, as the case may be. The band plays popular tunes, selections from operas, patriotic marches, and songs. At midnight, if permitted, there are fire-works. Before the trees and grass were planted in Jefferson Park, this place was very convenient for the frequent fire-works displays, and those Harlemites counted themselves fortunate who could have a box seat at these shows. The box seats were the fire-escapes on First avenue.

The streets immediately surrounding the center of these festivities, which are usually near the church or not far from it, are well lighted with glittering colored glass lamps—nowadays, with electric bulbs. The pomp, the lights, and the music help to create a truly festive spirit.

This particular holiday is also a day of happy family and friendly reunions, and general merry making. It is estimated that from thirty to forty thousand people come from the city and near-by boroughs, and some from even greater distances, to celebrate this great festal day. The shop keepers and peddlars also rejoice, since for them it is the biggest day of the year, financially speaking. Rain alone can mar the proceedings, but this has happened so rarely that many of the faithful believe that the usual good weather attending this feast day is brought about through divine intervention.

The Presepio and Saints' Days

Another distinctly Italian religious custom is the building of the famous Presepio at Christmas time. This consists of a miniature Bethlehem, and is built right in the home, usually in a corner of the living room on a table of some kind. With the materials available, the hills, the pastures, the star, the shepherds and the stable with Joseph, Mary and the Christ Child are reproduced. The effect is often very beautiful. The Italian Catholic churches always display on Christmas Eve, and for several days thereafter, a very realistic presepio. The American-born children, however, prefer their Christmas trees.

Many Saints' Days are celebrated at various times during the year, and there is a Saint for every day. If there is a Joseph in the family, St. Joseph's Day is celebrated very much in the same way as the American celebrates personal birthdays. Particular food seems to be intrinsically connected with certain holidays. On St. Joseph's Day *le zeppole di San Giuseppe* are eaten. These are marble-shaped doughnuts sprinkled with honey and infinitesimal seed-shaped confetti. On St. Lucy's Day egg noddles with macaroni are served, and so it is with many Italian holidays. Food plays a very important part of the celebrations.

Weddings and Christenings

Besides the holidays the Italians make a great celebration of their weddings. Even when they cannot afford it, they must hire a "hall," have music, dancing, expensive *dolci* (pastry), cordials, wines, and so on. The bride must have a perfect outfit; there must be an expensive church wedding, a High Mass, and all the attendent ceremony. These are occasions for great rejoicing. Those attending the wedding also vie with each other as to who will offer the most expensive gift. This eleborate display is impelled by a sentiment of pride and the desire for personal prestige. The Italians have a good name for this urge, *far figura* (make a good showing). Christening celebrations are often held in halls but more often in the homes. The gifts in this case are given to the baby. The godmother as a rule buys the whole baptismal outfit for the child who is to be christened, and ever after the two families involved address each other as *comare* and *compare*, meaning godfather and godmother. The northern Italian as a rule is not as ceremonious as the southerner; his celebrations are quieter and far more simple.

Funerals

Italian funerals like the weddings are elaborate. In the home no matter how straightened the circumstances there must be nothing lacking in the funeral set-up. The walls are usually covered with black or grey damask upon which are embroidered shining crosses of silver or gold, or it may be pictures of saints and other symbolic decorations. Stands with rows of candles remain lighted throughout the duration of the wake. The casket must be as beautiful as possible. The expense element does not bear weight with the majority of Italians at such a time. When friends and relatives arrive at the wake, their first duty is to kneel before the casket and say a prayer; after that they greet the members of the bereaved family. The closest friends and relatives arrange to stay throughout the wake. Preparation for the burial usually includes a High Mass at the church, since the majority of Italians are Roman Catholics. The funeral cortege usually includes many flowers (quantity depending upon the number of friends and relatives), a band playing sad and solemn music, and many automobiles with friends and relatives. Not so many years ago it was carriages, and the hearse was sometimes drawn by four horses instead of two. In the last decade the band is becoming less common in the funeral cortege.

The poorer families often go into debt in order to have everything as beautiful and as elaborate as possible. Underlying these funeral customs is the sentiment that it is the last thing that can be done for those who pass on and it must measure up to the memory of the dead.

Visiting and Serenading

Visiting is a form of leisure activity very popular among the Italians Sociability abounds in the tenements of all Little Italies as well as in East Harlem. In sickness, in trouble, as well as in normal times, the social spirit is paramount among these people. They share their sorrows as well as their joys. No one is quicker in lending a hand than the Italian, and he gives generously even when he has very little to give.

A custom which is prevalent in Southern Italy and which has also found a place in the Italian neighborhood is the serenade. A young man who loves a girl may serenade, not from the street as he would do in the "old country" but in the hallway. The girl who is serenaded is neither heard nor seen, but the young man in question knows that she knows he is there, and that is sufficient.

The Family as a Social Unit

Social interaction among the Italian immigrants is within families. For the Italian girl to go to a dance hall is a very rare occurrence. There is much dancing but it is done within family groups. Since Italian societies, lodges, and clubs have launched social programs, recreational activities are losing their domestic tone. More families are enjoying themselves outside of the home, but still it is the "family" that goes as a group.[2]

The whole life of the Italian centers within the family, and he guards it jealously. It is when forces are at work which tend to modify or threaten the family unity that his habitual cheerfulness withers within him. Add to unemployment, disease, and poverty, the perplexities which the second generation often cause their parents, and the Italian who may be so light-hearted and gay is also capable of plunging into the deepest despair. Keppel says, "There is an innate effervescent spontaneity flowing as much perhaps from the 'high variability' inherent in the fundamental capacities of the race as from anything else."[3] This "variability" is shown in the sudden temperamental changes which frequently occur among Italians and their descendants. Any teacher of Italian boys or girls has observed the extreme moods which are often displayed within a single class session.

It is often what the Italian immigrant finds in America which modifies his habitual cheerfulness. For instance, in Italy all classes of people "take time to live." One of the Americanisms that greatly

[2]In a meeting of the Y. W. C. A. International Center at 347 East 17th street, a girls' club worker from East Harlem asked the writer what she could do to get the girls out to their dances when the boys were invited. She claimed that the parents do not allow their girls to attend. The writer, who has been through the mill herself, offered the following suggestion. "Why not invite the parents or the mothers of these girls to your dances, and let them see for themselves that their girls are in good company and well chaperoned; approximate more nearly the family group situation and perhaps in time the girls may be permitted to attend your dances just as they do your other performances."

[3]Frederick P. Keppel, "The Italian at Columbia," *The Italian Intercollegiate,* Volume I, p. 8.

irritates the more intelligent and utterly bewilders the more ignorant of the race is the rate of speed which characterizes the activities of the American populace. In Italy the peasant works from sunrise to sunset, but witness the proverbial singing of the *contadini* on their way home at evenfall. There was no "boss" to shout "hurry up." One of the first expressions the immigrant learns in America is—hurry up. Again the Italian is used to courtesy, another habitual quality; here unfortunately he often meets with a brusqueness that has a decidedly chilling effect.

The adjustments which many of these immigrants are called upon to make have very frequently disastrous results. What is called an Italian community becomes unfortunately neither Italian nor American. The average second generation youth gets a smattering of both, which results in a conglomeration of distorted ideas of both cultures. The "product" is often a selfish individual who having absorbed the worst qualities of both groups has respect for neither. These children and youth fall a ready prey to gangster life and form the major element among the juvenile delinquents and youthful offenders of East Harlem.

There is, however, a hopeful aspect of the whole picture which is a direct antithesis to the one above; that is, the youth of Italian extraction who have absorbed the best that both American and Italian cultures have to offer. In this class are those who have become, and others who are in the process of becoming, leaders of the community. They are creating institutions which will act as constructive forces of American society. They sincerely seek to unite the qualities which are distinctly Italian contributions with the ideals which have come to be recognized as purely American. These "leaders" are themselves an exemplary product of the blending of the best in both cultures.

LANGUAGE DIFFICULTIES
OF IMMIGRANT GROUPS

When immigrants arrive in this country, one of the first difficulties they encounter is their inability to understand or speak the English language. Those immigrants, however, who settle in homogeneous communities where their mother tongue is spoken have no immediate problem. The Italian immigrant in any Little Italy may shop contentedly without the use of one English word. For those who must go outside the community to work the case is different, and a knowledge of English becomes a necessity. Often, however, the need for English depends on the nature of the work in which they engage. For instance, in 1905 a group of Messinesi (Sicilian) cabinet makers were working in the piano factories of Jacob Doll and Company located at 113th street—"over the bridge," the Harlemites used to call it. The foreman himself was a Sicilian. The workers all lived in upper East Harlem and formed a homogeneous group.

In the building line the same thing has happened. Groups of Italian workers were employed on different jobs. When the contractor was not an Italian, the foreman usually was, and he acted as spokesman for the group. In the last twenty-five or thirty years the builders with whom the Italian immigrant has come in contact have been Italians. Those workers, the ornamental plasterers and stone cutters, for instance, who were brought into frequent contact with native Americans, acquired a fair working knowledge of English within a comparatively short time. Wherever Italian tailors or dressmakers work together the same experience is repeated. In a machine shop downtown on Grand street, where 90 per cent of the workers were Italians from East Harlem, very few could speak English. They did not need it, they said.

The Italian community institutions of a decade or two ago helped to keep the Italian immigrant segregated and sufficient unto himself. The Italian churches, the Italian mutual benefit societies, the Italian newspaper, the Italian theatre and movie—every phase of community life which confronted him was carried on in his own language. What need, then, to learn English? To a lesser extent the same conditions exist today.

Seemingly, many Italian emigrants would feel no need for English, were it not for the problems growing out of the Americanization of growing children. Needless to say, the problems are greater in the home of non-English speaking parents. Notes from teachers require a knowledge of English, as do written requests to visit the school. While pupils may act as interpreters, varied indeed may be the interpretations.[4] This situation frequently leads to lying and deceit on the part of children and to the beginning of a rift between parents and children which may grow wider and wider, and end finally in disharmony or broken homes. Yet the majority of Italian parents do not seem to realize the seriousness of their position. While they live immersed in old-world customs and traditions, their children, through schooling and other contacts and associations, are acquiring a language and customs very unlike their own. Indeed, many parents are so far from seeing the need for acquiring English that when

[4]One child told her mother that "D" was considered a very fine mark, until the teacher sent for the mother and revealed the truth.

approached concerning it their reply is invariably that they do not need to know it, since their children who study the language may act as interpreters when necessary.

The more intelligent immigrant sees the advantage of learning the language of America as soon as he lands here, and tries in every way to gain this knowledge. But these are on the whole the Italian immigrants who become naturalized, who enter into American life naturally and who, accordingly, offer no problem of assimilation.

POLITICAL ASPECTS

In order to form an adequate conception of the political situation in such a community as East Harlem, it is necessary to know something of the favorable and unfavorable influences which affect immigrants. To begin with, the attitude of the native American in general has been hostile, especially in the manifestation of his superiority. This attitude as reported in the local foreign language press is usually distorted. The immigrants' experiences with employers and fellow-workers whose attitudes are hostile, rude and very often cruel, have a pronounced effect upon them. What they see and hear in their adopted country either greatly retards or greatly accelerates their political or civic sense. Consider the attitudes which the foreigner brings with him. The Italian immigrant, for instance, had no voice in the body politic in his own country, and possessed no political consciousness when he arrived here. (This, of course, does not apply to the Italian of today nor to the educated Italian of yesterday.) The bulk of Italian immigrants who arrived here up to 1914 were not, generally speaking, politically conscious.

The Italian immigrant as a rule first comes in contact with the political aspect of American life when the naturalization question looms up, which it usually does through union affiliations. He must usually understand English in order to understand what is going on, unless as is the case with the unions in the building line, tailors, dressmakers, and others, Italian branches are formed. Even when Italian is the official language spoken, the rules and regulations are laws of American labor organizations and as such the expression of an American institution. The trouble, however, from the point of view of the immigrant, has been that political bosses have monopolized many of these local unions, which has resulted in sectional blocs. In this way immigrants have been influenced and often compelled, through local organizations, to vote in city and state elections according to the will of the bosses, not knowing what they were voting for. Having come in contact with the corruption which exists in this city's politics, many have lost interest, and for many years a laissez-faire attitude has prevailed in all the Little Italies. Of late, however, there has been an awakening and widespread interest in politics, especially in Harlem's Little Italy. This is due to the intelligent leadership which has been active for the last decade and which has at last succeeded in creating public opinion. Many political clubs have sprung up and a majority of citizens both men and women are taking an active interest in civic affairs. The political picture of East Harlem in 1942 contrasts very favorably with that of 1930, and the situation is being watched with a great deal of interest by leading citizens of East Harlem.

ECONOMIC STATUS AS REFLECTED
IN HOUSING CONDITIONS

It is difficult to dissociate housing conditions from the economic status of the community. The East Harlem community as a whole has been characterized as a "slum." Generally, this means that the houses or tenements are old, dilapidated, dark, unclean, and overcrowded. Most of the people live in unsanitary, unhealthful and wretched conditions.

It used to be accepted generally, and still is by many, that the slums of our great cities are a product of the newer immigration. It would seem to be evident, however, that these newer immigrants were compelled by circumstances to settle in areas which were already in a dilapidated condition. Having no resources when they arrived, there was no alternative but to accept conditions as they found them. How, then, can one account for the wretched condition of the newer buildings which went up in East Harlem around 1900. Some reasons will be submitted later in this chapter. The writer has had opportunity to visit many of the homes in Harlem and remembers many changes which have taken place.

The most congested spot in Harlem was the one where Jefferson Park now stands. The writer's father used to describe it thus:

> There were many three-story wooden structures huddled together as it were. The old fashioned flats had been divided and subdivided into one room, two room, and three room apartments. The halls were dark, as were the rooms, only one room in the front and rear apartment having some light. There were no closets of any kind, but rough shelves had been put up for dishes and things. Sinks were in the halls and all the families shared them.

Toilets were out in the back yards. There were more old
and run down houses, facing these back yards. Hallways
were dark at night, and people used candles when going
up and down the stairs. Large families lived in two rooms.
One family which consisted of father, mother, and ten
children lived in two rooms, yet the home was immaculate; no one knew how it was done. There were plenty of
beer saloons and murders were not uncommon. The congested area had become such a menace to health and morals that a park was proposed. We were all mighty glad to
see all those "shacks" go down.

The houses in the vicinity of Jefferson Park were also old but in
better condition. On the whole all housing was, and much of it still
is, of the old-law flat type. Around 1892, however, a great many
houses began to go up in the empty lots. All the brick buildings on
113th Street between First and Second avenues were built about that
time. In 1898 there were still two empty lots at 107th and 108th
streets between First and Second avenues.

The houses that were built about this time were a great improvement over the older type. They had many more conveniences, including sinks, clothes closets, dish closets, stoves, washtubs in each flat,
and more light in all the rooms. The families who could afford to immediately moved into the new apartments. At 112th street whole
rows of buildings extending from First to Second Avenues went up
in 1900. And as soon as these new houses were built they were
promptly occupied. Enough houses could not be built between 1895
and 1905, and when all the lots were gone and there was no more
room, the Italian immigrants began to crowd out the Jews below
105th Street and the Irish on Second Avenue. The buildings on
Second Avenue were, and still are, of the old-law type. Now Second
Avenue in East Harlem is peopled by Italians. Only thirty years ago
it was a solid Irish section.

MOBILITY OUTWARD AND ITS SOCIAL EFFECTS

The buildings which were old and passable forty years ago are now
scarcely fit for human habitation. Yet this is where thousands of
children even today are getting their start in life. During the years between 1890 and 1910 the population of East Harlem's Little Italy
grew by leaps and bounds. In the meantime the second generation or
the American-born children of the first immigrant arrivals became of
age. With the prospect of marriage came also the desire to better their

condition. And so one witnesses the exit to the Bronx. The tendency of the Italians of Lower Manhattan is to move to the Boroughs of Queens, Brooklyn, Richmond, and New Jersey, while the majority of East Harlem Italians are inclined to move northward. Of the one hundred families interviewed in connection with this study in 1934 at least twenty-five have now moved out of Manhattan and five are known to own homes in the Borough of Queens.

The strong bonds which tend to keep the Italian immigrant in the Italian community do not hold for his American-born offspring. Especially is this true of the progressive second generation youth. They wish to identify themselves more and more with older Americans and consequently cling to the idea of getting out of the Little Italy as soon as finances permit. The desire of immigrant parents, however, to remain in the environment which offers them security and the desire on the part of their children to move out of the congested area is often the source of family conflict. This conflict usually occurs when parents have not kept pace with the social development of their children. The ambition of almost every Italian immigrant is to own a home. The frugal living and saving of many years in America has made possible the fulfillment of this ambition for many, and thousands of home owners in Greater New York, and especially in the Westchester section, are East Harlemites. Better transportation facilities have greatly accelerated Italian mobility, not only in East Harlem but in many other sections of Manhattan, facilitating movement to surrounding suburbs and boroughs.

A circumstance that lent great impetus to the movement northward was the fact that Italian contractors and their respective working men, such as stone masons, bricklayers, plasterers, carpenters, painters, plumbers, and laboreres, were putting up the apartment houses which went up in great numbers during the building boom of 1900 to 1910. Most of the apartment houses in the eastern portion of Fordham in the Bronx were built at this time. It was in the main these Italian workers who saw fit to move their families to these more desirable apartments and neighborhoods. And again, many thinking parents see the dangers of rearing their children in questionable environments and make it a point to move out of the congested sections as soon as they are able to afford the change.

Obviously those Italians who move out of the Little Italies are more or less of the progressive type. Consequently the moving out of a large number of Italians who possess the potentialities for leadership has not alleviated, but has rather aggravated, living conditions in Harlem's most congested districts. A local clergyman said to the writer, who he believed to belong to the group which he attacked,

"You people who might have contributed much to the life of this community moved out as soon as you acquired your education and position in life. We needed you right here to guide and lead our younger groups and to inspire the older groups with your courage and sympathy.[5]

The foregoing discussion presupposes different types of immigrants, and, indeed, the writer has often observed the effect caused by different inhabitants on buildings and streets which indicates, if it does not prove, that the type of the inhabitant has much to do with his dwelling and surroundings. We may assume that the immigrant who moves to the already run down neighborhood has no chance and so succumbs to the drab environment. But how does this affect the present character of the new buildings which went up in the nineties? The writer's family lived in 1896 at 322 East 107th street. The buildings (a whole row of them) were new. The families were all meticulously clean. The rent ranged from seven to nine dollars a month. The wages of workers in the building averaged about $2.50 a day. On the whole these houses were occupied by artisans and their families. With several empty lots across the street, and several trees on the block, 107th street was a fairly decent place to live. Only ten years later, however, when most of those families had moved out, the block was not recognizable; it had become a "street scene" of the slum. What had happened? The better class families had moved out when they felt the impact of the less privileged type of immigrant. Does this not seem to be a repetition of the older type of immigrant giving way to the newer type regardless of national origins? That this is so seems indicated by the fact that some of the old stone and brick dwellings, also old forty years ago, are still, apparently, in good condition. In this connection, mention may be made of the dwellings on 116th street between First and Second avenues, which used to be called "the doctor's street" because most of Harlem's physicians lived there. Their present good condition would appear to support the idea that the type of immigrant has much to do with the deterioration or maintenance of housing conditions.

The majority of Italian immigrants who came to the United States

[5]Remark made by the Reverend Amedeo Riggio, Jefferson Park Methodist Episcopal Church, 1932.

at the peak of the immigrant tide were from rural parts of Southern Italy. The Northern immigrant is by far in the minority, at least in New York City. In Cleveland, there is a large colony of Waldensians, Italians from the Alpine Valley, but this is unusual.

In Italy the peasants largely lived in the open air. Their houses had large rooms with stone floors which required no scrubbing. The washing of clothes was done at nearby creeks, streams, or even rivers. There were no stoves which required care. When these peasant immigrants arrived here, they naturally settled near their friends and relatives, who lived for the most part in already crowded areas. These sunshine-loving people were forced to live in more or less dark rooms; small ill-smelling wash-tubs replaced their outdoor creeks; pulley lines, their fresh green grass; wooden floors which require scrubbing, their hard stone floors. House-keeping here required the use of tools of which they had no knowledge. The writer has come in contact with many immigrant women who had never seen a scrubbing brush. When to these new experiences is added the strangeness of the new country, strange language, and the evils which necessarily accompany congestion, poverty, and the upbringing of American-born children, the wonder is that they adjust at all.

It is often said that the Italian immigrant has no desire to leave the congested district, that he is clannish and prefers to segregate himself from American influences. There is another side to the story, however, which, so far as the writer knows, is very rarely stated.

The number of Italians and Americans of Italian parentage who have been denied the rental of an apartment in non-Italian communities because they were considered foreigners is legion.[6] This has been a common occurrence for the last forty years among Italians, or American-born children of Italian parentage.

These facts would seem to indicate that the slums, as previously defined, are not a product of immigrants as such; rather they are, as in East Harlem, a direct outcome of social and economic forces over which the immigrant, for the time being at least, had no control.

---

[6]In this connection the writer will never forget the overwhelming rebellious reactions which followed a refusal of this kind when, being engaged in social work in Kips Bay district of this city and wishing to live as near her field of interest as possible, she tried to rent an apartment at 67th street and First avenue. She was met with a prompt refusal because the superintendent did not like her surname. In this case the applicant went to the owners of the building and finally obtained the apartment she wanted.

Italian Religious Institutions
in the East Harlem Area

Italian religious institutions in East Harlem, both Roman Catholic and Protestant, will be considered in this chapter, and an attempt will be made to ascertain the significance, if any, of their activities as a factor in adult education, as defined in this study.

There are many churches in East Harlem, but only those whose communicants are chiefly or wholly Italian, or of Italian descent, will be described. The Roman Catholic churches are (1) Church of Our Lady of Mount Carmel, (2) St. Lucy's Roman Catholic Church, and (3) St. Ann's Roman Catholic Church. The Protestant churches are (1) Jefferson Park Methodist Episcopal Church, and (2) Church of the Ascension (Presbyterian).

Italian Roman Catholic Churches in East Harlem

Since the majority of the people of Italy are members of the Roman Catholic church, it was natural that as soon as a community of Italian immigrants in the United States became large enough and prosperous enough to support a church of their own, a church was built. The development of the Roman Catholic church in the United States has paralleled the growth of Italian immigration. As Italians emigrated to the United States in ever increasing numbers in the late eighties, the problem for the Roman Catholic church grew in proportion. Since the greater number of Italians settled in the East, and especially in the metropolitan area of New York City, the problem was by far the most acute in that section.

In New York City the first Roman Catholic church to be fully supported by the Italians themselves was that of La Beata Vergine di Pompei, situated in the then thickest Italian-populated center, Bleeker and Carmine streets. It was founded by the Scalabrini Fathers, a religious order named after its founder, Monsignor Giovanni Battista Scalabrini.[7] In 1925 this church was rebuilt at a cost of $1,075,000.

In so far as has been possible, a Roman Catholic church has followed every Italian settlement in the United States.

[7] Perhaps Monsignor Giovanni Battista Scalabrini had more to do with the development of the Roman Catholic church in the Italian communities of New York City than any other one person. His activities began in Italy where, through lectures, the press, and publications, he succeeded in awakening wide missionary interest. In 1888 he founded a missionary school in Piacenza, Italy, for the training of young volunteer workers. Numerous Italian priests answered the call and the first workers arrived in America in 1888. Through their activities many churches were founded in the East Atlantic States.

CHURCH OF OUR LADY OF MOUNT CARMEL

As early as 1878 a group of Italian immigrants from Polla, province of Salerno (near Naples), settled in East Harlem, and began to organize what was to develop into the first Italian religious mutual aid society in New York City. The patron saint of Polla was the Madonna of Mount Carmel and the group called their organization "Congregazione della Madonna di Monte Carmelo." The first feast or celebration in honor of the patron saint was held in 1881. Since there was no church to house the statue of the Madonna, a temporary shrine was built in the back yard of one of the tenements in East Harlem and there the annual celebration took place. Three years later a priest who came from Rome "assumed charge of the rather spontaneous congregation. Feeling that it was a sacrilege to house the statue in a squalid tenement, he proceeded to raise funds for a church. The present structure . . . became the center of the festival of Our Lady of Mount Carmel, which takes place annually on July 16th.[8] Because of the unusual history of the founding of this church and the popularity and religious significances of the feast day for the Italians of New York City, Pope Leo XIII as one of the last acts of his life elevated the church to the dignity of a sanctuary.[9]

The Church of Our Lady of Mount Carmel, located at 447 East 115th street, is a large structure of gray Portland stone and cost over $200,000. The seating capacity is 2,000. It was completed in 1885, and shortly after a rectory was built which houses the staff of five priests. East of the church is a settlement house and a parochial school. The entrance to the school is on 116th street.

Membership

Although when the church was built, and for many years after, the congregation consisted of both American and Italian members, as more Italians came into the neighborhood, the American congregation was entirely displaced by Italians. For about twenty years the Italian services were held in the lower part of the church. The services for all children, however, were held in the upper or main part of the church.

[8]*The Italians of New York.* A Federal Writers' Project, p. 78.
[9]*Loc. cit.*, p. 78

An old resident of East Harlem says the following concerning the early Italian services:

> In 1886 the Italians in East Harlem lived within a radius of about a quarter of a mile. There was one church to go to and that was what we used to call the "American Church" at East 115th street. In those days we Italians were allowed to worship only in the basement part of the church, a fact which was not altogether to our liking. But as the neighborhood became more and more Italian and all the old residents moved out the church passed entirely into Italian hands. Now Our Lady of Mount Carmel Church is our very own.

By 1930 the membership of the parish was entirely Italian. It was in 1910 that the membership reached its highest peak when it numbered 6,800. Since that time there has been a steady decline, the reason for which has been described as follows:

> As soon as the people have money enough they move to the Bronx, to Queens, to Long Island. This leaves only the poorer people in the community which accounts for the fact that the parish has so little money to work with. There have been no changes in the character of the membership regarding economic status, occupation, or nationality.
>
> The Sunday School numbers seven hundred, about one-fourth are boys, and three-fourths, girls. The status of membership since 1910 is as follows:
>
> 1910 . . . 900
> 1915 . . . 850
> 1920 . . . 800
> 1925 . . . 750
> 1930 . . . 700
>
> The reasons given for this declining membership were the same as for that of the church; namely, that many families have moved out of the district.[10]

The decline in church membership continues, according to the priest interviewed in 1941. The activities are the same, but they are even less well attended than in 1930 because of the continued exodus of Italian communicants from the neighborhood.

[10]May Case Marsh, *The Life and Work of the Churches in an Interstitial Area*, Ph.D. thesis, New York University, 1932, p. 423 (unpublished mss.).

Activities

The social activities of the Church of Our Lady of Mount Carmel include the sponsorship of church societies, a social settlement, a parochial school, and, in 1932, a certain amount of welfare work.

Among the most important of the church societies are the following:

Junior Holy Name Society, for boys and young men from sixteen to twenty-one. Enrollment 80.

Senior Holy Name Society, for men. Enrollment 100.

Children of Mary, for girls. Enrollment 220.

The Society of Mount Carmel Congregation, for men and women. Enrollment 80.[11]

The Holy Name Society, the origin of which dates back to 1274, is a religious organization for boys and men. The aims of the Society are:

1. To honor the Name of God and of Jesus Christ by the example of a sensible religious life.
2. To spread and increase love for the sacred Name of Jesus.
3. To suppress blasphemy, profane and indecent language.
4. To prevent false oaths in and out of our courts.
5. To impart to Christian men courage in the profession of their faith.

Its duties are:

1. To abstain from every form of profane and unbecoming speech.
2. To safeguard the proper observance of Sundays and Holy Days of Obligation.
3. To receive Holy Communion with members of the Sosiety on the second Sunday of each month, or as often as the spiritual director of their own parish determines.
4. To cooperate generously under the direction of the spiritual director in every movement for the good of religion and in the parish where the Society is established.[12]

[11]Marsh, *op. cit.,* p. 423.

[12]From leaflet published by National Headquarters of the Holy Name Society, 884. Lexington Avenue, New York City. See also, Marsh, *loc. cit.,* p. 424.

In America the Holy Name Society is a national organization, so that the organizations of the local Roman Catholic church become branches of the larger organizations.

The Junior Holy Name Society of Mount Carmel holds two general meetings each month in the parish house. Once a month a talk is given by the spiritual director. Dues are twenty-five cents a month and are used for club expenses. The main purpose of the Society is to encourage boys and young men to live an upright and religious life. One of the rules of the organization is that all members must partake of Holy Communion once a month, and members who do not adhere to this rule are dropped automatically.

Social activities of the Junior Holy Name Society include one big dance a year and frequent social affairs in their meeting rooms. There are no specific drives for membership. Interested members usually invite their friends to join. The membership in 1942 remains about the same as in 1932. Most of the boys are second and third generation Italians.

The Mount Carmel Congregation was the original Italian mutual aid society. One of the most significant changes in the church's activities is the dying out of this organization in the latter 1930's. The church carries on the famous Annual Feast Day Celebration which was instituted by the Society. The celebration now lasts three days, July 14, 15, and 16, and there are special activities and parades for each day. The money collected on this occasion goes toward the support of the church.

Mount Carmel Settlement. The chief activity of the Settlement is a kindergarten which is under the charge of two Sisters. About one hundred children, ranging in age from two to five, are left here by working mothers, who pay twenty-five cents a week. The first and second floors of the house are used for this purpose. After school, from 3:30 to 5:30 P. M. classes in sewing and embroidery are held. From fifty to sixty girls, ages ten to fifteen years, attend these classes.[13]

The Parochial School of Mount Carmel was started in 1898. Classes are conducted in both Italian and English. It was in 1932 a 1A-6A grade school; but it has since become a 1A-8A grade school. Besides the regular subjects taught, the curriculum includes catechism and preparation for confirmation. The total enrollment in 1930 was 672 pupils, but according to the attending priest who was interviewed in 1941, the attendance has declined since 1932 from over seven hundred pupils to six hundred.

[13]Marsh, *op. cit.*, p. 426.

Other Church Organizations. According to the priest interviewed by May Case Marsh in 1931, the church is confronted with two great problems. The community does not answer the financial needs of the church, and if it were not for the offerings made at the shrine of Our Lady of Mount Carmel during the year, and especially at the annual celebration, the work of the church could not go on. And the second problem of the church in this neighborhood, which grows largely out of the first, is that of taking care of the American-born youth of Italian parents. "They must have religious instruction, for this will prevent crime. They must be taught respect for God and for parents, and to do no harm to anything or anybody."[14]

An interview in 1933 brought forth the following comments on church organizations:

> We have many church societies. However, most of them have to do only with religion. There is the Sacred Heart Society for older women. It is of a strictly religious nature. The Holy Rosary Society is a society for women of all ages but it too is purely religious. Likewise the societies of the Assumption and for the Souls of Purgatory are wholly religious. The Holy Name Society has two divisions. One is for the older men or senior members. The Junior Division is composed of young men. Not only are the interests of this group religious, but social as well. They play baseball and basketball. They're interested in athletics of all kinds. Frequently they hold dances in the Mount Carmel Hall. The young women belong to the Children of Mary Sodality. They have musicals, shows, and now and then a dance, as well as being interested in religion. The Mount Carmel Society (Congregation) is incorporated. Both men and women belong to it. It, too, is religious, however, it takes care as far as it is possible to supply their needs. At the Mount Carmel Hall, the young people of the Society hold dances, take part in athletics, and there is also a billiard room for those who wish to play.[15]

The priest further declared that the older people in general seemed to be more interested in their organizations, and that the women were more interested in the purely religious organizations than the men.

Welfare Work. A certain amount of welfare work was being carried on by the church in 1932. A volunteer worker, handled family

[14]Marsh, *op. cit.*, p. 339. From an interview with Father Mario Pascolido, in 1931.

[15]Interview by Rose Bergen, WPA worker, with Father Mario Pascolido, April 1933.

casework, in which she cooperated with the Association for Improving the Conditions of the Poor, the Charity Organization Society, the Catholic Charities, the Family Court, the Children's Court, and others. This volunteer worker, who was American born, was interviewed by May Case Marsh in 1931. The following is a quotation from that interview:

> The church is taking care of about eighty families a week. When she reports an especially needy case to the Father, he says, "I would gladly give them five dollars a week if I had it, but I haven't." The church collections are very poor. She told of some old ladies who stay all day long in the church because it is warm there. Father asked her to investigate these families and she found they had no fire and no food.
>
> When asked what she thought was the contribution of the church to the community, her reply was, "The church means a lot to the people. The priests respond to the call for service. The church gives money if it is needed." The Social worker investigates cases and refers them to the church and to other agencies. She keeps record cards for her own use. She is a free lance, and is not responsible to anyone. She also works at St. Lucy's Church, on Tuesdays and Thursdays.[16]

It will be noted from the above quotation that the welfare work of this church was of an informal kind. In 1942 the church no longer attempted case-work, but families in need were usually referred to the Catholic Charities organization.

Work with Adults, Other Than Religious Education. While no formal adult education or Americanization work is offered at Mount Carmel Church, an attempt is made to help members to obtain citizenship, and to help them to adjust to American ways.

> We don't attempt to teach them. However, when someone comes with a problem that troubles him, we never send him away without trying to help him. Sometimes we help them get their citizenship papers. They are constantly coming into conflict of some kind. The customs and ways are so different for them in America. We try to explain matters to them.

In an interview held in 1941, the priest interviewed had the following to say concerning adult education activities. "We refer our members to the evening public schools and the WPA centers for training in English and citizenship. We cannot afford to carry on other than our religious and, to some extent, our social activities. Indeed, it has been a hard struggle to maintain the existing activities."

[16]Marsh, *op. cit.*, pp. 426-427.

ST. LUCY'S ROMAN CATHOLIC CHURCH

As Italian immigration increased and crowded into Harlem's Little Italy, it soon became evident that Mount Carmel Church could not hold or take care of the increasing number of Roman Catholics. St. Lucy's which was founded in 1914, at the apex of the immigration tide, filled this immediate need, although a few years later even this second church was found to be insufficient.

St. Lucy's Church is located at 334-342 East 104th street. To the east of the church is the rectory, a four-story building which is connected with the church by an areaway on the second floor. The church was redecorated in 1925, and in 1928 a new heating system was installed. The property in 1931 was valued at $200,000.

The chief support of the church comes from contributions, but the people are poor and not able to give much. "The program of the parish is planned with the income in mind, so that the income is adequate to the present program. If there were a larger income, there would be a parochial school in connection with the parish."[17]

Membership

The membership of St. Lucy's Church consists of Italian immigrants and their children, most of whom are extremely poor and live in the immediate neighborhood. In 1931, the members of the church numbered 7,000. The newer members were young men and young women drawn from the church families. As was to be expected, the restrictive immigration laws had a deterrent effect on what had up to then been a steadily growing congregation. The movement of Italian families out of the East Harlem community was also a contributing factor in the declining membership.

According to the priest in charge of St. Lucy's Church in 1942, no appreciable changes have occured in the membership since 1931. He said concerning this point, "The population movement which still goes on in the Italian area of East Harlem is one of the chief causes of the decline in church membership." When questioned by the interviewer as to whether or not the East River Housing Project had affected the church constituency in any way, he said that financially very little might be expected of the residents there, since most of them were on relief and, furthermore, that no appreciable increase in membership was expected due to the fact that most of the residents in

[17]Marsh, *op. cit.*, p. 347.

the East River Housing Project were drawn from that neighborhood. He gave an added reason for the declining membership besides
the population movement; that is, that the second generation Italians were not having as many children as their Italian-born parents,
and that the third generation were having even fewer children than
their parents, if any at all. The future of the church depends to a great
extent upon the Spanish-speaking and colored population which
is invading the Italian area from the north, south, and east. If this
movement continues, perhaps in time Spanish churches will replace
the Italian.

The congested aspect of the immediate neighborhood remains, although the East River Housing Project has made some difference.
According to the priest interviewed, if more housing projects were
developed throughout the whole of the East Harlem area, great benefits would be obtained for all the residents there. If this happened
changes in the church's program might eventually have to be made.
He mentioned especially a possible parochial school.

Activities

On Sundays religious services are held every hour from 6:00 A. M.
to 11:00 A. M., and average attendance at each service is about 200.
The services are held in Italian for the older people, and in English
for the children and young people.

Sunday School. The largest organization in the church is the
Sunday School. Since 1931 when approximately 2,000 children were
registered, the Sunday School registration has dropped about forty
per cent. Although the membership has declined, there is in 1942 a
director of religious education, and an improvement is shown in
organization of subject matter and the quality of teaching. The
teachers are better trained. All volunteer their services. The graded
Bolton Sunday School Plan is used exclusively. The general aim of
the Sunday School is to prepare pupils for church membership.

There has been an appreciable increase in children's activities
since 1933. Cathechism classes which were previously held three
times a week are now held every afternoon after school. The special
purpose of these classes is to prepare pupils for first communion,
confirmation, and ultimately for church membership. A new feature
of the week-day program is the class in religious education being
held on Wednesday afternoons specifically for the elementary public
school children of the nearby public schools. This activity is carried
on in cooperation with the Board of Education of New York City

in connection with the recent policy of released time for religious education. There are ten teachers who volunteer their services for this particular activity.

Other Church Organizations. Other church organizations are:

> The Holy Name Society, for boys and men. Enrollment 150.
> The Holy Rosary Society, for women. Enrollment 300.
> St. Lucy's Society for Women. Enrollment 1,000.
> The Children of Mary, for girls. Enrollment 70.
> St. Aloysius Society, for boys. Enrollment 300.

The main objective of all the above organizations is "spiritual benefit."

The only recreational activities in connection with the church's program are those in which young people engage, such as dances and occasional socials. Emphasis is primarily on the religious work of the church.

Welfare Work. As at Mount Carmel Church, there is no welfare department at St. Lucy's, but needy families are referred to the Catholic Charities Organization. There was in 1931 a volunteer worker who gave two hours a week to the parish. When asked at that time about conditions in the immediate vicinity of St. Lucy's Church, she said:

> Conditions are worse than they were a year ago. There is a great deal of sickness around caused from lack of food. The greatest need is work. If this could be provided, they would not ask for money. The men in the parish are carpenters, day laborers, shovellers, and so forth. The workers think the difficulty is caused by President Hoover, that he should have work for them. They would do anything. The people are Italians, although the Spanish are moving in rapidly. They usually have seven or eight children and are very poor.

In speaking of a crime that had recently been committed in the neighborhood, the worker said, "If the people would only come to church there would be no crime and no racketeers." She also thought that the home was responsible for much of the juvenile delinquency prevalent in that area.

Due to the inadequate income of the church, it cannot afford to undertake community services which extend beyond its own religious organizations. It does, however, endeavor to direct families and individuals in the community to the social agencies able to help with their problems.

Adults who desire to learn English or who wish to prepare themselves for American citizenship are referred to the evening schools or to the Works Progress Administration classes which are held throughout the community.

ST. ANN'S ROMAN CATHOLIC CHURCH

As the Italian population increased, the need for a new church to fill the gap between Mount Carmel Church at 115th Street and St. Lucy's Church at 104th street became urgent. Thus, St. Ann's Roman Catholic Church was built. It is located on the south side of East 110th street between First and Second avenues. East of the church is the rectory, and adjoining this is the parochial school. The chief sources of financial support are contributions and church collections.

Membership

The members of St. Ann's Church are predominently Italian, although communicants in the immediate neighborhood include a few Puerto Ricans and Negroes. Like the members of Mount Carmel Church and St. Lucy's, the people are generally very poor. Most of the parish families live within the territory which extends from 107th street to 113th street, east of Madison avenue to the East River. Congestion in living quarters of a decade ago has been somewhat relieved, owing in part to the East River Housing Project, and also to the remodelling of old buildings. Many of the very old buildings have been condemned. A frequent sight in this section of East Harlem is boarded up condemned buildings.

The total membership of St. Ann's Church in 1932 was 20,000, including children. The average attendance in 1932 for all Sunday morning services was about 3,000, with an average attendance of 1,000 at the Children's Mass. The total average attendance for all Sunday services in 1942 is only 2,000; a reduction in attendance of one-third within ten years.

Services are held in English as well as Italian. An innovation in 1932 was the Young People's Mass in the English language. The Children's Mass has always been said in English.

The membership of St. Ann's Church exhibits the same tendency to decrease in number, as is shown for Mount Carmel and St. Lucy's. To some degree this may be attributed to population movement, although in 1942 comparatively few Italian families are moving out of the neighborhood of the church, since only the more prosperous can afford to move to better quarters. It was conceded, however, by the pastor interviewed, that the membership is becoming increasingly difficult to hold and that, perhaps, is one of the greatest problems the church is facing today. Reasons for this were given as the general social and economic change taking place everywhere. St. Ann's Church appears to be the only church of any denomination in the Italian community of East Harlem which does any advertising, and it is believed that it does help church attendance. Very little pastoral visiting is done, although it is believed that it has considerable bearing on church attendance.

The influx of Spanish-speaking peoples continues, especially from the southeastern part of the East Harlem area, but it was thought by the priest interviewed that it will be a long time before this will greatly affect the membership of St. Ann's Church. The economic outlook is not encouraging since the poor tend to remain in the neighborhood, while those who manage to improve their economic status will go elsewhere. Of the members, all of whom live in the immediate vicinity of the church, the priest interviewed said that approximately 40 per cent are still on relief in 1942.

Activities

Aside from the regular religious services, which are the same for all three Roman Catholic churches described, St. Ann's Church has the following organizations.

The Sunday School is the largest organization, the attendance figure given for 1932 being 3,000. In addition to the regular week-day program for children, religious education is given on Wednesday afternoons to the public school children of the neighborhood, under the "release time" provision, as noted. According to the Sister in charge, no other new activities have been added and no old activities dropped during recent years, although some recreational activities have been added in connection with the Works Progress Administration.

The Parochial School shows no decrease in membership, the daily attendance for 1942 being 500 pupils, the same figure as for 1932. The teachers are Sisters, with one exception. Religious education is an important part of the curriculum, which includes the regular elementary school subjects taught in the public schools.

The Holy Name Society of St. Ann's is an organization of elderly men, with an enrollment of sixty. The language spoken is Italian. Sometimes a prominent speaker drawn from the neighborhood addresses the Society on an interesting secular topic. The purpose and program of the Society are the same as those stated in the description given under Mount Carmel Church.

Girls Organization. The Saint Theresa and the Angel Society are girls' organizations. Besides religious instruction, their program consist of entertainment, plays and card parties. The head of the parish said in an interview in 1932 that he did not believe in dances, that they were too dangerous.

Boys' Organizations. There are also two boys' clubs—the Saint Aloysius Sodality and Saint Ann's Parish Club. The main purpose of both organizations is the maintenance of the boys' interest in the Roman Catholic religion. The social program of both clubs consists of athletic activities. In speaking of the boys' clubs, the priest said, "These young men are also given important duties connected with the church, such as ushering. The development of the 'sense of importance' has worked wonders with these boys. We also have a boys' choir."

St. Ann's Church, like the two other Roman Catholic churches described in this study, has limited its adult education programs to religious education. Services for adults are still conducted in Italian. Second and third generation Italians attend the services in English which have been instituted for them.

Influence of Italian Roman Catholic Churches in Adult Education

The Italian Roman Catholic churches in the East Harlem area do not extend any services to the community beyond those to their own church constituencies. The churches are not represented to any extent on social service committees in the community, nor are relief cases cleared through the Social Service Exchange. The three churches described have limited their adult education programs to religious education. No classes in English or civics for Italian immigrants have ever been held in connection with church programs. Individuals seeking help in citizenship problems are referred to immigrant education classes given under the auspices of the Board of Education of New York City. As has been shown, it is the policy of the three churches described to leave adult education as defined in this study to agencies outside the church.

Italian Protestant Churches in East Harlem

Although there are fifteen Protestant churches in the East Harlem area, only those two which have Italian congregations are described here.

JEFFERSON PARK METHODIST EPISCOPAL CHURCH

The Jefferson Park Church was the first Italian Protestant church to be organized in the East Harlem area. It had its beginnings in the first settlement house in East Harlem which was located at First avenue between 113th and 114th streets.

When the settlement was founded in 1890, teaching of the Protestant religion was the main objective of the institution, although social activities were included in the program. Among these activities was one for mothers, a sewing circle which attracted many of the Italian immigrant women in the vicinity. Later, these mothers and their husbands were urged to attend the first Italian religious services conducted by an Italian Protestant minister, who had about that time arrived from Naples. For several years, the services were held at the settlement, but soon the Methodist Episcopal Board of Home Missions of New York City became interested in the group of Italian converts and bought for their use a very old church at 112th street near Second avenue. The congregation grew steadily, due in part to the increasing Italian immigration. Before the end of a decade the small church could not hold the fast growing congregation and plans were made to build a new and larger church. Money was raised by both the congregation and the Methodist Episcopal Board of Home Missions for the new edifice. In 1906 the Jefferson Park Methodist Episcopal Church at 407 East 114th street was dedicated. For several years the new Italian Protestant church flourished. In 1912 when the writer was a member of that church there were approximately two hundred church members and about 175 children and young people in the Sunday School.

In 1914 a new pastor was installed, and while under his leadership the church made some gains, but the increase in membership in the years following 1912 was slow. This was due for the most part to the population movement outward which had already begun.

During the years immediately following the First World War there was, however, an expansion of the program of the Jefferson Park Church. One of the channels through which this expansion was made possible was the purchase of the old Wood Memorial Church at 319 East 118th street. The name was changed to Casa del Popolo (the house of the people). The Casa del Popolo soon developed into a social and religious center. Activities were many and varied and included a day nursery, a kindergarten, athletic and social clubs, classes in manual arts, homemaking and health classes for girls and women.

One of the most popular activities at the Casa del Popolo was a Sunday afternoon Vesper Service which drew a crowd of from four to five hundred children from the surrounding neighborhood at one meeting. The service consisted of moving pictures on religious themes, a Bible Story, hymn singing and a prayer.

During the peak of the Americanization movement in the early twenties, a "Civic School" for adults was also a very popular activity at the Casa del Popolo. For example, the director reported in a pamphlet, entitled "Growing to Be Bigger Men" and published by the church, that 342 Italian immigrants who had received instruction and aid at the "Civic School" became American citizens in 1921. With the advent of the depression in 1929 many of the activities at the Casa del Popolo had to be curtailed.

The Jefferson Park Methodist Episcopal Church is a four-story building at 407 East 114th street. It is on the north side of the street and faces Jefferson Park. Simplicity of design is expressed in the general architecture of the church building. The auditorium in which the religious services are held is on the first floor of the church. To the right as one enters is the Sunday School room. On the second floor is the kindergarten room. On the third floor are the various club rooms and offices for the pastor and church workers. The pastor and his family live on the fourth floor.

The community surrounding the Jefferson Park Church is the same as that described in connection with the Roman Catholic churches; that is, it is generally characterized by extreme poverty, congestion, a high rate of mobility, and a high rate of juvenile delinquency.

Environmental influences such as the population movement during the "boom" years (1920-1929) greatly affected the church constituency since members moving out of the neighborhood were not replaced by new ones. And again the restrictive immigration measures which went into effect in the early twenties also resulted in a reduced church constituency since there were fewer incoming Italian immigrants to draw from.

The population movement since 1932 has not been out of the neighborhood but within the neighborhood itself. Most of the people in the neighborhood have remained there because they could not afford to pay the higher rentals demanded elsewhere. The movement within the community has been caused by the condemning of some houses, and the remodelling of others, as well as the addition of the

East River Housing Project.

The church constituency, however, is not affected by this movement within the community; but it is being affected by the changes in population. Spanish-speaking and colored people are moving in above the Twenties and into the southern part of the community about 110th street. The movement is eastward. In the event of further housing projects in the neighborhood, it might mean the infiltration of colored people to occupy the houses vacated by Italians or the housing project themselves. A Negro succession is feared by many Italians in East Harlem. Should this occur, the Italian churches might be compelled to sell out to their successors.

Membership

All the members of the Jefferson Park Methodist Episcopal Church are Italian immigrants and their offspring. For the most part the congregation is made up of church families living in the immediate neighborhood, although there are a few individual members who have moved out of the community but maintain their membership. Whole families moving out of the community usually join a near-by church where the children may conveniently attend Sunday School and participate in other church activities. In 1932, although the membership of the church was not increasing, there had been no perceptible loss of members. At that time new members were drawn from the Sunday School, young people's church organizations, and from Italian families in the neighborhood. In 1942 the membership of 150 is still made up of Italian immigrants and their children. In some of the families the children have grown up and have work away from home. In other families, where the boys are serving in the armed forces, the family incomes already low have become lower.

The pastor admitted in 1941 that the congregation is declining, but offered no reason for it. When asked by the interviewer if he foresaw any possible changes in the church constituency in relation to the economic status or nationality, he replied that he was "not disturbed about the future."

Activities

The two religious services on Sunday are conducted in Italian. The average attendance at these services in 1932 was from fifty to sixty adults, and as stated above, there is a decline in membership, and therefore church attendance, since then. Communion services which take place once a month are usually better attended than the regular Sunday services. Special services held during Easter, Christmas, and other holiday seasons are always better attended than the regular services.

To assist the pastor there is a church worker whose duties include, besides the visiting of church members, club work (religious and social) among the young people and mothers. The most important duty of the church worker, however, is visitation among the members and prospective members. This has helped to maintain regular church attendance.

The young peoples' choir, which was started in the old church in 1902, sings English as well as Italian anthems. The number of members has varied from twelve to twenty-five, but there has always been a choir.

Among the most important of the activities of the church are the following:

The Sunday School is the most important educational organization. When the Sunday School was begun in 1895, the teachers were all non-Italian and were drawn from the near-by Protestant churches. About ten years later there were already four Sunday School teachers, children of Italian immigrant parents, who had joined the church as converts. In the last two decades, with one or two exceptions, the teachers have all been of Italian origin.

In 1932 there were 150 children enrolled in the Sunday School, and there were nine teachers, most of whom lived in the neighborhood. They had received no special training to teach, other than the training they had acquired through church organizations. One of the few changes brought about in the church's program since 1932 is the employment of a director of religious education, who is also superintendent of the Sunday School. The International Sunday School lessons are used. Since the teachers are not paid, the expenses of running the Sunday School is limited to the International Sunday School Quarterlies which are supplied to the teachers. The pastor of the church in 1942, who was also pastor in 1932, states that the regular Sunday School enrollment and attendance have been fairly constant through the years. In 1912 the enrollment was approximately 175; in 1932 it was 150, and in 1942 the enrollment is still 150. The usual age at which Sunday School members join the church is twelve.

On Wednesday afternoons, each week, classes in religious education are held especially for the public school pupils in near-by schools, in accordance with the "released time" provision of the

Board of Education. These classes rarely number more than thirty pupils, for most of the pupils in near-by schools are of Italian descent and are, for the most part, Roman Catholics.

The Kindergarten is maintained on the second floor of the church. About thirty children attend and two teachers are in charge. This educational activity has been going on uninterruptedly since it was started in the old church in 1900. It has always been free and open to all children in the neighborhood, regardless of their church affiliation.

Epworth League. Most of the young people of the church belong to the Epworth League, a religious organization for the training of young people in the ways of Christian living and the development of Christian leadership. There were in 1932, thirty-two members in this organization. The meetings are held on Sunday evenings.

Under the guidance and leadership of the director of religious education, the Epworth League has received a new impetus in the last few years. The writer has attended some of the Sunday evening meetings and has found enthusiasm and earnestness among the members which seemed lacking in 1932. The difference is not so much in the numbers attending as in the results being attained. The members are being trained to lead in the discussions, as well as to present problems for discussion.

Boys' Clubs. There are three athletic and social clubs for boys, one for each age group—junior, intermediate, and senior. The last named carry on their activities in the evening after working hours, while juniors and intermediates meet in the afternoon.

Recreational work with the boys' clubs has been increased in the last few years by a boys' worker supplied by the Young Men's Christian Association. Religious stereoptical pictures are shown and explained to members of the boys' clubs. Religious moving pictures are also shown when they can be obtained. Often these pictures are followed by discussion.

Girls' Club. The only club for girls is the Moentita Club which combines religious and social activities. Many activities such as sewing classes and home-craft classes, which were an important part of the church's social program, have been dropped since 1930. In 1942 the club activities are centered chiefly in defense work, such as Red Cross work. About fifteen girls between the ages of ten and sixteen belong to the club.

The Long Branch Fresh Air Home. In 1918 the Jefferson Park Church acquired a cottage in Long Branch, New Jersey, and subsequently fitted it to house about forty children. Later additional cottages were built. The property, including the cottages, was purchased by the Methodist Episcopal Board of Home Missions. The Home is supported by voluntary contributions of members and other groups. Very few of the many who go to the Home can afford to pay. After the first few years of experimentation, the summer fresh air work was so organized that trips were arranged for children and mothers alternately. The daily activities at the seashore include bathing, hiking, games, story hour, and singing. Each day begins with a religious service which everybody attends. On Sunday there is Sunday School and a church service.

THE CHURCH OF THE ASCENSION

There would perhaps have been no Church of the Ascension if in the summer of 1907 an Italian Presbyterian minister had not started preaching in a tent near the river front at East 106th Street. The pastor was assisted by two trained Christian workers who were in charge of the children's religious services and other activities. From the beginning the services were well attended. Children's twilight services, held every evening, were attended by approximately four hundred children. The adult services were not as well attended as the children's services, but there were always from two to three hundred present and on Sundays the tent was filled.

The Presbyterian Board of Home Missions became interested in this venture and, in 1909, rented a store at the corner of 106th Street and First Avenue in which to hold the services. Everything possible was done to give the store an ecclesiastical atmosphere. For several years, adult services were held on Sundays and during the week. In the church school there were about three hundred children and young people. There were also weekday classes in religious education.

In the summer this Protestant mission sent hundreds of children to the country through the Tribune Fresh Air Fund. Before 1910 there were very few social agencies and religious institutions which concerned themselves with sending children to the country. In Harlem's Little Italy the Italian Protestant churches were the only institutions which engaged in social welfare activities of this kind.

Another important activity in which this mission church engaged was the health service rendered to those who were not able to pay for medical care. Both children and adults in need of clinical services or hospitalization were taken to the free medical institutions by the church workers. For the adults the workers acted as interpreters.

Even though the mission was in the midst of a Roman Catholic community, where many of the people were hostile and openly registered their disapproval of the Italians who became Protestant converts, the church mission could not accommodate all those who wished to attend. It soon became apparent that the mission's greatest need was larger quarters. A group of interested men, who were also members of the Church Extension Committee of the Presbyterian Board of Foreign Missions, undertook to raise money for the building of a church for the congregation. It took several years to raise the necessary funds, but finally the church was built. It is called the Church of the Ascension and was dedicated on November 1912. The cost was approximately $100,000.

The Church of the Ascension is more ecclesiastical in appearance than the Jefferson Park Church and more nearly approaches the architectural beauty of many Roman Catholic churches. The auditorium seats approximately four hundred people. All the formal religious services are held there. The gymnasium in the basement serves for informal meetings and socials as well as athletics and games. On the upper floor of the church is a well-equipped kindergarten room. There are other rooms equipped for religious and social activities.

Membership

In 1932 the membership of about 400 had been fairly constant over a long period. There were 150 men and boys and 250 women and girls on the active files in 1938. The church constituency was entirely Italian. This included the children of Italian immigrants who were for the most part American born. When the church was first organized the main religious services were held in Italian, with the exception of the Sunday School. But as the children grew older, a special service in English was instituted for them.

In 1942 the Italian-speaking congregation is growing smaller, while the English-speaking congregation, comprised of the younger people who have grown up in the church, is growing larger. Due to this change, which has occurred also in other Italian Protestant churches in New York City,[18] the bilingual service has come into

[18]In two New York City churches known to the writer, the bilingual service has entirely replaced the Italian Sunday service: Holy Trinity Church in the Bronx, and the Italian Department of the Olivet Memorial Church in New York City.

use and is growing in favor. At the Church of the Ascension, the communion service as well as all the special services are conducted in the following manner: an Italian and an English sermon, Bible readings in both languages, Italian and English hymns and prayers are offered.

The economic status of the church members is the same as that described in connection with all other churches described in this chapter — congested population, much poverty, and juvenile delinquency. In reference to the problem of delinquency, the pastor of the Church of the Ascension had the following to say:

> People say when they read the papers about the racketeering that is going on, "It's the Italians." It's the Italians because they read Italian names. But it is not the Italians. It's the young Americans who are the children of Italians. They have grown up under the distressing conditions of the slums, and these conditions have had a great bearing upon these young American-born Italians. Had the parents remained in Italy the children would have been taking care of sheep and would never have become racketeers. The Italian is adventurous. He goes to the movies where crime is presented in an alluring way. He goes to the pool halls, and he sees much that is bad going on on the streets. If better living conditions could have been provided when the families came from Italy, instead of dirty, dingy rooms, there would not be so much crime now. I believe that society reaps what it shows.[19]

The pastor added that notwithstanding these conditions, "It is remarkable how many succeed and make a career for themselves. They go to universities, evening schools, and later they take up the professions."

The economic status of the church membership has not changed since 1932. According to the pastor of the church, at least two-thirds of the residents in Harlem's Little Italy were still on relief in 1942. The delinquency rate remains high.

A few changes in the physical structure of the community have taken place which may, according to the pastor of the Church of the Ascension, help to keep the residents there. The most notable of these is the new Benjamin Franklin High School. Families with prospective high school pupils may be induced to remain. Other inducements are the East River Housing Project, with its greatly improved living conditions, and the rehabilitation of old buildings.

[19]Marsh, *op. cit.*, p. 202. From an interview with the Reverend A. Stasio, pastor of the Church of the Ascension, April 1932.

Activities

The church services held on Sunday at the Church of the Ascension are for the most part informal. The average attendance at the Sunday morning service is approximately one hundred. At the communion and other special services the usual number who attended in 1932 was about three hundred, although in 1942 this number had declined about one-third.

A prominent part of the Sunday services is the hymn singing by the Congregation and anthems by the volunteer choir. The choir consists of twenty-five young men and women, who meet once a week for practice.

One of the changes which has occurred in the church's program since 1932 is the increase in the work with young people. As a consequence, more services are being conducted in English and the bilingual service is replacing the use of separate Italian and English services. The pastor of the church predicted the institution of the bilingual service for all services, and perhaps later the replacement of the bilingual by the all-English service if the limitations on immigration continue to exist.

Sunday School. There are four departments in the Sunday School — the senior, the junior, the primary, and the beginners class. One of the young men of the church is superintendent of the school. The teachers are young men and women who have themselves attended the school since they were children, and who have become leaders of the various organizations in the church. Only four or five of the fifteen Sunday School teachers have received special training in teaching. The International Sunday School lessons are used. Week-day and evening programs also provide religious education. A new activity of the church is the mid-week class for public school children, as the result of "release time" from school for religious education. This group numbers about forty children.

There were in 1932 two hundred children and young people in the Sunday School, and the attendance remains about the same in 1942. The young people who have married and dropped out have been replaced by younger children. According to the pastor, however, this may not be the case in the school of the future if the trend toward small families continues. Although some new members have been recruited through personal invitation of church members, the membership continues to be drawn mainly from the church constituency.

The Kindergarten. A kindergarten open to all children, regardless of church affiliation, has been carried on ever since the church was built. In 1932 there were forty children enrolled and two kindergarten teachers in charge.

Boys' Clubs. There are three clubs for boys, one for each age group —the junior, intermediate, and senior. The senior group limits membership to boys from fifteen to eighteen.

There is also an adult club for young men above eighteen years of age whose major interest is athletics and other social activities. A trend noted in 1942 is the growing popularity of inter-church (Protestant) athletic contests.

Girls' Clubs. Girls' and young women's organizations include The Ascension Pals, a club for girls from eleven to eighteen years, and the Sunshine Club, for younger girls from eight to eleven. They meet during the week for recreational purposes. There are in 1942 about sixty girls enrolled in these clubs.

The Young People's Society is an increasingly active organization. The conduct and management of the Society is entirely in the young people's hands. The Sunday program includes outside speakers as well as speakers chosen from their own leaders. All members are encouraged to participate in the discussions, and special topics are planned by the officers of the Society. In addition to their religious service, they have socials, entertainments, and summer camp activities. There are young people enrolled. The main objective of the organization is training for religious leadership.

The Women's Missionary Society is under the leadership of the pastor's wife. The chief aim of the Society is to serve the church by holding the constituency and recruiting new members. The women of this Society take care of most of the church visitation. A meeting is held once a month for discussion of social problems. Due to the increasing number of younger mothers in the congregation, the English language is being used more and more. Whereas formerly only Italian speakers were invited to address the Society, by 1941 English speakers had become frequent. The leader of the Society states that one of the changes which has occurred since 1932 is that the members have become increasingly concious of the social problems which obtain in the immediate neighborhood. Many members feel that more religious education, both for young and old, would solve these problems. The leader feels very strongly that religious education for every child would solve the juvenile delinquency problem. To substantiate this, she said that so far as she knew none of the children who had regularly attended the church school of the Church of the Ascension had ever been arrested or committed to any criminal institution.

Summer Camp Activities. For children and young people of the church is a summer camp chiefly supported by the Presbyterian Board of Foreign Missions. It is the American Parish Camp, located at Oakridge, New Jersey. It accommodates about sixty children and young people at one time, and during the summer there are usually from eight to ten two-week trips. The younger children whose parents cannot afford to pay for their board simply pay for their transportation. Those who can afford to pay are required to do so.

Influence of Italian Protestant Churches in Adult Education

The Church of the Ascension has taken advantage of every opportunity to cooperate with other agencies and institutions in the community, such as the Board of Health, the Community Service, the School Community Service, Social Service Exchange, and other churches, and the public schools.

The pastor of the Church of the Ascension sees great possibilities in the coordination of the work performed by the social and welfare agencies in the community. In his opinion, there are great obstacles in the way of its accomplishment, the greatest obstacle being the lack of a spirit of good-will by some of the social and religious institutions in the community. He thinks, however, that this and other obstacles are not unsurmountable and that the activities of the Community Service Committee of the Benjamin Franklin High School,[20] which are leading the way toward community organization, are especially commendable.

The only adult education carried on by the Italian Protestant churches, in addition to the regular church services, is of a religious type, as exemplified in the activities of the church organizations described. Classes in immigrant education which include the teaching of English and civics have never been given, with the exception of the work in the "Civic School" sponsored by the Jefferson Park Methodist Episcopal Church, which has been discontinued since 1929. As is true for the Italian Roman Catholic churches, the Italian Protestant churches described encourage church members or others who come to them for help in acquiring citizenship and a knowledge of the English language to attend the public evening schools in the

[20]The Community Service Committee is an organization of the Benjamin Franklin High School, whose chief purpose is to coordinate the social and welfare activities of the community so that they may function more efficiently among the people they are designed to help.

community, on the theory that the teachers in the public schools are trained for teaching and, consequently, are better qualified for the task than the members of the church staffs.

LEONARD COVELLO

AUTOBIOGRAPHY*

In the autumn of 1896, we arrived in America.

As a boy of nine, the arduous trip in an old freighter did not matter very much to me or to my younger brothers. A child adapts to everything. It was the older people who suffered, those uprooted human beings who faced the shores of an unknown land with quaking hearts.

My mother had never been further from Avigliano than the chapél just a few kilometers outside the town, where we went on the feast days of *La Madonna del Carmine.* Suddenly she was forced to make a long and painful trip from Avigliano to Naples, through interminable mountain tunnels where choking black smoke and soot poured into the railroad carriages. Then twenty days across four thousand miles of ocean to New York.

When the sea threatened to engulf us, she did not scream and carry on like the rest, but held us close with fear and torment locked in her breast—voiceless, inarticulate. And when finally we saw the towering buildings and rode the screeching elevated train and saw the long, unending streets of a metropolis that could easily swallow a thousand Aviglianese towns, she accepted it all with the mute resignation of *"La volonta di Dio,"* while her heart longed for familiar scenes and the faces of loved ones and the security of a life she had forever left behind.

We spent two days at Ellis Island before my father was aware of our arrival. Two days and two nights we waited at this dreary place which for the immigrant was the entrance to America. Two days and two nights we waited, eating the food that was given us, sleeping on hard benches, while my mother hardly closed her eyes for fear of losing us in the confusion. Once during a physical examination men and boys were separated for a short time from the women. My mother was frantic as the guard led me and my two younger brothers away. When we ran back to her, she clutched us convulsively. Still in her eyes there was the disbelieving look of a mother who never expected to see her children again.

The Heart Is The Teacher (New York: McGraw-Hill, 1958), pp. 19-45. Reprinted with permission of the author.

But her nightmare finally came to an end. We were on a small ferry boat crossing the lower bay of New York, going away from Ellis Island. My mother was standing at the railing with my father, and both of them happy—my father taller, more imposing than I remembered him, but still with his heavy mustache and short-cropped hair in the style of Umberto I. He held my younger brother by the hand and every once in a while glanced at me affectionately. The sunlight shone upon the water and upon the skyline of the city directly in front of us. I was standing with my brother Raffaele and a girl several years older than I who had accompanied my father to Ellis Island. She was dressed differently from the women of Avigliano, and her voice was pleasant and warm, and she could switch from our Italian dialect to English as she chose.

"You will like America," she chattered in Italian. "There are so many things to see. So many things to do. You will make many new friends. You will go to school. You will learn and maybe become somebody very important. Would you like that? "

My brother nodded vigorously. I was older. I only smiled. The girl now addressed herself to me. "Wouldn't you like that?"

I shrugged.

"Yes or no?" she teased.

"*Sì.*"

"Oh, but no! You must say it in English. Y—E—S, yes. Say it after me. Yes."

"Y—ess."

"Good! Bravo!" the girl laughed. "It is your first word in English and you will never forget it."

"Why?" I asked.

"Because I told you, foolish one! Because I told you, you will never forget the word and you will never forget me."

It was true. Mary Accurso was her name. It might have been possible for me to forget how I learned to say "yes" in English. But Mary Accurso—never.

Our first home in America was a tenement flat near the East River at 112th Street on the site of what is now Jefferson Park. The sunlight and fresh air of our mountain home in Lucania were replaced by four walls and people over and under and on all sides of us, until it seemed that humanity from all corners of the world had congregated in this section of New York City known as East Harlem.

The cobbled streets. The endless, monotonous rows of tenement buildings that shut out the sky. The traffic of wagons and carts and carriages and the clopping of horses' hoofs which struck sparks in the night. The smell of the river at ebb tide. The moaning of fog horns. The clanging of bells and the screeching of sirens as a fire broke out somewhere in the neighborhood. Dank hallways. Long flights of wooden stairs and the toilet in the hall. And the water, which to my mother was one of the great wonders of America— water with just the twist of a handle, and only a few paces from the kitchen. It took her a long time to get used to this luxury. Water and a few other conveniences were the compensations the New World had to offer.

"With the Aviglianese you are always safe," my father would say. "They are your countrymen, *paesani*. They will always stand by you."

The idea of family and clan was carried from Avigliano in southern Italy to East Harlem. From the River to First Avenue, 112th Street was the Aviglianese Colony in New York City and closest to us were the Accurso and Salvatore families. My father had lived with the Accursos during the six years he was trying to save enough for a little place to live and the money for *l'umbarco*. In fact, it was Carmela, wife of his friend Vito Accurso and mother of the girl who met us at the boat, who saved his money for him, untilthe needed amount had accumulated. It was Carmela Accurso who made ready the tenement flat and arranged the welcoming party with relatives and friends to greet us upon our arrival. During this celebration my mother sat dazed, unable to realize that at last the torment of the trip was over and that here was America. It was Mrs. Accurso who put her arm comfortingly about my mother's shoulder and led her away from the party and into the hall and showed her the water faucet. "Courage! You will get used to it here. See! Isn't it wonderful how the water comes out?"

Through her tears my mother managed a smile.

In all of her years in America, my mother never saw the inside of a school. My father went only once, and that was when he took me and my two younger brothers to *La Soupa Scuola* (the "Soup School"), as it was called among the immigrants of my generation. We headed along Second Avenue in the direction of 115th Street, my father walking in front, holding the hands of my two brothers, while I followed along with a boy of my own age, Vito Salvatore, whose family had arrived from Avigliano seven years before.

My long European trousers had been replaced by the short knickers of the time, and I wore black ribbed stockings and new American shoes. To all outward appearances I was an American, except that I did not speak a word of English.

Vito kept chanting what sounded like gibberish to me, all the while casting sidelong glances in my direction as though nursing some delightful secret.

"Mrs. Cutter cut the butter ten times in the gutter!"

"What the devil are you singing—an American song?" I asked in the dialect of our people.

"You'll meet the devil all right." And again, in English, "Mrs. Cutter cut the butter ten times in the gutter! Only this devil wears skirts and carries a stick this long. Wham, and she lets you have it across the back! This, my dear Narduccio, is your new head teacher."

Was it possible? A woman teacher! "In Avigliano we were taught by men," I bragged to my friend. "There was Maestro Mecca. Strong? When he cracked your hand with his ruler it went numb for a week. And you are trying to scare me with your woman teacher . . ."

I spoke with pride. Already "yesterday" was taking on a new meaning. I was lonely. I missed the mountains. I missed my friends at the shoemaker shop and my uncles and the life I had always known. In the face of a strange and uncertain future, Avigliano now loomed in a new and nostalgic light. Even unpleasant remembrances had a fascination of their own. Who had felt the blows of Don Salvatore Mecca could stand anything.

The Soup School was a three-story wooden building hemmed in by two five-story tenements at 116th Street and Second Avenue. When Vito pointed it out I experienced a shock. It appeared huge and impressive. I was ashamed to let him know that in Avigliano our school consisted of only one room, poorly lighted and poorly heated, with benches that hadn't been changed in fifty years. However, at this moment something really wonderful happened to take my thoughts from the poverty of our life in Avigliano.

Before entering the school, my father led us into a little store close at hand. There was a counter covered by glass and in it all manner and kinds of sweets such as we had never seen before. *"Candi!"* my father told us, grinning. "This is what is called *candi* in America."

"C-a-n-d-y!" know-it-all Vito repeated in my ear.

We were even allowed to select the kind we wanted. I remember how I selected some little round cream-filled chocolates which tasted like nothing I had every eaten before. It was unheard-of to eat sweets on a school day, even though this was a special occasion. Anyway, the only candy I knew was *confetti,* the sugar-coated almond confection which we had only on feast days or from the pocket of my uncle the priest on some very special occasion, and for which we kissed his hand in return. But today my father was especially happy. He ate a piece of candy too. The picture of us there on the street outside the Soup School eating candy and having a good time will never fade.

The Soup School got its name from the fact that at noontime a bowl of soup was served to us with some white, soft bread that made better spitballs than eating in comparison with the substantial and solid homemade bread to which I was accustomed. The school itself was organized and maintained by the Female Guardian Society of America. Later on I found out that this Society was sponsored by wealthy people concerned about the immigrants and their children. How much this organization accomplished among immigrants in New York City would be difficult to estimate. But this I do know, that among the immigrants of my generation and even later *La Soupa Scuola* is still vivid in our boyhood memories.

Why we went to the Soup School instead of the regular elementary public school I have not the faintest idea, except that possibly the first Aviglianese to arrive in New York sent his child there and everyone else followed suit—and also possibly because in those days a bowl of soup was a bowl of soup.

Once at the Soup School I remember the teacher gave each child a bag of oatmeal to take home. This food was supposed to make you big and strong. You ate it for breakfast. My father examined the stuff, tested it with his fingers. To him it was the kind of bran that was fed to pigs in Avigliano.

"What kind of a school is this?" he shouted. "They give us the food of animals to eat and send it home to us with our children! What are we coming to next?"

By the standards I had come to know and understand in Avigliano, the Soup School was not an unpleasant experience. I had been reared in a strict code of behavior, and this same strictness was the outstanding characteristic of the first of my American schools. Nor can I say, as I had indicated to Vito, that a blow from Mrs. Cutter ever had the lustiness of my old teacher, Don Salvatore Mecca. But what punishment lacked in power, it gained by the exacting personality of our principal.

Middle-aged, stockily built, gray hair parted in the middle, Mrs. Cutter lived up to everything my cousin Vito had said about her and much more. Attached to an immaculate white waist by a black ribbon, her prince nez fell from her nose and dangled in moments of anger. She moved about the corridors and classrooms of the Soup School ever alert and ready to strike at any infringement of school regulations.

I was sitting in class trying to memorize and pronounce words written on the blackboard—words which had absolutely no meaning to me. It seldom seemed to occur to our teachers that explanations were necessary.

"B-U-T-T-E-R—butter—butter," I sing-songed with the rest of

the class, learning as always by rote, learning things which often I didn't understand but which had a way of sticking in my mind.

Softly the door opened and Mrs. Cutter entered the classroom. For a large and heavy-set woman she moved quickly, without making any noise. We were not supposed to notice or even pretend we had seen her as she slowly made her way between the desks and straight-backed benches. 'B-U-T-T-E-R," I intoned. She was behind me now. I could feel her presence hovering over me. I did not dare take my eyes from the blackboard. I had done nothing and could conceive of no possible reason for an attack, but with Mrs. Cutter this held no significance. She carried a short bamboo switch. On her finger she wore a heavy gold wedding ring. For an instant I thought she was going to pass me by and then suddenly her clenched fist with the ring came down on my head.

I had been trained to show no emotion in the face of punishment, but this was too much. However, before I had time to react to the indignity of this assault, an amazing thing happened. Realizing that she had hurt me unjustly, Mrs. Cutter's whole manner changed. A look of concern came into her eyes. She took hold of my arm, uttering conciliatory words which I did not understand. Later Vito explained to me that she was saying, "I'm sorry. I didn't mean it. Sit down now and be a good boy!"

Every day before receiving our bowl of soup we recited the Lord's Prayer. I had no inkling of what the words meant. I knew only that I was expected to bow my head. I looked around to see what was going on. Swift and simple, the teacher's blackboard pointer brought the idea home to me. I never batted an eyelash after that.

I learned arithmetic and penmanship and spelling—every misspelled word written ten times or more, traced painfully and carefully in my blankbook. I do not know how many times I wrote "I must not talk." In this same way I learned how to read in English, learned geography and grammar, the states of the Union and all the capital cities—and memory gems—choice bits of poetry and sayings. Most learning was done in unison. You recited to the teacher standing at attention. Chorus work. Repetition. Repetition until the things you learned beat in your brain even at night when you were falling asleep.

I think of the modern child with his complexes and his need for "self-expression"! He will never know the forceful and vitalizing influence of a Soup School or a Mrs. Cutter.

I vividly remember the assembly periods. A long narrow room with large windows at either end, long rows of hard benches without backs, and the high platform at one end with a piano, a large table, several chairs, and the American flag. There were no pictures of any kind on the walls.

Silence! Silence! Silence! This was the characteristic feature of our existence at the Soup School. You never made an unnecessary noise or said an unnecessary word. Outside in the hall we lined up by size, girls in one line and boys in another, without uttering a sound. Eyes front and at attention. Lord help you if you broke the rule of silence. I can still see a distant relative of mine, a girl named Miluzza, who could never stop talking, standing in a corner behind Mrs. Cutter throughout an entire assembly with a spring-type clothespin fastened to her lower lip as punishment. Uncowed, defiant—Miluzza with that clothespin dangling from her lip . . .

The piano struck up a march and from the hall we paraded into assembly—eyes straight ahead in military style. Mrs. Cutter was there on the platform, dominating the scene, her eyes penetrating every corner of the assembly hall. It was always the same. We stood at attention as the Bible was read and at attention as the flag was waved back and forth, and we sang the same song. I didn't know what the words meant but I sang it loudly with all the rest, in my own way, "Tree Cheers for de Red Whatzam Blu!"

But best of all was another song that we used to sing at these assemblies. It was a particular favorite of Mrs. Cutter's, and we sang it with great gusto, "Honest boys who never tread the streets." This was in the days when we not only trod the streets but practically lived in them.

Three or four years after we had established ourselves in our first home in America, word got around that the city was going to tear down several blocks of tenements to make way for a park. The park took a long time in coming. Demolition was slow and many families stayed on until the wrecking crews were almost at their doors.

The buildings had been condemned and turned over to the city, and together with Vito and my other companions, I played in a neighborhood of rubble and debris and abandoned buildings. We stole lead from the primitive plumbing to sell to the junk man. We stole bricks and chipped off the old mortar and sold them again. And in order to do this, we had to scour around the area for old baby-carriage wheels to make carts in which to carry off the stuff that we stole.

My father worked as general handyman in a German tavern or cafe on 22nd Street. Downstairs there were bowling alleys, and during the winter he was kept pretty busy setting up pins along with his other work, but in summer business slackened and he was often without work for weeks at a time. When he did work he made seven or eight dollars a week and extra tips. But work or no work, money in our house was scarce. My mother kept saying, "What are we going to do ?" and my father would always answer, "What can I do?" If there is no work there is no work. You'll have to do the best you can."

It was a curious fatalistic attitude among our people in America that while they deplored their economic stuation they seldom tried hard to do anything about it. Generations of hardship were behind them. Life was such. *"La volontà di Dio!"* For them the pattern could never change, though it might, perhaps, for their children.

Our kitchen table was covered by an oilcloth with a picture of Christopher Columbus first setting foot on American soil. It was the familiar scene of Columbus grasping the flag of Spain, surrounded by his men, with Indians crowding around. More than once my father glared at this oilcloth and poured a malediction on Columbus and his great discovery.

One day I came home from the Soup School with a report card for my father to sign. It was during one of these particularly bleak periods. I remember that my friend Vito Salvatore happened to be there, and Mary Accurso had stopped in for a moment to see my mother. With a weary expression my father glanced over the marks on the report card and was about to sign it. However, he paused with the pen in his hand.

"What is this?" he said. "Leonard Covello! What happened to the *i* in Coviello?"

My mother paused in her mending. Vito and I just looked at each other.

"Well?" my father insisted.

"Maybe the teacher just forgot to put it in," Mary suggested. "It can happen." She was going to high school now and spoke with an air of authority, and people always listened to her. This time, however, my father didn't even hear her.

"From Leonardo to Leonard I can follow," he said, "a perfectly natural process. In America anything can happen and does happen. But you don't change a family name. A name is a name. What happened to the *i?*"

"Mrs. Cutter took it out," I explained. "Every time she pronounced Coviello it came out Covello. So she took out the *i*. That way it's easier for everybody."

My father thumped Columbus on the head with his fist. "And what has this Mrs. Cutter got to do with my name?"

"What difference does it make?" I said. "It's more American. The *i* doesn't help anything." It was one of the very few times that I dared oppose my father. But even at that age I was beginning to feel that anything that made a name less foreign was an improvement.

Vito came to my rescue. "My name is Victor—Vic. That's what everybody calls me now."

"Vica. Stricka. Nicka. You crazy in the head!" my father yelled at him.

For a moment my father sat there, bitter rebellion building in him. Then with a shrug of resignation, he signed the report card and shoved it over to me. My mother now suddenly entered the argument. "How is it possible to do this to a name? Why did you sign the card? Narduccio, you will have to tell your teacher that a name cannot be changed just like that . . ."

"Mamma, you don't understand."

"What is there to understand? A person's life and his honor is in his name. He never changes it. A name is not a shirt or a piece of underwear."

My father got up from the table, lighted the twisted stump of a Toscano cigar and moved out of the argument. "Honor!" he muttered to himself.

"You must explain this to your teacher," my mother insisted. "It was a mistake. She will know. She will not let it happen again. You will see."

"It was no mistake. On purpose. The *i* is out and Mrs. Cutter made it Covello. You just don't understand!"

"Will you stop saying that!" my mother insisted. "I don't understand. I don't understand. What is there to understand? Now that you have become Americanized you understand everything and I understand nothing."

With her in this mood I dared make no answer. Mary went over and put her hand on my mother's shoulder. I beckoned to Vito and together we walked out of the flat and downstairs into the street.

"She just doesn't understand," I kept saying.

"I'm gonna take the *e* off the end of my name and make it just Salvator," Vito said. "After all, we're not in Italy now."

Vito and I were standing dejectedly under the gas light on the corner, watching the lamplighter moving from post to post along the cobblestone street and then disappearing around the corner on First Avenue. Somehow or other the joy of childhood had seeped out of our lives. We were only boys, but a sadness that we could not explain pressed down upon us. Mary came and joined us. She had a book under her arm. She stood there for a moment, while her dark eyes surveyed us questioningly.

"But they don't understand!" I insisted.

Mary smiled. "Maybe some day, you will realize that *you* are the one who does not understand."

At what I nostalgically and possessively call *my* school—the Benjamin Franklin High School in East Harlem—there is a gold-medal award given at each graduation to the student who has been of greatest service to his school and his community. This is called the Anna C. Ruddy Memorial Award, and it commemorates a woman who, though not very well known to the outside world, was a tremendous influence in East Harlem during a lifetime devoted to the cause of the recently arrived immigrant and his children.

Miss Ruddy was the daughter of a Canadian pioneer from Ulster County, the Protestant stronghold in North Ireland. She came to East Harlem from Canada about 1890 to do missionary work among the Italians—a job for which she prepared herself by learning how to speak and read our language. She had no money. At first she had very little help of any kind, only an overwhelming desire to bring some measure of hope into the dinginess of the immigrant's very crowded tenement life.

Miss Ruddy preached the teachings of Christ. That she was Protestant did not make any difference to us. In general, our fathers looked upon religion through half-closed eyes while the women, with endless household chores and children to look after, found little time for regular church worship. The younger people were left pretty much to make decisions for themselves.

On Sunday afternoons when my father got together with his cronies for a game of cards and the wine flowed across the Christopher Columbus tablecloth, there were often arguments about religion. But no matter which way a religious argument turned, it always ended by someone mentioning the name of Miss Ruddy. Then a change took place. A quiet settled in the room as the card game got under way once more.

"A woman in a million," my father would say. "Protestant! Catholic! Egyptian! In the end, what difference does it make? Religion is a matter of the spirit and heart. I take my hat off to Signorina Ruddy."

His old friend Vito Accurso once said, "I am a freethinker, you all know that. I believe what I believe—that's the right God gave me when I came into this world. Some people are born idiots. Most people are born to a life which doesn't matter very much one way or the other. But every once in a while someone turns up that makes you stop and marvel. There you have La Signorina Ruddy. Special. Beautiful in her American way. She could have anything. Yet she spends her time here among us, taking care of our children and our sick, helping whenever she can. So God, if there is one, gave her the mind to call herself Protestant. For this, am I to deny my children the benefits of her teaching? Good is good and bad is bad, no matter how you name or color it . . ."

Many years of my life were spent under the influence of Miss Ruddy and the Home Garden, as her little mission was called. Yet, to catalog or classify it exactly is as difficult as it is to describe the unusual character of the woman who was its head. There was Sunday School and Bible reading—Miss Ruddy standing there, tall and imposing, her auburn hair swirling over her head and catching the sunlight which came through the windows of the small brownstone building which she had converted into a haven for the Italian children and young people of the neighborhood. She wore immaculately laundered blouses which buttoned close about her throat and a gold cross suspended by a fine gold chain—her only adornment. She read the Bible with the book settled loosely in the reading mostly from memory and only occasionally glancing down to reassure herself.

What meaning could Biblical verses and quotations have for the children of the slums of East Harlem? Who would listen to language that was like the ripple of water when in our ears rang the madness of the elevated trains and the raucous bellowing of Casey the cop above the cries of the fish mongers and fruit and vegetable peddlers as he chased us down the street?

"For what shall it profit a man if he shall gain the whole world and lose his own soul?"

"What do these words mean? You, Leanard Covello. Tell me what you think. Stand up. Don't be frightened."

"I'm not sure, Miss Ruddy. It's like somebody had a lot of money and at the same time he's no good."

"Exactly. If you hurt someone in the process of making money, what good is the money? You not only have done wrong but you have sinned against Jesus Christ and you have hurt yourself."

Away from the Home Garden we fought the Second Avenue gang with rocks and tin cans and used garbage-can covers for shields. We scavenged the dumps and the river front for anything we could sell to make a penny. We had a hideout under the tenement rubble where we played cops and robbers and took the fruit and sweet potatoes stolen from the pushcarts to cook in our "mickey cans." But at the same time we spent Sunday afternoon and several nights a week at the Home Garden with Miss Ruddy, where we formed another club called the Boys' Club. We read books, put on plays, sang songs. There was nothing strange about this duality, although it may seem so to people who have never been poor or lived in crowded big-city slums. For the Home Garden had much to offer tough little "street Arabs" like us.

In the unfolding of our lives, Miss Ruddy and the Home Garden filled a need we could find nowhere else. It was Miss Ruddy who gave me an idea of how important the influence of a teacher can be in the life of a growing boy. Of all of us who went to the Home Garden, not one, to my knowledge, ever became a criminal or ended "bad" in the usual sense of the word.

"Mother of the Italians," Miss Ruddy was called, because so many of our people ran to her with their troubles. When sickness or disaster fell she was always there to give help or comfort. Once, when someone asked her about her work among the Italians, she said, "They are like frightened bewildered children in a strange land. Where are they to turn for help if not to me or others like me?"

In Avigliano there were times when there was no food in the house. Then we bolted the door and rattled kitchen utensils and dishes to give the impression to our close neighbors that the noonday meal was going on as usual. After the *siesta* everyone went about his customary tasks and the outside world never knew exactly how it was with us. The intimate things of family life remained sealed within the family, and we created for ourselves a reserve both as individuals and as a group.

In America it was not much different. Our people had the worst possible jobs—jobs that paid little and were very uncertain. A stonemason worked ten hours a day for a dollar and a quarter—if there was work. When there was snow or rain or ice there was no work at all. During slack periods men just hung around the house or played *boccie* down in the vacant lot or played cards in the kitchen or in the cafe. They did not talk about their troubles, but their games did not have the usual gusto. The children especially could sense their feeling of helplessness in this land which offered little more than strangeness and hardship.

My mother lived in constant fear from the uncertainty of life. As the eldest child, I had been close to her in Avigliano. I was still closer to her here in America. There were now four boys in our family and my mother was expecting another child. I had to earn money somehow while I was going to school.

Miss Ruddy came to our assistance. One day after a Boys' Club meeting she called me into her office. She looked me over for a moment and then smiled. "How old are you, Leonard?"

"Twelve, ma'am."

"Would you like to work? If you had a job, that is? Are you strong enough?"

I could hardly control my excitement. "I'm as strong as any boy in the Home Garden. Is there a job for me?"

Miss Ruddy nodded. "Here, take this note to Mr. Griffin and let me know what he says."

I found out later that Mr. Griffin was one of the members of the Lexington Avenue Baptist Church that we attended with Miss Ruddy. Mr. Griffin owned a large bakery shop on 112th Street and Fifth Avenue. I hurried over to see him. He was seated in a large armchair in his office behind the shop. He was a well-built man, with gray, curly hair, a heavy mustache and a very friendly manner. He read Miss Ruddy's note and looked up at me.

"You're not much for size or weight," he said. "It's hard work, running around delivering orders early in the morning. And it's an all-year-around job—six days a week, except the Sabbath. People want their bread when they wake up. Five o'clock we begin. If you're willing, it's a dollar seventy-five a week with a cup of coffee and a roll thrown in to perk you up before you start working. You begin Monday."

"I'll be here, sir," I said.

He laughed and grabbed a loaf of bread and thrust it under my arm. "Here, fatten yourself up a little. I'll see you on Monday."

I literally leapt from his office in my excitement. I ran home to tell my mother and father that I had found a job and was ready to do my share in supporting the family. My mother put her hand on my shoulder. My father said, "Good. You are becoming a man now. You have grown up." I was only twelve, but I could feel that he was proud of me. And I was proud of myself because I had reached the age where I could do more than scrub floors and wash windows and look after my baby brothers. I could earn money and stand on my own two feet and help keep the family together, as I had been taught practically from the time I was born was my responsibility.

At four-thirty every morning I walked rapidly over to Fifth Avenue and 112th Street to the bakery shop. There the day's orders were waiting for me to put into bags for delivery. After a hurried cup of coffee and milk and a couple of rolls, I started out pulling a little wagon that I had constructed out of an old packing crate and baby carriage wheels.

Servicing the private houses was not so bad where there were only a few steps to climb. However, the apartment houses were quite different. The cellars were dark and I had to grope along, banging into walls, stepping on cats, hearing rats scurry out of my way, and always keeping a wary eye for janitors' dogs. Sometimes, in the beginning I carried a lantern, but this was awkward with the bags of bread, so I had to learn to make my way through the darkness in and out of serpentine alleys to the dumbwaiters where the coarse rope cut my hands as I whistled to facelsss customers who lived somewhere high up in the air like inhabitants of another planet.

It was rush, rush, rush, back and forth from the bakery until all the orders were delivered. Then I had to run home and get ready for school. For this work I received one dollar and seventy-five cents a week. It was not very much but it helped a great deal in days when meat was twelve cents a pound and milk six cents a quart. Thus, when I was twelve, work became an inseparable part of life.

Very early the essential difference between working hard in Italy and working hard in America became apparent to us who were young. In Italy it was work and work hard with no hope of any future. A few years of schooling and then work for the rest of one's life—no prospect of ever going beyond the fifth grade or ever becoming other than what one started out to be, in my own particular case, probably a shoemaker. But here in America we began to understand—faintly at first, without full comprehension—that there was a chance that another world existed beyond the tenements in which we lived and that it was just possible to reach out into that world and one day become part of it. The possibility of going to high school, maybe even college, opened the vista of another life to us.

This was the beginning of my work years—jobs after school and during summer vacation to help the family and in order to be able to continue in school. Next I worked for several summers in a baking powder factory downtown on Barclay Street, passing the bakery delivery job to my younger brother Ralph. The hours at the factory were from seven-thirty in the morning until six at night and from eight until three on Saturdays. The wages were three dollars, out of which came sixty cents a week for carfare and sixty cents a week for lunch. This left me with only one dollar and twenty cents to take home to my mother. But every penny counted and helped to keep us going.

Mrs. Cutter and the Soup School were behind me now, in time if not in memory. I was going to Public School 83 on 110th Street between Second and Third Avenues. What an impressive school that was to me! Five stories high. Hundreds of boys. Halls. Regular classrooms. And a teacher by the name of Miss Sayles who gave me twenty-five cents a week to run up to her home, a brownstone building at 116th Street and Lexington Avenue, to bring back her lunch.

Once a week the huge rolling doors which formed the classrooms were rolled back and we marched into assembly. As at the Soup School, everything was done in silence, in unison, and at attention. From a side door Mr. Casey, the principal, would emerge—bearded, impressive, wearing a black skull cap, stiff white collar and black tie, and a long, loose black coat with white laundered cuffs which stuck out from his coat sleeves. There was the usual flag salute and the Bible reading. Mr. Casey swallowed his words and I could never understand what he was saying, except one favorite expression, "Make a joyful noise unto the Lord!" This completely baffled me because everywhere, in the classrooms, in the halls, on the stairs, strict silence was the rule.

At one assembly I remember reciting a poem. I had recited it in class and then spent hours at home in front of a mirror saying it over and over, just as if I were standing in front of my uncle, Zio Prete, and he were sitting in his huge armchair with his cane at his side, listening impassively, critically. Waiting with my classmates to march into assembly, I was overwhelmed with fear. Mr. Casey finished the Bible passage, blew his nose into a large white handkerchief, folded it carefully away into a hidden corner of his coattail and announced, "This morning Leonard Covello of Class 4B will recite a poem for us. Leonard Covello."

A paralysis gripped me. I was unable to move.

Mr. Casey coughed. "Leonard Covello!"

My teacher tapped me on the shoulder. I managed to walk stiffly to the front of the assembly and face about. In a voice which I could not recognize as my own, I began: "I shall now recite a poem by Eugene Field."

Winken, Blinken, and Nod one night
Sailed off in a Wooden shoe—
Sailed into a sea of misty light,
Into a sea of dew . . .

I finished the poem and walked back to my seat, bewildered, but with a wonderful feeling of exhilaration. I had overcome a fear that had haunted me for weeks—fear of facing my more "American" classmates, fear of mispronouncing some of the difficult words, fear of my accent or of forgetting my lines. To my amazement, what had seemed so difficult was easy, much easier than I had ever dreamed—an experience which has repeated itself often during the course of my life.

The teaching at Public School 83 was thorough for those who could learn and who wanted to learn. Even in those days there was the truant officer, but he could hardly cope with the unwilling learner for whom school was no more than a prison or with the parent who considered too much schooling unnecessary. Two boys whose father had an ice and coal business were taken out of school at the age of twelve to help at home. It didn't bother them. In fact, they were happy about it.

The constant drilling and the pressure of memorizing, the homework, and detention after school raised havoc with many students. For me, this type of discipline seemed merely the continuation of my training in Italy. I wanted to go to school. School meant books and reading and an escape from the world of drudgery which dulled the mind and wore out the body and brought meager returns. I had seen it often with my father and his friends when they came home at night tired and dispirited.

"Nardo," my father repeated again and again. "In me you see a dog's life. Go to school. Even if it kills you. With the pen and with pen and with books you have the chance to live like a man and not like a beast of burden."

I was seldom absent from school and never late. Geography and history I mastered easily. I memorized with facility. I more than held my own in spelling and widened my English vocabulary by working diligently at the daily exercises and homework which the teacher called "meaning and use." This expression baffled me for a long time. We used to walk along the street, saying, "Hey, I gotta go home and study 'mean 'n yourself! " I did not worry about what the expression meant. I simply learned how to do it. The exercise involved a dictionary and a speller. We had to take five or six words from the speller, hunt for them in the dictionary, and then write a sentence illustrating their use.

Spelling bees were common in those days. The speller was graded with such words as "Mississippi" and "isthmus" in the lower classes and topped with words like "obliquity" and "Aix-la-Chapelle" and "aberration" and "capstone" in the upper class.

We memorized suffixes and prefixes, Latin and Greek roots, and we were required to give the meaings of words as they are used as well as their etymological meanings. Also each group of words had to be illustrated with "promiscuous examples." According to modern methods and educational theories, it was rough fare. But it had its values. It may not have been the best way to train the mind, but it did teach you to concentrate on mastering difficult jobs.

During the last year of grade school we had a period of German on Friday afternoon. As Professor Hoffstadter, the German teacher, stepped into the classroom, our regular teacher, Mr. Rosenthal, stepped out, and the fun began. Tall, slightly stooped, Professor Hoffstadter, like Mr. Casey, the principal, wore a beard and a Prince Albert coat, but Professor Hoffstadter's beard stuck straight out and came to a point and wagged up and down as he talked. For us it was the end of the week, and we waited impatiently to be off and away from school. For the itinerant professor it was the last of a long series of German lessons given day in and day out at various schools in the city. For both students and teacher there was only the desire to get it over with as quickly as possible.

Amid guffaws of laughter we sang

O Tannenbaum, O Tannenbaum
Wie grun sind deine Blatter . . .

After the song we had several German declensions of the definite article and a few German words to the question of:

"Was ist das?"
"Das ist ein Bleistift."
"Das ist der Kopf."

Only when Mr. Rosenthal sat in the classroom busy at some of his own work was it possible for the professor to do some teaching—usually what he had been trying to pound into our heads for some weeks.

"You are a rambunctious bunch of bums!" he would shout, his beard sticking straight out at us like the point of a rapier. We had no notion of what he was saying but the sound delighted us. "Rambunctious bums!" we yelled to each other. One boy, I remember, was so amused by the sound of German that he leapt out of his seat and into the aisle, holding his belly, convulsed with laughter, while poor Hoffstadter blustered and turned red in the face.

When I graduated and went to Morris High School I again found German on my school program. Who put it there I never knew. At that time I did not know that I could have chosen Latin or French. I just accepted the fact that I had to take German and that was that. Nor did my parents or the parents of other students question the choice. No one said, "If the German language is taught in the schools, why not Italian?"

During this period the Italian language was completely ignored in the American schools. In fact, thorughout my whole elementary school career, I do not recall one mention of Italy or the Italian language or what famous Italians had done in the world, with the possible exception of Columbus, who was pretty popular in America. We soon got the idea that "Italian" meant something inferior, and a barrier was erected between children of Italian origin and their parents. This was the accepted process of Americanization. We were becoming Americans by learning how to be ashamed of our parents.

One of my favorite teachers, Mr. Carlson, gave me a nickel one day and asked me to go to the bakery shop to get him a Napoleon. I looked at him dumfounded but, having learned to do what I was told, I went off. In the corridor I ran into my friend. "Hey, Vito," I said, forgetting that in school I was supposed to call him Victor. "Know what Mr. Carlson just did? He gave me a nickel to buy him a Napoleon. Napoleon was a general!"

"Sure, he conquered half the world."

Vito walked over to the bakery with me and waited outside while I went in and placed the nickel on the counter. I felt that Mr. Carlson, whom I respected, was playing a joke on me. I could hardly bear the thought of it, expecting at any moment that the woman behind the counter was going to laugh in my face. "Give me a Napoleon," I muttered through my teeth.

When she reached under the counter and took out a piece of cream-filled pastry, I felt a tremendous relief. My faith in people was once more reaffirmed.

And then at Public School 83 there was a Miss Quigley. She offered a prize to the boy who would do the best work in class. I was that boy, and the prize was a beautiful illustrated edition of the life of Abraham Lincoln. I read it again and again and cherished it, because in those days books were very precious. Miss Quigley lent me others and told me how I could borrow books from the Aguilar Library at 110th Street.

Today the library is housed in a beautiful multistoried building. At that time it was in a small store and there wre not many books. Still, to those of us who never owned any, it was a fascinating and wonderful place. From that day on, hardly an afternoon passed that I did not go there to pick up a book.

Now I was living what seemed like fragmentary existences in different worlds. There was my life with my family and Aviglianese neighbors. My life on the streets of East Harlem. My life at Home Garden with Miss Ruddy. Life at the local public school. Life at whatever job I happened to have. Life in the wonder-world of books. There seemed to be no connection, one with the other; it was like turning different faucets on and off. Yet I was happy.

III
Responses to American Life

INTRODUCTION

The responses of Italian immigrants to American society were as varied as the contexts in which they occurred; and the responses have not been easily defined or understood. There is a rather large literature extant which deals with Italian American and American society: this literature (essentially an investigation of intergroup relations) breaks down into a number of components, all interrelated to some degree.

Usually, the starting point of the investigations is a discussion of group relations among Italians; [1] and an application of what is discerned to an understanding of interethnic relations (*e.g.,* Italians and the Irish; Italians and the Jews).[2] The intricacies of American politics are explored (*vis à vis* interethnic relations) with elaborate explanations for Italian American failures or, at best, modest successes.[3] Inevitably, the greater conceptual themes of acculturation and assimilation are introduced, with notices of the adaptation of Italian Americans to American culture:[4] this greater framework presents difficulties, not only because of the very great sub-

---

[1]"When the Italians came to the United States, their differences were still fresh and unmitigated by the mixed marriages and cultural syncretism that have accompanied the recent massive internal migration taking place within Italy . . . The Italian mass migration to the United States began a mere ten years after national unification and reached its climax when the first generation of Italian citizens had barely reached adulthood. Hence, the migrants left Italy not as Italians but as Genoese, Venetians, Neapolitans, Sicilians, Calabrians, and the like, and continued to identify themselves as such for some time, if not for the rest of their lives." Joseph Lopreato, *Italian Americans* (New York: Random House, 1970), p. 101.

[2]See, for example, Rudolf Glanz, *Jew and Italian: Historic Group Relations and the New Immigration,* 1881-1924 (New York: Ktav Publishing Co., 1971).

[3]A good overview is in *Ethnicity in American Political Life: The Italian-American Experience* (New York: American Italian Historical Association: Proceedings of the First Annual Conference, October 26, 1968).

[4]See F. Cordasco, "Introduction," Irvin L. Child, *Italian or American? The Second Generation in Conflict* (New York: Russell & Russell, 1970; originally, Yale University Press, 1943).

tleties which attend any study of the acculturation of a people, but more precisely (in the case of Italian Americans) because of the intrusion into the discussions, ineluctably but fatefully, of the doleful problems of crime, delinquency, and deviant behavior. In a sense, the discussion of crime adumbrates even the study of prejudice and discrimination against Italians.

In explaining the failure of the Italians to make a larger impact on the New York City scene, Nathan Glazer and Daniel P. Moynihan offer the following explanation:

> The reasons are complex. But high among them would have to be listed the curse of the Mafia. In the 1960's the curse compounded. Not only did the Italian population continue to suffer from the exactions of its criminal element—a basic ecological rule being that criminals prey first of all on those nearest them—but also the charge, or fear, or presumption of "Mafia connections" affected nearly the entire Italian community. Injustice leading to yet more injustice: that is about what happened. During the 1960's the mass media, *and the non-Italian politicians,* combined to make the Mafia a household symbol of evil and wrongdoing. Television ran endless crime series, such as *The Untouchables,* in which the criminals were, for all purposes, exclusively Italian. Attorneys General, of whom Robert F. Kennedy was the archetype, made the "war against organized crime" a staple of national politics. As Attorney General, Kennedy produced Joseph Valachi, who informed the nation that the correct designation of the syndicate was not Mafia but "Cosa Nostra"—"Our thing." True or not, the designation was solemnly accepted by the media, with an air almost of gratitude for the significance of the information thus divulged. On the occasion that a reputed "family head" would pass away (often as not peaceably, amidst modest comfort in Nassau County), the *New York Times* would discourse learnedly on what the probable succession would be.
>
> This is rather an incredible set of facts. Ethnic sensitivities in New York, in the nation, have never been higher than during the 1960's. To accuse a major portion of the population of persistent criminaltiy would seem a certain course of political or commercial disaster. But it was not. The contrast with the general "elite" response to Negro crime is instructive. Typically, the latter was blamed on white society. Black problems were muted, while Italian problems were emphasized, even exaggerated. Why?[5]

[5]Nathan Glazer and Daniel P. Moynihan, *Beyond the Melting Pot: The Negroes, Puerto Ricans, Jews, Italians and Irish of New York City* (Cambridge, Mass.: M.I.T. Press, 1970), pp. lxvi-lxvii.

Glazer and Moynihan do not have the answer, except to suggest that "there may have been some displacement of antiblack feeling to Italians [and that] society needs an unpopular group around, and the Italians were for many reasons available."

At best, it is difficult to deal retrospectively with the multifaceted responses of Italians to American society; and it is too early to assess the new ethnic consciousness manifested by Italian Americans in the present period (what Nicholas Pileggi has called "Risorgimento: The Red, White, and Greening of New York"),[6] but there is some truth in Erik Amfitheatrof's observation: "Clearly, many Italian-Americans are today responding to the complicated forces loosed by their assimilation into the American mainstream. The children of Italian immigrants no longer feel Italian: They are American. In shedding a sense of apartness from American life, they have also relinquished their once-powerful emotional association with a remote Italian world that they knew secondhand, from family recollections and legends. A void has been created, and they are now beginning to reevaluate their ethnic past—which is Italian-American rather than Italian—because it is an inescapable part of what they think about themselves, and what they tell their children."[7]

The materials assembled in this section illustrate a variety of contextual responses by the Italians to the greater American society, and of reactions to their presence in the United States. Gino C. Speranza's commentary (1904) on assimilation ("How It Feels to Be A Problem") is a classic statement on the anguish of enforced acculturation; and his proposal that Italian-Americans be represented in the Italian Parliament, if furtively pursued, is a bizarre facet of the immigrant experience. Lilian Brandt's "Transplanted Birthright" (1904) is a wonderfully perceptive overview of a wide range of adaptive responses in the Italian community as viewed by a sympathetic outside observer. Paul J. Campisi's study of the Italian family in the United States is the proper setting from which Irvin L. Child's examination of the acculturative process of second generation Italian Americans can be best understood.

I have chosen to include Gino C. Speranza's "Giuseppe Petrosino

---

[6]Nicholas Pileggi, "The Risorgimento of Italian Power: The Red, White and Greening of New York," *New York*, vol. 4 (June 7, 1971); see also, Richard Gambino, "Twenty Million Italians Can't Be Wrong." *New York Times* (April 30, 1972) which is somewhat superficial, but itself a manifestation of the resurgence of *Italianità*. An excellent discussion of the new Italian consciousness is in Silvano M. Tomasi, *The Italians in America* (New York: Istituto Italiana di Cultura, Occasional Paper, July 1971).

[7]Erik Amfitheatrof, *The Children of Columbus: An Informal History of Italians in the New World* (Boston: Little, Brown, 1973), p. 324.

and the Black Hand," and Gaetano D'Amato's "The Black Hand Myth" as introductory pieces to Francis A. J. Ianni's "The Mafia and the Web of Kinship"; together, the pieces afford perspectives from which crime in the Italian community may be studied, and more properly related to the total societal contexts in which it occurred.[8]

The aggregate response of Italians and their progeny to the American milieu has been felicitously capsuled by Alexander DeConde:

> Despite the cruelty of their experience, the suffering, and the discriminations they endured, these people of Italian stock took a tenacious hold on life in the United States. Yet they came too late and were too inarticulate, without even a clear national heritage or command of a common language beyond some dialect, to impress deeply their own cultural traits upon the social structure of America. At times, out of shame for their origins or to lessen the sting of discrimination, some abandoned even the cultural identity that went with Italian names. But that practice faded as second, third, and fourth generations acquired a sense of security in their own status.
>
> Sociologists and historians have argued convincingly that immigration—unless the emigrating group has special reasons for cultural survival, such as resistance to persecution—breeds grave problems. Ultimately in such a case, the new nationality would be absorbed without leaving much of a legacy. Italians and their descendants in the United States seem to have gone through this process, but with neither the swiftness nor the completeness the theorists have postulated. Although it is true that immigrant peoples in the second and third generation largely lose their language and culture, are transformed by the pressures for conformity in American society, are stripped of their original attributes, and are recreated as something new, some, such as Italian-Americans, are still identifiable as distinctive groups.[9]

[8]Reference should be made to the important full-scale study by Joseph L. Albini, *The American Mafia: Genesis of a Legend* (New York: Appleton-Century-Crofts, 1971), which maintains that the history of organized crime in the United States long antedated the arrival of Italians. Related to the stereotypes of the Italian as a criminal, was the nativist fear of anarchists syndicalists which is best exemplified in the notorious Sacco-Vanzetti case which attracted world wide attention in the 1920's. Nicola Sacco and Bartolomeo Vanzetti were electrocuted on August 23, 1927 in Charlestown, Massachusetts, after conviction for a murder/robbery committed on April 15, 1920 in South Braintree, an industrial town twelve miles south of Boston. A vast literature has grown up around the Sacco-Vanzetti case which continues to deal with the innocence or guilt of the men. If the case is to be understood at all it must be related to the hysteria which surrounded the suppression of anarchist/syndicalist conspiracies by the frightened governments of the period, and the United States was not immune to the hysteria. See Herbert B. Ehrmann, *The Case That Will Not Die: Commonwealth vs. Sacco and Vanzetti* (Boston: Little, Brown, 1969).

[9]Alexander DeConde, *Half Bitter, Half Sweet: An Excursion into Italian-American History* (New York: Charles Scribner's Sons, 1971), pp. 379-380.

The resurgence of ethnicity in American society in our own time has not spared Italian Americans; if anything the new ethnic consciousness has unleashed vertiginous forces amongst Italian Americans as contrasting as the journalistic sensationalism of Nicholas Pileggi and the "godfather business" of Mario Puzo.

GINO C. SPERANZA

HOW IT FEELS TO
BE A PROBLEM*

*A Consideration Of Certain Causes Which
Prevent Or Retard Assimilation*

The American nation seems to like to do some of its thinking aloud. Possibly this is true of other nations, but with this difference, that in the case of the American, the thinking aloud is not suppressed even when it deals with what may be termed the "country's guests." Older nations, perhaps because they lack the daring, self-sufficiency of the young, prefer, in similar cases, to think in a whisper. All countries have problems to grapple with, economic, political or social; but with America even the labor problem is popularly discussed as if its solution depended on that of the immigration problem.

Now, considering the large percentage of foreign born in the population of the United States, it is a strange fact how few Americans ever consider how very unpleasant, to say the least, it must be to the foreigners living in their midst to be constantly looked upon either as a national problem or a national peril. And this trying situation is further strained by the tone in which the discussion is carried on, as if it applied to utter strangers miles and miles away, instead of to a large number of resident fellow citizens. Perhaps this attitude may be explained by the fact that to the vast majority of Americans "foreigner" is synonymous with the popular conception of the immigrant as a poor, ignorant and uncouth stranger, seeking for better luck in a new land. But poverty and ignorance and uncouthness, even if they exist as general characteristics of our immigrants, do not necessarily exclude intelligence and sensitiveness. Too often, let it be said, does the American of common schooling interpret differences from his own standards and habits of life, as necessarily signs of inferiority.

Charities, Vol. 12 (1904), pp. 457-463.

Foreignness of features or of apparel is for him often the denial of brotherhood. Often, again, the fine brow and aquiline nose of the Latin will seem to the American to betoken a criminal type rather than the impress of a splendid racial struggle.

Then there is another large class of "plain Americans" who justify a trying discussion of the stranger within the gates by the self-satisfying plea that the foreigner should be so glad to be in the "land of the free" that he cannot mind hearing a few "unpleasant truths" about himself.

This is not an attempt to show that the tide of immigration does not carry with it an ebb of squalor and ignorance and undesirable elements. It is rather an endeavor to look at the problem, as it were, *from the inside*. For if America's salvation from this foreign invasion lies in her capacity to assimilate such foreign elements, the first step in the process must be a thorough knowledge of the element that should be absorbed.

Many imagine that the record and strength of the American democracy suffice of themselves to make the foreigner love the new land and engender in him a desire to serve it; that, in other words, assimilation is the natural tendency. Assimilation, however, is a dual process of forces interacting one upon the other. Economically, this country can act like a magnet in drawing the foreigner to these shores, but you cannot rely on its magnetic force to make the foreign *an American*. To bring about assimilation the larger mass should not remain passive. It must attract, *actively attract*, the smaller foreign body.

It is with this in mind that I say that if my countrymen here keep apart, if they herd in great and menacing city colonies, if they do not learn your language, if they know little about your country, the fault is as much yours as theirs. And if you wish to reach us you will have to batter down some of the walls you have yourselves built up to keep us from you.

What I wish to examine, then, is how and what Americans are contributing to the process of the assimilation of my countrymen who have come here to live among them.

I have before me a pamphlet which a well-known American society prints for distribution among arriving immigrants. On the title page is the motto: *A Welcome to Immigrants and Some Good Advice*. The pamphlet starts out by telling the arriving stranger that this publication is presented to him "by an American patriotic society, whose duty is to teach American principles"—a statement which must somewhat bewilder foreigners. Then it proceeds to advise him. In America, it tells him, "you need not be rich to be happy and respected." "In other countries," it proceeds, "the people belong to the government. They are called subjects. They are under the power of some Emperor, King, Duke or other ruler," which permits the belief that the patriotic author of this pamphlet is conversant mostly with medieval history. There are some surprising explanations of the constitution, showing as wide a knowledge of American constitutional history as of that of modern Europe—but space forbids their quotation. "If the common people of other countries had faith in each other, there would be no Czars, Kaisers and Kings ruling them under the pretext of divine right." This is certainly a gem of historical exposition.

Then, in order to make the stranger feel comfortable, it tells him, "you must be honest and honorable, clean in your person, and decent in your talk." Which, of course, the benighted foreigner reads as a new decalogue. With characteristic modesty the author reserves for the last praise of his country: "Ours," he says, "is the strongest government in the world, because it is the people's government." Then he loses all self-restraint in a patriotic enthusiasm. "We have more good land in cultivation then in all Europe. We have more coal, and oil, and iron and copper, then can be found in all the countries of Europe. We can raise enough foodstuffs to feed all the rest of the world. We have more railroads and navigable rivers than can be found in the rest of the civilized world. We have more free schools than the rest of the world . . . So great is the extent (of our country), so varied its resources, that its people are not dependent on the rest of the world for what they absolutely need. Can there be any better proof that this is the best country in the world? Yes, there is one better proof. Our laws are better and more justly carried out."

Between such instruction and the welcome the immigrant gets from the immigration officials, he ought to feel that this is certainly the "best country in the world."

Perhaps the first impressions the foreigners receive are not a fair test of what it really feels to be a problem—because the initial adaptation to new and strange conditions is necessarily trying to any one.

The real test comes after—years after, perhaps—and it is this aftermath that I wish to examine. Perhaps I come from a hyper-sensitive race, and what I say of my people cannot apply to the immigrants of other nationalties, but close and constant contact with Italians of all classes on the one hand and twenty years of strenuous American living on the other, seem justification for voicing the sentiments of my countrymen among a people, many of whom look upon us as a menace. And the fact that though many suffer, yet few cry out, may be a further justification for one from their common average to speak for them.

Naturally, when one speaks of the Italian in America, the American thinks at once of the ubiquitous unskilled laborer. He thinks of him as a class or a mass composed or more or less picturesque elements, with no particular individual characteristics. This is especially true of the men who employ such a class. Through the padrone system of engaging men, the employer never comes to know the employed. He gives an order to the padrone to get him "five hundred dagoes." The men are supplied, they do their work and are passed on to other jobs. However practical this system may appear, it is based on a vicious mistake. The chief characteristic of the Italian is his individuality, and a system that treats him as one of a homogeneous mass is essentially wrong and cannot yield the best results. When the Irishman supplied the labor market in America, it may have been a simple thing to deal with him in masses; to apply that system to the Italian is to lose sight of elemental differences.

In endeavoring to graft the system employed in the case of Irish labor on the Italian, employers discovered a new element which they did not care to study or did not know how. So they tried to patch up the difficulty by the introduction of the padrone. This Italo-American middleman is for the laborer, to all intents and purposes, the real employer. How can you expect assimilation of this vast class of laborers when you uphold and maintain a system which completely isolates the class from its American superior? It may be argued that the padrone system is a necessity in dealing with large bodies of Italian laborers; but this is an argument which stops short in its conclusions. It is like claiming that an interpreter is necessary in addressing a foreigner; he is, unless you learn the foreign language. And, moreover, if you depend too much on the interpreter you will oftentimes find he is not interpreting correctly. Against this it may be urged that it is the business of the foreigner to adjust himself to his American employer; but how can he when you interpose a padrone?

Now, as a rule, padrones are of a type hardly calculated to teach their men what is best in American life. They are generally shrewd fellows with a good smattering of bad English and well versed in American boss methods. But they know their men well; they count on their ignorance and implicit confidence, on their helplessness and loyalty to the *compaesano*—be he right or wrong. Naturally, the padrone will endeavor to keep the laborer from all contact with his American superior; he will make himself the final arbiter and supreme power. I know of several instances where, in order to prevent an appeal to the contractor, the padrone has taught the laborer to fear his superior as a cruel and unapproachable person. Hence, this vast foreign mass touches at no point the American element or touches it in a way to make them desire to avoid it.

Is it a wonder that the intensely sociable Italian herds with his fellows and will not mix? Foreign urban congestion is a real problem, but may it not be that the remedy has to come from others than the foreigners? You begin by drawing a sharp line against him; you distinguish him from others. The cultured among you persist in seeing in him only a wearying picturesqueness with a background of mediaeval romance and Roman greatness; the uncultured among you see in every *meridionale* a possible *mafioso*, in every *settentrionale* one more mouth to fill from that "bankrupt Italy."

The better disposed tell us we are hard workers and earn every cent we make; but even these speak as from master to man. Perhaps it is our friends that make us feel most keenly that we are a problem. They take us under their wing, they are zealous in their defense, they treat us like little children. They speak of the debt the world owes Italy, they benignantly remind their countrymen that these foreigners have seen better days. It is extremely trying—this well-meant kindness that disarms criticism.

Of course, criticism by the stranger within your gates seems ungracious; but whenever it is attempted it is suppressed by this common question: "If you don't like it, why don't you go back?" The answer is never given, but it exists. For the majority of us this is our home and we have worked very hard for everything we have earned or won. And if we find matter for criticism it is because nothing is perfect; and if we institute comparisons it is because, having lived in two lands, we have more of the wherewithal of comparisons than those who have lived in only one country.

Then there is the American press. How is it aiding our assimilation? It would not be difficult to name those few newspapers in the United States which give space either as news or editorially, to nonsensational events or problems with which Europe is grappling. As regards Italy, there is such a dearth of information of vital importance that little, if anything, is known by the average American, of the economic or political progress of that country. Columns on Musolino, half-page headlines on the mafia, but never a word on the wonderful industrial development in northern Italy, never a notice of the financial policies that have brought Italian finances to a successful state!

What is the American press doing to help assimilate this "menacing" element in the republic?

"Why is it," was asked of a prominent American journalist, "that

you print news about Italians which you would not of other
nationalities?"

"Well, it is this way," was the answer, "if we published them about
the Irish or the Germans we should be buried with letters of protest;
the Italians do not seem to object."

It would be nearer the truth to say that they have learned the uselessness of objecting unless they can back up the objection by a "solid
Italian vote."

One result of the unfriendliness of the popular American press is
that it drives Italians to support a rather unwholesome Italian colonial press. Why should they read American papers that chronicle only
the misdeeds of their compatriots? Better support a local press which,
however poor and ofttimes dishonest, keeps up the courage of these
expatriates by telling them what young Italy is bravely doing at home
and abroad. But this colonial press widens the cleavage between the
nations, puts new obstacles in the way of assimilation and keeps up
racial differences.

To feel that we are considered a problem is not calculated to make
us sympathize with your efforts in our behalf, and those very efforts
are, as a direct result, very likely to be misdirected. My countrymen
in America, ignorant though many of them are, and little in touch
with Americans, nevertheless feel keenly that they are looked upon
by the masses as a problem. It is, in part, because of that feeling that
they fail to take an interest in American life or to easily mix with the
natives. And though it may seem far-fetched, I believe that the feeling
that they are unwelcome begets in them a distrust of those defenses to
life, liberty and property which the new country is presumed to put
at their disposal. They have no excess of confidence in your courts
and it is not surprising, however lamentable, that the more hot-head-
ed sometimes take the law into their own hands. You cannot expect
the foreigner of the humbler class to judge beyond his experience—
and his experience of American justice may be comprised in what he
learns in some of the minor tribunals controlled by politicians, and
in what he has heard of the unpublished lynchings of his countrymen
in some parts of the new land. What appeal can the doctrine of
state supremacy and federal non-interference make to him? Imagine what you would think of Italian justice if the American sailors
in Venice, in resisting arrest by the constituted authorities, had been
strung up to a telegraph pole by an infuriated Venetian mob, and the
government at Rome had said, with the utmost courtesy: "We are
very sorry and greatly deplore it, but we can't interfere with the auton-
omy of the province of Venetia!"

I am aware that the question is often asked: If these people are sensitive about being discussed as a problem and a menace, why do they come here? It is a question asked every day in the guise of an argument, a final and crushing argument. But is it really an argument? Is it not rather a question susceptible of a very clear and responsive answer. They come because this is a new country and there is a great deal of room here, and because you invite them. If you really did not want them you could keep them out as you have done with the Chinese.

I am not attempting to minimize the bad aspects of large numbers of aliens pouring into a new land; it is because I recognize such bad aspects and the necessity of using means to prevent harm, that I urge the study of the question from a neglected side. If assimilation is the only way out, then I say, do not follow methods that negative all efforts toward such a desired end. This new material in your body politic you call *dangerous;* why not be more precise in your definition and call it *raw?* One of the most intelligent American women I know, when told of my intention to write on this subject, said to me in all seriousness: "You must take your subject broadly. Go back to the time when your ancestors watched the Goths come over the mountains into what seemed to your ancestors to be their land." Of course, if you approach the question in that spirit, if you see a similitude between a barbaric invasion by martial usurpers bent on destroying a great civilized power, and the peaceable and natural process of emigration of civilized peoples from a land of classic civilization to a new country in its infancy, then there is little hope for an understanding. If you approach this raw material as dangerous, you will force it back on itself and perpetuate racial distinctions; you cannot, in the nature of things, deal fairly, calmly and scientifically with what you fear. Certainly you cannot deal with it in a sympathetic spirit. But look upon this foreign contingent as raw and crude material, and then the opportunity for infinite possibilities is within your grasp. What is dangerous demands destruction; but you can mould the raw. And with the possibility of tangible results in such moulding, is born hope and sympathy, optimism and enthusiasm.

Perhaps the hopefulness of this contention needs some proof of its reasonableness. In other words, what evidence is there that my countrymen, for example, should be considered rather raw material than a dangerous element? Let us study this point carefully, seeking arguments, if any there be, based not on the data of sentiment or from facts covering a short period or a small locality. Men and races cannot be judged by such standards. Let us rather examine historical, economical and political facts.

The racial traits and characteristics that have made Italy the "loved

Mother of Civilization" are not ephemeral qualities any more than is the cephalic index of the Mediterranean. They are qualities that persist and count; they may be dormant or the opportunity may be lacking for their display or action, but they must be counted as an asset in inventorying an Italian. There is more than a reasonable presumption that the race that achieved the dual political and spiritual supremacy in the Rome of Caesar and in that of Peter, that saved Europe from the eastern rule and found for it a new empire in the West, has the seeds of great possibilities. Those that crossed the mountains and brought light to Gallia, and those after them who, in a gentler age, crossed beyond to the land of your forefathers as heralds of that humanism that ennobled all that received it, were the ancestors of these people that flock to you now and whom some of you dread. Until you can show that the advent of these people has had a harmful influence upon new neighbors in the past, your conception of them as a menace has at least no historic basis. The evidence is all the other way.

Let us examine the political testimony in the case. Here we need not go very far back; the memories of living men suffice. By a tremendous and heroic effort, Italy achieved the dream of political unity in 1870. Such accomplishment meant the destruction of the results of centuries of well-entrenched oppression and foreign bondage. But Italy was united as much by the political sagacity of Cavour as by the heroic qualities of Victor II and Garibardi. It was the one country that justified its bloody struggle by the sanction of the political plebiscite. And ever since young Italy has patiently and bravely fought its way against tremendous odds toward its political ideals. Popular American belief to the contrary, as Dr. G. Tosti, one of the most scholarly of Italians in America, has shown, Italian financial policies have been so ably planned and handled that there has been a continuous rise in the value of Italian state bonds on foreign markets and a constant diminution in the rate of exchange.[1] Nor is it to be forgotten that, despite the heavy taxes imposed to meet the tremendous demands made upon her youth, united Italy has never admitted the possibility of bankruptcy and never paid her national debt in paper as, for instance, Russia has done.

Hence we see that the political and economic as well as the historic evidence tends to support an optimistic view of the possibilities of the Italian immigrant.

[1]"The Financial and Industrial Outlook of Italy," by Dr. G. Tosti in *American Journal of Sociology*, Vol. VIII, No. 1.

Not more relevant but more convincing, because more susceptible of direct and personal certification, is the evidence that the Ialian immigrant himself furnishes in this country. It is true that, as a nationality, Ialians have not forced recognition; though numerically strong there is no such "Italian vote" as to interest politians. They have founded no important institutions; they have no strong and well-administered societies as have the Germans and the Irish. They have no representative press, and well-organized movements among them for their own good are rare. Those who believe in assimilation may be thankful for all these things; for it could be held that it is harder to assimilate bodies or colonies well organized as foreign elements, then individuals held together in imperfect cohesion.

Yet the Italian in America as an individual is making good progress. In New York City, the individual holdings of Italians in savings banks is over $15,000,000; they have some four thousand real estate holdings of the clear value of $20,000,000. About ten thousand stores in the city are owned by Italians at an estimated value of $7,000,000, and to this must be added about $7,500,000 invested in wholesale business. The estimated material value of the property of the Italian colony in New York is over $60,000,000, a value much below that of the Italian colonies of St. Louis, San Francisco, Boston and Chicago, but, a fair showing for the great "dumping ground" of America.

But the sympathetic observer will find the most remarkable progress on what may be called the spiritual side of the Italians among us. It is estimated that there are more than fifty thousand Italian children in the public schools of New York City and adjacent cities where Italians are settled. Many an Italian laborer sends his son to Italy to "finish his education" and when he cannot afford this luxury of doubtful value, he gets him one of the *maestri* of Little Italy to perfect him in his native language. In the higher education you will find Italians winning honors in several of our colleges, universities and professional schools. I know of one Italian who saves money barbering during the summer and on Sundays, to pay his way through Columbia University. I know of another who went through one of our best universities on money voluntarily advanced by a generous and far-seeing professor. The money was repaid with interest and the boy is making a mark in the field of mathematics. I know of a third, the winner of a university scholarship, who paid his way by assisting in editing an Italian paper during spare hours; a fourth, who won the fellowship for the American School at Rome, and thus an American institution sent an Italian to perfect his special scholarship in Italy.

New York City now counts 115 Italian registered physicians, 63 pharmacists, 4 dentists, 21 lawyers, 15 public school teachers, 9 architects, 4 manufacturers of technical instruments and 7 mechanical engineers. There are two Italian steamship lines with bi-weekly sailings, 16 daily and weekly papers, and several private schools. Italians support several churches, one modest but very efficient hospital, one well-organized savings-bank and a chamber of commerce. They have presented three monuments to the municipality, one, the statue of Columbus, a valuable work of art. They are raising funds to build a school in Verdi's honor, under the auspices of the Children's Aid Society, and are planning to organize a trust company.

I have given the statistics for New York City because the Italian colony on Manhattan is less flourishing than those in other large American cities. So that what is hopeful for New York is even more promising in Philadelphia, St. Louis and Boston.

As regards the dependent and delinquent classes among Italians, a good deal of misapprehension exists. There is no such thing as a dependent *class* of Italians in the United States. Mendicancy, which is pointed out by the foreign traveler as one of the sores of Italy, is practically unknown among Italians here.

Of the delinquent class, some consideration is necessary. While it is true that many Italians are arrested for "violation of city ordinances," these arrests are often the result of ignorance—being the infraction of *mala prohibita* rather than of *mala in se*. The viciousness or weakness which results in drunkenness seldom manifests itself in Italians. In several years of practice at the bar, I have seldom seen an arrest for intoxication among them.

On the other hand, I am aware that Italians are often guilty of crimes of blood. But because these are mostly crimes of passion, committed without secrecy, they make excellent copy for the newspaper writers. As we read of these, while less exciting crimes fail to be chronicled, the popular belief is formed that more crimes are committed by Italians than by any other foreigners. I have yet failed to see any reliable statistical proof of this assertion. I do not seek to justify crimes of passion when I say that it is something to remember that an Italian will stab or shoot, but seldom poison. His hot-headedness prevents his committing crimes necessitating subtle and careful planning. One result is that by such "open crimes" he always pays the penalty of his misdeeds because proof of his overt act is always possible, whereas the carefully planned crimes of others often go unpunished from lack of evidence.

We have rapidly surveyed the conditions of the Italian among us —his historic background and the political and economic achievements of his brother at home. To consider him without his hereditary possibilities is to measure him by an unfair standard. The most highly civilized and desirable immigrant cannot adjust himself quickly to the environment of a new land; probably the only fair test of the value of any immigration is what it contributes to the new land through the second generation. If this is so, all discussion on the menace of Italian immigration would seem premature.

There is one more question that an Italian, speaking for his countrymen here, may urge upon Americans who are interested in the problem of assimilation. It is this: That you should make my countrymen love your country by making them see what is truly good and noble in it. Too many of them, far too many, know of America only what they learn from the corrupt politician, the boss, the "banchiere" and the ofttimes rough policeman. I have been in certain labor camps in the South where my countrymen were forced to work under the surveillance of armed guards. I have spoken to some who had been bound to a mule and whipped back to work like slaves. I have met others who bore the marks of brutal abuses committed by cruel bosses with the consent of their superiors. What conception of American liberty can these foreigners have?

This, then, is the duty upon those who represent what is good and enduring in Americanism—to teach these foreigners the truth about America. Remember these foreigners are essentially men and women like yourselves whatever the superficial differences may be. This is the simple fact far too often forgotten—if not actually denied. And this must be the excuse if you discuss these people as a menace, pitching your discussion as if we were beyond hearing, and beneath feeling, and sometimes even as if beyond redemption.

Make us feel that America has good friends, intelligent, clear-sighted friends; friends that will not exploit us; friends that will not be interested merely because of what Italy did in the past for all civilization, but friends that will extend to us the sympathy which is due from one man to another. You will thereby make us not merely fellow voters, but will prepare us for the supreme test of real assimilation—the wish to consider the adopted country as a new and dear Fatherland.

Italian East Harlem, New York City, late 1920's

Italian District, Lower East Side, New York City, 1920's

Our Lady of Mt. Carmel Feast Day, early 1930's.
Italian East Harlem, New York City

Italian East Harlem, New York City, early 1930's

Italian Street Vendor, Greenwich Village, New
York City, late 1930's

Italian Street Vendor, Italian East Harlem, New
York City, mid-1930's

Italian East Harlem, New York City, 1942

Italian Espresso Shop, New York City, mid-1930's

Italian Scavenger, Italian East Harlem, New York City, 1930's

Italian Fruit and Vegetable Vendor. Italian East
Harlem, New York City, 1930's

Italian District, Greenwich Village, New York
City, mid-1920's

March For Better Housing. Italian East Harlem,
New York City, early 1940's

Street Scene. Italian East Harlem, New York City, mid-1930's

Italian Grandparents and Child. Italian East
Harlem, New York City, late 1930's

Statue of Our Lady of Mt. Carmel. Our Lady of
Mt. Carmel R. C. Church, Italian East Harlem

Italian Women Outside Tenement. Italian East
Harlem, New York City, late 1930's

LILIAN BRANDT

A TRANSPLANTED
BIRTHRIGHT*

*The Development Of the Second Generation
of The Italians in an American Environment*

"Dear and most gracious Signora A———," wrote
Giulio, aged twelve, to his teacher in an industrial school
when she asked for letters containing certain information.
"My father has been two years in America, and he follows
the trade of carpenter, and . . . he would like to make
of me an honest, industrious boy, with, at the same time,
a trade better than his, and he sends me to school so that
when I am grown I may be an educated man and useful
to others.

"Later I wish to make machines for factories, and thus
to have better wages than others.

"Having nothing more to say I kiss my hand to you and
assure you that I am
Your
"Giulio."

This letter is typical. Its grace and courtesy, and the ambition it reveals, are characteristic of the Italian children in America. The
first two qualities are an inheritance that has come down to them
through the centuries; the third is developed, or at least given a chance
for expression, by American conditions.

Italian children, whether born in Italy or here, find America much
to their taste. They are prompt to adapt themselves to the freedom
of the new country and use all the facilities at their disposal for rising
to a higher economic level than their parents. Modification of their
names is one of the familiar external evidences of a disposition to become truly American, as it is also an example of the American tendency to make all things conform to our own ways. The transformation of Vincenzo Campobello to Jim Campbell, the general drop-

*Charities, Vol. 12 (1904), pp. 494-499.

ping of vowels and consequent condensation, are inevitable, and are
but a repetition of the changes that occurred when Goth and Roman
began to live together or when the Normans settled in England. But
because the American element which furnishes standards for the
Italians is usually of Irish origin, and because the Italian is actuated
by a deeper motive than mere convenience, the names of Patrick
O'Neill and Mike Mahoney are frequently borne by olive-skinned
Sicilian boys; and the soft-eyed Lucia, not yet a year from Naples, may
be heard to say, "Faith an' I won't then!" with the true Celtic in-
flection, thus bearing unconscious testimony to the assimilating
properties of the older and better established elements of the population. The boy or girl is seldom willing to go back to Italy. Mr.
Davenport, in his letters to the Brooklyn *Eagle*, has described the
misfits arising from the return of New York city public school products to an Italian village. In their enthusiasm for America, the children too often develop a tendency to despise the ways of their fathers
and lose their love of Italy and their pride in being Italians. Too often,
also, their sudden plunge into unaccustomed freedom has, as is ever
the case, its evil results. The removal of the old restraints, whether of
tradition or of law, before the self-governing power has been developed, is apt to produce an intoxication which makes the transition
period trying to all concerned. In the case of the Italians, it is especially trying to the parents, in American tenement neighborhoods,
who are completely at a loss as to how to deal with their children when
they are mischievous or unruly.

They are almost equally disturbed at assertions of independence
which are, to American minds, quite legitimate. They wish to keep
the children, and particularly the girls, close at home, and think them
"wild" if they show any desire to get out of the crowded rooms and
onto the street. Mothers do not want their daughters to go to evening
schools. "Why should she learn to write?" asked one of them,
"she'd only write to her 'fellas.'" The impossibility, under the conditions of New York life, of bringing up children according to traditional ideas of what is proper, is responsible for a large part of the
eagerness with which Italian parents seek to patronize institutions
for children.

The institution to them is not only a *collegio*, where good instruction is thoughtfully provided by an interested public, but
it is also too often a place where the child will be kept off the
streets, broken of his "wild" ways, and properly cared for until
he arrives at an age of self-support.

The most striking manifestation of the American spirit is, perhaps, found in the economic aspirations of the children. They are
rarely content to remain at their fathers' level. The ambition which

in Italy would have been kept dormant by social traditions, is roused in America by the all pervasive and generally effective idea of "getting ahead." It is the exception if the son of the immigrant who "works at shovel" or "goes with the hod" grows up to use the same tool. If the son of a bootblack chooses that profession, it is generally found that, while his father carried a kit, his idea is to advance at least to the dignity of a chair, which represents a certain amount of capital invested and a comparatively stable business. Another common instance of advancement by this evolutionary process is from fruit-peddling with a push-cart or even a basket, to the proprietorship of a corner stand. Children going out from the higher grades of the public schools generally hope for clerical positions; failing that, they choose factory work.

The four Italian schools of the Children's Aid Society in New York represent probably the poorest part of the Italian population of the city—the part with the least natural opportunity. The older children in these schools were asked, a few weeks ago, to write letters to their teachers, telling them what they would like to "be" when they grew up. As a result of this the writer has authentic records of the economic ideals of 143 Italian children between the ages of nine and fourteen. Some of them have been in America only a few months; others were born here: all are from families in which the struggle for daily existence is not uniformly successful. The fathers of these children are tailors, hod-carriers, laborers, street-clearners, boot-blacks, shoemakers, stone-cutters, peddlers, bricklayers, carpenters, rag-pickers, macaroni and candy makers, and bar-cleaners, with single representatives of such better-paid occupations as butcher, grocer, policeman and postman.

Of the 143 children, sixty-six are boys and seventy-seven girls. Four of the boys were undecided about the career they would choose and one pathetically confided, "My papa used to work in a laundry . . . He does not work for a long time because he is sick. When I can work I will do any work I can get because I have to help mamma because papa is sick."

Among the other sixty-one, ten of the younger boys elect to follow their fathers' calling. In two cases the father's occupation is not indicated in any way. The other forty-nine are all looking forward to something which seems to them higher. Four, whose fathers are a hod-carrier, a tailor, a bricklayer, and a macaroni maker, would be doctors, one adding confidently: "And I will learn very hard, for I like to be a good doctor, and I will make a lot money, and I will come to be a rich man and I will give my mother some money to buy a machine." Two, son of a street-cleaner and son of a tailor, propose to be lawyers. One wants to be a "music man and play mandolin and all the new songs, and play guitar"; another will be an artist; another, the heir of a day-laborer, says. "I am going to write books and people will say I am a smart man." One, whose father "goes all over with a street piano," hopes to "write in an office, write down numbers and count them up and write names." To "write in a bank" is the goal of another. A shoemaker's son aspires to be a "printer man, to printer the papers to sell—the *Journal*, the *Sun*, the *World*, the *Telegram*, the *Globe*, the *Mail and Express*, and lots of other papers, and our Italian *Bolletino della Sera*, that's the best work that I could do."

A fourteen-year-old, whose home is one of the most insanitary tenements of the city, and whose father is a peddler, writes, "If fortune favors me I shall continue my studies." The occupations of tailor, carpenter, bookkeeper, engineer, butcher, messenger, druggist, elevator-runner, truck-driver and store-keeper all have votaries. Seven of the boys indicate definitely that their choice is determined by the desire to "make a lot of money." A few, however, are actuated rather by pure love of glory or adventure; these are looking forward to being a policeman, a fireman (who will "blow out the fire") or even a soldier. Several show that they esteem respect and appreciation beyond gain, for they mean "to be called smart." An interesting declaration is this: "My father is a grocery, and I am going to be a farmer." Perhaps the most dramatic choice is that of twelve-year-old Luigi, His father is a coat presser, but Luigi spurns the colorless, hateful drudgery of the tailor shop, and will have a life of interest and excitement for he "would like to be a horso racing."

The seventy-seven girls show less variety and less individuality. The Italian girl, even more than the average girl, expects to be occupied, and at an earlier age than the average girl, with the care of her own household. Whatever her expectations, however, every girl indicates some one occupation as her choice. Forty-seven wish to be dressmakers and thirteen give their teachers the sincerest testimony of admiration by choosing that profession. Several of the would-be teachers explain that they will teach the children to sew, and one justifies her choice by the comment, "And then I will do as I please." Two would like to work in a candy shop, two in a tobacco shop, two would be hairdressers, two milliners, two "grocer girls." "My father shines," wrote one of these, "but I want to be a grocer girl." Another "would like to be a sister of the church," and the rest are attracted by the occupation of nurse, box-maker, "news-carrier," typewriter, cash girl, and "joiner"—whatever that last designation may imply.

On the whole, the work chosen by the girls is less indicative of ambition than of another prominent characteristic of the Italian children—their aptitude for handicraft. In book learning the general estimate of their teachers is that they are bright and quick when interested, but restless and lacking in continued application. Similarly, they are not always the greastest credit to their settlement friends, judged by the standard of regularity of attendance; for, as one head-worker expresses it, "a gang of Italian boys may start for the settlement in time for their club, with every expectation of being there, but be diverted on the way, and not show up."

In manual training, however, drawing, and whatever requires skilled fingers and artistic sense, they are easily leaders. It is not for nothing that they have lived for centuries in the land of beauty. Italy gives her children an instinctive knowledge of the beautiful in color and contour, which they unconsciously apply to practical affairs and which we others spend hours, and years, of effort to acquire. The attractive arrangement of fruit stands, the picturesque gayety of the Italian quarters in our cities, the groups of pilgrims from those far-away quarters who may be seen in the art galleries of Boston and New York on any "free" Sunday afternoon: these are familiar evidences of a racial characteristic which should be recognized as a distinct contribution to American life.

The girls in the evening schools of the Children's Aid Society—for some parents can be persuaded to countenance their daughters' attendance—are especially interested in tissue paper work, embroidery, and crocheting, and they work hard and show much ingenuity in making pretty things for their homes.

A teacher of drawing in the public schools of a New Jersey town which has a large Italian population, has found the Italian children far more talented, on the average, than the others. The first day that her classes were given brushes and paints, she noticed that the Italian children held the brushes correctly and handled them as if they had been using them for years, and that they scrupulously confined the paint they applied to the drawn outline, while the little Germans and Americans splashed cheerfully beyond the lines and seemed to find a paint brush as unfamiliar to their hands as Charlemagne's pen was to his. The teacher was surprised to find, also, when she gave a lesson on the principles of composition in pcitures—a lesson generally very difficult to comprehension—that the Italian pupils seemed to have an instinctive appreciation of what the others were obliged to accept on faith, and that they applied the rules with unerring judgment. These general observations seem more significant than individual instances of talent, since, as a small German girl objected when this teacher was commending the work of Antonio and Giuseppe and Tommaso, "But teacher, Max Schneider can draw too." Individual instances are, however, of interest, and might be cited indefinitely—the boy who filled a book with views of the school building and many architectural details; the one who, when the attitude of a little girl posed by the teacher for the class to draw did not seem to him, from his desk, wholly pleasing, deliberately walked up to the model and changed her position to suit him better; and the one who spent his evenings at the settlement in painting daffodils while his comrades revelled in exciting games.

The art sense of the Italians is one of the most valuable contributions they bring to their new country, because it is one of the qualities which we most conspicuously lack. At present, however, this contribution is largely wasted or misused.

It is misused when the parents, by reason of that most commendable trait, so often associated with the land of their adoption—the ambition to make money and "get on"—exploit their children while they are yet children. Italian boys and girls in institutions are demanded again by their parents as soon as they reach the legal working age, and are put to work at whatever offers. Tiny children are so deft with their fingers that they are kept working every day after school hours and at night at artificial flowers or feathercurling, or some similar occupation engaged in by their mothers at home.

The parents are responsible for a part of the waste, as well as for the exploitation, of their children's artistic ability. As for themselves and their own gifts, the struggle for a living makes choice impossible. But even when an opportunity offers for the proper education of a gifted child, the parents too rarely resist the temptation of an immediate advantage.

Another factor which contributes to the waste of these special gifts is the race prejudice which every new element in our population has had to encounter, from the day when the Indians saw, with dissatisfaction, the invasion of the first white men. There is in New York city a factory where ornamental brass and iron work of unusual beauty is done. The superintendent welcomes Italians, but his German foreman will have none of them. One young man, who did remarkably artistic work, was complained of again and again by the foreman, but no difinite charges were made. He insisted on the boy's dismissal. Finally the superintendent said, "Well, what is your objection to Rocco? Did you ever see him do anything wrong?" "O! no," replied the foreman, "he's too smart for that; but nobody could be as smart as that Rocco is and be all right."

Public school teachers do much, by calling to the attention of the older children the superior points of their Italian classmates, to break down these barriers of prejudice and disdain. The drawing teacher quoted above was recently given somewhat disconcerting evidence that her efforts in this direction had borne fruit. The town, it should be said by way of preface, is one in which the comtemptuous appellation of *Dago* is supplanted by the equally contemptuous *Ginney*. The teacher one day placed before the children a toy animal for them to draw and asked if any one knew its name. A little Irish girl, with all the courtesy at her command, vouchsafed: "I know that out in the park they call it an Italian pig."

The chief responsibility for the waste of this aptitude for artistic handicraft possessed by the Italians rests not on the parent's avarice nor on race prejudice, but on the American educational system and our failure to appreciate the value of what we are throwing away. The whole tendency of the public school system is to divert the children from manual work of any sort to clerical pursuits, and there is comparatively little instruction in a marketable kind of handiwork in the classes and clubs carried on by private enterprise to supplement the public school education. Manual training, as generally taught, is valuable rather as training the fingers and senses, furnishing entertainment, and suggesting possibilities of improving the home, than as supplying any education which would help toward earning a living. The explanation of this is to be found in the fact that there is practically no demand for hand work. Our age has little regard for beauty if it costs more, as it generally does, than ugliness. We must first, if we are to accept and use to our own advantage the gifts which the Italians come bringing, educate ourselves into an appreciation of those gifts. When that is done there will be a market for the things they can do better than we, and the provision for trade education will quickly follow.

The dismay with which we ordinarily contemplate any modification of "the American type" suggests that we are losing that sense of humor which we flatter ourselves is a conspicuous American characteristic. For surely an unprejudiced scrutiny of the American type does not establish the conviction that there is nothing further to be desired. There are points at which we are susceptible of improvement; there are qualities, of which we have now only a faint trace, for whose possession we should be justified in making some sacrifice. The Italians have a delight in simple pleasures, an appreciation for other things than mere financial success, a sense of beauty, a natural kindliness and social grace, which would be not wholly unendurable additions to our predominant traits. It rests with us whether we shall recognize these qualities, foster them, and assimilate them, or, by persistently ignoring and despising them, stamp them as undesirable, un-American, and mould the Italian immigrant in our own image.

GINO C. SPERANZA

POLITICAL REPRESENTATION OF ITALO-AMERICAN COLONIES IN THE ITALIAN PARLIAMENT*

During the past year discussion has been renewed in Italy on the suggestion made by some parliamentarians that the Italian colonies, outside of the Kingdom be allowed political representation at home.

This proposition is not devoid of interest for us, because by "colonies" in this case are included what we are in the habit of calling our "Little Italys."

The importance of New York, for instance, as an Italian colony, is growing every day. There are more Italians in this city than in any city of Italy except Naples, Milan and Rome. Nor is its importance merely a question of population. Its commercial and financial interests are actively on the increase. The irresponsible "bankers" who victimized the ingenuous immigrant are being supplanted by solid banks like Perera's on Wall street and Conti's on Broadway, and by well-financed institutions such as the Italian Savings Bank, the Italo-American Trust Company and the American branches of the Banco di Napoli.

The Italian Chamber of Commerce is aiding in the commercial development between Italy and America. Italo-American trade is making yearly gains, and represents, both in exports and imports, a very respectable amount.

Add to these conditions the fact that many Italians here return to the mother country and that an even greater number hold real property there and invest yearly, relatively large sums in farm lands at home, and the grounds for giving such expatriated Italians political representation in the home parliament becomes apparent. Indeed, it is quite probable that "Little Italy" in New York contributes more to the tax roll of Italy than some of the poorer provinces in

*_Charities_, Vol. 15(1906), pp. 151-152.

Sicily or Calabria. That the financial importance of the Italian colony in New York is being recognized was brought out in the course of a debate in Parliament in Rome, in which a deputy urged that steps be taken for the listing of Italian rentes on the American exchanges, and the Minister of Foreign Affairs pledged the government's interest to such proposition.

From the Italian standpoint, therefore, the proposition of colonial representation would seem to deserve practical consideration. Nor would it seem impossible to overcome many difficulties which obviously would arise in putting such a plan into practice. Whether we could prevent such a scheme is a debatable question. But that we should favor it, is even more doubtful. At first sight such a plan would seem a most powerful factor against American assimilation. Its effect might be to isolate even more completely the foreign element from American life, to render our "Little Italys" more than ever out of harmony with their American environment, and make amalgamation more than ever difficult. Yet, on the other hand, it might be urged that the Italo-American "colonist" would, as other colonists before him, hold his allegiance to the motherland as a purely sentimental tie, or as binding only in direct ratio with the material interests held by the mother country.

The experiment, for such it would be, would, however, deserve general interest in that it would be evidence of those new conditions and relations between different countries which tend to destroy the ancient sharp lines of demarcation between nations. A universal brotherhood may remain a utopian dream, but commercial interests, the "annihilation of time and space" by improved methods of transportation and the ebb and flow of travel, will render the old distinctions of nationalities and the parochial character of present-day patriotism, more and more an anachronism. The conception of citizenship itself is rapidly changing and we may have to recognize a sort of world or international citizenship as more logical than the present peripatetic kind, which makes a man an American while here, and an Italian while in Italy. International conferences are not so rare nowadays. Health, the apprehension or exclusion of criminals, financial standards, postage, telegraphs and shipping are today to a great extent, regulated by international action. Such action is bound to increase in scope and effectiveness. We have the Hague Tribunal and the Interparliamentary Union. The old barriers are everywhere breaking down. We may even bring ourselves to the point of recognizing foreign "colonies" in our midst, on our own soil, as entitled to partake in the parliamentary life of their mother country. Certainly it seems a suggestion worth studying.

PAUL J. CAMPISI

ETHNIC FAMILY PATTERNS: THE ITALIAN FAMILY IN THE UNITED STATES*

The changes in the Italian family in America can be visualized in terms of a continuum which ranges from an unacculturated Old World type to a highly acculturated and urbanized American type of family. This transformation can be understood by an analysis of three types of families which have characterized Italian family living in America: the Old World peasant Italian family which existed at the time of the mass migration from Italy (1890-1910) and which can be placed at the unacculturated end of the continuum; the first-generation Italian family in America, which at the beginning of contact with American culture was much like the first but which changed and continues to change increasingly so that it occupies a position somewhere between the two extremes; and, finally the second-generation Italian family which represents a cross-fertilization of the first-generation Italian family and the American contemporary urban family, with the trend being in the direction of the American type. Consequently, the position this family assumes is near the American-urban end of the continuum.

Since there are significant differences between the northern Italian and southern Italian families and since there are even greater differences between peasant, middle-class, and upper-class families, it seems expedient to single out one type of family for discussion and analysis, namely, the southern Italian peasant family. During the period of mass migration from Italy the bulk of the immigrants were from southern Italy (including Sicily)[1] These immigrants came

*American Journal of Sociology, Vol. 53 (May, 1948), pp. 443-449.

[1]During the decade of 1900-1910, of the 2,045,877 Italians who came to America, the majority were from southern Italy.

mostly from small-village backgrounds as peasant farmers, peasant workers, or simple artisans, and as such they brought with them a southern Italian folk-peasant culture. It is this type of background which the majority of Italian families in America have today.[2]

This paper cannot possibly present an adequate analysis of all the important changes observed in the Italian family. Therefore, a simple tabular form (see Table 1) is used to display the most important details.

The southern Italian peasant family in America.—At the time of the great population movement from Italy to America, beginning at the end of the nineteenth century, the southern Italian peasant family was a folk societal family. One of the chief characteristics of the folk society is that its culture is highly integrated, the separate parts forming a strongly geared and functionally meaningful whole[3]. This intimate interconnection between the various parts of a folk culture indicates that it would be artificial and fruitless to attempt to isolate, even for the sake of study and analysis, any one part, such as the family, and to proceed to discuss that as a discrete and distinct entity. All the characteristics of the Old World Italian peasant family are intimately tied in with such institutions and practices as religion, the planting and gathering of food, the celebrations of feasts and holidays, the education of the children, the treatment of the sick, the protection of the person, and with all other aspects of small-village folk culture. In the final analysis Old World peasant-family life meant small-village life, and the two were inseparable aspects of a coercive folk-peasant culture. This fact sharply distinguishes the Old World peasant family from the first-and second-generation families in America.

The first-generation southern Italian peasant family in America. —By the first-generation Italian family is simply meant that organization of parents and offspring wherein both parents are of foreign birth and wherein an attempt is made to perpetuate an Italian way of life in the transplanted household. This is a family in transition, still struggling against great odds to keep alive those customs and traditions which were sacred in the Old World culture. As a result of many

[2]The observations in this paper are based on the literature in the field, on my own specific research in America on the acculturation of Italians, and, finally, on personal impressions and conclusions as a participant observer. A visit to southern Italy and Sicily three years ago gave me an opportunity to come in contact with the Old World peasant-type family. While this type of family has changed considerably from the time of the mass migration to America, enough structural and functional family lags exist to make the reconstruction of it in this paper reasonably valid.

[3]See Robert Redfield, "The Folk Society," *American Journal of Sociology*, LII (1947), 293-308.

TABLE 1

DIFFERENCES BETWEEN THE SOUTHERN ITALIAN PEASANT FAMILY IN ITALY AND
THE FIRST- AND SECOND-GENERATION ITALIAN FAMILY IN AMERICA

Southern Italian Peasant Family in Italy	First-Generation Southern Italian Family in America	Second-Generation Southern Italian Family in America
A. General characteristics:		
1. Patriarchal	Fictitiously patriarchal	Tends to be democratic
2. Folk-peasant	Quasi-urban	Urban and modern
3. Well integrated	Disorganized and in conflict	Variable, depending on the particular family situation
4. Stationary	Mobile	High degree of mobility
5. Active community life	Inactive in the American community but somewhat active in the Italian neighborhood	Inactive in the Italian neighborhood, but increasingly active in American community
6. Emphasis on the sacred	Emphasis on the sacred is weakened	Emphasis on the secular
7. Home and land owned by family	In the small city the home may be owned, but in a large city the home is usually a flat or an apartment	Ownership of home is an ideal, but many are satisfied with flat
8. Strong family and community culture	Family culture in conflict	Weakened family culture reflecting vague American situation
9. Sharing of common goals	No sharing of common goals	No sharing of common goals
10. Children live for the parents	Children live for themselves	Parents live for the children
11. Children are an economic asset	Children are an economic asset for few working years only and may be an economic liability	Children are an economic liability
12. Many family celebrations of special feasts, holidays, etc.	Few family celebrations of feasts and holidays	Christmas only family affair, with Thanksgiving being variable
13. Culture is transmitted only by the family	Italian culture is transmitted only by family, but American culture is transmitted by American institutions other than the family	American culture is transmitted by the family and by other American institutions
14. Strong in-group solidarity	Weakened in-group solidarity	Little in-group solidarity
15. Many functions: economic, recreational, religious, social, affectional, and protective	Functions include semirecreational, social, and affectional	Functions reduced to affectional, in the main
B. Size:		
1. Large-family system	Believe in a large-family system but cannot achieve it because of migration	Small-family system
2. Many children (10 is not unusual)	Fair number of children (10 is unusual)	Few children (10 is rare)
3. Extended kinship to godparents	Extended kinship, but godparent relationship is weakened	No extended kinship to godparents
C. Roles and statuses:		
1. Father has highest status	Father loses high status, or it is fictitiously maintained	Father shares high status with mother and children; slight patriarchal survival
2. Primogeniture: eldest son has high status	Rule of primogeniture is variable; success more important than position	No primogeniture; all children tend to have equal status
3. Mother center of domestic life only and must not work for wages	Mother center of domestic life but may work for wages and belong to some clubs	Mother acknowledges domestic duties but reserves time for much social life and may work for wages
4. Father can punish children severely	Father has learned that American law forbids this	Father has learned it is poor psychology to do so
5. Family regards itself as having high status and role in the community	Family does not have high status and role in the American community but may have it in the Italian colony	Family struggles for high status and role in the American community and tends to reject high status and role in the Italian community

TABLE 1—*Continued*

Southern Italian Peasant Family in Italy	First-Generation Southern Italian Family in America	Second-Generation Southern Italian Family in America
C. *Roles and statuses—continued:* 6. Women are educated for marriage only	Women receive some formal education as well as family education for marriage	Emphasis is on general education with reference to personality development rather than to future marriage
7. The individual is subordinate to the family	Rights of the individual increasingly recognized	The family is subordinate to the individual
8. Daughter-in-law is subservient to the husband's family	Daughter-in-law is in conflict with husband's family	Daughter-in-law is more or less independent of husband's family
9. Son is expected to work hard and contribute to family income	Son is expected to work hard and contribute to family income, but this is a seldom-realized goal	Son expected to do well in school and need not contribute to family income
D. *Interpersonal relations:* 1. Husband and wife must not show affection in the family or in public	Husband and wife are not demonstrative in public or in the family but tolerate it in their married children	Husband and wife may be demonstrative in the family and in public
2. Boys are superior to girls	Boys are regarded as superior to girls	Boys tend to be regarded as superior to girls, but girls have high status also
3. Father is consciously feared, respected, and imitated	Father is not consciously feared or imitated but is respected	Father is not consciously feared. He may be imitated and may be admired
4. Great love for mother	Great love for mother but much ambivalence from cultural tensions	Love for mother is shared with father
5. Baby indulgently treated by all	Baby indulgently treated by all	Baby indulgently treated by all with increasing concern regarding sanitation, discipline, and sibling rivalry
E. *Marriage:* 1. Marriage in early teens	Marriage in late teens or early twenties	Marriage in early or middle twenties
2. Selection of mate by parents	Selection of mate by individual with parental consent	Selection of mate by individual regardless of parental consent
3. Must marry someone from the same village	This is an ideal, but marriage with someone from same region (i.e., province) is tolerated; very reluctant permission granted to marry outside nationality; no permission for marriage outside religion	Increasing number of marriages outside nationality and outside religion
4. Dowry rights	No dowry	No dowry
5. Marriage always involves a religious ceremony	Marriage almost always involves both a religious and a secular ceremony	Marriage usually involves both, but there is an increasing number of marriages without benefit of religious ceremony
F. *Birth and child care:* 1. Many magical and superstitious beliefs in connection with pregnancy	Many survivals of old beliefs and superstitions	Few magical and superstitious notions in connection with pregnancy
2. Delivery takes place in a special confinement room in the home; midwife assists	Delivery takes place generally in a hospital; may take place in home; family doctor displaces midwife	Delivery takes place almost always in a hospital; specialist, obstetrician, or general practitioner assists
3. Child illnesses are treated by folk remedies; local physician only in emergencies or crises	Child illnesses are treated partially by folk remedies but mostly by the family doctor	Child illnesses are treated by a pediatrician; much use of latest developments in medicine (vaccines, etc.)

TABLE 1—*Continued*

Southern Italian Peasant Family in Italy	First-Generation Southern Italian Family in America	Second-Generation Southern Italian Family in America
F. *Birth and child care—continued:*		
4. Child is breast-fed either by the mother or by a wet nurse; weaning takes place at about end of 2d or 3d year by camouflaging the breasts	Child is breast-fed if possible; if not, it is bottle-fed; same practice with variations regarding weaning	Child is bottle-fed as soon as possible; breast-feeding is rare; no weaning problems
5. No birth control	Some birth control	Birth control is the rule
G. *Sex attitudes:*		
1. Child is allowed to go naked about the house up to the age of 5 or 6; after this there is rigid enforcement of the rule of modesty	Variable, depending on the individual family's situation	This is variable, depending on the individual family; development of modesty is much earlier than in Old World peasant family
2. Sex matters are not discussed in family	Sex matters are not discussed in family	Sex matters increasingly discussed in family but not as freely as in "old" American family
3. Adultery is severely punished by the man's taking matters into his own hands	Adultery results in divorce or separation	Adultery may result in divorce or separation
4. Chastity rule rigidly enforced by chaperonage; lack of it grounds for immediate separation at wedding night	Attempts to chaperon fail, but chastity is an expectation; lack of it is grounds for separation, but there are few cases of this kind in America	No chaperonage; chastity is expected, but lack of it may be reluctantly tolerated
5. No premarital kissing and petting are allowed	No premarital kissing and petting are allowed openly	Premarital kissing and petting are allowed openly
6. Boys and girls attend separate schools	Schools are coeducational	Schools are coeducational
H. *Divorce and separation:*		
1. No divorce allowed	No divorce allowed, but some do divorce	Religion forbids it, but it is practiced
2. Desertion is rare	Desertion is rare	Desertion is rare
I. *Psychological aspects:*		
1. Fosters security in the individual	Fostered conflict in the individual	Fosters security with some conflict lags
2. The family provides a specific way of life; hence, there is little personal disorganization	Family is in conflict, hence cannot provide a specific way of life; yields marginal American-Italian way of life	Family reflects confused American situation, does not give individual a specific way of life, but marginality is weakened
3. Recreation is within family	Recreation is both within and outside the family	Recreation is in the main outside the family; this is variable, depending on individual family situation

internal and external pressures which have cut it off from its Old World foundations, the first-generation family is marked by considerable confusion, conflict, and disorganization. The uncertain and precarious position of the first-generation Italian family today is further aggravated by the loss of that strong family and community culture which had been such an indispensable part of the Old World peasant family. It is this loss in the first-generation family which pushes it away from the unacculturated end of the continuum to a position somewhere in the middle.[4]

The second-generation southern Italian family in America—This refers to that organization of parents and offspring wherein both the parents are native American born but have foreign-born parents who attempted to transmit to them an Italian way of life in the original first-generation family in America.

Among the significant characteristics of this type of family is the orientation which the American-born parents make to the American culture. This adjustment tends to take three forms. One is that of complete abandonment of the Old World way of life. The individual changes his Italian name, moves away from the Italian neighborhood and in some cases from the community, and has little to do with his foreign-born parents and relatives.[5] The ideal is to become acculturated in as short a time as possible. This type of second-generation Italian generally passes for an American family and is rare. A second form of generation Italian family is a marginal one. In this type there is a seriously felt need to become Americanized and hence to shape the structure and functions of the family in accordance with the contemporary urban American type of family. The parental way of life is not wholly repudiated, although there is some degree of rejection. This family is likely to move out of the Italian neighborhood and to communicate less and less with first-generation Italians, but the bond with the first-generation family is not broken completely. Intimate communications is maintained with the parental household, and the relationships with the parents as well as with immigrant relatives are affectionate and understanding. A third form which the second-generation family takes is of orientation inward toward an Italian way of life. This type of family generally prefers to remain in the Italian neighborhood, close to the parental home. Its interaction with the non-Italian world is at a minimum, and its interests are tied up with those of the Italian community. Of the three, the second type is the most representative second-generation Italian family in America. This is the family depicted in Table 1.

Table 1 reveals the movement of the first-and second-generation

---

[4]For an excellent analysis of the importance of a strong family and community culture see Margaret Park Redfield, "The American Family: Consensus and Freedom," *American Journal of Sociology*, LII (1946), 175-83.

[5]See Carlo Sforza, *The Real Italians* (New York: Columbia University Press, 1942), for an interesting account of Italian-Americans who change their names.

Italian families away from the Old World peasant pattern and toward the contemporary American family type. In this persistent and continuous process of acculturation there are three stages: (1) the initial-contact stage, (2) the conflict stage, and (3) the accommodation stage.

The initial-contact stage.—In the first decade of Italian living in America the structure of the Old World family is still fairly well intact, but pressures from within and outside the family are beginning to crack, albeit imperceptibly, the Old World peasant pattern. Producing this incipient distortion are the following: the very act of physical separation from the parental family and village culture; the necessity to work and operate with a somewhat strange and foreign body of household tools, equipment, gadgets, furniture, cooking utensils, and other physical objects, in addition to making an adjustment to a different physical environment, including climate, urban ecological conditions, and tenement living arrangements; the birth of children and the increasing contact with American medical practices regarding child care; the necessity to work for wages at unfamiliar tasks, a new experience for the peasant farmer; the attendance of Italian children in American parochial and public schools; the informal interaction of the children with the settlement house, the church associations, the neighborhood clubs, the neighborhood gang, and other organizations; the continuing residence in America and increasing period of isolation from the Old World; the acceptance of work by the housewife outside the home for wages; the increasing recognition by both parents and children that the Italian way of life in the American community means low status, social and economic discrimination, and prejudice; and the increasing pressure by American legal, educational, political, and economic institutions for the Americanization of the foreigner.

Nonetheless, the first-generation Italian family in this phase is a highly integrated one, as in the Old World. The demands of the American community are not seriously felt in the insulated Italian colony, and the children are too young seriously to articulate their newly acquired needs and wishes. The Italian family is stabilized by the strong drive to return to Italy.

The conflict stage.—In this period the first-generation family experiences its most profound changes and is finally wrenched from its Old World foundation. It is now chiefly characterized by the conflict between two ways of life, the one American and the other Italian, and by the incompatibility of parents and children. This phase begins roughly during the second decade of living in America—specifically, when the children unhesitatingly express their acquired American expectations and attempt to transmit them in the family situation and when the parents in turn attempt to reinforce the pattern of the Old World peasant family. Conflicting definitions of various family situations threaten to destroy whatever stability the family had maintained through the first period. This is the period of great frustration and of misunderstanding between parents and children. In this undeclared state of war between two ways of life it is the parents who have the most to lose, for their complete acceptance of the American way of living means the destruction of the Old World ideal.

The first-generation Italian family is also constantly made to feel the force of external pressures coming from outside the Italian colony. It is inevitable that the family structure should crumble under the incessant hammering. Not able to draw upon a complete culture and social system to support its position, the family pattern, already weakened, now begins to change radically: the father loses his importance, the daughters acquire unheard-of independence; in short, the children press down upon the first-generation family an American way of life.

Accommodation stage.—This period begins with the realization by parents and children that the continuation of hostility, misunderstanding, and contraventive behavior can result only in complete deterioration of the family. The ambivalent attitude of the children toward the parents, of great affection, on the one hand, and hostility, on the other, now tends to be replaced by a more tolerant disposition. This stage begins when the offspring reach adulthood and marry and establish households of their own, for by this time the control by the parents is greatly lessened.

Among the many factors which operate to bring about a new stability in the family are the realization on the part of the parents that life in America is to be permanent; the adult age of the offspring; the almost complete dependence of the parents on the offspring, including use of the children as informants, interpreters, guides, and translators of the American world; recognition on the part of the parents that social and economic success can come to the offspring only as they become more and more like "old Americans"; the conscious and unconscious acculturation of the parents themselves with a consequent minimizing of many potential conflicts; the long period of isolation from the Old World which makes the small-village culture and peasant family seem less real; the decision by the parents to sacrifice certain aspects of the Old World family for the sake of retaining the affection of the children; the acknowledgment by the children that the first-generation family is a truncated one and that complete repudiation of the parents would leave them completely isolated; the success of the first-generation family in instilling in the offspring respect and affection for the parents; and the gradual understanding by the children that successful interaction with the American world is possible by accepting marginal roles and that complete denial of the Old World family is unnecessary.

The accommodation between parents and offspring permits the second-generation Italians to orientate themselves increasingly toward an American way of life. The second-generation household, therefore, tends to pattern itself after the contemporary urban American family. Considerable intermarriage, the advanced age of the parents, the loosening of ties with the Italian neighborhood, and the development of intimate relationships with non-Italians make the transition of the second-generation family comparatively easy.

IRVIN L. CHILD

ITALIAN OR AMERICAN?*

Three types of reaction to the problems which the acculturative situation poses to the second-generation Italian have been discussed in detail. It is well now to consider briefly the relationships among these three types of reaction. One way of exhibiting the relationship is to compare the gains and losses accruing to an individual according as he consistently pursues one or another of the three types of reaction.

The rebel gains certain of the distinctive rewards that are offered for affiliation with the American group in the community. He continues to encounter the facts of prejudice against Italians at large. He tries to circumvent the barriers that are thus imposed by making himself out to be an exception and not really a member of the Italian group against which prejudice is felt. To the extent that the rebel reaction is successful, this exclusion of himself from the Italian group is accepted by his non-Italian associates, and the barriers against his feeling completely accepted by them may become very slight. The rebel loses the rewards that may be obtained through affiliation with the Italian group and he may at times regret the loss, but on the whole the gains that he makes seem to be an adequate compensation.

The gains made by the in-grouper are the complement of those made by the rebel. He, too, obtains the rewards of secure status as a member of a nationality group, but in his case it is the Italian group in the community instead of the American community at large. Although these rewards are from the nature of the social situation associated with a lower status than the rewards obtained by the rebel, they may well be more complete and satisfactory because acceptance by the Italian group is more thoroughgoing than acceptance by the American group. The in-grouper cannot get away from the American features of his environment nor, probably, from a consequent renewal in him of tendencies toward American participation and a

Italian or American? The Second Generation in Conflict (Yale University Press, 1943; reissued with an introduction by F. Cordasco, New York: Russell & Russell, 1970), pp. 188-200. Reprinted with permission.

constant reminder of the low status of the Italians. These conditions are frustrating; he does, however, gain a method of adjustment to the frustrations, for his affiliation with the Italian group gives him freedom to express hostility toward non-Italians at large and in particular.

The gains of the apathetic individual are of a different sort. He achieves not the successful pursuit of one set of goals relating to nationality, but an escape from the anxieties which are associated with those goals. By the lessening of the distinctiveness of the conflicting goals and of the strength of his desire for each of them, and by the cultivation of indifference to the barriers that stand in the way of their achievement, he gains the reward of not having the course of his life disturbed on the surface by conditions arising from the acculturative situation. He may of course achieve both sets of goals to a minor extent but he does sacrifice the fuller attainment of them that may be had through either the rebel or the in-group reaction. To the individual following the apathetic reaction the reward of escape from anxiety and conflict outweighs the loss of the other potential gains.

If each type of reaction leads to certain gains and certain losses, what determines the choice that an individual will make among the three? As with any complicated psychological phenomenon, it is fairly certain that the particular determinants of a similar mode of behavior will differ from person to person; some comments on this point with reference to the individual life histories will be made in the next section of this chapter. There are, however, some broad generalizations which follow from the theoretical interpretation of the three types of reaction and from a comparison of the present material with the findings of experimental studies of conflict behavior.

The conflict situation dealt with in this book has the general characteristics of what has been called a double approach-avoidance conflict. The individual is confronted with two alternative courses of action from each of which he anticipates both rewards and punishments. This situation is one of several types of situation which may induce conflict within the individual. Two other types of situation should be recalled here. One is the approach-approach conflict, in which the individual is confronted with incompatible alternatives from each of which reward alone is anticipated. The other is the avoidance-avoidance conflict, in which the individual must choose between two courses of action from each of which punishment alone is expected. Now under conditions of normal life, situations of these latter two types must be extremely rare. Attention to them, nevertheless, as types which may be to varying degrees approached in real situations is pertinent here.

Different consequences may be expected in the reaction to conflict depending upon whether the situation evokes only avoidance tendencies or only approach tendencies. When only avoidance tendencies are present, escape is to be expected if conditions permit it; if escape is not possible, then blocking or a fluctuation between a partial following of the one path and a partial following of the other may be predicted. When only approach tendencies are present, a fairly ready choice of one of the two paths and pursuit of it right up to the goal is to be expected. These predictions may be made from the theoretical structure outlined in Chapter III, with the additional assumption (already introduced in Chapter VI) that tendencies to approach and to avoid a situation both become increasingly strong as the individual draws near to it. It will be observed that the responses predicted for the avoidance-avoidance condition are substantially those which characterize the apathetic type of reaction as found in the second-generation Italians, and that the responses predicted for the approach-approach condition are very similar to those observed in the in-group and the rebel types of reaction. Even though all the second-generation Italians are faced with the choice of alternative paths each of which leads to both rewards and punishments, certain of them act very much as they would be expected to if only rewards were involved and certain of them act very much as they would be expected to if only punishments were involved.

These considerations relate directly to the question of why individuals choose particular types of reaction. Individuals differ in temperament and in the particular experiences they have undergone which are relevant to nationality groupings. As a result, the anticipation of reward may be far more conspicuous than the anticipation of punishment in the psychological significance of nationality grouping for one individual; for him the conflict situation will tend toward a pure approach-approach conflict. For another individual, the anticipation of punishment may far outweigh the anticipation of reward; he will find himself in something more akin to a pure avoidance-avoidance conflict. The latter individual is likely to adopt the apathetic reaction. The former individual is likely to adopt either the in-group or the rebel reaction; as between these two, the choice is presumably made according to the relative strength of the approach and avoidance tendencies in respect to the American and the Italian goals.

Comments on the Individual Life Histories

The picture of a given type of reaction does not give a complete or perfectly faithful picture of the response of any one individual to the acculturative situation. If serious misunderstanding of this point were likely, an individual life history might be presented at length to show the exent to which a description in terms of a type is or is not appropriate, and the extent to which a sample individual departs from a generalized picture of the type of reaction that he is said to represent. The investigator does not believe that the detailed presentation of a life history would contribute enough to this point to justify its conclusion. Use was made of life-history materials in formulating this book, however, and several comments are in order on their relation to the interpretations that have been made.

One striking fact about the individual life histories is the extent to which the essential features of the social situation are reflected in the single individual. In one of the life histories, for example, it was noted that every contrast between Italian and American culture that has been described in Chapter II was mentioned by the informant in connection with his own experience, in addition to many other cultural differences that are not referred to there. In the same life history the status of the Italians is seen to be substantially what was attributed to them in Chapter II, and most of the conditions of social organization that are cited in that chapter were mentioned explicitly by the informant.

The psychological significance of the acculturative situation, and the gains and losses to which particular types of reaction lead, are also shown very strikingly in the life histories. The demonstration is more striking than with the interview material because the significance of a particular event can be with greater certainty related to the long-term aspirations of the individual. The interpretations that can be made in the two life histories that have been most carefully studied by the investigator do not add a great deal to the interpretations that have been made in dealing with the more abstract types of reaction, and for that reason they will not be presented at length. The interpretations made in dealing with individuals are thoroughly congruent with the general character of the interpretations made in dealing with the types of reaction as represented in the more superficial data from the standardized interviews. Indeed, this congruence might be stated in reverse manner, for it was interpretations based on the investigator's experience in collecting life histories and in participant observation that originally suggested the treatment that is given to the data from the standardized interviews.

Another contribution that the life history of the individual might make is an increased understanding of the origins of a particular type of reaction. This expectation is confirmed with reference to the individuals concerned. It is possible to say with considerable certainty that consistent pursuit of the rebel reaction in one individual was aided by the attitude that his parents adopted toward the American schools. This informant was from early childhood unusually submissive to authority. His parents encouraged his transferring to his teachers his submissiveness to their own authority by, for example, urging him to respect and obey his teachers just as he did them. Partly through the cooperation of his parents he became highly responsive to the wishes of his teachers, and adopted rather early in life many goals derived from his perception of them and other Americans. When, after graduation from high school, he obtained a job in which his associates and his superiors were non-Italian, his accustomed submissiveness to authority increased the reward-value for him of conforming to their norms; in addition, the early training by his parents reduced the amount of anxiety that he felt in rebelling against them so long as he was still conforming to authority. This case may be compared with that of another life-history informant who shows predominantly the rebel reaction but also a good deal of the in-group reaction. The comparison suggests that the second informant was unable to rebel successfully against his parents, and therefore retained some of the in-group reaction, partly because his parents had not encouraged him to respond to his teachers as to themselves.

These and similar suggestions are not presented in detail here for the reason that they are, so far as the present evidence goes, purely individual phenomena and not capable of direct generalization. It seems probable that various individuals adopt a particular type of reaction because of quite different determinants in their own life histories. The interpretation that has been made here of each type of reaction shows what an individual gains or loses by adopting it. Except in the very general manner outlined in the previous section, it does not show why a particular individual chooses those gains or losses, and the detailed origins of the choice may be very different for different individuals.

The life histories are also useful because they suggest certain facts and interpretations that are not adequately represented in the data from the standardized interviews. The most striking instance is with reference to the rebel's feeling of affiliation with the Italian group. Persons who are fully recognized as members of the general American population may in various ways identify themselves with particular traditions deriving from their ancestry which do in a sense conflict with their American membership. For example, some descendants of early English settlers in New England identify themselves with an old tradition which does not quite jibe with the realities of American society today, and may even identify themselves with England as a contemporary nation more than they would be likely to do in the absence of an ancestral tradition. Similiarly the well-assimilated descendants of the French in Louisiana or of the Spanish in California are said to maintain some of their own traditions. The maintenance of these non-American traditions is often felt to enrich an individual's life and not to be inconsistent with his standing as an American. Does the young man of the second generation who rebels against his Italian background and seeks to become accepted as an American, similarly recognize his participation in a foreign tradition as enriching his life and not interfering with his status as an American?

Already in the chapter on rebel reaction there have been suggestions pointing in this direction. It was seen that knowledge of written Italian is fairly common among the rebels and that adherence to the Italian cuisine is surprisingly frequent. It is plausible that in both of these cases the Italian culture trait to which the individual adheres is chosen because conformity to it either is rewarded or is at least not punished by other members of the American group. It may be that just such traits are ones to which the successful rebel will cling as elements in a specialized cultural tradition, and that in doing so he will be more willing to recognize his Italian background than the rebel informants generally were in the course of the standardized interviews.

Further indication of a tendency in this direction comes especially from the life history of one informant who has been remarkably successful in pursuing the goals of the rebel reaction. He spontaneously attributes to himself certain characteristics which he traces to his Italian background. They are not the particular ones that have been mentioned in the paragraph above. They are a love of detail and color in architecture and painting, a liking for certain kinds of music (he explains his dislike for Grieg as being due to the contrast between Grieg's Scandinavian temperament and his own Mediterranean temperament), and certain personal characteristics, particularly individualism. The investigator would hazard the guess that this informant's willingness to attribute these "Italian" characteristics to himself is greater now that he feels successfully established as an American than it would have been during his period of struggle; but he cannot say for certain that this is true. The same informant also makes several statements which suggest that he is proud sometimes to point out his Italian origin because his present status represents all the more of an achievement in the light of his being a child of immigrants. He indicates that he feels closely identified with younger Italian-Americans of the second or third generation who are struggling to find a place in American society, and that his pride in himself as an example to them provides a further incentive for maintaining his own position. In all of these respects there can be seen in this informant at least the roots of a constructive synthesis of Italian origins with full acceptance in American society. Such a synthesis is likely to be a conspicuous accompaniment of the rebel reaction at the time of success rather than at a time of struggle, for it no longer leads to a serious threat of loss of status and it may even be a means of gaining special prestige.

THEORETICAL IMPLICATIONS

The specific theoretical intent of this book was to apply psychological principles and methods to the study of individual behavior in a complex social situation, that of an acculturating group. One significant finding is that types of reaction which may be analyzed in psychological terms and which with varying degrees of consistency characterize particular members of the second generation are related to culture change under conditions of acculturation. In general, the rebels report the least conformity with traits of Italian culture, the in-groupers report the greatest conformity, and the apathetic informants are intermediate. These differences are by no means found consistently but they are found to a sufficient extent to justify a tentative generalization. The investigator believes from the interviews and from his experience in participant observation that the differences hold true of behavior in a variety of situations and are not just a matter of willingness to admit cultural conformity to the interviewer. The generalization is put forward that the rebel reaction encourages a shift from the original culture of the immigrant group to American culture, that the in-group reaction favors retention of traits of the original culture, and that the cultural effect of the apathetic reaction is intermediate but depends upon the cultural adherence of the people with whom the apathetic individuals happen to associate.

This generalization could be applied to make predictions about the course of cultural change on the basis of psychological investigation of a sample of individuals in any group undergoing acculturation. Questionnaires or standardized interviews could be devised with a view to obtaining in a fairly brief time an estimate of the relative predominance of the various types of reaction. Comparison of the frequency of the types of reaction in samples from two *comparable* populations could provide a basis for predicting a differential rate of culture change.

A prediction could also be made that culture change would be more rapid during a historical period in which the social conditions were such as to predispose individuals toward the rebel reaction, and less rapid at a period when conditions predisposed individuals to the in-group reaction. Predictions can be made, for example, about the effect on culture change of the present state of war between Italy and the United States. If during the present period the general American population encourages people of Italian origin to regard themselves as Americans and really offers them the full rewards of membership in American society, the rebel reaction should be by far the most frequent, and adoption of American culture traits should therefore proceed at a tremendous rate. It is also predicted that if during this period of war the non-Italian members of the population uniformly suspect Italian-Americans of treasonable activity and do not offer them the full rewards of membership in American society, and if distinctively Italian groups offer a greater promise of security and group dominance, the in-group reaction will be very frequent and a revival of Italian culture will therefore appear.

The findings of this study also have some bearing on the problem of the differential modification of traits under conditions of acculturation. The evidence on this point is not very adequate but some suggestions may be made. One of the most persistent traits of Italian culture, regardless of the individual's type of reaction, is the cuisine. A major reason for its persistence may well be the frequently rewarding, and certainly nonpunishing, attitude of the American population at large. Dishes that are recognized by everyone to be of Italian origin are probably served occasionally in a large proportion of non-Italian households in the city. Italian dishes preserved in cans are a part of the standard stock of grocers throughout the city and are presumably bought by non-Italians rather than Italians. Many of the Italian restaurants secure a good part of their patronage from non-Italians. Italian families frequently invite non-Italian friends to their homes for an Italian dinner, and the usual response is enthusiastic apprecation. There is no other trait of Italian culture that receives anything like this treatment from the American population at large and that would, consequently, be so uniformly reinforced.

That the attitude of the non-Italians is an important determiner of the differential survival of the culture traits is suggested also by the tendency even in the rebels to wish to preserve the Italian language and to gain acquaintance with written Italian. That tendency was interpreted in Chapter IV as being due to the relatively high prestige attached in American society to acquaintance with standard Italian. The suggestion was also made that even for those who follow the in-group reaction the attitude of the American group may be an important determinant of trait selection. The high frequency among the in-group informants of expressed desire to speak good English was interpreted as the result of their perception that a poor command of English signifies low status in America and would hinder the movement toward dominance in American life of the Italian group with which they affiliate themselves.

What has been said so far in this section carries with it the assumption that the analysis made here of types of reaction will be found useful in the study of other acculturating groups. The author would broaden that assumption to include the study also of many situations to which the term "acculturation" would not generally be applied. These types of reaction seem very readily applicable to the behavior of persons faced with the problems of a possible change in their social-class status, in the region of their residence within the United States, or even in their club membership or political affiliation. The principal support for this assumption lies in the fact that parallel types of reaction are found in analyzing the responses of subjects in simple conflict situations in the psychological laboratory. Categories which fit the behavior of experimental subjects in the laboratory and the behavior of second-generation iItalians in relation to their fellows in daily life, are not likely to be entirely inapplicable to other human behavior.

In considering the generality of the sort of analysis made here, a distinction must be recognized between the three types of reaction, which refer only to response to conflict, and the more general theoretical scheme employed. The latter includes a number of basic principles of learning and motivation which have already proved useful in interpreting the behavior of both human beings and lower animals under controlled experimental conditions. The contribution that these principles have made to an understanding of the behavior of individuals as members of an acculturating group is an encouraging sign. It suggests that their validity extends far beyond the scene of their original conception and that they are useful in the analysis even of formidably complex social behavior. This work does not establish their validity. Conceptual models that will give a really good fit to the complexities of human social behavior have not yet been constructed. Methods must be developed, data must be gathered, but most of all systematic thinking must be done before such models can be built. Meanwhile, the present work may increase the presumption that basic principles of learning and motivation will appear either as parts of these models or as parts of their master tool.

Practical Problems

A number of practical problems are suggested by the conclusions of this study. One point that should be perfectly clear is that the special problem of adjusting to the American scene is not one that confronts immigrants alone. It also, certainly, confronts their children. The second generation may encounter conflicting cultural norms to an even greater extent than the immigrants. It also faces essentially the same conditions of status and pressures for affiliation as does the older generation. The status of nationality groups has of itself such an importance for the adjustment of the second gene-ration as to provide grounds for expecting that the third and fourth generations, even if removed from contact with an alien culture, will still have problems deriving from their nationality origin. Social workers and others who have practical experience with various na-tionality groups are already well aware of these facts. That they are not sufficiently impressed upon the general public should be clear from the frequent blame that is placed upon the descendants of immigrants for failure to adjust successfully to American life, as though there were nothing in the social situation to offer difficulties and as if the occurrence of difficulty indicated merely a personal inadequacy.

A point of which fewer people who have practical experience with the second generation may be aware is the diversity of individuals' reactions. It should be clear that social workers or others who are trying to aid in the adjustment of the second generation cannot succeed by making a uniform approach to all individuals. A person who displayed an in-group reaction would have to be appealed to in a very different way from the one who displayed a rebel reaction. Awareness of this diversity of response is undoubtedly valuable not only to the social worker but to the political propagandist, teachers, and especially all who are concerned with assisting in the American-ization of minority groups. In the planning of any practical work designed to modify the habits and attitudes of members of the second generation, individual differences need urgently to be considered.

This book may also serve a useful purpose if it makes Americans of all groups more aware of the importance today of the association of status with nationality origins, and if it thereby suggests to anyone desirable changes in his own behavior and attitudes. In particular it would be fortunate if people who are able to consider themselves in every respect Americans could perceive more clearly the consequences for our nation of not permitting descendants of recent immigrant groups always to share that feeling. A person who regards national unity as a desirable goal and at the same time shares the general prejudice against people with foreign-sounding names should consider the possible consequences for the country of the frequent occurrence of an in-group reaction, and may well take counsel with his conscience.

GINO C. SPERANZA

PETROSINO AND THE BLACK HAND*

The death of Giuseppe Petrosino, lieutenant in the New York Police Department, proves a new tragic fact that reforms seem impossible by the sacrifice of human lives; whether it be in sanitation and housing conditions, in industrial methods, or in the larger field of government, of social life and of international relations, men must die through avoidable sickness, through avoidable risks, through avoidable wars, before public sentiment becomes sufficiently aroused to patient examination and effective action.

Our country, young and powerful though it is, cannot hope successfully to cope, by its unaided and inexperienced strength, with the questions arising through the influx of a large element which is not bad or undesirable but alien to, and unprepared for our body politic, for our traditions and for our habits. Immigration, in its good and especially in its bad phases, is a matter of international concern and discipline; it cannot be treated as a national question which you and I and our fellow citizens may intelligently pass upon.

We have watched the European invasion, and in a daring but thoughtless spirit of youth, have said we could meet and turn it to our country's good. So we can. But not indiscriminately, not without taking due stock of the experience of our elders.

Lieutenant Petrosino went, single-handed, to fight a battle which can only be won by the patient planning and loyal co-operation of two civilized and friendly powers. He was a fearless man, a faithful servant; but he must have been ill-advised or ignorant of the means necessary to achieve the ends that he or his superiors sought.

What is the enemy he sought to fight? People on this side of the ocean have called it by various names—Mafia, Camorra, Black Hand. He was too well-informed an officer to follow popular or journalistic imaginary creations. He knew that the so-called black-handers belonged to no organization or society but had membership in that

Survey, Vol. 22 (1909), pp. 11-14.

class of evil doers who naturally, like birds of a feather, tend to gravi-
tate towards each other. *Mala Vita* is the Italian phrase for that evil and
socially parasitic class which we call the "criminal element" or the
"underworld." It exists in every country, and against it each nation
seeks to defend itself by its police systems and its courts.

What Officer Petrosino understood is what so many of us have
failed to appreciate, that if we wish to make our social defense against
alien criminals more effective we must learn the rules of war and seek
the co-operation of those strategists who know this special enemy and
its ways better than we do. The obstacles and difficulties in the way
are many.

First of all in our social defense against the criminal element, native or imported, we too often overlook that it has "brains." Several
years ago in writing on the social defense against crime I said:

> There is a great deal of misplaced sentimentality in re-
> gard to criminals and an erroneous popular belief as to
> their limitations for mischief. Criminologists, prison-war-
> dens and prosecutors tell us that many of the enemies of
> law and order are men of great cunning and daring, keen
> to adopt new methods and endowed with a "patient in-
> ventiveness" backed up by reckless audacity"; they have
> been known to wait a long time in the careful preparation
> of their misdeeds and have often shown remarkable ad-
> ministrative ability.

It is with this fact in view that countries older than ours have
called to their police service well-trained men and raised such service
to a profession and a career worthy of the ambition of cultivated men.
The prefects of police of continental Europe are government officials
of long training and high rank. Nor must we overlook that dishonest people as well as honest ones, criminals as well as missionaries, take advantage of the increasingly easier modes of communication and travel; that the under world, as well as the upper world,
feels the breaking down of national barriers—and is quick to profit
by it.

Secondly, when the social defense is against the criminal element
of a people different from our own, the advice and constant co-
operation of the government to which such peoples belong is indispensable. We have been suspicious of foreign co-operation and too
self-satisfied that our methods were "the very best." Why should
we be suspicious? Can anyone seriously maintain that Italy, for instance, has any interest in "dumping" her criminals abroad? Can
any thinking person really believe that Italian statesmanship could

be so inconceivably shortsighted that it would jeopardize the interests, safety and influence of millions of its honest immigrants by assisting or encouraging the exodus of its malefactors? As a matter of fact, what has Italy tried to do to check its criminals and to prevent their becoming international charges? Its criminal procedure, without the benefit of bail for the accused, and its absence of our refinements of legal presumptions and legal evidence, would shock us as too harsh against even a criminal; its penal system which makes a violator of the law a marked man for the police forces for practically the rest of his life and registers and controls his movements from place to place, would impress us by its severity. Its wonderfully organized police power centralized in the Ministry of the Interior, with its trained men of the *questura* and the admirable military-constabulary of the *carabinieri* corps would convince us, if we studied it, of its efficiency.

All this for protection at home. What for protection abroad? It was the Italian government that called an international conference to fight the anarchists when anarchy changed from philosophy to action. It was the Italian government of its own initiative that enacted stringent laws forbidding an emigrant from leaving the kingdom without a passport, which official certificate cannot be issued without an examination by the local authorities of the penal record of the applicant. It was the Italian government that proposed as far back as 1868 that our extradition treaty should stipulate that "The two contracting parties agree to communicate to each other, respectively, all sentences passed by tribunals or courts of the one state for crimes or offences of *whatever nature*, committed upon their territory by subjects or citizens of the other," a stipulation which now we see would have been all to our advantage but which Secretary Seward refused. It has been the Italian government that has repeatedly endeavored, at much expense, to extradite some of its criminals who have come here but whose surrender was rendered impossible by the strict interpretation given by our courts to the treaty provisions regarding the character of the evidence that must be presented. One of these alleged fugitives the day after his discharge applied to the federal courts for citizenship; the discharge of another (who has since disappeared) was hailed in the public press with head lines, "Italy Can't Have X," that sounded like the "triumph of the oppressed."

What should we do, for something must be done to check that most cowardly and sinister of crimes—blackmail and extortion? What should we do to strengthen our social defense against the *mala vita* from abroad that has been added to the problems of our native criminal element?

We must divest ourselves of our pride and of our prejudices. We must not send or allow brave officers to go to their death in inspiring but impractical skirmishes. Let us plan a warfare equal to the resourcefulness and power of the evil we seek to destroy. Let us be humble enough to accept allies, and unprejudiced enough to trust our allies in a cause that is of common interest. Wholesale restrictive immigration-measures will bar out the good; they have never kept out the bad. Let us rather make the existing laws less ingenuous; let us not ask the arriving immigrant to tell us "under oath" if he is a criminal; I believe the only Italian who said yes to such query was an honest immigrant who mistook his detention at Ellis Island as an incarceration, and gave that, as in fact it was, as his only criminal past. Let us ask for the official record of the immigrant as certified in the passport issued by a civilized government whom we should trust. And if a mountain-shepherd from the Abruzzi sails to New York from Hamburg, or Havre, or Marseilles instead of from the Italian port nearest to his town let us not consider it an invasion of the sacredness of personal privacy at least to inquire if not to watch. There is often a reason. Then, let us not be so sentimentally afraid of a "secret police"; the under world works in the dark and we must fight it in the dark. For Petrosino to sail on an Italian boat from New York where every dock laborer knew of his going was absurdly to undervalue the watchfulness of the enemy. A "secret police" and "secret" funds are absolutely necessary; we should trust the men we put in power to use such dangerous weapons with much judgement and care, or we should not clothe them with power.

We should have more and better trained men for detective and police duty among our alien population. The "drag net" that brings in a lot of "dangerously armed Sicilians" after a terrible tragedy like Petrosino's, makes good newspaper copy, inflames popular passion and prejudice, but leaves the battle unwon. It is too easy a way, and the only way to win is by hard-headed planning and patient, skillful operating.

Nor must we do our detective work in the newspapers, in the way that we are having trial of cases by the press.

Lastly, we must seek and offer cooperation. We should seek international conferences and agreements and give faith and credit to the requisitions and requests of other governments. Diplomacy is not a "smart game" but a means of facilitating the exchange of views, of understanding needs, and of finding means and ways.

The death of one brave man calls not for vengeance and passion but for thought.

GAETANO D'AMATO

THE "BLACK HAND" MYTH.*

It is not strange, perhaps, that most Americans believe that a terrible organization named the "Black Hand Society" exists in Italy, and is sending its members to establish branches for the purpose of plundering the United States, since nearly every newspaper in the country conveys that impression to its readers. One would think, however, that such men as Frank P. Sargent, Commissioner-General of Immigration, and Terence V. Powderly, Chief of the Division of Information of that Bureau, would inform themselves on a matter that pertains so closely to their duties. Nevertheless, both of these officials have put themselves on record as believing that such an organization exists. In his last annual report Mr. Sargent says, apropos of the suggestion that legislation be adopted requiring the presentation of a passport as a prerequisite to the examination of an alien applying for admission to the United States: "The current history of the perpetration of heinous crimes throughout the United States by foreigners domiciled therein, especially by the members of the 'Black Hand' and other like societies in evidence," etc. Again, in a recent article on "Undesirable Citizens," he refers to "the introduction into this free country of such hideous and terrifying fruits of long-continued oppression as the 'Black Hand' and anarchist societies."

Mr. Powderly is more specific. In an interview in the New York "Sun," he declared that he had learned in Italy last summer that "on its native heath the 'Black Hand' was organized for good," explaining further: "An Italian who wrongs a woman, and fails to right the wrong, is practically driven from among his fellows. The black hand of ostracism is raised against him. The 'Black Hand' in this country, brought into being for noble purposes across the sea, was prostituted and converted to ignoble purposes when transplanted to the United States." The "Black Hand" has scarcely even been heard of in Italy.

*North American Review, Vol. 187 (April, 1908), pp. 543-549.

It was never heard of until long after the term had been used in the United States, and then only as a distant manifestation of criminal activity regrettable because the good name of the Italians in the New World suffered by it. A society for the protection of women would be superfluous in Italy.

The name "Black Hand" is of Spanish origin, and the organization to which it referred was first described in 1889 by Major Arthur G. F. Griffiths, the English criminologist, in his work "Mysteries of Police and Crime." He wrote:

> "Not so very long since a wide-spread organization for evil was brought to light in Spain—the Society of the Black Hand, as it was called. In its origin, it consisted of missionaries who hoped to redress the balance between rich and poor; but it soon drew down to it many desperadoes who gladly accepted the openings it offered for carrying on their original trade. It became a very extensive and numerous society, existing in the provinces, each having its own centre and out branches, with a total of affiliated members exceeding 40,000."

In the United States, the "Black Hand society" is a myth, in so far as the phrase conveys the impression that an organization of Italian criminals exists in America, or that the Camorra or the Mafia has become naturalized here. By reason of the laxity of the immigration laws, there have crept into this country some thousands of ex-convicts from Naples, Sicily and Calabria, along with millions of honest and industrious Italians; and, owing to the inefficiency of the police in various cities where these Italians are domiciled, the criminals among them are able to live by robbery and extortion, frequently accompanied by murder, their victims being the more helpless of their fellow countrymen.

These fugitives from justice and gallows-birds, from whom it is America's duty to protect the law-abiding Italians who are doing yeoman service in the building of the Republic, are members of the Italian race that have brought disgrace upon the others, and upon whom the sensational press has conferred the title of "Black Hand Society." How many of these criminals there are in the United States it is impossible, for obvious reasons to estimate with any degree of accuracy. Lieutenant Petrosino, who is in charge of the little Italian Squad in the Police Department of New York and probably knows more about the predatory brotherhood than any one else, says that they may number as many as from three to four per cent of the Italian population. They are no more organized, however, than are the many thousands of lawbreakers of other nationalities in America. Indeed, Robert Louis Stevenson's playful but accurate characterization of the gangs of thieves that preyed upon nocturnal Paris three and a half centuries ago applies to the so-called "Black Hand" today —"independent malefactors, socially intimate, and occasionally joining together for some serious operation, just as modern stock-jobbers form a syndicate for an important loan."

Italian outlaws are enabled to reach this country to-day with almost the same facility as the honest Italian, so far as the laws of the United States are concerned. True, the ex-convict cannot obtain a passport from the Italian Government and sail on an Italian ship, but there is nothing to prevent his crossing the frontier and leaving from any port outside of Italy to which he may make his way. Many of the most dangerous of the Italian criminals in the United States have come here by way of England and Canada, and many others have shipped as sailors from Italian ports and deserted their ships on reaching this country.

The Neapolitan, Silcilian or Calabrian desperado, once he has reached these shores, finds the conditions ideal for levying tribute upon the feebler folk among his countrymen. In nearly all the larger cities, particularly of the East and Middle West, he will find them living in colonies by themselves. Besides the 500,000 Italians in New York, there are 100,000 each in Boston and Philadelphia; 70,000 each in San Francisco and New Orleans; 60,000 in Chicago; 25,000 each in Denver and Pittsburg; and 20,000 in Baltimore. In smaller cities are colonies that will number from 5,000 to 10,000.

Conditions are much the same in these colonies all over the country. They are generally located in a poor quarter of the town, which is not policed as well as those where the native American lives. The newcomers, moreover, are timid in their strange surroundings; they are ignorant of the law of the land; few of them can speak English, even if they dared to complain of outrages perpetrated upon them. And, when the humble and respectable Italians do appeal to the police and find that the law cannot, or will not, protect them, they are reduced to a pitiful extremity that has driven scores of potential citizens back to Italy, kept many an industrious resident in actual bondage to the lawbreakers, and in some instances even forced hitherto honest men to become criminals themselves.

Aside from the urban Italians, there are some 500,000 laborers of the race distributed throughout the United States, working in mines and vineyards and on railroads, irrigation ditches and farms, who are equally victims of their rapacious countrymen with the dwellers in cities. In fact, there is scarcely a point throughout the length and breadth of the country where a few Italians are gathered together that some criminals of the race have not fastened themselves upon them.

Every reader of the newspapers is familiar with the outrages that, in the name of the "Black Hand," have been perpetrated among the Italians, beginning some ten years ago and increasing coincidentally with the Italian immigration, but reaching a limit two or three years ago. Murder has been a common crime, and the dynamiting of houses and shops, the kidnapping of children, with every species of blackmail and extortion, was of so frequent occurrence that the mind became dulled to the enormity of these offences. In New York conditions have been worse than anywhere else; and yet, with half a million of Italians in the population, there are to-day only forty Italians in the Police Department. Along miles of street in New York there are no guardians of the people who understand the language of the residents. As Marion Crawford says, the employment of Irish policemen in Rome would be an analogous circumstance, since there are more Italians in New York than in the capital of Italy.

How little the police have understood the situation may be gathered from the fact that, during the height of the wave of Italian crime three years ago, respectable members of that race were not allowed permits to carry weapons of defence, even when their lives were threatened. Physicians whose nocturnal duties subjected them to particular peril; bankers and business men, at any time liable to the attentions of scoundrels who did not stop at murder; in fact, all persons with Italian names were prohibited absolutely from carrying arms. Wherefore the police aided and abetted the outlaws, all of whom carried knives and pistols, by making it impossible for the law-abiding Italian legally to prepare for defence in case of attack.

During twenty-nine years of residence in New York, I have found two causes that operate for the blackening of the Italian name in respect of crime: the sensationalism of the yellow press and the ignorance and recklessness of the police in recording arrests. Almost every dark-skinned European, not speaking English, who does not wear the Turkish fez, is put down on the police records as an Italian, and thus the Italian is condemned for much of the crime committed here by persons of other nationalities.

It is impossible to comprehend the attitude of a part of the American press with regard to the Italian, unless the theory is accepted that the truth is a consideration secondary to the publication of sensations that are calculated to increase the day's sales. Last spring, for instance, the newspapers manufactured a "Black Hand" scare, representing that the police were in despair of getting the lawless element under control. Two of the less sensational of the Sunday supplements had articles on the same day devoted to the subject, in each of which it was stated that an organization of Italian criminals under the name of the "Black Hand Society" existed in New York, and that it was growing in power so rapidly as to be an actual menace to the city.

One monthly magazine even published an alarmist article, actually signed with the name of Petrosino, the chief of the Italian Squad of the Police Department, entitled "Italian Mafia Has New York by the Throat," expressing views not held by the detective, who had never even heard of the article until it was shown to him in print. As a matter of fact, any reporter or writer who had made enquiries of Petrosino would have been informed that he was more encouraged than ever before to believe that he was at that very time bringing the Italians criminals under control.

A cruel bit of journalistic work that actually brought about fatal results came under my personal observation just after the assassination of King Humbert of Italy, in 1900, by the Italian anarchist Bresci, who had lived in Paterson up to a short time before the crime was commited. Newspaper reporters were swarming to New Jersey at that time, and one of them caught sight, in a barber shop in Hoboken, of the photograph of a well-known Italian merchant named Bianchetti, taken as he was saying farewell to some friends on board a steamer about to sail for Europe. The proprietor of the shop jokingly told this reporter that the man in the photograph was Bresei, whereupon the news-seeker bought it. I personally informed him that the photograph was that of a highly respected citizen of Hoboken and I gave his name. Nevertheless, the picture was published in a New York newspaper that afternoon, and afterward copied in the Italian newspapers, not only in America, but in Italy, the result being that many of Bianchetti's acquaintances, in the Mother Country as well as in the United States, believed that he was in some way involved in the assassination of the King. He died of a broken heart within a year.

The term "Black Hand" was first used in this country about ten years ago, probably by some Italian desperado who had heard of the exploits of the Spanish society, and considered the combination of words to be high-sounding and terror-inspiring. One or two crimes committed under the symbol gave it a vogue among the rapacious brotherhood; and, as it looked well and attracted attention in their headlines, the newspapers finally applied it to all crimes committed by the Italian banditti in the United States. Thus the press not only facilitates the commission of crime among the Italian ex-convicts, by making it appear that all the evil done by them is the successful work of a single organization, it aids the individual criminal by leading his ignorant countrymen, upon whom he preys, to believe that he makes his lawless demands on behalf of a powerful society.

In spite of the depredations of the thousands of Italian criminals whom this Government has allowed to enter the country and prey upon the honest and industrious of their own race here, the great body of that race has prospered. A quarter of a century ago, there were not more than 25,000 Italians in America, and their entire possessions would have been valued at a trifling sum. To-day, in New York alone, the estimated material value of the property in the Italian colonies is $120,000,000 aside from $100,000,000 invested by Italians in wholesale commerce, $50,000,000 in real estate, and $20,000,000 on deposit in the banks. I doubt whether any other nationality can show as good a record of twenty-five years of achievement.

Of the Italian as a good citizen, a valuable member of society, I may not write, but perhaps I may be allowed to quote the opinion of an American of Anglo-Saxon descent, James J. Starrow, of Boston. Mr. Starrow writes:

> "I believe the average Italian immigrant in physique the superior of the native New-Englander, and what other consideration is of more importance to us, or more surely lies at the base of a strong and vigorous race? The love of family is strong among Italians. What is more fundamental than this? The whole structure of modern civilization is based on the family group. If this goes to pieces, what matters it what the form of our Government may be? Can the native population point to any superlatively superior record in this respect? While the Italians consume a good deal of light wine, and occasionally too much, yet they are on the whole a very temperate race. The Italian drunkard hardly exists. Most important of all, the Italian women do not get drunk. The Italian seems to have a natural courtesy, which is not a mere surface indication, but, I think, springs, as all true courtesy does, from a certain affability of soul and regard for others."

In the United States, as everywhere, the Italian women are notably domestic. They are attached to home and family, and that tie they never break. They are never heard of in the divorce courts, and the President is not compelled to scold them about race suicide. Petrosino tells me that he has never seen an Italian woman "on the streets" in New York.

In the domestic life the Italian woman is at her best. She is a true helpmate to her husband; she works hard to help him, and saves for him, as, I think I may say, no woman of any other race does. It is due to her that the Italians in this country are growing so rapidly in wealth. It is due to her that the name of Italy is not associated with any suggestion of social vice in the Western World. While she retains her Old World ways she brings up her children as good and sound Americans, inculcating upon their minds the principles of thrift and economy which she herself learned in Italy.

Immigration into this country now averages about 100,000 per month the year round. Of these newcomers one in every five is from Southern Italy; and, as I have said, criminals are still coming in. The investigation made in Europe last summer by the Congressional Immigration Commission that reports to the present Congress ought to result in a law deporting all foreign ex-convicts in the United States, who cannot prove that they are making an honest livelihood, and establishing some form of consular inspection on the other side to prevent any more of the criminal class from entering.

FRANCIS A. J. IANNI

THE MAFIA
AND
THE WEB OF
KINSHIP*

One of the most extraordinary sociological puzzles of the times is the contrasting conceptions about the *Mafia* that have persisted for more than two decades, with seemingly no way of resolving almost diametrically divergent conclusions. On the one hand there are criminologists such as Donald Cressey, a consultant to a President's Task Force on Law Enforcement who talk of "a nationwide alliance of at least 24 tightly knit *Mafia* 'families' which control organized crime in the United States," the extent of which is estimated at "$50 billion per year with $15 billion in profit." On the other hand, there are writers, most recently Norval Morris of the University of Chicago Law School and his colleague, a visiting Australian criminologist, Gordon Hawkins who scoff at the evidence and the figures and, while readily admitting the presence of Italian-Americans in crime, are skeptical of the existence of a national crime syndicate or cartel. Government officials over the years have talked of the *Black Hand, The Unione Siciliana,* the *Mafia,* and, within the last decade of *La Cosa Nostra,* though the latter name was never used publicly before the disclosures of an Italian mobster, Joseph Valachi.

William James once said that wherever there is a contradiction it is the result of the fact that the parties to the dispute have failed to make relevant distinctions. My own feeling is that the questions about the Mafia have been wrongly put. To look at the problem in terms of whether a "syndicate" or "corporate organization" exists is to miss the most salient cultural facts about Italian, particularly south Italian life, and thus to misperceive the nature of the ties which do exist among Italian gangsters and shape the modes of their activity. If organized crime here, as Daniel Bell once put it, is an "Ameri-

Public Interest(Winter, 1971), pp. 78-100. Reprinted with permission.

can Way of Life," then one must look at the *Mafia*, not as a specific kind of organization, but as an aspect of an "Italian Way of Life"— and then see if this perspective can illuminate the picture.

In 1967 Francesco Cerase of the Institute of Social Research in the University of Rome and I decided to do just that, and with financial support from the Russell Sage Foundation we began a comparative field study of criminal syndicates in the United States and Italy. Our interest was in looking at them as secret societies rather than merely criminal organizations, and in seeing if there is a common model— some system of order or code of rules—which describes social controls within all such groups. We saw our task as the formulation of the system of implicit rules shared by the members of Italo-American criminal syndicates by examining how those members apply these rules. The central question of our research was: what is the code of rules that makes a criminal syndicate a social system and how do its members play the game?

For the last three years we have been observing and recording patterns of behavior and social relationship in several organized crime "families" in New York and we have attempted to identify the cultural patterns—both Italian and American—which underlie and activate this ordering of behavior.

Government studies invariably point to some organizational link between the Sicilian *Mafia* and Italo-American crime syndicates. But anyone searching out the origins of Italo-American criminal syndicates in Sicily and its *Mafia* finds problems on both sides of the Atlantic. In the first place, by no means all of the reputed *Mafia* members are Sicilians. Many, like Vito Genovese came from in and around Naples; some like Frank Costello, are from Calabria. But, significantly, all *are* from the south of Italy. The second problem is that while the Sicilian *Mafia* is well-known to Americans, each of the other two southern provinces—Calabria and the Campagnia (Naples and its environs)—also produced its own distinctive secret criminal society and there is no evidence of any organizational linkage among the three. These two facts, long known but largely ignored in studying the role of Italo-Americans in organized crime, are of fundamental importance when they are considered together and they are a basis for our answer to the question whether or not there is a *Mafia* in the United States.

The logic of our answer proceeds from field work in Italy which convinced us that *Mafia* is more than just a criminal organization; it is a generic form of social organization which developed in the south of Italy under particular social and cultural conditions. The *Mafia* is a social system in which power is distributed through a network of clan-like gangs which operate parallel to the law and which are held together by real and artificial kinship bonds. In order to deal with the problem of "the *Mafia*," one must turn first to southern Italy, and then consider whether or not the *Mafia*, or some variant of it, was transplanted in the United States.

II

There are, as almost everyone knows, two Italies—the urbane and economically-advanced north and the rural, still semi-feudal south. The northern Italian is a European; the spirit of capitalism and the acquisition of wealth motivate him as single-mindedly as they do the Swiss or the German. The southern Italian is a Mediterranean. The acquisition of material goods are secondary to him; the power to influence people—to command obedience and respect—are his primary concern. These differences are not superficial; they mold the behavior of the child; they shape all social relations. While beginning to change, these desires are still obvious in the three imperatives which shape southern Italian culture—the primacy of the family, the juxtaposition of church and state, and the ascendency of personal honor over statutory law. And these explain why the *Mafia* and other secret societies developed in the south.

Italy is a nation of families, not of individuals. In the south, especially, the family *is* the social structure and no social institution —not the state or even the church—has ever successfully challenged its supremacy. The family demands the southern Italian's first loyalty and within it he practices all of the virtues and self sacrifice which other men save for their church or state. The pattern of roles within the southern Italian family is recognizable from the model of the divine family in Catholicism. The authoritarian father is a patriarch who demands and commands immediate obedience. The true *paterfamilius*, he represents the family's power and status in the community. The mother is subservient to the father and her humility, and willingness to bear all burdens enshrine the honor of the family and win the respect of her children. Daughters, like mothers, are humble and their chastity is a matter of great moment to the family; in Italy wars have been waged over a daughter's honor. The son is obedient to his father and respects his mother. This pattern of relationship extends beyond the biological family by *comparaggio*—the practice of establishing fictive kinship with *compare* (godfathers) and *comare* (godmothers). Godparent-godchild relationships have far more potency in southern Italy than do the ceremonial godparent relationship we know in America.

Neither church nor state has ever been strong enough to challenge the family. The southern Italian treats government at any level with skepticism. He surrenders everything to the family but nothing to the state. And even those who are deeply religious do not really trust the church as an institution. In Italy, the church has always been an independent temporal power as well as a religious institution and this face of the church is distrusted just as much as any other government. It is this juxtaposition of church and state—a unified church to which all Italians belong and a weakly united state that few Italians serve—which has kept any strong political or religious authority structure from forming.

In southern Italy the rule of law is replaced by a familial social order which is regulated "invisibly." This social order is internalized in a code which exhorts each man, regardless of his age or rank, to protect the family's honor and to avenge any breech of that honor. The code is an integrative behavioral system which binds families to each other throughout each village and town in a ritualistic web difficult for the southern Italian to escape but just as difficult for the non-Italian to understand.

These major themes shape the culture of the south of Italy—a strong family, a weak political structure and a sense of honor which takes precedence over the law. Not only do they distinguish the southern Italian from his northern countrymen, they also explain how and why secret criminal societies formed in the south but not the north.

While the Sicilian *Mafia* is the best known of the Italian criminal societies (the Italians call them "delinquential" because not all of their activities are strictly criminal) the south of Italy has produced others as well. Throughout the south, the oppression by alien governments which preceded unification and the weakness of the central government which followed it, produced many bands of brigands whose aim ranged from profit-making to blood-revenge and even to reformist social justice. These social bandits—as Hobsbawm has described them—do not qualify as criminal secret societies in the *Mafia* sense because with few exceptions, they were *ad hoc* groups, with no past and a doubtful future. But they spring from the same cultural sources that produced the *Mafia* and other criminal secret societies, and in many ways they are ancestral to them.

In Calabria, the mountainous and remote province at the southernmost tip of mainland Italy, for example, an organization somewhere between social banditry and a criminal secret society seems to have existed almost unknown to the outside world (including the rest of Italy) for at least a century. Known colloquially as *'ndranghita* ("brotherhood" in Calabrian dialect), it is also called the *Onorata Società* (Honored Society). Although brigandage and smuggling were its primary functions, it became a powerful source of local, political and social control at the turn of the century. (The advent of fascism destroyed its political power.)

While the *Onorata Società* developed in the isolated mountain villages and then spread to the capital city of Reggio Calabria, another criminal secret society, the *Camorra,* was born in the city of Naples and then spread out to the villages and towns surrounding it. When the Camorra first became known in 1820 it was found only in the prisons of Naples where it had developed to the point that the control of the prisons was as much in the hands of *Camorristi* as it was of their Bourbon warders. Its influence spread outside the prisons, first into the city of Naples and eventually throughout the surrounding countryside. Discharged criminals formed the nuclei of the external *Camorra* gangs and for the next forty years, bands of *Camorristi* organized for robbery, blackmail, kidnapping and smuggling. Today, particularly in Naples, but elsewhere in the region as well, there are gangs and gangsters who smuggle cigarettes and gasoline (or, more frequently, expropriate them from NATO bases), extort money and operate the full range of familiar rackets. They are known to Italians as *Camorristi* or sometimes *"magliari"* (sledge hammers) but they retain little more than the aura of the old *Camorra.* The real *Camorra* required a weak government and social disorganization to flourish and, therefore, did not survive the first decade of fascism in Italy. If nothing else, Mussolini did bring strong, authoritarian government to Naples forcing the *Camorra* to go underground where it seems to have died.

The most famous of the secret societies of the south of Italy, the Sicilian *Mafia,* survived fascism. But what is alive and well are matters for conjecture. *Mafia* is a word which has at least two distinct meanings to Sicilians. When used as an adjective, it describes a state of mind and a style of behavior that Sicilians recognize immediately. It is bravura but not braggadocio. It bespeaks the man who is known and respected because of his contacts and ability to get things done. It suggests that he is unwilling to allow the merest hint of an insult or slight to go unanswered and it insinuates that he has means at his disposal to see that it doesn't. He is a "man of respect" who has "friends." In Palermo, even the style of dress, with the hat cocked to one side, the walk which we would call a self-assured strut, the manner of speech and the general air of self-reliance can mark a man as *mafioso* (the Sicilians actually say *mafiusu*). Such a man may or may not be a member of a formal organization in which he has a clearly defined role. Yet even in Sicily, the word *Mafia* also clearly denotes just such an organization when it is used as a noun.

Italians are trained from childhood to understand that things are not always what they seem. This use of double meaning has been a source of misunderstanding for years. The Italian scholar or journalist says *"mafia* is an attitude, not an organization." To the American this means that he is saying "there is no *Mafia*." He is saying nothing of the kind. He is suggesting that *mafia* as a pattern in Sicilian life exists regardless of the persistence of the *Mafia* as an organization, and that the organization would be impossible without the ethic. The distinction is subtle, but real. To the Sicilian it is impossible to separate the lower case state of *mafia* from the upper case powerful secret organization, *Mafia*. Both are part of the culture of Sicily which he learns from childhood.

The spirit of *mafia* derives from the fact that every man seeks protection for himself and his family. He cannot get this from the state, but only from a network of protection to which he finds himself bound. This network of friendship is a pattern of social obligation that has more permanence than religion and more legitimacy than law. Friendship becomes part of kinship. Each man and every family know what they owe to others and what is due from them. Favors become obligations and wrongs debts which demand redress; *"Si moru mi voricu; si campu t'allampu"* (If you kill me they will bury me; if I live, I will kill you). The spirit of *mafia* persists because it is born of this network and it is in turn the progenitor of the secret organization, *Mafia*.

In many ways, the term *organization* does not fit the Sicilian *Mafia*. European students of Mafia agree that there is no highly-centralized organization called the *Mafia* in Sicily (or anyplace else say the Italians); *Mafia* is a form of control over a particular community's life by a secret—or at least officially unrecognized, because everyone in the village knows who is involved—system of local groups. There is today an urban *Mafia* in Palermo that the Palermitani claim was brought back to Palermo by American gangsters who were deported to Sicily. But the true *Mafia* is overwhelmingly rural in origin and territory.

There is still a *Mafia* in western Sicily today but no one there calls it that. There, like its counterpart in Calabria, it has always been called the *Onorata Società*. It is also known by other names such as *la santa mamma* (the Holy Mother), or increasingly today, *gli uomini qualificati* (qualified men or specialists). Members do not call themselves *Mafiosi* and no one else calls them that. They are known simply as *gli amici*, the friends, or *gli amici degli amici*, the friends of friends.

Despite their secrecy we know enough about these societies to make a few generalizations about them as a form of social organization. First, *mafia* as a cultural model is not unique to Sicily although, like the southern Italian culture which produced it, it is most visible there. The Neopolitan *Camorra* and the Calabrian *Onorata Società*, though they differ from Sicilian *Mafia* in some features, are obviously of the same genus.

Mafia in the sense just described is more than a secret society. It is, as the Italians insist, a particular and peculiar state of mind. It is a basic form of social organization developed in the south of Italy to control or negotiate social conflict where there is a weak or absent state. The *Mafioso* operates as a middle man in a vacuum of political values, structures and organization. He is a broker—although not always an honest one—who operates as a network builder and monitor between and among elements in an unstable system. To the *Mafioso* and his clients, this seems to be the natural order of things. Given the weakness of the state and the insecurity of the poor living under it, he offers protection but also a form of representation to the populace who have no other means of negotiating with the power structure. The base of *Mafia* power is the personal relationship, for the *Mafioso* reduces every social relationship to a personal level, a level in which he can feel and perform in a manner superior to other men. Because he has "friends"—he is more of a man than others. Where justice is powerless, says the *Mafioso*, there the injured must have recourse to his own strength and that of his friends. When the state does become strong or authoritarian—as in fascism— the *Mafia* begins to fall apart. After the Allied Occupation it reappeared in western Sicily.

Just as there are many local *mafie* in Sicily rather than a unified central *Mafia*, so they serve many functions. It is involved in criminal activities and oppression but it is also an integrative system. It does serve as a means of social control, a mechanism for the management of social conflict (admitting that it generates some of the conflict itself) and for the provision of services to a community that would otherwise remain unserved.

The old world *Mafia*, thus, is an outgrowth of a rudimentary ideology and system or organizing society institutionalized in the culture of the south of Italy and particularly in Sicily for the management of specific forms of social conflict. It seems fair to assume that anywhere and everywhere southern Italians are found in large enough numbers to sustain the culture, the strength of this ideology and the cultural imperatives that produced it would lead them to respond to similar social conflict and disorganization by importing or resurrecting the *Mafia*.

III

In the decade from 1900 to 1910, a total of 2,104,000 Italians emigrated to the United States. Eighty per cent of them came from southern Italy and Sicily; most of these settled in eastern cities in self-contained "Little Italies" where each tenement re-established the old village square. The Italians succeeded in bringing their villages with them and that village culture—not any new Italo-American or even any emergent pan-Italian culture—set the standards for their beliefs and behavior. All of the facets of that village culture—the primacy of ties to kinfolk, the spell of religion and superstition and the disdain for extra-familial foreign laws—came with them and settled in the same urban villages. One question, of course, is this: Did *mafia* also come with them and is it also a part of what they have retained?

It is deceptively simple to answer this question with a well-documented "no." The Sicilian *Mafia*—or, for that matter, the Neopolitan *Camorra* or Calabrian *Onorata Società*—could not and did not migrate as organizations to the United States. It took hundreds of years for *mafia* to develop within the cultural values of the south of Italy and just as long for the behavior associated with it to be operationalized in viable organization. Despite strong cultural afinity, the Sicilian *Mafia*, for example, found the eastern end of Sicily inhospitable and so remained in the west. Why should it attempt to cross the ocean?

The conditions of the Italian migration to the United States also underwrite a negative answer to this question. It must be remembered that this was a proletarian emigration and was considered often a temporary move by most of the emigrants. At the time of the migration, *all* of the heads of the local *Mafie* in Sicily were men of some wealth, considerable power and prestige and hard-earned status. There was no reason for them to leave the island until Mussolini and his police prefect Cesare Mori began arresting and killing suspected *Mafiosi* in the 1920's. All of this is not to say that some few individual *Mafiosi* or *camorristi* did not come over as part of the emigration. Whole villages moved to America virtually *en masse* and minor *Mafiosi* and *Camorristi* probably were present among them, but they were few in number and almost certainly did not represent any potential leadership or they would have remained in Italy. What is more important is that they, like the vast majority of southern Italian immigrants, came as individuals and probably not to stay. The possibility that they were an advance party sent ahead to seek new territory and colonize is patently absurd to anyone who comprehends *Mafia*. The local *Mafie* were rooted in sentiment and power to the local community; neither was there any central organization or grand council that could make such a decision on a wider than local level.

Having set aside the contention that the *Mafia* or *Camorra* set up branch offices in the new world, it would be comforting as well as plausible to fall back on our distinction between *Mafia* and *mafia* and say that what the migrants did bring was some primaeval cultural sense of *mafia* with them which they used as a model for organizing crime. They did, and it has served them well, but that cultural model alone did not produce present-day Italo-American criminal syndicates. The emergence of Italo-Americans in a dominant role in organized crime is a post-1930 phenomenon. The strict diffusionist approach that sees only *Mafia* in Italo-American crime syndicates must therefore assume that the concept of *mafia* lay dormant among southern Italian immigrants for decades and then suddenly emerged as a model to organize Italo-American involvement in crime. Further, it must assume nothing was happening in the acculturative experience of Italo-Americans that allowed them to find better and already proven models in the native American setting. These assumptions do not bear up under analysis.

However potent the mafia model was in southern Italian culture, it had to be Americanized to be successful here. The social history of the Italo-Americans in the first thirty years of the century indicates the importance of southern Italian culture to the development of Italo-American criminal syndicates. However, social and economic conditions here were even more important.

IV

A number of social scientists have analyzed the relationships among ethnicity, organized crime and politics in American life. Daniel Bell describes the transfer in crime of one succession of European immigrants to another as the "queer ladder of social mobility;" in coming out of the slums, organized crime is one of the first few rungs. The Irish came first and early Irish gangsters started the climb up the ladder. As they came to control the political machinery of the large cities, the Irish won wealth, power and respectability through consequent control of construction, trucking, public utilities and the waterfront. The Irish were succeeded in organized crime by Jews and the names of Arnold Rothstein, Louis "Lepke" Buchalter and Jacob "Gurrah" Shapiro dominated gambling and labor racketeering for a decade. The Italians came last and did not get a commanding leg-up on the ladder until the late 1930's. They were just beginning to find politics and business as routes out of crime and the ghetto into wealth and respectability in the 1950's when the Kefauver hearings took place. Since then, the assumption seems to be that when they advance into business and politics, Italo-Americans somehow take the *Mafia* with them. Unlike the Jews and Irish before them, their movement into legitimate business and politics has not won them respectability. Instead, their presence indicates corruption and signals an attempt to "take over" control for illicit purposes.

In the early days of the Italian ghettos the crimes reported in the press were, in fact, *Italian* crimes. They were committed by Italians against other Italians. They were the traditional crimes of the *Mafia* and Camorra. And they were crimes which the Italians brought with them—extortion through threats of death and bodily harm, vendettas or blood feuds particularly between Neopolitans and Sicilians and kidnapping of brides. Almost as soon as they arrived, the Italians brought public notice to crime in the ghetto through the *Black Hand,* a series of threats, murders, maimings and bombings as a means of extorting money from fellow immigrants. *Black Hand* activities, however, were unorganized; they were the work of individual extortionists or small gangs and there is no evidence which suggests that there was any higher level or organization or any tie with the *Mafia* in Sicily or *Camorra* in Naples. Without the protective network of family and kindred, the immigrant was easy prey to anyone who appreciated his vulnerability and individual entrepreneurs or small gangs could operate freely in the police-less colonies. It is interesting that in the dozens of *Black Hand* letters we have seen, never once is there an explicit or implied threat that the *Mafia* or *Camorra* was in any way involved. What seems clear from all of the evidence is that the *Black Hand,* which lasted about 15 years (from the turn of the century to the first World War) was a cultural but not an organizational offshoot of *Mafia* and was completely Italian in origin and character.

It was the immigrants themselves who finally did away with the *Black Hand.* As was true in the earlier frontiers of the westward expansion, the lack of established patterns of social control and sanctioned codes of behavior provided an environment of "lawlessness" where conflict and violence were always just below the surface. Within the ghettoes, protection against crimes was left almost entirely to the immigrants as a result of that characteristically American attitude toward minority group crime which stands aloof so long as they keep it among themselves. Faced with an absentee government, the immigrants did just as they had done in Italy and just what a previous generation of American frontiersmen had done for the west. A rough and ready system of internal policing developed along with a set of "courts" which arbitrated disputes and meted out justice to wrong-doers. In Italy the custom had been to go to a "man of respect"—a leader in the *Mafia* or *Camorra*—for redress of ills and protection from the vagaries of peasant life; in the Italian-American ghetto it was the same and the informal courts held continue in diminished power even today. As recently as 1967, Mayor Lindsay of New York City found it expedient to call on members of an Italo-American criminal syndicate to "cool off" intergroup hostility between Italo-American and black gangs in Brooklyn. And they did it.

While the immigrants policed the ghetto, their sons guarded its boundaries. Just as the Irish and the Jews had done before them, they formed into street-corner gangs to escape overcrowded homes and to seek compatible peer-group relationships. One important function of these gangs was to protect the turf within the colonies from ma-rauding bands from outside. The bonds formed in these street gangs marked the first extra-familial socialization for Italian youngsters and they have persisted into adulthood.

There seems little question that all of the social conditions and the cultural imperatives that led to the formation of the *Mafia* and other secret criminal societies in the south of Italy did, in fact, exist in the American Little Italies by 1920. As we have seen, the immigrants brought the cultural imperatives through which fathers commanded and mothers were treated with respect. The social conflict produced by harsh and impoverished living conditions, exploitation by em-ployers, lack of access to routes of social mobility, the remoteness of governmental authority, all of which had plagued them in Italy, were present in the ghettoes as well. Yet no Mafia-type organization de-veloped prior to 1920 because two critical elements were missing. It had taken the *Mafia* and *Camorra* hundreds of years to develop in the friendly soil of southern Italian culture; twenty years was just not time enough for a new organization to take root in the United States. Neither was there the established pattern of relationship—the social system of *mafia*—because the migrants had come as individuals and, despite the affinities of co-villagers in the tenements, new links, new patterns of authority and new sources for power and profit had to be established. These same cultural and linguistic difficulties made it impossible for any emergent Mafia to operate outside the colony in these early years. As the son of a Sicilian immigrant who was a well-known *Black Hander* in New York's Lower East Side Italian colony in the early 1900's explained to us:

> Can you imagine my father going up-town to commit
> a robbery or a mugging? He would have had to take an in-

terpreter with him to read the street signs and say "stick
'em up" for him.

After 1920, however, two developments in this country and one in
Italy changed all this. In the United States the immigrant's children
were becoming Americans. Italo-Americans have managed to cling
to their familialism more tenaciously than any other ethnic group,
but culture contrast continues to loosen the grip for each succeeding
generation. Educated in American schools where individualism, not
family loyalty, was the basic lesson, they formed new friendships in
the street gangs. These new alliances crossed the old village and provincial lines and in some cases even reached out into other ethnic
groups. Then national Prohibition provided a new source for illicit
profits and so a new and accelerated route to riches for both immigrant and second-generation Italo-American. This new market provided the source for power and profit which allowed an American
Mafia to form in the ghettoes. Soon after Prohibition, small sweat-
shop stills were set up within the Italian colonies to distill the alcohol
essential to producing liquor. Italians had traditionally produced
their own wine and this "illegality" had been ignored by the American authorities before Prohibition. Converting home wineries to
home stills was not difficult and the immigrant alcohol cooker could
produce enough for himself and, if he was so inclined, enough to sell
to friends and neighbors. Some of the home distilleries became large
enough to make significant profits and the alcohol produced in these
larger stills, combined with that collected from smaller stills, became
an important source for the producers of illegal whiskey.

While the immigrants could produce and even organize collectives
for illegal alcohol, they were unable to move out of the colonies to
engage in the actual distribution process. Not so their sons who,
through membership in street gangs, were being initiated into the
world of the gangster. It is important to note that while the flamboy-
ance of Al Capone has given an Italian characterization to the popular stereotype of Prohibition era gangster, Italo-Americans by no
means dominated the rival bootleg gangs. The names of O'Bannion,
Moran and O'Donnell, and of Buchalter, Kastel, Lansky, Siegal,
Weiss, and Zwillman were far more important if less notorious than
those of Aiello, Capone, or Torrio. Italo-Americans more often filled
lower echelon, enforcer-type roles than leadership positions in gangs,
although some individuals, like Capone, did rise to prominence. The
role-model ideal for these aspiring underlings was not the old-
country oriented *Mafioso* or *Camorrista* who were contemptuously
called "greenhorns," "greasers," "handlebars" or "Moustache
Petes," but the more sophisticated Irish and Jewish mobsters who

had mastered the secrets of business organization. While the profits from bootlegging afforded the second-generation growth in the demi-world of organized crime gangs, they also produced important developments among the immigrants in the ghettos. Since the immigrants could not handle large scale distribution themselves, an informal alliance developed between immigrant and second-generation Italians and between the second-generation and non-Italian gangsters, particularly the Jews. Then, after Mussolini's brief honeymoon with the Sicilian *Mafia* ended in the mid-1920's Sicilian *Mafiosi* found their kinsmen in the United States a safe haven and a number of them did come reinforcing the Sicilian culture base among the immigrant bootleggers. By the mid-1920's all of the ingredients necessary for the formation of a new Italo-American *Mafia* were available in the ghettos and it remained only to mix them in the proper proportion within these protective walls. Just such an organization does seem to have developed.

V

The name most frequently associated with this emergent Italo-American *Mafia* is the *Unione Siciliana*. While the *Unione* is often cited in government reports, the origin of the name and the structure of the organization are lost in the nether world of law enforcement informants. In our own field work we often hear reference to it. One of our respondents, for example, a Sicilian-American involved in bootlegging activities in Brooklyn throughout the Prohibition era, told us:

> At that time (1928) all the old Sicilian "moustaches" used to get together in the backrooms of the club—it was a *fratellanza* (brotherhood) and they used to call it the *Unione*. They spent a lot of time talking about the old country, drinking wine and playing cards. But these were tough guys, too, and they owned the alky cookers and pretty much ran things in the neighborhood. They had all of the businesses in Red Hook locked up and they got a piece of everything that was sold. If some guy didn't pay up they leaned on him. Everybody paid them respect and if some guy caused trouble in the neighborhood they called him into the club and straightened him out.

The *Unione Siciliana* was an informal confederation of local groups of Sicilian-Americans involved in extortion and protection in the Little Italies and in bootlegging activities particularly in organizing the cottage-industry home-distillers in the ghettos. By the late

1920's this organization had all of the cultural and organizational features of a new *Mafia* in the United States. Like the *Mafia* in Sicily, it served the Little Italies as a means of social control, a mechanism for the management of social conflict (and again like the Sicilian *Mafia,* generated some of the conflict itself) and as a source for illegal services to a public which would otherwise remain unserved. Its link with the outside world was through the American-born or American-raised second-generation. The colonies could offer a culturally supportive base for the new *Mafia* but not the production-supportive substructure necessary to nurture the new social system.

By the end of the 1920's, however, the stage had been set for the inevitable clash between the immigrants of the *fratellanza* or *Mafia*-model *Unione* and the aspiring and rising second-generation Italo-American gangsters who were now moving into leadership roles in gangland. Once again changes in the general society intervened and hurried organizational change in crime. First the Great Depression and then the inevitability of the repeal of Prohibition forecast the end of an era of prosperity where there was enough illicit profit for everybody. With the end of Prohibition it became necessary to find new areas for exploitation to continue the flow of dollars. Some areas such as gambling and labor racketeering were reprehensible to the now-old "Moustache Petes" who saw such activity as unworthy of a man of respect. Other, less noble conflicts of interest and influence were also involved as various groups struggled in the inevitable quest for power. It was this conflict between the old *Mafia*-oriented *Unione* and the new American gang-oriented Italo-American syndicates which seems to have brought the situation to a head and destroyed the *Unione.*

The drama began in 1931 when Giuseppe Masseria, a Neopolitan prominent in the gang world of New York, issued orders to exterminate a number of Sicilian "old Moustaches" whose association was with the Mafia-like *fratellanza* groups. There had been continuing speculation as to the reason. Some say it was a conflict over future areas for exploitation, others that he was simply hungry for greater power. The move touched off a war in New York that eventually spread throughout the country. With Masseria were those non-Sicilian, Italo-Americans such as Vito Genovese, Joe Adonis and Frank Costello whose alliances with non-Italian (principally Jewish) mobsters had been forged in the world of the gangs. Opposed to Masseria were the old-time Sicilian-American leaders who had risen to prominence in the *Unione* many of whom had come from or around the small town of Castellammare del Golfo on the Western coast of Sicily. The Castellammare, including Joseph Bonnano, and other Sicilians such as Joseph Profaci and Gaetano Gagliano gathered behind Salvatore

Maranzano and each group launched attacks on the other.

The war raged throughout 1930 and the "old moustaches," particularly the Castellammare, were the most frequent victims. In one forty-eight hour period close to 40 of the old Sicilian leaders were killed in a purge that rivalled the "night of the long knives" in Nazi Germany. Despite his victories in these battles, Masseria lost the war and sued for peace, but Maranzano refused to come to terms. Masseria retreated to a heavily armed fortress in New York determined to hole up and hold out. His followers, however, seemed unwilling to go with him and five of his lieutenants—Genovese, Luciano, Livorsi, Straci and Terranova—surrendered to Maranzano and on April 20, 1930 the Castellammarese War came to an end as three of them executed Masseria in a Coney Island restaurant as they ate dinner together. Maranzano was assassinated by his own lieutenants on September 11, 1931.

Whatever else it was or did, the Castellammarese War brought the short melancholy life of the Italo-American *Mafia* to an end. The old "Moustache Petes," the custodians of the *mafia* tradition were either killed off or passed in obscurity. The younger immigrants and the second-and-succeeding-generations saw in the urban gangster, not the *Mafioso*, an American role-model filled with the excitement and promise their parents' nostalgic associations with social banditry of the *Mafia* and *Camorra* could no longer provide. They formed gangs of their own in the new form of urban criminal syndicates not the old rural brotherhoods. The new syndicates did not follow provincial lines, and working relationships with non-Italians, particularly Jews were established.

After 1930 the Italo-Americans succeeded the Jews as the major ethnic group in the ranks of organized crime. At about the same time that they reached prominence in organized crime, they also began to gain some political power in major cities particularly in the Middle Atlantic and northeast States which had been the settlement areas for a vast majority of sothern Italian immigrants. Now, the new judges, the new lawyers and prosecutors, councilmen and even police had grown up in the Little Italies along with the new leadership in organized crime. They had lived together as children and strong bonds had been established; still they kept the associations through friendship and marriage. Alliances of power, friendships and kin relationship all merged and today this presents a difficult if not impossible job of sorting out those which are corrupt or corrupting from those which merely express the strength of kinship relations among southern Italians and their descendants. Yet there is no question that family structure forms the basic network which ties Italo-Americans together in organized crime and that kinship is the pivot for that integration.

The Mafia-model *Unione* was a peculiarly southern Italian institution which could not and did not survive long in the new world. The acculturation process works in crime as elsewhere and the values which activated and informed the old *Mafia* model were no longer prized. But, for Italians at least, blood really is thicker than water and while the organizational form of *Mafia* disappeared, it has left a heritage of kinship which still integrates crime families and characterizes the involvement of Italo-Americans in organized crime.

VI

Since the hearings of the Kefauver Committee two decades ago, and increasingly since the report of the 1967 Task Force on Organized Crime of the President's Commission on Law Enforcement and Administration of Justice, government law enforcement agencies and their consultants have insisted that Italo-Americans in organized crime have, in fact, created a national organization.

La Cosa Nostra is the name government sources currently assign to this confederation of Italo-American criminals that they trace back through the *Unione* to the Sicilian *Mafia*. Whether the name is an invention by Joe Valachi or whether it is simply a term commonly used by members of Italo-American criminal syndicates to identify business activities of common interest it is not the name of a formal organization. The model which the Task Force report uses for the *Mafia* is a parody of the American corporate model. Leaving aside, for a moment, its international connections, *Cosa Nostra* seems not much different from the Bell Telephone System. Like Bell, it is described as a "nation-wide . . . cartel . . . dedicated to amassing millions of dollars' through the provision of services to the public. Unlike the Bell System, however, the services of *Cosa Nostra* are described as "illicit" and its ultimate aim is the corruption of "the basic economic and political traditions and institutions" of the country. Again like the Bell System, this national cartel is a confederation of local syndicates or "companies" which function with some independence at the local level but are subject to corporate policy decisions by a "national commission" which, structurally, at least, sounds like a board of directors. Just as "Ma" Bell rules over a family of local companies all of which provide the same service to their communities, so *Cosa Nostra* is made up of local units differentiated only by territoriality for each can "participate in the full range of activities (of) organized crime." Like any large corporation, this organization continues to function regardless of personnel changes because *Cosa Nostra's* local organizations are "rationally designed with an integrated set of positions geared to maximize profits." The descriptions of the local units or "families" continue the analogy in terms of positions, functions and authority structure. The position of *caporegima*, in the *Cosa Nostra*, for example, "is analogous to plant supervisor or sales manager" in a business organization and the *sottocapo* or "underboss" is "the vice-president" or "deputy." And like the Bell System, *Cosa Nostra* maintains contacts with its counterparts overseas. What this describes, of course, is the rational, deliberately designed *formal* organization constructed to achieve a set of specified goals. It sees "organization" as a chart describing positions, a hierarchy of jobs to be filled and carried out and as a blueprint which can be used to construct and reconstruct organizations everywhere.

Yet Italo-American crime "families" are *not* organizations in this sense at all. They are not rationally designed and consciously constructed; nor are they hierarchies of organizational positions which can be diagrammed or changed by merely redrawing the chart.

There is *no* formal organization or confederation of Italo-Americans in organized crime called *Mafia*, *Cosa Nostra* or anything else.

There are numbers of Italo-Americans who are involved in organized crime, they do form highly organized local syndicates (or "families") and the families do cooperate with each other in licit and illicit activities. But they are not held together by a national membership organization with a ruling council or even some shared conspiracy in crime. They are joined by the looser form of obligations and protections of the south Italian system of family and kinship.

Italo-American criminal syndicates are rightly called "families" because the relationships established within them produce kinship-like ties among members, ties which are given greater power when they are legitimated through marriage or godparenthood. Every "family" member knows that every other member has some duties toward him and some claim on him. Whether the relationships are based on blood or marriage as they often are, or are fictive as in the intricate pattern of ritual alliances through godparenthood, it is also kinship which ties generations together and allies lineages and "families."

Membership in a "family" is not like membership in a gang or an organization. A member does not receive a salary. He is usually engaged in his own activities. Members of families may even be competitive with each other. Nor does a member of a family necessarily give a share of his earnings to the head of the family. The closest model is a feudal one wherein a member swears fealty, receives protection and provides his services to protect others when it is asked.

It is this feature which sets Italo-American crime "families" off from the gangs in organized crime of previous ethnic groups. Every government report, after the *de rigeur* disclaimer that "of course, the vast majority of Italians in this country are god-fearing and hard-working" goes on to marvel at how tightly knit Italo-American crime families are and how closely structured the network among "families." The most frequently used term is "clannishness." One report describes this clannishness as "the cement that helps to bind the Costello-Adonis-Lansky Syndicate," another comments that a-mong Italo-American crime families, "a certain clannishness con-tributed to the retention of the custom of clannishness." Once again, the term is apt because, if one sets aside the literal view that clans are descent groups from a real or imagined common ancestor and takes the common sense view that they are alliances of lineages, then Italo-American criminal "families" are very much like clans.

While they do not maintain a fiction of descent from a common ancestor, Italo-American crime "families" are actually a number of lineages linked together into a composite clan. Like clans everywhere, these crime "families" enter into exchange relations with each other and form alliances which, once formed, are perpetuated. Like clans-men everywhere, members treat each other as agnatic brothers and acknowledge mutual rights and obligations on a kinship pattern how-ever remote they may be genealogically. Each clan has its own terri-tory. Some clans grow too large to maintain the kinship-like bond and divide, sometimes splitting through internal dissention, some-times sending off segments to new clan-territories. Some clans de-cline and die out or lose their territory in warfare. The clan, because of its kinship base and its territoriality, can establish and maintain its own rigid code of familial law and pass authority from one generation to another.

For over three years now, we have been looking at kinship relation-ships in Italo-American crime "families" in various parts of the country. The findings clearly indicate the role of kinship in integrat-ing individual "families" and in creating alliances among them which perpetuate power. In the New York-based Italo-American "family" which we have most closely examined, every one of the 15 members in leadership positions is related by blood or marriage and frequently by godparenthood as well. Data we have gathered on "fam-ilies" in other parts of the country show the same kinship-based organ-ization. The chart below, for example, traces relationships among the 20 leading "syndicate" families in a major mid-western city. Not only are *all* 20 families intermarried, they have also formed alliances through marriage with crime families in Buffalo, New York City and New Orleans.

MARRIAGE AND KINSHIP LINES AMONG 20 FAMILIES IN A MIDWESTERN CITY

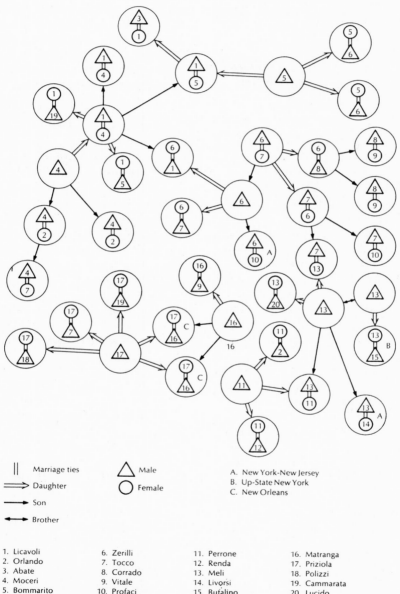

|| Marriage ties

⟹ Daughter

→ Son

↔ Brother

△ Male

○ Female

A. New York-New Jersey
B. Up-State New York
C. New Orleans

1. Licavoli
2. Orlando
3. Abate
4. Moceri
5. Bommarito

6. Zerilli
7. Tocco
8. Corrado
9. Vitale
10. Profaci

11. Perrone
12. Renda
13. Meli
14. Livorsi
15. Bufalino

16. Matranga
17. Priziola
18. Polizzi
19. Cammarata
20. Lucido

What the chart cannot show, however, is how intricately woven this web of kinship is and how it ties "families" in various parts of the country together. Consider just one alliance, that between the Tocco and Zerilli lineages. William Tocco married Rosalie Zerilli who is the sister of Joseph Zerilli. Joseph Zerilli's daughter Rosalie is married to Dominic Licavoli. Dominic Licavoli's brother Pete married Grace Bommarito. William Tocco and Rosalie Zerilli's son Anthony is married to Carmela Profaci, daughter of Joseph Profaci who was a "boss" of a "family" in New York City. Carmela Profaci's cousin is married to the son of Joseph Bonanno, a now-deposed former "boss" of another New York family. Profaci's other daughter Rosalie married the son of Joseph Zerilli. (Remember that Joseph Zerilli is the brother of Rosalie Zerilli who is married to William Tocco.) William and Rosalie Tocco's son Jack Tocco married Antoinette Meli who is the daughter of Angelo Meli. Antoinette's brother Salvatore Meli married Dolores Livorsi, the daughter of Frank Livorsi, who is a functionary in another New York area "family." Dolores' sister Rose is married to Tom Dio, a member of a New York family involved in labor racketeering. Jack Tocco's wife's (Antionette Meli) cousin Marie is married to William Bufalino, a leading member of an up-state New York "family." Jack Tocco's wife's brother Vincent Meli married Pauline Perrone, daughter of Santo Perrone. Pauline's sister is married to Augostino Orlando; her other sister, Mary Perrone is married to Carl Renda. This network of alliances intersects with several others which reach into "families" all over the country and is strengthened by an equally complex pattern of godparent-godchild relationships.

This same basic pattern of kinship organization occurs in every major syndicate "family" we have looked at in this country. Not only are individuals within "families" related, there is widespread inter-marriage among "families" throughout the country. Of the more than 60 "Mafia bosses" identified as participants at the famous Apalachin meeting in November 1957, for example, almost half were related by blood or marriage, and even more if godparenthood is included as a kin relationship. At one point, three of the five "bosses" of New York's "families"—Carlo Gambino, Vito Genovese, and Thomas Lucchese—had children who were inter-married.

These relationships are actually a series of complex alliances binding together lineages in the same "families" together for systematic exchange of services. And in all relations with outsiders, a man acts not simply as an individual but as a representative of his clan.

This clan pattern of organization also provides a common system of roles, norms and values which not only regulate the behavior within the "family" but also structures relationships among families. It is the universality of this clan organization and the strength of its shared behavior system which makes Italo-American criminal syndicates seem so similar and suggests a national or even international organization. Southern Italians really do not accept any collective larger than the extended kin group and so are reluctant to recognize any moral or social force outside the family. When the extra-familial institutions are alien, as they are in this country, the reliance on family-centered moral systems is re-inforced.

It is this shared, kinship-based moral code, rather than fear or coercion which defines behavior within Italo-American crime "families." And it is a collective amorality toward extra-familial authority structures which binds the "families" to each other and to the Italo-American community. The "code of silence," for example, is hardly an exclusive feature of *Cosa Nostra* or even *Mafia*. In our research on secret societies, we have yet to find one where secrecy is not part of the basic code. What is *different* about Italo-Americans involved in organized crime is that their secrecy and silence in the face of official inquiry are not conditions of membership in some organization but are ingredients of culture passed on through the socialization process.

VII

The kinship model which ties Italo-American criminal "families" together is now disappearing. After three generations of acculturation, the Italo-American family is losing its insistence on father-obedience and mother respect and the authority structure in the crime "families" is changing too. Newer, utilitarian alliances with power establishments in the larger society are replacing the traditional generational authority structure. As American culture continues to errode the strength of family and kinship in Italo-American culture, the "families" must weaken and will give way to the next wave of aspiring ethnics, just as the Jew and the Irish did before them.

The evidence of this displacement is already apparent. In New York City, for example, blacks, Puerto Ricans and Cubans are now displacing Italo-Americans in the policy or numbers rackets. In some cases, particularly in East Harlem and in Brooklyn this is a peaceful succession as the Italo-American "families" literally lease the rackets on a concession basis. The "family" supplies the money and the protection, the blacks or Puerto Ricans run the operation. In other cases we know of in central and west Harlem, however, the transition is not so peaceful and the Italian syndicate members are actually being pushed out. Current estimates are that upward to one-fourth of the control and operation of the policy racket in New York has already changed hands.

The outlook for the Italian crime "families" is not a promising one. Ethnic succession in organized crime will force them out, but their movement into legitimate business areas whether as "families" or as individuals is blocked because it comes at a time when interest in organized crime infiltration of business is at its height. They might, of course, go underground as the *Mafia* did in Sicily under Mussolini. But even if they do, there seems little chance they will re-emerge for Italo-American culture will not sustain them.

The "conspiracy" idea seems to be fading as well. Recently after a series of demonstrations and protests by Italo-Americans in the spring and summer of 1970, the Department of Justice dropped the terms *Mafia* and *Cosa Nostra* as generic for organized crime. Nixon administration spokesmen insisted that the decision was in no way related to the pressures of the demonstrations, which were, of course, attributed to the *Mafia* itself, but was the result of administration sensitivity to the argument that large segments of organized crime are obviously not Italian-dominated.

An era of Italian crime seems to be passing in large measure because of the changing nature of the Italian community and its inclusion in the society. To that extent, the pattern of Italian crime seems to be following that of previous ethnic groups described in Bell's essay "Crime as an American Way of Life." But what is distinctive about Italian crime is the "myth" that went with it, a myth that arose more out of the need of Americans, nourished in a populist politics, to believe in formidable conspiracies as a means of explaining reality. As I have tried to show, a *Mafia* did—and does exist; but its character is a compound of a cultural attitude and a web of kinships, which are attributes peculiar to the Italian scene, rather than the "big business" pattern, which is a projection of the American imagination.

IV
Employment, Health,
and Social Needs

INTRODUCTION

No literature is more graphic than that which describes the plight of the Italian worker in America; and no accounts are more poignant than those which delineate the conditions under which Italians lived in the congested enclaves they inhabited in American cities.

The exploitation of Italian workers in America and the health and social needs of the immigrant Italian family became *causes célèbres*, and generated a literature both of protest and reforms.[1] And, incongruously, while Italian immigrants provided a cheap source of labor, American nativists called for their exclusion. How strong the nativist impulse was in its rejection of the Italian is amply recorded by Eliot Lord who, writing in 1905, observed:

> It is urged that the Italian race stock is inferior and degraded; that it will not assimilate naturally or readily with the prevailing "Anglo-Saxon" race stock of this country; that intermixture, if practicable, will be detrimental; that servility, filthy habits of life, and hopelessly degraded standard of needs and ambitions have been ingrained in the Italians by centuries of oppression and abject poverty; that they are incapable of any adequate appreciation of our free institutions and the privileges and duties of citizenship; that the greater part are illiterate and likely to remain so; that they are lowering and will inevitably lower the American standard of living and labor and citizenship; that they are crowding out American laborers from avenues of employment; that their labor is no longer needed here for the development of the country; that a large percentage are paupers or on the verge of pauperism, and that the inevitable influence of their influx is pauperizing; that they make the slums in our large cities; that they burden our charitable institutions and prisons; and that there is no material evidence

[1]A good guide to the literature is Allen F. Davis, *Spearheads for Reform: The Social Settlements and the Progressive Movement, 1890-1914* (New York: Oxford University Press, 1967).

of progress and prospect of relief without the enforcement
of a wide ranging exclusion.[2]

The nativists were, of course, successful with the passage of the restrictive quota legislation of the 1920s; yet, the Italian worker endured all of the vicissitudes of the hostile American milieu, and survived. Specialized studies dealing with nativism show quite clearly that the opposition of organized labor (compounded by the anxieties caused by what was seen as a threat to a way of life) to southern and eastern European immigration was largely motivated by racial prejudice rather than by genuine economic competition.[3]

Fundamental to understanding the employment contexts of Italian immigrants is the *padrone* system which developed inexorably as an economic mechanism channeling Italian workers into the insatiable manufacturing (and changing agricultural) needs of an expanding America. Luciano J. Iorizzo and Salvatore Mondello have succinctly commented on the phenomenon: "Jobs in America were plentiful. American natives and immigrants from Northern and Western Europe were moving up along the industrial scale and were no longer available to fill menial positions. Every state in the Union came to depend on the southern and eastern European immigrants to perform the rough labor required in a rapidly growing nation. The newer immigrants were the chief source of common railroad labor by 1900. The Italians, the Poles, the Hungarians, and the Czechs dug and enlarged canals and waterways. They developed water-supply systems and carved out sewage lines in American towns and cities. They were sought in cutting timber. They harvested fruits, vegetables, and grains from sunbaked fields throughout the countryside. Newcomers worked in the iron and copper mines. They held the least desirable jobs in steel plants, and glass and shoe factories. And, of course, they traveled throughout the country providing the labor force for temporary and seasonal needs.

Many Italians were railroad and day laborers. Railroad work consisted of carrying cross ties, shifting track, laying new track, doing pick and shovel tasks, and acting as guards at grade crossings. On

[2]Eliot Lord, John J. D. Trenor, Samuel J. Barrows, *The Italian in America* (New York: B. F. Buck, 1905; Reprinted, San Francisco: R & E Research Associates, 1970), pp. 17-18.

[3]Barbara M. Solomon, *Ancestors and Immigrants: A Changing New England Tradition* (Cambridge: Harvard University Press, 1956) shows how New England Brahmins developed a basis for immigration restriction based on an ideology of race. See, particularly, Charlotte Erickson, *American Industry and the European Immigrant, 1860-1865* (Cambridge: Harvard University Press, 1957). See, also, important articles by Edwin Fenton, "Italian Immigrants in the Stoneworkers' Union," *Labor History*, vol. 3 (Spring 1962), pp. 188-207; and "Italians in the Labor Movement," *Pennsylvania History*, vol. 26 (April 1959), pp. 133-148.

the coal lines, the job of unloading the black cargo was particularly dirty and difficult. The day laboring jobs involved digging trenches for sewers and water pipes, preparing road beds for paving, excavating foundations for public works projects, and providing the raw labor for the countless construction jobs underway in America".[4]

There is a large literature available on the *padrone* system; and I have chosen Marie Lipari's short but incisively descriptive exposition as the best introduction to this aspect of American economic history. Gino C. Speranza's "Italian Foreman as a Social Agent" is a contemporary vignette (1903), itself more intelligible alongside the caustic earlier observations of S. Merlino on "Italian Immigrants and their Enslavement" (1893). Louise C. Odencrantz provides a carefully detailed study of Italian women in industry (1919), and I have included her poignant commentary, "Why Jennie Hates Flowers" (1917), "the story of little Italian children who are sweated to make buttercup wreaths at eight cents a dozen." John J. D'Alesandre's invaluable study of the occupational trends of Italians in New York City derives from that handful of studies undertaken by the short-lived Casa Italiana Educational Bureau in the 1930s.

Emily W. Dinwiddie furnishes a multifaceted picture of the housing and social conditions in which Italians lived at the turn of the century (1904), and the Philadelphia of the period was not unlike other cities in which Italians had settled; it is in these contexts that Daisey H. Moseley sketches her tableau (1922) of the social worker who ministered to the needs of Italian immigrants. The great scourge that was tuberculosis (and its endemic ravages in the tenements) is grimly recreated in the short articles (1908, 1910) of Dr. Antonio Stella and R. L. Breed.[5]

The health practices of South Italian immigrants, their transplantation to American cities, and the responses of American medical personnel and hospitals to immigrant health needs, are vividly depicted in a chapter entitled "Health and Hospitals" from *South Italian Folkways in Europe and America* by Phyllis H. Williams. An astute, sympathetic observer, Williams wrote (1938)

---

[4]Luciano J. Iorizzo and Salvatore Mondello, *The Italian Americans* (New York: Twayne Publishers, 1971), pp. 51-52.

[5]R. L. Breed was Assistant Secretary of the Committee [New York City] on Prevention of Tuberculosis. Dr. Antonio Stella was one of the leading tuberculosis specialists of the time, president of the New York City Italian Medical Society, and director of the Morgagni Tuberculosis Clinic. Stella was the author of a widely distributed small monograph issued by the prestigious medical publisher, William Wood: Antonio Stella, *The Effects of Urban Congestion on Italian Women and Children* (New York: William Wood, 1908).

in the preface to her work (intended as a handbook for social workers, visiting nurses, school teachers and physicians): "Americans are apt to assume that if an immigrant is given the opportunity to enjoy the advantages this country offers, sometimes almost for the asking, he will seize them with eager hands but this is not always true. The eager hands are not stretched out, and there is no gratitude for the offer. We conclude that he does not understand, because he is a foreigner, but it is more often we who do not understand what lies behind his refusal. Frequently the explanation lies in his folkways and mores, which cannot be changed by a single interview, nor yet within a year."[6]

[6]Phyllis H. Williams, *South Italian Folkways in Europe and America: A Handbook for Social Workers, Visiting Nurses, School Teachers, and Physicians.* With an introductory Note by F. Cordasco (New York: Russell & Russell, 1969; originally Yale University Press, 1938), p. xv. As an outsider, Williams steeped herself in the cultural background of the South Italian by drawing extensively upon the work of the physician-folklorist, Dr. Giuseppe Pitrè, *Biblioteca delle Tradizioni Popolari Siciliane* (25 vols., 1871-1913). Her use of Pitrè suggests that at the time her investigations were underway (the mid-1930s), no formal, organized body of material existed in English on southern Italian folkways and mores.

MARIE LIPARI

THE PADRONE
SYSTEM*

An Aspect of American Economic History

It has been charged repeatedly that the padrone system in the United States was one of the problems created by the influx of undesirable, low standard labor. Very little importance has been attached to the fact that it was our general internal economic structure which made possible the existence and growth of a padrone system. As a matter of fact, the so-called padrone methods were not novel when the padrone system among Italian immigrants developed here. Considering it in this light, perhaps a brief account of some of the previous and coincident methods of meeting the demand for labor in America will reveal the true relation of the padrone system to the general development of the country.

The majority of unskilled labor during our Colonial Period had come under pressure. Indentured service which lasted approximately 200 years (1619-1819) in America may be described as the use of labor under formal contract for a certain length of time in order that the worker could work out the cost of passage. This system accounted for about one-half of the immigration of the Colonial Period, according to Professor Commons. Political criminals, waifs, children of the poor classes, debtors, runaway apprentices and poor laborers in Europe, England and Germany especially, were collected and sent to America where they were to work out their debt for passage and other advances. Kidnaping of children for the purpose was not uncommon. Preference for the use of Negro slavery made the system extinct in the South before the end of the 18th Century. In the North, however, it continued until about 1819. According to Adams and Sumner, before 1650, the term of service for some was ten years or more and for many seven or eight years. After 1660, however, the term was permanently reduced to 4 years.

Italy-America Monthly, Vol. 2 (April 1935), pp. 4-10.

On the whole there is no doubt that the period of the indenture was often extended either because of the condition of the worker or because of connivance on the part of the employer. Although many servants who worked out their time became tenants or free-holders, the period of indenture of others became indefinite or continuous. The available free land was not always near at the expiration of their contract. Freedom of contract at the end of a period of indenture was only nominal, actually the employer could dictate the terms. Violence and physical force were often resorted to, to assure discipline. It will be seen later in this article that certain forms of the padrone system were very similar to indentured service, a very early American institution. Herman Feldman in his recent book, "Racial Factors in American Industry" defines the padrone system as an indirect form of indentured service.

Those who in the very early stages of Italian immigration to the United States collected children whose parents could not afford to support them in the small villages in Italy and took them here to work were known as *padroni*. This so-called padrone system among Italian children which preceded the padrone system described in the following pages was not at all unlike the system of indentured service among children during the Colonial days. Abuses of the apprenticeship system, which was common in the United States, until after the Civil War often resulted in conditions of indentured service or forms of the padrone system, although the former affected the skilled labor market. The working conditions and treatment of the apprentice depended upon the goodwill of the master. Furthermore, if the master neglected his obligation to teach his apprentice the trade, the latter was virtually working under "bondage" for a period of years.

In many cases, therefore, the basis of control of the master over the apprentice (a control in the labor market) was not essentially different from that of the padrone over the worker, child or adult. Apprentices were under contract for a certain number of years whether it took that long to learn the trade or not. According to Commons and Andrews, for the "time in excess of the time required to learn the trade he was in all but name an indentured servant."

Another device to assure employers a continuous and sufficient supply of labor, which developed parallel with the padrone system in the United States, was the practice of peonage, which the Supreme Court defined as "a status or condition of compulsory service based upon indebtedness of peon to master." The system had its beginning in the Southern states where it was feared emancipation would cause considerable migration of Negroes and therefore at least a temporary shortage of labor after the close of the Civil War. It was common to arrest Negroes and charge them with vagrancy. Employers would then pay the fines which were imposed, and then compel these vagrants to repay the debt through work. The worker became further indebted for provisions advanced him from the commissary, and charges made for transportation to the location of the work, and sometimes tools and uniforms. Wages were low and prices at the commissary exorbitant. Therefore these men were kept in constant debt. If they attempted to leave employment before the debt was fully repaid, in many states the employer could have them arrested on charges of "vagrancy", "extortion", or "intent to defraud." This was an extremely effective method of bringing them back to work. Their period of service, therefore, became continuous or indefinite.

Although peonage attained the greatest prominence in the South, when practiced against Negro labor, it was also practiced against white workers. There were instances of "compulsory service based on the indebtedness" in every state except Connecticut and Oklahoma, according to the Report on Peonage and Conditions of Work among Immigrants made by the Immigration Commission (1911). The system existed in lumber, turpentine, and various other kinds of labor camps. According to this report the most complete system could be found in the forests of Maine. Labor agents or brokers, only too willing to misrepresent working conditions, furnished the labor supply to work under such conditions. The operation of peonage was, therefore, in many cases identical with some forms of oppression which developed under the padrone system.

The close of the Civil War marked the beginning of a period of prodigious industrial and commercial expansion in the United States. This period was characterized by a development of longer railway lines; better regulation of water transportation; rapid changes in form of industrial organization and scale of production; the discovery and exploitation of new and abundant natural resources; and the rapid building up of the West from great stretches of wilderness into wealthy and powerful states. All this changed the setting of American life in every aspect. Even the South, which before the Civil War had relied almost solely upon foreign commerce and more especially upon its market for raw cotton abroad, began to exploit its resources and to show signs, however slight, of industrialization.

The rapidity and depth of this post war industrial expansion did not allow for any gradual adjustment of the domestic labor forces to the new situation. A brief consideration of what made up our total labor supply at the time will reveal the difficulty. Before this the United States had for many years enjoyed a continuous increase in native white population. During the period 1790 to 1830 only about 378,000 persons migrated to this country. The increase in white population from 7,862,166 in 1820 to 10,537,378 in 1830 was due mainly to the fecundity of the native stock. Although in the next decade the rate of natural increase of native white population had begun to decline, the immigration of one and one-half millions mostly from Ireland and Germany (as compared with a little over one-half million in the ten years previous) further increased our numbers. Between 1850 and 1860 the rate of natural increase declined still further, but an increase in total number of inhabitants was made possible by continued immigration from Northwestern Europe. After 1860 the Civil War was the first great factor accounting for the reduction in rate of total national increase of population because of direct losses due to hostilities, consequent decline in birth rate and almost complete cessation of immigration while the War lasted.

No consideration of our labor supply is complete without mention of the Negro population in the United States at that time. In certain Southern states Negro population had increased more rapidly than white population. Furthermore, in spite of laws prohibiting it, fresh importation of Negroes did not cease until 1880 or after. The Negroes as slaves had been an important portion of our total labor supply in the agricultural South. All the Northern states, where prosperity early began to depend upon industry, had freed their slaves by about 1804, but agricultural prosperity of the South after the introduction of the cotton gin ended all hopes of emancipation. According to Orth, in 1860 there were 4,441,830 Negroes in the United States, of whom only 448,070 were not slaves. Emancipation, therefore put the majority of the Negro residents on the labor market. However, this did not meet the growing demand for labor, since available Negro labor was not used immediately in the mine, railroad or industry.

It is true that some freedmen in the struggle to earn a livelihood which followed emancipation, found their way with great difficulty into occupations other than farming. In fact during the decade before the War (1850-1860) some slaves had been working in cotton factories, furnaces, iron mines and tobacco factories. However, those freedmen who became part of the industrial army represented a very small minority of the total labor supply.

It is also true that very early after the Civil War some slight movement of farm labor to industry, railroad or mine became apparent.

This was natural since by 1880 farming could already be considered a declining industry in the sense that an ever-decreasing proportion of people was needed to produce America's food.

Some domestic labor, both Negro and White, could be had, but not in sufficient amounts or at a low enough price to assure the ultimate success of the great industrial and commercial undertakings, which characterized the post Civil War expansion. The development of this country had always depended to some degree upon an influx of foreign born. During and immediately after the War employers of labor depended more than ever before upon foreign countries for their labor supply. This was reflected in the law passed by Congress in 1864, which made legal all contracts made in foreign countries by prospective emigrants to the United States, whereby these emigrants pledged their services in the United States for no longer than twelve months, in order to assure repayment of passage advanced them. This unqualified privilege to import foreign labor under contract fortified the position of the employers of labor, as sole guardians of the operating machinery of the labor market. Demand for labor determined what was to make up our labor supply, but there was neither time nor desire for coordination of efforts to organize the labor market. Each employing unit, under the existing laws of free competition chose the speediest and least expensive way of making its demands for labor effective.

The padrone system among Italian immigrants which first began to attract popular attention after the Civil War, may be traced to this lack of organization in our labor market in a period of excessive demand in relation to available domestic supply. It was one of the many and diverse methods which appeared for bringing demand for and supply of labor together. An American employer who sought labor could get it through a semi-Americanized Italian resident in America, who for a stipulated commission undertook to supply men in certain numbers and at a certain wage. This labor agent called padrone either went abroad himself or had a sub-agent abroad to recruit laborers. While the above mentioned law of 1864 remained in force, written labor contracts made before the sailing of the immigrant were usual. Even after its repeal in 1868, workers were brought here in companies or gangs under "almost open labor contracts." At that time importations were usually made for a certain specific job— such as the completion of a road, railroad or canal. Very often, though not always, entire groups were returned to Italy at the expiration of their contracts, which were seldom drawn for more than two or three years. Therefore, during the early stages of the padrone system the padrone acted solely as a middleman performing the eco-

nomic function of transfering labor. However, that is not the
padrone system among Italians as it is generally understood in
America, and perhaps with sufficient basis of fact, since immigration from Italy was at that time extremely small. In the period 1851-
1870, of a total of 4,913,038 immigrants, only 20,956 (less than one
half of one per cent) were furnished by Italy, including Sicily and
Sardinia. But according to Koren few Italians who came during
that time were not bound to service.

The speed and eagerness with which fresh supplies of laborers
were demanded made importations for specific jobs too cumbersome
a procedure. As early as the seventies and eighties the padrone had
already attained prominence as a labor broker in the labor market. In
order to be able to meet demands more promptly and to make larger
profits he induced his fellow countrymen to come to the United
States under contract to himself. This contract was usually a formal
agreement that upon their arrival he would find these men employment at a wage which seemed extremely high to the uninformed
peasants of Italy. He sometimes "contracted" for the labor of these
immigrants for a definite number of years (usually one to three). Of
course after the passage of the first alien contract labor law (in 1885),
designed to prohibit the importation of labor under contract, the
padrone became cautious. He continued to induce immigration by
offers or promises of employment, but great care was exercised to
conceal from the immigration authorities all evidence that any
workers were consigned to him. Formal contracts between padrone
and worker soon became the exception. In the absence of any specific
labor contract, the padrone could distribute these newly arrived
aliens to any employer who requested them, or as sometimes
happened, he could employ them himself, if he could undertake completion of a particular job on contract or subcontract. Therefore his
(the padrone's) headquarters became a labor reservoir from which
employers could draw at any time. This very often amounted to nothing less than the creation of a "labor reserve" for certain groups in
the employing class, an activity in the labor market which is somewhat comparable though not strictly similar to the speculative
feature of buying and holding for future use in the commodity market. This function remained unchanged even after greatly increased
influx of immigrant labor from Italy made it unnecessary for the
Italo-American padrone either to import laborers or induce immigration in order to readily meet demand. In fact although it was
not generally considered so, the padrone system was really a problem distinct from the general immigration question. Its perpetua-
tion did not depend upon continued immigration. Knowledge of

the market was and continued to be the basis of the padrone's control over certain kinds and amounts of labor.

It was perhaps this quasi-speculative feature of the padrone's function in the labor market that gave him the opportunity to take undue advantage of his "customers." The padrone was, of course, in business for profits, which were derived from various sources. As a rule, agreements were made whereby he paid passage for these emigrants in return for a promise on their part to pay the debt from their first wages in America. More often than not the amount the emigrant promised to repay was two or three times the actual cost of passage. If the emigrant had any property in Italy, the padrone took a mortgage on it at an exorbitant rate of interest in order to secure the loan. In addition to a commission allowed by the steamship company for the sale of tickets, the labor agent often, if he had a large enough number consigned to him, got a reduction on the passage rate. On the arrival of the laborers, he made an additional sum by boarding them at exorbitant prices until they were sent to their work. Those who were here for a period of time, he boarded between jobs. Some padroni owned or leased tenement houses at ports of entry for this purpose. The boarding debts were also to be paid when the laborer went to work. In addition to the commission received from the employer, the labor agent charged the immigrant a fee (called *bossatura*) for finding him employment. According to Koren this fee varied from one to ten dollars for a job lasting five or six months. The Ninth Special Report of the Commissioner of Labor in 1897 on conditions of Italians in Chicago revealed that of the 403 who said they worked for a padrone, twenty-four or 6% paid no commission, while 379 or 94% had paid a commission. An average of $4.84 per individual (of the number reporting) for an average working period of 11 weeks and 4 days was paid. Commissions were usually higher when work was scarce.

The location of the work was usually miles away in some remote section where a railroad was being built or a mine exploited. This turned out to be another source of profit since the padrone through the employing company could often get reduced railroad or steamtransportation and charge the laborer full first class passage or even more. If the employing company or contractor offered the men free transportation the padrone received the benefit; he charged the laborer. Transportation as well as "bossatura" expense was another item deductable from prospective wages which were sometimes much less than had been promised by the padrone, who often made jobs seem desirable by misrepresenting conditions of work and terms of employment. Quite often there were transportation facilities only a portion of the way, and where roads were impassable these workers were forced to walk many miles into the interior to their destination. By the time they arrived at the location of their work the immigrants were disappointed, if not thoroughly disillusioned. The misrepresentations of the padrone concerning general working conditions, if they had not suspected before, soon became apparent.

The privilege of supplying the men with food was usually granted the padrone upon agreement to pay the employing firm a certain percentage of gross receipts (usually five percent). Some padroni managed the stores themselves, but by far the greater number placed representatives in them. The men were forced to buy their provisions in these stores either by necessity, (the nearest town being miles away) or by threats of dismissal made by the padrone or his representative and carried out by the company. It was not uncommon for prices at these stores to be twenty to one hundred per cent higher than the prevailing market prices. In some cases men were compelled to buy provisions amounting to a certain fixed minimum daily. Failure to do so meant a heavy fine or dismissal. Some required payment of a certain minimum amount whether provisions were bought or not. The boarding privilege was also often bought by the padrone, sometimes for a certain flat amount per worker boarded. However, it was customary for the padrone to charge each worker one to three dollars per month for sleeping space without mattress or cover, even when this space was given to him free by the employing company. Oftentimes regular fees of about fifty cents a month for medical care, which was seldom if ever provided, were extorted from the workers.

The importance of all these charges lies in the fact that the laborer was unable to pay cash. He had started his job with debts, which were to be paid in installments from his earnings. Therefore, regular large deductions from his wages in payment of debts or for provisions advanced him from the company store left him at the end of a month's work almost penniless and dependent upon credit from the padrone at the company store to be paid out of the next month's wages. Accumulation of debts, therefore, was the basis of the padrone's control of the worker's earnings. Cases of forcible detention to compel a clearing of these debts were not uncommon. Some kept the workers constantly in debt by employing them one week and keeping them idle the next. Another plan used was to send workers on a job a week or two before they were needed in order to have them incur debts. Payments were assured the padrone by an arrangement with the employers not to pay the workers directly. The padrone or his agent received the wages, deducted what was due or sometimes more, and then gave what was left to the worker. Needless to say this was conducive to all kinds of petty extortions from the laborer. Disappearance of the padrone or his representative with all the wages of a whole group of workers was not infrequent.

Another not uncommon method of increasing profits practiced by the padrone was to discharge groups of men, on some pretext as soon as he felt he had made an ample return on his "investment," and to replace them with another group. This caused severe hardships if the worker's property abroad had been mortgaged, or if he had incurred debts to the padrone which remained unpaid at the time of his dismissal. However even more important than that is the fact that a high labor turnover served to further strengthen the position of the well informed element in the labor market, the employing class (acting through its labor brokers) in relation to labor, an uninformed group, which because of this lack of knowledge of the labor market very often found itself cut off from demand.

When a worker was dismissed he was dependent upon another labor broker, who was very likely just as unscrupulous as the last. Furthermore, change of jobs seldom meant improvement in conditions of work. Threats of dismissal were therefore the most effective weapons in the hands of padroni, although many did not hesitate to hire armed guards or severe overseers, who had no compunction to resorting to physical force or violence in order to assure discipline among the workers. Even the "thrift" for which Italians have always been noted was a source of profit for the padrone. Many padroni, if they were not immigrant bankers themselves, were connected with immigrant banks, which kept on deposit (without interest) the very meagre savings which some workers were able to accumulate in spite of all obstacles. These savings sometimes formed part of the capital on which the padrone operated. Heavy commissions were deducted for the services of sending money abroad to the worker's families. Quite often the "bank" was the padrone's headquarters. According to testimony brought before the Ford Committee there were in 1888 about 80 Italian immigrant banks through which men could be gotten in lots of fifty or one hundred.

It is extremely difficult to determine accurately how many were affected by the padrone system of transferring labor. In the Ninth Special Report of the Commissioner of Labor on conditions of Italians in Chicago in 1897, it was found that of 1860 men who were questioned 403 or 22% replied that they were engaged by a padrone. In the same year John Koren estimated that two-thirds of the Italian male population of "New York and adjoining municipalities were affected by the padrone system. Of course these estimates do not give a true picture of the extent of the system throughout the United States. There is no doubt that it permeated the country in every section. Furthermore, the padrone system did not affect Italians alone. According to the report of the Immigration Commission of 1911 some form of the system existed among all non-English speaking immigrant races.

Erroneous ideas are easily acquired but seldom changed. Koren opened his report on the padrone system, made for the Bureau of Labor in 1897, with the following statement as distorted as it is superficial: "Although the Italian Padrone discovered in the United States a field peculiarly suited to his activity he must be considered a distinct product of European soil, however much he for a time prospered under American conditions. His prototype is among the camorristi of Naples, perhaps, to be sought in the country whence he came, and a germ of the practice of extortion which has become known as the padrone system may be found in the custom of the Italian peasantry of seeking the goodwill of the padrone (master, landlord) and others whom they recognized as superiors by habitually making them presents in addition to required payments of fees." This idea expressed by Koren had been generally accepted even before his report. As late as 1921 during the House hearings before the United States Committee on Immigration and Naturalization, the padrone system was described as a type of serfdom imported from Italy, Turkey, and Assyria.

The economic problems presented by the padrone system were not essentially different from those presented by these other forms of exploitation of labor, such as indentured service, abuses of the apprenticeship system and peonage described above. These problems may be divided into three classes, those related to the supply of labor, those related to the demand for labor and those related to the operating machinery of the labor market. Poverty had always supplied the best reason for migration of labor either within a country or to some foreign country. Nevertheless the freedom of movement of labor had always been too limited to meet the excessive demand which had always characterized our economic development. Since labor did not flow in sufficient quantities to the places where it was needed, either from other sections of the country or from abroad, our employing classes resorted to coercive methods to draw upon available sources for their labor supply.

These forms of coercion had a common foundation characteristic of our economic structure—the inequality between employer and worker. These practices, deliberate or not, were in effect attempts to maintain a sufficient and permanent supply of propertiless wage earners. Even when natural resources were practically free, conditions of work among the victims of these various forms of exploitation were such that available land was always out of their reach. When land and natural resources were no longer free, but like other kinds of property, were still fairly inexpensive, these conditions of work prevented accumulation of sufficient capital for purchase. Thus, the proportion, who through labor alone, could acquire enough property or capital to become employers of labor or self-employed members of society was extremely limited.

The effects of the padrone system were more far-reaching than is generally recognized. The inevitable social consequences were various, persisting forms of maladjustment, which are condemned without any understanding of the underlying historical causes. The subject of social consequences, however, warrants a fuller treatment than is possible in this article. Although the padrone system as such has practically disappeared from the American scene, workers even today are in many places subjected to forms of exploitation characteristic of that system. The important thing to remember is that the improvement in general of the status of labor is a fundamental factor in the disappearance of these social maladjustments.

GINO C. SPERANZA

THE ITALIAN
FOREMAN AS
A SOCIAL AGENT*

*Labor Abuses in West Virginia and
Their Consequences To The Community*

In answer to several complaints of alleged abuses suffered by Italian laborers in West Virginia, the Society for the Protection of Italian Immigrants, decided to make an independent investigation and sent its corresponding secretary to study the situation on the spot.

Four counties (Kanawha, Raleigh, Clay and Wirt) were covered, many camps being visited and much evidence obtained. The testimony secured established the truth of the acts complained of in almost every instance. These may be summed up as follows:

I. Resort to practices bordering on fraud to get men to go to West Virginia.

II. Resort to intimidation ranging from isolation to armed surveillance to prevent laborers from exercising their rights as free men.

III. Well-established cases of brutal, cruel and unlawful conduct by employers or their bosses against laborers.

IV. Abuses of the commissary or camp-store through the indifference or neglect of contractors in letting out this privilege to improper persons.

I have elsewhere set forth in some detail examples coming under each of these heads, together with an explanation of certain geographic and economic conditions which to a certain extent explain, though they can be no means excuse, many and repeated acts of lawlessness, cruelty, and brutality.

There are some aspects and consequences of such unfortunate conditions as those existing in certain of these labor camps, which, irrespective of an appeal to our sympathies or our sense of justice, should

Charities, vol. 11 (1903), pp. 26-28.

be carefully considered. Men practically drafted from various centers of labor supply to strange localities, forced to work in many instances, not to save money, but to pay out their board and transportation, are very likely to become public charges. Dissatisfied, frightened, anxious to get away, these laborers brought to West Virginia from distant places, will naturally scatter at the very first opportunity; they will not say, "We will remain till we have saved enough to go home" but, like all men who fear immediate danger, will take chances, in flight. Thus, I have seen a number of cases where, Italian laborers, from lack of money for transportation (their savings all gone), walked long distances and became, temporarily at least, objects of charity.

The Italian in this country is seldom an applicant for charitable aid, yet conditions like those in West Virginia necessarily force him to mendicancy. Even in those cases it must have been an extreme necessity indeed, that drove Italians to become public charges. One group of about twenty walked from Charleston to Washington rather than beg transportation. Two that I found at the Washington workhouse were brought there because hunger and disease had driven them there.

Worse yet, the carelessness of some contractors as well as their brutality tends to increase the attendance at the public hospitals, which, in small towns, makes an appreciable difference in expense. Every workman assumes, of course, the risks and hazards of his employment, but the Italian laborers I visited in the hospitals were not there as the result of such risks and hazards, but of culpable negligence on the part of employers, if not of a brutal and inhuman treatment.

There is another important consideration which the abuses in the labor camps of West Virginia serve to clearly bring forth. It is not to be supposed that from even a business standpoint, contractors in that state wish to maltreat their workmen. If they do maltreat them, it is because they do not understand the men they handle. It can be said, for example, that to apply to Italian laborers, the methods of surveillance and direction applied to Irish laborers, is a vital mistake. It is fundamentally wrong because the Italian is essentially different from the Irish. The characteristic of the Italian is *personality*, he cannot be treated in *masses* but his characteristic views and feelings have to be considered individually. Courtesy is proverbial with him and he expects from others what he himself is ready to give. The cursing, the threats, and the blows of the foremen and bosses who cannot understand his nature will never get the best work from him.

Let us remember that thrifty and economical as these Italian workmen are, there are things that even the humblest of them hold dearer than money, and that no Italian laborer feels that he is fully paid by wages unaccompanied by the regard and consideration of his employer. This is the element—the new but hopeful element that is present-ing itself in the immigration problem and in the labor situation, so far as these refer to the Italians who come to us. The Italian laborer is here to stay, nor can we do without him. He, himself, is becoming aware that his work has a distinct value on the labor market and its great demand adds to such value. Let us help in his endeavor to reach a new estate, and whatever we do in this regard, will be repaid in staunch and loyal citizenship.

There is one way in which we can help towards the solution of this problem of Italian labor in America. It is to turn our efforts towards developing and encouraging a class of Italian foremen as a distinct species from the purely American, or Irish boss, or middleman. These should be young men sufficiently well versed in American business methods, who understand primarily the characteristics of the men under their charge—men who in the present period of transition and unrest, while we await for the second generation of Italo-American la-borer—will not merely get the best and steadiest work out of the em-ployed, but establish good relations between employed and employ-ers. As I said elsewhere: Wherever Italian labor is employed the Italian is at the mercy of the middleman, without any right of ap-peal. Whether it be the fraud of his own countryman, the banker-agent who sells his labor under false pretenses, or the extortion of his coun-tryman, the camp-storekeeper to whom the contractor lets the com-missary privileges; whether it be the "rake-off" of the foreman or the peculations of the paymaster; whether it be the brutality of the boss, or the unlawful order of the gang-foreman; no matter what the injus-tice may be, the laborer has no opportunity to appeal to his employer, either because the employer recognizes the decision of his middleman as final or because he will not bother with details.

Such a system is abhorrent to the finely adjusted character of even the humblest Italian, and the institution of middlemen that know the idiosyncrasies and characteristics of this class of laborers will result in good all around. That there is plenty of good material for such mid-dlemen is apparent to any one conversant with Italians in this country. There are among the younger laborers, honest fellows of remarkable intelligence who by a little help could become not merely foremen but spiritual leaders of their countrymen. They are men who will show their appreciation of any effort to help them to improve their condi-tions, not merely by gratitude, but by loyal service. The public mind has been so saturated with the journalistic idea that Italians are both frightfully ignorant and instictively criminal, that it never stops to consider that out of these people came some of the greatest leaders of civilization and the foremost of the Humanists.

Possibly my judgment may be biased by my kinship with them, yet it is a permissible and reasonable belief that the Republic, by extending a helping hand to the members of this sturdy southern race, will gather in a worthy element for our composite Americanism.

S. MERLINO

ITALIAN
IMMIGRANTS AND
THEIR ENSLAVEMENT*

I wish to present here a view of the Italian life in this country as it is. This is the best way to counteract the false impression of it that now prevails. My aim is not so much to call to the bar of public opinion those Italians who are responsible for the unparalleled oppression of their countrymen as to win for the victims the sympathy of honest and thoughtful Americans. Would that the attention now bestowed upon the descendants of the discoverers of America might be of some benefit to them!

It is not, however, exclusively in the interest of my down-trodden countrymen that I write this article, but in what I conceive to be the interest of the American workmen and of this country in general as well. For such is the unity of human society that the evils of a few are the evils of the many, and no society can be prosperous and happy which suffers some of its members to be oppressed. The working classes are especially interested in the removal of the evils I am about to describe, for it is by helping the more unfortunate that they themselves can rise to a higher standard of living, or at least hold their own. Workmen have yet to learn how dearly selfishness and discord cost in their struggle with strong and disciplined employers.

My only claim to attention is the fact that the statements made here are founded on my own observation, not on mere hearsay. I will choose two typical characters of Italian immigrants for study—the peasant and his born master. As a rule, the peasant has contrived by selling his little farm, or his mule, or some furniture, to bring over a handful of money. The *signore* brings nothing except, perhaps, a criminal record as a bankrupt merchant or commission-agent; or he may have been unsuccessful in one of the professions, or he may be a common adventurer. The farmer, with or without money, sets to work at once, and in his eagerness accepts almost any terms offered. The

Forum, vol. 15. (April 1893), pp. 183-190.

signore looks for a business which shall spare him the necessity of earning his bread by the sweat of his brow, and shall also enable him to gain more than bread alone. Since he has no chance to victimize the American workman, he looks on his humbler countryman as his legitimate prey.

Tradition, more than wealth, divides the Italian immigrants into laborers and contractors, and subjugates the laborers to the contractors. In the course of time some accidental changes may occur in the *personnel* of the two classes. The laborious and thrifty peasant of South Italy may become a shopkeeper and importer, and his son may graduate as a lawyer or a physician; the political exile from Romagna or Tuscany may become a saloon-keeper and a contractor; and teachers and members of other professions may turn streetsweepers or common laborers. Yet the initial differences in most cases become hereditary, and ultimately grow into social institutions.

The territorial divisions of Italy are reproduced by the distribution of the Italian immigrants through the States. The tailor from Naples and Palermo, the weaver from Lombardy, the hat-maker from Piedmont, all follow the tracks of those who have preceded them. When a workman earns enough to support a family and feels sure of steady employment, he generally buys a house on monthly payments and settles permanently in this country. But the common laborer—the house-painter, the stone-cutter, the job-printer—wanders from one State to another, contriving to live the whole year round on the small savings of a few working months. He has, therefore, little inducement to remain. The wages of the unskilled laborer are entirely arbitrary, the people from Southern Italy receiving as a rule lower wages than their Northern colleagues, even when working side by side with them.

The industry of the Italian laborer and the benefits to this country which accrue from his work cannot be disputed. He tills the soil, builds railroads, bores mountains, drains swamps, opens here and there to the industry of American workmen new fields which would not perhaps be opened but for his cheap labor. It is a mistake to believe that he causes the lowering of wages; this is due to the increase of the capitalists controlling great interests. It is equally unjust to speak of him as a pauper laborer. He becomes a pauper on landing because he receives no help, no guarantee of life and independence, and he necessarily falls a victim to the Italian contractor and the contractor's American partner or employer. There are people who would like to keep him out of this country; it would be more reasonable to keep out the contractor.

The Italian laborer does more than his share of work and receives less than his share of earnings; for as a matter of fact, the laws enacted with regard to this matter oppress the laborer and assist rather than hamper the contractor. Even supposing that the contractor does not succeed in importing contract labor, he finds in the market a large number of men entirely at his mercy, with not even the weak support of a promise to defend themselves against his greed. The few dollars which the immigrant posesses on landing are skillfully taken out of his pocket by the hotel-keeper before the hotel-keeper gives him a chance to work. When he is reduced to absolute indigence, the lowest kind of work imaginable is offered him and he has to accept it. He walks through Mulberry Street and sees a crowd around a bar in a basement. He enters the basement and finds a man employing men for a company. He adds his name to the list without knowing anything about the work he will be called upon to do, or about the place where he is to be transported, or about the terms of his engagement. Perhaps, however, he passes a banker's establishment and stops to read on a paper displayed at the window a demand for two hundred laborers, supplemented with the significant assurance that the place of work is not far distant. He enters, enlists, takes his chances, and falls in the snare set for him.

I once witnessed the departure of a party of laborers and I shall never forget the sight. In foul Mulberry Street a half-dozen carts were being loaded with bundles of the poorest clothes and rags. One man after another brought his things; women and children lounged about, and the men gathered together in small groups, chattering about the work, their hopes, and their fears. For these men *fear*. They have heard of the deceit practiced upon those who have preceded them and of their sufferings. Each man carried a tin box containing stale bread and pieces of loathsome cheese and sausage, his provisions for the journey. Some had invested whatever money they had in buying more of such food, because, as they told me, everything was so much dearer at the contractor's store. The sausage, for instance, which, rotten as it was, cost them four cents a pound in New York was sold for twenty cents a pound at the place of their work. Presently our conversation was interrupted by the appearance of the contractor; the groups dissolved, the men took leave of their wives and friends, kissed once more their children, and made a rush for the carts. Then the train started for the railroad station, where the laborers were to be taken to their unknown destination. Of course, this destination and the wages and the nature of the work have been agreed upon in some informal way. But the contract is a sham. I do not believe their is a single instance in which a contract was honestly fulfilled by the contractor. When we think of the law-breakers we instinctively refer to the lower classes. But the contractors are systematic law-breakers. As a rule, the laborer is faithful to the letter of his engagement, even when he feels wronged or deceived.

The contractor is sure to depart from the terms of the contract either as to wages, or hours of labor, or the very nature of the work. Contractors have been known to promise employment, to pocket their fees, and then to lead the men to lonely places and abandon them. Some employment agencies agree with the employers that the men shall be dismissed under pretext after a fortnight or two of work, in order that the agents may receive new fees from fresh recruits. As a rule, however, the men obtain more work than they want or can stand. The contractor, who has acted thus far as an employment agent, now assumes his real functions. Him alone the employer (a railroad or some other company) recognizes, and all wages are paid to him. He curtails these for his own benefit, first by ten or twenty per cent or more, and he retains another portion to reimburse himself for the money he has spent for railway fares and other items. Wages are generally paid at the end of the second fortnight; the first fortnight they remain unpaid till the end of the work, in guarantee of the fulfillment of the contract by the laborer. Meanwhile the men have to live, and to obtain food they increase their debt with the contractor, who keeps a "pluck-me store," where the laborers are bound to purchase all their provisions, inclusive of the straw on which they sleep. The prices charged are from twenty-five to one hundred per cent and upward above the cost of the goods to the seller, and the quality is as bad as the price is high. At sunset the work ceases and the men retire to a shanty, very much like the steerage of a third-class emigrant ship, the men being packed together in unclean and narrow berths. The shanty is no shelter from wind or rain. Only recently the shanty where the Chicago National Gas-Pipe Company huddled its Italian workmen, near Logansport, Ind., was blown down by a wind-storm and several men were killed. Neither the number nor the names of the dead were known, as Italian laborers are designated only by figures.

The brutality of the contractors toward their subjects baffles description. The contractor is a strongly-built, powerful man; he has acquired the habit of command, is well armed, protected by the authorities, supported by such of his employees as he chooses to favor, and, sad to say, by the people, who are hostile to the laborers. He often keeps guards armed with Winchester rifles to prevent his men from running away. His power has the essential characteristics of a government. He fines his men and beats and punishes them for any attempted resistance to his self-constituted authority. On Sunday he may either force them to attend church service or keep them at work. I have been told of contractors who taxed their men to make birthday presents to their wives. A feudal lord would not have expected more from his vassals.

There are numerous cases where the contractor objects to paying wages. One day last July, as I was walking in King's Bridge, near New York City, I met two laborers loitering in the rear of their shanty. They were evidently afraid to talk, and it was with much difficulty that I learned from them that they were the only members of a gang of about two hundred who had dared to strike work, because their contractor had employed them for three months without paying them. I made my way to the shanty and entered into conversation with a women who was engaged in cooking. She told me, with tears, that she had saved a little money and had invested it in feeding the men. "Now, if the contractor will not pay us," she said, "I shall be ruined." I denounced the outrage in the Italian press of New York, but ineffectually. A few days later some Italians who worked in a locality near Deal Lake, New Jersey, failing to receive their wages, captured the contractor and shut him up in the shanty, where he remained a prisoner until the county sheriff came with a *posse* to his rescue. I could mention a half-dozen more such cases, all recent. The latest came to my knowledge in Cleveland, Ohio. A contractor had run away with the money, and neither the press nor an attorney employed by the men succeeded in compelling the company which employed him to pay the workmen. Old laborers have the same tale to tell. Nearly all have the same experience. Every one will grant that robbing a poor man of his well-earned wages is a shameful crime; yet in no instance, to my knowledge, has a contractor been made to suffer for his fraud. He generally disappears for a few days and starts again in another place. In this way many, no doubt, have been enriched.

But this is not the worst form of outrage of which contractors are guilty. There have been cases where Italian laborers have suffered actual slavery, and in trying to escape have been fired upon by the guards and murdered, as happened not long ago in the Adirondacks. A similar case was told to me by one of the victims. He said:

> We started from New York on November 3, 1891, under the guidance of two bosses. We had been told we should go to Connecticut to work on a railroad and earn one dollar and seventy-five cents per day. We were taken, instead, to South Carolina, first to a place called Lambs (?) and then after a month or so to the 'Tom Tom' sulphate mines. The railroad fare was eight dollars and eighty-five cents; this sum, as well as the price of our tools, nearly three dollars, we owed the bosses. We were received by an armed guard, which kept constant watch over us, accompanying us every morning from the barracks to the mines and at night again

from the work to our shanty . . . Part of our pay went
toward the extinction of our debt; the rest was spent for as
much food as we could get at the 'pluck-me' store. We got
only so much as would keep us from starvation. Things
cost us more than twice or three times their regular price.
Our daily fare was coffee and bread for breakfast, rice with
lard or soup at dinner-time, and cheese or sausage for supper. Yet we were not able to pay off our debt; so after a while
we were given only bread, and with this only to sustain us
we had to go through our daily work. By and by we became
exhausted, and some of us go sick. Then we decided to try,
at the risk of our lives, to escape. Some of us ran away, eluding the guards. After a run of an hour I was exhausted and
decided to stay for the night in the woods. We were, however, soon surprised by the appearance of the bosses and
two guards. They thrust guns in our faces and ordered us
to return to work or they would shoot us down. We answered that we would rather die than resume our former
life in the mine. The bosses then sent for two black policemen, who insisted that we should follow them. We went
before a judge, who was sitting in a far-room. The judge
asked if there was any written contract, and when he
heard there wasn't, said he would let us go free. But the
bosses, the policemen, and the judge then held a short con-
sultation, and the result was that the bosses paid some
money (I believe it was forty-five dollars), the policemen
put the manacles on our wrists, and we were marched off.
At last, on April 1, we were all dismissed on account of the
hot weather. My comrades took the train for New York. I
had only one dollar and with this, not knowing either the
country or the language, I had to walk to New York. After
forty-two days I arrived in the city utterly exhausted."

Very little capital is required to establish an Italian bank in New
York. One has to rent a small place and advertise that money is received on deposit or for remittance to Italy. The illiterate laborer, who
is at work during the week when the post-office is opened and cannot
speak English, has no choice but to go to the banker on Sunday if he
wishes to send a small sum to his wife and children who are starving
in his native village of Calabria or Basilicata. The laborer brings
dollars and the banker pays Italian *lire;* the *aggio* on the exchange,
four or four and one-half per cent, as it may be, is appropriated by the
banker to himself. After a few weeks, the laborer calls to inquire
whether the receipt of money has been acknowledged. The banker receives him toughly and tells him, "The letter from Italy has not arrived yet." In spite of such a reception, nay, because of it, the
confidence of the laborer in his banker increases. The banker is a
signore from his own native province (there are as many banks in

Mulberry street as there are Italian provinces) and the laborer has an hereditary respect for him. Now he has saved a little money and brings it to the banker, foregoing any interest on it. Can he do otherwise? Can he take his savings with him? "He who keeps money on himself has death near him," a laborer once said to me. No wonder that murder may be resorted to as means to acquire it.

As a result of such circumstances the money flows to the bankers. The banker appropriates to his personal and speculative uses nine-tenths of every deposit, one-tenth being sufficient to meet eventual demands for reimbursement. The total amount of money so acquired by the Italian bankers of New York has been estimated by a trustworthy man (himself a banker) to be one million five hundred dollars. Yet there are bankers who are not satisfied with nine-tenths and contrive to get all the money of their customers. The Italian bankers, besides conducting a banking business, sell passenger tickets to and from Europe, exchange money, transact business as public notaries and attorneys, and deal in jewels and other commodities, regulating prices according to the ignorance and simplicity of their customers.

Some day a bank does not open. The neighbors begin to comment on the fact, the passers-by stop before the premises. A man complains that he has one hundred dollars in the bank. A new-comer has intrusted to it double that amount. The number of creditors increases at every moment; but the bank remains closed and the crowd becomes excited. The women cry, the men swear and make threats. At nightfall they all leave the place. Next morning or the following day it is announced that the banker has crossed the frontier to Canada, carrying with him the product of years of toil of hundreds of laborers.

There is one more device by which the people are fleeced—the lottery. This is a direct importation from Italy, a curious imitation of a governmental institution. Our home government extorts yearly more than sixty million *lire* from the poor, whom it promises to enrich. In Italy we look on the lottery as a heinous tax on distress and despair. Yet our lottery takes place only once a week. In New York people bet twice a day. In Italy five numbers are extracted out of ninety. Here twenty-four or twenty-six are extracted out of seventy. Both the chances and the temptation are greater than in Italy. In both countries the bet is made either on a single number or on a combination of two, three, etc. To take the simplest example: for one dollar you bet a single number; the winner receives two dollars, his own and one more as premium. In this case the chances of the individual bettor are to those of the banker as twenty-four to forty-six or as twenty-six to forty-four. The transaction is made in the rear of a shop, the real character of which is hardly disguised by a show-window simulating commerce. At every corner of Mulberry and the neighboring streets there is a betting-place bringing on an average a net revenue of two hundred dollars per day. The police know these places, and I have seen an officer of the law openly joining in its violation. The sum wagered is recorded on a piece of paper, payments are made regularly, and no one seems to doubt that the transaction is *bona fide*, although it does not take place publicly and solemnly as in Italy, and no one seems to know where and how it is done.

There are days of great excitement for the multitude of habitual bettors, and on dull days ingenious devices are tried, to kindle the enthusiasm and revive the faith in fortune. Printed books may be consulted about the destinies of numbers and their relations to the daily events of life, and ready-made combinations meet every event. The betting-places belong to individual bankers, who, however, have united in a mutual society to insure themselves against loss. The banker cannot lose money, neither is he in danger of arrest, as he never appears at the office, and all the business is transacted by his employees, who eventually are the scapegoats.

At best, the workman, after years of hard labor, saves just enough money to purchase his return ticket, or possibly a hundred dollars more to pay off the debts contracted in his absence by his family, or to buy up the small farm which was foreclosed by the government because he failed to pay the land tax. The boss or contractor, the hotel-keeper, the saloon-keeper, and the banker accumulate fortunes and buy villas or palaces in their native towns, whither they eventually return after the time has passed when their sentence to punishment is no longer valid, covered with all the honor and glory accruing from the possession of wealth.

LOUISE C. ODENCRANTZ

ITALIAN WOMEN
IN INDUSTRY*

Not so very many years ago society's chief interest in workers was in the amount of their earnings, and that largely as a source of taxes or a cause of pauperism. But the world has passed this stage of "it is nobody's business" policy in regard to its wage-earners, and the community is now generally ready to recognize that the conditions under which they work are matters of public concern. The manufactured products and the money returns are not the only interests of the public. It feels a responsibility for the human element—the producer.

INDUSTRIAL STANDARDS

There is now general agreement that industry should meet at least certain minimum requirements or standards in conditions of employment. Opinions differ as to the methods by which it may be made to live up to these standards, whether through the pressure of public opinion, the social education of employers and workers and voluntary action on their part, state regulation, or some other method. The principle of minimum requirements, however, is accepted as fundamental to social welfare and progress. The following statement embodies certain of these requirements and standards which have been accepted as a basis for measuring the welfare of the human factor in industry.[1]

*Italian Women In Industry: A Study of Conditions in New York City (Russell Sage Foundation, 1919), pp. 54-81.

[1]Odencrantz, L. C., and Potter, Zenas: Industrial Conditions in Springfirld, Illinois, P. 6. These are based upon a statement of Social Standards for Industry recommended in the report of the Committee on Standards of Living and Labor of the National Conference of Charities and Corrections in 1912.

"First and elementary among these matters are working conditions. These should be made as wholesome and safe as possible. Fire hazatds should be minimized, machinery guarded, sanitary conditions maintained, intrial diseases prevented, and good light and ventilation provided . . .

"Second, until children are sixteen years of age it is essential that they develop normally and receive training for the work of life. Any occupation, therefore, is objectionable which interferes with such development or training. Under fourteen, children should not be employed in gainful occupations.

"Third, hours of labor should not be so long as to injure health or to deny workers opportunity for self-improvement, the development of home life, and an intelligent interest in public affairs. Eight hours for a day's work is a standard which is now widely accepted.

"Fourth, every worker should have one day of rest in seven.

"Fifth, women and children should not be employed at night.

"Sixth, workers who give their full working time to an industry should receive as a very minimum a wage which will provide the necessities of life.

"Seventh, either the 'necessities of life' should include enough to allow workers to carry insurance and have something for old age or else industry should provide directly for the care of incapacitated workmen and for the dependents of workmen who are killed or used up at work through payment made by the employer,—the cost to be distributed over society by some form of insurance or other method.

"Eighth, irregularity of employment should be minimized, and when workers lose their positions adequate facilities should exist to help them find new places.

"Ninth, the bargaining power in settling the terms of the work agreement should be as evenly balanced as possible between the employer and the employe. This would recognize the right of employers and employes alike to organize or form unions."

Any industrial investigation in a center like New York City, with approximately 1,500,000 men and 600,000 women at work, is important because of the opportunity it provides to compare actual conditions with this program of minimum requirements. The value of such a study is increased when it deals with Italians and other immigrants whose entrance into industry, it is claimed, tends to lower standards of employment as well as those of living.

SOURCES OF INFORMATION

The 1,095 Italian women and girls investigated were found to be at the time of the interview or when last employed, in 734 different establishments covering 61 distinct industries.[2] The investigation of work places, however, was limited to 271 shops engaged in manufacturing in Manhattan. None was made of the work places of the few engaged in offices, stores, restaurants, or in private families. The dress and waist industry likewise was omitted as an investigation of it was being conducted at the time by the Wage Scale Board[3] of that industry, financed jointly by the Employers' Association and the trade union. Many establishments engaged in flower and feather making, millinery, and bookbinding had been covered in previous investigations of which reports had already been made.[4] Other omissions were due to the fact that some workers, especially those who could not speak English, were unable to give complete addresses. They knew how to get to their shop, but could not tell the name, street, or number. In other cases the shops had moved or failed.

In only 11 cases did the employer refuse the information desired. While some were naturally more interested and communicative than others, most of them tried sincerely to give what information they had. Many were interested in particular phases of their work, with little to say upon other problems; so that there was little uniformity in the kinds of information secured in the various establishments. One employer had given serious thought and much time to the problem of keeping his workers the whole year round. Another took no interest in this question, discharging workers when he didn't need them and advertising when he did. Some had had experiences, favorable or unfavorable, with trade union organizations which they were anxious to tell about; others showed not the slightest interest in the subject. Some answered only direct questions and could not be per-

[2]The following list will indicate how the original list of 734 was reduced to 271: Number of firms not engaged in manufacturing, 69; establishments covered in previous investigations, 55; establishments in dress and waist industry, covered by another investigation, 121; addresses incomplete, not found, etc., 198; information refused, 11; outside Manhattan, 9.

[3]The results of this investigation have been published as Bulletin 146 of the United States Bureau of Labor Statistics, Wages and Regularity of Employment and Standardization of Piece Rates in the Dress and Waist Industry of New York City (1914).

[4]Van Kleeck, Mary; *Artificial Flower Makers (1913), Women in the Bookbinding Trade (1913)*, and *A Seasonal Industry, a study of the millinery trade in New York* (1917). Russell Sage Foundation Publications.

suaded to show their shops or employes at work. Others escorted the visitor from basement to roof, explaining every detail of the work and conditions with a genuine interest in the purpose of the visit.

In 194 cases the owner or manager was interviewed and frequently the foreman or forewoman was called in to supplement their information. In other cases the manager or owner was inaccessible and the information was furnished by the forewoman or by someone in the office. The amount of information given varied with the interest and leisure time of the person interviewed; but the investigators were met with uniform courtesy, the interview not infrequently ending with an invitation to return for further information.

As the investigators went from shop to shop they were impressed with the diversity of the problems involved. Some Italians were in establishments which boasted of the highest industrial standards; others in sweat shops where workers were crowded together under

TABLE 5.—PROCESSES OF WORK PERFORMED BY ITALIAN WOMEN WORKERS IN MANUFACTURING INDUSTRIES

Process of work	Women
Operating sewing machines	222
Feeding and tending machines	64
Fine hand sewing	61
Medium-grade hand sewing	185
Coarse hand sewing	36
Hand and machine processes combined	27
Pasting	90
Branching (flowers and feathers)	45
Cutting	19
Hand stamping	7
Measuring and weighing	9
Sorting	15
Examining	12
Folding	7
Packing	48
Wrapping and tying	8
Ribboning	6
Pressing and cleaning	21
Processes peculiar to certain industries	76
Work incidental to manufacturing, such as supervising and stockkeeping	38
Work not stated further than as "general," or learning	31
Total	1,027[a]

[a] Of the 1,095 women investigated, 68 were not employed in manufacturing industries.

the worst conditions; some in places where everyone from owner to errand girl was Italian, and that the language of the shop; others where they were lost in a variety of nationalities and the employer could scarcely tell whether or not he had Italians on his payroll. It was exceptional to find shops where all the workers were Italian or, on the other hand, industries in which they were not represented at all. Of the 271 shops included in this investigation, 216 reported the number of Italian women employed and the proportion they formed of the regular force. In a total of 13,000 women employed, nearly one-third, or 4,600, were Italian by birth or by parentage. Table 6 shows how the numbers varied in different industries. Many employers frankly did not know how many or what proportion of their workers were Italian, so that the information cannot be given for 55 shops.

In the shops doing hand embroidery and laundry work, making men's clothing, women's tailored garments, and candy, more than half the women were Italian. Hand embroidery, with 94 per cent of the workers Italian, headed the list. Many of these were immigrants who had learned the trade in convents and private schools of Italy. At the time of the investigation, the fashion required that chiffon waists, dresses, and gowns should be elaborately embroidered with silks or beads. The fashion had come suddenly, as is the way of fashions, and no Americans or workers of other nationalities had been trained for this work, so that the Italians found a ready market for their skill, with few competitors.

The second largest proportion was in men's clothing factories, where 75 per cent of the women workers were Italian. In 22 out of 27 such shops, Italian was the predominant nationality. To the immigrant trained in fine hand sewing, the making of hand buttonholes offered an excellent field of work, and other women could quickly pick up the simple, coarse sewing like tacking and basting. For instance, in a men's clothing firm on Spring Street employing about 450 workers, practically all of the 150 women were Italian, many of whom could not speak English. Most of the work was simple, consisting of finishing, felling, turning straps, trimming off threads, cleaning, sewing on buttons, making pads, and basting, at which the women could earn from $6.00 to $10 a week. A few were working side by side with men operating machines and earning up to $26 a week; 15 were skilled hand buttonhole makers, earning up to $16 a week. No learners were taken, but unskilled help was used for such simple work as tacking and turning strips.

Almost as large a proportion of the women in shops making women's cloaks and suits was Italian. The work was for the most part finishing, as buttonholes were made by machines operated by men.

Great speed, however, combined with accuracy, is essential for a good finisher in this trade, and it usually takes about two years to become skilled. Consequently older women were employed. The major part of the work was done by men, and in the shops visited seldom as many as 10 women were employed. The trade was strongly organized for women as well as men, and in the busy season the earnings of the women soared up to $18, $20, or even $35 a week. A long slack season, however, cut down these high earnings, when some shops were closed entirely for three or four months, or only one or two women were kept for chance orders. Many of the Italian women who were married did not seek other work during the slack season but stayed at home. One employer thus explained the high wages of these women: "I believe it is because they have a way of working after they are married. As it takes some time to get started and efficient the longer trade life gives them the advantage."

Italians formed less than a fourth of the women in industries like the making of muslin underwear, corsets, children's clothing, umbrellas, linens, paper goods, and metal articles. In the making of straw hats, a highly skilled occupation where, according to some employers, only one in 20 succeeds in learning the trade, with wages ranging up to $30 or $40 a week during the busy season, over a third of the women were Italian in the shops investigated. One manufacturer said that the highest wage in the preceding week, $38, had been paid to an Italian. "Italian girls are very nice about their work and I am glad to get them when I can. They like perfection in their work." But in paperbox making, where the work was simple, easily learned, and wages rarely reached $10 a week, 44.5 per cent of the women were Italian.

Italians predominated in 112 out of 240 shops in which employers could state a prevailing nationality, but in every industry there were other shops where the majority were Americans, Hebrews, Germans, or Irish. In some industries the Italian's skill with the needle was a special asset, or her love for perfection and deftness of touch, while in other cases, because of her ignorance of the language and of how to get a job, she was forced to accept dirty, unskilled work.

EMPLOYERS' ATTITUDE

To the majority of employers a worker is a worker, irrespective of nationality. One employer stated that he had never noticed any special race characteristics in work but thought them individual. "Some Italians are excellent, and some are very poor." In some shops larger numbers were employed because the foreman or owner was Italian, or the shop was situated in an Italian neighborhood. One candy manufacturer would not employ an Italian who did not wear a hat, but came bareheaded or with a shawl over her head. Another employer in the cloak and suit industry stated, "We have only the better grade of Italians, born and educated here. They all speak English." Another in the same line said, "We never take Italians if we can help it. They make trouble with the other workers." "I'll take anybody who can do my work for me. I don't care what language they speak," said a manufacturer of boys' clothing. The crux of the matter was probably that if workers came up to the employers' standards of cleanliness, appearance, and ability to do the work, there was not much discrimination on grounds of nationality. Employers had no prejudice against the Italian girl who dressed like her fellow-workers and spoke their language. Her employment depended largely upon the individual employer, as one wanted only Italians, while his neighbor manufacturing the same kind and grade of goods objected seriously to her employment. Agreement was general that she earned the same wages as other workers in their shops. Some employers went further, declaring that Italians were unusually industrious and earned more, while others, with different experience, would agree with the employer who said that Italians ruin every trade they take up because "they will work for anything." Both extremes were rare, however, and the general verdict was that they were no worse and no better paid than the other workers in the shop.

WORKING CONDITIONS

Factory Buildings: Factories were housed in three types of buildings—the modern loft, the old loft, and the remodeled dwelling. The distinction between a modern and an old loft is based on structure rather than on equipment, so that a building housing a men's clothing firm, although it has introduced elevators and a sprinkler system, is still classed as an old loft because of the wooden floors and stairs and the limited window space. On the other hand, a five-year-old concrete building, built expressly for the firm occupying it, was classed as a modern loft in spite of the absence of elevators. The manager believed that a factory was a place to work in and did not wish his employes "joy-riding" in the elevator. Usually the formal entrance, the uniformed elevator man, and the concrete steps were evident in the modern loft buildings, while a freight elevator entered from the street, or worn wooden stairs ushered us into the old loft building.

The investigators found 54 shops occupying entire buildings, 74 more than one floor, 135 one floor, and the remaining eight less than an entire floor. The size of the shop, however, gives no indication of the number in the workroom. A firm occupying two adjacent lofts employed only eight women. Their work, spooling silk and cotton, required much space for the winding machines. Another firm, dealing in ladies' neckwear, occupied a very large main floor loft. They employed four girls as the neckwear was all made elsewhere. These four worked by artificial light in a small, dark room in the rear of the building.

The workrooms in remodeled dwellings were the most unsatisfactory. With wooden stairs, dark halls, inadequate lighting, and poor sanitary equipment these afforded little safety or comfort to the workers. In one case, 12 girls were crowded into the basement workroom of a candy shop on Varick Street with a damp cement floor, where they had to work by gaslight all day. On the other hand, modern brick buildings, such as the seven-story fireproof factory occupied by a tobacco company employing 1,500 women, were often equipped throughout with a sprinkler system, and fire drills were held each month. A factory for the manufacture of knee pants was located on the sixth floor of an old loft building which was not provided with an elevator, so that the 15 women and 50 men had to begin their day's work with a climb of five flights of wooden stairs poorly lighted. At the time of the visit a leak in the hall of one of the upper floors had caused water to drip down through the stairs. The rest of the building was occupied by a laundry and as the doors were left open the building was saturated with steam. However, as it was taller than its neighbors, the workers once upstairs had fresh air and good light. Only a few of the women were provided with chairs with backs, although they sat for eight and a half hours a day operating power machines or sewing on buckles by hand.

About three-fourths of the buildings were equipped with elevators. These were usually only freight elevators, rickety, slow traveling, and frequently decorated with the signs, "You travel on this elevator at your own risk." In the 55 buildings having no elevator service, 10 of the workrooms could be reached only by climbing three, four, or five flights of stairs; four others were situated in the basement. Not only is lack of elevators bad for the health of the workers but a menace in case of fire.

Fire Protection: While the present study could not cover the technical side of fire protection, which required more thorough examination and understanding of the problem than was necessary for the purpose of this inquiry, the investigators observed all degrees of fire protection or lack of it. One modern factory boasted the largest fire-escape in the world. In many cases, however, so crowded were the workrooms with piles of stock that escape in time of accident or fire would be doubtful. Some employers had regular monthly fire drills under trained supervision; others did not even know what a fire drill was. One owner of an underwear factory casually referred to a fire that had occurred in his factory on the preceding Sunday, when he had violated two legal provisions by allowing women to work seven days a week and permitting smoking in the workroom.

New York City has witnessed several horrible factory fires, one of the worst being the Triangle fire in 1912 in which 147 women lost their lives. Even with strict enforcement of the best regulations, serious accidents may occur. But workers should be protected as far as lies within human power. Narrow, wooden, unenclosed stairways such as were found in one loft after the other even where paper, cloth, and other highly inflammable materials are handled, provide inadequate and dangerous exits; piles of stock in front of windows and doors, the crowding together of machines and chairs, so that workers could not pass freely in or out; unprotected gas flames near inflammable material, and smoking increase the danger. It was obvious every day to the visitors that it is not enough to have laws upon the statute books providing protection against all these conditions; they must be enforced.

The workrooms represented every stage in the development of the factory system. In one instance three women sat making candy in what had formerly been a flat in an apartment house, while a few blocks away some 500 were employed in an eight-story building where they had the latest equipment in the way of an automatic sprinkler system, fire doors, excellent lighting, ample space, and a ventilating system. Employers ranged from the man who could scarcely understand a word of English, knew nothing of the problem of industrial betterment but only how the work should be done, was entirely unconcerned about conditions and recognized no personal responsibility for those in his workroom, to the man who had given time and thought to provide the best conditions possible for his workers, and who recognized a responsibility for their welfare as well as for payment of their wages.

Lighting and Sanitation: Good light conduces not only to better health but to better work. Some employers, however, had failed to grasp this relation, while others had installed the best lighting devices known. In nearly a sixth of the workrooms the investigator, even without any scientific analysis, could pronounce the light bad, while in others it was only fair and had to be supplemented by artificial means. Four of the shops required artificial lighting for all workers throughout the day; in others, only the workers in certain parts of the room were so handicapped. The matter is the more serious as two-thirds of the workrooms with bad lighting were in the needle industry, where practically every process is a strain on the eyes, from the incessant watching for nine hours a day, often on dark materials, of the rapidly moving needle of the sewing machine to hand sewing and finishing.

A large underwear factory was an example of good conditions. Here the majority of the work was done on the top floor where light came through large windows and skylights. Electric drop lights hung over the tables, so close together that when artificial lighting was needed no shadows were cast. Some employers who had made a serious study of the problem of lighting had not only installed the very latest devices, but had placed them to the best advantage of the work and the workers. In many cases, however, while the light was adequate, the employer had displayed little judgment in the placing of his workers, so that girls doing work requiring little eye-strain were seated by the windows with the best light, while others doing work requiring close application were farther back in the room. Not only in this respect but in others, with some thought and better management, conditions for the workers could have been much improved without extra expense.

Ventilation also received very little attention in most of the factories. Windows usually furnished the sole ventilating system, so that the temperature of the day and time of year determined whether workrooms were well ventilated or not. In only one of the factories seen in the needle trades was ventilation scientifically controlled. Fifteen of the Italian girls investigated were at work in this factory. The investigator, who was a physician, ascribed to this system their good physical condition. They seemed to enjoy their work in spite of its monotony. In marked contrast to the healthy look of these workers were the stooped shoulders and depressed air of women in other shops where windows could not be opened without creating a draft for someone, and were consequently kept closed. While employers were apt to lay the blame for bad air upon the workers who objected to open windows, yet they might have solved the problem by providing a better system. For instance, in one factory the panes of glass in some windows were so adjusted that they might be turned to admit air without a direct draft. With the installation of some such simple device, the welfare of large groups of workers could be materially bettered. It was frequently impressed upon the visitors that a very little thought and foresight in these problems of physical surroundings would have added much to the comfort, well-being, and efficiency of the worker.

The same lack of organization appeared in such a simple problem as the cleaning of the workrooms. About a fifth of the factories were recorded as "dirty" for the usual reason that there was no definite system of cleaning. Sometimes this devolved upon an errand boy who rushed through the work after the employes had gone. In some of the larger factories a man or woman was employed during the day to clean while the work was going on. One girl had complained that "in her place" the boy swept without dampening the floor, so that the workers sat in the dust. This particular "cleaning system" was seen in operation during one of the visits. In other cases the nature of the product rather than any concern for the workers required that the workroom be kept clean, and that this be done when the materials were not exposed.

Noise: The physical discomfort and actual effect of noise on the human machine varies. Workers often become accustomed to a constant noise and are disturbed when it ceases. Nevertheless, a person can do a higher grade of work when the function of the auditory nerve does not have to be suppressed. Young girls who try power-machine operating leave the work, even though they like it, because they cannot endure the noise. Where it cannot be eliminated it should be reduced to a minimum. More than half of the shops visited were noisy, and a large part of these were in the sewing trades, where the power machines pound away at great speed. That the noise can be largely controlled is shown by a special make of machine so constructed as to be practically noiseless. This machine suggests the possibility of improvement in the other machines.

Seats: New York State laws require that every person employing women in a factory shall, where practicable, provide and maintain suitable seats with proper backs; and where women are engaged in work which can be properly performed in a sitting posture, these seats shall be supplied and permission given to use them. Conditions, however, vary widely from the legal standards. In some industries, as for instance in the sewing trades, the nature of the processes requires that most of the workers must be seated, although in one underwear factory visited, only the machine operators and finishers were seated, while the examiners, packers, and pressers had to stand all day. In a petticoat factory a few blocks away all the women were sitting at their work, even the pressers and folders. It was the first time the visitor had ever seen pressers sit at their work. All the other pressers interviewed complained of the fatigue and strain due to continual standing. It is a curious thing that employers can devise reasons for customs that seem to have no basis. Regarding the hand chocolate dipping, one employer said, "Girls are obliged to stand to get the swaying motion of the body necessary to perform their work properly." But in a large factory nearby, 70 girls were doing a perfectly satisfactory job in this line, comfortably seated in chairs with backs. People might well do without the fancy curls on chocolates if they can be obtained only at the cost of the strain upon women who must stand continually at their work.

Factories were visited where women were required to stand, engaged in steaming or selecting feathers, packing feathers, crackers, candy, cigars or clothing, cleaning and sponging men's clothing, basting men's clothing, examining, pressing, mangling, cutting, fitting, boning corsets, drafting, grading and counting paper patterns, hand folding, hand stamping on stationery, hand labeling, weighing cereals, folding silk, filling and capping olive oil bottles, hand gathering of books, tending various kinds of machines, like weaving, winding, knitting, embroidery and labeling machines, and hanging curtains. The very name of the process indicates that the work in some cases cannot be done seated, such as fitting and serving as a model. Even when seats were provided they were frequently without backs, and hence did not adequately protect the women from strain and fatigue.

Lunch Rooms: The installation of a lunch room or some facilities for providing the workers with a proper lunch, is a good paying investment. Employers who had had enough initiative to give their workers a full hour at noon, with a chance for recreation, or who had provided an open space on the roof where the workers could walk about and get fresh air, showed themselves good business men, for the workers came back to their machines and work tables with renewed energy and interest. The same is true of the employer who, if he cannot provide a lunch room, at least arranges so that the workers may get something hot, like tea, coffee, cocoa or soup.

One underwear manufacturer provided a separate lunch room where employes could get soup and coffee at two and a half cents a cup and allowed no one to eat in the workroom, thus protecting his goods against stains. The shop of another underwear manufacturer was so crowded that he could not have a separate lunch room, but he had also found it profitable to provide tables for lunch in one part of the workroom, with a woman to make coffee at noon. No worker was allowed to eat at her machine. In a large corset factory on Broadway a lunch room with a counter where hot dishes were procurable, was situated on each floor. Shops with such facilities, however, were few. In most cases, a visitor happening in at lunch time would find the workers sitting at their machines or tables eating a cold lunch brought from home or bought from the factory peddler who deals largely in pies, pickles, apples, and candy. Occasionally a large, dirty coffee or tea pot provided by the workers supplied all with a cup of "something hot."

TYPICAL SHOPS

A description of certain typical shops will summarize more effectively than any mere generalization the actual conditions under which these Italian women toiled. A shop of the better class where all the 35 women employed were Italians was located on the seventh floor of a new 12-story loft building. The workroom was clean and well lighted and the workers, who were putting hand embroidery on dresses and waists, were provided with comfortable chairs with backs. In the fifty-four-hour week experienced women averaged about $12, although some earned as much as $15. The season lasted from September to May, and only 10 workers were kept during the slack period. "We lay off every worker we don't need," was the policy, the employer explained. "The Italians are wonderfully efficient in this work. We use only Italians. They seem to have the ability born in them and trained in them from their earliest childhood." This shop was visited because a fourteen-year-old girl was working a fifty-four-hour week at a wage of $5.00. She had no certificate and was employed in violation of the law that no person under sixteen may be employed without working papers, nor for more than forty-eight hours a week.

Only four of the 40 women employed in a certain chocolate factory on Greenwich Street were Italian. The employer explained that Italians could not get the uniformity necessary in hand dipping. "They seem to lack the knack of getting the same twist on the top of each chocolate." The workroom was light, clean, and well ventilated, and the floor was covered with sawdust and swept out every day. About 20 girls were sitting at tables, deftly dipping bonbons and cherries into chocolate. The girls earned $7.00 to $10 a week. Six girls were standing at a table placing each piece of chocolate in a round paper dish and packing 180 in a box. A rapid worker could pack 60 to 70 boxes a day. Two other girls were also standing as they labeled boxes, for which they were paid $6.50 a week. No girls under sixteen years of age were hired. The time schedule was a nine-hour day, or fifty-three and a half hours a week. Owing to the fact that the shop had been much disturbed by girls coming in late, a system of fines had been instituted whereby anyone five minutes late was fined for half an hour's time.

Italians, as has been already stated, were not found in unskilled work only. In a shop where 35 girls were doing fine engraving on stationery and checks, only two Italians were employed, but one of these was the most expert and best paid worker. Hand stamping, the most skilled process, requires at least a year's training, although each worker is taught all the processes, including machine stamping, examining, and packing. Experienced workers made $14 to $16 in the week of fifty-three and a half hours. The shop was in a well lighted, modern loft building.

Poor working conditions for women workers were found in a contractor's shop manufacturing boys' knee pants, situated in an old factory building with wooden stairs and dingy windows. Fifty men were busy operating power sewing machines and pressing, while near the windows in a corner sat six women "busheling," five of whom were Italian. In the fifty-four-hour week, the maximum allowed by law, they could make as high as $9.00, but usually their earnings fell below this. For instance, one girl seventeen years old had earned only $5.00 in the week before she was interviewed, although she had illegally worked sixty-one hours that week. The men had been able to organize, but the women had not.

Italians predominated in one of the best shops in the underwear trade, occupying a corner loft on East Sixteenth Street. Here 75 women were engaged in operating whirring power machines, finishing, ribboning, cutting out embroidery, or pressing stacks of dainty white muslin underwear. "Italians are very quick workers and I am glad to get them," said the superintendent. The workroom had excellent light, and the workers were so placed that they got the most benefit from it. There was a fire-alarm system and fire drills were held regularly under trained supervision. Although the shop was on a fifty-hour weekly basis, the employer managed to get his orders out without overtime or home work, and to keep his force together the year through. No one under sixteen years of age was employed, and the minimum wage for beginners was $5.00 a week. Sample makers could earn $15 a week steadily, while machine operators usually made between $12 and $15 at piece work. Even the two girls who had been interviewed, although only seventeen years old, were earning $10.50 and $14 a week. The work in this line was skilled and required training and practice.

Three other young girls had been less fortunate in the shops in which they had chanced to find work. All still under sixteen years of age, they had drifted into the shipping department of a factory where the sole work for the 75 girls employed was pasting on labels and packing into boxes the bolts of ribbon which came to the department complete except for this one process. The girls were paid $3.50 to $4.50 a week. It was a typical blind alley occupation where 50 new "learners" were engaged every year. This one process took only a few hours to learn, and the only requirement was that girls must know how to read in order to put on the correct labels of individual firms. Only four of the girls in the shop were as old as nineteen years. When girls asked for an increase they were encouraged to find better paying work, as the highest wage paid here was $7.00 a week. The force was kept busy all the year and the firm was constantly advertising for more. The only compensation for the blind alley nature of the work was the excellent workroom and a weekly schedule of only forty-four and a half hours. The crowd of young girls, standing or sitting around the long tables, many with their hair hanging in braids or curls, so that they looked like children, made the room appear little like a factory where workers might expect a well paid future. The majority of the girls were American born, with only 10 Italian born among them.

In a long, narrow room, down on Cherry Street, lighted only by a skylight, two Italian women were found standing and bending while they sorted bales of dusty waste paper. Neither could speak a word of English and neither knew that they were violating any law because they worked ten and a half hours every day, from seven in the morning until six at night. They only knew that at the end of a week's work the Italian owner, who was a friend, handed them each a five-dollar bill.

In an ostrich feather shop on Twelfth Street, owned by an Italian, almost all the 30 girls were Italian, some of whom could not speak English. They were seated at their work of selecting, scrapping, sewing, steaming, and curling feathers and plumes. In a week of forty-nine and a half hours the majority could earn $10 to $12, but they often supplemented their wages with earnings from overtime or home work. At other times, however, they might work only two or three days a week, but the entire force was kept. Although the workshop was located in a remodeled dwelling, the girls could get good light at their work and the place was fairly clean except for the usual litter that accompanies feather making.

One girl had been working for a year as examiner on sweaters in a loft on Wooster Street where she earned $10 to $11 a week. She was found busy at work among some 75 other women and girls of whom 10 or 12 were Italian. In the rear of the loft were weavers, and in the front sewing machine operators. In the middle were winders, who unfortunately had to work by gaslight all day in air filled with a fine dust from the yarn and worsted used. Although the dust had not caused any special disease the owner felt that it was probably injurious, but did not know how to get rid of it. Sewing machines were carefully provided with skirt guards and foot rests, and all workers who sat had chairs with backs. But women who were tending winding and knitting machines as well as examiners and folders, stood at their work through the day of eight and three-fourths hours. "We have about a fifty-one-hour week. Soon it will be the eight hour day and that will give the employes time really to live." Women were not yet organized in this trade, but the employer believed the time not far distant when they would be. With a minimum age of sixteen, a minimum wage of $5.00 when many of his competitors were still paying $3.50 or $4.00, a week of fifty-one hours and an attempt to keep his workers steadily, to safeguard the machinery and to provide the best work conditions he knew how, he offers an example of the employer who finds it compatible with his business principles to provide decent conditions as far as he understands them.

LOUISE G. ODENCRANTZ

WHY JENNIE
HATES FLOWERS*

"I HATE flowers," said Jennie, a little Italian girl of nine, as she bent over the pile of white daisy petals on the kitchen table. She was busily picking up the "peps," first dipping each stem in paste smeared on a piece of board, slipping a petal up each stem, and inserting it in one of the green tubes on the wreath.

Flowers to her did not spell green fields, pleasant odors, or something soft and agreeable to feel and handle. To this little girl, living in the crowded Italian district on the lower West Side in New York City, flowers meant piles of hideously colored petals of cambric, stiff with starch and dye, and smelling strongly of alcohol, glue and paste. These she had to fetch from the factory every day after school. Before school the next morning the family had to "manufacture" them into flowers.

Every one worked, all except the father, who declared that it was not "a man's work," and an older son, who was driver on a wagon truck. Even the baby, eighteen months old, could help by picking apart the petals. Maggie, four years old, was too young to go to school, but she could work the greater part of the day. Nardo, aged six, was an expert hand, although his mother complained that he wanted to play. Besides Jennie there was little Angelina, a hunchback of eleven years, who was really the forewoman of the group, seeing to it that each day's quota was faithfully done.

The account book showed that six dozens of wreaths, each with 39 flowers, were finished every night. The buttercup wreaths brought eight cents a dozen, and the daisies ten cents. For this work the family received $2.88 or $3.60 a week, according to whether they worked on buttercups or daisies.

From November until the end of April or May each year, the kitchen looked like a miniature factory. When I asked the mother whether the children could come to a club one afternoon a week, the answer was that they were all too busy. When I asked Angelina when she did her

*World Outlook, Vol. 3 (October 1917).

school homework, she replied, "In the morning when I get to school. First I do the writing, then I do the two times, then the three times. This morning I did the four times, so I won't have so much to do to-morrow." She was in the second grade. Later she volunteered, "I like school better than home. There are too many flowers. I don't like home."

The picture of this family is like that of hundreds of others that may be found in the Italian sections in New York City. Many of the homes would furnish a more lurid picture with longer and later hours, more crowded and less sanitary conditions, or children kept out of school entirely. In almost every tenement house some such homework is go-ing on, and in many of the apartments. If there is no homework, the reason is frequently that there are no children to do it. If the little hands are not making flowers, they are putting bristles in hair brushes, tying tags, tacking passementerie, or doing a variety of other kinds of work adaptable to children's hands.

Recently when the declaration of war brought a sudden demand for national emblem pins, children were found in the tenements engaged in fastening the pins on the emblem of democracy and freedom.

The Italians have practically a monopoly of homework in the city. An investigation of the men's clothing industry by the United States Government in 1910 showed that 98 per cent of the homeworkers in this trade in New York were Italian. The women did the finishing while the children pulled the bastings. In a study of the artificial flower industry in New York City by the Russell Sage Foundation in 1910 the investigators found that practically all of 110 families covered by them were Italian.

Child labor is one of the worst evils of the homework system, espe-cially in the artificial flower making industry. In fact, it is largely be-cause child labor is available in the tenements that the work can be carried on there profitably to the employer.

In the homes of the 110 families who were engaged in making arti-ficial flowers, a count of the workers showed that 10 per cent of the 371 homeworkers were under eight years of age and 37 per cent were under fourteen years of age. Children are forbidden by law in New York State to work within a factory before they are fourteen years old. In the tenements, however, children of all ages, ranging from mere babyhood until they are old enough to enter the factory, may be found at work with no limitation upon their hours or conditions of work.

In fact the work is so underpaid that only with long hours and the employment of every available child are the families able to earn even a small amount. One family of five—mother and four children—by working after school until ten at night could never make more than $4 a week.

"Making flowers at home is poor work, especially if you have only a few children to help you," complained the mother.

A visit to any of these homes in the afternoon or until nine or ten o'clock at night would show most of the children hard at work instead of studying their lessons or playing.

That "making flowers at home is poor work," even with the help of children, is indicated by a comparison of earnings in families with and without child workers. In the investigation of the artificial flower home workers, Miss Van Kleeck states that "the average weekly earnings of the families in which children were employed were $4.72. The average weekly earnings of the families in which no children were employed were $5.44."

What does such employment mean to the children?

Perhaps most serious is the effect upon the progress of these Italian children in school. It has been found in New York City that the proportion of retarded children in school is larger among Italians than in any other nationality. In this investigation of child homeworkers, the report states that "more than half the number of the child workers attending school were above the normal age for the grades in which they were enrolled." In other words, 51 per cent of the group were over age as compared with 30 per cent of over-age children among all the school children in New York City.

The results are not surprising. Such tedious, monotonous work done by a child after school hours cannot but interfere with his progress and dull his zest and interest in his school work. The child is prevented from doing the proper amount of home studying, or he must do it late at night after several hours of confining, uninteresting work. After sitting in a schoolroom five hours a day, the child should have an opportunity for physical action and play.

The serious interference that homework causes to school attendance and progress is the most urgent argument against the continuance of any system of homework. It always means child labor, and not only retardation in the child's school work, but in his career as a wage earner. When a child has had to spend every afternoon after school and his Saturdays doing such monotonous work, poorly paid, the idea of going to work and earning money must have lost its novelty. He has already learned what industry is and what the returns for his work may be.

Homework and premature employment are doubtless a contributing cause toward the tendency of young Italian boys to become loafers. Deprived of the opportunity for normal play and physical development in the open air, confined in the house and working in poorly ventilated rooms, often under pressure of speed, discouraged by poor progress in school through no fault of their own, the children do not have a fair start when they enter their wage-earning careers.

The homework system in New York City means largely the employment of Italian children in the home. Until the system is abolished there is little hope that these small Italian children will be released from their bondage. For thirty-four years the State has been trying to regulate the system, by forbidding the manufacture of certain articles for the protection of public health. Children in the tenements used to shell nuts, sometimes helping the work along by cracking an obstinate one with their teeth. Articles of food, dolls, children's and infants' clothing are no longer allowed to be handled in the tenements because sometimes they were found in homes where there was sickness. The dangers to public health convinced the legislators that such work must be stopped.

As no one, however, has yet proved to the legislature any relation between public health and artificial flowers, passementerie and such articles, Italian children by the hundreds are allowed to work at any age any number of hours in their homes, making these things. Forbidding children to help their parents at this work in their homes is of no avail, as a man's home is his castle and inspection is almost impossible.

Perhaps some day a Solomon may appear who can explain and convince that until all tenement manufacture is forbidden, the child laborers will be with us.

JOHN J. D'ALESANDRE

OCCUPATIONAL
TRENDS OF
ITALIANS IN
NEW YORK CITY*

INTRODUCTION

Those of us who have been working with and among Italian groups, whether it be with the first—or second—generation Italians, or both, in order to better understand the problems of their adjustment, have often felt a need for information concerning occupational activities of Italians in the United States. The material herein is presented for the value it may possess to the many teachers interested in knowing the occupational distribution and trends that affect the children of Italian parents. Many leading educators feel that it is important to have a more comprehensive vocational guidance program for the children in our schools, which should be incorporated into our school curriculum. It is generally recognized that this would to a great extent act as a corrective to many problems which the schools are at present unable to cope with. The occupational analysis of this group may be of value to those who are trying to devise a vocational or educational guidance plan for a group. It may be of value also to social workers or personnel workers who are giving advice concerning a choice of occupation.

An analysis of vocational choices made by high school boys of Italian origin in an unpublished study by the Casa Italiana Educational Bureau, shows that the choice is often unintelligent, and in many cases is not directed; nor has it any continuity toward a definite aim in life. This has been shown to be frequently true in many studies of occupational activities. Whereas, in the United States there are actually

* Occupational Trends of Italians in New York City (New York: Casa Italiana Educational Bureau, Bulletin No. 8, 1935).

417

several thousand occupational activities, these boys mentioned less than two hundred. Furthermore, their choice was not well distributed even among the two hundred lines of work. To further emphasize the limited distribution of choice, the choice of the boys was concentrated in about ten leading occupations. There was a marked preponderance of a choice for the professions. Of course, it is to be expected that a high school group would seek a high level in occupation.

The discrepancies between the choice of vocations and the status of workers now employed can be traced to many causes. Youth is always hopeful and optimistic, and inclined to look forward to great things. Most children are ignorant of the conditions existing in the occupational world. They have little or no conception of the many types of work, or of the qualifications needed by the worker for the work. Youth is influenced by the prevalent social attitude which glorifies certain kinds of work as "white collar" vocations and deprecates the more "menial" occupations. On the other hand there is the sad fact to be reckoned with that the choice of occupation is often determined by stern necessity and the need to accept whatever employment may be offered, whether or not it may be suitable or according to the interests of the boy.

When dealing with the young people as part of a guidance program, it is valuable to know the occupation of the parent, since it may affect the future of the child in one or more of the following ways:

1. The occupation of the parent generally determines his earning power and often the economic status of the family. Obviously, this exerts a direct influence upon a boy's chances for a prolonged schooling.

2. The father may try to influence his son to follow his own line of work.

3. As more frequently happens, the father may react against his own occupation, and may try to have his son trained along some line which is entirely different.

4. In these days of scarcity of employment opportunities, we must know of any possibility of employment for a boy, and whether or not the father can give him help in finding his first job.

5. If we know the father's occupation, it gives us one more clue concerning the environment in which the boy is growing up.

6. If the occupational background of the parent is limited along certain lines, it may suggest what occupational information or misinformation the boy may have received, and hence what type of information is most needed from us.

PURPOSE OF THE SURVEY

This first and partial analysis of some of the material gathered by the Casa Italiana Educational Bureau was made with the hope that it might prove to be of value to those who have indicated a need for and an interest in occupational information concerning the Italian in New York City. We hope to arouse a recognition for the need of a body of facts that can be further developed, studied, compared, and analyzed by those who are interested in our Italian population and its many problems of adjustment in a modern complex urban civilization. This is an initial attempt. There are many lists, compilations, charts, and tables that are still available for more complete study and analysis of the occupational problem. The main purpose of this study shall have been achieved if it will have stimulated in the student of social and economic life of the Italian in our country an interest in the social and economic implications which more comprehensive data might reveal.

TECHNIQUES

It is of the utmost importance in a project of this sort that the material be scientifically and uniformly gathered, compiled, and analyzed and that the resultant material need as little explanation and weighing as possible to make comparison valid. We have attempted to fill these requirements. We hope that the method and technique used in presenting and analyzing the following material has been reduced to such form as to make it of interest and value to the general public.

The matter of the classification of occupations is a very difficult one to handle. There is no satisfactory and generally accepted classification. For this reason we have made no attempt to group the occupations studied, except in the cases of the professions and clerical occupations. The Millbank Foundation Classification of 1900, the Census Classification, the Counts Social Status Scale, the Barr Scale of Occupational Intelligence, Menger's Social Status Scale, the data compiled from Army Mental Tests or any other material do not permit of comparative analysis or study because of the different methods and techniques used in obtaining and classifying occupations. Largely because of the variety of these classifications we were in this study unable to make any analysis, comparable with the aforementioned studies.

TABLE VII.—PERCENT DISTRIBUTION OF ITALIANS IN PROFESSIONAL AND CLERICAL OCCUPATIONS FROM BIRTH, MARRIAGES AND DEATH RECORDS, NEW YORK CITY, 1916 AND 1931

	Births				Deaths				Marriages			
	1916		1931		1916		1931		1916		1931	
	No	%	No	%	No	%	No	%	No	%	No	%
Professional	380	1.2	266	1.6	34	1.4	64	1.7	108	1.5	80	2.1
Clerical	224	.7	327	1.9	44	1.8	81	2.1	149	2.0	155	4.1

SCOPE OF DATA

These data were selected because they were the only available information on occupations offering so large a sampling of the Italian population in New York City.

The statistical compilation was made from the total number of birth, marriage, and death certificates of New York City residents for the years 1916 and 1931 as contained in the original records of the Department of Health for the City of New York. The occupations from the birth certificates were those of the father if either or both parents were born in Italy. The marriage records used were cases where either the bride or groom or both were born in Italy. The occupation was of the groom. The death records used were of the males of either Italian birth or Italian parentage. The occupation of the deceased as recorded on the death certificate was taken for this study.

LIMITATION OF THE STUDY DUE TO THESE CONDITIONS

Cognizance is taken of the fact that the study contains many conditions that have not as yet been investigated and evaluated. The birth and marriage records, obviously, do not include the unmarried males who are engaged in occupations. The age-group distribution of the 1916 groupings as compared to the 1931 groupings, because of the immigration problem explained herein, would tend to make the 1931 grouping older and may be a factor in explaining some of the changes in the occupational ranks, numbers, and percentages. The immigrants who make up the 1916 group contain an older age-group distribution than a cross section of a population group with a normal percentage of infants, children, and youths.

While it is true, for example, that a person may have been married in New York City in 1916 and 1931; or given birth to children both in 1916 and 1931, this possibility of duplication in the listing of the recorded occupations on birth and marriage record is negligible.

Another factor to be considered is that changes have occurred within industry during these fifteen years. Regardless of nationality grouping, a knowledge of such change is very important and a study is necessary of the total situation to make a thorough and valid analysis of occupational trends in New York City.

The death records were filled out and sent to the Board of Health by doctors and undertakers. The recording of births was dependent upon the filling in of the information by doctors and midwives. In the marriage records, the personal factor might enter more than on the other records. The prospective groom in stating his occupation might try to raise his occupational status. Moreover, the occupation as recorded in all these records does not mention the industry.

Due to the method of recording, it has been difficult to classify these occupations into skilled, semi-skilled, and unskilled. Undoubtedly many among the unskilled may have changed the nomenclature of their particular work. There is less likelihood of a change of occupation and of nomenclature in the recorded listings of skilled and professional occupations. All these factors affect the accuracy of these records.

In presenting the following tables, I to VI inclusive, the following steps were taken:—The transcribed birth, marriage, and death records were each arranged in alphabetical order, according to name of occupation. The numbers in each occupation were then totaled and listed. Because the birth records of 1916 numbering 31,556 were the largest group, the occupations containing 100 or more cases in that series were selected as the basis of comparison for all six series. Since the number of occupations here was 36, we have included the first 36 occupations for all the tables even though they represent less than 100 cases.

In reading Tables I and II, it will be seen that "Laborer," the largest grouping for both years, formed 50.4 per cent in 1916 and 31.4 per cent in 1931 of the total cases in these respective series. This may be interpreted to mean that our immigration laws had a decided effect on this grouping. In 1917 the act to restrict illiterate immigrants was passed. The Emergency Quota Act of 1921 limited the number of immigrants to three per cent of the number of each nationality living in the United States in 1910. This, however, was not quite as effective in reducing Italian immigration as the Johnson Act of 1924 which reduced the percentage from three to two and changed the basis on which the number was calculated from the 1910 census to the 1890 census, and provided for further restriction after 1927. The economic depression in our industries, especially building and construction, since 1929 and the advance in the mechanization of our industries, (e.g. steam shovels, automatic machinery, etc.) may have lessened the demand for laborers causing them to go into other types of employment. This may explain the decrease of nineteen per cent in the number of laborers.

"Shoemaker" retained the rank of fourth position, but the percentages were 2.9 and 3.7 for 1916 and 1931 respectively. The difficulty of nomenclature applies throughout this study. For example, there were listed Cobbler, Heel Maker, Shoe Worker, etc. However, because it seemed to us that any arbitrary grouping or combining would be largely subjective, we adhered to the name of occupation as given. The status of the unionized factory "shoe worker" and the "cobbler" who maintains a small shop would be different in their economic, social, and occupational levels.

"Carpenter" dropped from fifth to sixth in its rank among occupations, but increased from 2.1 per cent in 1916 to 2.5 per cent for 1931. It would be significant to carry on a further study of these differences and the causes of them in view of the fact that building for 1931 materially decreased and there was a decrease in the use of wood in the building industry in New York City. It may mean that some of the unskilled workers of 1916 have entered the skilled field of carpentry.

"Drivers" showed a change in rank from seventh to eighteenth but the change in percentage was not so great. Here again we encountered a number of various classifications that might have been included in "Driver," e.g. Milk Wagon Driver, Teamster, Truckman and Chauffeur.

TABLE VIII—PROPORTION OF ITALIAN BIRTHS, MARRIAGES, AND DEATHS TO TOTALS RECORDED IN NEW YORK CITY, 1916 AND 1931

	Italian	Total	Percentage of Italian to Total
Births—1916	31,556	137,664	22.9
Births—1931	16,945	115,621	14.7
Deaths—1916	2,504	77,801	3.2
Deaths—1931	3,778	77,418	4.9
Marriages—1916	7,341	54,782	13.4
Marriages—1931	3,785	61,574	6.1

"Longshoreman" showed a change of from sixth to eleventh in ranking. The difference in percentage was slight. The percentage for 1916 was 1.9 and for 1931, 1.5. Most of the longshoremen are unionized and their remuneration is fairly high. There are among them those skilled or experienced in proper handling, storing, tying slings, fastening nets, and the use of the winches.

"Coal man" changed in ranking from eighth to one hundred seventy-second. There were 325 or 1.0 per cent for 1916 and 4 or .02 per cent for 1931. The decrease in the use of the coal stoves probably accounts for most of this change.

"Business Man" ranked ninth in 1916 and twenty-third in 1931. There were 289 (.9 per cent) in 1916 and 130 (.8 per cent) in 1931. "Business Man" is a classification which may include anyone from a proprietor of a small one-man business to the head of a large organization. The various "dealers" may or may not be classified as business men.

"Mechanic" held its ranking fairly well. There were 289 for 1916 and 383 for 1931. Their percentages vary greatly in that they were .9 per cent and 2.1 per cent respectively. "Mechanic" may include a wide range of skilled occupations as Electrician, Machinist, Maintenance Man, and others.

"Street Cleaner" ranked twenty-sixth in 1916 and seventieth in 1931. There were 143 (.4 per cent) in 1916 and 22 (.1 per cent) in 1931.

"Piano Maker" showed a great decrease in rank, number, and percentage. It would be interesting to determine all the factors influencing these changes. The development of the Victrola, and later the radio, was an important factor.

The decrease of "Bartender" may be attributed to the prohibition laws.

Tables III and IV give the occupations of the grooms as gathered from the 7,341 New York City marriage records of 1916 and 3,785 New York City marriage records of 1931.

"Laborer" in the marriage records (See Tables III and IV) showed 32.5 per cent for 1916 and 10.6 per cent in 1931.

"Tailor" changed in ranking from second with 6.8 per cent in 1916 to fourth with 3.7 per cent in 1931.

"Barber" in the marriage series again as in the birth series maintained a fairly constant rank and percentage.

"Shoemaker" dropped in rank from fourth in 1916 to fifth in 1931, with the percentage changing from 3.5 to 2.9.

"Driver" as in the birth records again shows a great decrease in per cent and ranking. "Chauffeur" showed an opposite trend.

Notice particularly the variation in rank or percentages or both for the following occupations: Carpenter, Machinist, Fruit Dealer, Long-

TABLE I — LEADING OCCUPATIONS: ITALIAN FATHERS OF CHILDREN BORN IN NEW YORK CITY IN 1916†

Rank	Occupation	Number	Per cent	Rank in Table II
	Total	31,556	100.0	
	36 Leading Occupations	27,209	86.2	
1	Laborer	15,905	50.4	(1)
2	Tailor	1,697	5.4	(3)
3	Barber	1,667	5.3	(2)
4	Shoemaker	909	2.9	(4)
5	Carpenter	651	2.1	(6)
6	Longshoreman	596	1.9	(11)
7	Driver	546	1.7	(18)
8	Coal Man	325	1.0	(172)
9	Business Man	289	.9	(23)
10	Mechanic	278	.9	(9)
11	Cook	258	.8	(22)
12	Baker	257	.8	(14)
13	Painter	256	.8	(8)
14	Bricklayer	237	.8	(16)
15	Printer	214	.7	(25)
16	Fruit Dealer	199	.6	(20)
17	Plasterer	198	.6	(10)
18	Presser	195	.6	(19)
19	Bootblack	192	.6	(37)
20	Butcher	191	.6	(15)
21	Waiter	176	.6	(33)
22	Proprietor	167	.5	(32)
23	Musician	155	.5	(30)
24	Merchant	151	.5	(41)
25	Salesman	147	.5	(13)
26	Street Cleaner	143	.5	(70)
27	Machinist	140	.4	(29)
28	Mason	137	.4	(34)
29	Piano Maker	131	.4	(261)
30	Clerk	130	.4	(12)
31	Operator	125	.4	(129)
32	Grocer	118	.4	(39)
33	Bartender	112	.4	(287)
34	Porter	108	.3	(44)
35	Ice Man	106	.3	(17)
36	Chauffeur	103	.3	(5)
	All other occupations	4,092	13.0	
	Unknown	255	.8	

†The source of the data in this table is the birth certificates on file at the Division of Vital Statistics, Department of Health, New York City.

TABLE II — LEADING OCCUPATIONS: ITALIAN FATHERS OF CHILDREN BORN IN NEW YORK CITY IN 1931

Rank	Occupation	Number	Per cent	Rank in Table I
	Total	16,945	100.0	
	36 Leading Occupations	13,700	80.5	
1	Laborer	5,321	31.4	(1)
2	Barber	850	5.0	(3)
3	Tailor	713	4.2	(2)
4	Shoemaker	633	3.7	(4)
5	Chauffeur	608	3.6	(36)
6	Carpenter	429	2.5	(5)
7	Ice Dealer	392	2.3	*
8	Painter	379	2.2	(13)
9	Mechanic	363	2.1	(10)
10	Plasterer	306	1.8	(17)
11	Longshoreman	257	1.5	(6)
12	Clerk	253	1.5	(30)
13	Salesman	250	1.5	(25)
14	Baker	231	1.4	(12)
15	Butcher	228	1.3	(20)
16	Bricklayer	216	1.3	(14)
17	Ice Man	192	1.1	(35)
18	Driver	180	1.1	(7)
19	Presser	170	1.0	(18)
20	Fruit Dealer	142	.8	(16)
21	Ice and Coal	139	.8	*
22	Cook	133	.8	(11)
23	Business Man	130	.8	(9)
24	Peddler	116	.7	*
25	Printer	114	.7	(15)
26	Trucking	101	.6	*
27	Plumber	99	.6	*
28	Electrician	93	.5	*
29	Machinist	93	.5	(27)
30	Musician	89	.5	(23)
31	Contractor	88	.5	*
32	Proprietor	88	.5	(22)
33	Waiter	87	.5	(21)
34	Mason	76	.4	(28)
35	Foreman	73	.4	*
36	Cabinet Maker	69	.4	*

* Does not appear in leading occupations Table 1.

	All other occupations	3,053	18.4	
	Unknown	117	.7	
	Unemployed	75	.4	

Leading occupations in 1916 (Table I), which do not appear in Leading Occupations for 1931 (Table II)

Rank in 1931	Occupation	Number	Per cent	Rank in Table 1
37	Bootblack	68	.4	(19)
39	Grocer	59	.3	(32)
41	Merchant	56	.3	(24)
44	Porter	49	.3	(34)
70	Street Cleaner	22	.1	(26)
129	Operator	9	.1	(31)
172	Coal Man	4	—	(8)
261	Piano Maker	2	—	(29)
287	Bartender	1	—	(33)

shoreman, Salesman, Plasterer, Musician, Cigar Maker, and Hatter.

The data concerning marriages in 1916 and births in 1916 may well be taken as typical of the parents of children now in our High Schools—ages 14 to 18. This data, therefore, should be particularly interesting to a vocational counselor at the present time.

Tables V and VI give the occupations of the deceased as recorded in the death certificates for 1916 and 1931, respectively. The listing of occupations was taken from those records that gave Italy as the birthplace of the deceased, or of one, or both, of the deceased parents.

The death records represent an older age group. The age-group distribution for 1931 show greater concentration toward the older ages than was shown in 1916.

The increase in the number of the "Retired" from 1916 to 1931 is to be expected in view of the above statement. They were only 2.4 per cent in 1916 and 7.1 per cent of the total group in 1931.

"Laborer" in Tables V and VI, again ranks number one, but did not show as great a difference in per cent as "Laborer" in the figures for births and marriages.

It may be surmised that the "Unknown" group variance is due to greater care and further instructions in filling out the death certificates in 1931.

The total number of cases in the birth records were 31,556. In listing the occupations for 1916, there were 580 different listed occupations given as the occupation at which the parent was employed. In listing the 1931 births there were 488 occupations reported for the 16,945 cases.

The occupations listed for the years 1916 and 1931, combined, showed 851 separate or differently-named occupations. These were obtained by listing alphabetically the occupations for 1916, then listing the occupations for 1931, combining these lists and eliminating all duplications. The 48,501 cases found in these two series thus list 851 different occupations.

In the marriage records of 1916, for a total number of 7,341 there were 403 separate occupations listed. For the year 1931 there were 481 occupations listed from the 3,783 cases. The combined occupations listed for the years 1916 and 1931, showed a total of 664 occupations for the total of 11,127 cases.

In the death compilations for 1916, of the 2,504 cases, there were 243 occupations. In 3,778 cases for the year 1931, there were 295 occupations. For the years of 1916 and 1931 combined, there were listed 388 occupations from 6,282 death records.

As explained before, the writer made no attempt to combine or alter the occupations as actually written in the transcripts. It must be recognized, therefore, that with proper reporting this number would be

TABLE III — LEADING OCCUPATIONS: ITALIAN BRIDEGROOMS NEW YORK CITY, 1916

Rank	Occupation	Number	Per-cent	Rank in Table IV
	Total	7,341	100.0	
	36 Leading Occupations	5,671	77.4	
1	Laborer	2,389	32.5	(1)
2	Tailor	498	6.8	(4)
3	Barber	342	4.7	(3)
4	Shoemaker	255	3.5	(5)
5	Driver	200	2.7	(20)
6	Carpenter	152	2.1	(12)
7	Clerk	117	1.6	(6)
8	Machinist	115	1.6	(23)
9	Cook	104	1.4	(13)
10	Waiter	104	1.4	(17)
11	Presser	89	1.2	(14)
12	Coal Dealer	85	1.2	*
13	Painter	78	1.1	(7)
14	Chauffeur	76	1.0	(2)
15	Ice Dealer	73	1.0	(16)
16	Piano Maker	71	1.0	*
17	Mechanic	70	1.0	(8)
18	Fruit Dealer	68	.9	(29)
19	Butcher	66	.9	(15)
20	Longshoreman	64	.9	(63)
21	Salesman	64	.9	(9)
22	Baker	56	.8	(10)
23	Printer	55	.7	(18)
24	Bricklayer	50	.7	(19)
25	Mason	49	.7	(36)
26	Plasterer	48	.7	(11)
27	Musician	47	.6	(49)
28	Grocer	43	.6	(28)
29	Cigar Maker	39	.5	(69)
30	Operator	34	.5	(21)
31	Bootblack	33	.4	*
32	Merchant	33	.4	*
33	Electrican	27	.4	(25)
34	Hatter	27	.4	(72)
35	Cabinet Maker	25	.3	(26)
36	Candy Maker	25	.3	(40)
	All other occupations	1,315	17.8	
	Unknown	355	4.8	

* Does not appear in occupation reported by Italian bridegrooms in 1931.

TABLE IV — LEADING OCCUPATIONS: ITALIAN BRIDEGROOMS, NEW YORK CITY, 1931

Rank	Occupation	Number	Percent	Rank in Table III
	Total	3,785	100.0	
	36 Leading Occupations	2,495	66.3	
1	Laborer	402	10.6	(1)
2	Chauffeur	224	5.9	(14)
3	Barber	186	4.9	(3)
4	Tailor	140	3.7	(2)
5	Shoemaker	108	2.9	(4)
6	Clerk	105	2.8	(7)
7	Painter	99	2.6	(13)
8	Mechanic	94	2.5	(17)
9	Salesman	92	2.4	(21)
10	Baker	79	2.1	(22)
11	Plasterer	76	2.0	(26)
12	Carpenter	71	1.9	(6)
13	Cook	60	1.6	(9)
14	Presser	60	1.6	(11)
15	Butcher	59	1.6	(19)
16	Ice Dealer	55	1.5	(15)
17	Waiter	54	1.4	(10)
18	Printer	50	1.3	(23)
19	Bricklayer	46	1.2	(24)
20	Driver	46	1.2	(5)
21	Operator	43	1.1	(30)
22	Ice Man	41	1.1	*
23	Machinist	40	1.1	(8)
24	Plumber	33	.9	*
25	Electrician	31	.8	(33)
26	Cabinet Maker	22	.6	(35)
27	Upholsterer	20	.5	*
28	Grocer	19	.5	(28)
29	Fruit Dealer	18	.5	(18)
30	Fruit Store	18	.5	*
31	Laundry Worker	18	.5	*
32	Restaurant Worker	18	.5	*
33	Auto Mechanic	17	.5	*
34	Contractor	17	.5	*
35	Cutter	17	.5	*
36	Mason	17	.5	(25)
	All other occupations	1,415	33.2	
	Unknown	20	.5	

* Does not appear in leading occupations in Table III

LEADING OCCUPATIONS IN 1916 (Table III), WHICH DO NOT APPEAR IN LEADING OCCUPATIONS FOR 1931 (Table IV)

Rank in 1931	Occupation	Number	Per cent	Rank in Table III	Rank	Occupation	Number	Per cent	Rank in Table III
40	Candy Maker	15	.4	(36)	72	Hatter	8	.2	(34)
49	Musician	13	.3	(27)		Coal Dealer	0	0	(12)
63	Longshoreman	10	.3	(20)		Piano Maker	0	0	(16)
69	Cigar Maker	8	.2	(29)		Bootblack	0	0	(31)
						Merchant	0	0	(32)

TABLE V — OCCUPATIONS OF ITALIAN MALES, DECEASED IN NEW YORK CITY, 1916

Rank	Occupation	Number	Per cent	Rank in Table VI
	Total	2,504	100.0	
	36 Leading Occupations	1,663	62.5	
1	Laborer	658	22.3	(1)
2	Student	233	9.3	(2)
3	Barber	94	3.8	(4)
4	Tailor	88	3.5	(3)
5	Longshoreman	44	1.8	(7)
6	Driver	40	1.6	(28)
7	Shoemaker	38	1.5	(5)
8	Shoe Worker	34	1.4	(15)
9	Carpenter	33	1.3	(6)
10	Clerk	30	1.2	(10)
11	Painter	28	1.1	(8)
12	Peddler	25	1.0	(13)
13	Porter	22	.9	(16)
14	Grocer	20	.8	(19)
15	Junk Dealer	20	.8	(30)
16	Merchant	19	.8	(40)
17	Baker	18	.7	(11)
18	Bootblack	16	.6	(18)
19	Cook	16	.6	(17)
20	Waiter	15	.6	(36)
21	Bricklayer	14	.6	(20)
22	Janitor	13	.5	(50)
23	Mason	13	.5	(35)
24	Printer	13	.5	(21)
25	Salesman	13	.5	(12)
26	House Worker	12	.5	(46)
27	Machinist	11	.4	(31)
28	Musician	11	.4	(25)
29	Butcher	10	.4	(24)
30	Fruit Dealer	10	.4	(23)
31	Bartender	9	.4	(167)
32	Jeweler	9	.4	(51)
33	Proprietor	9	.4	(33)
34	Watchman	9	.4	(29)
35	Blacksmith	8	.3	(49)
36	Cigar Maker	8	.3	(54)
	All other occupations	416	20.5	
	Unknown	365	14.6	
	Retired	60	2.4	

TABLE VI — OCCUPATIONS OF ITALIAN MALES, DECEASED IN NEW YORK CITY, 1931

Rank	Occupation	Number	Per cent	Rank in Table V
	Total	3,778	100.0	
	36 Leading Occupations	2,488	65.0	
1	Laborer	840	22.2	(1)
2	Student	276	7.1	(2)
3	Tailor	134	3.5	(4)
4	Barber	130	3.4	(3)
5	Shoemaker	100	2.6	(7)
6	Carpenter	69	1.8	(9)
7	Longshoreman	62	1.6	(5)
8	Painter	61	1.6	(11)
9	Chauffeur	56	1.5	*
10	Clerk	55	1.5	(10)
11	Baker	50	1.3	(17)
12	Salesman	50	1.3	(25)
13	Peddler	43	1.1	(12)
14	Ice Man	37	1.0	*
15	Shoe Worker	37	1.0	(8)
16	Porter	34	.9	(13)
17	Cook	33	.9	(19)
18	Bootblack	30	.8	(18)
19	Grocer	28	.7	(14)
20	Bricklayer	27	.7	(21)
21	Printer	27	.7	(24)
22	Plasterer	26	.7	*
23	Fruit Dealer	23	.6	(31)
24	Butcher	22	.6	(29)
25	Musician	22	.6	(28)
26	Helper	21	.6	*
27	Contractor	19	.5	*
28	Driver	19	.5	(6)
29	Watchman	19	.5	(34)
30	Junk Dealer	18	.5	(15)
31	Machinist	18	.5	(27)
32	Mechanic	18	.5	*
33	Proprietor	18	.5	(33)
34	Cabinet Maker	17	.4	*
35	Mason	17	.4	(23)
36	Waiter	17	.4	(20)
	All other occupations	801	22.1	
	Retired	268	7.1	
	Unknown	221	5.8	

* Does not appear in leading occupation in Table v.

LEADING OCCUPATIONS IN 1916 (Table V), WHICH DO NOT APPEAR IN LEADING OCCUPATIONS FOR 1931 (Table VI)

Rank in 1931	Occupation	Number	Per cent	Rank in Table V
40	Merchant	16	.4	(16)
46	House Worker	13	.3	(26)
49	Blacksmith	12	.3	(35)

Rank	Occupation	Number	Per cent	Rank in Table VI
50	Janitor	12	.3	(22)
51	Jeweler	12	.3	(32)
54	Cigar Maker	9	.2	(36)
167	Bartender	1	—	(31)

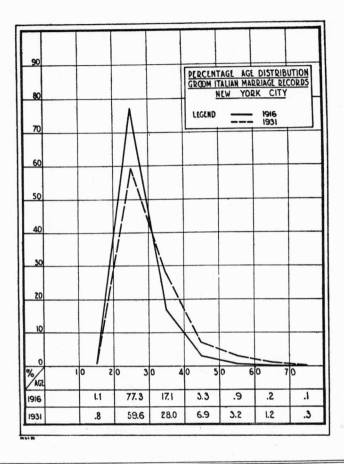

%/AGE	10	20	30	40	50	60	70
1916		1.1	77.3	17.1	3.3	.9	.2	.1
1931		.8	59.6	28.0	6.9	3.2	1.2	.3

PERCENTAGE AGE DISTRIBUTION
GROOM ITALIAN MARRIAGE RECORDS
NEW YORK CITY
LEGEND ——— 1916
       - - - 1931

TABLE IX

PERCENTAL TREND IN CONCENTRATION IN LEADING OCCUPATIONS OF ITALIANS IN N. Y. C.

	From Birth Records				From Marriage Records				From Death Records			
	1916		1931		1916		1931		1916		1931	
	%	Cumulative %	%	Cumulative %	%	Cumulative %	%	Cumulative %	%	Cumulative %	%	Cumulative %
5 leading occupations	66.1	66.1	47.9	47.9	50.2	50.2	28.0	28.0	40.7	40.7	38.8	38.8
Next 5 occupations	6.4	72.5	10.9	58.8	8.1	58.3	12.4	40.4	7.0	47.7	8.0	46.8
Next 5 occupations	3.9	76.4	7.2	66.0	5.5	63.8	8.7	49.1	4.6	52.3	5.7	52.5
Next 21 occupations	9.8	86.2	14.5	80.5	13.6	77.4	17.2	66.3	10.2	62.5	12.5	65.0
All other occupations	13.0	99.2	18.4	98.9	17.8	95.2	33.2	99.5	20.5	83.0	22.1	87.1
Unknown	.8	100.0	.7	99.6	4.8	100.0	.5	100.0	14.6	97.6	5.8	92.9
Unemployed			.4	100.0								
Retired									2.4	100.0	7.1	100.0

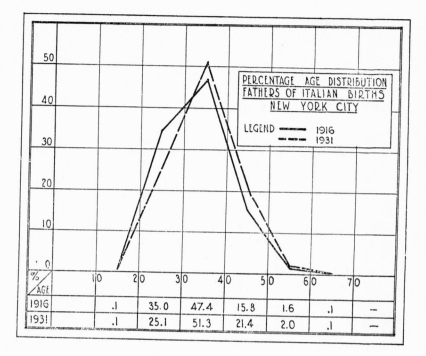

PERCENTAGE AGE DISTRIBUTION FATHERS OF ITALIAN BIRTHS NEW YORK CITY						
%/AGE	10	20	30	40	50	60	70
1916	.1	35.0	47.4	15.8	1.6	.1	—
1931	.1	25.1	51.3	21.4	2.0	.1	—

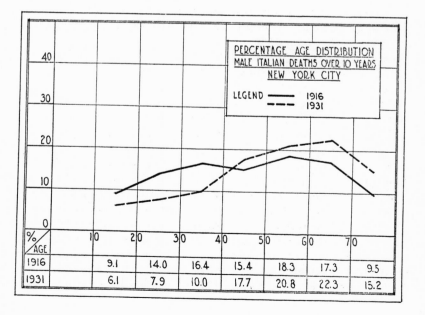

PERCENTAGE AGE DISTRIBUTION MALE ITALIAN DEATHS OVER 10 YEARS NEW YORK CITY						
%/AGE	10	20	30	40	50	60	70
1916	9.1	14.0	16.4	15.4	18.3	17.3	9.5
1931	6.1	7.9	10.0	17.7	20.8	22.3	15.2

somewhat reduced. For example, the listings of Auto Tester, Auto Mechanic, Auto Repairer, Auto Ignition Man, might reasonably have been included under one classification.

CONCLUSIONS AND SUGGESTIONS FOR FURTHER STUDY

It has often been asserted that the newer immigrants have inferior intelligence, figure more prominently in crime, and in general present greater social problems than the older stocks who immigrated to this country prior to 1880. Careful studies of the occupational trends for these ethnic groups may contribute to a clearer understanding as to the truth of such assertions. For example, if intelligence *as measured by our tests,* is a result of, rather than a cause of, differential levels in occupations, then the trend of an ethnic group from occupations of a lower level to a higher level should also show an increase in the general "intelligence" level for that group. The examination of such an assumption would, of course, require the carrying out of a testing program on a scale commensurate with that carried out in the last war.

This investigation, despite the limitations, indicates clearly that the distribution of Italians in the occupations is by no means static. Significant is the percental decrease in the classification of laborers. On the other hand, there is a definite increase in the diversification of leading occupations engaged in.

Both in 1916 and 1931, the following six occupations appeared among the first fifteen, as shown in all six series:—Laborers, Tailors, Barbers, Shoemakers, Carpenters, Painters.

In 1931, four new occupations appeared among the first fifteen in all three lists:—Chauffeur, Clerk, Salesman, Baker.

Three others appeared on the two most significant lists:—Mechanic, Plasterer, Butcher.

It seems reasonable to conclude that this is an indication of a definite tendency for Italians to follow the occupational pattern set by the total population in New York City as reported in the U.S. census of 1930.

This investigation has, it may be hoped, added somewhat to the common fund of knowledge relating to the occupational activities of the Italian immigrant population in New York City. It has set forth a considerable body of data from which certain generalization might be tentatively drawn and certain tendencies traced. Furthermore, some of the results of this and similar studies may be of direct use to the many social agencies working with immigrant groups. Such material, for example, as that relating to the number of workers in an occupation, and the changing distribution of the leading occupations, might well be taken into account in determining the social agencies' attitude toward their clients as regards programs for guidance in educational and occupational fields.

Nevertheless, neither this nor any other study provides the material for a fully rounded guidance policy. For such a policy would, necessarily, have to rest on the answers to a series of questions which cannot be answered on the basis of existing data. What are the conditions that affect vocational choices? Which are environmental? How may we learn more of social status of an occupation? How may we determine the intelligence status of workers? These are some of the questions the answers to which may furnish the basis for a well-rounded social guidance program. Anything approaching adequate answers to these queries can not be derived from this study. Most of these topics must wait upon more extensive enumerations and more thorough analyses than have yet been completed.

The present fund of statistical information relating to occupations —extensive as it is—cannot, therefore, be accepted as in any way providing an adequate statistical background for a well-rounded occupational program. It furnishes certain material, however, that may be of use in formulating a program. But it derives perhaps its greatest value from the fact that it calls attention to the importance of the problems; that it indicates the questions that must be elicited, the inadequacy of the present materials, and the need for a unified and coordinated plan; and that it suggests the paths that may be followed in seeking to answer these problems.

EMILY WAYLAND DINWIDDLE

SOME ASPECTS OF ITALIAN HOUSING AND SOCIAL CONDITIONS IN PHILADELPHIA*

Philadelphia's "Little Italy" is one of the most picturesque sections of the city. For about thirty-five blocks the Italians are closely packed together. One can walk the streets for considerable distances without hearing a word of English. The black-eyed children rolling and tumbling together, the gaily colored dresses of the women and the crowds of street vendors all give the neighborhood a wholly foreign appearance. The rag shops and macaroni factories are an important feature of the district.

An overwhelming majority of Italians was found in one block in which every house was visited. Classed according to the nativity of the father, or of the mother where the father was dead, of the 366 families here 358 were Italian; 4 were Russian; 2 American; 1 German; and 1 Swiss. The Russian and German families were all Jewish.

The principal occupation of the heads of families, given in the order of the number of persons engaged in each, were those of laborers, shopkeepers, rag-pickers or rag-dealers, tailors or engaged in tailoring trades, peddlers and vendors, unskilled employes in factories and stores, barbers, street cleaners, cobblers and shoemakers, and musicians.

Of the special work carried on within the apartments rag-picking took the lead. Next came tailoring and cobbling and last scissors sharpening and umbrella mending.

Though not the subject of special study, some general information in regard to amusements was gathered. Gambling in various forms was frequently seen. Social drinking in the homes was not uncommon. A large proportion of the houses had casks or barrels of wine in the cellars. Drinking in the saloons seemed less frequent. Of

Charities, vol. 12 (1904), pp. 490-494.

the 180 buildings of every kind in the block investigated, two were saloons. This did not seem a large proportion of the total of eighty-one stores and places of business. The Italian marionette theatre is crowded every night with men and boys, who hang in breathless attention upon the continued stories acted there from evening to evening. In spite of the reeking tobacco smoke, the jammed and uncomfortable condition of the audience and the absence of women in the assembly, a more orderly or better disposed gathering could scarcely be found. The church festivals are also attended by great crowds and form a striking part of the neighborhood life.

Aside from the character of the population the district itself is full of interest. Like most of the older parts of the city it is intersected by small alleys in such a way that the interiors of the blocks are covered over with numbers of rear houses. Of the 167 occupied dwellings visited in the block previously spoken of, seventy-three were rear buildings. Where back yards are covered over in this way the space left for light and air is sometimes dangerously small. One row of seven alley houses, back to back with another row so that all ventilation from the rear was cut off, received such light and ventilation as it had from a court, four feet three inches wide, with buildings on the opposite side extending almost the entire length of the court. The occupants of these houses were obliged to keep lamps burning all day.

That overcrowding by land areas is much greater here than in other parts of the city is proved by the census statistics, which show that the Second, Third and Fourth wards, within which nearly all the Italian district lies, contain more than one-sixteenth of the total population of the city in less than one one-hundred and fiftieth of the area.

Overcrowding per room, however, is a much more serious evil than overcrowding by number of persons to the acre. In one tenement house 30 Italian families, 123 persons, were living in 34 rooms. Of 366 families visited considerably more than one-fourth had only one room each. It is difficult to imagine what this means without having seen life under such conditions. In some cases as many as seven persons cook, eat and sleep in one room. Except in freezing weather the members of the family who are able to do so stay out of doors until midnight because the rooms are unendurable. Cleanliness is impossible and decency is utterly disregarded.

Much of the overcrowding is due to the common practice of taking lodgers, and the fact that the adult occupants of the rooms are often not related to each other in any way makes the promiscuous herding together even worse in its influence upon morals than in its effect on health. There was difficulty in ascertaining the separate rental of the living quarters of each family visited, as some rented a shop and several living rooms together and could not give a clear account of the proportion paid for each. Definite statistics were obtained in regard to 335 families. Of these 34 owned their living quarters, 2 occupied their apartments rent free in return for janitor's services, 16 families stated that they paid no regular rent, being relatives of the owner or sub-landlord of the house. Of the remainder 26 were sub-landlords, leasing entire houses, occupying one apartment and subletting others; 75 rented and occupied whole houses used solely as dwellings; and 182 had each a separate apartment in a house tenanted by two or more families.

The average monthly rent of a house used solely as a dwelling for one family was $7.99. The average rent for a single apartment in a house occupied by two or more families was $5.51. It will be seen that the rent per apartment is less in the houses containing several families than in the one family buildings. The rent per room, however, is greater in the houses occupied by several families. In these the average is $3.33 per room, as opposed to $2.28 in the one family dwellings. The reason for this is in the fact that the great majority of single family houses are rear buildings with small rooms and without water in the house or conveniences of any kind, while the buildings having two or more families are usually on the street, have larger rooms and are better fitted up. This accounts for the greater per room rent in the latter. The smaller rent per apartment is because of the smaller number of rooms occupied by the families in these houses.

The figures given above take no account of the amount of rent repaid by lodgers within the apartments, doing no independent housekeeping. The number of these is very large, as has been previously stated.

Lack of space not infrequently leads to the use of cellars for living purposes. One cellar kitchen seen lacked only a few inches of being entirely below ground and had no ventilation except by two doors. The door which communicated directly with the outer air, the tenants informed me, was kept closed and fastened up during the entire winter. The filthiest room I visited in the district was a cellar bedroom which the family above let to lodgers for ten cents a night.

Many of the cellars which were not inhabited were in an unhealthful condition. One had a stream of considerable size flowing through the middle from a broken water pipe in the yard. It had worn a fairly deep channel in the earth floor and the tenants said that it had been pouring through for over a month. This cellar, however, was less offensive than others, where the leakage consisted of foul water and sewage instead of fresh water.

As if the human occupants of the house did not furnish sufficient life, some of the families kept fowls or animals of one kind or another. During a visit to one house the door from the inside cellar steps was pushed open and a goat stalked in to join the family circle, having apparently grown weary of the dark cellar. The worst case was that of a slaughter house and dwelling in one building. About 30 sheep were kept on the second floor, which was reached by an inclined plane. Downstairs a room was used for slaughtering and about one hundred sheep were killed every Saturday besides numbers every day. The butcher and his wife lived in the house and had a kitchen on the ground floor. This was in a closely built up block with houses adjoining on every side.

Lack of cleanliness in the rooms was not surprisingly bad in view of the overcrowding and the inadequate water supply. It was frequently the case that the living rooms and especially the bedrooms were much cleaner than the halls, cellars and yards.

The insufficient water supply would excuse much. I have found eleven families, having as sole water supply one court hydrant for the whole number. Ten other families used another hydrant in common. Considerably less than one-third of the Italian families visited had exclusive use of one or more water fixtures each. In the block specially investigated, counting in all fixtures from which water could be drawn—yard hydrants, sinks, baths, stationary tubs and basins—there were in all 237 fixtures for 366 families and 81 stores and places of business.

The number of baths was of course small, yet 17 out of 167 houses had one each. For the whole block the average was one bath for each 22 families, 102 persons to a tub. Five of the tubs were said not to be used for bathing purposes and three more were reported to be so used only in summer. This appeared to be due to their location and condition rather than to lack of appreciation on the part of the tenants. One tub, for example, was in the middle of a large bedroom, without enclosure of any kind. In another case a family of eight had one room and a bath. They used the bath compartment as a sleeping room, the tub serving as a sink. The three tubs used only in summer were in extension rooms which were extremely cold, so that the pipes froze in winter.

No attempt to describe conditions found in the district would be complete without some special notice of the evils of the tenements and rear houses. It is often said that Philadelphia has no tenement-house problem, yet of 167 dwellings in one block, forty-one, or nearly one-fourth, were each occupied by three or more families doing cooking on the premises and so came under the legal definition of a tenement. These tenement houses are nearly all buildings apparently intended for private residences but used without alteration or with only slight changes for three or more families. The families in most cases have no fire protection. They are overcrowded. They have miserably inadequate sanitary accommodations of every kind. There is very little oversight. A special janitor or housekeeper is almost unknown.

In the rear houses evils of a slightly different kind are found. The buildings are small, usually containing only three tiny rooms. As many houses as possible are crowded together on the lots so that a large proportion have no yard space at the rear or side. The houses which have yards usually have to throw them open to the entire court because they contain the hydrants or other accommodations for all the buildings. Frequently they have only surface drainage and where they are defectively paved and graded, slops and filth remain stagnant under the windows of the buildings. One row of rear houses has already been spoken of as containing seven buildings back to back with another row and getting all their light and air from a space in front, four feet three inches wide. This same row had one hydrant for all the houses, but last fall the hydrant got out of order and the water supply was cut off, remaining cut off for several months, during which time all the tenants went to a neighboring house to borrow water. The occupants of most of the houses were very neat and kept their rooms clean, but the alley was filthy. It received the drainage from a stable at one side and a tenement at the end, so that the gutter, which occupied a large part of the passageway, was constantly foul.

Thus far I have spoken of the bad conditions found, but it must not be thought that the picture is altogether dark. Some comfortable houses, equipped with modern conveniences and occupied by one family each, were seen. A large proportion of the worst houses were occupied by recent immigrants who had not had time to work their way up to living in more expensive dwellings and did not know where to seek redress for the discomforts they suffered from in their present quarters, if they knew or desired anything better.

DAISY H. MOSELEY

THE CATHOLIC SOCIAL WORKER IN AN ITALIAN DISTRICT*

The Catholic social worker who finds her opportunity for service in family case work among the Italian poor in the United States is fortunate. As a Catholic she has a distinct right to this particular service, because, whether we Catholics of America will or not, the problems of the Italian immigrant and his family are our problems, and their solution is in some measure our responsibility. The sense of possessing the right to this heritage is an asset to the social service worker, and the heritage is a wonderful one. Most of our Italian poor are industrious, lovable and generous, with great potentialities for good, but they are confronted with difficulties which are made more serious by the strangeness of our language and customs, and their mode of living causes them to be exposed to numerous dangers, physical and moral. Hence they are often in need of the aid of trained social workers.

Sympathy is the keynote of fortunate approach in Italian social work. It takes much knowledge of resources, great common sense and firmness, and a certain gift for lucid speech and direction to treat a case successfully. Possibly a true understanding of her clients' attitude is much to demand of the family case worker, but she can at least study enough of their national psychology and customs, and of their ordinary manner of living, to enable her to comprehend why certain conditions exist, and what is the Italians' attitude towards them.

The student of social service looks in vain for an adequate literature descriptive of conditions in our congested Italian districts. The social literature in which the "Little Italys" of America are depicted, usually contains atmosphere and little else; it is redolent of macaroni and tomato sauce; it echoes the music of hurdy gurdies and the

*Catholic World, Vol. 114 (February, 1922), pp. 618-628.

laughter of dancing children; it makes, in fact, delightful reading, but contains little definite information. This atmosphere has an Old World charm which tempts the lover of the quaint, but the love of the quaint tends to grow less as the long black tenement stairs grow longer. If she would not lose her zeal, the worker must have a foundation more solid than atmosphere on which to build.

This solid foundation is knowledge of facts, and there is much available printed matter, not literary or artistic, but brim full of facts. Studied in the light of one's particular interest in conditions among Italians in America, the reports of the Department of Labor, Bureau of Immigration, and the United States Census reports become fascinating reading. In the card index of a library of sociology or religion can be found the titles of various valuable studies of phases of Italian life in our cities; and the reports of societies which have been devoted to work among them throw many side lights. Other information which aids in contact with one's clients is information about Italy itself. The Italian speaks lovingly of his *"paese,"* the part of Italy in which he lived, and if the visitor is sufficiently well read or well traveled to enable her to discuss that native heath, its beauties or industries or some interesting fact about it, she and her client have a common interest for conversation. Time spent in general conversation may not prove time wasted. For with no other group is it so essential to have a friendly, leisurely approach as with the Italians. They are naturally social and disinclined to haste, and hasty dictatorial treatment is distasteful to them. One may find it irksome to spend an hour or longer in a first visit, and more irksome to have to see innumerable wedding and confirmation photographs, but such a visit has tremendous psychological value.

Probably most of the Italians in America live in sections peopled almost entirely by their compatriots; thus the social service worker among them finds herself grappling with only one national psychology because her group of clients is homogeneous. This tendency to congregate presents, however, some difficulties for the American worker: it lessens the necessity of the immigrant for the language of the country and, in consequence, he often fails to learn English. It also tends to preserve traditions and customs little in accord with American life.

When she enters upon life in a crowded section, the intelligent worker realizes that she is to meet with every question known to modern philanthropy and, during her first day in an Italian district, she learns that most of these problems will be quadrupled in complexity by one cause: language. Relatively few social workers who have Italian clients speak pure Italian or one dialect, not to mention the difficult dialects of Piacenza and Calabria and parts of Sicily. Their clients are, as a rule, ignorant, and frequently can read no language. They have heard almost as little English as they would have heard in Italy, and most of the women, save the very young ones, have lived so entirely among their compatriots that they speak no English; others speak and understand so imperfectly that one cannot judge how incorrectly they may report a conversation. How small a chance the American visitor and the client have to comprehend each other! Children, even were it right to employ them as interpreters, and it is not, are inexact; and they know neither language in its entireness. If an interpreter must be the medium, the Italian woman prefers to choose her own, usually a friend whom she trusts. The visitor may find this person less gifted than someone she would choose herself, but if she is wise she will not substitute a stranger.

Each individual must solve the dilemma for herself, but the visitor who knows a few phrases of Italian, expedites and facilitates her work. If she can ask the baby's name and age in the mother's native tongue and understand the answer given, she progresses far more quickly in her acquaintance with mother and baby, for friendly inquiries are chilled by translation.

A serious problem which evolves from the language difficulty is a child problem; it contains the germ of many present and many future sufferings, and therefore it is a point to attack if social workers are not to be entirely baffled in their efforts to prevent delinquency among their young clients. The immigrant family comes to America and settles in an Italian district. The father finds work as a rule among his fellow-countrymen; the mother keeps the home in a tenement inhabited by other Italians. Neither is so situated as to learn to speak English. The children, however, are quickly discovered by the school authorities, and are required to attend school; they are often placed in ungraded classes which are devoted exclusively to the study of English. After about three months spent in such a class the little Italian has mastered a good speaking knowledge of English; he has imbibed a vast amount of American patriotism, and knows about George Washington's unwillingness to prevaricate and Abraham Lincoln's splitting the rails. With childish enthusiasm he has become American, and with childish weakness he has perhaps grown ashamed of his Italian parentage.

It is indeed well that he should become American, but his parents are Italian, and if they are to retain necessary parental control, he must not be allowed to lose respect for Italy, to forget his father's language, or to feel that he is his father's superior because he can serve as family interpreter and perhaps swear a little in English.

No one who knows these fascinating children will fail to see dangerous elements in their behavior at home—elements which bode ill for society in the future. The social worker who evolves means of keeping her clients and their children in touch with each other and who inspires in them mutual respect, is helping to overcome these dangers.

Granted that difference in language constitutes perhaps the greatest national difference, and presents the most tangible difficulty, the varying customs and traditions merit equal consideration. Many of these Old World peasant prejudices seem worse than nonsense to a modern young American, but there is no means to estimate the unhappiness a zealous young woman may cause when she attempts to direct the destiny of a member of a family and defies the customs and prejudices of others of the family and their neighbors. To avoid this she must be acquainted with the customs. There are books descriptive of Italian peasant customs, and the social worker in America can derive much useful knowledge from case records of Italian clients of charitable organizations and courts.

Perhaps the most evident difficulties which evolve from the customs have to do with the privileges of women. Not to consider at all the married woman, take the question of recreation for adolescent girls and young women. The young social worker thinks herself, as a rule, privileged to lead her own life; she goes almost wherever she pleases and with whomsoever she chooses within certain bounds of convention. She would advocate such independence for the bright, attractive Italian woman of her own age. But should she encourage the Italian girl in such a course until the latter defies the customs of her family and goes perhaps to the moving pictures with a man unchaperoned, that girl may meet with all the horrors of being disowned by her family, scorned by the neighbors, not desired as a wife by any compatriot, and eventually cast out entirely from the society of her own group, because it is a tradition that an unmarried woman should not go unchaperoned.

It is not necessary that the social worker should be converted to the wisdom of this tradition, but she must recognize its existence, and respect its dictates. Truly, the problem of the fun-loving Italian girl who wishes to spend her hours of freedom as the American girls among whom she works spend theirs, is a serious one. Here is an opportunity for constructive and preventive work, because the desire to be a normal American doubtless leads many a pretty girl of Italian parentage into shocking her family and her friends by some action in itself perfectly harmless, and their attitude towards her may cause her to drift into actual delinquency.

The physical problems which prevail wherever there are crowded and poor living conditions, are prevalent among the Italians in the great cities, because they live usually in thickly congested sections. Certain aspects of these problems may be peculiar to one group, but on the whole they can be treated as in other groups. Here again, however, the social service visitor will realize that the homemakers, not the young ones as a rule, but the middle aged, are so handicapped by their ignorance of English that they cannot always avail themselves of employment bureaus, clinics, milk stations, hospitals, dispensaries, or other agencies established to aid the poor. If the visitor makes the contact between her client and one of these agencies, she can be sure that the client will avail herself of its services and teach her neighbors to do so. This is especially true in regard to hospitals and dispensaries.

Other assets in treatment of Italian cases can be relied on in the solving of financial problems. Financial problems are, of course, numerous. They are largely the result of seasonal occupation, day's work, piecework and other means of subsistence which yield irregularly. There is often no fixed income, and sickness or lockouts carry distress in their wake. Among other groups the social worker frequently finds herself facing a financial crisis with a friendless family. It may strike the uninitiated as odd, but one seldom finds an isolated family in an Italian district in America; careful inquiry will almost invariably reveal that the client has relatives or friends within the district or within reach, who can help and advise. The Italian usually belongs to an Italian Benefit Society, and he usually carries a small insurance policy for each member of his family. Another matter worthy of comment is, that in cases of financial distress it is seldom necessary to give the frequently demoralizing direct relief of food and money. The case worker can take reasonable time to procure medical aid or employment or a regular weekly allowance or whatever kind of assistance the family requires, because she knows generous Italian neighbors in the tenement will slip in with food and clothing; will perhaps lend a month's rent in advance; will exercise the privileges of neighborly charity.

Many isolated questions present themselves, such as the establishment of rights to mothers' pensions, and the deportation of families or individuals, but they are the various problems of aliens and not peculiar to Italians. The trained social worker knows her resources in such instances. There are peculiar problems, however, which no social worker can ignore: these relate to religion.

It has been said advisedly that no social worker can ignore the religious problems among the Italians. The successful non-Catholic case worker knows fully as well as the Catholic that the average Italian is essentially Catholic; if she sees that her clients are neglecting the sacraments, expecially if she finds that they fail to have their children baptized, she is aware of signs of danger; she fears to hear of other serious lapses not only from formal religion, but from morality.

The wise social service worker knows that she is not as a rule qualified to give spiritual advice; she is equally certain that her clients need such advice; Italian clients may be especially in need of it if, through failure to understand the customs and language of the new country, they have drifted away from their religion. In ordinary cases the Catholic social worker can refer the difficulty to the pastor; it is her privilege to be the link between the new country and customs and the old long-treasured religion, and to help entire families to safeguard their Faith.

One hears much of the dangers of proselytism among our Italian poor, and they are grave—but one hears little of a more prevalent danger: civil marriage with no religious ceremony. Why this habit of being married only by a magistrate should have gained such ground among our younger Italians is a puzzle, but the fact remains that unnumbered young, energetic Italian couples who have their children baptized, whose homes are adorned with holy pictures, who are Catholics at heart, are living under the ban of excommunication. The causes and results of this difficulty are manifold: that it should exist so largely among the young Italians who have grown up in America seems to point to previous inadequate religious instruction among Italian children, or to a lapse of religious care during the drifting and acquisitive age of adolescence. The harm has already been done, in most cases, before the social worker meets them. However, when she meets with couples who have not been married in the Church, she must attempt to prevent further evils by getting the couple properly married. This is not so easy a task as having the baby baptized—and many are the weary hours she will work before she accomplishes her purpose. If she is wise, she realizes that these are hours spent in preventive work—and in that highest of labors: the prevention of evil and the furthering of good.

All Catholics are aware of the danger attendant upon neglecting the religious instruction of children, and, of course, where numbers of Catholic children go to the public schools as our Italians do, the danger is great. Here again, however, the Italian custom is a great asset. As the Italian mother insists on baptism, so does she insist on the child's making his First Communion and being confirmed—and should she not the child would in all likelihood do so himself, for

Confirmation and First Communion days are great days in the Italian child's life.

The Catholic social worker can, of course, aid in preparation for the Sacraments, but the great need for the trained case worker's care comes at a later period in the child's career: in the age of adolescence. The trying years which intervene between the time of First Communion and the time of settling to a regular vocation, are years in which the adolescent crave excitement. In gratifying this craving the young people often get into difficulties, and the problems peculiar to this age which present themselves to the social worker are numerous; the religious problems are not the least among them. The social worker comes into contact with her young client perhaps through the Juvenile Court or Probation Officer or through the school authorities, persons who, though trained in their particular duties, may understand neither Catholicism nor the Italian temperament, and therefore seek the aid of the social worker who specializes in work among Italians. The Catholic social worker is especially fitted to give this aid. She it is who can most readily renew the child's contact with his church and pastor, and help him to get a new start.

The possibility that an Italian girl may drift into delinquency through her parents' lack of comprehension of American customs has been mentioned. Another possibility is that young Italians may drift into deceit through a desire to work. A lie to obtain working papers may be the foundation on which a dishonest career is builded— and this temptation to lie exists in a great degree for Italian youth among the poor. Italian families are usually large, and the financial returns of the average family are irregular. By the time a girl is twelve or thirteen years old there are often several other children at home, and she is requisitioned to help care for them, to cook and wash and sweep. For this she receives, of course, no remuneration. She probably has been deft with her needle since her eighth or ninth year, and knows that needlework in shops and factories brings money and gives respite from household cares. The temptation to lie about her age and get her working papers is sometimes too great. This deceit becomes a religious problem to the Catholic social worker; she realizes its significance in the child's future life. It is an exceedingly difficult problem to handle when the social worker meets with it where great poverty exists, where the child's earnings are really needed. In such instances, if the social worker is resourceful and tactful, she can help form a splendid character; if she blunders, and perhaps she may blunder by too severe treatment of the moral aspect of the case, forgetting the insidious temptation, she may cause the child to drift away from a religion which dictates absolute honesty, may even precipitate her into a career of religious doubt.

The wise social worker will insist on making the case known to the proper authorities, even though she may happen upon it quite accidentally, but she will convince the child that it is best to do so, and she will find means to tide the ambitious girl or boy over the year or two which must pass before he or she can work under the law.

It is to the adolescent, perhaps, that Protestant proselytism is most dangerous, and the average Catholic who thinks of Italian districts thinks simultaneously of proselytism. The Catholic social worker meets with a few serious difficulties when she encounters the zeal of the Protestant workers for converts among the Italians. She must be careful not to overrate the difficulties nor to underrate the Protestant proselytizers.

Visits to Catholic and avowedly Protestant institutions in a given Italian district will impress one fact indelibly upon the mind: the average Italian is essentially Catholic or he would avail himself more of the creature comforts of the Protestant institutions; he must realize something of the dangers of proselytism, or he must feel that the Protestant atmosphere is too chill, else one would certainly find greater numbers of Italians in Protestant settlements. In New York, where a few Catholic Italian Settlements exist, one finds them thronged with children; the happy noise is so great that one wonders how the hard-worked teachers can instruct in sewing and perhaps in catechism; it is a strange contrast to the orderly precision and perhaps lonely emptiness of the Protestant settlement.

However, among her clients the Catholic worker will almost invariably discover some who, apparently for no reasons save material ones, frequent Protestant churches and settlements. The task of convincing these clients that they are weakening their faith by their own deceitful action is a delicate one: these settlements offer pleasures which Catholic settlements do not offer, and one has no substitute to suggest to the client. Of course, the only solution here is Catholic education, and to this end endowed Catholic settlement houses will be a great aid.

In the course of her work the Catholic will meet with capable, self-sacrificing Italian Protestant ministers and social workers, who are equipped with knowledge of both English and Italian, and who have large sums of money at their command. These Italians are not always renegades from the true faith; in some cases their ancestors were Protestants. With such ministers and social workers the Catholic must, of course, treat as frankly of her problems with her clients as she would with Americans. She will find that they also recognize her right as a Catholic to work among Italian Catholics.

If the worker finds among her clients Italians who have forsaken

Catholicism for Protestantism and investigates the history of the case thoroughly, she will probably find marriage or divorce associated with that history; or desire for worldly success in a "Protestant country" may have been responsible. Of course such families, which she believes should be Catholic, are problem families for the case worker. She may be the means of restoring to such a family its precious Catholic heritage.

One group for which proselytism has few dangers is that of the aged Italians, but the aged may give the case worker grave concern. In many Italian homes one finds the grandmother or grandfather, not so old in years perhaps, as in days of unceasing hard work and poverty. This old person is a pitiful member of the household: childish, and afraid or unable to go out alone, he or she sits in the home year after year. The discovery of such a person and the alleviation of his wants, spiritual and physical, is often possible to the social worker. By a simple word to the pastor, she may enable the client to receive the sacraments regularly.

In dealing with religious problems among the Italian poor, the Catholic social worker is certainly assisted by mutual belief in Catholic doctrine, and it is not too much to say that this kinship of Catholicism, aids her in approaching every problem, whether spiritual or physical. Yet this very kinship offers another and dangerous aspect, in that an American well instructed in her faith may think she finds cause for scandal among Italian Catholics. She would be astounded to be told that it was Pharisaical scandal—but, before she condemns her clients as bad Catholics, she must consider what are and are not the essentials of religion—and she must not forget the circumstances of her clients' lives. For example, it is a commandment of the Church that Catholics hear Mass on Sundays, but an Italian woman who has a number of very small children near the same age— and no one with whom she may leave them if her husband's work as barber or waiter or laborer takes him away in the early morning—has a great temptation not to leave the home, would perhaps do wrong did she leave. Instead of being scandalized by this very prevalent phase of life, the social worker will recognize that the mother must be aided in this difficulty. Day nurseries are established for the care of children whose mothers work, and perhaps some such temporary Sunday morning care may be given to children whose mothers are at Mass.

The deprivation suffered by a Catholic who cannot hear Mass on Sunday can scarcely be comprehended by a Protestant, and this is only one of the problems which a Catholic can most readily understand. Even in this limited discussion of the problems of the Italian poor, it will be seen that they are difficulties which should appeal primarily to the Catholic woman—and especially to the Catholic social service worker.

Through the ages of Christianity, the Church has invariably responded to the needs of the times by the establishment of orders or societies to meet those needs. In our age she recognizes the necessity for trained social workers among the sick and poor, and it is to be hoped that many lay women who respond to her call, will recognize the necessity for specialized training for work among the Italian poor, work which cannot fail to reward the laborer.

ANTONIO STELLA

TUBERCULOSIS AND THE ITALIANS IN THE UNITED STATES*

In spite of the traditional renown of Italy as the paradise of Europe and one of the most healthful countries on earth, notwithstanding the fact that she really yields less victims annually to consumption than any other nation on the continent under similar demographic conditions, it is an undoubted fact, and a truth sadly brought daily to the attention of physicians, social workers, and others in a position to know, that tuberculosis is very prevalent among the Italians emigrated to these shores.

To have an idea of the alarming frequency of consumption among Italians, especially in the large cities of the Union, one must not look for exact information to the records of the local boards of health and the registry of vital statistics; they are, for the very reason of the mobility of the Italian emigration, very fallacious, and show a low figure; but one must follow the Italian population as it moves in the tenement districts; study them closely in their daily struggle for air and space; see them in the daytime crowded in sweat-shops and factories; at night heaped together in dark windowless rooms; then visit the hospitals and dispensaries; and finally watch the outgoing steamships, and count the wan emaciated forms, with glistening eyes and racking cough, that return to their native land with a hope of recuperating health, but ofttimes only to find a quicker death.

This desire and tendency on the part of all Italians, whether rich or poor, to go back to their homes as soon as informed that they are affected with phthisis, is the chief cause of the discrepancy between the *actual high* number of consumptives existing among the Italians in the United States and the *official low* figures of the various health boards.

In fact, in a recent table of the New York Health Department as to the mortality from consumption among the different nationalities between the ages of fifteen and forty-five years, we find that the Ital-

Charities, vol. 12 (1904), pp. 486-489.

449

ians occupy only the tenth place in the list, losing but 149.9 per 10,000 population, as against 548.4 and 428.0 lost, respectively, by the negroes and the Irish, who lead the way. On the contrary, Italians come second in the table, where the mortality is considered below the fifteenth year of life (children generally being allowed to die here); and the same high percentage would certainly be found for the adult generation, were the statistics arranged not according to the death-rate, but according to the infection-rate, which is simply appalling.

From some tenements in Elizabeth and Mulberry Street, there have been as many as twelve and fifteen cases of consumption reported to the Board of Health since 1894.[1] But how many were *never* reported? How many went back to Italy? How many moved away to other districts?

My personal experience with some of the houses in that particular neighborhood is that the average has been not less than thirty or forty cases of infection for each tenement yearly, the element of house-infection being so great. I remember some rear houses in Elizabeth street, and one in Mott street, now torn down, through the operations of the new tenement law, that yielded as many as twenty-five cases in the course of a year to my personal knowledge alone.

And how could it be otherwise?

When we consider the infectious character of tuberculosis on the one side, and the overcrowded and filthy conditions of some tenements on the other, where a population of men, women and children is herded together at the rate of eight and ten in every three rooms (in some "flats" on Elizabeth street this number can often be doubled), a population, besides, made up chiefly of agriculturists, fresh yet from the sunny hills and green valleys of Tuscany and Sicily, abruptly thrown into unnatural abodes and dark sweat-shops—a population, at that, overworked, underfed, poorly clad, curbed with all the worries and anxieties of the morrow, and only free, thank God!—from the worst ally of consumption—alcoholism—where could the Koch bacillus find victims more prepared, where a soil more fertile than among such surroundings?

We know now-a-days that the penetration of a pathogenic germ into our system is not sufficient to cause a disease. It must find our body in a state of temporary paralysis of all its natural defenses, to be able to give rise to certain morbid processes, the evolution of which constitutes a disease.

No one will deny that the integrity of our respiratory organs depends

[1]See diagram, "Italian Quarter." Handbook on the Prevention of Tuberculosis. published by the New York Charity Organization Society, p. 90.

chiefly on the quantity and quality of air we breath. Every individual in normal condition should have at least 35 cubic meters of air as it is reckoned for hospitals, and the air we breathe in should not contain more than one per cent of all the expired air (Rubner). In many tenements, on account of the overcrowding, the quantity of air left for each person is reduced to three or four cubic meters, and the expired air in the sleeping-rooms represents one-half or one-sixth of all the air available. We can well say, then, that the atmosphere of those places is largely made up of the emanations from the bodies of the various persons living together.

What deleterious effect on the lungs and on the system in general the sojourn and sleep in these rooms must have, is beyond all calculation. The haematosis and oxygenation are first affected and then appears that train of obscure and insidious symptoms (persistent anaemia, progressive fatigue, emaciation, etc.), which represent the ante-tubercular stage, and actually prepare the ground for the bacillary invasion.

Those that feel this change most keenly, and fall victims to tuberculosis with marked rapidity, are not the second generation of immigrants, as generally believed, but the very first arrivals, especially those coming from the rural districts of Italy, unaccustomed yet to the poisoned atmosphere of city life.

Among those—and they are the large majority—who seek work in factories and shops, instead of pursuing their natural occupations in the open air, the stigmata of progressive physiological deterioration and general low vitality are most apparent. Six months of life in the tenements are sufficient to turn the sturdy youth from Calabria, the brawny fisherman of Sicily, the robust women from Abruzzi and Basilicata, into the pale, flabby, undersized creatures we see, dragging along the streets of New York and Chicago, such a painful contrast to the native population! Six months more of this gradual deterioration, and the soil for the bacillus tuberculosis is amply prepared.

For the Italians, though, besides the abrupt passage from rural to urban life, and the unsanitary housing accommodations, which stand among the foremost influences responsible for the spread of tuberculosis among them, another potent factor must be mentioned, and this refers to certain trades and occupations, that are especially favored by our countrymen, and which may well be called phthisiogenic, on account of the important role they play in the development of tuberculosis.

Suffice it here to mention the rag-sorters, sweepers, bootblacks, hotel cleaners, continually exposed to the inhalation of dust contaminated with dried tubercular sputum; the plasterers, marble and stone cutters, cigar makers, printers, pressmen, upholsterers, cabinet makers, barbers, tailors, brass and glass workers, who all stand near the head of the list in the mortality from consumption, and among whom we find thousands of our Italian immigrants.

In many of those occupations, besides the direct irritation to the bronchial mucous membrane from the inhalation of dust, the work itself requires a sitting position (cigar makers, tailors), in which the chest is bent forward, and thus prevents the expansion of the lungs, and directly interferes with the proper aeration of the pulmonary apices.

Still worse is the condition where the sweat-shop system flourishes at home, either as extra work, done late in the night, by young men and women already exhausted by ten hours of work in a crowded factory, or as a regular practice, by poor housewives, desirous of adding to their husbands earnings.

Words can hardly describe the pathetic misery of these Italian women, compelled to sew two or three dozen of pants for forty cents, using up their last spark of energy to make life better, when in fact they only accomplish their self-destruction. For their health is usually already drained by a too-productive maternity and periods of prolonged lactation; they live on a deficient, if not actually insufficnt, diet; they sleep in dark, damp holes, without sunshine and light, and have already had enough to exhaust them, with the raising of a large family and the strain of hard housework.

This practice explains in a measure the somewhat higher death-rate from phthisis of Italian women than men, especially among Sicilians, and the fact that we often find among them consumption in the quick form, that is, miliary tuberculosis of the sub-acute or the very acute type, which, rather than a clinical rarity, is of quite common occurrence in this class of patients.

And this high susceptibility is not due to any inherent lack of vitality in the race. The Italians otherwise show the most wonderful elements of resistance and recuperation, as may be seen in the favorable manner they react to surgical operations, extreme temperature, and all sorts of trials. Nor is it dependent upon any individual hereditary predisposition, for while the younger generation, emigrated to America, die rapidly, their parents at home live to a surprising old age. Their rapid fall is due solely to an ensemble of deleterious causes, acting simultaneously, steadily and forcibly on their constitution, and in a manner so complete, that the fertilization of the ubiquitious Koch bacillus must result of necessity.

The pulmonary form, however, while by far the most prevalent, is not the only manifestation of tuberculosis among the Italians in the

United States. Tuberculosis of the peritoneum and intestines, of the bones and glands, is seen very frequently among adults, in contrast with the common experience elsewhere that it is chiefly prevalent in early life; in the same way you will hear from physicians of large hospital practice, that many obscure conditions in the pelvis and adnexa, in the brain, kidney and other internal organs, occurring among Italians, prove at the pathological investigation to be tubercular, when everything else would have pointed to a different cause.

In view of these facts and the present state of our emigration, we must then consider the prevalence of tuberculosis among Italians as a function of their special economic and social conditions in their new environment, and if any remedies can be expected in the future to stop the spread of the scourge among them, they must be found in the betterment of those conditions and a thorough change of their present aspirations.

The statistics show that the higher we move up in the social scale, the lower the mortality from consumption; or as Gebhard puts it, "the death-rate from tuberculosis among the various classes, in large cities, is in inverse ratio to their individual income." This inequality of fortune in our modern society plays really the most important role in the spread of tuberculosis, and as long as present conditions prevail, we shall always find tuberculosis to be "the disease of the masses," par excellençe, and the inseparable ally of poverty.

Now every one knows that the Italians in this country represent almost exclusively the working class, and in some quarters the very poor class. To raise them to a higher social level, economically speaking, besides being a matter of slow evolution, implies a problem of such magnitude and such distant realization at the present, that we can only hint at it in passing by, and leave the social workers and economists the full discussion of it.

R. L. BREED

ITALIANS FIGHT
TUBERCULOSIS*

The Italian Committee on the Prevention of Tuberculosis, just organized in New York, has a large task before it. Not only has New York a larger Italian population than any other city except Naples and Rome, but tuberculosis attacks the Italian in America with particular success. His move from country to city, from warm to cold climate, from outdoor farm work to indoor work or to unhealthy construction camp, with his thrifty tendency to crowd into cheap tenements and to eat insufficient food, all render him susceptible. Moreover, the majority of Italian immigrants are between fourteen and forty-five years old—the very period when tuberculosis most prevails in all races. Too often six months in the tenements or in the camps suffice to shrivel the sturdy youth of Calabria, the brawny fisherman of Sicily, the robust peasant of Abruzzi, into the pale, flabby creature seen in "Little Italy."

The committee has been made representative of every province of Italy from the Swiss Alps to Sicily, in recognition of the broad area from which New York Italians come. The chairman is Lloyd C. Griscom formerly ambassador at the Quirinal, who greatly endeared himself to the Italian people, especially in his administration of the relief sent from America after the Messina earthquake. The vice-chairman is Dr. Antonio Stella, one of the leading tuberculosis specialists of the city, president of the Italian Medical Society and director of Morgagni Tuberculosis Clinic. Dr. Stella, as the special representative of the king of Italy, was successful in securing the next meeting of the International Tuberculosis Congress for Rome, 1911. The Italian government is represented on the committee by G. Di Rosa, acting consul general, and Bernardo Attolico, Italian inspector of emigration for the United States, who is a doctor of laws from the Roman University, and was a member of the First National Committee on Tuberculosis in Italy. Associated with these public men are V. G. DeLuca, a labor

*Survey, Vol. 23 (February 12, 1910), pp. 702-703.

contractor who employs several thousand men on construction work; Dr. F. Fortunato and Dr. A. Maroni of the Italian Hospital; Dr. Antonio Pisani, a member of the Board of Education; C. Piva, president of the Italian Benevolent Institute; Joseph F. Francolini, president and founder of the Italian Savings Bank; F. Tocci, a banker and one of the oldest Italians in New York; Emanuel Gerli, a prominent silk importer and director of the Italian Benevolent Institute; Ernesto G. Fabri, president of the Society for Italian Immigrants, Vito Contessa, president of the Sons of Columbus and interested in many social movements, and Lawrence Veiller, director of the Department for the Improvement of Social Conditions of the Charity Organization Society. Until an Italian secretary is selected, Frank H. Mann, secretary of the Committee on the Prevention of Tuberculosis of the Charity Organization Society, will serve as acting secretary.

The committee will divide the Italian colony into districts and follow out all the tried and successful preventive measures—distribution of literature, a weekly press service for Italian newspapers, illustrated lectures and exhibits. It expects to undertake a campaign for the better ventilation of homes and work shops, and to make an investigation into the peculiar needs of the Italian tubercular poor, to be followed by the establishment of special clinics.

The committee announces that it "hopes to set the ideal for less talk and discussion with regard to the 'problem of Italian immigration,' and more active and organized effort in their behalf; less oratory against the foreign peril and more active friendliness, for this committee believes that those who have already contributed so largely to our material greatness are destined to make large contributions to our intellectual pre-eminence if they be met with kindness and helpfulness. An intelligent Italian workman summed up his fellow immigrants' needs the other day as 'a chance to work and kindness.' "

PHYLLIS H. WILLIAMS

THE SOUTH ITALIANS: HEALTH AND HOSPITALS*

Our South Italian immigrants had two means of coping with illnesses in their native land. Ancient tradition furnished them with a mass of folklore relating to organic and mental disorders and their cure. In particularly trying cases, they could be doubly sure by calling in one of the local specialists in such beliefs and practices—a witch, a barber, a midwife, or an herbalist. From modern science they had gleaned but few notions, and those in a vague form. They looked with considerable question upon that upstart, the book-trained physician.

Small towns usually had one physician, paid by the state or by the commune in which he practiced. He earned a fixed salary and in some places free use of a house through treating the poverty-stricken and those not so poor, and supplemented these returns with what fees he could charge private patients. These practitioners did not, however, stand always in good repute. Their services were valued in true South Italian style on the basis of the idea that "when it don't cost anything you might know it is no good." The following notes on a cholera epidemic, written by an eyewitness,[1] illustrate the status frequently held by these professional functionaries of a state or commune:

> They resist and resent every effort to purify and ventilate their houses, and the most natural and simple precautions are neglected. As for the physicians, provided for them at the public expense, they look upon them with horror, and it is dangerous for them even to walk the streets. About a week since Dr. C————, on his way to visit a patient, ex-

---

South Italian Folkways in Europe and America (Yale University Press, 1938; reissued with an introductory note by F. Cordasco, New York: Russell & Russell, 1969), pp. 160-182. Reprinted with permission.

[1]Harriette Matteini, *Letters from Florence, Italy, in 1866* (New Haven: Fanny Winchester Hotchkiss, 1893) pp. 52-59.

cited a veritable tumult. "Give it to him! give it to him,"
was cried out from the infuriated crowd, "He is one of the
doctors paid by the municipality to poison the poor pe-
ple," and had not the carabineers interfered for his protection, he would have been torn in pieces.

In addition to these local practitioners of questionable popular
repute, modern scientific advice and health treatment were also available on a more extensive scale in such large cities as Palermo and Naples. The peasant—isolated from the blessings of civilization and
content with his primitive answers to health problems—had little
opportunity to test the validity of such notions.

Folk medicine had one great advantage among others in the eyes of
the peasantry: it cost little or nothing. The peasant could make diagnoses and prescribe the pills and potions he compounded from the
abundant materials available in the fields and woods. Since the herbalist competed with every good housewife, he was in demand only to
meet the most unusual emergencies, to supply pills and potions of
mysterious content. The barber's role as a bloodletter was firmly established. In competition with the legitimate physicians, some of the
old magicians and witches tended to take on airs, to develop into
what in commonly called in this country a quack or charlatan. References in the following discussion develop our conception of the
work of these specialists.

The traditions of folk medicine shed significant light upon the
processes of cultural evolution and upon the functioning of the human mind. Despite their variance from the findings of scientists,
their efficacy makes their persistent survival no great source of wonder. The following excerpts from a defense of the primitive healer[2]
places the whole matter in a sympathetic, a more accurate,
perspective:

Scientific medicine is oriented to deal with biologically
induced or "organic" ailments. It leaves socially or mentally induced or "functional" complaints largely to others—to psychiatrists, to faith healers, to quacks. The
orientation of primitive medicine was exactly the reverse.
Few of the shaman's patients suffered from organic disease; the vast majority came to him with some social or
psychological problem to solve. Although phrased, to be
sure, in terms of witchcraft or some similar theory of super-
natural causation, these problems were ordinarily soluble
by a person possessing insight and an intimate knowledge
of personalities and personal relationships in a small
community. Even with us, the general practitioner in a

[2] "Give the Medicine Man His Due," *Bulletin of the Associates in the Science of Society*, New Haven, March 1937, Vol. VI, No. 3, pp. 6-8, pp. 7-8 quoted.

small town often succeeds, through personal familiarity
with his patients and with the community situation, where
a better trained but impersonal city specialist fails. The
shaman has all the advantages of the "family doctor."
Like the latter, he is more than a physician; he is a practical student of human relations . .
If medicine has a lesson to learn from anthropology, it
is this: that scientific medicine will begin to approach the
art of the shaman in effectiveness when it becomes not only
a biological, but also a social and psychological, science.

Faith in their practices or in the magical power of the witches made
up, in many cases, for the inadequacy of their procedures.

Folk diagnoses were typically based on superficial external characteristics, formed into folk sayings. One group of the more general of
these bore resemblance to the saying that the "wicked look like devils,
and the good like angels." These pat statements of relationships included the following: "The red-haired are hot-tempered and deceitful." "There were two faithful ones with red hair, Jesus Christ and
the Calf of Sorrento." (The latter was the heifer that kept the Christ
Child warm in the manger. A statue of it stands at Sorrento.) Hair on
the body denoted strength, but too much hair gave one the characteristics of a savage. "The eye that does not see bespeaks the heart that
does not feel." "Tall men have little enterprise." (The ethnocentrism
of this latter statement is apparent.) "The face without color is false."
"God save us from a hairy woman!" "He who has long ears will live
long." "The fat woman is sterile." A hooked nose in a livid face was
the most outstanding indication that a person had the Evil Eye. Thick
lips indicated sensuality, and a large mouth, greed. A person with a
long neck was thought susceptible to tuberculosis. Small hands signified long life.

All knew these sayings. The ones that did not check with a type of
experience that was immediate and real at least were of a type bolstered
by striking coincidences, the sort of thing that substantiates beyond
question so many other folk superstitions. Since they exerted a powerful influence in defining the "man as he should be," they are highly
useful to social workers in more ways than merely in connection with
folk medicine. They furnish a means for fathoming the otherwise in-
explicable antipathies that issue forth in the remark, "I disliked him
from the very first."

The maladies known to the amateur practitioners of folk medecine
were somewhat limited in number. The respiratory diseases, especially tuberculosis, bronchitis, and pneumonia, while relatively rare,
were among the most dreaded. The early stages of tuberculosis were
seldom recognized, and an accurate diagnosis was thus possible only

when the patient had reached the last stages, beyond all help. On this account, Sicilians call it the *male sottile* (insidious sickness). A well-known remedy consisted of a decoction of fleas taken from the bed of the suffer—a device that suggests the modern theory of inoculation with one's own germs. Peasants popularly supposed that this malady was tansmitted through the blood. The people so feared tuberculosis that one who suspected that he had it tried to dissimulate the characteristic signs. He would not use a receptacle for his sputum but would spit rather on the floor (usually earthen) in the usual manner of healthy persons. The hot dry air and bright sunshine of the southern climate prevented the disease from becoming more general.

Various maladies involving high fever, such as malaria, typhoid (commonly confused with typhus), and rheumatic fever, were of common occurrence. Their causes were not understood. This situation is characterized by the fact that they believed "the symptoms are the illness itself."[3] When symptoms appeared that they could recognize, they were ready to treat the disease itself, not to attempt to prevent its further development.

Contagious diseases of childhood were quite prevalent in Italy. As in many other countries, mothers looked upon them as inevitable and even desirable experiences for their children. They therefore exposed them to such sicknesses in order to produce a "mild attack." This was done in the case of measles, chicken pox, and scarlet fever. Smallpox was so general that the peasants thought no one could escape it. A Sicilian proverb states that "a girl cannot be termed beautiful until she has had smallpox"; that is, until one could determine whether or not it would destroy her beauty.[4] Of the non-infectious diseases, cholera infantum and other intestinal ailments were the most common. Though children were nursed for two or more years, they were also given the same food as adults after a few months—a diet predisposing them to this type of sickness.

Two cures were current for children that had chronic illness. One, known as measuring, consisted in taking the child—the nature of the cure necessitated that it be a young child—and bringing its right leg up to its left arm and its left leg up to its right arm . The other treatment was to dress the patient in a miniature copy of the black habit of Saint Anthony, the patron of children. One sent to America from Italy by a child's grandmother was of black homespun wool and had a small hood. It was a dress rather than a habit, but this may have been

---

[3]Giuseppe Pitrè, *Biblioteca delle Tradizioni Popolari Siciliane* (Torino-Palermo; Palermo; Carlo Clausen, (1896) Vol. XIX, p. 189.

[4] *Ibid.*, p. 250.

because the patient was a girl. The child wore it ritualistically for a part of each day for several weeks.

Sometimes a woman who had a chronic disease would go from door to door to ask for money. The humiliation of this begging, which may or may not have been necessary, had a sacrificial connotation. When she collected enough, she took the money to a priest to have a mass said for her recovery. If a patient was too ill for such a "begging pilgrimage," some member of her family did it for her.

According to popular theories, many diseases—both external and internal—were caused by an excess of acid or salt in the system or by the accumulation of too much blood in one place: an inflammation. Another fundamental tenet in their philosophy of sickness was that every disease had to run a certain course; their lore definitely set the number of days for each illness. The people believed, therefore, that it was dangerous to give anything but very mild treatment lest the ailment be driven inward before the period had ended. Tradition, of course, furnished prescriptions for each disorder, and, when symptoms were so obvious that even the patient's family could recognize them, the matter was comparatively simple. When a diagnosis could not be made, however, various specifics were available for trial one after another. Provided that the patient did not die in the process—a confirmation, not a refutation, of popular theory—a remedy might finally be discovered. Following its administration, recovery always set in. When the remedy was successful, a suitable diagnosis might then be worked out. It never seemed to enter anyone's mind that death might be due to the conglomeration of treatment or that recovery took place in spite of them. Italians believed vaguely that the effects of all the wrong pills, potions, and charms were nullified by the application of the correct one. A physician, when called in, frequently had to content himself with competing with family experimentation.

The sources of cures in folk medicine were vegetable, animal, and mineral, ranking in number and alleged value in the order given. Among vegetables, the most common were olive oil, lemon juice, wine, vinegar, garlic, onion, lettuce, wild mallow, flour in the form of bread, rue, and tobacco, known as the *erba santa* (sacred plant). Sometimes the whole of an animal was utilized; sometimes only part. The principal creatures figuring in folk prescriptions were the wolf, chicken, viper, lizard, frog, pig, dog, mouse, and sea horse, all of course indigenous to Italy. The minerals valued included most commonly salt in the form of rock salt rather than sea salt, and such others as sulphur, a prized remedy found in great abundance in the mines along the south coast of Sicily. Certain bodily secretions, principally saliva, urine, mother's milk, blood, and ear wax, were also commonly employed. Saliva was thought most efficacious when taken from the mouth early in the morning before any food had been eaten. This was called "fasting spittle." Mothers used it to bathe the eyes of children with conjunctivitis. "Fasting spittle" from the mouth of a seventh male child was alleged to be a cure for impetigo. To ward off the Evil Eye, one spit three times behind the back of a woman of ill repute who has just kissed a newly born infant or behind a hunchback or a priest with an ugly face. To ward off contagion when visiting the sick, one had to spit at the house door with great force. If a woman was in labor and the process did not advance rapidly enough, a neighbor had to spit out of the window of the room. All ritual spitting had the power to break any magic spell that might have brought sickness or ill fortune of any kind.

Baldness was treated with an application of warm cow's urine. Sulphur and lemon juice were mixed as an ointment for scabies. A live frog fastened to the temple near the afflicted organ was thought to cure certain eye diseases. A slice of garlic held near the eye to make it water also served somewhat the same purpose. Slices of lemon or potato were bound on the wrists to reduce fever, a disorder that Italians looked upon as an illness unrelated to any other symptom. They thought that fever might be brought on by fright, a draught of air, disappointment, or sorrow—a theory that played some part in making Italian parents indulgent toward their young children. Sufferers from erysipelas wore a dried sea horse as an amulet. This disease was so dreaded that it was never mentioned by name. He who dared to mention it would promptly contract the ailment himself. People spoke of it merely as "the ugly beast." Like Saint Vitus' dance or chorea, erysipelas was believed to result from the entrance of an evil spirit into the body. It was cured by the repetition of magic formulas, one of the most typical of which is the following from Modica in Sicily:

> Lisina (erysipelas)! Going round the world,
> Dressed in red, walking in red.
> Lisina, where are you going?
> I am going to the sea, where I shall cast away the erysipelas
> of men.
> Go! Throw it in the thorns! Throw it in the sea,
> So that it may melt away as salt melts in water.

The wearing of a red scarf was a cure for this disease as well as for measles. Black silk scarfs were often put around the necks of those suffering from sore throat, held to be a forewarning of sickness. Neither the silk nor the warmth of the scarf was significant; the color served much the same function as the wearing of black for mourning, as an avoidance practice. There was no illness for which there was not required some oil, water, or a miraculously effective loaf of bread of peculiar design.

Bleeding, cupping, and scarifying were common therapeutic measures. Barbers carried out the first of these operations with a lancet or leeches. They also performed, with no other authority than that granted by traditional usage, such commonplace surgical operations as vaccination, cautery, the setting of fractures, the treatment of minor dislocations, and the opening of abscesses.

Tumors were spoken of as "closed melons," the true nature of which could not be ascertained. According to popular opinion, cancer was an animal that crept through the body and devoured the flesh on its way. Since they did not believe such internal growths could be cured, no interference with them should be attempted. This notion survives in this country in the strong opposition of old-fashioned Italians to hospital treatment for these disorders. External growths, on the other hand, were a different matter. They required varied but immediate attention.

Venereal diseases were called the "French sickness" or the "woman's sickness." Because of their nature, in Italy as in this country the advice of quacks and magicians was more frequently sought by victims than that of a legitimate physician. Contact with a virgin was held to be an unfailing cure for gonorrhea. In Sicily, however, the problem that confronted sufferers was where to find a virgin who would have intercourse with a man outside of wedlock. The faithfulness of Sicilian women was proverbial, and their daughters were strictly supervised in all that they did. Dr. Giuseppe Pitrè,[5] the Italian folklorist and physician, states that the only two instances of this treatment to come under his observation involved definitely feebleminded girls.

Worms were a common complaint among children. This was probably due to the use of night soil as a fertilizer. Many cases were also diagnosed as worms that were actually some other type of stomach or intestinal disturbance. The following Sicilian charm was used as a specific against such ailments:

> Saint Cosimo and Damiano,
> You are the sovereign doctors.
> Saint Elias was also a heavenly doctor.
> The worms in this circle [drawn about a child's stomach]
> Are all evil creatures.

[5]*Ibid.*, p. 463.

Kill them all.
Keep them from his little heart.
For Jesus' sake,
Cast them out and let them come no more.[6]

Cosimo and Damiano were twin saints who were supposed to have been physicians and were therefore regarded as the patrons of medicine. Their aid was frequently invoked in troublesome illnesses. A cross made in ink on a child's abdomen was another valuable specific against worms.

Nervousness, hysteria, and mental diseases of all kinds were attributed to the entrance of an evil spirit into the body. It lived in the body until it was cast out by making its abiding place so unpleasant that it was constrained to leave. This prompted the physical abuse of the sufferers, shaking and beating them and making horrible faces at them. In earlier times, the treatment was even more drastic. Doctor Pitrè,[7] upon witnessing the driving out of spirits in this way in 1898 in the Church of San Filippo de Calatabianco, was divided between a violent desire to laugh at the facial contortions of the populace and a sense of horror at the cruelty of the whole proceeding. If he laughed, he knew full well that the people would stone him.

If girls past puberty exhibited nervousness, their relatives thought it due to their need for a husband; the cure was to find one as soon as possible. Since a certain amount of nervous instability was not unusual in adolescent girls, this method of dealing with it was one of the considerations that prompted early marriage among Italians.

The South Italians believed that the intellect was the gift of God. When a person became insane through its removal, God had taken back his gift as a punishment. Insanity, however, might also be due to such an influence as that of the Evil Eye. In such a case, a witch who had the particular knowledge necessary to cope with the situation was called in. Some of the charms she would use had an obviously Christian origin, as has this example:

In the name of the Father and of the Holy Trinity.
Two eyes have harmed you,
May three person relieve you:
Father, Son, and Holy Spirit.
Away with envy and iniquity,
May they scorch and burn in the flaming fire.
Drive away all evil.
In this house there are four evangelists:
Luke, John, Mark, and Matthew.

[6]*Ibid.*, p. 397.
[7]*Ibid.*

It is significant that "Luke the Physician" was mentioned first; the usual order is, of course, Matthew, Mark, Luke, and John.

With all these possibilities for cure within comparatively easy reach, it is not a matter for surprise that the South Italian did not accept the physician with any eagerness. The populace reasoned that when it was a question of seeking advice regarding their health, they would be foolish to pay money only to learn something unpleasant. The sick and healthy alike thus surrounded themselves with all manner of devices and precautions with which to avert evil influences and unsalutary contacts. They drew, for instance, upon their almost endless stock of folk cures when friends and relatives fell ill. When death came despite all their cures and charms, they attributed it either to their failure to find the correct remedy or to the all-embracing will of God. For the latter, there was no alternative but patient and devout submission.

The South Italian feared greatly any exposure to draughts and chills. He thought these caused not only lung diseases but nervousness and even insanity. He was, nevertheless, even more fearful of the so-called *donne di fuora* (witches) who were always on the lookout for an open window to obtain entrance to a house, as the preceding chapter points out. Having entered, the mischief they could do knew no limits. They might leave the father and mother wracked with rheumatism when they awakened the next morning or the children scarred with some relic of their presence. Chapter IX describes the methods used for coping with these dangers.

An affliction traditionally confined to men was that known as *lupuminaru*. This changed them, under certain conditions, into a *lupo mannaro* (werewolf). After saying goodbye to his wife, a man might go out on Christmas Eve and be immediately transformed into such a wolf. When he met someone then on the street, he bit and even killed and sometimes ate him. The best defense against these persons so unwillingly made into horrible monsters was to carry a stick with a nail or pin in the end. When one stuck this stick into a werewolf and made the blood run, he was at once restored to his human form. And here is the "catch" that placed this fantasy upon a plane where it could not readily be tested: when discovered, the afflicted man always begged that his identity should not be revealed. A wife who knew her husband's condition always prepared a tub of cold water so that when he returned home he might duck his head in it and thus regain his former shape.

Although South Italians were afraid of hospitals, these have long been a part of the social life of their homeland. In fact, compared with these institutions, the well-trained physician was a much more recent addition. The general antipathy of Italians to hospitals was derived, therefore, from factors other than any that might be associated too closely with novelty. The first institutional care of the sick was provided in Italy by monks and nuns in monasteries. The sick who came under their care, however, were not those who had homes or relatives to look after them but were the wanderers, the homeless, the lepers— in short the dregs of mankind. Not infrequently, some of these patients were demented persons who might have homes and friends but had been turned out because of their supposed possession by evil spirit. The monks and nuns took them in out of sheer pity rather than because they were equipped in any way to cure them or to alleviate their sufferings except to the extent that kindness and shelter might help. Their openhandedness, of course, varied according to the extent to which some prince or noble had subsidized them or to which their establishment depended upon its own internal economy alone. Under such conditions, any sort of care was thought good enough for their patients.

Hospitals had their popular status lowered in numerous ways. The menials about such monasteries and convents were usually *orfano-trofi* (female orphans) from asylums who performed rough tasks in return for a scanty living and a small dowry. Without the latter, many of these unfortunate girls might never have been able to marry. During the past century in Sicily, too, in an effort to stamp out the profession of female mourners who forced their services contrary to law upon bereaved families, "the government sentenced persons detected in this practice to three months service in the hospital of the Cubba," in Palermo.[8] That many hospital attendants were thus once criminals did not add to the repute of the institutions.

The South Italians' attitude toward charity also helps to clarify the hospital situation. Nature had been grudging to them, and their labor often brought forth little or no result. They started out therefore with the philosophy that "what don't cost anything ain't no good," even though they bitterly realized that many things that did cost something were also frequently no good—unless one took into account the self-discipline afforded. Charity as dispensed by the rich and noble of the old times was given from a superfluity; it could not be doled out upon the basis of a sentiment that an Italian would think so foolhardy as he would this slogan of the Community Chest in this country: "Give Till It Hurts." Charity, as a result had little value to poor Italians, for the gifts were apt to be intermittent, irregular in amount, and frequently unsuited to the needs of recipients. This connotation of charity car-

---

[8]*Ibid.,* (Palermo; L. Pedone Lauriel di Carlo Clausen, 1889) Vol. XV, p. 238.

ried over into the popular attitude toward hospitals. Rationalizing that physicians naturally want something in return for skilled attention, peasants believed that free care was given only so that the bodies of the patients might thus be used experimentally. This notion, as we shall see, has been carried over to America.

In Sicily, a hospital for the insane was called an *ospizio* or *ospedale*, and therefore "when a man went to the hospital it signified he was insane."[9] The word *ospizio* also meant a convent or asylum, in the sense of an institution for the poor and dependent. An old Neopolitan curse runs, *Pozz' fini in dint ospedale"* ("May you end your days in the hospital"). This was held to be the worst fate that could befall a human being. News that a friend was going to the hospital elicited the cry, *"O Dio! Sant' Anton'!* How dreadful!" This reaction had no connection with the degree or nature of the patient's ailment.

The beliefs regarding death furnished still other reasons for antipathy toward hospitals. The souls of those who died in hospitals did not pass on at once to Purgatory because those establishments were believed to interfere with the proper funeral rites. These ghosts haunted the buildings where lay the sick and dying and struck terror into their hearts. When a patient talked in delirium, people thought he was conversing with the ghosts of former patients. This notion also gathered impetus from the fashion in which these institutions were forced to dispose of bodies. When a dead person's home was some distance away, Italy's climate necessitated such speedy burial that all was over in many instances before relatives arrived. Peasants believed, too, that when—especially during epidemics—a hospital became too crowded, nurses merely administered a draught reputed to have been the favorite poison of Catherine de' Medici, prepared for the purpose by accommodating physicians and apothecaries. An English woman,[10] living near Lecce in Apulia, illustrated this belief in 1881 with the following incident:

> During an epidemic of diphtheria . . . so many sufferers died, that one of our servants (a peasant) being attacked, we hoped to save her from a like fate by sending her to the hospital in the town. She was there delivered over to the care of the good nuns, who presided as hospital nurses; but such was her horror of the dreaded hospital, that she effected her escape, and, to our dismay, we beheld her returning on foot from the place—eight miles off—to which she had been conveyed, in an apparently dying condition, that very morning.

[9] *Ibid.*, (Torino-Palermo; Carlo Clausen, 1896) Vol. XIX, p. 428.

[10]"Country Life in Italy," *Cornhill Magazine*, 1881, p. 615.

Great stigma thus attached to hospitals in the South Italian peasant's mind not only because they were charity institutions and accepted all sorts of inmates, but still more because of the superstitions
he connected with them. When as a last resort a patient was coerced
into entering a hospital, he was generally near death, and the strain
of the long journey to the nearest institution plus his superstitious
dread of the place often hastened his inevitable end. "You only go to
the hospital," they asserted, "to die."

The *ospedoli* (hospitals) of Italy included then several different
types of institutions that served varied purposes and sprang from
disparate sources. They included the free hospitals for the poor that
compared in reputation to the sick wards of town poorhouses in New
England, though in many places their condition was far superior.
Three of the largest *ospedali* in Naples were the *Gesù e Maria*, the
Ospedale della Pace, and the *Dei Pelligrini*. Another, the *Incurabili*
(for incurables) was affiliated with the University of Naples. The
hospitals for the insane, such as the *Ospedale Santa Maria della
Pieta per le Malattie mentale* in the province of Rome, bore the same
generic label. The establishment for the care of the aged poor, however, was called the *Ospizio per i Vecchi* (Hospice for the Old) or
Ricoveri, a more modern term. When the inmates of this institution
became ill, they had to be sent to the free hospitals. These institutions
had two great advantages from the Italian standpoint, not found in
the corresponding organizations in this country: hospital visiting
was not restricted to certain hours of the day, and food might be
brought to the patients.

Those who could pay their rates had the privilege of suffering in
institutions that were not called *ospedali*. These were the *cliniche
private* (private clinics) and *case di salute* (sanatoria). The dispensaries for outpatients were free and called *cliniche,* but no one who
could pay would attend them or, for that matter, be permitted treatment in them. When a person who could afford medical treatment
was well enough to walk, he went to his physician's office; if not,
the physician called at his home, as in America. Private clinics were
named for the head surgeon in attendance who also acted as director.
The nurses were highly trained women who had to have attended both
high school and college. Such training might or might not be required of the nuns who nursed in the *ospedali,* many of whom were
French and belonged to the Order of Saint Vincent.

Generally speaking, then, clinics for inpatients were paid institutions; for outpatients, free dispensaries; and hospitals were always
free and for the very poor only.

IN AMERICA

The attitude of the first-generation immigrant toward medical care is much the same as it was in Italy. He came to this country well equipped, as he thinks, with the best of medical knowledge and of ideas on the preservation of his family's health. When his ideas are ridiculed, he examines the substitute offered, finds it far beyond his grasp, and rejects it as unsuited to his needs. The first concessions he makes are in part due to his inability to procure materials, such as wolf bones, from which to compound accustomed remedies. He can, however, wander into American fields and woods and return with a burden that includes a bewildering array of mushrooms and other foods as well as of plants, berries, and barks for his medicine cupboard. Wild fennel, deadly nightshade, wild mallow, mullein, dock, and sorrel are all grist to his mill. Plants that do not grow wild, like basil and rue, are cultivated either in his garden or in little wooden boxes and pots that he sets on his porch or fire escape. Such herbs, dried and mixed with powdered palm leaves or salt, are worn as amulets or, soaked in that powerful repellent of evil, olive oil, are used to massage dislocations and rheumatism, and for worms in children.

One learns about these things quite simply through exhibiting a sympathetic interest in what immigrants are raising or have hanging up to dry. One can thus gain an insight into an aspect of their lives that is little known but quite valuable to social workers, physicians, visiting nurses, etc. How else can one learn of the faith of Italian immigrants in a wild-mallow brew and in chicken soup for treating intestinal disturbances? They value the latter as a cathartic rather than as an easy source of nourishment for the ill. How else can one prepare oneself to cope with the disturbing belief of these immigrants that fever sufferers should be given hot rather than cooling drinks? This question involves, of course, a type of magic—the homeopathic—that has also prompted them to treat spider and snake bites by feeding a part of the creature itself to its victim.

Strangely enough, people who in Italy went so readily to a barber for bloodletting, strenuously object in this country to blood tests. The idea that blood drawn off by a barber is supposed to be unhealthy figures in this paradox. When tests are made in American clinics, on the other hand, the needle is inserted in a healty arm. The Italian has the conception of the connection between soul and blood found in Leviticus: "for the life of all flesh is the blood thereof." An epileptic declared that he had never had a convulsion until he gave some blood to a friend for a transfusion. This gave an evil spirit its chance to get into him. Italian children, like their parents, are very much afraid of spilling their blood and cry out loudly when pricked with a pin. Mothers often hesitate to have their children's blood tested because they know their offspring will be so terrified at the experience as to become ill. A mother who wished to cooperate with the school nurse suggested that each child have a sample of its blood drawn behind a screen; thus the other children would not see the blood. Another reason that enters into this antipathy is touched on in the first part of this chapter. Italians do not see the sense in meeting something unpleasant halfway through taking blood tests for diphtheria, syphilis, and tuberculosis. They argue that, since diseases largely run their own course anyway, it is better to leave all investigation into health questions until a condition becomes so obvious that it cannot be neglected. They use traditional precautions and hope for the best until action is practically forced upon them. The notion fits in well with their fatalistic ideas. *"Pazienza!"* they caution, "one should not expect too much of life!"

Dentists meet this obstacle, modified to relate to the teeth. Italians believe that it is useless to give dental care to first teeth, and, so far as second teeth are concerned, they are more likely to impute caries to "poor American air" than to incorrect diet. At any rate, when a tooth has reached a stage of decay where it demands treatment, it is soon enough to consider doing something about it. When a child lost his incisors in Italy, peasants blamed it on eating too much cheese!

Italians still keep sicknesses secret as long as they can. This applies especially to afflicted daughters. They are ashamed to let neighbors know of an incident that may impair the social status of a member of their family. A reputation for poor health affects unfavorably the value of girls as potential wives. This notion applies only mildly to boys. After all, boys need not worry about their "marketability." Anything that might impair the fertility of girls, however, may make even a satisfactory dowry useless.

The old ideas regarding pregnancy have undergone slight but significant variations in this country. The notion that a mother does not conceive while nursing continues to be held, as is a theory that bolsters this one: that a woman who does not conceive at regular periods during her child-bearing years will develop tumors. This prevents prolonged nursing from restricting reproduction and minimizes its own chances of being exploded as an inaccurate generalization. An American obstetrician suggests that the tumor theory may well be due to the fact that conditions militating against conception are unhealthy and not infrequently of a malignant nature. "It is funny," one hears young mothers lamenting, "how the old-fashioned women with large families seldom suffer from the ailments that we present-day women do." In further support of the tumor theory's application, a doctrine teaches that continence produces uterine disease, and gives rise to the conclusion that contraceptive practices bring on various unhealthy conditions, especially nervousness. This theory is related to the idea that the best cure for nervousness among adolescent girls is marriage. The prevalence of birth-control notions in this country and the social pressures that force them upon immigrants, whether they will or no, have given these theories considerable significance.

The posterity policy of these immigrants continues to affect the men, as well, in a way noteworthy in this connection. They believe that continence produces tuberculosis in them. The following incident illustrates the sort of problem presented by this belief:

> An Italian woman whose condition obliged her to observe absolute continence for a set period in order to regain her health, was finally prevailed upon to tell her husband of her need. After hearing the physician's report, he promised to do his best. After a few weeks, however, he arrived at a tuberculosis clinic with a specimen of sputum for examination. Fortunately, there was an enlightened person in authority at the clinic who took the man's belief at face value and promised further examination so long as the man continued to bring in specimens. Each examination, being negative, greatly relieved the Italian.

A physician's success in persuading children of Italian parentage to take medicine depends to a large extent on the trust the mother has in him. Since an Italian physician generally understands something of her cultural inhibitions she is more tractable in his hands than in an American's. Physicians of other cultural backgrounds, however, may succeed as well by sensing the nature of her defenses and using sympathy and patience to win her over. They must realize in particular that Italians believe that children—like animals—know instinctively what is good for them. When a child is forced to take medicine or food that is strange or even disagreeable, he is injured by it. This does not mean that all the old remedies of folk medicine were pleasant to take, but the mothers were so persuaded of their beneficial qualities that they were able to convince their children.

Italians have even less faith in those American specialists in ills of the psyche, the psychiatrists, than they have in our medical practitioners. Most first-generation immigrants place the psychiatrist on a level with their own witch doctors, the *maghi*. Some are afraid of him, and a few merely think it a waste of time to go and answer what they term a "lot of silly questions." The following instances may be regarded as typical of the former group:

> A woman consented to a psychiatric interview, even though she had no faith in the physician. She did so purely because she was fond of the visiting nurse and wished to please her. She arrived at the clinic with a large handbag clutched in her arms with which she was greatly preoccupied. Nothing could persuade her to part with it. "I tell you after," she confided mysteriously and went into the psychiatrist's office. When she came out, she opened the bag and exhibited a quantity of amulets against the Evil Eye. She had added all she could borrow from her neighbors to those possessed by her family. "The doctor," she triumphantly asserted, "he no hurt me."

Psychiatrists informed in the vagaries of Italian folklore can aid greatly in coping with problems that arise in this and other connections. Social workers, for example, soon discover that many Italians believe a "problem case" in a family brings more consideration and frequently more relief than might otherwise be expected. As an experienced woman frankly put it, "if you pretend you're nervous, you get more help."

The continuance of belief in the malevolence of witches in this country even unto the second and third generations, as the preceding chapter brings out, makes this a highly significant factor to be dealt with in medical and psychiatric treatments. Witches figure chiefly in explanations of ill-health among children. The following instance, told by the mother of a five-year-old girl who had had infantile paralysis followed by other illnesses, is instructive:

> The mother took her daughter to a *maga* (witch) and told what had happened. The child hid her face, and the *maga* pointed out, "I look like a devil to her, and she is frightened of me." This *maga*, said the informant, had lost two children and had sold her soul to the devil in return for the power to cure other people's children. The *maga's* purpose for doing this seemed rather vague, but the mother explained it as being due to her discontent with human limitations, a reason that is often advanced by Italians. "She talks with devils, but I think God will forgive her and give her back her soul for the good she does to others," the mother insisted.
>
> She told the *maga* that her little girl had been in the habit of sleeping between her parents. Apparently the

witches or, as the Neapolitans call them, the *iannare* had come in through the window and cast a spell on the child. "They would have harmed me and my husband, too," the mother sagely noted, "but they could not, because one of my ancestors once caught one of them and would not let her go until she promised not to harm my family for seven generations. I am the seventh. When we woke in the morning, my husband and I, we were black with bruises where the *iannare* had pinched us."

The *maga* rubbed the little girl with some salve, "mumbled something," and told the mother that at the crisis her child would have a sort of fit or spell. This all happened. The next night the child had a fit, and there was a frightful noise outside the window to which the mother listened in terror. Her husband slept through it all. The little girl was also under treatment by an Italian physician at the time who merely laughed at the witch's efforts, but the child recovered, and her parents gave the entire credit to the *maga*. They had only gone to the physician because the nurses at the hospital where the child had been treated at the time of the paralysis insisted upon it.

Americans who do not know the history of Italian hospitals can never fully appreciate the deep mistrust that these immigrants feel toward the corresponding institutions in this country. The red tape connected with admission and discharge adds to their bewilderment and makes the separation from the solicitude of relatives even more painful. The culmination of the admission process in the removal of their clothes not seldom fills them with despair. The diet then increases their discomfiture. When ill, they believe that the eating of some particularly attractive food—regardless of its ingredients—aids the cure. Even the attempts of well-meaning hospital dietitians fall short of their expectations. An actual South Italian dish would be too strong smelling for the modern hospital ward. A woman who had been in a hospital for some time without appearing to gain much headway confided to a friend that she "was being slowly poisoned by the meals."

Despite the arguments of nurses and physicians, Italians frequently take their relatives home or transfer them to a different hospital. Only in the case of public charges does this sometimes become known. Particularly when it becomes obvious to a person's connections and friends that an Italian will not recover, he is taken home as soon as possible. "Be sure to take him home," they caution; "you must not let him die in the hospital." This aversion to death in an institution includes even patients in private wards. Even though the latter might be thought to have the status of patients in Italian *cliniche private,* old ideas cannot be quickly uprooted, possibly because in America both charity and paying patients are usually housed under one roof. Hospitalization in a private room, however, generally arouses less opposition than in wards. Families not otherwise able to finance such a luxury even taken out loans at burdensome rates (42 per cent per annum) in order to meet the expense. They invest such debts with the superstitious notion that failure to repay them speedily may "bring the sickness back." These loans frequently lie at the bottom of the family situation which sends people to the "family welfare."

When a social worker attempts to coerce a family into sending a member to a hospital, an obstacle arises in more than a few cases that the following example illustrates:

> A man whose wife was quite ill could not bring himself to make the decision alone to send her to a hospital. His physician urged the move, but he went to his favorite brother for counsel. The latter advised against it, much to the regret of the social worker on the case. Discouraged at her failure, she went to the man's brother herself to see if she could find and answer his objection. He listened at length and apparently with understanding to her story and then gave this as his opinion: "Perhaps you are right. Who can say? But me, I cannot advise it. People would say I was jealous and trying to get rid of my sister-in-law. If she died, everyone would blame me."

Mutual suspicion and jealousy, so marked a trait of Italian culture, thus play fundamental roles again here in the rationalizations of these people.

One outstanding exception to the culturally determined dread of hospital care crops out in this country in the case of childbirth. Although many women still prefer the family physician or a midwife and home confinements, even some among those Italian women who appear to be most retarded in adjustment to American mores are eager to have their babies born in hospitals. They want to leave shortly after delivery, nevertheless, even though nurses argue, "Why did you come to the hospital? We thought you understood that you would have to stay at least a week." The nurses do not understand one of the prime reasons for these women coming to the hospital. A hospital confinement furnishes a means of avoiding the traditional sexual intercourse rites at the onset of labor—a practice rarely seen nowadays. When the time for this dangerous procedure has passed, an additional stay in the hospital merely means a longer period of subjection to a strange and annoying routine.

Despite the old derogatory beliefs regarding hospitals, the high cost of institutional care is one of the chief deterrents to its wider adoption by the Italian. Equally important is the fact that he has by no means become accultured to institutional care either in sickness or in old age. He has a strong feeling that the most significant moments of his life should take place under his own roof. To him the bed and the house remain symbolical of family life, and to dissociate them from such important occurrences as birth, marriage, and death is to undermine the very foundations of his culture.

V

Education

The Italian Child in the American School

INTRODUCTION

The immigrants of the "new migrations" (1882-1921) differed not only in language and customs from earlier American residents, but arrived during those decades when the American "common school" had largely evolved into its framework of a "genuine part of that [American] life, standing as a principal positive commitment of the American people."[1] The Italian immigrant child was the child of his own immigrant subcommunity within the American city in which his parents had settled. In this immigrant subcommunity, the child was securely related to an organized social life which largely duplicated the customs and mores which his parents had transplanted to America.

It was the American school which saw its role essentially as one of enforced assimilation. Cubberley, the educational historian and a leading educational theoretician for the period, makes this vividly clear: "Everywhere these people [immigrants] tend to settle in groups or settlements and to set up their own national manners, customs and observances. Our task is *to break up* their groups and settlements, to assimilate or amalgamate these people as a part of the American race, and to implant in their children, so far as can be done, the Anglo-Saxon conception of righteousness, law, order, and popular government, and to awaken in them reverence for our democratic institutions and for those things which we as people hold to be of abiding worth."[2]

The American school has not been spared in the new attentions and scrutinies which are recasting the text of American history in

[1]Lawrence A. Cremin, *The American Common School: An Historic Conception* (New York: Bureau of Publications, Teachers College, Columbia University, 1951), p. 219.

[2]Ellwood P. Cubberley, *Changing Conceptions of Education*(Boston: Houghton Mifflin, 1909), p. 16.

the revisionist examinations which have begun to appear. Colin Greer has brilliantly repudiated the myth which suggested that American schools took the backward poor, the ragged, ill-prepared immigrant children who huddled in the cities, educated them, and molded them into the homogeneous productive middle class that is America's strength and pride. The documentary record indisputably establishes the unfortunate truth of Colin Greer's observations:

> Every schoolchild and certainly every education major learns the same heart-warming story about the history of our public schools. The public school system, it is generally claimed, built American democracy. It took the backward poor, the ragged, ill-prepared ethnic minorities who crowded into the cities, educated and Americanized them, and molded them into the homogeneous productive middle class that is America's strength and pride. But that story is simply not true. Worse yet, the "Great School Legend" is largely responsible for today's schools' resistance to needed change. Having examined the records of a number of major urban school systems, I will attempt to report here the facts obscured by this legend, and to suggest the consequences of our misguided faith in the schools. The rate of school failure among the urban poor, in fact, has been consistently and remarkably high since before 1900. The truth is that the immigrant children dropped out in great numbers--to fall back on the customs and skills their families brought with them to America. It was in spite of, and *not* because of, compulsory public education that some eventually made their way.[3]

[3]Colin Greer, *The Great School Legend: A Revisionist Interpretation of American Public Education* (New York: Basic Books, 1972), pp. 3-4. In a foreword to the Greer book, the sociologist Herbert J. Gans notes: "Today, only the successful immigrants are remembered, which is why we can indulge in a romantic view of the old lower East Side and other historic slums, ignoring that they were terrible places, probably more terrible than they are today," and Gans relates the immigrant experience to the problems of the contemporary poor: "Moreover, one of the most important implications which can be drawn from Colin Greer's study is that in the past, poor people did not succeed economically through the school, but that as they succeeded economically, they could exert pressure on their children—and the teachers—to make sure that their children would succeed in school. This is also one of the implications of the Coleman Report, and suggests that educational success follows upon economic success, not the other way around. Consequently, unless the schools are able to reverse their historic role, which I doubt, the only way today's poor can escape is through the economy, and only then will they be able to see to it that their children can succeed in school. Educators like Colin Greer need an educational strategy against poverty, but for those of us who are concerned with an overall strategy, his book reconfirms the belief that such a strategy must be mainly economic. Poverty is likely to be eliminated only if the economy and the federal government jointly create decent, secure and well-paying jobs for today's unemployed and underemployed, buttressed by whatever on-the-job training is necessary and backed up by adequate income grants for adults who can not work. Only when such a program has created a generation of economically secure graduates from poverty will it be possible for the public school to do the job that the great school legend so wrongly claims it once did."

No overall programs were developed in the schools to aid any particular group. Although there was little agreement as to what Americanization was, the schools were committed to Americanize (and to Anglicize) their charges. Ellwood P. Cubberley's *Changing Conceptions of Education* (1909), which Lawrence A. Cremin characterizes as a "typical progressive tract of the era,"[4] saw the new immigrants as "illiterate, docile, lacking in self-reliance and initiative and not possessing the Anglo-teutonic conceptions of law, order, and government" and the schools' role was (in Cubberley's view) "to assimilate and amalgamate." As I have noted elsewhere:

> The schools reflected the attitudes prevalent at the time of the great immigrations which, in essence, held that the immigrant was a one-generation problem. Assimilation was an educational process, and if immigrant children got a "good" education, the parents would be assimilated with them. In the process, parents and community were neglected if not ignored. There is some doubt that the school acted as the main device through which the child was assimilated, and if so, it did its job poorly. Certainly, the schools did not ameliorate the plight of the immigrant parent. If anything they provided little opportunity to the immigrant parent to obtain information as to what the aims and objectives of the schools were, and in this respect the schools and the parent were in continuing conflict. If New York City was typical, the urban schools provided no system-wide policy which dealt with the educational needs of immigrant children; and where programs were fashioned to meet these needs, there was no attempt made to differentiate between immigrant groups (e.g., the experience of Italian and Jewish children in New York City strongly documents this failure); instead children were lumped under the rubrics "native-born," or "foreign-born". If one discounts the multiplicity of disfunctional programs, rampant discrimination, authoritarian prejudice, it is still difficult to attribute the general patterns of failure to immigrant children or their parents. The blame for the failure lies almost wholly within the school and the dominant society which shaped its programs and articulated its cultural ideals.[5]

[4] Lawrence A. Cremin, *The Transformation of the School: Progressivism in American Education, 1876-1957* (New York: Alfred A. Knopf, 1961), p. 68.

[5] F. Cordasco, "The Children of Immigrants in the Schools: Historical Analogues of Educational Deprivation," *The Journal of Negro Education*, vol. 42 (Winter 1973), pp. 52-53. This article is a somewhat revised version of the introductory essay prepared for the reissue of *Children of Immigrants in Schools*, vol. 29-33 of *Report of the Immigration Commission:* 41 vols. (Washington: Government Printing Office, 1911; Republished Metuchen, N. J.: Scarecrow Reprint Corp., 1970), a vast repository of data on the educational history of immigrant children in America, with detailed analyses of backgrounds, nativity, school progress, and home environments of school children in 32 American cities.

It is against these backgrounds that the materials in this section have been assembled. The anonymous "America's Interest in the Education of Italian Children" (1907), grimly poses the question: are Italian children a menace to America? A generation later, the question remained unanswered;[6] and Leonard Covello's "A High School and Its Immigrant Community"(1936) recast the question by relating it to the community-centered high school he was developing in the Italian community of East Harlem; and the conclusions from the investigations (1942) of Joseph W. Tait clearly suggest, even at this late date, that a pervasive uncertainty surrounded the relationships of the American school and the minority child. It is in the chapter drawn from Leonard Covello's classic work, *The Social Background of the Italo-American School Child* (1944), that the complexities of the encounters of the Italian child and the American school are most fully delineated. Covello provides a complete discussion of southern Italian family mores, and the effect of these customs as transplanted to America on the school situation in the United States, as typified in East Harlem, New York City. It is the very substance out of which the contexts of conflict and acculturation evolve for the Italian child in the American school, and the matrix in which the responses of the immigrant child are to be understood.

[6]In 1924, the New York Association for Improving the Condition of the Poor issued a monograph on *The Growth and Development of Italian Children in New York City* (Publication No. 132) which reported on the physical condition of Italian children (*i.e.*, stature; weight; dentition; seasonal variation in growth) with the clinical objectivity and thoroughness of a veterinarian atlas. Typical conclusions: "So far as average height and weight of children at particular age periods may be relied upon as evidence of physical development, we may therefore conclude that Italian children in New York City are retarded in their development, for they are both shorter and lighter than the common run of children throughout the country. Moreover, these children are less underweight than underheight. Indeed when we consider average weight for given height, the Italian children are actually heavier up to ten years of age. The retardation, therefore, is chiefly in skeletal growth.

"The apparent underdevelopment of the Italian children is probably due to two factors, one concerned with heredity and the other with environment. Practically all of the parents of these children are natives of Southern Italy where people of short stock predominate, so that it is fair to assume that the children have inherited a short, stocky build. The district in which these children live is one of the most congested in New York City. While few of the families are actually destitute, family income in most cases is inadequate to supply a proper standard of living. Inadequate income and the inability of Italian immigrants to adjust themselves to living conditions in American cities have militated against the health of the children. Thorough physical examinations of large numbers of these children have revealed serious physical defects. In early childhood rickets of a severe form is unusually prevalent. Nearly forty per cent of the children are found on the doctor's diagnosis to be undernourished. Pneumonia and other respiratory diseases are unusually prevalent and result in a large number of deaths of children under five. Therefore, while presumably inheriting a short, stocky build, the Italian children living in congested quarters of New York City because of adverse living conditions are retarded in their growth and development." (pp. 17-18)

AMERICA'S INTEREST
IN THE EDUCATION
OF ITALIAN
CHILDREN *

Of all the nationalities represented in our regular influx of immigrants the Italian has, beyond a doubt, been the object of the most varied discussion. While not blind to his virtues, it has been his faults that have been most vigorously asserted. During the past year or two the Italian periodicals have been taking up the discussion, pro and con. A noteworthy contribution to this discussion which is very favorable to the Italian immigrant appears in the *Rassegna Nazionale* (Florence). The author severely criticises the Italian in the United States for his lack of loyalty to his fellows and of pride in his nationality. In the article there are some interesting statistics.

Of the Italian emigrants who land in New York, 45 per cent are males between fifteen and forty-five: more than 45 per cent come from southern provinces, and among the men 45 per cent are unskilled laborers. Now, owing to various peculiar conditions in America (compulsory education, which keeps boys in school until they are fourteen years old and turns them out too "educated" to be willing to do manual labor, the immense amount of gigantic constructions of subways, office-buildings, bridges, etc.), the demand for unskilled labor in America is practically unlimited. These workmen, therefore, obtain work without the necessity of going more than 200 or 250 miles from New York, and prosper accordingly at once. From among these, however, come the fluctuating class of southern Italians, who, by their inveterate love of country, cannot settle here definitely. They spend eight or nine months in America and return to Italy for the rest of the year. In 1903 more than 98,000 returned to Italy, and in 1904 more than 134,000. The permanent class that remains is the bulk of Italian-American citizens which need to be reckoned with as a factor in the future of Amer-

*Review of Reviews, vol. 36 (1907), pp. 375-376.

ica. Among them, although they are often very illiterate, there are no anarchists, no members of the Black Hand or other criminal societies, and almost no criminals of any kind. They are ignorant, but almost without exception honest. That the knowledge of the alphabet is no guarantee of virtue is shown by the fact that between January 1 and March 31, 1905, there were arrested in New York 44,014 persons, of whom only 1175 were illiterate, or only 2.6 per cent.

THE TESTIMONY OF STATISTICS

The author refutes positively, by means of statistics, those who condemn Italians as degenerate, drunken, lazy, dirty, and prone to crime. If those accusations were true anywhere, he says, they would be true in New York, where there are crowded together 450,000 Italians. He then makes a comparison between these 450,000 Italians and the 300,000 Irish resident in New York.

To begin with the accusation of pauperism, in 1904 there were on Blackwell's Island 1564 Irish paupers and only sixteen Italians. Of suicides eighty-nine were Irish and twenty-three Italians. On May 1, 1902, there were in New York 282,804 Irish and 200,549 Italians. Which of the two varieties of adoptive citizens contributed more to crime? For drunkenness 1281 Irish were arrested and only 513 Italians. Next to the Russian Jew, the Italians are the most temperate of all nationalities immigrating to this country.

The author admits that in one class of crimes the Italians have an unenviable priority,—in deeds of violence committed without premeditation, from jealousy or anger.

Nevertheless, in the main, all the statistics show them to be a law-abiding people. The Sicilian Mafia and the Black Hand Society form the only exception to this rule; and the power and extent of these coalitions are grotesquely exaggerated in the popular fancy of the Americans. As to the filthy habits attributed to Italians, this charge is for the most part unwarranted. The municipal inspectors of tenement houses in New York report that Italian tenement houses are much cleaner than those of the Jews or the Irish. One of the typical Italian quarters is inhabited by 1075 families, but is kept in a state comparatively hygienic, since the rooms contain on an average but one or two persons. "As far as the social evil goes, the Italian women are pre-eminently virtuous. Out of 750,000 emigrants to America during the last four years only one woman has been arrested for immoral conduct."

ARE ITALIAN SCHOOL CHILDREN A MENACE TO AMERICA

On the face of it an article on the hygienic condition of the common schools in Italy would be of no interest to Americans, but when it is remembered that there are arriving every day at our ports hundreds and thousands of children and adults who bear on them and bring to us the results of those schools it will be seen that their condition is of grave concern to us.

In particular those interested in the anti-tuberculosis campaign will find a painful interest in an article in the *Nouva Antologia* (Rome) by Signor Alessandro Lustig. He reports the results of an investigation undertaken by him at the request of the Anti-Tuberculosis Congress which recently convened in Milan. The schools investigated were chosen from every region of Italy.

The state of the schools is in almost every case disheartening, and even alarming. Any one who knows the lack of hygienic knowledge and equipment in the Italian schools will not be surprised to learn that in the matter of statistics of mortality for consumption the students of Italy stand first of all. Not only do the schools fail to aid the pupils in their healthy development; they positively injure it.

Very few of the school-buildings were constructed for that purpose, and only 50 per cent of the majority have been adapted in the slightest to their present use. The few buildings constructed expressly for school purposes are often not well adapted for children, and are used for other purposes as well. As for the others, they are generally indecent, crowded, airless, and located in positions unfavorable to the health and morals of their inmates. In one province, out of 217 buildings, 84 (or 35 per cent.) are excessively damp. In some provinces there are many schools where there is no water in the school buildings, nor any form of water-closets. In one province 70 per cent. of the buildings have none. Almost without exception, the schoolrooms in the elementary schools have insufficient cubic air-space, are badly lighted, and filled with germ-laden dust. In one province 70 per cent

of the schoolrooms have no means of warming them, are
without light, damp and dirty, and 81 per cent have no
water. The seats are instruments of torture, the cause of
many curved spines and of eye troubles, which are very
prevalent in the secondary schools. There is no chance
for physical education, since almost none of the schools
have proper playgrounds, which are neither dusty nor
wet.

Such being the state of the schools, it is not surprising that sanitary
supervision by the state is unknown. The law indeed makes some
provision for state regulation. These regulations demand that (1)
every school shall be thoroughly disinfected at least once a year, and
(2) that every school shall be visited at least once a month in ordinary
times and oftener if necessary by a government health inspector.
These regulations are, as a rule, totally disregarded. The author says
that it is not to be hoped that a radical transformation can take place
at once, nor even for a long time, though he sketches lightly the program that would be desirable,—school lunches, recreations, hospitals, Alpine colonies, and a better instruction in school hygiene for
teachers. But certain elementary improvements should be made at
once, and must be made if the rapid spread of tuberculosis among
school-children is to be checked.

GOVERNMENT EFFORTS TO LOWER THE
PERCENTAGE OF ILLITERACY

In an article in the *Nuova Antologia* (Rome) Signor Maggiorino
Ferraris, deputy in the Italian Chamber, writes of the earnest efforts
which are made in Italy to combat the evil of illiteracy. He says:

For many years Italy, with its ignorant masses, has fed
the lowest levels of the great cities of the world, of Europe
and of the United States. At the present day, in the press,
in books, and sometimes even in the foreign legislatures,
there has been discussion of the comparative merits of
Italian emigration and of that of the yellow and black
races. This is a hard truth brought home to many of our
fellow-countrymen in foreign lands: and in Italy it is only
ignored by the rhetoricians, who do not travel, who do
not know foreign languages, who do not read,—and even
boast of this,—a single newspaper or a single book pub-

lished beyond the Alps. This does not depend upon any inferiority of race; far otherwise. The Italian emigrant who has studied or who has at least grown up among intelligent surroundings, wherever he may go, will become a capable workman, a merchant, an active member of the community, and will do honor both to himself and to his native land.

Signor Ferraris regards an annual expenditure of 5 lire per capita as an irreducible minimum to assure adequate primary instruction. At present the communes expend annually 80,000,000 lire and the state 17,000,000. In order to reach the sum of 5 lire per capita, the state must provide each year 65,000,000 lire additional.

LEONARD COVELLO

A HIGH SCHOOL
AND ITS IMMIGRANT
COMMUNITY—
A CHALLENGE AND AN
OPPORTUNITY*

In New York City, the public-school system occupies not only an important strategic position but also a unique position in the life of the community. It is the only social agency that has direct contact with practically every family within the community and the education law makes this contact with the family compulsory from the early childhood to the late adolescence of every boy and girl. This is important when one realizes that the public school system functions in a city which has a population of close to seven million people, of whom one million two hundred thousand go to school.

In a city of the size of New York, with a population made up mainly of comparatively recent migrations from every nook and corner of the world, a study of the composition and characteristics of the population is a vital necessity.

The total population of New York City, according to the United States Census for 1930, was 6,930,446. An analysis of the population figures of this Census brings out certain significant and educationally important facts, as follows:

Native stock
1,505,200 or 21.7 per cent of the population
is *native white* of *native parents*

Foreign stock
2,788,625 or 40.2 *per cent is native white* of
foreign-born parents
2,293,400 or 33.1 per cent is *foreign born*
343,221 or 5.0 per cent is Negroes and others

Journal of Educational Sociology, vol. 9 (February, 1936), pp. 333-346.

The fact that 73 per cent of the population of New York City is of foreign stock is, of course, very significant.

In general the composition and characteristics of the population of New York as shown by the United States Census of 1930 are true for the East Harlem community in Manhattan in which the main building of the Benjamin Franklin High School is located. The high school draws its student body largely from this community whose total population is 233,400, according to the United States Census of 1930. Of this total 20,888 or 9.0 per cent are native white of native parents. Of the foreign stock, 13,000 or 5.6 per cent are Porto Rican; 86,174 or 35.7 per cent are native white of foreign parents; 83,345 or 36.9 per cent are foreign born; 29,422 or 12.7 per cent are Negroes; and 571 or .1 per cent other groups. As these figures show, in the section where the Community Advisory Council of the school is concentrating its efforts, 78.2 per cent of the residents is of foreign stock. It is estimated that about a third of the population is of Italian origin. There is also a rapidly increasing population of Spanish-speaking peoples, mainly Porto Rican, while there is, and has been, a correspondingly rapidly diminishing population of people of Jewish, Irish, and German stock.

These facts are educationally important. The school, in order to be effective, must keep constantly in mind the fact that it is dealing with a heterogeneous population, new to American soil, transplanted here in haste, and only now beginning to take root. This new immigration is still struggling with a bilingual problem, is still facing all types of difficulties in trying to adapt itself to the varying, quickly shifting, and confusing standards of social behavior. It is still living under emotional stress because it has been unable to adjust itself adequately to the speed and complexity of our industrial and commercial life. It is still incapable of adjusting itself to the tempo of American life. This condition is further aggravated by the fact that these communities are often isolated from the more wholesome forces in our American life. These things create problems difficult to solve and present both an obligation and an opportunity to the school.

The problem of juvenile delinquency, for example, is one that baffles all the forces of organized society. The police, the home, the church, and the school seem helpless in meeting the situation. The causes of delinquency are many and varied but one fact seems constantly evident, viz.: that the highest rate of delinquency is characteristic of immigrant communities. This fact obtrudes into every consideration of this problem. It is true, however, that the delinquent is usually the American-born child of foreign-born parents, not the immigrant himself. Delinquency, then, is fundamentally a *second generation* problem. This intensifies the responsibility of the school, the one organization most definitely charged with the duty of molding youth into a better type of citizen. In juvenile delinquency and crime, the economic problem is an extremely important factor but it is not, by far, *the* most important factor. The most important cause is to be found in the weakening of social controls in these communities—controls that were operative in the homelands and in the communities from which the foreign born came. That fact has definitely increased juvenile delinquency and it has drawn into the criminal class more and more of the youth of the country.

In these immigrant communities, composed of foreign-born parents and American-born children, the most critical period in the life of the family is that in which the children reach adolescence and on through the adolescent period. This is the high-school age. It is the age when the so-called American idea of "living one's own life," which the immigrant-born children have absorbed from their American environment, begins to clash with the European idea of family solidarity, of obedience, of respect for elders, and of subservience to family needs and requirements.

The real educational problem lies in the emotional conflicts that are particularly tormenting to the boy or girl whose parents still have both feet planted firmly and deeply in centuries of European tradition and custom. With these established traditions and customs, the younger generation is often in conflict. There is often a feeling of scorn and shame in the children of the foreign born because of the pressure of adverse opinion from without their own racial group. This often produces an anti-social attitude that is dangerous to the boy and dangerous for the community. This antisocial attitude is largely the fertile breeding ground for the crime and delinquency that present such a disturbing problem for school and society.

THE SCHOOL AND FORTY MILLION NEW AMERICANS

The situation thus briefly outlined is not peculiar to any one community alone. Conditions of this nature prevail not only in many communities in New York City but in practically all industrial centers where the new immigrant has sought work and tried to found a home. Out of a total population of about 125,000,000, approximately 40,000,000—or one third of the people of the United States—are of foreign stock. For these people in their foreign communities a more wholesome community life must be evolved. It is difficult to do this, particularly at this late stage. The problem of assimilation and

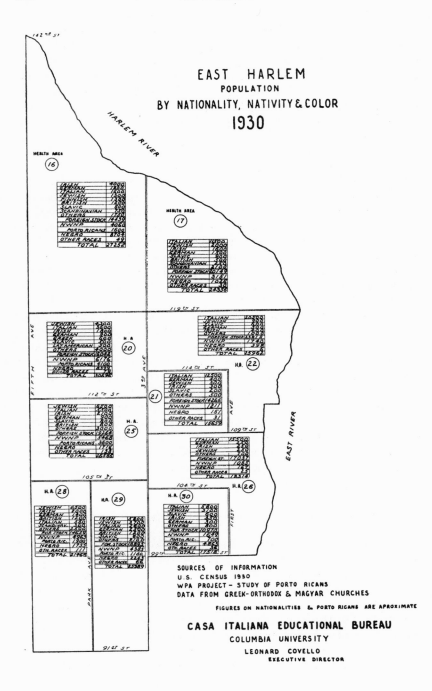

EAST HARLEM
POPULATION
BY NATIONALITY, NATIVITY & COLOR
1930

SOURCES OF INFORMATION
U.S. CENSUS 1930
WPA PROJECT — STUDY OF PORTO RICANS
DATA FROM GREEK-ORTHODOX & MAGYAR CHURCHES

FIGURES ON NATIONALITIES & PORTO RICANS ARE APROXIMATE

CASA ITALIANA EDUCATIONAL BUREAU
COLUMBIA UNIVERSITY
LEONARD COVELLO
EXECUTIVE DIRECTOR

of cultural harmony, the development of a wholesome national consciousness in the midst of great cultural diversity, the clash of racial and nationality interests are really basic problems—and they must be the chief concern of the school because to the school is entrusted the education of the future citizens.

Unfortunately, the school, in the past, has failed to realize fully the importance of these problems; neither has it perceived definitely the extent of its influence in arriving at a happy solution of the difficulties peculiar to the immigrant's unfixed and unrecognized American status.

Let us for a moment ask: What role has the public school played in immigrant or foreign communities in which it is located? What role is it playing today? Has the school really felt the life of the community pulsating beyond its four walls? Has it made an attempt to realize the problems and the difficulties with which the immigrant neighborhood is faced? Has it answered the community call for help and its need and longing for guidance? To what extent has the school penetrated into the community, analyzing, encouraging, and developing its latent educational forces, and helping to counteract the forces of disorganization that apparently even the highly organized society of today seems unable to curb even in the better ordered communities?

The answer to all these questions, unfortunately, is very discouraging. The school, in the past, has met few, if any, of these problems. However, there seems to be at present an awakening sense of duty and of opportunity that may produce a changed outlook and a stronger influence for progress in the future. The school is reaching out for the contacts and the program that will provide a basis for effective work. To function successfully, it must know not only the social and educational background of its boys and girls, but it must also go one step further; it must strive to understand the individual child in his social relationships outside of school. More important still, it must play an active and aggressive part in the affairs of the community. The school must assume the role demanded by its very nature; it must be the leader and the coordinating agency in all educational enterprises affecting the life of the community and, to a certain extent, the pivot upon which much even of the social and civic life of the neighborhood shall turn. There can be no denial of the fact that there are, outside the school, vital, powerful, and compelling forces that are constantly educating the boys and girls of the community in spite of, or contrary to, the school ideal. The surging life of the community as a whole, its motion-picture houses, its dance halls, its streets, its gangs, its churches, its community houses, its community codes of behavior and morals—these will either promote or destroy the work of the school.

The Benjamin Franklin High School soon realized this fact and set about organizing a Community Advisory Council. This Council proposes to bring to the aid of the school all the constructive forces within the East Harlem district so as to combat the many disruptive forces of the community. The main building of the high school itself is in the heart of an immigrant community that seems to have suffered from an almost malevolent concentration of those factors in modern industrial life that warp human development. Unsanitary dwellings, congested housing, lack of play space, unsightly streets, low economic returns for the wage earner, exploitation of the worker and often of his whole family, lack of proper opportunities in all the varying phases of life—all these things have contributed to the deterioration of the East Harlem neighborhood into what is known as a "tough" district among those who are unfamiliar with the potential human values basic in the people and in the life of the community. The fact that there is a widespread lack of understanding of these inherent values in the immigrant centers throughout the Nation creates problems that should be of interest to progressive educators.

A COMMUNITY-CENTER PROGRAM

The Benjamin Franklin High School is merely feeling its way toward what may be a proper solution of these problems. The school naturally sought, from the beginning, to identify itself closely with the social and educational agencies in the community. Members of the faculty were asked to serve on committees of the Yorkville Civic Council and the East Harlem Council of Social Agencies. The principal of the school was elected vice-president of the latter organization, while the main building of the school was used for the yearly meeting of the East Harlem Council of Social Agencies for 1935. At this meeting the program of the school and the scope and work of the school's Community Advisory Council were discussed fully.

Concurrently with the opening of the day high school in September 1934, the school, in cooperation with the East Harlem Council of Social Agencies and the Civil Works Administration, set up an afternoon community playground from 3:30 until 6:00, for the children of the neighborhood. An evening community center for adults, open from 7:30 until 10:00, was established also in an effort to place all the facilities of the school at the service of its neighbors from early morning until late at night. The Community Advisory Council, as may be seen from the charts reproduced here, has called upon every community organization that comes in contact in any way whatsoever with the people of the neighborhood.

The school, and the cooperating agencies in the neighborhood, are centering attention and effort upon certain fundamental aspects of the educational problems of the community because of a conviction that to correct the causes of maladjustment is patently the task of any school that wishes to aid in transforming these communities of foreign-born people into an integral part of the larger American community to which they should, for the good of all concerned, belong fully and happily. To accomplish this, it is necessary first to allay the distrust and the antagonism that have arisen out of misunderstanding and indifference. Disruptive forces must be replaced with a spirit of friendliness and intelligent cooperation in the building of wholesome social and civic relationships. There must be a spirit of tolerance, and of mutual give and take between the immigrant and his children and the native born and his children. The immigrant and his children must be made to feel that they "belong to America. They must be made to realize that America does not regard them as inferiors and that all that is not American is not to be scorned. They must be encouraged to feel that "a knowledge of and a pride in" their foreign cultural heritage is natural and just—something desirable for themselves, for the America of today, and the America of tomorrow.

These children of the foreign born must be given the pride and the sense of equality that are absolutely essential to their well-being, because personal dignity cannot be founded on shame or fear. For such shame and fear, the school must substitute ambition and self-respect that will lead these boys and girls to make a real contribution to America through lives that are well ordered, happy, and constructive. Furthermore, these children of the immigrant must be made to feel that the school is a symbol of the finer things of life. Warmth, friendliness, interest in the individual that knows no limitations of race, creed, politics, temporary adversity, or of social misfortune— these are the important things, particularly in dealing with youth. Too often they are omitted because of the complexities of modern living; too often the inability to find time for friendly individual contacts and for a real understanding of the needs of youth defeats the most zealous and well-meaning plans for educational and social betterment.

The Benjamin Franklin High School is dedicated to the task of building a finer citizenship and a better community life for all. Whatever may be the measure of its success, no matter how many may be the obstacles and the discouragements, the school will continue to try to meet its larger responsibility and its larger opportunity. In doing this every agency and every influence will be marshaled into the service of the community. In order that citizenship may be made vital to the boys of the district every resource and every facility will be merged in a comprehensive program for the future.

THE COMMUNITY ADVISORY COUNCIL

Already five major committees, which will work in the five major fields for improving the citizenship of the boys and of our community, have been formed. They are the Health Committee, the Citizenship Committee, the Parent Education Committee, the Correction and Guidance Committee, and the Racial Committee. Last year a limited survey of the social and educational agencies in the district was made. This survey will be continued more intensively this year and will be regularly included in the yearly school program in an effort to assemble all available data for use in the proposed plan for coordinated community education, with the school as the center of activity. The school must know its community intimately in order to work out an intelligent and effective program.

To ensure full neighborhood participation, generous use will be made of languages other than English. A great many of the older people in the community do not use English but speak instead some foreign language. This makes it necessary to interpret American life to them not only in the English language but in their own languages as well. Plans are being made also to reach the numerous racial and national societies through languages with which they are familiar. The students of the language department of the Benjamin Franklin High School will give plays from time to time in foreign languages, and in English also for these foreign-language-speaking groups. There will be musical programs, and questions of citizenship, child guidance, health, and other personal, social, and community problems will be discussed. We feel, moreover, that the contact of the boys of the school with the older groups will tend to create a sense of responsibility in these boys and will aid in developing the latent leadership that certainly exists among them. That this is true has been proved in the past by results obtained by some of us who have been doing, successfully, work of this kind for a great many years. It is still needed and we shall continue it intensively and with larger means than has been possible in the past.

Educating youth is not the sole task in a foreign community like that of East Harlem; parent education is an equally vital need. There

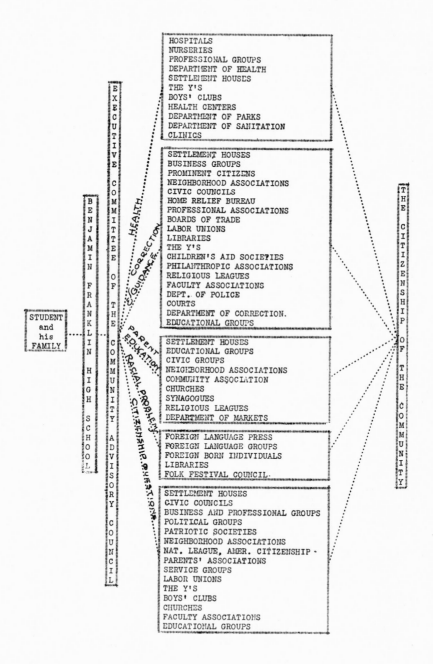

ORGANIZATION OF THE
COMMUNITY ADVISORY COUNCIL
of the
BENJAMIN FRANKLIN HIGH SCHOOL

BENJAMIN FRANKLIN HIGH SCHOOL

Leonard Covello -- Chairman

EXECUTIVE COMMITTEE

Harold Fields -- Chairman

EDUCATIONAL
Members of Board of Education
The Superintendent of Schools
Assoc. & Asst. Superintendents
Members of Local School Boards'
Principals of Local Public Schools
Principals of Parochial Schools

PROMINENT CITIZENS OF THE COMMUNITY

BENJAMIN FRANKLIN HIGH SCHOOL
Parents' Association
Alumni Association
Faculty Club

CIVIC GROUPS
Patriotic Societies
Neighborhood Associations
Nat. League, Amer. Citizenship
Civic Councils
Home Relief Bureaus
Parents' Associations

FOREIGN LANGUAGE SOCIETIES AND FOREIGN LANGUAGE PRESS
Societies
Press
Folk Festival Council

MUNICIPAL DEPARTMENTS
Parks
Health
Hospitals
Clinics
Sanitation
Markets
Police
Courts
Correction

SOCIAL AGENCIES
Settlement Houses
Libraries
Community Associations
The Y's
Children's Aid Society
Philanthropic Assn.
Scouts   Health Centers
Boys' Clubs   Nurseries

RELIGIOUS GROUPS
Churches
Synagogues
Religious Leagues
Affiliated Church Organizations

BUSINESS & PROFESSIONAL GROUPS
Professional Associations
Boards of Trade
Service Groups - Lions, Rotary, etc.
Labor Unions

are special aspects to this program also, if the real problems are to be intelligently met. The Parents' Association into which all members of the community are welcomed will be developed more fully along racial lines because it is felt that the foreign-born parent must know the school and what it offers. Use of languages other than English— as well as English—makes it easier for the non-English speaking parent to realize the difficulties that face his children and aids, therefore, in establishing more wholesome and harmonious relations in the home. A great deal of our time during each day at the school is taken up by interviews with parents who do not speak English and who are helpless, therefore, in coping with situations that arise between them and their children. The school acts as a medium of harmony whenever and wherever it is possible to serve in this way. Our Student Aid Committee, through its home visiting, is working along these same lines.

EDUCATION FOR CITIZENSHIP

The work of the Citizenship Committee of the Benjamin Franklin High School offers proof of how civics can be taught through a practical program rather than merely through textbooks.

In an endeavor to interest the boys of our school in the citizenship of their parents, we have instituted a naturalization drive for the benefit of their parents and relatives and neighbors. We have organized a corps of speakers from among our own students who will present to the boys of the school the reasons why they should be concerned about the citizenship of their parents. The movement in this way becomes an expression of interest on the part of the boys rather than one that is imposed upon the students by the teachers.

To aid in creating further interest, letters in English and in several foreign languages are sent by the teachers to advise the parents of this citizenship drive and to urge them to become citizens for their own sake and for the sake of their children. A form asking for their citizenship or alien status accompanies these letters. When this form has been returned a second letter to parents seeking naturalization is sent out informing them where and when they can receive training in citizenship and complimenting them upon their interest in becoming citizens of the United States.

At a designated time a group of naturalization secretaries who have been gathered from associated agencies in this field will report at the school to assist personally these alien parents. As a matter of interest, the students are being urged to accompany their parents on these evenings. Application forms are filled out free of charge, citizenship questions are answered, and immigration matters are discussed.

The result of all this has been a greatly increased interest in citizenship among the boys and a closer cooperation between the school and the patriotic, civic, and welfare organizations of the community. Likewise, the boys have become more genuinely interested in the affairs of their parents. At the same time, the parents have been made to feel that the school exists to serve them as well as their children. This has brought about a better understanding generally and has made possible a program of related activities beneficial to all. Moreover, the elementary schools and the junior high schools have been drawn into closer cooperation with the high school. The principals of these other schools are also notifying parents of the opportunity to prepare for citizenship, thus creating a desire for participation on the part of the entire community.

SOCIAL-WELFARE ACTIVITIES

The social agencies in the community have already been indexed by institution and type of service and the school will make this information available through the boys for their families. Whenever necessary the information will be translated into the language which the parents understand and, if need be, connections with these agencies will be established by the Student Aid Committee of the school which has been already actively in touch with many of these agencies.

To combat the prevalence of truancy and delinquency which has been rather marked in this district, we plan, in cooperation with interested citizens of the community, to establish a "Big Brother" movement in the district. Teachers, parents, and others will assist in this phase of the work, which will be done not only by the adults of the community but by some of the older boys of the school as well. Experience in this type of service leads me to believe that these young men will render excellent service.

A joint program in the study of housing conditions has been carried out with the Lenox Hill Neighborhood Association, which has prepared a very interesting exhibit of charts, graphs, and models which the students of the Benjamin Franklin High School visited during school hours. The housing exhibit was then transported to the school library and for over a week was made available for study and discussion to all the students in the school. The English social science, and art departments took up in their classes the question of housing.

Discussions of housing, compositions on better houses and model houses and even model villages were included in this program which has led to an intelligent and real appreciation of housing and its effect on the community.

Another venture centers about individual aid for students. Many of the boys desire to secure information about opportunities in different lines of work or in careers they wish to follow. To meet their needs, we arranged a series of assembly meetings dealing with the opportunities open to boys today in various professional and nonprofessional fields. The discussion leaders were men and women of the community who had succeeded in their particular lines of work. In this way we will be able to assist our students as a body; and, in specific cases, refer them to properly qualified individuals who will study their cases and recommend their entrance into the field of activity for which they seem best qualified.

The advisability of establishing a series of adult forums using English and foreign languages is under consideration. Through these we hope to reach the parents of the boys. Our ultimate hope lies in the fact that if these forums prove successful, we can convey to the parents and to other adults in this neighborhood an understanding of what we are trying to accomplish and we can help them in arriving at a more sympathetic approach of the problem of raising their American-born child of foreign heritage.

As for myself, I am firmly of the conviction that America, which began as an experiment in democratic institutions, can only continue and grow as a democracy if democracy will concern itself particularly with these forty million people of foreign stock in the country—the forty million new Americans of whom a goodly number are concentrated in isolated immigrant communities, "for democracy cannot rise any higher than the level of the mass of its citizens."

Surely by working thus upon a plan for better, finer community life, as well as for better education, the school justifies itself more fully. Out of this intelligent widening of its activities and influence may come the fulfillment of the hopes and dreams that have spurred some of us to ceaseless thought and effort in behalf of the youth of today.

JOSEPH W. TAIT

SOME ASPECTS OF THE EFFECT OF THE DOMINANT AMERICAN CULTURE UPON CHILDREN OF ITALIAN BORN PARENTS*

The purpose of the study reported in the preceding pages was to ascertain in what direction and to what extent, if any, children, 11 to 15 years of age, of Italian-born parents are affected by differenmt amounts of contact with the dominant American culture.

The method employed was to compare groups of Italian children attending schools of varying percentages of foreign enrollment. The number of Italian children studied was 734. These were distributed among five large public schools of the following percentages of foreign enrollment: 100, 75, 55, 40, and 30. In an effort to clarify and supplement the results of the study the reactions of a group of 360 children of native American parents, and of a similar age range, were also studied.

The character traits of Italian children which were studied were: inferiority feeling, attitude toward the foreign background, awareness of rejection, adjustment, ascendance-submission, extroversion-introversion, and emotional stability. Rejection of foreign children by native American children was also studied.

The background traits, which it was felt at the outset might influence the results and which, therefore, were considered throughout the study, were: socio-economic status, bilingual home environment, total foreign influence, intelligence, mental age, and chronological age.

The published tests and questionnaires used in the study were: Pupil Portraits, Aspects of Personality, the Hoffman Bilingual

Some Aspects of the Effect of the Dominant American Culture Upon Children of Italian Born Parents(New York: Teachers College, Bureau of Publications, Columbia University, 1942), pp. 49-55. Reprinted with permission.

Schedule, and the Pintner General Ability Tests. In addition, three questionnaires, styled "How-I-Feel—A," "How-I-Feel—B," and "How-I-Feel—C," were constructed and validated by the experimenter to indicate intensity of inferiority feeling, reaction against the foreign background, awareness of rejection, rejection of foreign children by children of American-born parents, and lack of social contacts between children of foreign-born parents and children of American-born parents.

Throughout the study group mean differences were tested for statistical significance by the Neyman-Johnson method.

In Part A of the study the mean score of each school for each trait was compared in turn with all the others. This gave ten different school comparisons. Many of the school mean differences were not statistically significant, but if there was a consistency in the direction of the differences, it was assumed that there was, at least, a suggestion of a tendency.

The interpretation of a tendency is in terms of increasing amounts of contact with native American children on the assumption that the percentage of native American enrollment in the school is a fair indication of the amount of contact between the two groups.

The following is the evidence afforded by the data for the various traits for Part A of the study.

INFERIORITY FEELING

There is a suggestion in the findings that Italian children experience a somewhat higher degree of inferiority feeling, the more they associate with native American children.

ATTITUDE TOWARD THE FOREIGN BACKGROUND
AND AWARENESS OF REJECTION

The data for attitude toward the foreign background and awareness of rejection provide no convincing evidence of a consistent effect on Italian children of increasing amounts of contact with native American children. There is a suggestion, however, that Italian children living in a community of approximately 100 per cent foreign population reject the foreign background and are aware of rejection to a somewhat higher degree than Italian children living in a community in which the population is in part native American.

ADJUSTMENT AND EMOTIONAL STABILITY

There is a suggestion in the data that Italian children have a somewhat better adjustment and are slightly more emotionally stable, the less they associate with native American children.

ASCENDANCE-SUBMISSION AND EXTROVERSION-INTROVERSION

There is a suggestion in the findings that Italian children become slightly more ascendant and more extrovert, the more they associate with native American children.

Part B contains a report of correlations between background traits and those which were the main objects of study and of sex and age group comparisons. It also reports the results for Schedule B, Section III, which was designed to find out whether Italian children knew the names of famous Italians in this country and in Italy.

All correlations for background traits were negligible or low.

The data for age group comparisons give some support to the hypothesis that when Italian children are divided into age groups differing by approximately two and four years, there is a tendency for increasing "goodness" of trait to be associated with increasing chronological age. In every comparison the mean difference was favorable to the older group.

Sex mean differences were favorable to the girls for all traits studied, except ascendance-submission, and were statistically significant for attitude toward the foreign background, awareness of rejection, and adjustment. The only difference favorable to the boys was that for ascendance-submission and this difference was statistically significant.

Attitude toward the foreign background correlated to the extent of—.47 with adjustment. Awareness of rejection had a correlation of —.40 with adjustment and .58 with attitude toward the foreign background.

The indication of the data is that children of Italian-born parents know surprisingly few names of famous Italians in this country and in Italy. It would seem as though their instruction lays little or no stress on the national origin of successful Italian men and women.

Part C contains a report of correlations between rejection of foreign children and socio-economic status, intelligence, mental age, chronological age, and lack of social contacts between Italian and native

American children. It also reports sex and socio-economic group differences for rejection of foreign children.

All the correlations, except one, were negligible or very small. The coefficient of .63 for rejection of foreign children and lack of social contacts indicates a tendency for greater tolerance to be found where there is knowledge and acquaintance.

The sex and socio-economic group differences were not statistically significant, but were in the direction of slightly greater tolerance in the girls and in the high socio-economic group.

A FIELD OF VITAL AND CHALLENGING PROBLEMS

An important consideration is whether or not the findings of this study provide corroboration for the often repeated assertions by writers that the children of foreign-born parents in this country are passing through a harrowing experience because of rejection by native Americans of their culture and of themselves as social equals, and that they tend to develop serious personality conflicts. When the question is approached from the standpoint of averages, it seems likely that certain broad trends toward unfavorable character traits are present. However, there is nothing in the data of this study to warrant any generalized assertion that children of foreign-born parents in the process of assimilation are experiencing "mental agonies" or passing through a "harrowing struggle." Personality development is a very individual process and is conditioned by myriad considerations both within and without the home. Among the many factors which may cause serious maladjustment in individual cases, nationality prejudice and other assimilation difficulties may play an important role. To discover this role might well be the object of an intensive case study.

A second worth-while consideration is the extent to which the findings of the present study support those of Young and Brown, reviewed in Chapter II. Pauline Young found only 10 per cent of her subjects who believed there was no conflict in their homes between New and Old World standards. Even if her subjects were competent to judge what constituted a cultural conflict, there would be no necessary relationship between the cultural conflict and the cahracter traits of the children. The data of the present study indicate that cultural conflicts do occur in many foreign homes, but that they occur in as high as 90 per cent of these homes is open to well-founded doubt.

Brown found no personality differences between Slovak and American children, except what could be accounted for by differences of socio-economic status. This is not in accord with the trends of the present study, insofar as Slovak and Italian children are subjected to the same or similar cultural pressures.

An ever present difficulty in studies which use paper and pencil questionnaires is that of securing frankness on the part of the subjects. Very few children or adults are motivated by a sincere desire to aid the cause of research, especially when such aid entails the making of assertions which place them in an unfavorable light. Frequently the person who is smarting under a grievance may make some commitments, but the person who is mildly aggrieved reacts to a questionnaire much in the same way as a person who is perfectly adjusted. There can be, therefore, no assurance that a picture of conditions obtained by the questionnaire technique will be a true portrayal of the facts. A statement which can be made with reasonable assurance is that such a picture of conditions will be better than the facts. It seems altogether likely that the Italian children used in the present study are more adversely affected by cultural pressures than their scores indicated and also that the American children reject foreign children to a greater degree than they admitted. If this argument is sound, then the trends of the data are more significant than the mathematics of the scores indicates.

The field of personality differences and difficulties of the children of national minorities in this country has been very much neglected. A great host of fundamental questions await solution. A few suggested themselves during the course of the present study.

When children had a choice of seats, even in schools where there was little written evidence of rejection or awareness of rejection, they invariably chose to sit with friends of their own national stock. The present study was concerned primarily with the presence of traits, but the causes of differences are of more fundamental importance. The variation of personality traits among the different national minority groups would be worthy of intensive study. Why do children of foreign-born parents have American Christian names in nine times out of ten? Were they so christened or did the pressure of the environment make it expedient for them to acquiesce in American usage? What is the influence of the teacher in making the path of assimilation hard or easy? Does Moreno's "saturation point" in the relations of Negroes and whites apply also to other minority groups? Do cultural conflicts make for greater delinquency among the children of the foreign-born?[1] These and many other questions would be worth the time and attention of the sociologist and the psychologist.

A matter of practical consideration is what are we to do about the cultural conflicts which it is so generally asserted exist in the foreign-born, and especially in their children. Would education and a broad and sympathetic understanding make easy the path of assimilation for these newcomers to our shores? Undoubtedly they would, if the education included a knowledge of the intimate life of the foreign community and the sympathetic understanding were based on an appreciation of the values in the foreign culture.

No society can remain dynamic, if its culture becomes static. History has witnessed the waxing of nations which appropriated the best in the cultures of many lands and added to this by their own creative genius. It has witnessed the waning of nations which shut their doors to the best influences from abroad. "There is much of art and beauty," says Thaddeus Sleszynski, "among our foreign folk that should be preserved for future generations. Their music and folk songs have a rhythm and a beauty all their own. We have nothing in America quite like the dances which they all danced together at the village festivals in Europe. There is an appreciation of opera and good music among the common people found only among Americans of education and training. More of their books deserve to be translated into English for the profit and enjoyment of all. There is a hospitality and a spirit of neighborliness among our foreign-born which we of this day have somehow lost. There is a feeling of pride in their work felt by artisans who have had their training in the small towns of Europe that is not often found among American workmen. All these things and many more should be passed on to become the heritage of future generations.[2]

It may be that the best solution of the problem of culture conflict is to implant in the hearts and minds of native Americans through the media of our schools and other educational institutions a knowledge of and respect for the real values in the cultures of other lands and in the achievements of their peoples and, at the same time, to encourage in our new Americans a pride in their national origin and their heritage. Such a course would bring to them contentment and self-respect and need not be inconsistent with the development of an even greater pride in the culture and traditions of America to which they have made and are making a worth-while contribution. There

---

[1]For a study in which cultural conflict is ascribed as an important factor in crime, see E. T. Glueck, "Cultural Conflict and Delinquency." *Mental Hygiene*, 21, 1937, 46-66.

[2]Thaddeus Sleszynski, "The Second Generation of Immigrants in the Assimilation Process," *Annals of the American Academy of Political and Social Science*, 93, 157-58.

is little doubt but that culture conflicts, where they exist, have their best hope of extinction in an atmosphere of mutual trust and esteem.

LEONARD COVELLO

THE INFLUENCE OF SOUTHERN ITALIAN FAMILY MORES UPON THE SCHOOL SITUATION IN AMERICA*

THE ITALIAN CONTADINI AS A GROUP IN THE "NEW" IMMIGRATION

The wave of immigration that began to reach the shores of the United States around the turn of this century deposited here a variety of ethnic, or cultural, groups from all corners of the world but predominantly from eastern and southeastern Europe. Each of these groups contributed to the material growth of their land of adoption. Each of them left an imprint on the economic, political, social, and cultural life of this country. They all—some more, some less— affected the pattern of American culture as it existed prior to their coming. In turn, each of these immigrant groups was influenced by the American way of life through a give-and-take process, which inevitably led in some degree to its cultural modification.

Some of the groups which constituted the "new" immigration,[1] whose cultural background was in many ways compatible with, or even complementary to, the existing American cultural patterns underwent comparatively rapid and substantial changes in their way of life. Political patterns in their native land, or language idioms, or occupational status, or a variety of other elements in the cultural baggage of such immigrant groups, may have been comparable, either in single elements or in a combination of them, to those in

---

*The Social Background of the Italo-American School Child: A Study of the Southern Italian Family Mores and their Effect on the School Situation in Italy and America. Edited and with an Introduction by F. Cordasco (Leiden: E. J. Brill, 1967), pp. 275-327

[1]The "New" immigration applies to immigrants who came from eastern and southeastern Europe and included such countries as Italy, Greece, Balkans, Poland, Russia and the Near East. This mass migration to the United States began about 1880.

America. And such particular elements may have contributed toward lessening *a priori* the unavoidable conflict between immigrant groups and the American environment with which they came in contact in various situations. This factor, alone, may have favorably launched them on the road toward assimilation; i.e.,

> A process of interpenetration and fusion in which persons and groups acquire memories, sentiments and attitudes of other persons or groups, and, by sharing their experience and history, are incorporated with them in a common cultural life.[2]

In this process many members of such groups, or even groups as a whole, may have steadily undergone a cultural transition which removed them more and more from the cultural inheritance that they brought with them from their native land, and which consistently led them to greater and greater absorption of American cultural life. They, in short, were in the process of becoming Americans not only politically but culturally as well.

CULTURAL DISSIMILARITY OF ITALIAN CONTADINO AS A BASIS FOR CONFLICT IN THE UNITED STATES

There were, however, among the "new" immigration groups, some whose cultural heritage was lacking in elements that would make the reduction of conflicts possible. Their adjustment to life in America became, for this reason, a difficult process, and a cultural fusion occurred only on some points and, usually, only on the surface. In the category of cultural groups that show a definite lag in assimilation belong the Italians in the United States, who in 1930 numbered 4,456,875, 60 per cent or 2,667,445 of whom lived in urban areas.[3] These figures include Italian immigrants and their American-born children. Specifically, the group that is conspicuous for its retardation in the process of assimilation is composed of Italians from southern Italy, including their American born children, who constituted the bulk of Italian immigration to the United States.[4]

[2]Robert E. Park and Ernest W. Burgess, *Introduction to the Science of Sociology*, p. 736.

[3]Leonard Covello, *The Italians in America* (New York: Bulletin 6, Casa Italiana Educational Bureau, Columbia University, 1934.)

[4]*Annual Report of the Commissioner of Immigration*, Fiscal Year ending June 30, 1903, Washington, D.C., p. 546, indicated 83.97 per cent for Italian immigrants from the south as against 16.03 per cent for those from the north of Italy.

And most prominent among the southern Italian immigrants, insofar as the difficulty of their adjustment to life in America is concerned, are those of the *contadino*, or peasant, class who contributed the greatest share of Italian immigration to the United States.

United States immigration reports for 1903 identified 0.2 per cent of southern Italian immigrants as having had professional occupations in Italy; 12.7 per cent as former workers in trades and industries. The remainder is distributed between farmers and farm laborers (64.9 per cent), and a group with no indicated occupation, actually women and children (22.2 per cent).[5] On the assumption that this occupational distribution was average for the period of mass immigration, and that women and children were proportionately distributed among the first three categories, it may be concluded that farmers, or more precisely, southern Italian peasants, comprise at least 78 per cent of all Italians in the United States. And thus any problem involving Italians in America will, because of the numerical aspect alone, concern itself primarily with the particular immigrant group from southern Italy that was, in its native milieu, identified as the *contadino* class.

Some of the elements of the cultural background of this particular group have been described in Part I of this study. As has been suggested therein, these people were in a peculiar stage of cultural evolution which made even their identification with the concept of "Italy"—a country whose economic and social norms were those of a modern society—unjustifiable and certainly misleading. The difficulty of this group in adjusting itself quickly and in an appreciable degree to life in America must be accepted as an *ipso facto* premise. Their folkways and mores in the realms of religion, social life, economic organization, and education abounded in vestiges of a civilization of by-gone eras; ancient customs and practices were survivals, "not merely as symbolical residues of the past but retained the force of primeval verities."[6]

With a cultural background that deviated sharply from the norms applicable to Italy as a whole, the southern Italian peasant was, to paraphrase Brown's statement, neither adjusted in his own country, nor was he therefore likely to be equipped for adjustment in a foreign land.[7] Acute conflicts between the American cultural milieu and the cultural tradition of the southern Italian *contadino*

[5]*Loc. cit.*

[6]Raffaele Riviello, *Costumanze, Vita e Pregiudizi del Popolo Potentino*, p. 102.

[7]Lawrence Guy Brown, *Immigration*, p. 161.

were in order because of much more dissimilarity than likeness between the two. In comparison with most other immigrant groups there was hardly an aspect of the southern Italian tradition that was not in contrast to the existing American patterns. Even their adherence to the Roman Catholic faith constituted, because of unorthodox practices, rather a source of conflict than a point of coincidence.

An old Italian resident of East Harlem in New York City, relates for example,

> In 1886 the Italians in East Harlem lived within a radius of about a quarter of a mile. There was one church to go to and that was what we used to call the "American Church" at East 115th Street (now the renowned Church of Our Lady of Mt. Carmel). In those days we Italians were allowed to worship only in the basement part of the Church, a fact which was not altogether to our liking.[8]

The full impact of a religious conflict is revealed, however, by an Irish old-timer, who states:

> These Italians were strange people, very strange to us . . . That they were dressed in a manner unaccustomed among us, that their language was nothing like what had been told us about the sonority of Italian speech, that they were noisy and ill mannered mattered little . . . We even had pity for them. But, for God's sake, when they began to come to our church and made a market place of it, we were sure that they were the people whom the Lord chased from the temple. In those days we were quite sure, and even today I don't see how they have the nerve to call themselves Christians when they are not.

ASSIMILATIVE LAG OF SOUTHERN ITALIAN CONTADINO IN THE UNITED STATES

A cultural fusion was therefore likely to be an extremely protracted process. Even rudimentary forms of accommodation[9] to the American environment progressed with unusual slowness. More-

[8]Marie Concistrè, *Education in a Local Area: A Study of a Decade in the Life and Education of the Adult Italian Immigrant in East Harlem, New York City.* An unpublished Ph.D. dissertation, New York University, 1943, p. 273.

[9]That is, a process of adjustment in which social relations and attitudes are organized only for the purpose of preventing or reducing conflicts and to maintain a basis of security.

over, all tendencies toward accommodation denoted attempts to establish a replica of a southern Italian milieu which would assure a measure of security against demoralization. In the midst of a strange and overtly hostile environment, the natural tendency to create a socio-cultural refuge led to the creation of "Little Italys" and, therefore, to isolation. This tendency toward isolation within an Italian cultural and geographic shell was a natural phenomenon.[10] As a compensatory mechanism to overcome the difficulties of adjustment to an American environment, it inevitably channelled the process of accommodation toward adjustment in terms of southern Italian social values and southern Italian customs. This manner of adjustment acted inevitably to hinder the process of accommodation to the American milieu and often resulted in open hostility to American patterns.

As an illustration, the slow progress that Italians have made in learning to speak English[11] may be cited. A lag in this specific area of accommodation is due not to inability but more probably to unwillingness and, most certainly, to lack of any incentive to conceptualize the practical purpose of learning English.

An Italo-American who immigrated in 1906 makes the following unequivocal statement.

> Before I sailed to America our local priest attempted to scare us by telling about the difficulty of learning English. But we knew better; we knew that there would be no need to torture oneself with a strange language . . . When I arrived in New York I went to live with my *paesani.* I did not see any reason for learning English. I didn't need it for everywhere I lived, or worked, or fooled around there were only Italians . . . I had to learn some Sicilian, though, for I married a girl from the province. Sicilian helped me a great deal in my family and in my work . . . I don't speak much English but that never bothered me.

With the tendency toward establishing a replica of the old world milieu, it was inescapable that the family became the central institution around which all community life was built. Whereas the physical isolation of an Italo-American community provided means of accommodation for the Italians as a group, the individual could find a safeguard against personal disorganization and insecurity only

---

[10]Brown, *op. cit.,* p. 213.

[11]The United States Census for 1930 and 1940 attest to the fact that Italians occupy first rank among those unable to speak English.

within the orbit of family life. In Italy, primary group life—that is, the family—and to some extent the village, exercised a definite control over the attitude and behavior of an individual, while little conflict and the utmost conformity to the folkways resulted in little social disorganization and little personal demoralization. In America, however, the Italian immigrant, who came mostly as a single individual, faced a situation in which he was suddenly compelled to "live his own life," to act and think and to believe in his own way. His social training in Italy had not prepared him for such a drastic change. Brown, though referring to the European peasant in general, was likely to have had in mind the southern Italian peasant when he wrote:

> In Europe his situation was dominated by flora and fauna; here he lives in a world of machines. In his original habitat customs and traditions were controlling forces . . . In rural Europe his attitudes, beliefs, ideas, and fears were tied up with nature; here they fail to find their counterpart. His subjective personality does not find its objective aspect in reality.[12]

To achieve a state of adjustment in which his "subjective personality" could survive the hostility of his new environment, he needed first of all a familiar tradition; not as a cherished memory—for that would only increase his conflicts—but as an overt manifestation of his traditions that would represent to him a concrete mooring. And just as in Italy the common pattern of family life, entrenched in tradition and upheld by the weight of universal conformity, conditioned every member of the *contadino* class so that he had a clear conception at all times of what he and the others must be and do in their society, so the family has become in the Italo-American communities that institution which gives the communities moral content in a concrete and satisfactory manner. Just as in Italy, all social control was based on no other moral categories than those of the family, so any social consciousness of Italo-Americans within "Little Italys" appertains primarily to sharing and adhering to the family tradition as the main motif of their philosophy of life.

That the retention of this cultural "basis" is essentially the source of their retarded adjustment, is a position taken by many sociologists. The retardation is not, however, as Sutherland suggests, "because of the immigration of the family into a heterogeneous district"[13] but,

[12]Brown, *op. cit.*, p. 222.

[13]Edwin H. Sutherland, *Principles of Criminology*. p. 93.

on the contrary, because family life gave impetus to the establishment of a high degree of homogeneity in Italian communities in America.[14] And because of this, the Italo-American family continues to be the repository of the old-world cultural inheritance and the locus of a cultural transfer upon the American-born generation.

ACCOMMODATION TO SCHOOL EDUCATION AS AN ASPECT OF THE ASSIMILATIVE PROCESS

For this reason, the assimilative process of Italians in America is basically tantamount to a modification of their familial background. Any investigation of problems concomitant with, or "suspected" of being related to, the process of acculturation must of necessity seek areas where cultural changes are not only observable but where they can be observed not as isolated phenomena but as interrelated aspects of the process. "Most facts," says Thrasher, "have meaning and significance only as they are defined by the cultural background in which they occur."[15] It has been shown that within the Italian family resides a great degree of the cultural totality of the group.

The basic assumption of this study—that children of Italian parentage in our public schools are, as a "problem" element, the product of an ill-adjusted cultural group, whose familial mores may, because of great divergence from the dominant mores of America, be detrimental to the formal educational process—derives from the evident influence which the Italo-American parental home exerts upon the social and cultural orientation of the children. The familial and societal mores of the Italo-American communities,[16] which sustain the character of social exclusiveness of the family and which *ipso facto* contributed toward upholding the separative barriers between the Italian milieu in America and the broad American community, produce a specific influence on the habits, attitudes and behavior of an American-born child when he approaches other groups, or when

[14]The Italian section of East Harlem comprising about 70,000 Italians has, according to investigations of the Benjamin Franklin High School in 1936, only about 12 per cent non-Italian residents.

[15]Frederic M. Thrasher, Social Backgrounds and Informal Education, *Journal of Educational Sociology*, Vol. VII, No. 8, (April, 1943), p. 470.

[16]The great majority of Italians in America are located in urban centers of the North Eastern United States. In each large city the Italians are confined to locally self-sufficient neighborhoods (natural areas). The Italian population of New York City, for example, is distributed among eight major Italian communities. William B. Shedd, *Italian Population in New York*. Bulletin Number 7, Casa Italiana Educational Bureau. (New York City: Columbia University, 1934).

the child comes into contact with that broad milieu which can be defined as America: its people, its way of life, its institutions. As any family, anywhere, determines the pattern of the child's behavior in outside group life, so the Italo-American family leaves a strong imprint upon the child's social orientation and supplies him with a definite set of social and moral values that will to a great extent govern the child's future life in broader groups. So, also, this Italo-American family greatly influences the child in its process of adjustment to American society: in regard to his feeling as part of the big outside world; in regard to appreciating and understanding people unlike himself; in regard to his tendency to assume or to reject certain roles in that other group.

CONSPICUITY OF ITALO-AMERICAN CHILDREN IN THE PUBLIC SCHOOLS OF NEW YORK CITY

An investigation into the proposition that peculiar Italian family mores produce peculiar and conspicuous behavior and attitude patterns in school must obviously proceed from evidence that such peculiarities, regardless of causes, are indeed observable. But in spite of an apparent possibility of ascertaining the existence or non-existence of such a phenomenon by objective means and by no complex methodology, there is no information available. The main obstacle to the accumulation of such data is the manner in which school records are conceived. Disinterestedness heretofore on the part of the school in environmental factors of student background makes assemblage of data on the basis of ethnic differentiation a very difficult undertaking. Likewise difficult is the position of the investigator who attempts to acquire even subjective information from persons with authoritative positions in our schools.[17] With the exception of the rather numerous publications of I.Q. test measurements, which are probably the main avenue of disseminating information regarding the conspicuity of Italo-American school children, and a few statistical works on leisure time preferences, motion picture attendance, and rejection of the parental culture, there are no extant data upon which to base an assumption relative to this question.

The main source of material available to support the *de facto* conspicuity of Italo-American school children must of necessity be that

---

[17]The investigator sent out a number of simply worded, unprovocative questionnaires to principals and teachers as to their subjective experiences with Italian parents and their children in school. The responses were 100 per cent non-commital.

consensus which confronts an investigator in private, eye-to-eye conversation, second hand gossip, occasional newspaper reportage, and similar *vox populi* pronouncements. Substantially, the circulating opinions are correct as to the singular position children of Italian origin occupy in our public schools. All objective evidence available to the investigator, who has spent many years as a participant observer in the school and in the Italian community of East Harlem, points to the "problem" of Italo-American school children as being out of proportion to their population ratios, both in school and the entire city of New York. Further, the frequency with which Italo-American school children figure in the category of problem students is also incongruous with the comparatively long sojourn of the Italian-born parents in the United States.[18]

On the whole the conspicuity of Italo-American school children shifted during the last fifteen or twenty years from the elementary school to the junior and senior high schools.[19] In former years, elementary school teachers rather frequently expressed their perturbation that

> . . . Italian children were usually more crude in manner, speech, and dress than non-Italian children . . . It was common for Italian boys and girls to leave school to help out the family income. Parents were openly opposed to the long educational period of the elementary school . . . Boys and girls were truants . . . These children, especially the boys, were a source of constant irritation to teachers . . . These children were disliked both by teachers and non-Italian pupils . . . they created difficulties for the school.

The situation in the elementary schools seems to have changed for the better, and this is being attested by a great number of teachers. One states, for example:

> In retrospect, certain things stand out as I compare our present Italo-American pupils with those that have come to us over a nineteen-year period. They are much less unlike the non-Italian children than their oldest brothers and sisters were . . . Except for the difficulty of making Italo-American children bring their parents to visit the

[18]Research done at the Benjamin Franklin High School under the supervision of the investigator reveals that the average length of residence in America among Italians in East Harlem is about 40 years.

[19]Paranthetically this shift may, to some extent, be taken as a criterion of their cultural advancement or acculturation.

school, there is practically no reason to accuse Italo-American pupils of being different from the rest.

Parallel with these changes in the elementary schools, the role of Italo-American students as "problem cases" becomes pronounced in the secondary school. Over-all evidence of this is contained in the statistics of the United States Census for 1940 on the educational status of the American people. Thus, for Health Area 21,[20] of New York City, a typical Italian section of East Harlem with the most homogeneous Italian population in the area, it is possible to obtain a comparison of the ratio of school attendance with that for New York City as a whole, as is shown in Table VII.

Table VII

Comparison of School Years Completed for Both Sexes. Twenty-five Years and Older, in Health Area 21 (In East Harlem) and in New York City as a Whole, According to United States Census, 1940 [21]

Number of School Years Completed	Health Area 21 Per cent of total population	New York City Per cent of total population
No schooling at all	18.96	7.63
Grade School 1-4 years	21.39	7.19
5 or 6 „	12.29	7.75
7 or 8 „	32.76	40.88
High School 1-3 years	6.68	12.69
4 „	2.85	12.38
College 1-3 years	0.77 [22]	3.69
4 years or more	0.96 [22]	5.63
Not reported	3.34	2.16
Total	100.00	100.00
Median school years completed	6.3	8.3

While the proportion of the population that completed the eighth grade (32.76 per cent of the total population in Health Area 21, as against 40.88 per cent for New York City as a whole) presents a fairly comparable situation, it is apparent that the proportion who gradu-

[20]Health Area—a section having an average population of about 25,000 into which the city of New York has been subdivided for statistical local administrative purposes.

[21]Compiled from data of the 16th United States Census 1940, in monograph on *Population and Housing Statistics for Health Areas, New York City.* (Washington, D. C.: United States Government Printing Office, 1942) pp. 6 and 112.

[22]This group consists mainly of non-resident professional people practicing within the area.

ated from high school in Health Area 21 (2.85 per cent) compares unfavorably with that for New York City (12.38 per cent). This denotes a comparatively high rate for Italo-American children who drop out of high school, a conspicuous aspect of high school attendance in the East Harlem community.[23]

A study[24] made by the High School Division of the New York City Board of Education in 1926 shows that an average of 42.2 per cent of all high school students in New York City graduate. It is of immediate interest to contrast this with the results obtained in a study made in 1931 which showed that only 11.1 per cent of Italo-American high school registrants graduate.[25]

Truancy, absence, cutting classes, lateness, and disciplinary infractions are problems of much greater frequency among high school students of Italian origin than among non-Italians. Something of the degree of their conspicuity in these problem areas is given in Table VIII. In this table are condensed the findings of a series of

Table VIII
Ratio of Non-Italian to Italian Students at School X, in the Frequency of Truancy and Other Problems for 1930-1932

	Ratio of Non-Italian to Each Italian Student	
School Population [26]		8 : 1
Truancy 1931	2.3 : 1	
Truancy 1932 [27]	1.8 : 1	
Absence 1930	4.6 : 1	
Absence 1931	4.3 : 1	
Cutting Classes 1932	3.0 : 1	
English	1.8 : 1	
General Science	1.0 : 1	
Mathematics	1.2 : 1	
Shop	2.0 : 1	
Assembly	2.3 : 1	
Lateness 1930	3.7 : 1	
Habitual Lateness	1.2 : 1	
Disciplinary Cases 1930	2.7 : 1	
Disciplinary Cases 1932	2.3 : 1	
Recidivists 1932	1.8 : 1	

[23]Of interest is the average number of school years attended. The above health area denotes 6.3 years, as against 8.3 years for the entire city.

[24]The investigator was unable to obtain a copy of the pamphlet describing this study, but knows hat the fact reported above is correct.

[25]This study was made by the investigator at the De Witt Clinton High School in New York City in 1931. A careful analysis was made of all Italian boys who registered between the years 1901 and 1925.

[26]The median register for the entire school during 1930-1932 was about 10,500, of which 11.1 per cent were Italians (1170 students).

[27]Among non-Italian truants 12.8 per cent were chronic truants; among Italians, 31.6 per cent.

studies made by the investigator in 1931, 1932, 1933, and 1934 which attempted to compare the above problems among non-Italian students and those of Italian parentage in a particular high school.

In spite of the crudeness of the figures in Table VIII, it is revealed that students of Italian parentage are prominent in the most overt aspects of problems connected with "attending" high school, and that the frequency with which the schools perceive or register their non-conformity to social roles expected of a student are far in excess of their true population ratio, which is one Italian student to eight non-Italian students. The degree of such non-conformity can only be surmised. The true situation in the high schools in 1944 would be difficult to ascertain,[28] but in the absence of available objective data, it is of interest to note that the consensus among high school teachers is to the effect that "during the last ten years there has been an improvement in the school attitude and behavior of Italian students."[29] Changes, if any, appear, however, to be so imperceptible as to be scarcely measurable. Up to the beginning of the Second World War the situation remained, in comparison with 1930-1934,[30] and for all practical purposes, the same. This latter situation applies to students who live within the centers of Italian cultural survival; i.e., the large Italo-American communities. Significantly enough, reports from culturally heterogeneous areas of New York City indicate "a rather rapid disappearance of an Italian type of student who used to be outstanding in doing just the opposite of what an average high school boy ought to do."[31]

CONFLICT BETWEEN THE AMERICAN SCHOOL AND THE EDUCATIONAL CONCEPTS OF THE CONTADINO

The conspicuity of Italo-American children in the school, when viewed from the point of school administration, may appear as ab-

[28]The Second World War is undoubtedly exerting a specific influence upon Italo-Americans in regard to school education. While realizing the desirability of a study of Italo-Americans under war conditions—a study which undoubtedly would contribute further toward understanding their assimilative process and the schooling problem as well—this investigator finds it impossible to throw any light upon the situation as of today.

[29]Opinions were polled through informal approach by a non-teacher at the Benjamin Franklin High School in 1943.

[30]See Table VIII.

[31]Conversations with teachers in a suburban area where Italians have never achieved the establishment of a "Little Italy."

normal. Contrarily, from the point of view of the assimilative, or accommodation process, of Italians in America, and especially those from the homogeneous Italo-American communities, the school problem is anything but incomprehensible. In the light of an assimilative retardation, such a situation—both in the elementary and in the high schools—lends itself to a plausible interpretation.

The educational inheritance of the southern Italian immigrant—the concepts of and attitudes toward education—has been described in Chapter VIII, in sufficient detail to give a general idea of its significance in his process of accommodation. From the immigrant's point of view there was no obvious need for more than a trifling amount of formal education. All practical arts and skills should be acquired at an early age by working either in the parental household or through apprenticeship. Knowledge beyond the every-day requirements was a privilege and necessity for the "better" classes. His concept of wisdom had nothing in common with categories of knowledge and learning that are acquired in the school. In Italy, his knowledge, his various skills and work techniques, had been comparatively static; they were simple and required no elaborate process of transmission from generation to generation. The moral code in his simple and homogeneous society had also been simple. A uniform body of rules and behavior was learned in daily contacts with relatives and neighbors. All moral customs, unshaken for centuries, were effectively transmitted without any stimulation of critical and logical faculties. School learning was, therefore, at a great distance from popular comprehension and consumption.

Even when and where there existed some degree of appreciation of school learning, the Italian immigrant's concepts of education excluded the possibility of expanding school attendance beyond childhood years and beyond the most elementary schooling. At best, school attendance beyond a few years was justified only if a boy—girls were never considered—was determined to establish himself in one of the professions. Another reason for the immigrant's aversion to prolonged school education was the fear of family dissolution and disorganization which would follow school attendance through the absorption by youthful members of the family of modern ideas, incompatible with the desire to preserve the good old family tradition.

Such an attitude toward school education inevitably found itself in conflict with the prevailing American mores that govern education and, particularly, with the compulsory character of school education in America. The impulse to resist compliance, which meant the exposure of his children to a world of strange ideas, was rooted in the desire to entrench them in parental ways of thinking and doing things. School education in America, as the southern Italian peasant found it, not only had no appeal to him; it was conceived to be an institution demoralizing youth and disorganizing their traditional patterns of family life.

An Italo-American, a former physician in Sicily, gives concrete expression to this reaction to the American system of compulsory school attendance.

> Most people believe that Italians came here mainly for economic reasons. But it is erroneous to overlook that in America they sought to find freedom from various deviltries of the Italian government. Among these were the attempts (not always successful) to introduce compulsory education which the peasant in southern Italy considered more of a burden than a blessing. So when here in America he was confronted with compulsion to send his children to school, regardless of sex, age or the financial background of the home, he showed a tendency to resist, especially when this compulsion was accompanied by the fear that the children might be imbued by the school with ideas antagonistic to the traditions of the parents . . . If they sent them to school at all, they did so because they did not want to appear as barbarians.

Economic Aspect of the Conflict

There was undoubtedly fear of indoctrination of alien concepts, and the peasant felt rather keenly the danger to his traditions. But the most overt area of conflict arose in the economic and social patterns of family life. For next to the difficulties of the parents themselves in making the necessary economic and social adjustments, the prospects of compulsory school education for their children threatened the very foundations of orderly family life.

Under the southern Italian cultural patterns, all children were useful and effective members of their families from an early age. As the child became older and increased in physical strength and experience, in judgement and dependability, he performed more numerous and more difficult tasks and shared more and more fully in the counsels of the family group. There were no sharp age divisions; each shaded into the older and younger. So general was the pattern of life where children fitted into family life and its economy that all people were divided into two groups: children and adults. There was no adolescent group, so to speak. There were helpless infants and playful tots, young men and women, feeble folk, but there was never a group of adolescents.

The first reaction to the American school system was based on the immigrant's discovery in America of a group which, though evidently adult in physical growth, was a child-group since it attended school and indulged in childish activities, such as playing ball. The status of American youth amazed him but also filled him with apprehension. Whereas in Italy young people in their teens found all their needs satisfied by the home and the simple relationships of the villages, in American society, youth, as the *contadino* saw it, lives in a profoundly different world. The fear of the possibility that his child might follow in the footsteps of American youth derived from the drastic change he himself was undergoing. Home industry was gone. One and often both parents had to work outside the home. American laws and economic conditions were obviously sentencing their children to idleness for a long span of years. Boys, and even girls, were compelled to go to school up to a certain age regardless of parental feelings, the child's aptitudes and desires. Below a certain age, work by children was prohibited. And when the child neither goes to school nor attends to useful work, the enforced leisure and idleness detach the child from the orbit of family life and remove him from the wholesome influence of the familial tradition.

Loss of Children as Economic Assets

This imposed idleness to which the Italian parent reacted acutely, and often with a sense of frustration, was probably the most keenly felt conflict between the family tradition and the American school education. The economic implications were of primary significance. The southern Italian peasant was traditionally unaccustomed to the idea of supporting a boy of, let us say, twelve years of age. On the contrary, the boy was expected to contribute to the household economy. The need to support such a boy was inconceivable, and the parent could not with ease undergo in America a change in this direction.

A first generation Italo-American from Basilicata who came to the United States about thirty years ago is still unreconciled to the idea of supporting children of school age.

> In our family (in Italy) every member of the family worked for the family. Even children did their share when they were five years old, watching the little lambs. There were no wages and no pay day . . . Three times a

year, all the older members of the family—including the
married ones—received about ten cents . . .
That's where you really worked. There was no playing.
In America it's all play, and I see young men who should
be contributing to their families, still going to school and
playing ball in the streets . . . And the shameful thing
is they expect their parents to support them.

The drastic change of status of youth in America resulted in the loss
of children as an economic asset. Although the Italian parent was compelled to accommodate himself to the prevailing American mores in
regard to school education—and to make a concession to the inevitability of his children's being condemned to a life of idleness—he
never removed from his tradition the role of the child as a material
supporter of the family. As will be shown later, the old pattern remained an aspect of his culture, quite invulnerable to assimilation.

The reaction of a typical immigrant peasant to the economic uselessness of his son is revealed in the following extract from a life history. An Italo-American born near Reggio, Calabria, in Italy about
1882 (precise age is unknown to informant) relates:

I and my twelve-year-old son Joe, came to New York in
1907. In the old country I earned my living grinding and
sharpening tools . . . Having scraped together some
money, about forty dollars in all, we arrived in New York
with about four dollars in cash and my set of professional
instruments.[32] . . . My first lodging place was in Coney
Island among my *paesani* from the south of Calabria.
Each day, except Sunday, we started from home at about
nine o'clock and set out for Bensonhurst . . . would continue with our work till about sunset. Financially I was
making out all right. On Sundays and at other occasions
Joe went shining shoes and made quite good money.
Things went so that I figured making a second grinder
for Joe and let him cover another route. In this way, I
figured, enough money could be earned in a couple of
years, and we could return to Italy where I intended to
open a small business . . . Joe had great business talent.
I intended to put him in business there in Italy.
Those were my plans. And then one day my whole life
was changed and bitterness crept into my soul. One day
a policemen approached me and started asking something
about Joe. I could not understand the cop, so I called to
a fellow Italian who acted as interpreter. At first the whole
thing made no sense to me. Even now after so many years,

[32]Although the informant was born of *contadino* parents and his wife was a *contadino* woman, he prides himself in having been a *mastro*, i.e., an artisan. Though illiterate, he prefers to speak of his trade as a profession.

after having become an American citizen and all that, the incident is fresh in my memory. I was asked, how come my boy is not in school. To tell the truth, I was told about it by my *paesani* who warned me about the American law which compels all smart and all dopey ones to go to school, regardless of whether they want to or need it. But I did not think this law applied to me for I intended to return to Italy. Besides, Joe only looked small; as a matter of fact he was over twelve years old. I told no lies to the cop, I just told him how things stood . . . I thought the storm was over. But in a couple of days there came a kind of detective and said that Joe had to go to school . . . I felt sorry for myself and all my good plans, but I felt sorry also for Joe who was crying, and who was not made to be a scholar . . . .

We moved near the former racetrack at Gravesend Avenue but that did not help me any. If Joe went out to work he would be caught sooner or later; my envious enemies among my *paesani* would see to it that it happened. And what good would it do if Joe sat home and I worked? Was it really necessary for me to take Joe all the way from Italy in order to let him sit at home and be helpful in no other way than by cooking a dish of macaroni? It was wrong, very wrong but I could do nothing about it. So I went to work alone, and Joe had to go to school. And instead of helping me and thus, his family, Joe had to be supported by me. Mind you, a fellow who was thinking of girls and was strong as a good sized tree could gc to school as if he were a nobleman's son, while his poor father was breaking his back.

I was disgusted with the situation. Joe was of no use to me. And I did not care whether he went to school or not. The only consolation I had was the knowledge that he could not be kept in school after he became fourteen years old. However, even in this I was disappointed. Joe was a son of a gun; he liked the idea of being supported by me; the American ideas went to his head. If at times he earned some money, he spent it all on himself, and never contributed to the burden . . . When Joe was fourteen he quit school but he was not the same Joe anymore. The two years that he spent at school did him no good. The school rather harmed him, and ruined my entire life. All the respect and obedience he had before, he lost in the school which did not teach him anything good. Whenever he gave me some money he always tried to give me as little as possible . . .

When my wife and my two other children came to America, I knew in advance what to expect. It was a bitter pill to swallow when your own children were of little use to you. But since I did not rely upon them anymore, as I used to on Joe, I was not upset when my other thirteen year old boy

went to school and we parents, had to wait patiently till
the school years were over . . . . I regret the day that my
thought of taking Joe to America was born.

More acute was the parental reaction where it concerned school
education for girls. In itself, this aspect of the American school situation seemed to the Italian absurd, since the education of girls was
contrary to the economic and social role of a *contadino* woman. It
had almost no precedents in southern Italy. The economic dislo-
cation within the family, due to the necessity of tolerating a new
disruptive activity by the boys, was great. But the separation of the
girl from her customary functions within the home was, from the
Italian peasant's point of view, economically disastrous. The old
family equilibrium in which the adolescent girl fitted well, and in
a useful way, into the family structure and its economy had entirely
broken down; girls were hardly any longer an integral part of the
Italian family institution. A girl, who was in school from the age
of seven to fourteen, was a source of constant irritation and anger to
her parents.

An Italo-American mother born in Sicily, thirty-seven years in the
United States makes a common complaint.

> Boys had always more privileges than girls and so
> the idea of their going to school instead of helping us
> (parents) was only half bad. Boys somehow managed to
> make a penny or two, and in this way kept peace with my
> husband . . . But when girls at thriteen and fourteen
> wasted good time in school, it simply made us regret our
> coming to America.

Bitter opposition to sending girls to school may have been motivated also by reason of the effect upon the social position of the
mother, who as a result frequently had to work outside the home.
The gist of the complaint, though usually made with reluctance,
had been frequently voiced by Italian mothers.

> In our old village (near Caltanisetta, in Sicily) it was
> shameful for a wife to do outside work. When I came to
> America I never believed I would have to go to work out-
> side of my own home. But look what happened! My hus-
> band made a meager living, so what are children for if not
> to help their parents. I realized that my son Carlo would
> not be able to help till the age of twelve, for that was in
> 1901 when a boy could not get working papers unless
> he was that old. I hoped Jennie, my oldest daughter would
> help me. But no, they changed the law and Jennie had to go
> to school till she was fourteen.

What was I to do? With Carlo in school it was bad enough. Without Jennie's help, who spent the better part of the day in school, I was compelled to go to work myself . . . Thank God, I managed to squeeze out a day here and there so that Jennie could stay home and work on pieces of embroidery which was well paid for by—(name of firm). I was lucky the school inspector (obviously a truant officer) was a nice man.

Opposition of the Contadino Family
to Compulsory School Attendance

The above document suggests that the *contadino* parent took recourse to ignoring the attendance law whenever possible. Lax enforcement of the school attendance law in the 1900's; lack of fear of losing prestige in the community (for school education was entirely unrelated to the mores of a "Little Italy"); absence of any counteracting influence through such institutions as the church or mutual aid societies; all were conducive to a way of least resistance: girls—and less frequently boys—were simply discouraged from attending school.

Evidence of this evasion of the compulsory education law is overwhelming; a few extracts from life histories are revealing of the situation.

My uncle and his wife saved sufficient money to go into the restaurant business. But before opening a business of his own he brought from Italy his parents, two brothers and a sister. This he did in the interest of himself for his relatives could be relied upon as trustworthy and industrious helpers. But he did this also in the interest of his family, for, as he said, he provided jobs for his relatives at good wages and, what's more important, a chance to work within the family . . .

His wife and their two children were required to work hard. Josephine, the girl, helped a great deal though she was only eight years old. As a matter of fact, she did more work than her brother Nick who was fourteen years old. When Josephine was ten years old, the father forbade her to go to school. In his estimation, she could read and write, and that was enough for any Italian girl. The father insisted that she was big enough to give real help to her parents.

He made up different excuses before attendance officers who somehow let him alone (that was around 1910) . . . Josephine is forty-two years old today, married, a mother of five children, and almost illiterate.

Nickey, the boy, was encouraged to go to school, but was

expected to work also in the father's restaurant. Nickey soon lost interest in the school and quit it. Later he demanded from his father a greater allowance, and when this was refused he went to work as a furrier.

A public school teacher's report is illustrative of the prevailing attitude of the southern Italian immigrant toward the loss of his children's earning power.

This was years ago . . . I was amazed at the frank statements by Italian pupils who when absent from school gave as an excuse, "My mother told me to stay home," or "My parents cannot afford to send me to school every day," or anything to this effect . . .

In my conversations with the parents I became convinced that they did not uphold the worth of education nearly as much as the worth of the child's earning power to eke out the parental income.

From the life history of a third-generation Italo-American:

My mother was born in America. She had only two years of elementary school, because the death of her mother (also born in America) necessitated her remaining at home—being the eldest child. How she managed to get away with only two years at a New York Public School, I never could find out.

A very common situation, in which the main aspects of the conflict are evident, is revealed in the following extract:

One woman (twenty-four years old) of the T—family, who was born in 1914 in East Kingston, New York, told me she had never been to school because her mother did not believe girls should be educated except at home and in church. When the truant officer came around, the little girl would hide and the mother would tell the officer that she had only three children although she really had ten. The officials, moreover, were very lax in their duties, and the Italians were able to keep their children home from school so that they could work them all day long at household tasks. This American-born woman still cannot speak good English.[33]

[33]This and the preceding document are of significance for they substantiate the opinion among students of Italo-American communities that there is a group of American born children—usually girls of Italian parentage—who for all practical purposes are illiterate.

The opposition on economic grounds to compulsory school attendance beyond a "reasonable" number of years was a manifestation of
a cultural conflict between the mores of the Italian peasant and the
American mores which governed school education of youth.
Changes in the attendance law which increased the duration of compulsory schooling were therefore apt to increase the antagonistic
attitudes of Italians to a much greater degree than would be expected
on the part of American communities or immigrant groups who were
more conditioned to accept changes than the Italians. It was probably unfortunate, therefore, that the many changes since 1903 coincided with the most acute period of accomodation of Italians to their
American environment. Thus while the 1896 law, which was operative at the height of Italian immigration and which permitted children to obtain working papers at the age of 12,[34] was severe from the
Italian point of view, the subsequent changes were more drastic insofar as American educational concepts developed more rapidly than
Italians could acculturate to them. Consequently the conflict not
only did not lessen, but instead grew, and contributed to the retention of an antagonistic attitude toward compulsory school attendance. Thus the new law of 1903 which extended the compulsory
school age from fourteen to sixteen gave additional impetus to the
Italians to regard the law and American schools as a force which, as
an Italo-American expresses it, "ruined all our hopes of a decent
living, kept us poor and destroyed the sanctity of the home." Or, as
one irate mother stated when she was told that her fifteen-year-old
son had to attend high school regularly, *"La legge e fatta contra la
famiglia."* (The law is made against the family).

Economic conditions among Italians in the United States, though
on a low level, have rarely been so drastic that an Italian family
could not support its school-age children. In comparison with prevalent economic norms of the United States, they appear to be afflicted by pauperism. Yet from the point of view of southern Italian old-
world standards of living, their situation in America is incongruous
with the notion of poverty. They themselves attest to this. A typical
statement, without much variation, applies to nearly all Italians.

> In Italy we were poor, always on the verge of starvation
> . . . Who could afford to eat spaghetti more than once
> a week? Who could afford a luxury like a pair of city
> shoes? In America no one starved, though a family

[34]*Statistical Reference Data Showing School Background Conditions, Factors,
Trends and Problems*, Part I. Board of Education of the City of New York, Bureau of
Reference, Research and Statistics, (January, 1936). Publication No. 27, pp. 184-
189.

> earned no more than five or six dollars a week . . .
> Don't you remember how our *paesani* here in America
> ate to their heart's delight till they were belching like
> pigs, and how they dumped mountains of uneaten food
> out of the windows? We were not poor in America; we
> just had a little less than the others.

The same informant states in the same breath, however, that "the schools made of our children persons of leisure—*signorini* (little gentlemen)—they lost the dignity of good children to think first of their parents, to help them whether they need it or don't need it . . . America took from us our children." This expression "America took our children," or "the school took our children," is repeated so often and so consistently that a mere emphasis on an economically induced conflict between the patterns of the family and the American school seems to offer insufficient explanation of the problem. Absence of poverty *per se* and a simultaneous accusation of the school as a source of economic ruination suggest that the conflict was based on a totality of cultural divergence, and that economic motives had validity only insofar as they were the most overt cultural manifestation of a peasant society in a state of maladjustment to a foreign environment.

As in any attempt to explain the causes of their emigration from Italy, the Italians think of no other reason but that of poverty—which may have very likely been only a rationalization, and the true causes may have been of a different sort—so the Italian immigrant evaluated or rationalized his status in America, and his difficulties, primarily in terms of economic values. Any cultural modification, any change in the family pattern, any change in social status of the groups or the individual are measured by him mainly by the degree of material benefits or losses accompanying the process of change. This is not to say that he is unaware of other values, other criteria; however, the sphere of economic interest, at least within his family, is to him the mainspring of his accommodation. And to follow up the changes that the Italian family in America experienced relative to the schooling of children, it appears expedient to examine first the changes caused by economic adjustments, and hence to proceed to the more general aspect of a cultural conflict and accommodation.

THE EFFECT OF ECONOMIC ADJUSTMENT ON FAMILY MORES, IN RELATION TO THE SCHOOLING PROCESS

The impact of the industrial character of American economic life was strong enough to cause dislocations in the family pattern of any immigrant group; even the old American stock must have felt it.

Amidst a world of machines the Italian was the most affected by it,[35] since, among the other immigrant groups, he was probably the least adept at adjusting himself. Within the framework of the Italian family, there had to occur a drastic permutation of the roles of all members of the inclusive primary group.

Contrary to the nominal role of the father in Italy as breadwinner of the family, in America he actually had to assume this role *de facto*. The wife who in Italy was constrained exclusively to activities of the household economy became in America a "cash earner" by dividing her energy between her loyalty to her family and "toil for others, but for the sake of her household." A change in the economic function of the mother and thus the acquisition of a new social status within the precincts of the family was in itself significant enough to cause a structural reorganization of the *contadino* family.

The most important change, and probably a contributing factor in the above modification, was the change in the economic significance of the child. Inability of the parent to utilize the child, especially a boy, in a home industry; difficulty in fitting a child into a steady and gainful activity without detaching him from the surveillance of the parental home; the constant pressure to comply with the school attendance law, these led him toward a process of accommodation. Childhood, as a definite stage of development, was gradually becoming accepted not as a concession to the prevailing American concepts but as an adjustment to his own newly created situation. "In an accomodation," say Park and Burgess, "the antagonism of the hostile elements is for the time being regulated and conflict disappears as overt action although it remains latent as a potential force.[36] Indeed, the Italian parent accepted the span of childhood as of longer duration, but he accepted it in a spirit of fatalistic resignation; the traditional attitude remained latent and the antagonism was never wholly dissolved. He never conceptualized "childhood" more or less in conformity with the American patterns; he retained the traditional attitude which under specific conditions, as will be shown later, leaves its latent state and assumes the full force of a *modus vivendi*.

It should not be overlooked that the process of accommodation in the above aspect was greatly affected by the cardinal problem of whether the immigrant considered America as a permanent abode or only as temporary expediency to secure a better financial status in his homeland. For it must be obvious that those Italians who came here as temporary wage earners could hardly be expected to entertain any

[35]Brown, *op. cit.*, p. 222.
[36]Park and Burgess, *op. cit.*, p. 665.

other but an antagonistic attitude toward complying with American statutory laws if they interfered with their economic interest. Likewise, as long as the average Italian immigrant oriented his interests in the direction of the homeland, as long as he cherished the hope of returning to Italy, he could hardly be expected to make vital concessions to the prevailing American patterns. A continuous hesitancy between remaining in America as a permanent place of residence and repatriation to Italy had to give way either to deliberate choice or to a spirit of resignation before a more definite attitude toward education in America could "jell." It appears, in fact, that the general trend to abandon any design of returning to Italy became noticeable in the early 1920's, and this period coincided with a noticeable change in the accommodation process of Italians, and, particularly, in their attitude toward availing themselves and their children of education.[37]

For example an Italo-American relates:

> We, my family, came here with the intention of earning as much money as possible and then returning to Sicily. As long as I had brothers and a sister living in Italy—my parents had died—I always had a longing to return, or at least, to go back for a visit. But when all my brothers and my sister came to this country for good, I lost my former interest to return to Italy. The few friends of my childhood are still there, but I can be without them as long as all my relatives are in America.

Having accepted America as the land "where one will be buried," the Italian parents accepted also the new economic pattern of the family, and with it a prolonged "childhood." This had a profound influence so far as the schooling process is concerned, and furnishes the clue to an understanding of the present day differences between the elementary school situation and the problem of Italo-American children in the high school.

The Prolongation of Social Infancy of the Italian Child in America

With the end of childhood shifted several years ahead, at least up to the "working-paper" age, and with the realization by the parents of their inability to regard the child in his early teens as an economic asset, the loss of the family's significance as an economic unit inevita-

---

[37] The investigator bases his conclusion upon several factors of which the most important seems to have been the introduction of literacy tests for immigrants which gave a strong impetus to bring from Italy as many relatives as possible before the quotas and "grace periods" expired, and thus to settle the *famiglia* upon American soil for good. With the establishment of numerically strong familial units, all social interests became centered in America.

bly was associated with the peril of a breakdown, or lessening of the social inclusiveness of the family which was to the Italian a satisfactory social world. In fact, the family was the only world the parent knew that gave him a safe mooring and kept him from disorganization and demoralization. And therefore, though the parent acquiesced in prolonged childhood, he retained a basic antagonism toward the American school as one of the primary sources of family "ruination." To be sure, he complied with the necessity of sending his children to elementary school; but not because of any realization of moral value or material prospects—but solely because he had "no use for his children" at a certain age. But he also realized the potential danger in that his children themselves might become imbued with the sense of material uselessness to their parents, a principle which from his point of view endangered all moral and social values of family life. So while he upheld the letter of the compulsory attendance law, he never gave in to its spirit. He merely accommodated; he did not undergo a cultural change in the sense of assimilation. All his attitudes toward education in America were nurtured by the very same familial mores which governed his educational concepts in Italy. His desire to preserve the family tradition could not preclude the abandonment of the economic role of the child. On the contrary, he clung to the tradition with persistence for he realized not only the moral worth but also the factual possibility of retaining the above principle at a later stage of the child's development. While his children were attending elementary school, he paved the way for their acceptance of economic responsibility on grounds of their approaching maturity.

As has been indicated in Chapter VII, the driving of the child toward early social maturation constituted an important element of the family mores in southern Italy. And in the retention of the Italian cultural background in America, this aspect protrudes in any situation that has bearing upon the adjustment process in America, particularly in the school situation. Having acquiesced in the uselessness of children at the early stages of school education, there was at least no open manifestation of a conflict between the Italian parental home and the American school laws. On the surface there seemed to be even approbation and stimulation of school attendance on the part of the parents. It is probable that at the elementary school age level, there came a reasoned acceptance of the child as a "child." Since no economic significance could be attached to the boy or girl, and since no benefits could be derived from them save some help with domestic chores, going to school came to be regarded as a moral activity, for even in Italy, the parents rationalized, a *child* went to school.

An Italian-born mother sums up this acceptance of the situation as follows:

> We in our family were never accustomed (in Italy) to sending our children to school. The school building was far away and we would be always in fear of something happening to our boy. Joe who was born in Italy, once disappeared for two days. We decided not to send him to school any more.
>
> Here in America it's different. The school is on the next block . . . so we are glad the children go to school. Besides, what could they possibly do at home? They are just a nuisance hanging around without doing anything worthwhile. They are, you know, *Americani* children; so what can one expect from them? It is just as well that they go to school. At least I know that for several hours my heart is at ease.

But notwithstanding an apparent acquiescence, there was and still is a deep-rooted conflict; for as social maturity of the child approaches—a stage of development which has shifted from about ten years of age for the girl and about twelve for the boy in Italy to twelve for the Italian girl and fourteen for the Italian boy in America—the conflict comes out into the open. The economic and familial functions of the child, covering a series of duties and responsibilities which at a certain age traditionally relegate all child activities such as play and even school attendance to memories of childhood, again enter the considerations of the parents. Here is what an Italian-born mother of a fourteen-year-old boy told the judge of the juvenile court.[38]

> Nick no wanta work. He big man, fourteen and wanta play ball all the day. Father say, "You go today and work in restaurant with your uncle . . . " He make faces, cusses, laughs, and runs out to play ball . . . He very bad boy . . . He no wanta work . . . He like nothing but ball . . . The father work hard. Have heart trouble. Nick ought to help. His father work hard when he was only eleven years old. That would be right way for Nick.

As the children grow older, and as the working-paper age looms ahead, the justification for sending them to school as well as the need

---

[38]Report of Causes of Crime, *National Commission on Law Observance and Enforcement.* (Washington, D.C.: 1931) Vol. II, No. 3, pp. 4-5.

to comply with the compulsory school attendance law becomes less and less obvious to them.

> Frank R. student of the M. Vocational high school has been absent from school practically all term. When he does attend, he refuses to remain more than one-half day . . . Father states that Frank is a very nice, obedient son. He knows that Frank dislikes school and has difficulties with his teachers. He thinks Frank has no scholastic ability and it would be best for all concerned if Frank got his working papers. The father knows that the boy is only fifteen, but insists that other boys of even less than Frank's age got their papers, and that *such things could obviously be arranged*, if one really wishes to help the family.

If there was at the elementary school age level a semblance of parental stimulation of attendance, there appears, as the child nears the newly conceptualized maturation point, a definite attitude of passivity. Or, if there was previously an attitude of tolerance, it is superseded by open hostility toward the prospect of "further wasting the time at school."

This is the case of Lily D, fifteen years old, pupil of a public school in the Bronx, New York City, whose father came from the *contadino* class in Italy and who is now a barber in his own establishment. Her mother works as a factory hand.

> The teacher reported that the girl had not reported to school this term and that she was being kept at home to keep house . . . When we called at Mr. D's barber shop, he stated emphatically that the only conditions under which he would send Lily to school would be if the city contributed to his family income the same amount that his wife earns ($17.00) so that his children (the family consisted of eleven members) could have what he considers the necessities of life and his wife could stay at home and take care of them . . . The family is not on home relief and Mr. D. thinks they would not be eligible for it even without his wife's earnings.

With each advancing year, the normal unwillingness of the child to go to school, his absence, truancy, poor scholarship, and so forth, are met with less and less parental disapproval. The gradual nonconformity of the child with schooling regulations is rationalized by the parents as a symptom of over-age; i.e., the approach of maturity which is incompatible with going to school.

Anthony V., sixteen years old, attending public school, who formerly was an obedient boy and a regular attendant at school has started to show a truancy pattern and a defiant attitude toward school . . . Father feels that the son should be given a mechanical education if school is to be of any use to Anthony. Otherwise, the father feels that the boy is very mature and that naturally his mind is set on going to work and not on attending school.

The Shift of Conception of Social Maturity to Working-paper Age

It is at this stage that the parents begin to speak openly of their own poverty, of the duties of the children toward the family, of the child's being "too old" for school, of "not having the necessary brains," and so on—inculcating in the children the traditional concepts of social responsibility and conditioning them to the acceptance of the traditional role as economic supporters of, or contributors to, the material welfare of the family.

In a recent interview with a mother and her son who had been a truant and was failing all his subjects, I turned to the boy and said to him: "Why you are a full-grown man. Just think of it, sixteen years of age, tall, well-built, strong . . . " and before I could finish, the mother interrupted and said, "Why he should have been a man and acted like a man when he was thirteen years of age. His father went to work when he was nine years old, as a stone mason. By the time he was thirteen he was earning almost a man's wage. He had to work hard, out-of-doors, in all kinds of weather, and sometimes not too sure of even getting his wages at the end of the job."

In almost every interview that we have with Italian parents when they are called in to discuss either the school work, school attendance or the behavior of their children, there is a recurring theme which crops up: that the father when he was eight, nine, or ten years old was practically doing a man's work and assuming adult responsibility. This information is not only given to the boys in the presence of the teacher, but is the topic of conversation in the home and particularly around the dinner table. This statement is often made boastfully and also, at times, derogatory to the American system which keeps boys and girls in school to an age at which, when in Italy, the mother and father were probably either married or on the way to assuming full family responsibility.

They begin to impose upon the children a variety of functions regardless of whether or not they interfere with school attendance and school duties.

> Mother said that her husband is no longer a young man (52 years now) and needs rest. She herself is quite ill, therefore she is taking the boy out of school so that he can take over the operation of the father's newspaper stand.

In this respect they also show an overt leniency toward infractions committed by their children in the school and meriting parental disapproval. Case of L. V., high school boy, age fourteen and a half years, follows:

> Leo has been reported as a very obnoxious student in his class . . . He refuses to obey the teacher, is openly rebellious, uses vile language . . . The mother received me with cordiality and tried to pooh-pooh all complaints about her son. "I don't mind if he goes to school," she told me. "I would be very proud to have a learned man in our family. But then again, I am against his being tortured. The teachers have no sympathy for him; they don't realize that it is hard for Leo to sit in class with babies around him . . . Leo is coming of age, he is almost fifteen years old; the teachers should know that . . . If it pleases the school I shall tell my husband to beat Leo up, though I don't see that Leo is a bad boy. I think he is a very dutiful son, very considerate of us. Tell Mr. Covello that we will do our best; it won't be long now. Leo will have a good job."

The ambivalent attitude of the parents which is noticeable at the earlier stage and which is, undoubtedly, the manifestation of a conflict between their tradition and the American point of view, gives way to open disapproval of the imposition upon them of undesirable customs. Whereas a parent at an earlier stage may have voiced loudly his approbation of schooling but at the same time constantly reminded his child of the duties and responsibilities toward the family, he now emphasizes only the latter element. Or for example, as long as the child is under sixteen, that is, the compulsory age limit, the Italian parent professes a willingness to cooperate with the school. Parents will concede that education is their concern, though "it takes *too* many years of the youngsters' lives." But when the age of sixteen is reached a drastic change occurs; the parent suddenly shifts the entire responsibility of a decision for further schooling upon the child himself.[39] As if to emphasize the social maturity of the boy which is now being recognized by the American school, the parents suddenly profess not to have any say in such matters. "It is up to the boy, himself," they usually say. "He is big enough, so let him decide for himself whether he wants to go to school or not. We wash our hands of this affair."

Take for example the case of J. R., age fifteen, of Italian parents.

> (The mother) wants both her sons to graduate. However, if their mind isn't to it, she does not believe in forcing them.

From the parental point of view, social maturation is the point of departure for all their rationalizations, attitudes and decisions in the schooling of their children. All pressures exerted by the parents in inculcating the old tradition find their moral validation by invoking the maturity angle. Thus the demands of parents that children render economic assistance in support of the family have a tendency to be based not on the principle of "Children *must* help their parents," as was traditional in Italy, but on the principle, "Children who reach maturity, and are therefore aware of their obligations toward the family, *are expected* to help the family." The difference between the two formulas is the difference between the child as "property of the parents" and the child as an "individual member of the family," which is essentially a criterion of the degree of accommodation of the Italian parents to American values.

A mother of seven children, six of whom were born in America, epitomizes the concern of the Italian parent over the late maturation of children in America.

> It is difficult to bring up children in this country. In the old country children somehow knew, without being taught, that they should help the family . . . In America all children are much younger; they have neither the understanding nor the physical strength that children in Italy have. Here a family has to wait a long time till the children get sense and make up their minds that there is nothing finer in the world than to take interest in the affairs of the family. Maybe it is the weather, maybe it is the bad food. I don't know. But children grow here very slow. And because they grow so slow one cannot be sure that they will be obedient children.

[39]This pertains, however, only to a boy, for the girl, according to the familial tradition is not invested with the power to make decisions of her own.

This is how another woman expressed the same concern:

> I came from Italy with my mother when I was fourteen
> years of age. At fifteen I was married and in the course of
> my married life, have had sixteen children, eleven of
> whom are still living. My daughters were married later
> than I was. In fact they married in their early twenties but
> I trained them in housework at an early age, and once
> they got through elementary school, in the good old days
> (in America) when boys and girls could leave school at
> the age of thirteen, I sent them to work so they could make
> a contribution to the family. So that when they were
> married, they really were grown up and had some sense in
> their heads.
>
> But my grandchildren, fourteen, fifteen, sixteen, and
> even seventeen years of age, are just like children and I am
> much disturbed because I don't know when they are ever
> going to grow up. They do not want to learn any of the
> household duties and their chief concern is playing,
> movies, and boy friends. It is a bad country where child-
> ren, boys and girls, but particularly girls, are not trained
> to work with their mothers in the home. I have tried to do
> something with my grandchildren but their mothers and
> fathers have taken on American ways and I make no head-
> way with them at all.

The change in attitude, if it were common to all parents, would denote a substantial cultural modification and, in school matters,
would definitely stimulate a still greater lengthening of childhood
and prolong the schooling period. However, all evidence points to
the fact that the original principle has still great weight; and that the
prolonged process of social maturation has merely produced a
chronological shift.

Aware of the conflict between the parental mores and the school,
the parent asserts himself in no unmistakable terms lest the school's
influence over the child is contrary to parental designs.

Take for example, the case of J. S., junior high school student, age
fifteen:

> The father was born in Italy. He settled in Hartford,
> Conn., where he and his wife were earning good money in
> a silk mill, and had not time to go to school, but raised
> two daughters and one son. The father made out well, but
> in the depression, lost the store he owned and $200.00 in a
> bank account. The girls had to postpone, therefore, the
> plan of marrying and had to work in order to put the
> family back on its feet. Joe, the son, left the second year of

junior high school, also to help the father, who was more eager to see Joe quit school than Joe himself. A school teacher who tried to persuade the father to let Joe finish was told by the father how much he regretted the step taken. He assured the teacher that the $200 lost in the bank was, in truth, the money put aside for Joe's education. However, since this money was gone, the father could not see the possibility of supporting Joe even in such matters as carfare and school lunch.

Further investigation revealed that the family neither applied for nor was entitled to relief. The pooled earnings of the family with the exception of Joe, amounted to over $60 weekly. The father's desire to have Joe quit school, therefore, had no economic justification.

Take also the case of V. C., age fifteen:

Mother did not think Vincent would be back to school in the fall since he'll be sixteen the week after school opens. Times have been hard with her and she's been on relief until it was stopped, then she was left without support. Vincent is a good boy and feels that he has a responsibility to shoulder in looking after his mother and sister.

The following case illustrates a definite uneasiness on the part of the mother when confronted by a high school social worker who might sway her boy against parental wishes:

Visitor (social worker) inquired concerning Vincent's failure to attend school. The mother told the worker that her husband, who is quite advanced in years, wishes to retire from any active work. A recent change occurred in the household in that a daughter, who has been working, married and is no longer part of the family group. The loss of her income is very serious to the family in which there are five members at present. Mrs. C. (the boy's mother) refuses to send the boy to another school for it is too far from home. She is willing to do her share to let Vincent go to Benjamin Franklin if he will be given nothing else but lessons in printing. This, in the mother's opinion, is the only education that the boy wants and needs . . . But Vincent must continue working under any circumstances because his money is needed in the family. The boy keeps only $2 for himself. A certain day was set for an appointment with Vincent. The mother made certain that the visitor understood that she wished to be present so that Vincent would not be exposed to the influence of the social worker without the benefit of the mother's judgment.

Within the home the parents, especially the father, use every occasion to indoctrinate the children with the moral basis of support for the parents. There are few homes where the mother or the father does not remind the children of how "things used to be in olden days," when boys and girls considered duty toward the family as a cardinal virtue. Work by children at an early age, even though inimical to school education, is regarded as the surest conditioning mechanism to bring about the desired behavior of the child.

> I went to school for a few years in Italy, but while going to school, I learned the barber's trade. When I was ten and a half years old, my uncle took me to America. I found myself working in a barber shop where I earned $1.50 a week with board . . . When I was about thirteen, I made nine trips back and forth from New York to Liverpool on a boat as a barber, where I not only made good money but considerable tips. I often tell my children this because I think they ought to understand that life is not just trying to get things from your father and your mother; that you have got to work and work hard . . . I also tell them that I had only been in America a few weeks when I began to send money to my parents in Italy, because I was a good son and wanted to make sure that not only my parents and family, but the rest of the *paesani* knew what I was doing. Here in America we bring up our children to depend upon their parents far too much and far too long. The children here want to do nothing but play . . . I believe in children working at an early age so that they learn responsibility and duty toward their parents and toward their family. That is what we mean when we say in Italian, to live like *Cristiani* (Christians).

Such a parental attitude is typical and denotes the unavoidable subordination of schooling to the economic interest of the family. It is therefore very common to observe a state of great disappointment in the parents when their concession to American educational patterns results in no definite benefits. This applies both to the boys and girls, though the parental reaction toward the educational career of the daughters is more acute than toward the sons.

> We regulate our actions by what we see is happening around us. We note a family that has sent its daughters to high school and college. The family has provided everything; food, clothing, carfare, *unearned* money

in her pocketbook to spend in so many foolish ways—
even money for cigarettes. The girl is over twenty years
of age. She graduates, gets her diploma and then marries. Then she finds a job and, what is worse, she continues to work even though her husband is working. Tell
me, what benefit does the family, the father and mother,
get out of all this? It seems to me that the parents bring
up children with many sacrifices, send them to school
and then they all live by themselves and for themselves.
It's not so bad with boys for they at least, make some contribution to the family, but in my opinion, as soon as a
girl gets enough schooling so as not to get in trouble with
the law, she should go to work and help her family until
she marries. For when she marries, she belongs to her
husband and her husband's family and you cannot expect anything from her.

A teacher of Italian *contadino* parentage in the New York City public school system states:

My parents knew that education was a compulsory thing
in America and so they took it as a matter of course. But
when I expressed my intention of continuing with high
school and finally with training school education
(teaching as a profession), my parents, especially my
mother, raised an indescribable fury. Seven more years of
schooling! Whoever heard of such a thing! A girl should
think of home, etc. . . . For the seven years that followed
I had a hard time. I could never ask my parents for a nickel
for carfare. I certainly could not ask them for lunch money or anything of that sort. I could not complain to them
about how hard my work was for that was just what they
were praying for me to say. *Then they could rightfully
force me to quit.*

An Italo-American college student, who probably describes the situation in her own home, offers this observation:

The girls have a much harder time than boys . . . The
boys were and still are the favored ones in Italian families. They are catered to, hand and foot . . . If they
have a good job and bring in a good salary, their privileges are greatly augmented. With regard to education,
again the boys are favored. Girls are meant to take care
of the home, cook, and get married.
I know of a family of five boys and a few girls. The oldest
girl decided she wanted to become a teacher. Everything
under the sun was done to discourage her from following
her desires but of no avail . . . The daughter couldn't

ask for carfare even in the worst weather for she never got it. In fact the father always cursed the day he came to America, because if he had stayed in Italy, no daughter of his would have the desire to become a teacher. She would have to work on the farm and in the house.

But only little different is the attitude of parents concerning a son who managed to acquire a school education beyond the elementary grades. A father of two sons, both born in America, complains: (the following is a paraphrase).

My oldest son C was always a very obedient son. I cannot remember a single instance when we had reason to complain about him. He was always a hard worker and gave us every penny he earned. Even while in school, he managed to bring home from two to seven dollars a week. At the age of fourteen he began to lose interest in school. We could see he was not made to be a scholar so I got him a job at the docks . . .

He is a married man now, but even now—just last week— he gave me a couple of dollars. You ask me about my youngest son? Well, that fellow is different. I begged him, my wife begged him to work with his brother at the docks where they pay a man's wages. But no, his mind was set to continue school after he was fifteen years old. Now he has the diploma. What good is it to him? What good is it to his parents? While he was a *boya* (boy) he gave very little to his mother. Then for three years that he went to high school, all he gave us was twenty-two dollars . . . At least he had the decency not to ask me for money.

He is now in the Army and keeps all the money for himself. What he will do with his diploma I don't know. I know only that his high school cost me at least three hundred dollars, for that is what he could have contributed to our home.

Criticism of the past school attendance of a boy, which was unjustifiable from the point of view of familial mores, is also voiced in the following manner by an Italo-American woman.

I feel sorry for Mrs. T—the way her family cannot manage their boy C. The fellow is big enough to be married and have children . . . A good-for-nothing! A bad, very bad example for the rest of the children in the neighborhood. He has the brain of a cockroach. He knows it; everybody knows it. Yet he insists upon going to college . . . He has no consideration for his poor parents. He exploits

> their good nature and takes from them, the chance to have
> a good meal . . .

> If he were my boy, I would know what to do, No, mister,
> such boys must work and work hard. So he went to high
> school. So what? He'll never amount to anything anyway.
> And look at his poor parents. They slave for him, while
> it should be the opposite.

The old-world attitude toward sons and daughters as the source of material benefits regardless of their school status and their educational interests must *ipso facto* be considered as a definite impediment to Italo-American children in making school adjustments. Obviously preoccupation of the parents with the economic role of children, though they have ceased to be integral parts of the household economy, prevents the development by the parents of an attitude which would contain elements of duty toward their children, at least in the sphere of school education. Parental obligation toward children as a concept did not exist in Italy. Supplying the child with clothing, food, shelter, and so forth, was essentially an investment by parents which would yield returns sooner or later. And since the child started as a useful member of the household—or more precisely, the parental economy—at an early age, the returns were immediate and concrete. In America, the same attitude among the *contadino* immigrants remains in force, with the only modification that the returns on the investment have become a matter of the future.

An Italian from Sicily explains this in the following way: (a paraphrase).

> A child (in Italy) was earning his upkeep. If he was sick
> so that he could not work at all, then his other brothers
> and sisters had to assume the sick share of the sick one.
> Parents would occasionally remind a girl or a boy: "That
> is enough; but don't go for you have to do your sick
> brother's share." When the child got well, he made up to
> his brothers and sisters for what they did for him. All
> children were worth the clothing they wore and the food
> they ate . . . When there was nothing for a boy to do at
> home, he was leased out to another family where, though
> he may have been only six or seven years old, he either
> watched the goats, or picked nuts or did any other work.
> And the parents of the boy would be paid by the other
> family. Seldom in money, for it was not considered that
> a boy of such an age is worth money. But in products or
> in reciprocal work . . . It was so in Italy; everything
> very nice. The parents stuck to the children and the child-
> ren stuck to their parents.

In America things are not that simple. Here a parent has to wait long years till everything that was spent on the child comes back . . . Some parents even keep track of what the upbringing of a particular child costs them, and they tell the amount to the son or the daughter so that they know how much is expected from them. Some parents are bitterly disappointed when things turn out differently than they expected. There are children who never pay back . . .

I, myself, don't think much of giving an education to a girl for there is no chance to be repaid. Everything she earns in later life belongs to her husband. With a boy it is different. One can take a chance even on his going to school for, *if he is an obedient son*, he will return the cost of his upkeep with interest . . .

But as I say, you have to wait and be watchful all the time.

Backed by the force of old-world tradition, the Italian in America— and that means the former *contadino*—is least likely to "invest" in the education of his children, which, as precedents have shown him, does not necessarily insure a status that would permit the son or the daughter to repay, more easily and more willingly, the sacrifices of the parents. There is nothing in the economic aspects of the southern Italian cultural background which would stimulate willingness to subscribe to an educational adventure for their children. A basic lack of a parental sense of duty toward children permits no trifling with expenditures on behalf of children. It is therefore not surprising that the average immigrant parent from southern Italy is averse to supplying his school child with what one customarily refers to as an "allowance." Several of the already cited cases indicated it. Although the evidence which points to the existing practice of giving children either none at all, or only minimum allowance for personal needs, pocket money, or school expenses,[40] does not reveal such a practice as deliberate discouragement of school attendance; the situation must be regarded nevertheless as an additional economic factor which negatively affects the schooling process of Italian children. "In my home," says a high school student, "a nickel for carfare has to be bargained out." Another says, "My chances of high school education are directly proportional to the proximity of the school." Wrathful at her son who had cut school to go to the movies, and who was both a truant and a failure at school, a mother exclaims:

Why, I give him twenty-five cents a day—every day of his life! I don't know why I do it for he should earn this

[40]The observation is made also by Consistrè, *op. cit.*, p. 340.

> money himself. He's no baby—fifteen years old. He does
> no work. He says that he can't study and go to work at the
> same time. I think his studies are playing ball and the
> movies. It's no use—work will cure him.

Such are, naturally, extreme cases. Yet the old pattern prevails, and
the formula: "You go to school, so *you* must meet the expenses,"
leads to situations where a school child, especially of high school
age, is compelled to rely on devious methods to secure a semblance of
parity with other children in the school. There are comparatively
few families who grant an allowance to their children unless the
children themselves earn it.

> I make six to eight dollars a week working on Saturdays
> in a pet shop. Most of the money I earn by pigeon deals on
> the side . . . All my money I give to my mother and she
> hands me $1.50 for the week. I tried to plead with her ex-
> plaining that five carfares to school are a quarter, five
> lunches about seventy-five cents. So what is left to me?
> "That's your business." she tells me.

> What else can I do but chisel the money out? I simply give
> her less than I earn.

When the Italo-American boy uses the term allowance, he means
the money that he has earned and which in part has been returned to
him for personal needs.

CONFLICT BETWEEN THE AMERICAN SCHOOL AND THE CULTURAL
TRADITION OF THE CONTADINO

Thus far the attempt has been to throw some light upon the problems of school children of Italian parentage only so far as they are affected by economic factors within the parental home. However
significant is the above factor, the problem requires further examination. Ostensibly the preoccupation of the parents with the economic
aspects of family life is not necessarily derived from the actual economic situation within the home. For, as several of the above cited
documents denote, the parental insistence upon support of the home
by the child occurs rather frequently where there is no justification
for giving priority to the child's earning over his schooling. The
consistent association of the child's economic role with either his
maturity status or his behavior in reference to the moral content of
the family tradition suggests the need to examine the conflict be-

tween parental designs and the American school as the product of a totality of cultural conflict, in which the economic elements, though important, are probably only a subordinate factor. Indeed, on the basis of an assimilative lag on the part of the former *contadino*—brought about by communal isolation, limited interaction with the American milieu, and accommodation to a changed Italian, rather than American, environment—it would seem to be evident that the retention of basic southern Italian cultural norms within their family life in America necessarily follows the preservation in large degree of the basic concepts and practices in regard to schooling, which in Italy sharply conflicted with the mores and folkways of the *contadino* family. Unacquainted or, at best, only slightly influenced by the principles of formal education and its compulsive aspects in Italy, the immigrant *contadino* could not but sense the American school as an "animosity" to his immediate interests which in America, as in Italy, were primarily the safeguarding of the traditional family code of living.

The School as a Social Institution

Among all American institutions the school was probably the most vital area where the mores of the *contadino* clashed with those of America, for it was primarily in the school that the child of the immigrant made a contact with America that had, so to speak, an official character. All previous contacts were for the most part vicarious experiences, since the social world of the child constituted only his family, and the Italo-American community. Even these contacts, because of restriction of the child's movements in the process of his upbringing, seldom reached out beyond the immediate tenement house stoop or, at the most, the social block. Even the play group of the child was limited because of restrictions imposed upon the choice of playmates. All pre-school contacts with America produced no direct impact upon the child, who remained fully under control of the parental tradition.

A jarring note in the harmony of the family was struck when the child began to go to school. It was at this moment that the parents felt the impact of an alien culture upon the child and very directly upon themselves. At this moment they clearly sensed the conflict between themselves and the American school. They became aware of the peril to their familial tradition and realized that the school implants into the child a different tradition; so different that there were only a few points of coincidence. If the school in Italy was an institution imposed upon their mores, in America the school became not only an alien institution but one that jeopardized the safe moorings of family life. Whereas in Italy the danger, emanating from the school, of family disorganization, individualization of its members, and so on, were only latent—since the *contadino* because of neglect or concessions to his way of life was comparatively free from complying with compulsory school attendance—in America this very principle stood in opposition to the preservation of the old-world family patterns. The American school because of this, constituted an institution in which the Italian had no share; neither was it an institution toward which he could look with great tolerance. If there are indications of modified attitudes toward the school, there still remains this basic evaluation of the school as a danger to the Italian familial organization tantamount to its well being. To be sure, school teachers report a considerably greater *rapport* between the school and the Italian parents than in former years. A teacher from a school in the East Harlem community observes:

> . . . we don't find any more of the old aloofness. Italian mothers—though almost never fathers—are frequent visitors to our school; they aren't any more the shy women who would not speak even though you addressed them in their native tongue . . . It is still difficult to make them join the Parent Teachers Association. But I must say, most of the mothers come at least to offer some excuse why they can't join . . . They are gradually responding to our invitation to make themselves feel at home . . . Occasionally they even come up with complaints against the laxity of our school discipline.

Other reports, however, suggest that in spite of an apparent bridging of the gap, the elementary school remains an institution remote from the every-day interests of Italian parents. For example, a report of a visiting teacher reads:

> After visiting several Italian families I must conclude that the indifference of the parents to their children staying out of school is due to the fact that they do not understand the laws and customs of this country too well and do not know the penalty of wilfully allowing their children to stay from school without cause.

A further example of the indifference to the school is given in the following report:

> After conversations with many Italian parents I came across only one Italian father who realized that as a tax-

payer he is supporting the school. All other Italians pro-
fessed no interest in knowing who pays for the schools.
They listened with incredulity to the explanation of how
their rentals help to keep our schools open.

One of my conversants offered the following statement:
"Maybe it is so. And if it is so, why don't they ask us what
kind of schools we would like. If as you say, *we* pay for
the schools, then I say we pay too much for all the useless
stuff that is being taught."

Obviously, the elementary school still represents an institution
which is too remote from the mores of present day Italians to be free
from a cultural conflict with both the Italian parents and their children, at least to an extent which would make the school an integral
part of the Italo-American community. Although the elementary
school has become an accepted institution, it still lacks for them social and moral authority which are essential to real schooling.[41]
Militating against such an acceptance of the elementary school is
the cultural background of Italians in America from which, in spite
of significant accommodation, advancement is still characterized by
mores incapable of being adjusted to the prerequisites of American
society. And the very intention of the parents to preserve the family
tradition causes them to regard the school as an institution which
has quite definitely alienated—and continues to alienate—the child
from the social, economic, and moral foundations of family life. The
parents sense with misgiving the influence of the school upon the
whole structure of familial relationships. A statement by Julius
Drachsler is much to the point:

The fear of losing the children haunts the older generation. It is not merely the natural desire of parents to retain
influence over the child . . . It is a vague uneasiness
that a delicate network of precious traditions is being
ruthlessly torn asunder, that a whole world of ideals is
crashing into ruins; and amidst this desolation the fathers and mothers picture themselves wandering about
lonely in vain search of their lost children.[42]

"The school takes our children away from us" is still heard. And
although, as has been previously suggested, the economic aspects
play an emphatic role, the indignation and the fear element that ac-

[41]Charles H. Judd, "Specialization, the Bane of Secondary Education," *The
Bulletin of the Department of Secondary School Principals of the National Education Association*, (March, 1938), Vol. XXII, p. 15.

[42]Julius Drachsler, *Democracy and Assimilation*, p. 80.

company such outbursts indicate that the accusation of "having taken the child away" goes deeper than economic rationalizations of
the parents would imply. It is a fear that the school will indoctrinate
the child with ideas contrary to all Italian codes of proper family life
and thus prove detrimental to all members of the family.

Since the most acute stage of a cultural conflict between the
Italian parental home and the American school occurs during the
child's attendance of the elementary school, the parents, particularly
the mothers, are keenly concerned over the activities of the child relative to grade school attendance. A public school teacher of Italian
origin describes the situation thus:

> I was born in Italy and went there through grammar and
> high school. Some peasant children went to school, the
> majority did not. Children walked as far as one and a half
> miles to reach the school, and I never saw the mothers
> accompanying them. Even seven-year-old girls walked
> the distance all by themselves; that is either alone or in
> the company with another girl, but never in company
> with boys.

> But look what they do here in America! The mothers take
> their children to school in the morning, even if its only a
> block or so. They don't leave immediately, though surely
> they have their home chores to do. No, they wait till
> everything indicates that the school is in session; only
> then do they go home. In the afternoon they are back at
> the school, long before classes are dismissed. When
> children begin pouring out of the school gates, the
> mothers actually pounce upon their children and in a
> moment you see them being dragged off toward home.
> There is such eagerness to bring the children home that
> makes no sense to the outsider.

> The fact is that the mothers are afraid lest their children,
> especially the girls, are contaminated by contact with
> other children, spend too much time among strangers in
> the next block, and are away from supervision . . .

Another informant, also a teacher of Italian origin, states that

> . . . in our public school, Italian mothers come some-
> times without being called. Our principal attributes this
> to their interest in the scholastic problems of their child-
> ren. I suspect a different motive, for as one mother put it,
> "I came to find out whether Tony eats his sandwich I give
> him each morning or whether he throws it away. You
> people in school have no interest in that. You will even

> probably tell him that he does not have to listen to his mother. You have different customs here; and if I let Tony do as you tell him, I cannot control him. You, Mr. Teacher, are an Italian yourself, and you know what bad ideas are being put into our children."

It is therefore quite probable that the apparent willingness on the part of Italian mothers to "cooperate" with the elementary school is derived not from any interest in the school *per se*, but solely from a desire to counteract the detrimental influence of the school. Such behavior, basically of an antagonistic nature, bespeaks the remoteness of the school from the parental patterns of life. Despite the acceptance of the principle of compulsory attendance and the apparent familiarity of the parents with the particular school which is attended by the child, even the elementary school is hardly a social institution in a sense that it is complementary to the mores governing the informal aspects of education at home. Rather, one must emphasize the conflict between the two.

Yet, whereas on the level of elementary schooling there is the possibility of expecting parental compliance with attendance and some form of cooperation with the school, the parental attitude toward secondary education is one of latent animosity and of overt disinterestedness. As against some form of *rapport* at the elementary school level, there is none at all between the parental home and the high school. The remoteness of secondary education from the everyday life interests of the southern Italian, the retention of the old-world educational concepts and practices make the high school a much more alien institution than the elementary school.

> Italian parents have come to consult me about their children who were in other schools—not only high schools remote from the East Harlem community, but elementary schools in the district. Rarely does the parent know the name of the school, and even more rarely, the name of the principal or teachers in the school. It is *la scuola* (the school)—nameless—with teachers without names, remote, inaccessible, where confusing things happen and situations develop *"che tormentano i genitori e la famiglia e dove non si capisce niente,"* (that torment the parents and the family and where all is confusion).

While animosity toward the elementary school is somewhat blunted by formal educational precedents in Italy, and the acceptance of elementary schools may be regarded as tantamount to some accultur-

ation, the attitudes toward high school education are on the whole
the same as the Italian immigrant showed toward the elementary
school at the early stage of immigration. The high school is being
conceptualized as a social institution even less than was the elementary school. Its authority has no points of coincidence with the Italian milieu in America. And, therefore, neither the compulsory aspects of high school (or junior high school) attendance, nor its
curriculum, nor its moral content press themselves upon the parents
as social norms that must be complied with. On the contrary, all
evidence points toward a pronounced rejection of high school as a
whole.

It is pertinent, however, to state at this point that the above generalization is valid only for the *contadino* parents and, more specifically, for those who brought no formal educational experience with
them from Italy. Those who were in the class of "literates," and were
by this factor alone stimulated toward greater accommodation and
even assimilation, cannot be characterized by rejection of secondary
education. Many instances indicate a rather complete acceptance on
their part of the high school. But, under a cloak of conformity with
American educational norms, there almost constantly lurks some of
the elements in the southern Italian family tradition which either ne-
gate or offset the full value of secondary school education. The individualization process in such families did not go far enough to
permit great changes of familial patterns; acceptance of high school
and even higher education is the result of accommodation, and the
conflict therefore, though less overtly than in the case of the illiterate *contadino*, exists nevertheless.

Here is a statement, by a mother who comes from the *artigiano*
class, showing overt antagonism to higher education:

> Well, my daughter wanted to be a teacher. I sacrificed
> everything to send her to high school and college. I did
> not send her to a factory or a shop to help along the fami-
> ly income, much as the family needed it. And now after
> all the worries and sacrifices, she can't get a job in any
> school (in New York City). Send her away from home?
> Don't even mention the idea. That's impossible. Who
> would look after her? A girl cannot go out alone into the
> world away from her family. The Americans who send
> their girls away from home don't know what they are do-
> ing. We Italians oppose that idea—all of us. A girl must
> sleep under her own family roof. Even if my daughter
> wanted to go badly enough, which I doubt because she
> was not brought up that way, our whole family and rela-
> tives would not permit it. It is simply impossible.

Well we did send our children to high school and college and followed the American way and *che mi conchiude?* (what does it amount to?) Did they make anything out of it? We should have followed *i buoni costumi del nostro paese* (the good customs of our native village). Send them to work soon to help out the family and then arrange for them to *sistemarsi* (get settled and raise a family). Everybody would have been much better off. I stay awake nights thinking of the terrible mistake my husband and I made.

Intellectual Interests of the Contadino in Relation to High School Education

Basic to the "non-recognition" of formal education beyond the compulsory age limits, and the lack of encouragement to children, is undoubtedly the retention of the old-world concept that any knowledge above the wisdom of the group leads to family dissolution and disorganization. Any category of knowledge that, if acquired by the child, may result in lowering the prestige of the parents is still viewed with suspicion and alarm. Latent antagonism toward the school is shown in the following statements:

My grandmother always maintained that the American schools had transformed me from an exemplary Italian child to a girl with questionable attitudes and ideas. Close contact with my mother-in-law has revealed that she entertains the same viewpoint concerning the American school system. I have often discussed with her, the problem of what the school should inculcate in the minds of young students. Wistfully remarking that "in Italy it was different" she goes on to speak about manners and morals. When pressed to explain the definite meaning of such terms she stated that children should be taught to respect their parents and relatives. They should never question their authority, nor disobey with a shrug of the shoulders as they are accustomed to do here in America. To keep quiet, listen and absorb the wisdom of their elders is the duty of children. These are the things they should be taught.

My parents did not even like my ability to speak English. As a junior high school boy I was smart enough to act as interpreter between my Italian speaking parents and social investigators from the Home Relief Bureau. My father did not like the idea at all. I realized that my acquisition of a voice in family affairs was irksome to my parents, especially my father whom I deposed from his high pedestal of authority.

My parents marvelled at the progress that I made in school, and considered it a great honor and a great point of pride that I knew so much. But I must say my parents somehow felt hurt when they realized that we children became their superiors.

Philip needs experiences to widen his interests. The father does not approve of reading in general, saying that too much reading causes confusion in one's head. There are plenty of wise men among the relatives of the family, says the father, who can advise better than any book or newspaper.

(Report of Guidance Laboratory: Remedial Reading. Teachers College, Columbia University to Benjamin Franklin High School, May, 1943).

In the two documents which follow, two Italian fathers speak of the futility of high school education and deplore the high school career of their children:

My son Joe graduated from high school at the age of nineteen. His older brother quit school at fifteen. Now both are working as plasterers. Tell me, please, was it worthwhile to go to all the trouble? Joe isn't at all smarter than his brother. But he got ideas in his head that he is smarter. And the result? He is a nuisance in my family. He does his share but he also demoralizes the rest of the children. I am afraid that high school went to his head and now he is good for nothing.

My two boys went to school against my will. And what do I see now? By having forced them to learn things they do not need, their health is gone, and they are just two stupid donkeys, who cannot take care of themselves; have no use for what they learned and even forgot long ago whatever they did learn in school.

In Italy they would have been healthy young men, with a sense of dignity; responsible men. *Men*, I say, because this schooling made them children.

High school education in the eyes of parents should yield concrete results. There is bitterness and disillusionment when high school education proves a blind alley. The by-product of such education—the experience of intellectual broadening—is in itself meaningless to the illiterate or semi-illiterate parent. It must always result in definite material returns commensurate with the time, money, and effort expended.

Mother wants me to become either a lawyer or an importer of Italian food products. Father thinks my tongue is not loose enough to be a lawyer. He thinks a lawyer has to be first of all an orator. He therefore thinks a career as a real estate broker is the best for me.

But beneath all this talk of theirs, they don't care as long as I make a good living. When I told them that I was asked in school what my ambitions are, my mother said, "Just say you want to be a lawyer. What you will become no one can tell. What difference how you earn your money as long as you earn it honestly." My parents don't want to influence me—at least, that's what they say. They expect me to make up my mind all by myself. They tell me that since I know so much more of American conditions than they, I ought to be able to make a better decision than they would.

At the same time they remark, especially my father, that the money one needs for a lawyer's education could very well be used in establishing a good importing business. They also remark that in five or six years I could be in business all for myself. All our relatives would support me with money, help and advice. Whereas it is doubtful if our relatives would be interested in my law career.

The old-world system still retains its ancient hold. There is still the feeling that higher learning, a profession, is not for the son or daughter of a former *contadino*. On the other hand, however, the process of accommodation undoubtedly stimulates in the parents a desire to see their children get such an education provided they achieve the desired status quickly, without much mental effort and without greatly upsetting the familial pattern. But the realization that under the present system of education it takes from fourteen to sixteen years of unceasing mental and financial strain to become a lawyer or physician leads to a situation where the majority of Italo-Americans in the free professions are almost exclusively drawn from the non-*contadino* group; i.e., from the former *artigiani* and *galantuomini*. A high school diploma is therefore the limit to which a parent will aspire. But even this limit is in no case outside the scope of familial interests. The parent has discovered that high school education is not necessarily associated with material benefits or higher prestige, unless such education reaches the higher stages which lead to the respected professions of doctor, lawyer, and engineer. Thus, high school education has in itself neither vocational or professional significance. And since it has no bearing upon a specific vocation or specific income prestige, the parent views the high school as nothing but a place where "one's brains are being stuffed without any future use." The recurrent theme runs as follows: "P is a good painter but never went to high school. D went to high school and became a painter. What is the difference between the two?"

Even the vocational curriculum of the high school has little appeal to the parent, because it is commonly voiced among Italians, that "A trade can be learned only by actual work, which is the only school." The customary rationalization:

> A (a girl) quit school at fourteen and went into a dress shop. B studied dressmaking for three years. Four years of school and B earns twenty-two dollars and A earns, at the same time, thirty dollars. And all that B knows she learned from A.

This line of parental reasoning is rather frequently the means by which the child is dissuaded from relying on the educational validity of the school. A high school student relates:

> My mother was always of the opinion that I had the weakest brains among all the children of our family. So when I entered this school both my mother and father shook their heads saying: "If it were within our power we would save you the time and the difficulties which are ahead of you."
>
> When I was fifteen and still eager to continue in high school, my parents became extremely angry. They wanted to know definitely what I was studying for. When I told them that I was taking sign designing and painting and intended to make this my life's vocation, my father got very angry, but then he softened up and started to show me how useless it was to waste time in school for such things.
>
> He offered me a bet that within six months I would know more about sign painting than the school could teach me in six years. "Why," he told me, "don't you know that your godfather is working for a man whose brother is a very wealthy sign painter? Your godfather has a duty toward you and our entire family; he will fix things up so that even your apprenticeship won't cost you anything."
>
> A week later my godfather came himself and told me to get ready; everything was fixed. I refused to go. I spoke of sign painting as an art; I mentioned the importance of a high school diploma . . .

> I hope to graduate next year. My father is still angry and
> I try to placate him by giving him a couple of packs of
> cigars every week. My mother has no reason to feel that
> way for I give her at least eight dollars every week. But
> both still insist that this foolishness of mine is against
> their wishes. My father says he won't come to my gradua-
> tion. He promises to be drunk on that day so that he can
> forget the insult my family will suffer from me.

A negative attitude toward the high school derives also from the
perception of the school as a source of weakening of the morals of the
children. The retention of the southern Italian idea that the school
must at least support the sanctity of family life and uphold the pattern of relationships between family members increases the conflict
between the parents and the school. Absence of religious instruction
in the American school, which in Italy was a source of great consolation to the parents insofar as the "dangers" of schooling were concerned, is not necessarily met with disapproval, yet it constitutes an
additional conflict. The Italian father, who in America is a persistent
church absentee, may not give much attention to this. But the Italian
mother who in America became the "keeper of the moral tradition"[43] and is also the upholder of the religious cult, views the absence of religious instruction with misgivings. At elementary school
level the concern for religious instruction is felt less keenly, for at
that age the accepted immaturity of the child makes it imperative for
the mother to subject the child to a variety of religious and ritualistic performances, either at home or in the church. Upon reaching
the state of maturity, the mother has less control over the religious
orthodoxy of her children, especially over the boys; and in the absence of any communal solidarity in matters of church attendance, or
of adherence to the old religious practices—which in Italy was obligatory and an article of social control—the grown-up boy (though
seldom the girl) becomes completely detached from the observation
of the religious tradition. This results in the rather frequent complaint about the amoral character of the high school. An excerpt
from a mother's letter to the principal of a high school follows:

> . . . Forgive my writing but the matter is important,.
> Perhaps I shall have to come and see how my son Joseph
> behaves in school. He is now seventeen years old and
> therefore, independent, so I cannot talk to him much.
> Please help me . . . When he comes home he does no-

---

[43]In juxtaposition to the father who is absorbed primarily in the preservation of
the economic patterns of family life.

thing but eat and drink; he bathes every night . . .   He drinks mostly milk.

I ask you to convince Joseph that he should never listen to friends, that some friendships bring one to the mad-house. He never used to be interested in friends, but since he goes to your school he spends most of his time with his friends whose correct address he won't tell me . . .

Please make Joseph go to church on Sunday and on Holy Days of Obligation. It is five years since he has gone to church. At least if he went once a month to Mass . . . Please make a rule that all high school boys should be faithful to their religion. They should be taught religion. All boys in high school should be made to go to church, receive the Sacrament and confess themselves at least once a month . . . They should bring a receipt from the priest that they were in church.

This is an expression of a parental wish to have the school render support to the mores of the Italian family. This particular mother's appeal is based on her remembrance of the moral support that the school in Italy used to give her. The frantic appeal seems to empha-size the conflict between the cultural tradition of her home and the boy's trend toward breaking away from this tradition. Even the fact that the boy "bathes every night" seems to have moral content, and is taken by the mother as a portent of bad things to come.

The complaint against the amorality of the high school also de-rives from the apparent unwillingness of the school to inculcate in the children the respect for family values. The following excerpts from documents are illustrative of this parental point of view.

My parents always lament the fact that whereas in the old country the schools taught manners and respect for their elders, the American schools appear not to be concerned with these matters.

My father and mother tell me always about the advantage of living in America. But I know also that they are still unreconciled to many things in America, especially the school (I am now attending) . . . The school, in their opinion, is the place where children are taught *not* to re-spect their parents. They often say: "Nothing good comes from going to school here. You learn many things, but you forget many more," meaning the things that parents teach their children.

A few years ago a discussion took place between approximately three hundred representatives of Italian societies, and teachers of Italian origin in New York City, on the question, "What does the American public school expect of the Italian parent and what does the Italian parent expect of the American public school?"

One parent decried the fact that even though the American school had such marvelous equipment and kept children for such a long period in school, the end result was, in many respects, deplorable for the Italian parents and for the Italian family; that *la morale* (morals) were neither studied nor practiced, and that, above all, they were totally lacking in respect and obedience to parents and elders. His exact words were: "The American school takes our children away from us and the time comes when these children of ours go to the east and we the parents go to the west."

The undertone of the whole meeting in terms of parental attitude toward the school was one of frustration, a feeling of hopelessness and helplessness before forces which were not understood and against which they were powerless.

Lack of Penal Measures in the High School as a Source of Complaint

A factor which clinches all parental arguments against the high school is its lack of any authority to administer punishment to transgressors of school rules. It is not that they justify punishing a truant, a late comer or one guilty of some disciplinary violation. Their attitudes of futility toward high school education, or even antagonism, provide them with no incentives to invoke retribution. What makes the school alien to their deep-rooted concepts of school education is the absolute absence of penal measures. A school that compels children to attend, yet has not the authority to punish, is a misnomer to them, for, as they say, "Teaching is to make things remembered. And memory requires a scar or two on your body." Or as one Italian puts it: "My younger brother works for me on a delivery wagon. Since I pulled out some of his hair, he remembers all streets and all addresses. The bald spot on his head is better than having studied a map of the city."

There is nothing naive about their inability to understand the laxity of the school. For in their traditional background, the formula—authority equals the power to punish—applies to any situation, to any institution.

When discussing witha group of Italians the penal measures of the church and the school in Italy, there was no
disagreement as to the power of both. "If you did not obey
the church rules and the priest hinted at the possibility of
punishment, you trembled with fear. The priest could fix
things so that you wished you were dead.

"And the school? We, of course, did not go to school. The
children went, and believe me, the teacher used his fists
good and often. In our estimation he had the right to do
it and there was nobody who would object."

Italians therefore never quarrelled with the right or wrong of punishment. And the teacher in Italy, by administering severe punishment, did not detract anything from his prestige or that of the school
as an institution; he rather enhanced it. The situation in America,
contrary to that in Italy, quite definitely induced the former *contadino* to regard the American school as lacking in authority and indirectly contributing to the lessening of parental control over their
children.

An Italian from Calabria, thirty-two years in the United States, the
father of seven children, states:

There are many good things in America. But there are also a great number of bad things which fill me with nostal-
gia for the land where I was born. Among these bad
things is that I came to learn that I have almost no power
over my own children . . . Oh, how often I know too
well, that a good spanking can cure bad habits of my
children. Yet I must think twice before I do this. Here in
America I may be taken to court for having administered
punishment on my own son. And mind you, the children
know this. They even have the nerve to dare me to beat
them, saying, "Papa, you surely will land in jail if you
touch me."

What a shame! A father must give his children a lesson
when no witnesses are around for fear of having the police on his head!

And the schools? Are they helping me in any way to bring
up my children in the right manner? The teachers say
they don't believe in corporal punishment, so they do
nothing—just talk and talk. And if I give my son a spanking, I know the difference between spanking and making
one lame—what happens? The teacher sides with my boy.
He is o.k., and I am not.

Frank, a shoemaker, over thirty years in America, speaks English with a decided accent but uses a vocabulary far beyond that of an Italian who has had no schooling in America. His wife speaks English fluently, having had American schooling. Their son is in the Navy, training as an ensign. When asked about American schools, Frank stated emphatically:

> The American school is bad, very bad. They teach a lot of things that don't help nobody. You have got to educate first and then the child will learn. A child who is *educato* will learn. He will learn easily because he is obedient, has respect for parents, has good manners. He is home with his family. He has *buona educazione* and *educazione* must always come before *istruzione*. The family, of course, must give *educazione* but the school must do it too. The school does not do it. Too many women teachers. Boys should have men all the time and men should give the boys this *educazione* that was so well done in my town in Italy. Here they do not even scold a child much less give him a good *bastonate* (beating) so we are left helpless and the children do as they please.

Recreational Education of the School as a Source of Complaint

Another factor which intensified the conflict between the parental home and the school, and contributed to non-recognition of the school as a social institution, was the element of recreation—to be exact, play—directly associated with the school activities of a child. As has been indicated in previous chapters, the concept of play as diversion did not exist among southern Italian peasants. School education in Italy was a strictly formal process into which no form of recreation could be fitted. So when the Italian in America perceived the emphasis of the school on play activities, it became impossible for him to reconcile his old-world attitude toward schooling as an *attivita seria* (a serious activity) with what he considered an element of frivolity.

At the elementary school age level, play though basically condemned is regarded with some tolerance because of the acceptance of a prolonged childhood. Play activities of high school children, however, evoke unmistakable, irreconcilable bursts of indignation and anger. In the first place, their tradition is rigid in condemning any activity even slightly reminiscent of childish play if the person who indulges in it has reached a status of comparative maturity. *Il giuoco della palla* (any game using a ball)—baseball, basketball, football,

golf, tennis—is, in the attitude of parents, incongruous with the
duties and responsibilities that a young man of fourteen or a girl of
thirteen should assume toward their family and the status they
occupy within their immediate community. In the second place, any
kind of sport or game that requires expenditure of physical energy is
an undignified, wasteful thing to do; it is fraught with the possibility
of physical injury and injury to health in general. Such sports as
football for boys—or basketball and tennis for girls—are frowned
upon also because of the waste of time and material for clothing or
shoes that are required to organize a team. When such activities
emanate from the school, their inability to associate a "scholar" with
"child interests" results in antagonism directed toward the school.

> Why, these boys and girls—particularly the boys—do
> nothing but play ball, morning, noon and night. The
> school should give our children definite tasks to do in the
> home. But one cannot expect very much from the school
> because it is the school that encourages play.

Very typical is the following comment of an Italian mother:

> It is very, very bad that the little children are taught in
> school to do nothing else but play ball. But I cannot un-
> derstand how it is possible for a high school to do the
> same thing . . . When my boy went to high school, I
> was pleased that one in our family may become a learned
> man. But I was disappointed . . . They accuse my boy
> of having lost interest in learning, but I don't blame him.
> How can he learn when they compel him to play more
> than to study? Imagine they called me to school to ex-
> plain why my son does not want to attend his playing
> lessons! I did not go, because I brought up my boy well. I
> did not teach him to play; the school taught him that . . .
>
> I always thought of the school as a place where one has to
> study. But play? *Questo giuoco e la rovina della famiglia*
> *(this play business is the ruination of the family).*

THE SOUTHERN ITALIAN CONCEPT OF THE ROLE OF THE STUDENT

In the early days of the Italian experience in America when some of
the Italian boys were beginning to go to high school, the role that
the young student should play in the home and in the community

was a subject of much controversy. In the days when the compulsory age law did not compel all children to attend a secondary school, going to high school was an important and a serious step in the Italian immigrant family. The decision to go was the result of much family deliberation. The boy so designated had to take on the role of a real student—European type—and the final goal was not just merely an educational experience. It had to result in the achievement of a profession which would bring prestige and economic returns of the family. This placed upon the young man definite responsibilities. He had to be a student in every sense of the word—strict application to his books and his studies; no such undignified behavior as "hanging around a corner," or playing games in the street. He was considered to be, and had to act with all the dignity of a young adult. Stories and anecdotes were current in the immigrant home of the rigorous life of the student in the higher school in Italy; long hours of study, difficult examinations, severe discipline, and even suicides of students who failed or whose families could no longer support them financially in their studies. Suicide, in such a case, was not condemned—in fact, it was extolled.

Working one's way through school—the American method—was not looked upon with favor. A student should not demean himself or his family by engaging in manual labor. He should devote himself to his studies and have the members of his family support him financially—even to his spending money. The family underwrote the complete professional career—even though it meant a medical course involving four years of high school, pre-medical school, medical school, internship, and the setting up of a medical office.

A secondary school education is still, in the eyes of the Italian immigrant, a serious undertaking only for those students who seek to carve out a career for themselves. It is not an incident in the growing-up period of the child. To insist upon a high school education for all children, regardless of the ability or the willingness of the child, is the height of absurdity. It is an encouragement to truancy and the demoralization of the child. Once past the elementary level, formal schooling is for the real student. The school is the center for learning, frequented by students with a serious purpose, and not a playful interlude preceding the world of work. This is a most persistent attitude and is the cause for many conflicts between parent and child and school.

Bibliography
of
Selected References

BIBLIOGRAPHY
OF SELECTED
REFERENCES

I. BIBLIOGRAPHIES

The fullest bibliography is Francesco Cordasco, *Italians in the United States: A Bibliography of Reports, Texts, Critical Studies and Related Materials* (New York: Oriole Editions, 1972) which is a partially annotated bibliography of 1462 items on all aspects of the Italian experience in America (*i.e.*, Bibliographies; Emigration; Italian American History and Regional Studies; Sociology of Italian American Life; Italian American in the Politico-Economic Context; Belles-Lettres and the Arts). Considerable bibliography is found in many of the entries in the following classified list, and this is indicated for some of the entries. An excellent bibliographical essay on extant sources is Silvano M. Tomasi, *The Italians in America* (New York: Istituto Italiana di Cultura, Occasional Paper, July, 1971); and notices of recent works are in F. Cordasco, "The Children of Columbus: The New Italian-American Ethnic Historiography, *"Phylon: The Atlanta University Review of Race & Culture* (September, 1973). Reference should also be made to:

BADEN, ANNE L. *Immigration in the United States: A Selected List of Recent References.* (Washington, D. C.: Government Printing Office, 1943).

DORE, GRAZIA. *La Democrazia italiana e L'emigrazione in America.* (Brescia: Morcelliana, 1964). Bibliography, pp. 389-493. A major work.

FIRKINS, INA TENEYCK. "Italians in the United States," *"Bulletin of Bibliography*, v. 8 (January, 1915), pp. 129-133.

New York Public Library. [The] *ITALIAN PEOPLE IN THE UNITED STATES.*(New York: the Library, 1936). 2 vols. [A collection of clippings and pamphlets.]

"A selected list of bibliographical references and records of the Italians in the United States," *ITALIAN LIBRARY OF IN-*

FORMATION [New York]. Outline Series. Series 1., No. 5 (August, 1958), pp. 1-19.

VELIKONJA, JOSEPH. *Italians in the United States.* Occasional Papers, No. 1. Department of Geography, Southern Illinois University. (Carbondale, Illinois: 1963). [See *Review* (corrections), Joseph G. Fucilla, *Italica* vol. 41 (June 1964), pp. 213-216.] Awkwardly arranged, but a valuable pioneer compilation and list on the Italian experience in the United States. No annotations; includes an author index. Some copies of the mimeographed list are miscollated.

II. ITALIAN EMIGRATION TO AMERICA

A. General Studies and Reports

BECCHERINI, FRANCESCO. *Il fenomeno dell'emigrazione italiani negli Stati Uniti.* (San Sepoloro: Tip. Boncompagni, 1906).

D'AMBROSIO, MANLIO. *Il Mezzogiorno d'Italia e l'emigrazione negli Stati Uniti.* (Roma: Athenaeum, 1924).

DORE, GRAZIA. *La Democrazia italiana e L'emigrazione in America.* (Brescia: Morcelliana, 1964). Bibliography, pp. 389-493. A major work.

FOERSTER, ROBERT F. *The Italian Emigration of Our Times.* (Cambridge: Harvard University Press, 1919. Reissued with an introductory note by F. Cordasco, New York: Russell & Russell, 1968).

LIVI-BACCI, MASSIMO. *L'immigrazione e l'assimilazione degli italiani negli Stati Uniti secondo le statisiche demographiche Americane* (Milano: Giuffrè, 1961). [Estimates that there were in 1950 in the U. S. no fewer than 7 million people, belonging to three generations, who had at least one Italian grandparent. Other estimates have run as high as 21 million and over.] See Giuseppe Lucrezio Monticelli, "Italian Emigration: Basic Characteristics and Trends," in S. M. Tomasi and M. H. Engel, eds., *The Italian Experience In The United States* (1970), pp. 3-22.

UNITED STATES IMMIGRATION COMMISSION. *Report of the Immigration Commission.* 41 vols. (Washington: Government Printing Office, 1911). *Index of Reports of the Immigration Commission,* S. Doc. No. 785, 61st Congress, 3rd Session, was never published. [Abstracts, vols. 1-2; includes statistical review of immigration; emigration conditions in Europe; dictionary of races or peoples; immigrants in industries; immigrants in cities; occupations of immigrants; fecundity of immigrant women; children of immigrants in schools; immigrants as charity seekers; immigration and crime; steerage conditions; bodily form of descendants of immigrants; federal immigration legislation; state immigration and alien laws; other countries; statements and recommendations.] The restrictive quotas derive from this work.

VILLARI, LUIGI. *Gli Stati Uniti d'America e l'emigrazione italiana.* (Milano: Fratelli Treves, 1912).

B. Special Studies

BONACCI, GIOVANNI. *Calabria e emigrazione.* (Firenze: Ricci, 1908).

CATTAPANI, CARLO. "Gli emigranti italiani fra gli Anglo-Sassoni," *Atti, Congresso Geografico Italiano* [Palermo, 1911], pp. 143-162.

CERASE, FRANCESCO P. "A Study of Italian Migrants Returning from the U.S.A.," *International Migration Review,* Vol. I. New Series (Summer, 1967), pp. 67-74.

"Character Of Italian Immigration." *New England Magazine,* n.s., 35 (1906), pp. 216-220.

DORE, GRAZIA. "Some Social and Historical Aspects of Italian Emigration to America," *Journal of Social History* (Winter 1968).

DICKINSON, JOAN Y. "Aspects of Italian Immigration to Philadelphia," *Pennsylvania Magazine of History and Biography,* vol. 40 (October 1966), pp. 445-465.

FOERSTER, ROBERT F. "A Statistical Survey of Italian Emigration," *Quarterly Journal of Economics,* v. 23 (November 1908), pp. 66-103.

GANS, HERBERT J. "Some Comments on the History of Italian Migration and the Nature of Historical Research," *International Migration Review,* Vol. I New Series (Summer 1967), pp. 5-9.

GILKEY, GEORGE R. "The United States and Italy: Migration and Repatriation," *Journal of Developing Areas* (1967), pp. 23-35.

HALL, PRESCOTT F. "Italian Immigration," *North American Review,* v. 163 (August 1896), pp. 252-254.

HAUGHWONT, FRANK G. "Italian Emigration," *U.S. Consular Reports,* v. 11 (December, 1883), pp. 364-366.

HUNTINGTON, HENRY G. "Italian Emigration to the United States," *U. S. Consular Reports,* v. 44 (February, 1894), pp. 308-309.

MONTICELLI, G. LUCREZIO. "Italian Emigration: Basic Characteristics and Trends with Special Reference to the Last Twenty Years," *International Migration Review,* Vol. I, New Series (Summer 1967), pp. 10-24.

SENNER, JOSEPH H. "Immigration from Italy," *North*

American Review, v. 162 (May 1896), pp. 649-656. Reply by
P. F. Hall, v. 163 (August 1896), pp. 252-254.

SPERANZA, GINO C. "Our Italian Immigration," *Nation,* v.
80 (1905), p. 304; also, "The Italian Emigration Department in
1904," *Charities,* v. 15 (October 21, 1905), pp. 114-116.

STELLA, ANTONIO A. *Some Aspects of Italian Immigration
to the United States; Statistical Data Based Chiefly Upon the
U.S. Census and Other Official Publications.* (New York:
Putnam's Sons, 1924, Reprinted, San Francisco: R & E Research
Associates, 1970).

C. Miscellaneous

BARKER, FOLGER. "What of the Italian Immigrant?" *Arena,*
v. 34 (August 1905), pp. 174-176.

BODIO, LUIGI. *Protection of Italian Immigrants in America.*
U.S. Bureau of Education (1895), v. 2, pp. 1789-1793.

CORSI, EDWARD. *In The Shadow Of Liberty: The Chronicle
of Ellis Island.* (New York: Macmillan, 1935).

LOPREATO, JOSEPH. *Peasants No More* (San Francisco:
Chandler, 1967). [Social change in southern Italy as a consequence of emigration.]

MERLINO, S. "Italian Immigrants and Their Enslavement,"
Forum, v. 15 (April, 1893), pp. 183-190.

TOMASI, SILVANO M. *An Overview of Current Efforts and
Studies in the Field of Italian Immigration.* (Staten Island,
New York: Center for Migration Studies [*circa* 1968]).

TOSTI, GUSTAVO. "Italy's Attitude Toward Her Emigrants," *North American Review,* v. 180 (May 1905), pp. 720-
726.

VELIKONJA, JOSEPH. "Italian Immigrants in the United
States in the Mid-Sixties," *International Migration Review,*
Vol. I., New Series (Summer 1967), pp. 25-37.

VON BOROSINI, VICTOR. "Home-going Italians," *Survey,*
v. 28 (September 28, 1912), pp. 791-793.

III. ITALIAN AMERICAN HISTORY AND REGIONAL STUDIES

A. General Studies

AMFITHEATROF, ERIK. *The Children of Columbus: An
Informal History of the Italians in the New World.* (Boston:
Little, Brown, 1973).

CLARK, FRANCIS EDWARD. *Our Italian Fellow Citizens in Their Old Homes and Their New* (Boston: Small, Maynard, & Co., 1919).

DeCONDE, ALEXANDER. *Half Bitter, Half Sweet: An Excursion into Italian-American History* (New York: Charles Scribner's Sons, 1971).

GROSSMAN, RONALD P. *The Italians in America* (Minneapolis: Lerner Publications, 1966).

IORIZZO, LUCIANO J. and SALVATORE MONDELLO. *The Italian Americans* (New York: Twayne, 1971).

LOPREATO, JOSEPH. *The Italian Americans* (New York: Random House, 1970).

LORD, ELLIOT, JOHN D. TRENNER, SAMUEL BARROWS. *The Italian in America* (New York: B. F. Buck and Company, 1906. Reprinted, San Francisco: R & E Research Associates, 1970).

MUSMANNO, MICHAEL A. *The Story of the Italians in America* (New York: Doubleday, 1965).

PISANI, LAWRENCE FRANK. *The Italian in America. A Social Study and History* (New York: Exposition Press, 1957).

ROLLE, ANDREW F. *The Immigrant Upraised: Italian Adventurers and Colonists in an Expanding America.* (Norman, Oklahoma: University of Oklahoma Press, 1968). Bibliography, pp. 351-371.

ROLLE, ANDREW F. *The American Italians: Their History and Culture.* (Belmont, California: Wadsworth, 1972).

ROSE, PHILIP M. *The Italians in America.* (New York: George H. Doran Co., 1922).

SCHIAVO, GIOVANNI E. *Italian-American History* 2 vols. (New York: Vigo Press, 1947-49).

SCHIAVO, GIOVANNI ERMENEGILDO. *Italians in America before the Civil War.* (New York: G. P. Putnam's Sons, 1924. [1934]).

TOMASI, SILVANO M. and M. H. ENGEL, eds. *The Italian Experience in the United States.* (Staten Island, New York: Center for Migration Studies, 1970). [Includes extensive bibliographies.]

B. Reminiscences, Biographies and Narratives

ARRIGIONI, LEONE SANTE. *Un Viaggio in America.* Impressioni. (Torino: Tipografia Salesiana, 1906).

BARZINI, LUIGI. *Americans Are Alone in the World.* (New York: Random House, 1953). See also, *The Italians.* (New York: Atheneum, 1964).

BIAGI, ERNEST L. *The Purple Aster, a History of the Order Sons of Italy in America.* (New York: Veritas Publishing Co., 1961).

CONTE, GAETANO. *Dieci anni in America. Impressioni e ricordi.* (Palermo: G. Spinnato, 1903).

COVELLO, LEONARD (with GUIDO D'AGOSTINO). *The Heart is the Teacher.* (New York: McGraw-Hill, 1958). Reprinted with *An Introduction* by F. Cordasco (New York: Littlefield & Adams, 1970 [*The Teacher in the Urban Community: A Half Century in City Schools*]).

FALBO, ERNEST S., ed. [and Trans.]. Count Leonetto Cipriani, *California and Overland Diaries from 1853-1871.* (Portland, Oregon: Champoeg Press, 1961).

FERRARI, ROBERT. *Days Pleasant and Unpleasant in the Order Sons of Italy; The Problem of Race and Racial Societies in the United States. Assimilation or Isolation?* (New York: Mandy Press, 1926. Reprinted with a new Foreword by F. Cordasco, Clifton, N. J.: Augustus M. Kelly, 1974).

GALLENGA, ANTONIO CARLO NAPOLEONE. *Episodes of My Second Life. American and English Experiences.* (Philadelphia: J. B. Lippincott, 1885).

IAMURRI, GABRIEL A. *The True Story of an Immigrant.* Rev. ed. (Boston: Christopher Publishing House, 1951).

MAZZEI, PHILIP. *Memoirs.* Trans. by H. R. Marraro. (New York: Columbia University Press, 1942).

NEIDLE, CECYLE S. *The New Americans.* (New York: Twayne, 1967). Includes notices of Leonard Covello, Angelo Pellegrini, Constantine Nunzio, Edward Corsi and Pascal d'Angelo.

PANUNZIO, CONSTANTINE M. *Immigrant Crossroads.* (New York: The Macmillan Co., 1927).

PANUNZIO, CONSTANTINE M. *The Immigrant Portrayed in Biography and Story: A Selected List with Notes.* (New York: Foreign Language Information Service, 1925).

PANUNZIO, CONSTANTINE M. *The Soul of an Immigrant.* (New York: The Macmillan Co., 1922 [1924; 1934]).

PEEBLES, ROBERT. *Leonard Covello: An Immigrant's Contribution to New York City.* Unpublished doctoral thesis, New York University, 1967.

PELLIGRINI, ANGELO M. *Immigrant's Return.* (New York: Macmillan, 1951).

PELLEGRINI, ANGELO M. *American by Choice.* (New York: Macmillan, 1956).

SPERANZA, GINO C. *The Diary of Gino Speranza, Italy, 1915-1919.* Edited by Florence Colgate Speranza. (New York: Columbia University Press, 1941) 2 vols. [Gino Charles Speranza, 1872-1927].

TORIELLI, ANDREW JOSEPH. *Italian Opinion on America as Revealed by Italian Travelers, 1850-1900.* (Cambridge, Mass.: Harvard University Press, 1941).

C. Regional Studies

a. Northeast

ADAMS, CHARLOTTE. "Italian Life in New York," *Harper's Monthly,* v. 62, no. 371 (April, 1881), pp. 666-684.

ALTARELLI, CARLO C. *History and Present Conditions of the Italian Colony at Paterson, N.J.* (New York: Columbia University Studies in Sociology, 1911).

BARRESE, PAULINE J. "Southern Italian Folklore in New York City," *New York Folklore Quarterly,* XXI (September 1965), pp. 181-193.

BETTS, LILLIAN W. *The Italian in New York.* (New York: University Settlement Studies, 1904-1905).

CORDASCO, F. and R. GALATTIOTO. "Ethnic Displacement in the Interstitial Community: The East Harlem [New York City] Experience," *Phylon: The Atlanta University Review of Race & Culture,* vol. 31 (Fall 1970), pp. 302-312; also in *Journal of Negro Education,* vol. 40 (Winter 1971), pp. 56-65. [Notices of the Italian community.]

CORDASCO, F. *Jacob Riis Revisited: Poverty and the Slum in Another Era.* (New York: Doubleday, 1968). [Italians in New York. Riis' photographs of the Italian subcommunity in New York City (1890-1905?) are in the Jacob A. Riis Collection, Museum of the City of New York.]

IRWIN, GRACE. "Michelangelo in Newark," *Harper's Magazine,* v. 143 (September 1921), pp. 446-454.

MANGANO, ANTONIO. *Italian Colonies in New York City.* (New York: Columbia University Studies in Sociology, 1904).

PILEGGI, NICHOLAS. "Little Italy: Study of an Italian Ghetto," *New York,* Vol. 1 (August 12, 1968), pp. 14-23.

RIIS, JACOB A. "The Italian in New York," *How the Other Half Lives. Studies among the Tenements of New York.* (New York: Charles Scribner's Sons, 1890).

SHEDD, WILLIAM B. "Italian Population in New York City," *The Casa Italiana Educational Bureau,* Bulletin No. 7 (1934); [Also published in *Atlantica,* September 1934].

U.S. Federal Writer's Project. New York City. *THE ITALIANS OF NEW YORK*. A survey prepared by workers of the Federal Writer's Project. Work Progress Administration in the City of New York. (New York: Random House, 1938). [Published also in Italian]

b. The South

"A Model Italian Colony in Arkansas," *Review of Reviews*, v. 34 (September 1906), pp. 361-362.

BRANDFON, ROBERT L. "The End of Immigration to the Cotton Fields," *The Mississippi Valley Historical Review*, vol. 50 (March 1964), pp. 591-611. [On attempts to replace Negroes with Italian agricultural workers.]

CUNNINGHAM, G. E. "Italians: A Hinderance to White Solidarity in Louisiana, 1890-1898," *Journal of Negro History*, vol. 50 (January 1965), pp. 22-36.

HEWES, LESLIE. "Tontitown: Ozark Vineyard Center [features of the predominantly Italian community and how it developed]," *Economic Geography*, vol. 29 (April 1953), pp. 125-143.

"Italians in the South;" "The South Wants Italians," *Outlook*, v. 87 (1907), pp. 556-558.

LANGLEY, LEE J. "Italian as a Southern Farmer, Striking characterization of Their Success and Value to the Community," *Manufacturers' Record* (August 1904).

LANGLEY, LEE J. "Italians in Cotton Field. Their Superiority over Negroes Shown on an Arkansas Plantation, *"Manufacturers' Record* (April 1904).

PHENIS, ALBERT. "Italian Immigration to the South," *Manufacturers' Record* (May 1905).

RAMIREZ, M. D. "Italian Folklore from Tampa, Florida," *Southern Folklore Quarterly*, vol. 13 (June 1949), pp. 121-132; also, pp. 101-106.

c. Midwest

BOYER, BRIAN. *"Chicago's Italians," Midwest,* [Chicago Sun Times] (July 14, 1968), p. 6+.

La PIANA, GEORGE. *The Italians in Milwaukee, Wisconsin: General survey, prepared under the direction of the Associated Charities.* (Milwaukee, Wis.: 1915. Reprinted, San Francisco: R & E Research Associates, 1970).

NELLI, HUMBERT S. *The Italians in Chicago: A Study in Ethnic Mobility.* (New York: Oxford University Press, 1970). [Considerable documentation and bibliographies.]

SCHIAVO, GIOVANNI. *The Italians in Chicago: A Study in Americanization.* (Chicago: Italian American Publishing Company, 1928).

SCHIAVO, GIOVANNI. *The Italians in Missouri.* (Chicago: Italian American Publishing Co., 1929).

U.S. BUREAU OF·LABOR. *The Italians in Chicago.* A social and economic study. Ninth Special Report of the Commissioner of Labor. Prepared under the direction of Caroll D. Wright. (Washington, D. C.: Government Printing Office, 1897).

VECOLI, RUDOLPH J. *Chicago's Italians Prior to World War I: A Study of Their Social and Economic Adjustment.* [Unpublished doctoral thesis. University of Wisconsin, 1963.]

VECOLI, RUDOLPH J. "Contadini in Chicago: A Critique of *The Uprooted,*" *Journal of American History,* vol. 51 (December 1964), pp. 404-417.

VISMARA, JOHN C. "The Coming of the Italians to Detroit," *Michigan History Magazine,* v. 11 (January 1918), pp.110-124.

WRITERS' PROGRAM [Nebraska] *The Italians of Omaha.* (Omaha: Independent Printing Co., 1941).

d. The West

BOHME, FREDERICK G. "The Italians in New Mexico," *New Mexico Historical Review* (April 1959), pp. 98-116.

CRESPI, CESARE. *San Francisco e la sua catastrofe.* (San Francisco, Tipografia internazionale, 1906).

LA VOCE DEL POPOLO [1868-1905]. Microfilm. (San Francisco: R & E Research Associates, 1970). [The first Italian Newspaper in California].

RADIN, PAUL. *The Italians of San Francisco: Their Adjustment and Acculturation.* California, Relief Administration. Cultural Anthropology Project. (San Francisco, 1935. Reprinted, San Francisco: R & E Research Associates, 1970).

ROLLE, ANDREW F. "Italy in California," *Pacific Spectator,* v. 9 (Fall 1955), pp. 408-419.

ROLLE, ANDREW F. "Success in the Sun: Italians in California," *The Westerners.* Los Angeles Corral. Los Angeles: Brand Book, 1961.

ROLLE, ANDREW F. "The Italian Moves Westward: Jesuit Missionaries Formed the Vanguard of Italy's Many-sided Impact on the Frontier," *Montana* [the Magazine of Western History], Vol. 16 (January 1966), pp. 13-24.

SCHIAVO, GIOVANNI. "The Italian Fishermen in California," *Vigo Review* (December 1938).

SPERONI, CHARLES. "The Development of the Columbus Day Pageant of San Francisco," *Western Folklore,* vol. 7 (1948), pp. 325-35; "California Fisherman's Festivals," *Ibid.,* vol. 14 (1955), pp. 77-91.

e. Miscellanea

BANFIELD, EDWARD C. *The Moral Basis of a Backward Society*. (New York: Free Press, 1958). [On Southern Italian society.]

CARR, JOHN FOSTER. "The Italian in the United States," *World's Work*. v. 8 (1904), pp. 5393-5404.

CARR, JOHN FOSTER. "The Coming of the Italian," *Outlook*, v. 82 (February 29, 1906), pp. 419-431.

COVELLO, LEONARD. "Italian Americans." Francis J. Brown and Joseph S. Roucek, eds. *Our Racial and National Minorities. Their History, Contributions, and Present Problems*. (New York: Prentice Hall, 1937).

COVELLO, LEONARD. *The Italians in America*. (New York: Casa Italiana Education Bureau. Bulletin No. 6 [1932?]).

DAVID-DUBOIS, RACHEL, ed. *Some of the Contributions of Italy and Her Sons to Civilization and American Life*. (New York: Casa Italiana Educational Bureau, Bulletin No. 3 [1935?]).

FANTE, JOHN. "The Odyssey of a Wop," *American Mercury*, v. 30 (September 1933), pp. 89-97.

GLANZ, RUDOLF. *Jew and Italian: Historic Group Relations and the New Immigration*, 1881-1924. (New York: Ktav Publishing Co., 1971).

JENKINS, HESTER. "And We Have Been Calling Them 'Dagoes,'" *World Outlook*, v. 3 (October 1907), p. 61.

MARINACCI, BARBARA. *They Came From Italy: The Story of Famous Italian-Americans*. (New York: Dodd, 1967). [Text for Grades 8 and up.]

MONDELLO, SALVATORE. "The Magazine *Charities* and the Italian Immigrants, 1903-14," *Journalism Quarterly*, vol. 44 (Spring 1967), pp. 91-98.

PECORINI, ALBERTO. "Our Italian Problem," *Review of Reviews*, v. 43 (1911), pp. 236-237.

PECORINI, ALBERTO. "The Italians in the United States," *The Forum*, v. 45 (January 1911), pp. 15-29.

PILEGGI, NICHOLAS. "How We Italians Discovered America and Kept It Pure While Giving It Lots of Singers, Judges, and Other Swell People," *Esquire*, Vol. 69 (June 1968), pp. 80-82.

PILEGGI, NICHOLAS. "The Risorgimento of Italian Power: The Red, White and Greening of New York," *New York*, vol. 4 (June 7, 1971), pp. 26-36.

PUZO, MARIO. "The Italians, American Style," *New York Times Magazine* (August 6, 1967).

SEXTON, PATRICIA. *Spanish Harlem*. (New York: Harper & Row, 1965). [Italian community.] See also, F. Cordasco, "Spanish Harlem: The Anatomy of Poverty," *Phylon: The Atlanta Review of Race & Culture*, vol. 26 (Summer 1965), pp. 195-196.

SPERANZA, GINO. *Race or Nationality: A Conflict of Divided Loyalties.* Indianapolis. [1920?]

TOMASI, LYDIO F., ed., *The Italian in America: The Progressive View, 1891-1914.* (New York: Center for Migration Studies, 1972). Articles out of the progressive journal *Charities* (1894-1913) which deal with the Italian immigrant.

VELIKONJA, JOSEPH. "The Italian Born in the United States, 1950," *Annals of the Association of American Geographers,* Vol. 51 (December, 1961), p. 426.

IV. SOCIOLOGY OF ITALIAN AMERICAN LIFE

A. Social Structure: Conflict and Acculturation

CAMPISI, PAUL J. "Ethnic Family Patterns: The Italian Family in the United States," *American Journal of Sociology,* v. 53 (May 1948), pp. 443-449. Also published as, "The Italian Family in the United States," Milton L. Barron, *American Minorities.* (New York: Alfred Knopf, 1957).

CHILD, IRVIN LONG. *Italian or American? The Second Generation in Conflict.* (New Haven: Published for the Institute of Human Relations by Yale University Press, 1943. Reissued with an introduction by F. Cordasco, New York: Russell & Russell, 1970). [originally, Ph.D. dissertation, Yale University, 1939]

DOUGLAS, DAVID W. *Influence of the Southern Italian in American Society.* Columbia University Studies in Sociology. (New York: Columbia University, 1915).

GANS, HERBERT J. *The Urban Villagers.* (New York: Free Press, 1962). [Italian-American community of Boston].

GLAZER, NATHAN and DANIEL P. MOYNIHAN. *Beyond the Melting Pot: The Negroes, Puerto Ricans, Jews, Italians, and Irish of New York City,* 2nd ed. (Cambridge: M.I.T. Press. 1970). [The section on Italians was written by Glazer].

NELLI, HUMBERT S. "Italians in Urban America: A Study in Ethnic Adjustment," *International Migration Review,* Vol. I. New Series (Summer 1967), pp. 38-55. [See entries for R. J. Vecoli for different view.]

SPERANZA, GINO C. "How It Feels to be a Problem: A Consideration of Certain Causes Which Prevent or Retard Assimilation," *Charities,* v. 12 (May 7, 1904), pp. 457-463.

STEINER, EDWARD A. "The Italian in America." *On the Trail of the Immigrant.* (New York: Fleming H. Revell, 1906).

WHEELER, THOMAS C. *The Immigrant Experience: The Anguish of Becoming an American.* (New York: Dial, 1971). [Narrative by Mario Puzo].

WHYTE, WILLIAM F. *Street Corner Society: The Social Structure of an Italian Slum.* 2nd edition. (Chicago: University of Chicago Press, 1955). [Revision of Ph.D. dissertation, University of Chicago, 1943].

WILLIAMS, PHYLLIS H. *South Italian Folkways in Europe and America: A Handbook for Social Workers, Visiting, Nurses, School Teachers, and Physicians.* (New Haven: Published for the Institute of Human Relations by Yale University Press, 1938. Reissued with An Introductory note by F. Cordasco, New York: Russell & Russell, 1969).

B. Education

AYRES, LEONARD P. *Laggards in Our Schools.* (New York: The Charities Publication Committee [of the Russell Sage Foundation], 1909). [Useful data and information on Italian school children].

Children of Immigrants in Schools. vols. 29-33 of *Report of the Immigration Commission.* 41 vols. (Washington: Government Printing Office, 1911). Republished with *An Introductory Essay* by F. Cordasco (Metuchen, N. J.: Scarecrow Reprint Corp., 1970). [A vast repository of data on educational history of immigrant children in America. Detailed analysis of backgrounds, nativity, school progress and home environments of school children in 32 American cities.] See also, Morris I. Berger, *The Settlement, the Immigrant and the Public School* (unpublished doctoral thesis, Columbia University, 1956); and F. Cordasco, "Educational Pelagianism: The Schools and the Poor," *Teachers College Record,* vol. 69 (April 1968), pp. 705-09.

CORDASCO, F. "The Challenge of the non-English Speaking Child in American Schools," *School & Society* (March 30, 1968), pp. 198-201. [On the enactment of the bilingual amendments (Title VII) of the Elementary and Secondary Education Act.]

CORDASCO, F. "The Children of Immigrants in the Schools: Historical Analogues of Educational Deprivation," *Kansas Journal of Sociology,* vol. 6 (Fall 1970), pp. 143-152. [Italian children in American schools.]

COVELLO, LEONARD. "Language Usage in Italian Families," *Atlantica* (October-November 1934).

COVELLO, LEONARD. "A High School and its Immigrant Community," *Journal of Educational Sociology,* vol. 9 (February 1936), pp. 333-346. [Benjamin Franklin High School, East Harlem.]

COVELLO, LEONARD. *The Social Background of the Italo-American School Child. A Study of the Southern Italian Family Mores and Their Effect on the School Situation in Italy and America.* Edited and with an introduction by F. Cordasco. (Leiden, The Netherlands: E. J. Brill, 1967). [Revision of doctoral thesis, New York University, 1944.]

CONCISTRE, MARIE J. *Adult Education in a Local Area: A Study of a Decade in the Life and Education of the Adult Immigrant in East Harlem, New York City.* Unpublished doctoral thesis. New York University, 1944. [A major study of the Italian community].

GOLDEN, HERBERT H. "The Teaching of Italian: The 1962 Balance Sheet," *Italica*, vol. 39 (1962), pp. 275-288. [A significant statement on the decline in Italian language instruction in the U.S.]

MATTHEWS, SISTER MARY FABIAN. *The Role of the Public School in the Assimilation of the Italian Immigrant Child in New York City 1900-1914.* Unpublished doctoral thesis, Fordham University, 1966.

MAY, ELLEN. "Italian Education and Immigration," *Education*, v. 28 (March, 1908), pp. 450-453.

PATRI, ANGELO. *A School Master in the Great City.* (New York: Macmillan, 1917).

TAIT, JOSEPH W. *Some Aspects of the Effect of the Dominant American Culture Upon Children of Italian-Born Parents.* (New York: Columbia University, 1942 [Teachers College Contributions to Education]. Reprinted with a Foreword by F. Cordasco, New York: Augustus M. Kelley, 1971).

THOMPSON, FRANK V. *Schooling of the Immigrant.* (New York: Harper, 1920). See also Alan M. Thomas, "American Education and the Immigrant," *Teachers College Record*, vol. 55 (1953-54), pp. 253-67; also, F. Cordasco, "Summer Camp Education for Underprivileged Children," *School & Society*, vol. 93 (Summer 1965).

WHEATON, H. H. *Recent Progress in the Education of Immigrants.* (Washington: Government Printing Office, 1915). See, in this connection, *Bibliography of Publications of the U.S. Office of Education 1867-1959.* With an introductory Note by F. Cordasco. (Totowa, N. J.: Rowman and Littlefield, 1971).

C. Health and Related Concerns

BREED, R. L. "Italians Fight Tuberculosis," *Survey*, v. 23 (February 12, 1910), pp. 702-703.

BREMNER, ROBERT H., ed. *Children and Youth in America: A Documentary History*, vol. I (1600-1865); vol. II, 1866-1932: Parts 1-6; Parts 7-8. (Cambridge: Harvard University Press, 1970-71).

DINWIDDIE, EMILY W. "Some Aspects of Italian Housing and Social Condition in Philadelphia," *Charities*, v. 12 (May 1904), pp. 490-494.

GEBHART, JOHN C. *Growth and Development of Italian Children in New York.* (New York: The Association for the Improvement of the Condition of the Poor, 1924).

MOSELEY, DAISY H. "The Catholic Social Worker in an an Italian District," *Catholic World,* v. 114 (February 1922), pp. 618-628.

STELLA, ANTONIO. *The Effects of Urban Congestion on Italian Women and Children.* (New York: William Wood, 1908).

STELLA, ANTONIO. "Tuberculosis and the Italians in the United States," *Charities,* v. 12 (May 7, 1904) pp. 486-489.

STELLA, ANTONIO. "The Prevalence of Tuberculosis among Italians in the United States," *Transactions of the Sixth International Congress on Tuberculosis.* Washington, September 28—October 5, 1908, v. 1—5. (Philadelphia: W.F. Fell, 1908).

STELLA, ANTONIO. "[Tuberculosis] among the Italians," *Charities,* v. 21 (November 7, 1908), p. 248.

STELLA, ANTONIO. *La lotta contro la tubercolosi fra gli Italiana nella citta di New York ed effetti dell'urbanesimo.* (Rome: Tip. Colombo, 1912).

D. Religion and Missionary Work.

BANDINI, ALBERT. "Concerning the Italian Problem," *Ecclesiastic Review,* v. 62 (1920), pp. 278-285.

BROWNE, HENRY J. "The 'Italian Problem' in the United States, 1880-1900," *U. S. Catholic Historical Society, Historical Records and Studies,* v. 35 (1946), pp. 46-72.

FELICI, ICILIO. *Father to the Immigrants. The Life of John Baptist Scalabrini.* (New York: P. J. Kennedy & Sons, 1955).

FEMMINELLA, FRANCIS X. "The Impact of Italian Migration and American Catholicism," *American Catholic Sociological Review,* vol. XXII (Fall 1961), pp. 233-241.

McLEOD, CHRISTIAN. [Anna C. Ruddy]. *The Heart of the Stranger. A Story of Little Italy.* (New York: Fleming H. Revell Co. 1908). [The life of Italians in East Harlem, New York City, written by a social religious reformer who founded the Home Garden (1901) later to become LaGuardia Memorial House.)

MANGANO, ANTONIO. "The Associated Life of the Italians in New York City," *Charities,* v. 12 (May 7, 1904), pp. 476-482.

MANGANO, ANTONIO. *Religious Work for Italians in America: A Handbook for Leaders in Missionary Work.* (New York: Immigrant Work Committee of the Home Missions Council [c. 1915]).

MANGANO, ANTONIO. *Sons of Italy: A Social and Religious Study of the Italians in America.* (New York: Missionary Education Movement of th United States and Canada, 1917. Reprinted with a Foreward by F. Cordasco, New York: Russell & Russell, 1972).

MONDELLO, SALVATORE. "Protestant Proselytism among the Italians in the U.S.A. as Reported in American Magazines," *Social Sciences,* vol. 41 (April 1966), pp. 84-90.

PALMIERI, AURELIO. *Il Grave Problema Religioso Italiano negli Stati Uniti.* (Florence, 1921). [major work]

SARTORIO, ENRICO C. *Social and Religious Life of Italians in America.* (Boston: The Christopher Publishing House, 1918. Reprinted with a Foreword by F. Cordasco, Clifton, N. J.: Augustus M. Kelly, 1974).

TOMASI, SILVANO M. "The Ethnic Church and the Integration of Italian Immigrants in the United States," S. M. Tomasi and M. H. Engel, *The Italian Experience in the United States* (Staten Island, New York: Center for Migration Studies, 1970), pp. 163-193.

VECOLI, RUDOLPH J. "Prelates and Peasants: Italian Immigrants and the Catholic Church," *Journal of Social History,* vol. 2 (Spring 1969), pp. 217-268. [considerable bibliography]

E. Crime, Delinquency, and Social Deviance

ALBINI, JOSEPH L. *The American Mafia: Genesis of a Legend.* (New York: Appleton-Century-Crofts, 1971). [Basic work]

ANDERSON, ROBERT T. "From Mafia to Cosa Nostra," *American Journal of Sociology,* vol. 71 (November 1965), pp. 302-310.

D'AMATO, GAETANO. "The Black Hand Myth," *North American Review,* v. 187 (April 1908), pp. 543-549.

"Death of Joseph Petrosino," *Current Literature,* v. 46 (1909), pp. 478-480.

HOWERTH, I. A. "Are the Italians a Dangerous Class?" *Charities Review,* vol. 4 (November 1894).

IANNI, FRANCIS A. J. "The Mafia and the Web of Kinship," *The Public Interest* (Winter 1971), pp. 78-100. [a major contribution]

SCHIAVO, GIOVANNI E. *The Truth about the Mafia and Organized Crime in America.* (New York: Vigo Press, 1962).

TALESE, GUY. "The Ethics of Frank Costello," *Esquire* (September 1961): also "Joe Bonanno, *Ibid.* (Aug., Sept., Oct., 1971) ["Joe Bananas"]; also, *Honor Thy Father.* (New York: World, 1971).

V. ITALIAN AMERICAN IN THE POLITICO-ECONOMIC CONTEXT

A. Labor and the Padrone System

BAILY, SAMUEL L. "The Italians and Organized Labor in the United States and Argentina: 1880-1910, *International Migration Review,* vol. I, New Series (Summer 1967), pp. 56-66.

CIOLLI, DOMINIC T. "The 'Wop' in the Track Gang," *Immigrants in America Review*, v. 11 (July 1916) pp. 61-64.

D'ALESSANDRE, JOHN J. "Occupational Trends of Italians in New York City," *Italy-America Monthly*, v. 2 (February 25, 1935), pp. 11-21. *Casa Italiana Educational Bureau*, Bulletin No. 8, 1935.

FENTON, EDWIN. "Italians in the Labor Movement," *Pennsylvania History*, v. 26, no. 2 (April 1959) pp. 133-148.

IORIZZO, LUCIANO J. "The Padrone and Immigrant Distribution," S. M. Tomasi and M. H. Engel, eds., *The Italian Experience in the United States* (Staten Island, N.Y.: Center for Migration Studies, 1970), pp. 43-75.

LIPARI, MARIE. "The Padrone System: An Aspect of American Economic History," *Italy-America Monthly*, vol. 2 (April 1935), pp. 4-10.

NELLI, HUMBERT. "The Italian Padrone System in the United States," *Labor History*, vol. 5 (Spring 1964), pp. 153-167.

ODENCRANTZ, LOUISE C. *Italian Women in Industry: A Study of Conditions in New York City.* New York: Russell Sage Foundation, 1919.

PHIPARD, CHARLES B. "The Philanthropist Padrone," *Charities*, v. 12 (May 7, 1904), pp. 470-472.

SPERANZA, GINO C. "The Italian Foreman as a Social Agent," *Charities*, v. 11 (July 4, 1903), pp. 26-28.

B. Politics and Government

BONE, HUGH A. "Political Parties in New York City," *The American Political Science Review*, April 1946. [Material on Italians in New York City politics.]

COXE, JOHN E. "The New Orleans Mafia Incident," *Louisiana Historical Quarterly*, v. 20 (1937), pp. 1066-1110. (Bibl. pp. 1109-1110).

EHRMANN, HERBERT B. *The Case That Will Not Die: Commonwealth vs. Sacco-Vanzetti.* (Boston: Little, Brown, 1969).

FELIX, DAVID. *Protest: Sacco-Vanzetti and the Intellectuals.* (Bloomington, Indiana: Indiana University Press, 1965).

KARLIN, ALEXANDER J. "New Orleans Lynching of 1891 and the American Press," *Louisiana Historical Quarterly*, v. 24 (1941), pp. 187-204.

MANN, ARTHUR. *LaGuardia Comes to Power, 1933.* (Philadelphia: Lippincott, 1965).

MANN, ARTHUR. *LaGuardia, A Fighter Against His Times, 1882-1933.* (Chicago: University of Chicago Press, 1969).

MONTGOMERY, ROBERT H. *Sacco-Vanzetti—The Murder and the Myth.* (New York: Devin, 1960).

PARENTI, MICHAEL J. *Ethnic and Political Attitudes—A Depth Study of Italian Americans.* Unpublished doctoral thesis. Yale University, 1962.

RUSSELL, FRANCIS. *Tragedy in Dedham.* (New York: McGraw Hill, 1962). [Sacco-Vanzetti case]

[Sacco-Vanzetti Case] *Transcript of the Record of the Trial of Nicolà Sacco and Bartolomeo Vanzetti in the Courts of Massachusetts.* (New York: Henry Holt, 1928-1929).

SCHAFFER, ALAN. *Vito Marcantonio, Radical in Congress.* (Syracuse: Syracuse University Press, 1966). [Originally, Ph.D. dissertation, University of Virginia, 1962]

SPERANZA, GINO C. "Political Representation of Italo-American Colonies in the Italian Parliament," *Charities,* v. 15 (1906), pp. 521-522.

C. Agriculture (Rural Settlement)

BENNET, ALICE. "Italians as Farmers and Fruit-Growers," *Outlook,* v. 90, no. 2 (September 12, 1908), pp. 87-88.

BENNET, ALICE. "The Italian as a Farmer," *Charities,* v. 21 (October 3, 1908), pp. 57-60.

MEADE, EMILY F. "The Italian Immigrant on the Land," *Charities,* v. 13 (March 4, 1904), pp. 541-544.

MEADE, EMILY F. "Italians on the Land," *U.S. Labor Bureau. Bulletin.* No. 14 (May 1907), pp. 473-533., [Hammonton settlement]

PALMER, HANS C. *Italian Immigration and the Development of California Agriculture.* Unpublished doctoral thesis, University of California [Berkeley], 1965.

PECORINI, ALBERTO. "The Italian as an Agricultural Laborer," *Annals, American Academy of Political and Social Science,* v. 33 (1909), pp. 380-390.

[Rossi, Adolfo.] "Italian Farmers in the South" [An interview with Adolfo Rossi by Gino C. Speranza]. *Charities,* v. 15 (1905), pp. 307-308.

SCOTT, CHARLES. "Italian Farmers for Southern Agriculture," *Manufacturers' Record,* v. 48 (November 9, 1905), pp. 423-424.

"Tontitown: An Italian Farming Community," *Service Bureau for Intercultural Education* [New York], Publications (1937).

TOSTI, GUSTAVO. "The Agricultural Possibilities of Italian Immigration, *Charities,* v. 12 (May 7, 1904), pp. 472-476.

INDEX

INDEX

917.3   70087
C
Cordasco, Francesco

The Italians

Date Due

OCT 2 6 1979			
DEC 6 1979			